6394456

D1525233

NORTH DAKOTA
STATE UNIVERSITY

SEP 1 7 2007

SERIALS DEPT.
LIBRARY

I & II KINGS

THE OLD TESTAMENT LIBRARY

Editorial Advisory Board

WILLIAM P. BROWN
CAROL A. NEWSOM
DAVID L. PETERSEN

Marvin A. Sweeney

I & II Kings

A Commentary

Westminster John Knox Press
LOUISVILLE • LONDON

© 2007 Marvin A. Sweeney

All rights reserved. No part of this book may be reproduced or transmitted in any form or by any means, electronic or mechanical, including photocopying, recording, or by any information storage or retrieval system, without permission in writing from the publisher. For information, address Westminster John Knox Press, 100 Witherspoon Street, Louisville, Kentucky 40202-1396.

Book design by Jennifer K. Cox

First edition
Published by Westminster John Knox Press
Louisville, Kentucky

This book is printed on acid-free paper that meets the American National Standards Institute Z39.48 standard. ♾

PRINTED IN THE UNITED STATES OF AMERICA

07 08 09 10 11 12 13 14 15 16 — 10 9 8 7 6 5 4 3 2 1

Library of Congress Cataloging-in-Publication Data

Sweeney, Marvin A. (Marvin Alan), 1953–
    I & II Kings : a commentary / Marvin A. Sweeney.—1st ed.
        p. cm. — (The Old Testament library)
    Includes bibliographical references.
    ISBN-13: 978-0-664-22084-6 (alk. paper)
    ISBN-10: 0-664-22084-3 (alk. paper)
    1. Bible. O.T. Kings—Commentaries.   I. Title.

    BS1335.53.S94 2007
    222'5077—dc22   2006052994

For
my maternal aunts and uncles
and their families

David W. Dorman
Carol
Philip and Annette, Cody and Colton
Matthew and Angela, Kayla

Deanne Voss z"l and William H. Voss
Trudy
Judson and Lynn
Jared and Therasa

R. Michael Dorman and Barbara Dorman
Adam
Marcy

CONTENTS

PREFACE

It has been a privilege to work with 1–2 Kings over the past six years. Although my work on this volume began in 2001, my earlier work in the prophetic and historical literature of ancient Judah and Israel, particularly my study *King Josiah of Judah: The Lost Messiah of Israel* (Oxford and New York: Oxford University Press, 2001), provided the foundation for my understanding of the history of the kings of Israel and Judah.

I would like to express my appreciation to those who made this work possible. My student assistants, Ms. Hye Kyung Park and Mr. Gi-Soo Song, played invaluable roles in helping to gather research materials for this volume. The Claremont School of Theology provided research leaves in the spring 2001 and fall 2004 semesters that enabled me to concentrate more fully on this work. Professor Antony J. Campbell, S.J., my former teacher and now Emeritus Professor of Old Testament at the Jesuit Theological College, Parkville, Australia, discussed many aspects of Kings and read drafts of the introduction during the course of several sabbaticals spent in Claremont. Volume editor, Professor Carol Newsom, Candler School of Theology, read the manuscript carefully and made many suggestions for its improvement. Any problems that remain are my own responsibility. My colleagues in Hebrew Bible, Kristin De Troyer and Tammi Schneider, are always ready to provide judicious insight into scholarly (and other!) issues and continue to set new standards in collegiality. My M.Div. and M.A. students at the Claremont School of Theology, my rabbinical and cantorial students at the Academy for Jewish Religion California, and my doctoral students at the Claremont Graduate University have enlivened and enriched the study of this literature in the many classes that I have taught over the years. Finally, my wife, Muna, and our daughter, Leah, make everything possible with their love and constant reminders of life's deepest joys.

I would like to dedicate this volume to my maternal aunts and uncles and their families: my Uncle David; the memory of my Aunt Deanne and Uncle Bill; and my Uncle Michael and Aunt Barbara.

San Dimas, California   Iyyar 5766 / May 2006

In keeping with some streams in Jewish tradition, I have employed the terms YHWH, G-d, L-rd, and so on, to render the Divine Name.

ABBREVIATIONS

ABD	*Anchor Bible Dictionary.* Edited by D. N. Freedman. 6 vols. New York, 1992
AfO	*Archiv für Orientforschung*
AION	*Annali dell'Istituto Orientali di Napoli*
AJBI	*Annual of the Japanese Biblical Institute*
AJSL	*American Journal of Semitic Languages and Literatures*
ANEP	*The Ancient Near East in Pictures Relating to the Old Testament.* Edited by J. B. Pritchard. Princeton, 1954.
ANET	*Ancient Near Eastern Texts Relating to the Old Testament.* Edited by J. B. Pritchard. 3d ed. Princeton, 1969.
ARAB	*Ancient Records of Assyria and Babylonia.* Daniel David Luckenbill. 2 vols. Chicago, 1926–1927.
ASORDS	American Schools of Oriental Research Dissertation Series
ASTI	*Annual of the Swedish Theological Institute*
ATSAT	Arbeiten zu Text und Sprache des Alten Testament
AThANT	Abhandlungen zur Theologie des Alten und Neuen Testaments
BA	*Biblical Archaeologist*
BASOR	*Bulletin of the American Schools of Oriental Research*
BDB	Brown, F., S. R. Driver, and C. A. Briggs. *A Hebrew and English Lexicon of the Old Testament.* Oxford, 1907
BETL	Bibliotheca ephemeridum theologicarum lovaniensium
BHS	*Biblia Hebraica Stuttgartensia.* Edited by K. Elliger and W. Rudolph. Stuttgart, 1983
Bib	*Biblica*
BibSem	The Biblical Seminar
BJS	Brown Judaic Studies
BR	*Biblical Research*
BWA(N)T	Beiträge zur Wissenschaft vom Alten (und Neuen) Testament
BZAW	Beihefte zur Zeitschrift für die alttestamentliche Wissenschaft
CAH	Cambridge Ancient History

CANE	*Civilizations of the Ancient Near East.* Edited by J. Sasson. 4 vols. New York, 1995
CBQ	*Catholic Biblical Quarterly*
CBET	Contributions to Biblical Exegesis and Theology
CBQMS	Catholic Biblical Quarterly Monograph Series
ConBOT	Coniectanea biblica: Old Testament Series
CTA	*Corpus des tablettes en cuneiformes alphabétiques découvertes à Ras Shamra-Ugarit de 1929 à 1939.* Edited by A. Herdner. Mission de Ras Shamra 10. Paris, 1963
*DDD*²	*Dictionary of Deities and Demons in the Bible.* Edited by K. van der Toorn et al. 2d ed. Leiden, 1999
DJD	Discoveries in the Judaean Desert
Dtr	Deuteronomic
DtrH	Deuteronomistic History
EA	El-Amarna tablets. According to the edition of J. A. Knudtzon. *Die el-Amarna-Tafeln.* Leipzig, 1908–1915. Reprint, Aalen, 1964. Continued in A. F. Rainey, *El-Amarna Tablets, 359–379.* 2d revised ed. Kevelaer, 1978
EDB	*Eerdmans Dictionary of the Bible.* Edited by D. N. Freedman et al. Grand Rapids and Cambridge, 2000
EncJud	*Encyclopaedia Judaica.* 16 vols. Jerusalem, 1972
ErIsr	*Eretz-Israel*
EvT	*Evangelische Theologie*
FAT	Forschungen zum Alten Testament
Fest.	Festschrift
FOTL	Forms of the Old Testament Literature
FRLANT	Forschungen zur Religionen und Literatur des Alten und Neuen Testaments
GKC	*Gesenius' Hebrew Grammar.* Edited by E. Kautzsch. Translated by A. E. Cowley. 2d ed. Oxford, 1910
HALOT	Koehler, L., and W. Baumgartner. *Hebrew and Aramaic Lexicon of the Old Testament.* 5 vols. Leiden, 1994–2000
HAR	*Hebrew Annual Review*
HBD	*HarperCollins Bible Dictionary.* Edited by P. J. Achtemeier et al. 2d ed. San Francisco, 1996
HSM	Harvard Semitic Monographs
HSS	Harvard Semitic Studies
HTR	*Harvard Theological Review*
HUCA	*Hebrew Union College Annual*
IBT	Interpreting Biblical Texts
IDB	*The Interpreter's Dictionary of the Bible.* Edited by G. A. Buttrick. 4 vols. Nashville, 1962

IDBSup	*The Interpreter's Dictionary of the Bible: Supplementary Volume.* Edited by K. Crim. Nashville, 1976
IEJ	*Israel Exploration Journal*
IOS	*Israel Oriental Society*
JANESCU	*Journal of the Ancient Near Eastern Society of Columbia University*
JAOS	*Journal of the American Oriental Society*
JARCE	*Journal of the American Research Center in Egypt*
JBL	*Journal of Biblical Literature*
JCS	*Journal of Cuneiform Studies*
JJS	*Journal of Jewish Studies*
JNES	*Journal of Near Eastern Studies*
JNSL	*Journal of Northwest Semitic Languages*
JR	*Journal of Religion*
JSOT	*Journal for the Study of the Old Testament*
JSOTSup	Journal for the Study of the Old Testament: Supplement Series
JSS	*Journal of Semitic Studies*
JTS	*Journal of Theological Studies*
KAI	*Kanaanäische und aramäische Inschriften.* H. Donner and W. Röllig. 2d ed. Wiesbaden, 1966–1969
Kleine Schriften	*Kleine Schriften zur Geschichte des Volkes Israel.* By Albrecht Alt. 3 vols. Munich: C. H. Beck, 1953.
LHBOTS	Library of Hebrew Bible/Old Testament Studies
LXX	Septuagint
MT	Masoretic Text
NEAEHL	*The New Encyclopaedia of Archaeological Excavations in the Holy Land.* Edited by E. Stern. 4 vols. Jerusalem, 1993
OBO	Orbis biblicus et orientalis
OPIAC	*Occasional Papers of the Institute for Antiquity and Christianity*
OTL	Old Testament Library
OTP	*Old Testament Pseudepigrapha.* Edited by J. H. Charlesworth. 2 vols. New York, 1983
OTS	*Oudtestamentische Studiën*
PEQ	*Palestine Exploration Quarterly*
POS	Pretoria Oriental Studies
SAS	State Archives of Assyria
SAAS	State Archives of Assyria Studies
SBLDS	Society of Biblical Literature Dissertation Series
SBLMasS	Society of Biblical Literature Masoretic Studies
SBLMS	Society of Biblical Literature Monograph Series

SBLSBS	Society of Biblical Literature Sources for Biblical Study
SBS	Stuttgarter Bibelstudien
SBT	Studies in Biblical Theology
SHANE	Studies in the History of the Ancient Near East
SOTSMS	Society for Old Testament Studies Monograph Series
TA	*Tel Aviv*
TGUOS	Transactions of the Glasgow University Oriental Society
TRu	*Theologisches Rundschau*
VT	*Vetus Testamentum*
VTSup	Supplements to Vetus Testamentum
WMANT	Wissenschaftliche Monographien zum Alten und Neuen Testament
ZAW	*Zeitschrift für die alttestamentliche Wissenschaft*
ZDPV	*Zeitschrift des deutschen Palästina-Vereins*

BIBLIOGRAPHY

Text Editions

Baillet, M. *Les "Petites Grottes" de Qumran.* DJD 3. 2 vols. Oxford: Clarendon, 1962.

Brooke, Alan England, et al. *The Old Testament in Greek.* Volume 2 of *The Later Historical Books.* Part 2: *1 and 2 Kings.* London: Cambridge University Press, 1930.

Elliger, Karl, and Wilhelm Rudolph, eds. *Biblia Hebraica Stuttgartensia.* Stuttgart: Deutsche Bibelgesellschaft, 1977.

Gottlieb, Hans. *The Old Testament in Syriac according to the Peshitta Version.* II/4: *Kings.* Leiden: Brill, 1976.

Rahlfs, Alfred. *Septuaginta.* Stuttgart: Wurtemburgisches Bibelanstalt, 1935.

Sperber, Alexander. *The Bible in Aramaic. The Former Prophets according to Targum Jonathan.* Leiden: Brill, 1959.

Ulrich, Eugene, et al. *Qumran Cave 4. IX: Deuteronomy, Joshua, Judges, Kings.* DJD 14. Oxford: Clarendon, 1995.

Weber, Robert, OSB. *Biblia Sacra iuxta vulgatum versionen.* Stuttgart: Deutsche Bibelgesellschaft, 1983.

Commentaries

Benzinger, I. *Die Bücher der Könige.* Kurzer Hand-Commentar zum Alten Testament 9. Tübingen: Mohr Siebeck, 1899.

Brueggemann, Walter. *1 & 2 Kings.* Smyth & Helwys Bible Commentary. Macon, Ga.: Smyth & Helwys, 2000.

Buis, P. *Le livre des Rois.* Sources bibliques. Paris: Gabalda, 1997.

Burney, C. F. *The Book of Judges and Notes on the Hebrew Text of the Books of Kings.* New York: KTAV, 1970.

Cogan, Mordechai. *1 Kings.* Anchor Bible 10. New York: Doubleday, 2001.

Cogan, Mordechai, and Tadmor, Hayim. *II Kings.* Anchor Bible 11. New York: Doubleday, 1988.

Cohn, Robert L. *2 Kings.* Berit Olam. Collegeville, Minn.: Liturgical, 2000.

DeVries, Simon J. *1 Kings.* Word Biblical Commentary 12. Waco, Tex.: Word, 1985.

Fritz, Volkmar. *1 & 2 Kings.* Continental Commentary. Translated by Anselm Hagedorn. Minneapolis: Fortress, 2003.

Gray, John. *I & II Kings: A Commentary.* OTL. 2d ed. Philadelphia: Westminster, 1970.

Hobbs, T. R. *2 Kings.* Word Biblical Commentary 13. Waco, Tex.: Word, 1985.

Hochberg, Reuven, and Rosenberg, A. J. *The Book of Kings.* Judaica Books of the Bible. 2 vols. New York: Judaica, 1998, 1993.

Jones, G. H. *1 and 2 Kings.* The New Century Bible Commentary. 2 vols. Grand Rapids: William B. Eerdmans; London: Marshall, Morgan, and Scott, 1984.

Kittel, Rudolph. *Die Bücher der Könige.* Handkommentar zum Alten Testament 1/5. Göttingen: Vandenhoeck & Ruprecht, 1900.

Klostermann, August. *Die Bücher Samuelis und der Könige.* Kurzgefasster Kommentar zu den heiligen Schriften Alten und Neuen Testamentes A/3. Nöordlingen: C. H. Beck, 1887.

Long, Burke O. *1 Kings, with an Introduction to Historical Literature.* FOTL 9. Grand Rapids: William B. Eerdmans, 1984.

———. *2 Kings.* FOTL 10. Grand Rapids: William B. Eerdmans, 1991.

Montgomery, James A., and Gehman, Henry Snyder. *The Books of Kings.* International Critical Commentary. Edinburgh: T & T Clark, 1951.

Mulder, Martin J. *1 Kings.* Vol. 1. *1 Kings 1–11.* Historical Commentary on the Old Testament. Leuven: Peeters, 1998.

Nelson, Richard D. *First and Second Kings.* Interpretation. Atlanta: John Knox, 1987.

Noth, Martin. *Könige 1. I. Könige 1–16.* Biblischer Kommentar, Altes Testament 9/1. Neukirchen-Vluyn: Neukirchener, 1968.

Provan, Iain W. *1 and 2 Kings.* New International Bible Commentary. Peabody, Mass.: Hendrickson; Carlisle: Paternoster, 1995.

Robinson, J. *The First Book of Kings.* The Cambridge Bible Commentary. Cambridge: Cambridge University Press, 1972.

———. *The Second Book of Kings.* The Cambridge Bible Commentary. Cambridge: Cambridge University Press, 1976.

Šanda, A. *Die Bücher der Könige.* Exegetisches Handbuch zum Alten Testament 9. 2 vols. Münster: Aschendorff, 1911–12.

Seow, Choon-Leong. "The First and Second Books of Kings." Pages 1–295 in *The New Interpreter's Bible.* Vol. 3. Edited by L. E. Keck et al. Nashville: Abingdon, 1999.

Slotki, I. W. *Kings.* The Soncino Books of the Bible. London: Soncino, 1990.

Thenius, Otto. *Die Bücher der Könige.* Kurzgefasstes exegetisches Handbuch zum Alten Testament 9. Leipzig: Weidmann, 1849.

Walsh, Jerome T. *1 Kings.* Berit Olam. Collegeville, Minn.: Liturgical, 1996.

Würthwein, Ernst. *Die Bücher der Könige.* Das Alte Testament Deutsch 11/1–2. Göttingen: Vandenhoeck & Ruprecht, 1977.

Books and Monographs

Ahlström, G. W. *Royal Administration and National Religion in Ancient Palestine.* SHANE 1. Leiden: Brill, 1982.

Auld, A. Graeme. *Kings without Privilege.* Edinburgh: T & T Clark, 1994.

Barré, Lloyd M. *The Rhetoric of Political Persuasion.* CBQMS 20. Washington, D.C.: Catholic Biblical Association, 1988.

Barrick, W. Boyd. *The Kings and the Cemeteries: Toward a New Understanding of Josiah's Reform.* VTSup 88. Leiden: Brill, 2002.

Beck, Martin. *Elia und die Monolatrie.* BZAW 281. Berlin and New York: Walter de Gruyter, 1999.

Bergen, Wesley J. *Elisha and the End of Prophetism.* JSOTSup 286. Sheffield: Sheffield Academic Press, 1999.

Bietenhard, Sophia Katharina. *Des Königs General.* OBO 163. Freiburg: Universitäts-Verlag; Göttingen: Vandenhoeck & Ruprecht, 1998.

Bohlen, Reinhold. *Der Fall Nabot.* Trierer Theologische Studien 35. Trier: Paulinus, 1978.

Brenner, Athalya, ed. *A Feminist Companion to Samuel and Kings.* The Feminist Companion to the Bible 5. Sheffield: Sheffield Academic Press, 1994.

Brichto, Herbert Chanan. *Toward a Grammar of Biblical Poetics: Tales of the Prophets.* New York and Oxford: Oxford University Press, 1992.

Bronner, Leah. *The Stories of Elijah and Elisha: As Polemics against Baal Worship.* POS 6. Leiden: Brill, 1968.

Campbell, Antony F., S.J. *Of Prophets and Kings. A Late Ninth-Century Document (1 Samuel 1–2 Kings 10).* CBQMS 17. Washington, D.C.: The Catholic Biblical Association, 1986.

Campbell, Antony F., and Mark A. O'Brien. *Unfolding the Deuteronomistic History: Origins, Upgrades, Present Text.* Minneapolis: Fortress, 2000.

Carr, David McLain. *From D to Q: A Study of Early Jewish Interpretations of Solomon's Dream at Gibeon.* SBLMS 44. Atlanta: Scholars Press, 1991.

Cogan, Morton. *Imperialism and Religion.* SBLMS 19. Missoula, Mont.: Scholars Press, 1974.

Coote, Robert B., ed. *Elijah and Elisha in Socioliterary Perspective.* Semeia Studies. Atlanta: Scholars Press, 1992.

Debus, Jörg. *Die Sünde Jerobeams.* FRLANT 93. Göttingen: Vandenhoeck & Ruprecht, 1967.

Dietrich, Walter. *Prophetie und Geschichte.* FRLANT 108. Göttingen: Vandenhoeck & Ruprecht, 1972.

Dutcher Walls, Patricia. *Narrative Art, Political Rhetoric: The Case of Athaliah and Joash.* JSOTSup 209. Sheffield: Sheffield Academic Press, 1996.

Eissfeldt, Otto. *Der G-tt Karmel.* Berlin: Akademie, 1954.

Eynikel, Erik. *The Reform of King Josiah and the Composition of the Deuteronomistic History.* OTS 33. Leiden: Brill, 1996.

Fohrer, Georg. *Elia.* Abhandlungen zur Theologie des Alten und Neuen Testaments 53. 2d ed. Zurich: Zwingli, 1968.

Fox, Nili Sacher. *In the Service of the King: Officialdom in Ancient Israel and Judah.* Monographs of the Hebrew Union College 23. Cincinnati: Hebrew Union College, 2000.

Galil, Gershon. *The Chronology of the Kings of Israel and Judah.* SHANE 9. Leiden: Brill, 1996.

Gerbrandt, Gerald Eddie. *Kingship according to the Deuteronomistic History.* SBLDS 87. Atlanta: Scholars Press, 1986.

Gooding, D. W. *Relics of Ancient Exegesis: A Study of the Miscellanies in 3 Reigns 2.* SOTSMS 4. Cambridge: Cambridge University Press, 1976.

Görg, Manfred. *G-tt—König—Reden in Israel und Ägypten.* BWANT 105. Stuttgart: W. Kohlhammer, 1975.

Gugler, Werner. *Jehu und Seine Revolution.* Kampen: Kok Pharos, 1996.

Handy, Lowell K., ed. *The Age of Solomon: Scholarship at the Turn of the Millennium.* SHANE 11. Leiden: Brill, 1997.

Harrington, Daniel J., and Anthony J. Saldarini. *Targum Jonathan of the Former Prophets: Introduction, Translation, and Notes.* Aramaic Bible 10. Collegeville, Minn.: Liturgical, 1987.

Hauser, Alan J., and Russell Gregory. *From Carmel to Horeb: Elijah in Crisis.* JSOTSup 85. Sheffield: Almond Press, 1990.

Hentschel, Georg. *Die Elija-erzählungen.* Erfurter Theologische Studien 33. Leipzig: St. Benno, 1977.

Hoffmann, Hans-Detlef. *Reform und Reformen.* AThANT 66. Zurich: Theologischer Verlag, 1980.

Honor, L. L. *Sennacherib's Invasion of Palestine: A Critical Source Study.* New York: AMS, 1966.

Hrozný, Heinrich. *Die Abweichungen des Codex Vaticanus vom hebräischen Texte in den Königsbüchern.* Leipzig: W. Drugulin, 1909.

Hurowitz, Victor (Avigdor). *I Have Built You an Exalted House.* JSOTSup 115. Sheffield: Sheffield Academic Press, 1992.

Jepsen, Alfred. *Die Quellen des Königsbuches.* Halle (Salle): Max Niemeyer, 1953.

Keinänen, Jyrki. *Traditions in Collision: A Literary and Redaction-Critical Study on the Elijah Narratives 1 Kings 17–19.* Publications of the Finnish Exegetical Society 80. Helsinki: The Finnish Exegetical Society; Göttingen: Vandenhoeck & Ruprecht, 2001.

Kenik, Helen A. *Design for Kingship.* SBLDS 69. Chico, Calif.: Scholars Press, 1983.

Keulen, Percy S. F. van. *Manasseh through the Eyes of the Deuteronomists.* OTS 38. Leiden: Brill, 1996.

———. *Two Versions of the Solomonic Narrative.* VTSup 104. Leiden: Brill, 2005.

Knoppers, Gary N. *Two Nations under G-d: The Deuteronomistic History of Solomon and the Dual Monarchies.* HSM 52–53. Atlanta: Scholars Press, 1993–94.

Lehnart, Bernhard. *Prophet und König im Nordreich Israel.* VTSup 96. Leiden: Brill, 2003.

Levin, Christoph. *Der Sturz der Königin Atlaja.* SBS 105. Stuttgart: Katholisches Bibelwerk, 1982.

Lowery, R. H. *The Reforming Kings.* JSOTSup 120. Sheffield: Sheffield Academic Press, 1991.

Marcos, Natalio Fernández. *Scribes and Translators: Septuagint and Old Latin in the Books of Kings.* VTSup 54. Leiden: Brill, 1994.

Mazar, Benjamin. "The Aramaean Empire and Its Relations with Israel." Pages 151–72 in *The Early Biblical Period: Historical Essays.* Jerusalem: Israel Exploration Society, 1986.

McKay, John. *Religion in Judah under the Assyrians.* SBT 2/26. Naperville, Ill.: Allenson, 1973.

McKenzie, Steven L. *The Trouble with Kings: The Composition of the Books of Kings in the Deuteronomistic History.* VTSup 42. Leiden: Brill, 1991.

Minokami, Yoshikazu. *Die Revolution des Jehu.* Göttingen Theologische Arbeiten 38. Göttingen: Vandenhoeck & Ruprecht, 1989.

Moore, Rick Dale. *G-d Saves: Lessons from the Elisha Stories.* JSOTSup 95. Sheffield: Sheffield Academic Press, 1990.

Mulzer, Martin. *Jehu schlagt Joram.* ATSAT 37. St. Ottilien: EOS, 1992.

Nelson, Richard D. *The Double Redaction of the Deuteronomistic History.* JSOTSup 18. Sheffield: JSOT Press, 1981.

Nental, Jochen. *Trägerschaaft und Intentionen des deuteronomistischen Geschichtswerks.* BZAW 297. Berlin and New York: Walter de Gruyter, 2000.

Noth, Martin. *The Deuteronomistic History.* JSOTSup 15. Sheffield: JSOT Press, 1981.

O'Brien, Mark A. *The Deuteronomistic History Hypothesis: A Reassessment.* OBO 92. Freiburg: Universitätsverlag; Göttingen: Vandenhoeck & Ruprecht, 1989.

Otto, Susanne. *Jehu, Elia, und Elisa.* BWANT 152. Stuttgart: W. Kohlhammer, 2001.

Polzin, Robert M., and Eugene Rothman. *The Biblical Mosaic: Changing Perspectives.* Semeia Studies. Philadelphia: Fortress; Chico, Calif.: Scholars Press, 1982.

Provan, Iain W. *Hezekiah and the Books of Kings.* BZAW 172. Berlin and New York: Walter de Gruyter, 1988.

———. *1 & 2 Kings.* Old Testament Guides. Sheffield: Sheffield Academic Press, 1997.

Rahlfs, Alfred. *Septuaginta-Studien.* 3 vols. Göttingen: Vandenhoeck & Ruprecht, 1904–1911.

Rofé, Alexander. *The Prophetical Stories.* Jerusalem: Magnes, 1988.

Rösel, Hartmut N. *Von Josua bis Jojachin.* VTSup 75. Leiden: Brill, 1999.

Rüterswörden, Udo. *Die Beamten der israelitischen Königszeit.* BWANT 117. Stuttgart: W. Kohlhammer, 1985.

Särkiö, Pekka. *Die Weisheit und Macht Salomos in der Israelitischen Historiographie.* Schriften der Finnischen Exegetischen Gesellschaft 60. Helsinki: Finnische Exegetische Gesellschaft; Göttingen: Vandenhoeck & Ruprecht, 1994.

Schäfer-Lichtenberger, Christa. *Josua und Salomo.* VTSup 58. Leiden: Brill, 1995.

Schenker, Adrian. *Älteste Textgeschichte der Königsbücher.* OBO 199. Fribourg: Academic Press; Göttingen: Vandenhoeck & Ruprecht, 2004.

———. *Septante et Texte Massorétique dans l'Histoire la plus ancienne du Texte de 1 Rois 2–14.* Cahier de Revue Biblique 48. Paris: Gabalda, 2000.

Schmitt, Hans-Christoph. *Elisa.* Gütersloh: Gerd Mohn, 1972.

Schweizer, Harald. *Elischa in den Kriegen.* Studien zum Alten und Neuen Testaments, 37. Munich: Kösel, 1974.

Shenkel, James Donald. *Chronology and Recensional Development in the Greek Text of Kings.* HSM 1. Cambridge: Harvard University Press, 1968.

Spieckermann, Hermann. *Juda under Assur in der Sargonidenzeit.* FRLANT 129. Göttingen: Vandenhoeck & Ruprecht, 1982.

Stavrakopoulou, Francesca. *King Manasseh and Child Sacrifice.* BZAW 338. Berlin and New York: Walter de Gruyter, 2004.

Steck, Odil Hannes. *Überlieferung und Zeitgeschichte in den Elia-Erzählungen.* WMANT 26. Neukirchen-Vluyn: Neukirchener, 1968.

Stipp, Hermann-Josef. *Elischa—Propheten—G-ttesmänner.* ATSAT 24. St. Ottilien: EOS, 1987.

Sweeney, Marvin A. *King Josiah of Judah: The Lost Messiah of Israel.* Oxford and New York: Oxford University Press, 2001.

Tagliacarne, Pierfelice. *"Keiner war wie er" Untersuchung zur Struktur von 2 Könige 22–23.* ATSAT 31. St. Ottilien: EOS, 1989.

Talshir, Zipora. *The Alternative Story: 3 Kingdoms 12:24 A–Z.* Jerusalem Biblical Studies 6. Jerusalem: Simor, 1993.

Talstra, E. *Solomon's Prayer.* CBET 3. Kampen: Kok Pharos, 1993.

Thiele, Edwin R. *The Mysterious Numbers of the Hebrew Kings.* Grand Rapids: Kregel, 1983.

Timm, Stefan. *Die Dynastie Omri.* FRLANT 124. Göttingen: Vandenhoeck & Ruprecht, 1982.

Toews, Wesley I. *Monarch and Religious Institution in Israel under Jeroboam I.* SBLMS 47. Atlanta: Scholars Press, 1993.

Trebolle Barrera, Julio C. *Centena in Libros Samuelis et Regum.* Madrid: Consejo Superior de Investigaciones Científicas Instituto de Filología, 1989.

———. *Jehú y Joás. Texto y composición literaria de 2 Reyes 9–11.* Institución San Jerónimo 17. Valencia: Institución San Jerónimo, 1984.

———. *Salomon y Jeroboan.* Institución San Jerónimo 10. Valencia: Institución San Jerónimo, 1980.

Vanoni, Gottfried. *Literarkritik und Grammatik. Untersuchung der Wiederholungen und Spannungen in 1 Kön 11–12.* ATSAT 21. St. Ottilien: EOS, 1984.

Van Seters, John. *In Search of History.* New Haven, Conn.: Yale University Press, 1983.

Volgger, David. *Verbindliche Tora am einzigen Tempel.* ATSAT 61. St. Ottilien: EOS, 1998.

Wächli, Stefan. *Der weise König Salomo.* BWANT 141. Stuttgart: W. Kohlhammer, 1999.

White, Marsha C. *The Elijah Legends and Jehu's Coup.* BJS 311. Atlanta: Scholars Press, 1997.

Articles and Chapters in Books

Aberbach, Moses, and Leivy Smolar. "Aaron, Jeroboam, and the Golden Calves." *JBL* 86 (1967): 129–40.

Ackroyd, Peter R. "An Interpretation of the Babylonian Exile: A Study of II Kings 20 and Isaiah 38–39." *Scottish Journal of Theology* 27 (1974): 329–52.

Alt, Albrecht. "The Monarchy in the Kingdoms of Israel and Judah." Pages 311–35 in *Essays on Old Testament History and Religion.* Garden City, N.Y.: Doubleday, 1967.

Barrick, W. B. "On the Removal of High Places in 1–2 Kings." *Bib* 55 (1974): 255–57.

Becking, Bob. "Jehoiachin's Amnesty, Salvation for Israel? Notes on 2 Kings 25,27–30." Pages 283–93 in *Pentateuchal and Deuteronomistic Studies.* Edited by C. Brekelmans and J. Lust. Leuven: Leuven University Press, 1993.

Begg, Christopher T. "The Significance of Jehoiachin's Release: A New Proposal." *JSOT* 36 (1986): 59–66.

———. "Unifying Factors in 1 Kings 1.2–17a." *JSOT* 32 (1985): 75–86.

Ben Zvi, Ehud. "The Account of the Reign of Manasseh in II Reg 21,1–18 and the Redactional History of the Books of Kings." *ZAW* 103 (1991): 351–74.

Bloch Smith, Elizabeth. "Who is the King of Glory? Solomon's Temple and Its Symbolism." Pages 18–31 in *Scripture and Other Artifacts: Essays on the Bible and Archaeology in Honor of Philip J. King*. Edited by M. D. Coogan et al. Louisville, Ky.: Westminster John Knox, 1994.

Brettler, Marc Z. "The Structure of 1 Kings 1–11." *JSOT* 49 (1991): 87–97.

Carroll, Robert P. "The Elijah-Elisha Sagas: Some Remarks on Prophetic Succession in Ancient Israel." *VT* 19 (1969): 400–415.

Claburn, W. Eugene. "The Fiscal Basis of Josiah's Reforms." *JBL* 92 (1973): 11–22.

Cogan, Mordechai. "Israel in Exile: The View of a Josianic Historian." *JBL* 97 (1978): 40–44.

Cohn, Robert L. "Form and Perspective in 2 Kings V." *VT* 33 (1983): 171–84.

———. "The Literary Logic of 1 Kings 17–19." *JBL* 101 (1982): 333–50.

———. "Literary Techniques in the Jeroboam Narrative." *ZAW* 97 (1985): 23–35.

Cross, Frank M., Jr. "The Themes of the Books of Kings and the Structure of the Deuteronomistic History." Pages 274–89 in Frank Moore Cross Jr., *Canaanite Myth and Hebrew Epic*. Cambridge: Harvard University Press, 1973.

Dietrich, Walter. "Josia und das Gesetzbuch (2 Reg. XXII)." *VT* 27 (1977): 13–35.

Dozeman, Thomas. "The Way of the Man of G-d from Judah: True and False Prophecy in the Pre-Deuteronomic Legend of 1 Kings 13." *CBQ* 44 (1982): 379–93.

Fewell, Dana N. "Sennacherib's Defeat: Words at War in 2 Kings 18.13–19.37." *JSOT* 34 (1986): 79–90.

Finkelstein, Israel. "The Archaeology of the Days of Manasseh." Pages 168–87 in *Scripture and Other Artifacts: Essays on Bible and Archaeology in Honor of Philip J. King*. Edited by M. D. Coogan et al. Louisville, Ky.: Westminster John Knox, 1994.

Friedman, Richard E. "From Egypt to Egypt: Dtr[1] and Dtr[2]." Pages 167–92 in *Traditions in Transformation: Turning Points in Biblical Faith*. Edited by B. Halpern and J. Levenson. Winona Lake, Ind.: Eisenbrauns, 1981.

Frisch, Amos. "The Exodus Motif in 1 Kings 1–14." *JSOT* 87 (2000): 3–21.

———. "Shemaiah the Prophet versus King Rehoboam: Two Opposed Interpretations of the Schism (1 Kings XII 21–4)." *VT* 38 (1988): 466–68.

———. "Structure and Its Significance: The Narrative of Solomon's Reign." *JSOT* 51 (1991): 4–14.

Frost, Stanley Brice. "The Death of Josiah: A Conspiracy of Silence." *JBL* 87 (1968): 369–82.

Gooding, D. W. "The Septuagint's Rival Versions of Jeroboam's Rise to Power." *VT* 17 (1967): 173–89.

Gordon, Robert P. "The Second Septuagint Account of Jeroboam: History or Midrash?" *VT* 25 (1975): 368–93.

Gross, W. "Lying Prophet and Disobedient Man of G-d in 1 Kings 13: Role Analysis as an Instrument of Theological Interpretation of an Old Testament Narrative Text." *Semeia* 15 (1979): 97–135.

Halpern, Baruch. "Jerusalem and the Lineages in the Seventh Century BCE: Kingship and the Rise of Individual Moral Liability." Pages 1–107 in *Law and Ideology in Monarchic Israel.* Edited by B. Halpern and D. W. Hobson. JSOTSup 124. Sheffield: JSOT Press, 1991.

Halpern, Baruch, and David Vanderhooft. "The Editions of Kings in the 7th–6th Centuries." *HUCA* 62 (1991): 179–244.

Haran, Menahem. "The Empire of Jeroboam ben Joash." *VT* 17 (1967): 267–324.

Hauser, Alan J. "YHWH versus Death—The Real Struggle in 1 Kings 17–19." Pages 9–89 in Alan J. Hauser and Russell Gregory, *From Carmel to Horeb.*

Hayes, John H., and Jeffrey K. Kuan. "The Final Years of Samaria (730–720 BC)." *Bib* 72 (1991): 153–81.

Hays, J. Daniel. "Has the Narrator Come to Praise Solomon or to Bury Him? Narrative Subtlety in 1 Kings 1–11." *JSOT* 28 (2003): 149–74.

Ishida, Tomoo. "The People of the Land and the Political Crises of Judah." *AJBI* 1 (1975): 23–38.

Jepsen, Alfred. "G-ttesmann und Prophet. Anmerkungen zum Kapital 1. Könige 13." Pages 171–82 in *Probleme biblischer Theologie.* Edited by H. W. Wolff. Munich: Chr Kaiser, 1971.

Jobling, David. "Forced Labor: Solomon's Golden Age and the Question of Literary Representation." *Semeia* 54 (1991): 57–76.

Knoppers, Gary N. "Prayer and Propaganda: Solomon's Dedication of the Temple and the Deuteronomistic Program." *CBQ* 57 (1995): 229–54.

———. "'There Was None Like Him': Incomparability in the Books of Kings." *CBQ* 54 (1992): 411–31.

LaBarbera, Robert. "The Man of War and the Man of G-d: Social Satire in 2 Kings 6:8–7:20." *CBQ* 46 (1984): 637–51.

Lasine, Stuart. "Jehoram and the Cannibal Mothers (2 Kings 6:24–33): Solomon's Judgment in an Inverted World." *JSOT* 50 (1991): 27–53.

———. "Manasseh as Villain and Scapegoat." Pages 163–83 in *The New Literary Criticism and the Hebrew Bible.* Edited by J. C. Exum and D. J. A. Clines. JSOTSup 143. Sheffield: JSOT Press, 1993.

Lemke, Werner. "The Way of Obedience: 1 Kings 13 and the Structure of the Deuteronomistic History." Pages 301–26 in *Magnalia Dei/The Mighty Acts of G-d.* Edited by F. M. Cross Jr. et al. Garden City, N.Y.: Doubleday, 1976.

Levenson, Jon D. "From Temple to Synagogue: 1 Kings 8." Pages 143–66 in

Traditions in Transformation: Turning Points in Biblical Faith. Edited by Baruch Halpern and Jon D. Levenson. Winona Lake, Ind.: Eisenbrauns, 1981.

———. "The Last Four Verses in Kings." *JBL* 103 (1984): 353–61.

———. "Who Inserted the Book of Torah?" *HTR* 68 (1975): 203–33.

Levin, Christoph. "Joschiaja im deuteronomistischen Geschichtswerk." *ZAW* 96 (1984): 351–71.

Liverani, M. "L'histoire de Joas." *VT* 24 (1974): 438–53.

Lohfink, Norbert. "The Cult Reform of Josiah of Judah: 2 Kings 22–23 as a Source for the History of Israelite Religion." Pages 459–75 in *Ancient Israelite Religion.* Edited by P. D. Miller et al. Philadelphia: Fortress, 1987.

———. "Die Bundesurkunde des Königs Josias." *Bib* 44 (1963): 261–88.

———. "Kerygmata des deuteronomistischen Geschichtswerks." Pages 87–100 in *Die Botschaft und die Boten.* Edited by J. Jeremiah and L. Perlitt. Neukirchen-Vluyn: Neukirchener, 1981.

———. "Zur neuer Diskussion über 2 Kön 22–23." Pages 24–48 in *Das Deuteronomium: Entstehung, Gestalt und Botschaft.* Edited by N. Lohfink. BETL 58. Leuven: Peeters, 1985.

Long, Burke O. "A Darkness between Brothers: Solomon and Adonijah." *JSOT* 19 (1981): 79–94.

Lundbom, Jack R. "Elijah's Chariot Ride." *JJS* 24 (1973): 39–50.

———. "The Lawbook of the Josianic Reform." *CBQ* 38 (1976): 293–302.

Malamat, Abraham. "Aspects of the Foreign Policies of David and Solomon." *JNES* 22 (1963): 1–17.

———. "Josiah's Bid for Armageddon." *JANESCU* 5 (1973): 268–78.

———. "The Kingdom of Judah between Egypt and Babylon: A Small State within a Great Power Confrontation." Pages 117–29 in *Text and Context.* Edited by W. Classen. JSOTSup 48. Sheffield: JSOT Press, 1984.

———. "A Political Look at the Kingdom of David and Solomon and Its Relations with Egypt." Pages 189–204 in *Studies in the Period of David and Solomon and Other Essays.* Edited by T. Ishida. Winona Lake, Ind.: Eisenbrauns, 1982.

———. "The Twilight of Judah in the Egyptian-Babylonian Maelstrom." *VTSup* 28 (1975): 123–43.

McConville, J. G. "1 Kings viii 46–53 and the Deuteronomic Hope." *VT* 42 (1992): 67–79.

McKenzie, Steven L. "The Books of Kings in the Deuteronomistic History." Pages 281–307 in *The History of Israel's Traditions: The Heritage of Martin Noth.* Edited by S. L. McKenzie and M. P. Graham. JSOTSup 182. Sheffield: Sheffield Academic Press, 1994.

———. "The Source for Jeroboam's Role at Shechem (1 Kings 11:43–12:3, 12, 20)." *JBL* 106 (1987): 297–300.

Meyers, Carol L. "Jachin and Boaz in Religious and Political Perspective." *CBQ* 45 (1983): 167–78.

Miller, J. Maxwell. "The Elisha Cycle and the Accounts of the Omride Wars." *JBL* 85 (1966): 441–54.

———. "The Rest of the Acts of Jehoahaz (1 Kings 20. 22,1–38)." *ZAW* 80 (1968): 337–42.

Montgomery, James A. "The Supplement at the End of 3 Kingdoms 2 (1 Reg 2)." *ZAW* 50 (1932): 124–29.

Na'aman, Nadav. "The Historical Background to the Conquest of Samaria (720 BC)." *Bib* 73 (1990): 206–25.

———. "The Kingdom of Judah under Josiah." *TA* 18 (1981): 3–71.

Nelson, Richard D. "Josiah in the Book of Joshua." *JBL* 100 (1981): 531–40.

———. "Realpolitik in Judah (687–609 B.C.E.)." Pages 177–89 in *Scripture in Context II: More Essays on the Comparative Method.* Edited by W. W. Hallo et al. Winona Lake, Ind.: Eisenbrauns, 1983.

Olley, John W. "Pharaoh's Daughter, Solomon's Palace, and the Temple: Another Look at the Structure of 1 Kings 1–11." *JSOT* 27 (2003): 355–69.

Otto, Susanne. "The Composition of the Elijah-Elisha Stories and the Deuteronomistic History." *JSOT* 27 (2003): 487–508.

Parker, K. I. "Repetition as a Structuring Device in 1 Kings 1–11." *JSOT* 42 (1988): 19–27.

———. "Solomon as Philosopher King? The Nexus of Law and Wisdom in 1 Kings 1–11." *JSOT* 53 (1992): 75–91.

Porton, Bezalel. "The Structure and Theme of the Solomon Narrative (1 Kings 3–11)." *HUCA* 38 (1967): 93–128.

Plein, Ina. "Erwägungen zur Überlieferung von 1 Reg 11,26–14,20." *ZAW* 78 (1966): 8–24.

Preuss, Horst Dietrich. "Zum deuteronomistischen Geschichtswerk." *TRu* 58 (1993): 229–64, 341–95.

Rad, Gerhard von. "The Deuteronomic Theology of History in I and II Kings." Pages 205–21 in *The Problem of the Hexateuch and Other Essays.* London: SCM, 1966.

Rainey, Anson F. "Compulsory Labor Gangs in Israel." *IEJ* 20 (1970): 191–202.

Römer, Thomas, and Albert de Pury. "L'historiographie deutéronomiste (HD): Histoire de la recherché et enjeux du débat." Pages 9–120 in *Israël construit son histoire.* Edited by Albert de Pury et al. Geneva: Labor et Fides, 1996.

Roth, Wolfgang. "The Story of the Prophet Micaiah (1 Kings 22) in Historical-Critical Interpretation." Pages 105–37 in *The Biblical Mosaic.* Edited by Robert Polzin and Eugene Rothman. Philadelphia: Fortress, 1982.

Schenker, Adrian. "Jéroboam et la division du royaume dans la Septante ancienne. LXX 1 R 12,24a–z, TM 11–12; 14 et l'histoire deutéronomiste." Pages

193–236 in *Israël construit son histoire*. Edited by Albert de Pury et al. Geneva: Labor et Fides, 1996.

Schniedewind, William S. "History and Interpretation: The Religion of Ahab and Manasseh in the Book of Kings." *CBQ* 55 (1993): 649–61.

Scott, R. B. Y. "Solomon and the Beginnings of Wisdom." *VTSup* 3 (1969): 262–79.

Sekine, M. "Beobachtungen zu der josianischer Reform." *VT* 22 (1972): 361–68.

Seow, Choon Leong. "The Syro-Palestinian Context of Solomon's Dream." *HTR* 77 (1984): 141–52.

Smelik, Klaas A. D. "King Hezekiah Advocates True Prophecy. Remarks on Isaiah xxxvi and xxxvii/II Kings xviii and xix." Pages 93–128 in K. A. D. Smelik, *Converting the Past: Studies in Ancient Israelite and Moabite Historiography.* OTS 28. Leiden: Brill, 1992.

———. "The Portrayal of King Manasseh: A Literary Analysis of II Kings xxi and II Chronicles xxxiii." Pages 129–89 in K. A. D. Smelik, *Converting the Past: Studies in Ancient Israelite and Moabite Historiography.* OTS 28. Leiden: Brill, 1992.

Solomon, Ann. "Jehoash's Fable of the Thistle and the Cedar." Pages 114–32 in *Saga, Legend, Tale, Novella, Fable. Narrative Forms in OT Literature.* Edited by G. W. Coats. JSOTSup 35. Sheffield: Sheffield Academic Press, 1985.

Stade, B. "Anmerkungen zu 2 Kö 15–21." *ZAW* 6 (1886): 172–86.

Steck, Odil Hannes. "Die Erzählung von JHWH's Einschreiten gegen die Orakelbefragung Ahasjas (2 Kön 1,2–8,17)." *EvT* 27 (1967): 546–56.

Sweeney, Marvin A. "The Critique of Solomon in the Josianic Edition of the Deuteronomistic History." *JBL* 114 (1995): 607–22.

———. "King Manasseh of Judah and the Problem of Theodicy in the Deuteronomistic History." Forthcoming in *Good Kings, Bad Kings*. Edited by L. L. Grabbe. JSOTSup. Sheffield: Sheffield Academic Press.

———. "On the Literary Function of the Notice concerning Hiel's Reestablishment of Jericho in 1 Kings 16.34." Pages 104–15 in *Seeing Signals, Reading Signs: The Art of Exegesis.* Edited by M. A. O'Brien and H. N. Wallace. JSOTSup 415. Sheffield: Sheffield Academic Press, 2004.

———. "Synchronic and Diachronic Considerations in the Portrayal of the Demise of Solomon's Kingdom." Forthcoming in an untitled Festschrift for Shalom Paul. Edited by B. J. Schwartz et al. Winona Lake, Ind.: Eisenbrauns.

Tadmor, Hayim. "The People and Kingship in Ancient Israel: The Role of Political Institutions in the Biblical Period." *Cahiers d'histoire mondiale* 11 (1968): 3–23.

Talmon, Shemaryahu. "The Judean 'Am ha'Areṣ in Historical Perspective." Pages 71–76 in *Fourth World Congress of Jewish Studies. Papers.* Volume 1. Jerusalem: World Union of Jewish Studies, 1967.

Thackeray, H. St. John. "The Greek Translators of the Four Books of Kings." *JTS* 8 (1907): 262–78.

Tomes, Roger. "Our Holy and Beautiful House: When and Why Was 1 Kings 6–8 Written?" *JSOT* 70 (1996): 33–50.

Trebolle Barrera, Julio C. "Jeroboam y la Asamblea de Siquen." *Estudios Biblicos* 38 (1979–80): 189–220.

Van Seters, John. "Solomon's Temple: Fact and Ideology in Biblical and Near Eastern Historiography." *CBQ* 59 (1997): 45–57.

Van Winkle, D. W. "1 Kings xiii: True and False Prophecy." *VT* 39 (1989): 31–43.

Viviano, Pauline A. "2 Kings 17: A Rhetorical and Form Critical Analysis." *CBQ* 49 (1987): 548–59.

Walsh, Jerome T. "The Context of 1 Kings xiii." *VT* 39 (1989): 355–70.

Weippert, Helga. "Die deuteronomistischen Beurteilungen der Könige von Israel und Juda und das Problem der Redaktion der Königsbücher." *Bib* 53 (1972): 301–39.

White, Marsha C. "Naboth's Vineyard and Jehu's Coup." *VT* 44 (1994): 66–76.

Whitley, C. F. "The Deuteronomic Presentation of the House of Omri." *VT* 2 (1952): 137–52.

Williams, David S. "Once Again: The Structure of the Narrative of Solomon's Reign." *JSOT* 86 (1999): 49–66.

Williamson, H. G. M. "The Death of Josiah and the Continuing Development of the Deuteronomistic History." *VT* 32 (1982): 242–48.

Wolff, Hans Walter. "The Kerygma of the Deuteronomic Historical Work." Pages 83–100 in *The Vitality of Old Testament Traditions*. Edited by W. Brueggemann and H. W. Wolff. Atlanta: John Knox, 1975.

Wright, George E. "The Provinces of Solomon." *ErIsr* 8 (1967): 58*–68*.

INTRODUCTION

First and Second Kings presents a narrative history of the kingdoms of Israel and Judah from the conclusion of the reign of King David ben Jesse and the ascent of his son Solomon ben David to the throne (ca. 960 B.C.E.) through the release of King Jehoiachin ben Jehoiakim from prison during the Babylonian exile (ca. 560 B.C.E.). These books include accounts of the reigns of all the kings of Israel and Judah, from the united kingdom of David and Solomon, through the revolt of northern Israel from the house of David ca. 920 B.C.E., the destruction of northern Israel by Assyria in 722/721 B.C.E., and the destruction of Judah by the Babylonians in 587/586 B.C.E. Although 1–2 Kings appears as a coherent, self-contained literary unit, it is a component of a larger narrative history of Israel's and Judah's life in the land of Israel including the books of Joshua, Judges, 1–2 Samuel, and 1–2 Kings, known in Jewish tradition as the Former Prophets. These books trace the history of the Israelite people and their relationship with YHWH their G-d from the time of their entry into the land of Canaan under the leadership of Joshua ben Nun, Moses' successor, through the Babylonian exile. They are especially concerned to explain why the people of Israel and Judah were attacked and exiled from their land in order to provide a firm theological foundation for returning to the land and rebuilding their life there in the aftermath of exile.

It is important from the outset to understand the character and meaning of a historical account. History is not simply a recounting of the events or facts of the past. History is written to address the needs of the present and future by studying and learning from past experience to aid in charting a course for present and future action. No history can realistically be expected to account for all events or facts; it must be selective in choosing *what* and *how* to present the past. Any history therefore represents an interpretation of history that is guided by the questions and concerns that motivate the study of history in the first place. The choices made in the presentation of history, the questions and concerns that guide these choices, and the ideological, political, social, and theological perspectives that prompt these questions and concerns constitute the core of historiography. Insofar as historiographical principles are to some degree inherently subjective, the reader of history must come to understand the historiographical perspectives that inform a historical composition in order to assess the view of the past that it presents and the lessons that may be derived from it. The reader runs the risk of error in such an assessment, but that is an obstacle faced in practically every human undertaking. The reader must therefore constantly engage in a self-critical assessment of his or her own reading of history to ensure the fullest possible understanding of the historical narrative and the events upon which it is based. This does not undermine the writing or reading of history; it simply puts the assessment of both on as secure an epistemological foundation as may be possible.

Such concerns are particularly important in reading biblical historical narrative, because the religious truth claims associated with the Bible so frequently influence the historiographical viewpoints of its readers. Because the Bible is generally understood in Western religious tradition to represent divine truth, readers of the Bible throughout history have been reluctant to analyze or to question its truth claims. And yet the age of Enlightenment with its emphasis on empirical observation and rational skepticism as the basis for evaluating truth claims posed precisely such questions to biblical narrative. The archaeological discovery and analysis of material remains from the ancient world and the deciphering of ancient Near Eastern texts from Mesopotamia, Egypt, Aram, and Israel itself have frequently revealed realities and perspectives that might substantially confirm or challenge biblical narrative. Even the Bible presents historical narratives, prophetic and liturgical texts, and other materials that sometimes differ among themselves. These factors prompt a great deal of tension in the field as many scholars, based on their adherence to or rejection of the Bible's truth claims, take extreme positions in reading the Bible's historical literature. Those who defend the Bible's truth claims tend to accept its historical claims at face value, and look for evidence to confirm the veracity of its historical presentation.[1] Those who question the Bible's truth claims often see in the challenges offered by archaeology, ancient Near Eastern literature, and the Bible itself support for their claims that the Bible must be viewed strictly as fiction and therefore discount it as a historical source.[2]

This dichotomy in the field represents a failure to come fully to terms with the purposes of biblical historical literature, particularly insofar as the competing interpretations in the field are based so strictly on the question of whether the events portrayed in the Bible actually took place as described. Instead, readers of biblical historical literature must adopt a middle way in assessing a work

1. E.g., William G. Dever, *What Did the Biblical Writers Know and When Did They Know It? What Archaeology Can Tell Us about the Reality of Ancient Israel* (Grand Rapids: Eerdmans, 2001); Baruch Halpern, *The First Historians: The Hebrew Bible and History* (San Francisco: Harper and Row, 1988).

2. E.g., Thomas L. Thompson, *The Mythic Past: Biblical Archaeology and the Myth of Israel* (London: Basic Books, 1999); Keith W. Whitelam, *The Invention of Ancient Israel: The Silencing of Palestinian History* (London and New York: Routledge, 1996).

like 1–2 Kings. The reader must be prepared to evaluate archaeological sources, ancient Near Eastern texts, and the overall literary presentation of 1–2 Kings to ask how history is presented and how that presentation corresponds to other sources both within the Bible and without. If the account in Kings corresponds with the evidence presented by other sources, Kings likely presents a verifiable account of the past. But when it differs, the reader must ask why. The reader must be attentive to theological and historiographical perspectives worked into the text—that is, to what extent and why does it take up matters of theology, divine purpose, human observance of the will of the divine, and so forth? And to what extent and how does the narrative serve that historiographical or theological agenda?

First and Second Kings does not simply offer a historically verifiable account of the past. First and Second Kings is designed to answer the question of why Israel and Judah were exiled by arguing that the people of Israel and Judah, particularly their monarchs, failed to observe YHWH's Torah, and thereby called divine punishment upon themselves. In making such a presentation of history, 1–2 Kings is sharply critical of the kings of Israel and Judah for prompting the people to forgo observance of YHWH's expectations. First and Second Kings must therefore be recognized not simply as a work of history, but as a work of theodicy as well, insofar as it defends the notion of divine righteousness by arguing that the people and especially its kings—and not YHWH—were at fault for the destruction and exiles of Israel and Judah. In making such a presentation, 1–2 Kings also lays a foundation for the restoration of the people to the land. By pointing to the demise of the kings of Israel and Judah and by consistently calling for the observance of YHWH's expectations as expressed in divine Torah, 1–2 Kings lays a foundation for the restoration of the people to the land, based on divine Torah. The foundation of such a restored community based on Torah and centered on the temple in Jerusalem by Ezra and Nehemiah represents an attempt to implement the lessons of the past learned from 1–2 Kings and the Former Prophets at large.

Such an agenda is evident in the final form of 1–2 Kings and the Former Prophets (a.k.a. Deuteronomistic History or DtrH) as a whole.[3] There is evidence of earlier editions of 1–2 Kings and its role in the Former Prophets. These

---

3. Martin Noth, *The Deuteronomistic History* (JSOTSup 15; Sheffield: JSOT Press, 1981), developed the hypothesis that the Former Prophets constituted a Deuteronomistic History (DtrH) that presented an account of Israel's history based on the theological perspectives of the book of Deuteronomy; see Steven L. McKenzie, "Deuteronomistic History," *ABD* 2:160–68; Horst Dietrich Preuss, "Zum deuteronomistischen Geschichtswerk," *TRu* 58 (1993): 229–64, 341-95; Thomas Römer and Albert de Pury, "L'historiographie deutéronomiste (HD): Historie de la recherché et enjeux du débat" in A. de Pury et al., eds., *Israël construit son histoire* (Geneva: Labor et Fides, 1996), 9–120; Marvin A. Sweeney, *King Josiah of Judah: The Lost Messiah of Israel* (Oxford and New York: Oxford University Press, 2001), 21–32.

editions include a final exilic edition of the DtrH from the mid-sixth century B.C.E. that sought to address the problems posed by the Babylonian exile by pointing to the kings of Israel and Judah as a source for divine punishment; a Josianic edition of the DtrH from the late seventh century B.C.E. that sought to identify the sins of the northern kings of Israel as the source for divine punishment and the reign of the righteous Josiah as the means to address that issue; a Hezekian edition of the DtrH from the late eighth century B.C.E. that sought to explain the suffering of northern Israel based on its inability to produce competent and righteous rulers and to point to Hezekiah as an example of the leadership needed; a Jehu edition of Samuel–Kings from the early eighth century B.C.E. that saw the rise of the house of Jehu as the means to ensure the security of the nation and to restore the past glories of the age of Solomon; and finally a Solomonic edition of Samuel–Kings from the late tenth century B.C.E. that sought to present the house of David as the key to the well-being of the united people of Israel and Judah. Each of these editions is treated in the following pages.

The Exilic Edition of 1–2 Kings in the Context of the Deuteronomistic History

The present form of 1–2 Kings in its entirety functions as an important element of the exilic edition of the Deuteronomistic History.[4] This statement does not mean that the entire text of 1–2 Kings or the DtrH for that matter was written by an exilic author, but it does mean that the entire present text of 1–2 Kings was redactionally incorporated into the exilic edition of the DtrH. Although some elements of the text were composed as part of the exilic edition of 1–2 Kings and the DtrH, most of the text appears to have constituted an earlier edition of the work, which calls for consideration of both the synchronic and the diachronic dimensions of the text.[5] It functions synchronically or ahistorically as a literary whole regardless of the settings of its composition or the intentions of its authors. It functions diachronically as a historically conditioned text that reflects both the concerns of its various authors and the settings of its composition.

4. For discussion of exilic editions of the DtrH, see Noth, *Deuteronomistic History*; Rudolph Smend, "Das Gesetz und die Völker. Ein Beitrag zur deuteronomistischen Redaktionsgeschichte," *Probleme biblischer Theologie* (Fest. G. von Rad; ed. H. W. Wolff; Munich: Chr. Kaiser, 1971), 494–509; Walter Dietrich, *Prophetie und Geschichte* (FRLANT 108; Göttingen: Vandenhoeck & Ruprecht, 1972); Timo Veijola, *Das Königtum in der Beurteilung der deuteronomistischen Historiographie. Eine redaktionsgeschichtliche Untersuchung* (Helsinki: Suomalainen Tiedeakatemia, 1977).
5. For the distinction between synchronic and diachronic readings, see my "Form Criticism," in *To Each Its Own Meaning: An Introduction to Biblical Criticisms and Their Application* (ed. S. L. McKenzie and S. R. Haynes; Louisville, Ky.: Westminster John Knox, 1999), 58–89.

As a component of the DtrH, 1–2 Kings provides an account of the concluding stage of Israel's existence in the land of Israel. Joshua, Judges, and Samuel each form a self-standing component of the larger literary work. Joshua relates Israel's entry into the land under Joshua. Judges provides an account of Israel's premonarchic period. First and Second Samuel provides an account of Israel's establishment of a central monarchy, first under Saul and later under David. First and Second Kings provides an account of the history of that centralized monarchy from the reigns of David and Solomon, through the dissolution of the centralized monarchy into the kingdoms of Israel and Judah, the destruction of the Israelite kingdom by Assyria in the late eighth century, and the destruction of the Judean kingdom in the early sixth century.

This highly theologized account of Israel's and Judah's history attempts to explain why Judah and Israel—or more properly, the Davidic monarchy—came to an end and how this lesson might influence any attempt to restore Israelite or Judean life in the land. The account in Joshua through Kings is highly dependent on the book of Deuteronomy and the understanding of divine Torah expressed there. Deuteronomy presents a series of addresses by Moses to the people of Israel on the eve of their entry into the land of Canaan, in which Moses reiterates the divine Torah revealed at Mount Sinai and the need to observe that Torah as the basis for life in the land. The blessings and curses in Deut 28–30 make this especially clear—namely, if the people observe YHWH's will, they will be secure in the land; if they fail to observe YHWH's will, they will suffer foreign invasion and exile. Readers should note that Deuteronomy does not consider exile to be the end of the matter. Deuteronomy 30 anticipates that exile will lead to repentance on the part of the people and subsequent restoration once the punishment has run its course.

The account of Israel's history in Joshua through Kings emphasizes throughout the importance of the people's adherence to YHWH's expectations as expressed through divine Torah or instruction. When they observe YHWH's Torah, they dwell securely; when they do not observe YHWH's Torah, they suffer. This theological perspective appears at key points throughout the history—for example, Joshua's initial speech to the people in which he adjures them to observe YHWH's Torah as they prepare to take possession of the land (Josh 1); Joshua's speech to the people at Shechem as he reiterates the covenant and reminds them of their obligation to observe YHWH's Torah (Josh 24; see also Josh 23); the narrative portrayal of YHWH's decision to punish the people in the premonarchic period when they turned to other gods and to deliver them when they repent (Judg 1–2); Samuel's speeches to the people in which he reminds them of their obligation to observe YHWH's will at the inauguration of the monarchy (1 Sam 8; 12); Nathan's adjuration that David and his sons must observe YHWH's will at the foundation of the Davidic dynasty (2 Sam 7); Solomon's speech emphasizing the need for observance of divine Torah at the foundation of the temple (1 Kgs 8); the narrative sermon explaining the fall of the northern kingdom of Israel as a result of the failure of the northern kings and their people to observe divine Torah (2 Kgs 17); and the repeated references to YHWH's decision to destroy Jerusalem as a result of Manasseh's failures to abide by YHWH's expectations (2 Kgs 21:10–15; cf. 23:26–27; 24:3–4).

The present form of 1–2 Kings clearly expresses this theological view of history in its presentation of the experience of the Israelite and Judean monarchies. Its culmination in the Babylonian exile points to the ultimate concerns of this work, namely, to explain the Babylonian exile as an act of divine punishment for the people's failure to observe divine Torah. The text thereby constitutes a form of theodicy insofar as it absolves YHWH, the divine patron and protector of Israel, from responsibility for the Babylonian exile and instead focuses on the wrongdoing of the people as the fundamental cause of the disaster. One must note that 1–2 Kings does not end with the exile per se, but with an account of the release of King Jehoiachin ben Jehoiakim from prison by the Babylonian monarch, Evil Merodach (Amel Marduk), the son of Nebuchadnezzar, who ruled during the years 562–560 B.C.E. prior to his overthrow by Nergalsharrezer in a coup. One must also note that the text blames King Manasseh ben Amon alone for the destruction of Jerusalem, whereas material prior to the account of Manasseh's reign in 2 Kgs 21:1–18 takes a far more collective stance, that is, the kings led the people in turning away from YHWH's expectations. The concluding chapters of Kings show a marked interest in individual monarchs of the house of David in relation to the question of the Babylonian exile.

Interpreters are accustomed to considering 1–2 Kings as a history of Israel and Judah or as a history of the kings of Israel and Judah, but 1–2 Kings is formulated specifically as a history of the house of David from the conclusion of David's lifetime and Solomon's accession to the throne through the reign of Jehoiachin ben Jehoiakim, the last monarch of the Davidic line. The kings of northern Israel also figure prominently, but they drop from view in 2 Kgs 17 following the destruction of northern Israel, serving more as foils for the presentation of the Davidic kings who dominate the work from beginning to end. The concerns with the Davidic monarchy are expressed in the earlier books of Deuteronomy and the Former Prophets as well. Deuteronomy calls for worship of YHWH at only one site, which was the pattern for worship in Davidic Judah centered at the temple in Jerusalem. The portrayal of Joshua in the book of Joshua is dependent upon the portrayal of the Davidic monarch Josiah ben Amon,[6] who in turn is portrayed as the ideal Davidic monarch of the Former Prophets. Judges emphasizes the failures of the northern judges in their attempts to unify and protect the nation, and ultimately prepares the reader for the introduction of Judean Davidic kingship as the means to overcome the failures of

---

6. Richard D. Nelson, "Josiah in the Book of Joshua," *JBL* 100 (1981): 531–40.

the northern tribes.[7] First and Second Samuel presents an account of the rise of David to kingship following the failure of the Saulide monarchy.[8]

Consideration of the literary form of 1–2 Kings demonstrates this fundamental concern with the house of David against the backdrop of the Babylonian exile, which brought the dynasty to a conclusion. First and Second Kings is formulated as a distinctive and coherent literary block within the Former Prophets. Although it builds upon 1–2 Samuel, 1–2 Kings has its own literary introduction. First and Second Samuel concludes with a block of material in 2 Sam 21–24 that presents diverse elements, including David's role in handing over the sons of Saul to Gibeon for execution, David's psalm of thanksgiving, his last words, a roster of his warriors, and narratives concerning David's census of Israel and the selection of the site for the future temple. These materials stand outside the narrative structure of 1–2 Samuel and are generally regarded as appendices. But their placement at the end of Samuel also clears the way for 1–2 Kings to begin with a new introduction that both establishes continuity with the books of Samuel and prepares the reader for a very new stage in Israel's history. The narrative begins in 1 Kgs 1:1–2:11 and 2:12–46a with accounts of the means by which Solomon was designated as the successor of the aged King David and followed David's advice to secure his hold on the throne. Many scholars identify this material as the conclusion to the so-called Succession Narrative or Court History in 2 Sam 9/11–20, but such a view is based strictly on a diachronic reading of the presumed compositional history of the text. First Kings 1:1–2:11; 2:12–46a build upon the earlier material by focusing on David's sons, Nathan, Bath Sheba, and Solomon, all of whom figure prominently in 2 Samuel. But having been set off from the earlier narrative by the appendices in 2 Sam 21–24, 1 Kgs 1:1–2:11; 2:12–46a introduce the history of the kings in 1–2 Kings insofar as 1 Kgs 1:1–2:11 provides an account of David's death and Solomon's selection as his heir and 1 Kgs 2:12–46a provides an introduction to the reign of Solomon with an account of his actions to secure his father's throne. These segments fill this introductory role far more capably than they function as a conclusion to Samuel or the Succession Narrative. They lay the groundwork for the future of the house of David from the time of Solomon on, precisely the concern of 1–2 Kings.

Following 1 Kgs 1:1–2:11, the series of subunits in 1 Kgs 2:12–46a; 2:46b–4:20; and 5:1–14:20 together present an account of Solomon's reign and its consequences, namely, the revolt of the northern tribes against the house of David. Beginning with the reign of Rehoboam ben Solomon in 1 Kgs 14:21 and continuing through the conclusion of the book with the reign of Zedekiah ben

7. Marvin A. Sweeney, "Davidic Polemics in the Book of Judges," *VT* 47 (1997): 517–29.

8. Antony F. Campbell, S.J., *1 Samuel* (FOTL 7; Grand Rapids and Cambridge: Eerdmans, 2003), 167–294; Campbell, *2 Samuel* (FOTL 8; Grand Rapids and Cambridge: Eerdmans, 2005), 15–86.

Josiah and its consequences in 2 Kgs 24:18–25:30, the literary structure of
1–2 Kings is constituted by a sequence of regnal reports, which present and
evaluate the reigns of each of the kings of Israel and Judah according to a stereotypical generic form.[9] Although individual examples of the regnal report vary
widely, they adhere to a rather rigid standard form that includes three elements.
The first is the introductory regnal formula that includes the name of the king,
his age at accession, the years of his reign, and an evaluation of his reign in the
eyes of YHWH. The second is the body of the regnal account, which is a freely
composed narrative that provides an account of the major events of the king's
reign. The third is the concluding regnal formula, a standardized element that
makes reference to the rest of the acts of the king in the Chronicles of the Kings
of Israel or Judah, the death of the king, his burial, and his successor on the
throne. This basic form constitutes the literary structure of the narrative from
1 Kgs 14:21 through the conclusion of 2 Kgs 25:30. There are a few instances
of narratives that stand outside of the standard form, but these instances must
be regarded as appendices to the preceding regnal account. The following dia-
gram illustrates the literary structure of 1–2 Kings:

I. The Death of David and Designation of Solomon
      as His Successsor   1 Kings 1:1–2:11
II. Regnal Account of Solomon ben David   2:12–14:20
    Solomon Secures His Throne   2:12–46a
    Solomon's Subsequent Rule   2:46b–4:19
    Solomon's Reign and Its Consequences   4:20–14:20
      Solomon's Wealth and Power   4:20–5:32
      Solomon's Construction of the Temple Complex
        and Royal Palace   6:1–9:9
        Palace and Temple Complex   6:1–7:12
        The Construction of the Temple Implements   7:13–51
        Solomon's Dedication of the Temple   8:1–66
        Solomon's Second Encounter with YHWH   9:1–9
    The Rise of Solomon's Adversaries   9:10–11:40
      Introduction   9:10
      Solomon's Association with Hiram of Tyre   9:11–28
      Solomon's Association with the Queen of Sheba   10:1–29
      Solomon's Apostasy   11:1–25
      The Rise of Jeroboam ben Nebat   11:26–40

9. Contra many scholars who argue that the structure of 1–2 Kgs includes segments on Solomon
in 1 Kgs 1–11, the downfall of Israel in 1 Kgs 12–2 Kgs 17, and the downfall of Judah in 2 Kgs
18–25 (e.g., Richard D. Nelson, *The Historical Books* [IBT; Nashville: Abingdon, 1998], 129–31).
For discussion of the regnal account form, see Burke O. Long, *1 Kings, with an Introduction to Historical Literature* (FOTL 9; Grand Rapids: William B. Eerdmans, 1984), 158–65, 259.

This structure of 1–2 Kings highlights its concern with presenting a history of the house of David, insofar as it begins and ends with the first and last monarchs of the Davidic line. It also treats the various dynasties that ruled northern Israel, but these appear as foils to the house of David insofar as the northern kingdom emerges in revolt against the house of David and disappears from the scene well before the conclusion of the work. Indeed, 1–2 Kings portrays the emergence of the northern kingdom as the result of dissatisfaction with the rule of Solomon, both by the tribes of Israel, who regard him as an oppressive monarch, and by YHWH, who regards him as an apostate monarch. Although the revolt of the northern tribes is divinely sanctioned, the pagan religious practice of Jeroboam ben Nebat, the first northern king, provides the basis for a pattern of apostasy in the northern kingdom that results in the condemnation of every northern king and Assyria's ultimate destruction of the northern kingdom of Israel.

Interpreters have been largely content to note that northern Israel serves as a foil or model for the southern kingdom of Judah, while contending that 1–2 Kings is concerned fundamentally with presenting a history of all the kings of Israel and Judah.[10] But such a position overlooks the literary role played by the northern kingdom in undermining the house of David well beyond its disappearance in 2 Kgs 17, which occurs by means of the linkage between the northern house of Omri and the house of David. The remarkable charge in 2 Kgs 21:10–15 that King Manasseh ben Hezekiah was solely responsible for the destruction of Jerusalem and Judah stands in stunning contrast to the portrayal of royal wrongdoing and punishment in the balance of the book.[11] There the apostate northern (and southern) kings lead their people into wrongdoing with the result that the entire nation is held accountable for the ensuing punishment. But Manasseh breaks this pattern; he causes Judah to sin, but YHWH's decision to destroy Jerusalem and Judah is consistently presented as the result of *Manasseh's* sins, not those of the people. First and Second Kings therefore calls for close attention to his reign.

That the text makes an explicit comparison of Manasseh's apostasy with that of Ahab ben Omri of northern Israel (2 Kgs 21:3) is striking. Since most interpreters correctly observe that Jeroboam ben Nebat sets the pattern for apostasy among the northern kings, Ahab's mention here has attracted little attention. Ahab is the primary monarch of the house of Omri, which is condemned to complete destruction by the prophet Elijah as a result of Ahab's murder of Naboth of Jezreel in a bid to appropriate his vineyard (1 Kgs 21). Insofar as the house of Omri is overthrown by Jehu in 2 Kgs 9–10, one would seemingly not need to be concerned with the house of Omri again. But while all male members of the house of Omri are killed in Jehu's revolt, Ahab's sister Athaliah bat Omri

10. E.g., Frank M. Cross Jr., "The Themes of the Books of Kings and the Structure of the Deuteronomistic History," in *Canaanite Myth and Hebrew Epic* (Cambridge: Harvard University Press, 1973), 274–89.

11. Marvin A. Sweeney, "King Manasseh of Judah and the Problem of Theodicy in the Deuteronomistic History," in *Good Kings, Bad Kings* (ed. L. L. Grabbe; JSOTSup; Sheffield: Sheffield Academic Press, forthcoming); cf. Sweeney, *King Josiah,* 52–63.

survives because she is married to King Ahaziah ben Jehoshaphat of Judah. She nearly destroys the entire house of David in her bid to seize the throne of Judah, but her infant son, Joash ben Ahaziah, survives to reclaim the throne after Athaliah herself is overthrown in a coup led by the priest Jehoiada.

This incident is crucial to the history of the house of David. From the time of Joash on, the entire house of David is also descended from the house of Omri. The house of David therefore becomes subject to the judgment pronounced by Elijah against Ahab and the house of Omri (1 Kgs 21:17–29), which helps to explain the explicit parallel drawn between the actions of Ahab and those of Manasseh, who follows in the tradition of his Omride ancestral line. It also helps to explain the portrayal of the death of his righteous grandson, Josiah ben Amon, who is granted the right to die in peace by the prophet Huldah before the judgment against Jerusalem and Judah is carried out (2 Kgs 22:11–20). Just as Ahab was granted the right to die before seeing the destruction of his house because of his repentance, so Josiah's repentance won him the right to die before seeing the destruction of Jerusalem and Judah. The fate of the house of Omri was ultimately realized in the fate of the house of David in 1–2 Kings.

The fundamental relationship between the house of David and the house of Omri in 1–2 Kings also comes to expression at the beginning and the end of the work. The problems in the house of David begin with Solomon, who is portrayed as apostate in his efforts to establish sanctuaries for the gods of his foreign wives in 1 Kgs 11. Indeed, his marriage to foreign women violates one of the fundamental instructions of Deuteronomy to avoid marriage with the Canaanite nations because they will lead Israel to serve foreign gods (Deut 7:1–6). Solomon's wives included more than just the standard listing of Canaanite nations from Deuteronomy; 1 Kgs 3:1–2; 7:8; 9:16, 24; and 11:1 highlight his marriage to the daughter of Pharaoh, the very embodiment of the enemy of YHWH as portrayed in Deuteronomy. The text also recounts his efforts to impose forced labor on his people to build the temple and his own palace, to trade with Egypt in chariots and horses, and to send Israelites back across the Red Sea in pursuit of trading relations. In short, Solomon effectively becomes a pharaohlike figure during his reign. He violates every prohibition required of a righteous king in Deut 17:14–20, the so-called Torah of the King that prohibits the king from leading the people into apostasy; from amassing to himself wives, silver, and gold; and from returning the people to Egypt.[12] It is no accident that Solomon's second vision of YHWH in 1 Kgs 9:1–9 reiterates the command to observe YHWH's will or suffer the consequences: removal of the

12. Pekka Särkiö, *Die Weisheit und Macht Salomos in der Israelitischen Historiographie* (Schriften der Finnischen Exegetischen Gesellschaft 60; Helsinki: Finnische Exegetische Gesellschaft; Göttingen: Vandenhoeck & Ruprecht, 1994); Marvin A. Sweeney, "The Critique of Solomon in the Josianic Edition of the Deuteronomistic History," *JBL* 114 (1995): 607–22.

Davidic monarchy from the throne and exile from the land. At the very outset of the history of the Davidic dynasty, 1–2 Kings anticipates the exile and the removal of the Davidic house in keeping with the perspectives of Deuteronomy.

Finally, one must consider the conclusion of 1–2 Kings with its accounts of the destruction of Jerusalem, the capture and exile of King Zedekiah ben Josiah, and the release of King Jehoiachin ben Jehoiakim from Babylonian prison. The portrayal of Jehoiachin's release has been interpreted both as a representation of the end of the Davidic line and as an expression of hope for Judah's restoration.[13] Although the latter interpretation might be attractive as an indication that the DtrH looks to the future as well as to the past, the intertextual links between this final episode in Kings and elsewhere in the DtrH call for acceptance of the former interpretation. Jehoiachin is viewed as the last legitimate, ruling monarch of the Davidic line, insofar as his uncle Zedekiah was installed as a Babylonian puppet following Jehoiachin's exile. The release from prison offers a sense of hope for the future, but it is crucial to note that Jehoiachin never returns to Jerusalem or to royal authority as he continues to live in Babylon supported by the Babylonian king. None of Jehoiachin's descendants ever regains the throne in Jerusalem. The history of the Davidic dynasty ends with Jehoiachin regardless of the role the house of David plays in the conceptualization of messiahs in later Jewish or Christian tradition.[14]

Zedekiah's fate also demands consideration. He is clearly a puppet king who was unable to control his own population. The resulting revolt against Babylon was a disaster that saw the end of Jerusalem and the Davidic house. It is striking that Zedekiah makes a bid for escape from the doomed city only to be captured by the Babylonians on the Araboth or plains of Jericho. Although interpreters tend to focus on his judgment at Riblah, his capture at Jericho is especially noteworthy because of its role in expressing Israel's possession of the land of Israel and because of Jericho's role in expressing the decline of Israel under the Omride dynasty. Jericho is the first Canaanite city captured by Joshua upon Israel's entry into the promised land (Josh 6), and it thereby marks the first stage in Israel's possession of the land. Joshua 6:26 notes that the man who rebuilds Jericho will do so only at the cost of his sons. The seemingly irrelevant notice in 1 Kgs 16:34 that Hiel of Beth El rebuilt Jericho at the cost of his own sons marks the reign of Omri and points to the ultimate exiles of Israel, Judah, and Jerusalem, culminating in the reign of Omri's descendant Zedekiah. Zedekiah's

13. For readings of Jehoiachin's release from prison as a sign of judgment against the house of David, see Noth, *Deuteronomistic History*, 12, 74, 98; Hans Walter Wolff, "The Kerygma of the Deuteronomic Historical Work," in *The Vitality of Old Testament Traditions* (ed. W. Brueggemann and H. W. Wolff; Atlanta: John Knox, 1975), 85–86. For a reading that emphasizes potential restoration of the monarchy, see Gerhard von Rad, *Studies in Deuteronomy* (SBT 9; London: SCM, 1947), 74–91.

14. Cf. Mephiboseth, the son of Jonathan and grandson of Saul, who likewise eats at David's table (2 Sam 9:13) and renounces any claim to his father's/grandfather's inheritance (2 Sam 19:5–31).

capture at Jericho indicates that Israel has come full circle, namely, possession of the land begins and ends at Jericho.[15]

The portrayal of the end of the Davidic dynasty through the capture of Zedekiah at Jericho and the submission of Jehoiachin to Evil Merodach justifies the exilic setting for the composition of the final edition of the DtrH. Evil Merodach (Amel Marduk; r. 562–560 B.C.E.) was the son of Nebuchadnezzar and the last king of Nabopolassar's dynastic line. The narrative seems to know nothing of the coup d'état that swept Amel Marduk from the throne. The composition of the exilic DtrH must be dated to the reign of Evil Merodach. With its portrayal of the demise of the house of David, the exilic edition of 1–2 Kings would be read in relation to the acceptance of Persian rule as an expression of the will of YHWH in Ezra–Nehemiah.[16] As part of his effort to implement YHWH's Torah as the foundation for Judean life under Persian rule, Ezra recites the history of the nation, including the history that comes to expression in the DtrH as a whole. This constitutes recognition in Ezra–Nehemiah of the lessons taught by the DtrH; the kings of Israel and Judah, most notably the house of David, failed to prompt the people to observe divine Torah and thereby to secure their hold on the land as promised by YHWH. In setting up a restored nation in Jerusalem, centered at the temple and based upon divine Torah, Ezra implements the lessons of the DtrH in a bid to try again.

The exilic edition of the DtrH draws heavily on the earlier Josianic edition of the work, but various elements point to exilic editing and composition. Scholars have noted the distinctive formulation of the regnal evaluations in the regnal accounts of Jehoahaz ben Josiah (2 Kgs 23:31–35), Jehoiakim ben Josiah (2 Kgs 23:36–24:7), Jehoiachin ben Jehoiakim (2 Kgs 24:8–17), and Zedekiah ben Josiah (2 Kgs 24:18–25:30).[17] The distinctive forms and content of these compositions mark them as the work of the exilic edition of the DtrH. The regnal accounts of Manasseh ben Hezekiah (2 Kgs 21:1–18) and Amon ben Manasseh display similarities with these accounts as well, which suggest that they too were edited by the exilic DtrH.[18] Furthermore, the present forms of the reg-

15. Marvin A. Sweeney, "On the Literary Function of the Notice concerning Hiel's Reestablishment of Jericho in 1 Kings 16.34," in *Seeing Signals, Reading Signs: The Art of Exegesis* (ed. M. A. O'Brien and H. N. Wallace; JSOTSup 415; Sheffield: Sheffield Academic Press, 2004), 104–15.

16. Ezra–Nehemiah portrays Ezra's return to Jerusalem as a fulfillment of the book of Isaiah (see Klaus Koch, "Ezra and the Origins of Judaism," *JSS* 19 [1974]: 173–97), and follows the view expressed in the final form of the book of Isaiah that Cyrus—and not a Davidic monarch—serves as YHWH's temple builder and messiah in place of the Davidic monarch (see Marvin A. Sweeney, "Isaiah and Theodicy after the Shoah," *Strange Fire: Reading the Bible after the Holocaust* [BibSem 71; ed. T. Linafelt; Sheffield: Sheffield Academic Press, 2000], 208–19).

17. Helga Weippert, "Die 'deuteronomistischen' Beurteilungen der Könige von Israel und Juda und das Problem der Redaktion der Königsbücher," *Bib* 53 (1972): 301–39.

18. Sweeney, *King Josiah*, 36.

nal accounts of Manasseh ben Hezekiah (2 Kgs 21:1–18) and Josiah ben Amon (2 Kgs 22:1–23:30) both anticipate the destruction of Jerusalem. The expression of such a concern therefore indicates that they have been subject to exilic redaction, even though much of the narrative may have been originally composed as part of the Josianic DtrH.[19]

First and Second Kings in the Josianic Edition of the DtrH

Although the present form of 1–2 Kings and the Former Prophets at large ultimately focuses on the problem of the Babylonian exile, considerable evidence survives of literary and conceptual tension within these works that points to the existence of earlier editions of 1–2 Kings and the DtrH. One of the most cogent hypotheses for an earlier edition is the proposed Josianic edition of 1–2 Kings and the DtrH.[20] A variety of grounds exist for this proposed edition.

One of the most important bases for the proposed Josianic DtrH is the tension in the presentation of the Babylonian exile and the reign of King Josiah ben Amon of Judah (2 Kgs 22:1–23:30). Despite the overriding emphasis on the coming Babylonian exile in the regnal accounts of the last kings of Judah, the account of Josiah's reign presents a monarch who appears to function as the ideal monarch of the Davidic line and all of the kings of Israel. He engages in temple reform that both centralizes the worship of YHWH among the people of Israel/Judah and purifies it of pagan influence in keeping with the commands of Deuteronomy. He dismantles the various pagan religious installations placed in Jerusalem, Judah, and Israel by earlier kings, including the horses dedicated to the sun, the altars on the roof of the upper chamber of Ahaz, the altars of Manasseh in the temple courts, the high places around Jerusalem built by Solomon for his foreign wives, the altar at Beth El established by King Jeroboam ben Nebat of Israel, as well as many other high places, cultic pillars, asherim, and so forth, in an effort to purify the cultic practice of his nation. Indeed, his temple reform and reconstitution of the covenant is based on the discovery of a book of Torah found during the course of temple renovations that appears to be Deuteronomy or at least an early version of

19. Although the regnal account of Hezekiah ben Ahaz is well known for its concluding prophecy by Isaiah that Hezekiah's sons would ultimately be carried off to exile in Babylon, this work seems to have anticipated an earlier edition of Manasseh's regnal account (for discussion, see the commentary). The portrayal of Solomon's second vision of YHWH in 1 Kgs 9:1–9, in which YHWH tells Solomon that his dynasty could come to an end, that the temple might be cast away, and that the people might be exiled for failing to observe divine Torah also points to exilic retouching of an earlier narrative (see commentary below).

20. Cross, "Themes"; Richard D. Nelson, *The Double Redaction of the Deuteronomistic History* (JSOTSup 18; Sheffield: JSOT Press, 1981); Gary N. Knoppers, *Two Nations under G-d: The Deuteronomistic History of Solomon and the Dual Monarchies* (HSM 52–53; Atlanta: Scholars Press, 1993–94); Sweeney, *King Josiah*; Antony F. Campbell and Mark A. O'Brien, *Unfolding the Deuteronomistic History: Origins, Upgrades, Present Text* (Minneapolis: Fortress, 2000).

the book insofar as his program is so closely aligned with Deuteronomic law. Furthermore, his destruction of the Beth El altar and his death at Megiddo indicate an effort to reunite Israel and Judah around the worship of YHWH in the Jerusalem temple and under the rule of the house of David as in the days of Solomon. Cross observes that the sins of all of the kings of northern Israel, beginning with Jeroboam ben Nebat, provide a counterpoint to the righteousness of Josiah.[21] Josiah emerges as the monarch who corrects the sins of all the past monarchs of Israel and Judah.[22]

The DtrH builds the reader's expectations for Josiah. As noted above, the book of Joshua presents Joshua as an ideal leader, whose portrayal appears to be based on that of Josiah. He unites the people in the land of Israel, purges the people of moral and cultic wrongdoing by calling for observance of YHWH's Torah, and engages in a covenant ceremony much like that of Josiah's; moreover, he and Josiah are the only leaders of Israel to observe Passover. When Jeroboam ben Nebat builds the illegitimate altar at Beth El and offers incense at it, an unnamed prophet announces that one day a son of the house of David named Josiah will destroy the altar (1 Kgs 13:1–10), a prophesy that is fulfilled in the account of Josiah's reign. Josiah is hardly unique among those kings of Judah who are considered righteous. But the formulaic qualifications that "he did not turn aside to the right or to the left" (2 Kgs 22:2) and that "before him there was no king like him who turned with all his heart, with all his soul, and with all his might according to all the Torah of Moses" (2 Kgs 23:25) surpass the praise granted to righteous kings by drawing respectively on language employed in Deut 17:20 and Josh 1:7 (cf. Deut 6:5) to describe the ideal conduct expected of the king. This language puts him on a par with Moses and Joshua, an evaluation that not even David enjoys in the DtrH. Indeed, David's adultery with Bath Sheba and murder of her husband Uriah points to a flaw in David that Josiah does not share.

With such a resounding and well-grounded buildup for Josiah, it is difficult to understand the presentation of his early death at Megiddo and the ultimate destruction of Jerusalem and Judah by the Babylonians. Josiah's righteousness is clearly recognized and anticipated throughout the DtrH, but it is not enough to overturn YHWH's decision to destroy Jerusalem on account of the sins of Manasseh. Wrongdoing in the DtrH was always presented as a collective issue, that is, Israel as a whole sinned even though they were led into such action by the idolatrous kings of northern Israel. By contrast, Jerusalem and Judah were destroyed because of the sins of one man, King Manasseh of Judah. The portrayal of Josiah's early death comes as quite a surprise; he has been touted throughout the DtrH as the epitome of Israelite righteousness, his reform mea-

21. Cross, "Themes," 278–85.
22. Sweeney, *King Josiah,* 21–177.

sures realize all of the goals of Deuteronomy, and his reign appears to be the culmination of Israel's history, but he dies at Megiddo at the hands of Pharaoh Necho of Egypt (the very nation from which Israel is delivered in Deuteronomy!). Twenty-two years later, Jerusalem and Judah are destroyed, and the people are exiled from the land.

Considerable literary tension points also to a redactional reworking of a Josianic DtrH into the present exilic narrative. The introductory regnal formulae for all of the monarchs following Josiah—namely, Jehoahaz, Jehoiakim, Jehoiachin, and Zedekiah—all display a distinctive form, "and he did evil in the eyes of YHWH according to all that his fathers/father/Jehoiakim did."[23] This form differs from the formula applied to pre-Josian kings, which makes no such reference to the fathers. A similar formula appears for Amon, which refers to his own father Manasseh. Of course, the present form of Manasseh's regnal account has been composed in relation to the exilic edition insofar as it claims that Jerusalem's and Judah's destruction is due to his sins. An original Josianic DtrH would have begun in Deuteronomy and continued through the reign of Josiah, including earlier versions of the regnal accounts of Manasseh, Amon, and Josiah in 2 Kgs 21–23. The Josianic DtrH portrayal of Josiah would have presented him as the ideal monarch of the Davidic line, who finally achieved the ideal of a united Israel, based on the observance of YHWH and YHWH's commands as expressed in Deuteronomy, centered at the Jerusalem temple, and ruled by a righteous Davidic king.

Some elements of 1–2 Kings and the DtrH have been edited or composed in relation to the Josianic DtrH. Such elements include the book of Joshua, the account of David's affair with Bath Sheba and murder of her husband Uriah the Hittite in 2 Sam 10–12, Solomon's apostasy in 1 Kgs 11, the account of the anonymous prophet's condemnation of Jeroboam ben Nebat in 1 Kgs 13, elements of the DtrH sermon concerning the fall of Israel in 2 Kgs 17, elements of Hezekiah's regnal account in 2 Kgs 18–20, and early forms of the regnal accounts of Manasseh, Amon, and Josiah in 2 Kgs 21–23.

Although the account of Israel's entry into the land in Joshua presupposes and employs earlier traditions, the image of Joshua is constructed to establish a parallel with King Josiah. The language of Josh 1:7–8, in which YHWH instructs Joshua to meditate and act upon divine Torah not turning to the right or the left, reiterates the instructions for the ideal king in the Dtr Torah of the king in Deut 17:14–20 and the regnal evaluation of Josiah in 2 Kgs 22:2; 23:5. The concern with observance of Torah appears again in Joshua's exhortation speech to Israel in Josh 23 (see esp. v. 6). Joshua conducts a covenant ceremony for the people at Shechem in Josh 8:30–35 in which he writes a copy of the Torah like that mentioned in the Torah of the King (Deut 17:18) and then reads

---

23. Weippert, "Die 'deuteronomistischen' Beurteilungen," 333–34.

it to the people as instructed in Deut 31:9–14. These actions anticipate those of
Josiah in 2 Kgs 23:1–3. Joshua observes Passover at Gilgal upon crossing the
Jordan River in Josh 5:10–12, whereas Josiah is the first monarch to observe
Passover since the days of the Judges (2 Kgs 23:21–23). Finally, Joshua acts as
leader of all Israel, which anticipates Josiah's efforts to reunify the nation. Altogether, these elements indicate an effort to portray Joshua both as the ideal
leader of a unified Israel and as a model for King Josiah. Such an effort facilitates the presentation of Josiah as the ideal monarch of the Davidic line.

Many interpreters presuppose that David is the ideal monarch of the DtrH,
but such a view fails to account for David's adultery with Bath Sheba and his
role in the murder of her husband, Uriah the Hittite (2 Sam 10–12). Although
YHWH forgives David, his actions remain a blot upon his record (see 1 Kgs
15:5). David is the foundational figure of a secure and united Israel, but his marriage to Bath Sheba ultimately produces his heir Solomon, whose own actions
play such an important role in splitting the people of Israel after his death. Josiah
corrects the problems introduced by Solomon (and the other kings) as part of
his own efforts to reunite the people of Israel around the Jerusalem temple and
the house of David. When considered in relation to David's adultery and murder, Josiah emerges as an ideal monarch in relation to the founder of the dynasty
as well. Although the account of the Bath Sheba affair and murder of Uriah is
frequently associated with the so-called Succession Narrative or Court History
of 2 Sam 9/11–20; 1 Kgs 1–2, it is a relatively self-contained pericope that has
little influence on the balance of the narrative in 2 Sam 9/11–1 Kgs 2.[24] Even
when Bath Sheba reappears in 1 Kgs 1–2, there is no hint of her adultery with
David or the murder of her first husband. She is simply one of David's wives
who acts to ensure that her own son Solomon attains the throne. With the
removal of 2 Sam 10–12, David emerges as an all-too-lenient father whose
indulgence leads to tragedy within his family, not as a criminal in need of pardon from YHWH. The narrative does not require 2 Sam 10–12 for any reason
but to cast aspersions on the characters of David, Bath Sheba, and to a lesser
extent, Solomon. But such aspersions aid in building the case that Josiah—not
David—is the ideal Davidic monarch.

The presentations of Solomon and Jeroboam ben Nebat are keys to the presentation of Josiah in the Josianic DtrH. Solomon is revered as the temple
builder, but he is also charged with responsibility for the division of Israel as a
result of his worship of the gods of his foreign wives. Jeroboam ben Nebat, as
the first king of northern Israel, bears responsibility for the continued apostasy
of the northern tribes as a result of his establishment of Beth El and Dan as sites

---

24. See J. W. Flanagan, "Court History or Succession Document? A Study of 2 Sam 9–20 and
1 Kings 1–2," *JBL* 91 (1972): 172–81, who argues that 2 Sam 11:2–12:25 (and 1 Kgs 1–2) are a
later redactional reworking of an earlier court history; cf. Campbell, *2 Samuel,* 97–102, 173–83.

for the worship of the golden calf. Both Solomon and Jeroboam are temple founders in the Josianic DtrH, and Josiah must correct the problems introduced by both. Josiah removes the pagan religious installations erected for his foreign wives (2 Kgs 23:13–14; cf. 1 Kgs 11:1–13). Josiah also destroys the altar at Beth El (2 Kgs 23:15–20; cf. 1 Kgs 12:25–33; 13:1–34).

The presentations of both Solomon and Jeroboam serve the interests of the Josianic DtrH, but they also show signs of redactional shaping. Apart from the presentation of his apostasy in 1 Kgs 11, Solomon is a wise monarch who brings wisdom, wealth, and power to Israel, and who builds the Jerusalem temple as the religious center of a unified nation. Although there is a great deal of innuendo in 1 Kgs 1–2; 3–10, these narratives are largely adulatory, whereas 1 Kgs 11 raises explicit questions about Solomon's adherence to YHWH. Solomon's apostasy leads directly to Jeroboam's kingship in 1 Kgs 11. The northern tribes revolt not out of outrage at Solomon's religious practice but as a result of Solomon's heavy taxation of the northern tribes. Without the presentation of Solomon's apostasy in 1 Kgs 11, Solomon emerges as an ideal monarch, whereas the northern tribes rebel against the son of a king who brought them prosperity and security. Jeroboam's own religious apostasy becomes an issue in the DtrH only after he has become king of Israel, and indeed it becomes the basis for the condemnation of all of the northern monarchs who are uniformly charged with following in his sins. The Josianic interests in this presentation of Jeroboam are clear in 1 Kgs 13:1–2, which explicitly mentions Josiah as the figure who will one day destroy the altar. Both the Solomon and Jeroboam narratives have been retouched to reflect Josianic interests. Solomon's apostasy in 1 Kgs 11 presents him as a foil to the righteous Josiah, and indicates that the chapter represents a redactional reworking of an otherwise laudatory presentation of an ideal king. Jeroboam's apostasy is of a different character insofar as it is foundational to the presentation of the northern kings who are uniformly condemned in the DtrH. Nevertheless the reference to Josiah in 1 Kgs 13:1–2 indicates at least some redactional work by the Josianic DtrH.

Similar observations can be made in relation to the sermon on the fall of northern Israel in 2 Kgs 17 and the regnal account of Hezekiah ben Ahaz in 2 Kgs 18–20. Although 2 Kgs 17 is formulated as the regnal account of King Hoshea ben Elah, who ruled northern Israel at the time of its final destruction by the Assyrians, much of the chapter is an anonymous reflection on the reasons for northern Israel's downfall, focusing especially on northern Israel's apostasy following on the example of its first king Jeroboam. Jeroboam's apostasy is key to the Josianic edition, but discussion of the Hezekian and Jehu editions of the work indicates its importance to these earlier editions as well. The mention of foreign worship at Beth El in the aftermath of the Assyrian destruction in vv. 24–34a refers to a problem that exists "until this day," that is, until the time of the Josianic reform that would eliminate their influence from the land. The account of Hezekiah's reign focuses primarily on his attempt to revolt against the Assyrians, and indeed, it portrays Hezekiah's reign as a success insofar as Hezekiah's piety resulted in YHWH's actions to destroy the Assyrian invader. His piety also provides an appropriate contrast to the apostasy of Jeroboam and the northern kings that called for Josiah's attempt at reform and restoration. It is well known that the idyllic picture of Hezekiah's success against the Assyrians is the product of later redaction that would emphasize Hezekiah's turn to YHWH as the key to his victory/survival and present him as a model for future action. Of course, Hezekiah's efforts provide a model for Josiah's own actions in the Josianic DtrH.

Finally, the current presentations of Manasseh, Amon, and Josiah are the product of the exilic DtrH, but each monarch would have had a regnal account suitable to the Josianic DtrH. Manasseh's account in 2 Kgs 21:1–18 may have originally included the portrayal of his repentance after having been dragged in chains to Babylon to appear before the Assyrian king like that of 2 Chr 33:10–17. Such a narrative would have provided a model for Josiah's own repentance on finding the Torah scroll in the Jerusalem temple. It is unlikely that Amon's account in 2 Kgs 21:19–26 would have been changed much, since he was assassinated after only two years on the throne. Josiah's regnal account would have included much of 2 Kgs 22:1–23:30, which focuses on the discovery of the Torah and his efforts at reform. Huldah's oracle would have differed markedly, however, since she would not have announced Josiah's death. It is instead likely that she would have delivered an oracle supportive of Josiah's efforts, perhaps a version of YHWH's promise never again to cause the feet of Israel to wander from the land that now appears in 2 Kgs 21:10–15. Unfortunately, modern readers will never be certain, nor will they know how the Josianic edition might have ended following the conclusion of Josiah's reforms in 2 Kgs 23:30. Perhaps it would have included a summation of Josiah's accomplishments, particularly his reunification of the nation around the Jerusalem temple and the Davidic monarchy in keeping with YHWH's Torah. Josiah's early death precluded such a conclusion.

First and Second Kings in the Hezekian Edition of the DtrH

The literary and conceptual tensions within 1–2 Kings and the Former Prophets has prompted widespread acceptance of the proposed Josianic DtrH. Nevertheless, the tension within this literature is hardly limited to the question of proposed Josianic and exilic editions of the DtrH. Once the texts associated with these editions are removed from consideration, indications of even earlier editions remain. Interpreters must exercise due caution in attempting the redaction-critical reconstruction of supposed earlier texts that are now some three or more editions removed from the present form of the DtrH. Despite the difficulties, these tensions and their implications for understanding the compositional history of the DtrH demand attention.

Recent studies have begun to note literary and thematic signs that point to a culmination in the regnal account of King Hezekiah ben Ahaz of Judah in 2 Kgs 18–20. The present form of the narrative clearly serves the interests of the proposed Josianic and exilic editions of the DtrH insofar as it focuses on Hezekiah's turn to YHWH as the basis for the defeat of Sennacherib's siege of Jerusalem and points to the Babylonian exile. Nevertheless, interpreters have noted the very remarkable statement in 2 Kgs 18:4 that Hezekiah removed the high places (*bāmôt*) from the land and broke down the masseboth and the Asherah.[25] The concern with high places is pervasive throughout 1–2 Kings prior to Hezekiah's regnal account. Northern Israel's apostasy against YHWH through its adherence to the high places, masseboth, and asherim is cited as one of the fundamental causes for the destruction of the northern kingdom (2 Kgs 17:9–12) from the time of Jeroboam ben Nebat on (1 Kgs 12:31). It always provides a basis for the critique of most of the Davidic monarchs prior to Hezekiah (including some who are otherwise judged to be righteous), such as Solomon (1 Kgs 3:2–15; 11:1–8); Rehoboam (1 Kgs 14:23); Asa (1 Kgs 15:11–15); Jehoshaphat (1 Kgs 22:44); Joash (2 Kgs 12:4); Amaziah (2 Kgs 14:4); Azariah (2 Kgs 15:4); Jotham (2 Kgs 15:35); and Ahaz (2 Kgs 16:4). Despite Hezekiah's removal of the high places, 2 Kgs 21:3 states that his son Manasseh rebuilt them following his father's reign only to have them removed once again by Josiah (2 Kgs 23:8–9). Second Kings 18–20 therefore portrays Hezekiah as the figure who initially resolves a major problem in Judah—and one of the major problems that resulted in the destruction of northern Israel. Hezekiah's action is undertaken during the course of temple renovation, but his efforts are cut short by Assyrian invasion. Such a portrayal suggests that Hezekiah's regnal account may once have formed the culmination of an earlier edition of the DtrH.[26]

Other indications suggest that Hezekiah's regnal account may once have formed the culmination of an earlier DtrH edition. The placement of Hezekiah's regnal account immediately following Hoshea's regnal account in 2 Kgs 17, which discusses the fall of northern Israel, is not simply due to historical chronology; it contrasts the righteous Hezekiah with the purportedly sinful monarchs of northern Israel. Whereas Israel is destroyed by Assyria for apostasy initiated by its kings, Jerusalem is spared as a result of Hezekiah's repentance and turn to YHWH. Indeed, 2 Kgs 18:5 states that he was an ideal monarch of the Davidic

25. E.g., Iain W. Provan, *Hezekiah and the Books of Kings* (BZAW 172; Berlin and New York: Walter de Gruyter, 1988), 82–89.

26. So ibid., who argues that the culmination in the account of Hezekiah's reign represents a Josianic edition of the DtrH; see also Weippert, "Die 'deuteronomistischen' Beurteilungen," 307–23, who notes that the formulaic regnal patterns point to a redactional culmination in the account of Hezekiah's reign.

line: "there was none like him among all the kings of Judah, nor among those who were before him."

Formulaic patterns must be considered as well. Distinctive patterns in the regnal formula for the kings of Judah and Israel reach their conclusions with the reigns of Ahaz of Judah (2 Kgs 16:2b, 4, "and he did not do what was right in the eyes of YHWH like David his father . . . and he sacrificed and burned incense at the high places") and Hoshea of Israel (2 Kgs 17:22, "and they walked in all the sins of Jeroboam . . ."). The Judean pattern shifts to a different formula beginning with Hezekiah (2 Kgs 18:3: "and he did that which was right in the eyes of YHWH . . . like all that David his father did"). The formulas for the northern kings come to an end with Hoshea. On this basis, Weippert suggests that a later redaction of the DtrH begins with the account of Hezekiah.[27] There is also a change in the concluding regnal accounts, particularly the burial notices and the identifications of the royal mothers. Judean kings through Ahaz are buried in the city of David, but the pattern is disrupted beginning with Hezekiah, who lacks a burial notice. Manasseh and Amon are buried in the garden of Uzzah, and later kings from Josiah on show no consistent pattern. Queen mothers from Amon on are identified by name, patronym, and place of birth, whereas there is no consistency in the identification of the mothers through Manasseh. In both cases, the formulaic evidence points to a shift in formulation beginning with Hezekiah. Halpern and Vanderhooft therefore argue that these signs point to a Hezekian edition of the DtrH that presented Hezekiah as the ideal monarch of the Davidic line.[28]

Apart from the account of Hezekiah's reforms in 2 Kgs 18:1–8, no major narrative focuses on Hezekiah's reign as an ideal time in Judah's or Israel's history. The present narrative focuses on Sennacherib's invasion, which would have impeded any efforts on Hezekiah's part to exercise ideal kingship. One may speculate that Hezekiah sought to restore the Solomonic ideal by reuniting Judah and the remnants of Israel under Davidic rule around the Jerusalem temple. Such a move might be expected in the aftermath of the destruction of northern Israel, particularly for a monarch whose grandfather and father (Jotham and Ahaz) had shown loyalty to the Assyrians at the time of the Syro-Ephraimitic War. When the Assyrians proved to be obstacles for such efforts, Hezekiah revolted. The consequences of that revolt preclude any such pretensions. Although Hezekiah remained on the throne, he continued to be an Assyrian vassal, and any efforts to reunite the country would have come to an end. Any culminating narrative that pointed to Hezekiah's ideal reign over a reunited Israel and Judah is now lost.

---

27. Weippert, "Die 'deuteronomistischen' Beurteilungen," 323–33.

28. Baruch Halpern and David Vanderhooft, "The Editions of Kings in the 7th–6th Centuries," *HUCA* 62 (1991): 179–244.

Nevertheless, further evidence exists for a Hezekian edition in the account of northern Israel's revolt against Rehoboam ben Solomon in 1 Kgs 12, the presentation of the period of the Judges, and the presentation of Israel and Judah following the collapse of the northern Jehu dynasty in 2 Kgs 15–17. Each case indicates a fundamental problem among the northern tribes, namely, they show little capacity for just self-government. Only the house of David provides a basis for righteous rule among all the tribes of Israel. This is not to say that the theme of northern apostasy so characteristic of the Josianic DtrH is absent. But the attempt to demonstrate that the northern tribes are unable to organize effective self-government or to recognize righteous Davidic rule differs from the uniform presentation of northern apostasy in the Josianic DtrH.

Such a concern is evident in the account of northern Israel's revolt against Rehoboam in 1 Kgs 12:1–24. Whereas 1 Kgs 11 focuses on Solomon's apostasy as the cause for the split in the kingdom, 1 Kgs 12:1–24 focuses on northern concerns that Rehoboam will govern as harshly as Solomon. When Rehoboam travels north to Shechem to confirm his kingship over the northern tribes, they put the question to him in v. 4, "Your father made our yoke heavy. Now therefore lighten the hard service of your father and his heavy yoke that he placed on us, and we will serve you." The question refers to the burdens in Solomon's reign of building the temple, the royal palace, the store cities, and so forth. After consulting with both his father's advisors and his own advisors, here called the "children" with whom he had grown up, Rehoboam informs the northerners in rather crude terms that he would be even harsher than his father. Upon hearing the blustering answer of the clearly immature king, the northern tribes revolted against the house of David and appointed Jeroboam ben Nebat as their king. When considered in historical terms, the northerners' response reflects the undue burdens placed on them. Solomon seems to have acted like a Judean Pharaoh in unduly burdening the northern tribes while requiring little or nothing from his own tribe of Judah. While masking the abuse of the northern tribes, 1 Kgs 3–10 emphasizes the wisdom, wealth, and power of Solomon's kingdom. The northern tribes may have done all or most of the work, but they fail to recognize what they had gained, a secure and wealthy kingdom. When considered in relation to the laudatory account of Solomon's reign of unprecedented peace, prosperity, and power, the northern tribes emerge as whining ingrates. Such a portrayal would clearly serve Davidic, specifically Hezekian, interests, and point to one of the fundamental reasons for the split in the kingdom: the northerners didn't realize how good they had it. When left to their own rule, they ultimately met disaster. Hezekiah would then emerge as the righteous monarch who would reinstitute unity and purity of worship. The northern tribes would likely have seen things differently, but from a Davidic perspective, no other Davidic monarch from Solomon through Hezekiah presents such an opportunity for political and religious unity—for either northern Israel or the house of David.

Similar concerns permeate the presentation of premonarchic Israel in the book of Judges.[29] Although past interpreters treat Judges primarily as a historical presentation of the premonarchic period, awareness has grown regarding the historiographical concerns that shape that presentation. Noth's initial study of the DtrH noted the fourfold pattern articulated in Judg 2:11–22 that shapes the presentation of each major judge: apostasy by Israel, YHWH's appointment of an oppressor to punish Israel, Israel's repentance, and YHWH's appointment of a judge to deliver Israel. This pattern establishes a framework for the book as a whole that takes up earlier traditions about individual tribal or local deliverers and relates them to the history of all Israel. But other patterns are at work as well. The evaluation formula, "and Israel did what was evil in the eyes of YHWH," anticipates the regnal evaluation formulas of 1–2 Kings. Judges' emphasis on the increasing Canaanization of the tribes and the deteriorating position of women in Israel points to a progressive decline throughout the book.[30] Such an interest in asserting Israel's decline during this period appears in conjunction with an interest in portraying the inability of the northern tribes, particularly Ephraim and Benjamin, to provide effective leadership for the nation. Such polemics support an overall interest in promoting Judah and the house of David as the source for desperately needed leadership in Israel.

This agenda is evident from the initial presentation in Judg 1–2, which portray the failure of the tribes under the leadership of Joshua to drive out the Canaanites from the land. Such a failure results in the above-noted pattern of apostasy, oppression, repentance, and deliverance because of the continuing influence of the remaining Canaanites. Judges 3–16 emphasizes that the Canaanites will continue to exercise this influence throughout the period of the judges. The first judge, Othniel, is Judean and effectively unites Israel to defeat Cushan Rishathaim (Judg 3:7–11). The presentation of the following judges, all of whom are from northern tribes, displays a progressive deterioration of Israel due to Canaanite influence and inability, particularly by Benjamin and Ephraim, to assert effective leadership. Ehud of Benjamin defeats Eglon of Moab, but he is only able to do so by deceit (Judg 3:12–30). Deborah of Ephraim defeats Sisera, but she is unable to unite all of the tribes, and Jael again employs deceit to kill Sisera (Judg 4–5). Gideon of Manasseh, originally known as Jerubbaal ("let Baal be magnified"), is the son of a Baal worshiper and ultimately engages in Canaanite practice himself. He defeats the Midianites, but he is threatened by the Ephraimites who demand to know why they were not called to lead the battle. His own son, Abimelech, plunges the nation into civil war when he tries to seize power (Judg 6–9). Jepthah of Gilead (Gad and Manasseh) defeats the Ammonites, but he sacrifices his

29. See Sweeney, "Davidic Polemics."
30. For discussion of the deteriorating position of women in Judges, see esp. Tammi J. Schneider, *Judges* (Berit Olam; Collegeville, Minn.: Liturgical, 2000), passim.

daughter in a manner reminiscent of pagan practice, and is attacked by Ephraim for his failure to call them into battle (Judg 10–12). Samson of Dan humiliates the Philistines, but never defeats them. His marriage to a Philistine woman (see Deut 7:1–6) ultimately undermines him and results in the loss of Dan's tribal territory (Judg 13–16).

The chapters of Judges 17–21 are generally considered as appendices, but they present the culmination of Judges' major concerns. The section emphasizes the need for a righteous and effective king in Israel, but undermines northern claims in favor of those of Judah. Judges 17–18 relates how the tribe of Dan moved north following its displacement, pointing to the establishment of the sanctuary at Dan by a man who stole money from his own mother and corrupted a Levite from the Judean town of Beth Lehem, the home of David. Judges 19–21 relates the murder of a Levite's concubine from Beth Lehem by the men of Gibeah. Gibeah is in Benjamin, and it served as Saul's capital. When Benjamin refused to bring the perpetrators to justice, the other tribes declared war on Benjamin while meeting at Beth El (the site of the other northern sanctuary), and nearly destroyed the tribe. Benjamin was saved only by a decision to allow its men to seize maidens dancing in the vineyards during the festival at the Shiloh sanctuary, which again raises questions about Benjamin's character. The narrative ends by expressing hope for a king in Israel to bring order to the nation.

Judges prepares the reader for the rise of David to replace the ineffective Saul. It also prepares the reader for the demise of the northern kings in 1–2 Kings and the potential restoration of Davidic kingship over all Israel. The deterioration of northern Israel and Judah in 2 Kgs 15–17 is crucial. Following the idyllic portrayal of a unified Israel under King Jeroboam ben Joash (2 Kgs 14:23–29), 2 Kgs 15 portrays a series of royal assassinations in northern Israel, the rise of the Assyrian empire as a threat to Israel, and northern Israel's attempts to threaten Judah. Second Kings 16 portrays Ahaz ben Jotham's submission to Assyria as a result of his attempts to defend Judah in the Syro-Ephraimitic War. Second Kings 17 relates the fall of northern Israel, and argues that this resulted from Israel's apostasy. Overall, these chapters continue the themes of Judges, continuous apostasy in the north and the rise of an oppressor, but repentance is lacking. The result is disaster, and only Judah and the house of David are left to pick up the pieces.

Ultimately, Hezekiah emerges as the figure who might deliver Israel from Assyrian oppression. Although 2 Kgs 18–20 serves the interests of the Josianic DtrH, the fundamental accounts of Hezekiah's and Jerusalem's deliverance in 2 Kgs 18–19 and his healing from illness in 2 Kgs 20:1–11 point to Hezekiah as the monarch whose piety and righteousness save Jerusalem. Only in 2 Kgs 20:12–19 is Hezekiah called into question when Isaiah announces that his reception of the Babylonian envoys will result in the exile of his sons. Apart from this episode, Hezekiah is the deliverer of Israel from Assyria in 2 Kgs 18:1–20:11. Historically, the Assyrians continued to dominate Judah well beyond the reign of Hezekiah and into the early years of Josiah. Nevertheless, the DtrH contends that the Assyrians never again threatened Israel or Judah. Such a contention would clearly serve the interests of the courts of Hezekiah and perhaps Manasseh, which appear to have submitted to Assyria to keep the nation safe.

The Jehu Dynastic History

Although the exilic, Josianic, and Hezekian DtrH editions take us deep into the hypothetical redaction history of 1–2 Kings, literary tension points to even earlier stages. Campbell and O'Brien have put forward one of the most cogent proposals for an earlier stage in the compositional history of the DtrH known as the Prophetic Record.[31] The Prophetic Record presents a history of Israel from the inauguration of the monarchy under Samuel and Saul through Jehu's overthrow of the House of Omri in 1 Sam 1–2 Kgs 10. It is fundamentally concerned with the role of prophets in establishing and overthrowing the royal houses of Israel. Because Jehu's overthrow of the house of Omri constitutes the culmination of the proposed work, the Prophetic Record is a late-ninth-century work, formulated in prophetic circles gathered around Elisha and his successors, that legitimizes the House of Jehu as the choice of YHWH.

The hypothesis is also based on several sets of literary observations. The first pertains to the prophets' involvement in the anointing of Saul, David, and Jehu. Each of these monarchs was designated by a prophet in remarkably similar circumstances in 1 Sam 9:1–10:16; 1 Sam 16:1–13; and 2 Kgs 9:1–14a. Each is anointed by a prophet: Saul by Samuel (1 Sam 10:1), David by Samuel (1 Sam 16:13), and Jehu by an agent of Elisha (2 Kgs 9:6). Each is anointed in relative privacy (Saul, 1 Sam 9:27; 10:14–16; David, 1 Sam 16:2–3, 13; Jehu, 2 Kgs 9:6, 11). Each prophet attributes the anointing to YHWH (1 Sam 9:15–17; 10:1; 1 Sam 16:1, 3, 7–9, 12; 2 Kgs 9:3, 6). Each anointee is designated as "king designate (*nāgîd*)," "king-to-be," or simply "king (*melek*)" (1 Sam 9:16; 10:1; 1 Sam 16:1; 2 Kgs 9:3, 6). In each case, the anointing has empowering consequences: Saul sees signs that G-d is with him (1 Sam 10:7, 9), David is gripped by the spirit of YHWH (1 Sam 16:13), and Jehu's destruction of the house of Omri fulfills Elijah's judgment against Ahab (2 Kgs 9:7–9a).

31. Campbell and O'Brien, *Unfolding the Deuteronomistic History*; Antony F. Campbell, S.J., *Of Prophets and Kings. A Late Ninth-Century Document (1 Samuel 1–2 Kings 10)* (CBQMS 17: Washington, D.C.: The Catholic Biblical Association, 1986); Mark A. O'Brien, *The Deuteronomistic History Hypothesis: A Reassessment* (OBO 92; Freiburg: Universitätsverlag; Göttingen: Vandenhoeck & Ruprecht, 1989); cf. Bernhard Lehnart, *Prophet und König im Nordreich Israel* (VTSup 96; Leiden: Brill, 2003), who argues for a ninth–eighth-century northern prophetic tradition that includes Samuel, Elijah, and Elisha.

The second set demonstrates the interrelationships of the narratives concerning prophetic judgment in relation to Jeroboam, Ahab, and Jehu in 1 Kgs 14; 1 Kgs 21; and 2 Kgs 9. Each of these narratives includes reference to YHWH's bringing evil on the royal house (1 Kgs 14:10a; 1 Kgs 21:21a; but 2 Kgs 9 lacks such reference); each calls for extirpation of the royal house (1 Kgs 14:10b; 1 Kgs 21:21a; 2 Kgs 9:7a, 8a); each refers explicitly to the cutting off of every male of the house (1 Kgs 14:10a; 1 Kgs 21:21b; 2 Kgs 9:8b); the latter two narratives refer back to the fate of the house of Jeroboam (1 Kgs 21:22a; 2 Kgs 9:9a); and each refers to the fate of those who die in the city or the country (1 Kgs 14:11; 1 Kgs 21:24; 2 Kgs 9:26, 36). These elements form a core apart from characteristic Dtr elements, and demonstrate a pre-Dtr pattern that constitutes the basis for the Prophetic Record in 1 Sam 1–2 Kgs 10. Similar patterns appear in 1 Kgs 16:1–4 concerning Baasha and the prophet Jehu ben Hanani, although the lack of a full narrative like those concerning Jeroboam, Ahab, and Jehu suggests a later Dtr composition.

Campbell and O'Brien acknowledge gaps, particularly the lack of such patterns for Solomon. There is no prophetic designation of Solomon that matches those for Saul, David, or Jehu, nor is there judgment for Solomon that matches those for Jeroboam, Ahab, and Jehu. Although they concede that an earlier Solomon narrative may once have appeared in the Prophetic Record,[32] they omit the present Solomon narrative and argue that the Prophetic Record appears in two parts. The first concludes in 2 Sam 8:15 with its summation of David's rule, and the second resumes at 1 Kgs 11:26 with Jeroboam's rise to kingship.

The presentation of Solomon points to an important dimension of the narrative that requires further work, that is, the need to account for a narrative that presents a period of prosperity, power, and peace as the culmination of at least one part of the proposed Prophetic Record. It is no accident that the Solomon narrative appears between the two portions of the Prophetic Record as identified by Campbell and O'Brien since it presents the culmination of the first part of the narrative in which David supplants Saul to rule over a unified Israel. David is designated by Samuel after Saul's failure; David is clearly favored by YHWH; but David spends his entire life acquiring his empire and establishing his rule, whereas Solomon is able to organize that empire and reap its benefits. Solomon represents a stage of political, religious, and cultic attainment. He is not judged in the largely laudatory narrative in 1 Kgs 3–10. That only comes in 1 Kgs 11, which is identified as a Josianic composition. Instead, the kingdom dissolves after Solomon's death not due to his apostasy in worshiping the gods of his foreign wives but due to both the unwillingness of the northern tribes to accept the burdens of a powerful and centralized monarchy and the incompetence of Solomon's son Rehoboam.

---

32. Campbell and O'Brien, *Unfolding the Deuteronomistic History,* 336.

Indeed, the question of the northern tribes' fitness to rule themselves is the subject of the second half of the Prophetic Record. Jeroboam ben Nebat plays little role in the revolt, but is appointed as king only after the revolt is successfully completed. His first act is one of apostasy insofar as he establishes illegitimate worship of the golden calves, illegitimate priests, and illegitimate festivals at Beth El and Dan. Ahab fares little better as the key figure of the house of Omri. After marrying the Phoenician princess Jezebel and establishing the worship of her god Baal Melqart in Israel, he proceeds to kill the prophets of YHWH, murder Naboth of Jezreel, and seize Naboth's property. Jehu's revolt reverses the problems of the houses of both Jeroboam and Omri by eliminating the influence of foreign gods and reestablishing YHWH as G-d of Israel.

And yet the work of purification is not completed with Jehu's revolt in 2 Kgs 9–10. Various elements are left unresolved. Elisha is Elijah's successor, and Jehu is now king, as indicated in YHWH's instructions to Elijah in 1 Kgs 19. But Elisha remains active through the reign of Jehu's grandson Joash according to 2 Kgs 13:14–21. YHWH's message to Elijah also called for anointing Hazael as king of Aram. But Hazael does not begin to afflict Israel until the end of the reign of Jehu (2 Kgs 10:32–33), and he continues until his death in the reign of Jehoahaz. Only Jehoash ben Jehoahaz finally contains the Arameans (2 Kgs 13:22–25). Although Jehu's revolt is an important milestone in the narrative, there are too many loose ends. Narrative resolution appears only in the account of the reign of Jeroboam ben Joash in 2 Kgs 14:23–29, who finally reestablishes Israel's boundaries from Lebo-Hamath in the north to the Sea of the Arabah in the south and restores the glory of Israel as known in Solomon's time. Jeroboam's kingdom is restored in accordance with the word of YHWH as spoken through Jonah ben Amittai (2 Kgs 14:25). Jeroboam ben Joash then emerges as the deliverer of Israel.

The hypothesis of a Prophetic Record proposed by Campbell and O'Brien must be modified. It is concerned with the interaction of prophets and kings, but it is not concerned solely with the anointing and undermining of dynasties. The hypothesis is also concerned with the attainment of peace, wealth, power, and divine blessing in the reigns of Solomon and Jeroboam ben Joash. Written from the perspective of the house of Jehu, it therefore represents a Jehu Dynastic History rather than a Prophetic Record. It dates to the first half of the eighth century B.C.E., prior to the Assyrian invasions, when northern Israel reached the apex of its power under the Jehu kings.

There are important indications that the Jehu Dynastic History is itself a composite work. Campbell and O'Brien note the presence of two basic blocks in their proposed Prophetic Record, the one pertaining to Saul, David, and Jehu, and the other to Jeroboam, Ahab, and Jehu. The Jehu narrative ties the two blocks together, but the culminating roles of the Solomon narrative in each block must also be considered. The Solomon narrative brings the Saul and David block to a close, insofar as Solomon's ascension to the throne confirms the rise of the house of David to kingship. Only after Solomon's lifetime is completed does the future of the dynasty come into question with the revolt of the northern tribes. Although the future of the house of David in Judah is confirmed, the revolt of the northern tribes launches a new chapter in the history of (northern) Israelite kingship that only comes to resolution with the rise of the house of Jehu. Even then, full resolution is only achieved in the reign of Jeroboam ben Joash.

The Saul, David, and Solomon block clearly serves Davidic interests, with little hint of northern interests or grievances until the aftermath of Solomon's reign. Likewise, the Jeroboam, Ahab, Jehu, and Jeroboam block gives clear voice to northern interests, and portrays the house of Jehu as the means to address the problems of the northern monarchy. It would seem then that the proposed Jehu Dynastic History is a composite work in which an earlier narrative concerning the rise of the house of David—culminating in the reign of Solomon—has been taken up and expanded with a history of the northern kings from Jeroboam ben Nebat through Jeroboam ben Joash. Although the Davidic/Solomonic history would present Solomon as the culmination of Israel's quest for just and secure leadership, the newly formed Jehu history would present the houses of Saul and David as failed milestones together with the houses of Jeroboam, Baasha, Zimri, and Omri, in the quest to establish just and secure leadership in northern Israel.

The narrative pertaining to the northern dynasties would have been written as part of the Jehu Dynastic History, including the histories of the kings from Jeroboam ben Nebat to Jeroboam ben Joash in 1 Kgs 12–2 Kgs 14, with the exception of 1 Kgs 13 earlier identified as a Josianic composition. The Elijah and Elisha cycles form a part of the Jehu Dynastic History, although they appear to have an independent compositional history prior to being taken up and edited into the Jehu history.[33] Indeed, the Elijah narratives appear to be based on earlier ninth-century traditions now extant in 1 Kgs 17–19; 21; and 2 Kgs 1–2, combined with traditions concerning anonymous prophets in 1 Kgs 20, 22, which

33. Contra Steven L. McKenzie, *The Trouble with Kings: The Composition of the Books of Kings in the Deuteronomistic History* (VTSup 42; Leiden: Brill, 1991), 81–100, and Georg Fohrer, *Elia* (2d ed.; AThANT 53; Zurich: Zwingli, 1968), who argue that the Elijah and Elisha cycles are later compositions. Their arguments rely heavily on the lack of Dtr influence in the Elijah-Elisha narratives and affinities with Jeremiah and Ezekiel. But earlier traditions worked into a DtrH framework need not display Dtr characteristics. The affinities with Jeremiah and Ezekiel demonstrate only common narrative forms and visionary aspects (cf. Keith W. Carley, *Ezekiel among the Prophets* [SBT II/31; Naperville, Ill.: Allenson, 1974], who demonstrates Ezekiel's dependence on earlier prophetic traditions).

serve as an introduction to the block of material concerning Elisha in 2 Kgs 2/3:1–8:15.[34] Such redaction would have taken place in conjunction with their inclusion in the Jehu narrative in the early to mid-eighth century B.C.E.

The composite nature of the Jehu Dynastic History has implications for the Davidic-Solomonic history in 1 Sam 1–1 Kgs 10. Insofar as the Jehu history posits Rehoboam's immaturity together with the northern tribes' unruliness as causes of the revolt, David's leniency toward his sons in 2 Sam 9–20; 1 Kings 1–2 emerges as a key issue. David fails to discipline his sons, even when they rape a sister, murder a brother, and revolt against the father's rule. Such fatherly neglect is consistent with the portrayal of Rehoboam, who relies on the advice of the "boys" with whom he grew up in making decisions that ensure the dissolution of his empire.

The portrayal of David's relationship with his sons builds upon the portrayal of his relationship with his father-in-law Saul. David undermined the rule of his father-in-law by going over to the Philistines, building his own power base, marrying Saul's daughter Michal, refusing to produce a Saulide heir, and consistently claiming that he was not at fault. Absalom likewise undermined David as he prepared for revolt while sulking at his father's house, assembled an entourage to accompany him throughout Judah and Israel as he built a power base among the people, and ultimately took David's concubines. Similar considerations pertain to Amnon. Just as David built his kingdom by taking the women who would lead him to power over Saul—that is, Michal, Abigail, and others—so Amnon took by force the woman to whom he felt entitled as the firstborn of the king. But in Amnon's case, the woman turned out to be his half-sister Tamar. His rash action resulted in his murder by Tamar's full brother Absalom, which ultimately triggered the revolt. Finally, Adonijah presumptuously claimed the throne prior to his father's death, later demanded David's concubine, and ultimately died as a result of his failure to prepare a power base. His presumption mirrors David's own sense of entitlement, but his lack of preparation for such a power contest confirms David's failure to educate or discipline his son. Second Samuel 9–20 and 1 Kgs 1–2 portray David's failures as a father as a form of retribution for his failure to serve as a good son-in-law to Saul. These chapters build the case for the portrayal of Rehoboam in the narrative concerning the revolt of the northern tribes in 1 Kgs 12. Although the northern tribes would have submitted to him had he made the proper choice, his rash answer to their demands for more lenient rule shows his failure to follow in the footsteps of his wise father—namely, his father never passed on any of his wisdom.

---

34. See, most recently, Susanne Otto, *Jehu, Elia und Elisa* (BWANT 152; Stuttart: W. Kohlhammer, 2001).

The Solomonic History

The preceding discussion of the Jehu history points to an even earlier narrative history that culminates in 1 Kgs 3–10 with the reign of Solomon ben David.[35] These chapters present Solomon's reign as a period of unprecedented peace, power, prosperity, and stability that sees the construction of the royal palace complex and the Jerusalem temple. Solomon's reign marks the true beginning of the Davidic dynasty, insofar as he successfully succeeds his father David.

Although many elements of this narrative serve as the basis for later critique of Solomon in the Josianic DtrH, they appear here as indications of his great power and wealth. The initial notice concerning Solomon's marriage to the daughter of Pharaoh in 1 Kgs 3:1 marks his importance, insofar as his marriage signals an alliance with one of the world's great superpowers of the day. Although Gibeon is identified as a Canaanite city in Josh 8–9, David's defense of Gibeon against Ish-boshet provided him with the power base that enabled him to establish his own kingdom in Jerusalem, Benjamin, and Judah. Solomon's dream at Gibeon therefore does not raise questions, but points unequivocally to him as a wise monarch whose power and wealth were granted by YHWH. His ability to organize his kingdom to produce wealth and to support the royal court and its building projects, particularly the temple and royal palace complex, are not cause for revolt among the northern tribes but a testimony to the benefits that Solomon's rule brought to Israel. His trading expeditions to Egypt and the Red Sea, his wedding gift of Gezer from Pharaoh, and his relationship with the queen of Sheba all mark the spectacular wealth and power of his reign. When removed from the context of condemnation of Solomon and the revolt of the northern tribes, 1 Kgs 3–10 presents Solomon as a great monarch, who turned his father's kingdom into a powerful empire based on the house of David and the Jerusalem temple.

First Kings 3–10 hardly stands alone. First Kings 1–2 plays an important role in marking the transition from David's to Solomon's rule, tying the account of Solomon's reign into the account of David's rise to power in 1 Sam 1–2 Sam 24. The anti-Saul and pro-Davidic concerns expressed in Judg 19–21 suggest that this narrative—or some version of it—may have stood as part of the proposed Davidic or Solomonic history. There is also a clear Davidic or Solomonic interest, however, in the portrayal of the demise of the house of Saul in 2 Sam 9–20 (minus the Josianic material in 2 Sam 10–12), which is crucial for the rise of Solomon to power. Following the rise of Solomon to the throne, the house of Saul never again is a factor in the royal succession of Israel. But until the

---

35. Cf. Bezalel Porton, "The Structure and Theme of the Solomon Narrative (1 Kings 3–11)," *HUCA* 38 (1967): 93–128.

ascension of Solomon to the throne, the house of Saul has a very clear claim to rule. David rules over Israel as a member of the house of Saul, by virtue of his marriage to Saul's daughter Michal and the elimination of Saul's sons as contenders to the throne. Saul's presumed successor, Jonathan, dies with Saul and his brothers Abinadab and Malchishua in battle against the Philistines at Mount Gilboa (1 Sam 31). Saul's son, Ish-Bosheth (Esh Baal), who takes the throne after his father's death, is never able to exercise full power and is assassinated by two Gibeonite army officers during his failed war against David and the Philistines (2 Sam 2; 4). Jonathan's son, Mephibosheth, is described as lame and eats at David's table (2 Sam 9), a clear sign of his submission to his aunt's husband. Following the failure of Absalom's revolt, Mephibosheth gives up all claim to his father's inheritance (2 Sam 16; 19). Shimei, a member of the house of Saul, curses David during Absalom's revolt (2 Sam 16), and Solomon later puts him to death (1 Kgs 2), thereby ending any threat to his throne from surviving elements of the house of Saul. Although Sheba ben Bichri has no clear relationship to the house of Saul, his Benjaminite identity might indicate a pro-Saulide motivation for his failed revolt against David in 2 Sam 20:1–22. Saul's remaining sons and grandsons are handed over by David to the Gibeonites for execution in 2 Sam 21 on grounds that are not entirely clear. David's son Amnon, born to his wife Ahinoam, who in turn is sometimes identified as Saul's former wife, dies at Absalom's hand following his rape of his half-sister Tamar (see 2 Sam 13). Only David is left, and his refusal to have relations with his wife Michal ensures that no Saulide heir will ascend the throne (2 Sam 6).

With the elimination of the house of Saul, the way is clear for Solomon to ascend to the throne. Thus the history of David also serves as the history of Solomon's rise to the throne. Altogether, 1 Sam 1–1 Kgs 10 (minus 2 Sam 10–12; 21–24) constitutes the Solomonic history, which presents the history of the house of David culminating in the magnificent reign of Solomon. There is little indication of post-Solomonic interests in this narrative, which would suggest that it was written during the reign of Solomon himself, perhaps following the completion of the temple, in the mid-tenth century B.C.E. Remaining literary tension in the Samuel traditions suggests that the Solomonic history is based on an earlier Davidic history that reaches its culmination in 2 Sam 8, but that question is beyond the scope of this commentary.

Textual Versions of 1–2 Kings

The Masoretic Version

The Hebrew Masoretic text (MT) was produced during the Middle Ages by Jewish specialists known as *baʿălê hammasôrâ*, "masters of the tradition," or "Masoretes," who standardized the system of vowel pointing and accentuation of the well-established text of the Tanakh, that is, the Jewish Bible.[36] The MT is based on a Tiberian system of vowel pointing and accentuation that was developed in the sixth–eighth centuries C.E. Although some suggest that early Masoretes were Karaites, the earliest known masoretic manuscripts from the ninth–eleventh centuries were written by the renowned scribes of the ben Asher family, who are identified with the rabbinic tradition. The earliest known manuscript is the Cairo Codex of the Prophets (896 C.E.), which was copied and pointed by Moshe ben Asher.[37] The Aleppo Codex (915 C.E.) was produced by Aaron ben Asher.[38] The Aleppo Codex was identified by Maimonides as the most authoritative manuscript of the Bible known in his day, although it was partially destroyed in 1948 during the anti-Jewish pogroms in Syria. The Leningrad or St. Petersburg Codex (1009 C.E.), the oldest known complete Masoretic Bible, is the basis for modern critical editions of the Hebrew text.[39]

The Masoretic vowels provide a standardized interpretation of the words or semantic dimensions of the Hebrew text, and the accentuation provides a standardized grammar or syntax for reading the sentences and phrases of that text. Textual blocks are defined by the introduction of gaps in the Hebrew text. Larger sections are defined by an open gap, that is, one that extends from the last word of the text to the end of the line, called *pārāšâ pĕtûḥâ*, "an open section," to indicate a major structural unit within the larger text. Smaller sections are defined by a closed gap, that is, one that begins with the concluding word of the previous section and ends with the first word of the new section, called *pārāšâ sĕtûmâ*, "a closed section," to indicate a subunit within the larger *pārāšâ pĕtûḥâ* or "open section." Masoretic manuscripts display a great deal of variation in the placement of *pĕtûḥôt*, "open sections," and *sĕtûmôt*, "closed sections."

Hebrew Manuscripts from Qumran

The Judean wilderness manuscripts of 1–2 Kings include 4QKings, 5QKings, and 6QKings.

---

36. Israel Yeivin, *Introduction to the Tiberian Masorah* (SBL MasS 5; Missoula, Mont.: Scholars Press, 1980); Aaron Dotan, "Masorah," *EncJud* 16:1401–82; Dominique Barthélemy et al., *Josué-Esther* (vol. 2 of *Critique textuelle de l'ancien Testament*; OBO 50/1; Göttingen: Vandenhoeck & Ruprecht; Freiburg: Universitätsverlag, 1982), i–cxvi; Christian D. Ginsburg, *Introduction to the Massoretico-Critical Edition of the Hebrew Bible, with a Prolegomenon by Harry M. Orlinsky* (New York: KTAV, 1966); Emanuel Tov, *Textual Criticism of the Hebrew Bible* (Minneapolis: Fortress; Assen: Royal Van Gorcum, 2001), 21–79.

37. F. Pérez Castro, *El codice de Profetas de el Cairo* (8 vols.; Madrid: CSIC, 1979–92).

38. Moshe H. Goshen-Gottstein, *The Aleppo Codex I. Facsimile* (Jerusalem: Magnes, 1976); cf. Goshen-Gottstein, "The Aleppo Codex and the Rise of the Masoretic Bible Text," *BA* 42 (1979): 145–63.

39. David Noel Freedman et al., *The Leningrad Codex: A Facsimile Edition* (Grand Rapids: Eerdmans, 1998).

4QKings (4Q54) includes seven small fragments of text from a manuscript written in a late Hasmonean book hand dated to the mid-first century B.C.E.[40] The fragments include material from 1 Kgs 7:20–21 (frag. 1); 7:25–27 (frag. 2; cf. 1 Chr 28:12); 7:29–31 (frags. 3–4); 7:31–42 (frag. 5; 2 Chr 4:11); 7:51–8:9 (frag. 6; 2 Chr 5:3, 7–8); and 8:16–18 (frag. 7; cf. 2 Chr 6:5–6). The text appears to be a premasoretic version of Kings, but it has been influenced by readings from corresponding texts in 1–2 Chronicles.

5QKings (5Q2) includes three fragments of 1 Kgs 1:16–37, including elements from 1 Kgs 1:1 (frag. 1); 1:16–17 (frag. 2); and 1:27–37 (frag. 3).[41] The manuscript appears to be premasoretic, but the relative absence of text leaves other possibilities open. Milik dates the manuscript to the Hasmonean period in the mid-second century B.C.E.

6QKings (6Q4) includes eighteen identifiable fragments and seventy-seven other unidentifiable pieces with single words or letters of a papyrus scroll of 1–2 Kings.[42] The contents of the manuscript include 1 Kgs 3:12–14 (frag. 1); 12:28–31 (frags. 2–4); 22:28–31 (frag. 5); 2 Kgs 5:26 (frags. 6–7); 6:32 (frags. 8–9); 7:8–10 (frags. 10–14); 7:20–8:5 (frag. 15); 9:1–2 (frag. 16); and 10:19–21 (frag. 17). The manuscript includes several textual variations from the MT that correspond to features evident in some Greek, Latin, Syriac, and Aramaic manuscripts, but the variations do not indicate that this text should be identified with any of the major versions. Baillet dates the manuscript to the second half of the second century B.C.E.

The Septuagint Version and Related Greek Recensions

The Septuagint is the standard Greek version of the Christian Old Testament.[43] The Alexandrian version of the Septuagint is believed to have originated in the Greek-speaking Jewish diaspora communities of Egypt from the mid-third century B.C.E. According to the second-century B.C.E. Letter of Aristeas,[44] the Ptolemaic Egyptian king, Ptolemy II Philadelphus (r. 285–247 B.C.E.) commissioned a Greek translation of the Torah as part of his efforts to collect all of the world's major literary works. Aristeas states that seventy-two Jewish scholars worked

40. Julio Trebolle Barrera, "4Q Kgs," in Ulrich et al., *Qumran Cave 4. IX: Deuteronomy, Joshua, Judges, Kings,* 171–83.

41. J. T. Milik, "I Rois," in M. Baillet et al., *Les "Petites Grottes" de Qumran* (2 vols.; DJD 3; Oxford: Clarendon, 1962), 1:171–72.

42. M. Baillet, "Livres des Rois," in Baillet et al., *Les "Petites Grottes,"* 1:107–12.

43. Henry Barclay Swete, *An Introduction to the Old Testament in Greek* (New York: KTAV, 1968); Sidney Jellicoe, *The Septuagint and Modern Study* (Oxford: Clarendon, 1968); Emanuel Tov, *The Text-Critical Use of the Septuagint in Biblical Research* (Jerusalem Biblical Studies 8; Jerusalem: Simor, 1997); Melvin K. H. Peters, "Septuagint," *ABD* 5:1093–1104.

44. See R. J. H. Shutt, "Letter of Aristeas," *OTP* 2:7–34; cf. Jellicoe, *Septuagint,* 29–58.

on the island of Pharos, and completed the work in seventy-two days. Later patristic tradition maintains that each worked independently, but the completed translations were identical because of the scrupulous care employed in rendering the Hebrew text into Greek.

The Septuagint likely originated in the practice of providing Greek translation for liturgical and study purposes among the highly assimilated Greek-speaking Jews of Ptolemaic Egypt. The Torah was translated as early as the mid-third century, and employs Egyptian Greek terminology. The references to the Prophets in the prologue to Ben Sira indicate that these books were known in Greek by the second century B.C.E. Citations of the Septuagint in Philo, the New Testament, and Josephus indicate that it was well-known by the first century C.E.

No manuscript of the original Alexandrian version of the Septuagint is known to exist, and the many corrections and modifications found within the extant Christian manuscripts indicate that the Septuagint has undergone extensive revision to correct errors, translational and stylistic features, interpretative features, and apologetic elements that were introduced into the text. A variety of Greek recensions were produced during the early patristic period in an effort to present a standardized and authoritative Greek text. Aquila, a former student of Rabbi Akiva and a convert to Christianity (sometimes identified with the translator of Targum Onkelos), undertook a literal Greek rendition of the Hebrew text ca. 128 C.E. Symmachus, identified either as an Ebionite Christian or a Samaritan convert to Judaism, produced a Greek edition of the text in the late second century C.E. that combines literal accuracy with good idiomatic Greek. Theodotion, identified as an Ephesian convert to Judaism or an Ebionite, produced a distinctive text in the late second or early third century. In an effort to pursue apologetics against Jews, Origen in 230–240 C.E. collected Aquila, Symmachus, Theodotion, the Septuagint, the Hebrew text, and a Greek transliteration of the Hebrew to produce the six-column Hexapla, which in turn provided the basis for the production of authoritative Septuagint manuscripts in the fourth century C.E.[45]

The Lucianic recension is of particular importance for Kings.[46] Lucian had a reputation as a learned biblical scholar at Antioch, and ultimately suffered martyrdom at Nicomedia under Maximin in 311–312 C.E.[47] He worked together with a Hebrew scholar by the name of Dorotheus to produce an Antiochian revision of the Greek Bible that would bring the Greek text into closer conformity with the Hebrew. The Lucianic version was first identified in the Syro-Hexaplar, where the Syriac letter *lamadh* (L) marks 4 Rgns/2 Kgs 9:9, 28; 10:24, 25; 11:1; 23:33, 35 as Lucianic readings. These readings also appear in the cursive Greek

45. Peters, "Septuagint," *ABD* 5:1099.

46. See esp. Alfred Rahlfs, *Septuaginta-Studien* (3 vols.; Göttingen: Vandenhoeck & Ruprecht, 1904–1911).

47. Swete, *Introduction*, 82–85.

manuscripts 19, 82, 93, 108 (=Brooke and McLean mss. boc$_2$e$_2$). The readings of these manuscripts correspond to citations by Chrysostom and Theodoret, both of whom are Antiochian scholars who would cite from the Lucianic text. Greek cursive manuscript 118 was also recognized as a Lucianic text. Modern discussion has attempted to identify and clarify the nature of the Lucianic text, but many questions remain open.[48] Rahlfs's study of the Lucianic recension for 3–4 Reigns/ 1–2 Kings argues that Lucian brought the Old Greek into conformity with the Hebrew.[49] Barthélemy, based on Thackeray's contention that 2 Rgns/2 Sam 11:2–3 Rgns/1 Kgs 2:11 and 3 Rgns/1 Kgs 22–4 Rgns/2 Kgs 25 in Codex Vaticanus represents the work of a later translator, contends that the Lucianic manuscripts represent the old Greek in 1 Kgs 1:1–2:11 and 1 Kgs 21–2 Kgs 25.[50] Barthélemy maintains that the other manuscripts previously thought to represent the old Greek are actually the second-century C.E. *kaige*-Theodotion recension, which he identified on the basis of a variety of textual features, most notably the use of Greek *kaí ge* to render Hebrew *wĕgam*. Cross argues that the Lucianic manuscripts represent two layers, namely, a Lucianic substratum revised toward a Hebrew text and a superimposed layer of Lucianic corrections.[51] Tov contends that the Lucianic manuscripts include two layers with Lucianic revisions.

The earliest known Septuagint manuscripts were written by Christian scribes. The most complete version of the Greek Bible is the fourth-century C.E. Codex Vaticanus (Vatican Greek Manuscript 1209).[52] Codex Alexandrinus (British Library Royal I.D.) dates to the fifth or sixth century and contains many corrections, which may represent the source materials of the scribe.[53] Codex Venetus (St. Mark's Library, Venice), which once formed a complete Christian Bible with Codex Basiliano-Vaticanus (Vatican Greek 2106), dates to the eighth or ninth century C.E., and includes 3–4 Reigns.[54] The Lucianic manuscripts of 3–4 Reigns are discussed by Rahlfs.[55]

The Septuagint and its various recensions bear witness to a premasoretic Hebrew text tradition. Although the underlying Hebrew text is earlier than the present form of the MT, interpreters must exercise appropriate caution in accept-

48. See Tov, *Septuagint* 152 n. 13, for a summary of discussion.

49. Rahlfs, *Septuaginta-Studien III*.

50. Dominique Barthélemy, *Les Devanciers d'Aquila* (VTSup 10; Leiden: Brill, 1963); H. St. John Thackeray, "The Greek Translators of the Four Books of Kings," *JTS* 8 (1907): 262–78.

51. Frank Moore Cross Jr., "The History of the Biblical Text in Light of Discoveries in the Judean Desert," *HTR* 57 (1964): 281–99; Cross, "The Contribution of the Qumran Discoveries to the Study of the Biblical Text," *IEJ* 16 (1966): 81–95.

52. For discussion of Codex Vaticanus, see Swete, *Introduction*, 126–28; Jellicoe, *Septuagint*, 180–83.

53. For discussion of Codex Alexandrinus, see Swete, *Introduction*, 125–26; Jellicoe, *Septuagint*, 183–88. For a facsimile edition, see *The Codex Alexandrinus (Royal MS. 1 D v–viii) in Reduced Photographic Facsimile* (London: British Museum, 1936).

54. Swete, *Introduction*, 131–32; Jellicoe, *Septuagint*, 197–99.

55. For discussion of the Lucianic manuscripts, see Rahlfs, *Septuaginta-Studien III*, 7–18.

ing all differences between the LXX and MT as evidence of earlier Hebrew readings. In many cases, the differences represent attempts at interpretation of the underlying Hebrew or stylistic modifications intended to produce an esthetically pleasing Greek rendition of the text. Indeed, some of the major differences noted between the Greek and Hebrew text may be later features. The chronological differences of the Lucianic and LXX texts in reckoning the reigns of the Israelite and Judean kings appear to be the results of errors in calculating the reigns or attempts to correct problems in the text. The celebrated additions in 1 Rgns 2:35a–n, 46a–l; 12:24a–z; 16:28a–h; and 2 Rgns 1:18a–d, which purportedly represent an earlier text tradition of each episode, apparently represent midrashic-style rewritings designed to elaborate upon or correct problems in the Hebrew text.

The Peshitta and Syriac Versions

The Peshitta functions as the primary version of sacred Scripture for the eastern Syriac churches, including the Syrian Orthodox Church, the Maronite Church, and the Church of the East.[56] It is written in Syriac, an eastern Aramaic dialect spoken widely throughout western Asia until it was supplanted by Arabic. The term "Peshitta," derived from the root, *pšṭ,* "to stretch out, make straight," means "simple" or "common." It refers to the "common" version of the Bible, much as the Latin term "Vulgate" indicates the "common" version of the Bible in Western Christianity. Because *pšṭ* also functions in reference to "interpretation," it may be analogous to the Arabic term *tafsir,* "interpretation, translation," which is employed for Arabic versions of the Bible.

Although the term "Peshitta" is known only from the ninth century C.E., it originates in earlier times. Weitzman confirms that the Peshitta dates to the first or second century C.E., and he maintains that it originated in Edessa among nonrabbinic Jewish groups that ultimately adopted Christianity.[57] The Peshitta has affinities with the Targums, insofar as it served the needs of an Aramean-speaking Jewish or Christian community. The Peshitta is influenced by Septuagint, but it adheres far more closely to the proto-masoretic text.

The Peshitta divides 1–2 Kings differently than the MT. First Kings 1:1–2 Kgs 2:18 is identified as 3 Kings in the Peshitta tradition, and 2 Kgs 2:19–25:30 is identified as 4 Kings. In many manuscripts, 3 Kings/1 Kgs 16:29–2 Kgs 2:18 is identified as "the book concerning Elijah," and 4 Kings/2 Kgs 2:19–13:21 is identified as "the book concerning Elisha." The principal manuscript employed in the critical edition of 3–4 Kings is Manuscript B. 21 Inferiore, folios 114a–132b, of the Ambrosian Library in Milan, produced in a facsimile edition

56. See Michael Weitzman, *The Syriac Version of the Old Testament: An Introduction* (Cambridge: Cambridge University Press, 1999); Peter B. Dirksen, "The Old Testament Peshitta," in Martin Jan Mulder, ed., *Mikra* (Assen/Maastricht: Van Gorcum; Philadelphia: Fortress, 1988), 254–97.

57. Weitzman, *Syriac Version,* 206–62, esp. 248–58.

by A. M. Ceriani (1876–1883).[58] The manuscript is written in an Estrangela script, and dates to the seventh century C.E. The other primary manuscript is Bibliothéque nationale, Syriac manuscript 341, folios 84a-101a, also written in Estrangela, which dates to the eighth century C.E.[59]

Another Syriac version of the Bible is the Syro-Hexaplar, an early-seventh-century translation of the Bible into Syriac based largely on the fifth column (Septuagint) of Origen's Hexpla.[60] The Old Testament portion of the work was translated in Alexandria in 613–617 C.E. by Paul of Tella with assistance by Thomas of Harkel. Manuscripts of the Syro-Hexaplar version of Kings appear among the Nitrian manuscripts of the British Library, and the Bibliothéque nationale includes a manuscript of 4 Kings. Fragments of a Palestinian Syriac version translated from the Septuagint include 3 Kgs 2:10–15; 9:4–5.[61]

Targum Jonathan

Targum Jonathan on the Prophets is an Aramaic version of the Prophets, including Joshua; Judges; Samuel; Kings; Isaiah; Jeremiah; Ezekiel; and the Twelve Prophets.[62] The Talmud identifies this version as "the Targum of the Prophets that was composed by Jonathan ben Uzziel from the mouth of Haggai, Zechariah, and Malachi" (*b. Meg. 3a*). Jonathan ben Uzziel was a student of Rabbi Hillel (*b. Sukkah 28a; B. Bat. 134a; ʾAbot R. Nat. A14, 29a*), which places him in the late first century B.C.E. through the early first century C.E. Theodotion, who produced an early Greek translation of the Bible, might be a Graecized form of the name Jonathan.[63]

Targum Jonathan arose in the social setting of synagogue worship and study as an interpretative translation of the Bible into Aramaic, the vernacular language spoken by Jews in western Asia from the late Second Temple period through the Islamic conquest. Many note the reference in Neh 8:7 to the Levites who interpreted Ezra's reading of the Torah to the people. This event hardly represents the origins of the Targum per se, but it does point to the social background in which Targumic tradition developed by the first century C.E.[64]

Targum Jonathan presupposes the MT, but it takes liberties. It frequently changes names; contemporizes place names in the Bible to names employed in

58. Hans Gottlieb, *The Old Testament in Syriac according to the Peshitta Version. II/4: Kings* (Leiden: Brill, 1976), v–viii.

59. Ibid., viii–ix. See iii–ix for discussion of other manuscripts.

60. Swete, *Introduction*, 112–14; Jellicoe, *Septuagint.*

61. Swete, *Introduction*, 114–15.

62. See Philip S. Alexander, "Jewish Aramaic Translations of Hebrew Scripture," *Mikra*, 217–53; Pinkhos Churgin, *Targum Jonathan to the Prophets* (New York: KTAV, 1983); Leivy Smolar and Moses Aberbach, *Studies in Targum Jonathan to the Prophets* (New York: KTAV, 1983).

63. Barthélemy, *Devanciers*, 148–56.

64. See Charles Perrot, "The Reading of the Bible in the Synagogue," *Mikra*, 137–59.

the first–second centuries C.E.; introduces changes of word and phrase to clarify or interpret the Hebrew text; modernizes statements of practice; substitutes literal for metaphoric language; takes great care in depicting G-d and human relations with G-d; and adds midrashic, halakhic, and other interpretations.[65]

The basic manuscript of Targum Jonathan employed by Sperber in his critical edition is British Library Oriental manuscript 2210, a fifteenth–sixteenth-century Yemenite manuscript of the Former Prophets, which reflects the early fourth––fifth-century Babylonian vocalization.[66] Other important manuscripts are Codex Reuchlinianus of the Badische Landesbibliothek in Karlsruhe, a western Tiberian manuscript that dates to 1105. Manuscript p. 116 of the Jews College in London includes the western Tiberian text of 1 Samuel–Malachi, dated to 1486.

The Vulgate and Other Latin Versions

The Vulgate was produced by Jerome (ca. 347–420 C.E.), who was commissioned in 382 by Pope Damasus to produce a standard Latin text of the Bible.[67] Jerome's work was motivated by the same problems discussed above in relation to the Hebrew, Greek, Syriac, and Aramaic versions, namely, there was a variety of text types circulating in the ancient world that would have challenged the authoritative role of sacred Scripture in both Christianity and Judaism.

Western Christianity turned increasingly to Latin translations of the Bible since Latin was widely spoken in regions dominated by Rome. The Vetus Latina or Old Latin text appeared during the first Christian centuries, but this version is known only from patristic quotations, fragmentary and palimpsest manuscripts, liturgical texts, and so on.[68] Preliminary analysis of the Vetus Latina for 1–2 Kings indicates that it must be used with caution since it diverges widely from its Greek Vorlage. A full text-critical examination of the Vetus Latina remains to be completed.[69]

The Vulgate adheres closely to a premasoretic Hebrew text, although it is influenced by the Septuagint, the other Greek versions, and the Old Latin. Jerome consulted Jewish authorities throughout the process of translation. Despite his efforts at philological accuracy, he sometimes introduces his own theological perspectives into the translation. Following the affirmation of this version's authenticity at the Council of Trent in 1546, it became known as the Vulgate.

---

65. See Daniel J. Harrington and Anthony J. Saldarini, *Targum Jonathan of the Former Prophets: Introduction, Translation, and Notes* (Aramaic Bible 10; Collegeville, Minn.: Liturgical, 1987), 4–13.

66. See Alexander Sperber, *The Bible in Aramaic. III. The Latter Prophets according to Targum Jonathan* (Leiden: Brill, 1962), v–vi; Harrington and Saldarini, *Targum Jonathan*, 2.

67. See Benjamin Kedar, "The Latin Translations," *Mikra*, 299–338.

68. See Natalio Fernández Marcos, *Scribes and Translators: Septuagint and Old Latin in the Books of Kings* (VTSup 54; Leiden: Brill, 1994).

69. Marcos, *Scribes*, 71–87; cf. N. Fernández Marcos and J. R. Busto-Saiz, *El texto antigueno de la Biblia Griega II: 1–2 Reyes* (Textos y estudios Cardenal Cisneros 53; Madrid: CSIC, 1992).

The oldest known manuscript of the Vulgate is Codex Amiatinus, an eighth-century manuscript written in Northumbria and now located in Florence. Codex Amiatinus and Codex Cavensis, an eighth- or ninth-century Spanish manuscript now housed in Salerno, serve as the manuscript bases for critical editions of the Vulgate.[70]

The Question of Chronology

One of the most difficult problems in the interpretation of 1–2 Kings is the chronology of the kings of Israel and Judah. The regnal accounts provide information concerning each king's age at accession to the throne, the corresponding year of his Judean or Israelite counterpart, and the years of his reign. Unfortunately, the MT, LXX, and Lucianic recensions vary considerably.[71] Studies that defend the chronology of the MT face serious problems in reconciling the inconsistencies of the MT system. They adjust the dates of individual monarchs, argue for different systems of reckoning accession years in the north and south, and argue that some reigns must overlap due to coregencies.[72] Although the LXX and Lucianic systems make far more sense than the MT, studies that defend the Greek chronologies have been at a loss to explain why the MT would modify the system of the Greek text to produce a convoluted chronology.[73]

The following summarize the chronological data for the kings of Judah in the MT and the LXX/Lucianic texts:

Kings of Judah	Age at Accession	Accession Date	Years of Rule
David	30	NA	40
(2 Sam 5:4; 1 Kgs 2:11; 2 Rgns 5:4; 3 Rgns 2:11)			
Solomon	NA	NA	40
(1 Kgs 11:42; 3 Rgns 11:42)			
Rehoboam	41/41/16	NA	17
(1 Kgs 14:21; 3 Rgns 14:21; 12:24a)	(1 yr. Jeroboam?)		
Abijah	NA	18 yr. Jeroboam	3/6
(1 Kgs 15:2; 3 Rgns 15:2)			

70. See Samuel Berger, *Histoire de la Vulgate pendant les premiers siècles du moyen age* (New York: Franklin, 1958), 14–15, 37–38.

71. For overviews, see G. H. Jones, *1 and 2 Kings* (2 vols.; The New Century Bible Commentary; Grand Rapids: William B. Eerdmans; London: Marshall, Morgan and Scott, 1984), 9–28; Gershon Galil, *The Chronology of the Kings of Israel and Judah* (SHANE 9; Leiden: Brill, 1996); James Donald Shenkel, *Chronology and Recensional Development in the Greek Text of Kings* (HSM 1; Cambridge: Harvard University Press, 1968); and Edwin R. Thiele, *The Mysterious Numbers of the Hebrew Kings* (Grand Rapids: Kregel, 1983).

72. E.g., Thiele, *Mysterious Numbers*; Galil, *Chronology*.

73. Jones, *1 and 2 Kings*; Shenkel, *Chronology and Recensional Development*.

Asa	NA	20/24 yr. Jeroboam	41
(1 Kgs 15:10; 3 Rgns 15:10)			
Jehoshaphat	35/35/35	4 yr. Ahab/	25
		4 yr. Ahab/	
		11 yr. Omri	
(1 Kgs 22:42; 1 Rgns 22:42; 1 Rgns 16:28a)			
Jehoram	32	5 yr. Joram	8
(2 Kgs 8:16–17; 4 Rgns 8:16–17)			
Ahaziah	22	12/11 yr. Joram	1
		12/11 yr. Joram	
(2 Kgs 8:25–26; 9:29; 4 Rgns 8:25–26; 9:29)			
[Athaliah]	NA	NA	6
		(1 yr. Jehu?)	
(2 Kgs 11:3; 4 Rgns 11:3)			
Jehoash	7	7 yr. Jehu	40
(2 Kgs 12:1–2; 4 Rgns 12:1–2)			
Amaziah	25	2 yr. Joash	29
(2 Kgs 14:1–2; 4 Rgns 14:1–2)			
Azariah/Uzziah	16	27 yr. Jeroboam	52
(2 Kgs 15:1–2; 4 Rgns 15:1–2)			
Jotham	25	2 yr. Pekah	16
(2 Kgs 15:32–33; 4 Rgns 15:32–33)			
Ahaz	20	17 yr. Pekah	16
(2 Kgs 16:1–2; 4 Rgns 16:1–2)			
Hezekiah	25	3 yr. Hoshea	29
(2 Kgs 18:1–2; 4 Rgns 18:1–2)			
Manasseh	12	NA	55
(2 Kgs 21:1–2; 4 Rgns 21:1–2)			
Amon	22	NA	2
(2 Kgs 21:19; 4 Rgns 21:19)			
Josiah	8	NA	31
(2 Kgs 22:1; 4 Rgns 22:1)			
Jehoahaz	23	NA	3 mos.
(2 Kgs 23:31; 4 Rgns 23:31)			
Jehoiakim	25	NA	11
(2 Kgs 23:36; 4 Rgns 23:36)			
Jehoiachin	18	NA	3 mos.
(2 Kgs 24:8; 4 Rgns 24:8)			

Zedekiah   21   NA   11
(2 Kgs 24:18; 4 Rgns 24:18)

The following presents the chronological data for the kings of Israel according to the MT and LXX/Lucianic versions:

Kings of Israel	Age at Accession	Accession Date	Years of Rule
Jeroboam	NA	NA 1 yr. Rehoboam?	22/NA/24?
(1 Kgs 14:20; NA; cf. 3 Rgns 15:9)			
Nadab	NA	2 yr. Asa	2
(1 Kgs 15:25; 3 Rgns 15:25)			
Baasha	NA	3 yr. Asa	24
(1 Kgs 15:33; 3 Rgns 15:33)			
Elah	NA	26 yr. Asa/ NA	2
(1 Kgs 16:8; cf. 3 Rgns 16:8)			
Zimri	NA	27 yr. Asa/ NA	7 days
(1 Kgs 16:15; cf. 3 Rgns 16:5)			
Omri	NA	31 yr. Asa NA	12
(1 Kgs 16:23; cf. 3 Rgns 16:23)			
Ahab	NA	38 yr. Asa/ 2 yr. Jehoshaphat	22
(1 Kgs 16:29; 3 Rgns 16:29)			
Ahaziah	NA	17 yr. Jehoshaphat	2
(1 Kgs 22:52; 3 Rgns 22:52)			
Jehoram	NA	18 yr. Jehoshaphat/ 18 yr. Jehoshaphat/ 24 yr. Jehoshaphat	12
(2 Kgs 3:1; LXX 4 Rgns 3:1; Luc 4 Rgns 3:1)			
Jehu	NA	NA (1 yr. Ahaziah/Athaliah?)	28
(2 Kgs 10:36; 4 Rgns 10:36)			
Jehoahaz	NA	23 yr. Jehoash	17
(2 Kgs 13:1; 4 Rgns 13:1)			

Jehoash	NA	37 yr. Jehoash /	17
		37 yr. Jehoash/	
		40 yr. Jehoash (c_2)	
(2 Kgs 13:10; 4 Rgns 13:10; cf. c_2)			
Jeroboam	NA	15 yr. Amaziah	41
(2 Kgs 14:23; 4 Rgns 14:23)			
Zechariah	NA	38 yr. Azariah/	6 mos.
		38 yr. Azariah/	
		28 yr. Azariah	
(2 Kgs 15:8; LXX 4 Rgns 15:8; Luc 4 Rgns 15:8)			
Shallum	NA	39 yr. Uzziah	1 mo.
(2 Kgs 15:13; 4 Rgns 15:13)			
Menahem	NA	39 yr. Azariah	10
(2 Kgs 15:17; 4 Rgns 15:17)			
Pekahiah	NA	50 yr. Azariah	2/2/10(e_2)
(2 Kgs 15:23; 4 Rgns 15:23; see e_2)			
Pekah	NA	52 yr. Azariah	20
(2 Kgs 15:27; 4 Rgns 15:27)			
Hoshea	NA	12 yr. Ahaz	9
(2 Kgs 17:1; 4 Rgns 17:1)			

The above tables demonstrate a number of variations between the chronological data of the MT and the LXX/Lucianic. Major conclusions follow.

The MT presents an impossible chronology. With regard to the northern kings, Omri's accession to the throne in the thirty-first year of Asa (1 Kgs 16:23) hardly follows from the seven-day reign of Zimri which began in the twenty-seventh year of Asa (1 Kgs 16:15). Omri's twelve-year reign beginning in the thirty-first year of Asa (1 Kgs 16:23) can hardly allow for Ahab's accession to the throne in the thirty-eighth year of Asa (1 Kgs 16:29). The forty-year time span for the reigns of Nadab, Baasha, Elah, Zimri, and Elah calls for the second year of Jehoshaphat in keeping with the reading of the LXX text. The LXX text also eliminates the accession dates for Elah, Zimri, and Omri, all of which are problematic. Ahab's twenty-two-year reign beginning in the thirty-eighth year of Asa (1 Kgs 16:38) can hardly allow for Ahaziah's accession to the throne in the seventeenth year of Jehoshaphat (1 Kgs 22:52); it must be the ninth year of Jehoshaphat, but if one places the beginning of his reign in the second year of Jehoshaphat with the LXX, then Ahaziah's reign must begin in the twenty-fourth year of Jehoshaphat in keeping with the Lucianic text of 4 Rgns 3:1. Jehoahaz's seventeen-year reign beginning in the twenty-third year of Jehoash cannot begin in the thirty-seventh year of Jehoash of Judah (2 Kgs 13:1), but must begin in the fortieth year of Jehoash of Judah as stated in the Lucianic manuscript c_2. Jeroboam's forty-one-year reign beginning in the fifteenth year of Amaziah of Judah (2 Kgs 14:23) cannot allow for Zechariah's accession in the thirty-eighth year of Azariah (2 Kgs 15:8), which must take place in the twenty-eighth year of Azariah in accordance with Lucianic texts. Hoshea's nine-year reign beginning in the twelfth year of Ahaz (2 Kgs 17:1) is impossible and calls instead for the fourth year of Ahaz (cf. *BHS* note). The MT's impossible chronology is corrected at virtually every step by LXX and the Lucianic text.

The MT chronology of the Judean kings requires one major correction. Abijah's three-year reign beginning in the eighteenth year of Jeroboam (1 Kgs 15:2) appears as a six-year reign in LXX/Lucian (2 Rgns 15:2). A related statement is 1 Kgs 15:10, which claims that Asa ascended the throne in the twentieth year of Jeroboam, whereas 4 Rgns 15:10 states that Asa ascended the throne in Jeroboam's twenty-fourth year. According to MT 1 Kgs 14:20, Jeroboam reigned only for twenty-two years, but LXX lacks this text as well as any other statement concerning the length of Jeroboam's reign. Interpreters overlook the exegetical problem that prompts the change. MT 1 Kgs 15:6 states that "and there was war between Abijam and Jeroboam all the days of his life," which is impossible since Rehoboam is already dead. But if Abijam has a six-year reign, then Rehoboam's seventeen-year reign and Abijam's six-year reign call for a twenty-four-year reign for Jeroboam. The change takes place when the *lamedh* from the word *šālôš,* "three," in 2 Kgs 15:2 drops out, leaving only the consonantal base for *šēš,* "six," which stands behind the Greek text of 3 Rgns 15:2. Interestingly, the statement in 2 Kgs 15:6 concerning war between Abijam and Jeroboam drops out of the LXX text together with the notice concerning David's treatment of Uriah the Hittite in 2 Kgs 15:5b. This may be a case of homeoteleuton based on the appearance of the phrase "all the days of his life" at the end of both vv. 5b and 6, but the disappearance of vv. 5b–6 eliminates the problem that prompted the changes in the first place. It also eliminates an unpleasant reminder of David's sin from a context that otherwise praises him.

These examples demonstrate that the MT chronology makes little sense, but there is no cause to posit that the masoretic scribes modified a sensible chronology that now appears in the LXX and Lucianic texts. It makes far more sense to posit that the LXX and Lucianic texts reflect efforts to correct the proto-MT. Unfortunately, we may never possess a full understanding of the true chronology of the kings of Israel and Judah.

COMMENTARY

I. The Death of David and Designation of Solomon as His Successor 1 Kings 1:1–2:11

The first major unit of 1–2 Kings is the account of David's death and designation of Solomon as his successor in 1 Kgs 1:1–2:11. Scholars generally define the larger unit as the account of Solomon's reign in 1 Kgs 1–11, the account of Solomon's succession in 1 Kgs 1–2, or the like (e.g., Long 11–32; Campbell and O'Brien 324–25), but these decisions are based on models of compositional history that do not take full account of the synchronic form of the text.[1]

First Kings 1:1–4 introduces the unit, beginning with a nominative clause that relates David's old age, and provides the basis on which the following account of the designation of David's successor proceeds. First Kings 1:5–49 then relates Adonijah's unsuccessful attempt to have himself designated as David's successor together with Nathan's and Bath Sheba's successful efforts to prompt David to designate Solomon as king. First Kings 1:5–49 begins with a nominative clause that identifies Adonijah as the principal actor, and each of its seven constituent subunits likewise begins with a nominative clause that identifies the major character or characters of each constituent episode (1 Kgs 1:5–10, 11–14, 15–27, 28–31, 32–37, 38–40, and 41–49). The third major unit in 1 Kgs 1:50–2:10 provides an account of Adonijah's fear, again introduced by a nominative clause in v. 50, and David's final instructions to Solomon in 1 Kgs 2:1–9 prior to the report of the old king's death in 1 Kgs 2:10. The fourth major unit, the summation of David's reign in 1 Kgs 2:11, brings the account of David's reign to a close.

The general bloodbath that follows Solomon's succession to the throne raises questions about Solomon, even though he was counseled to act in this manner by David on his deathbed.[2] The narrative goes to special lengths to portray

---

1. Lucianic versions place a superscription between 1 Kgs/3 Kgdms 2:11 and 2:12 to mark the beginning of 3 Kgdms; see Rahlfs's note to 3 Kgdms 2:11 (*Septuaginta* [Stuttgart: Wurtembergisches Bibelanstalt, 1935] ad loc.). Many scholars follow Leonhard Rost, *Die Überlieferung von der Thronnachfolge Davids* (BWANT 42; Stuttgart: W. Kohlhammer, 1926), who argues that 2 Sam 9–20; 1 Kgs 1–2 constitute a single tenth-century B.C.E. literary work that attempts to justify Solomon's ascension to the throne.

2. Delekat, for example, opens the question of such anti-Solomonic tendencies (Lienhard Delekat, "Tendenz und Theologie der David-Salomo-Erzählung," in *Das Ferne und Nahe Wort* [Fest. L. Rost; ed. F. Maass; BZAW 105; Berlin: A. Töpelmann, 1967], 26–36; cf. Sophia Katharina Bietenhard, *Des Königs General* (OBO 163; Freiburg: Universitäts-Verlag; Göttingen: Vandenhoeck & Ruprecht, 1998), 212–28.

Solomon as David's choice to succeed him, but it is never clear that David had the right to make such a decision. Earlier portrayals of the selection of monarchs, including both Saul (1 Sam 8–12) and David (1 Sam 16; 2 Sam 2–5; 7), emphasize the role of the Deity and the people in choosing the king (cf. Deut 17:14–20). The narrative at no point indicates YHWH's approval of the choice of Solomon (or Adonijah), other than to place divine oaths and blessings concerning the succession of David's son in the mouths of the principal characters, such as Nathan, Bath Sheba, David, and so on. Confirmation that such statements do indeed come from YHWH never appear in this narrative. The acclamation of the people takes place only after David makes his decision, and by that point, it is largely irrelevant to the decision as the people simply accept the designation of Solomon by David. YHWH ultimately approves Solomon in 1 Kgs 3, but this does not mitigate the impression that Solomon came to the throne improperly.

First Kings 1–2 is a redactional block that provides the transition from 2 Samuel to 1 Kings. By raising questions about Solomon, these chapters lay the foundation for the critique of Solomon in 1 Kgs 11, as well as the critique of the monarchy throughout 1–2 Kings. Such a concern fits well with the Josian DtrH, in which Josiah functions as a foil to Solomon by correcting the problems in Israelite worship instituted by Solomon. This concern also serves the exilic edition of the DtrH, which attempts to explain the destruction of Jerusalem and the temple, the fall of the Davidic monarchy, and the Babylonian exile.

1:1 And King David was old, advanced in years, and they covered him in garments, but he was not warm. 2 So his servants said to him, "Let there be sought for my lord, the king, a young virgin woman, who will stand before the king,[a] and be an attendant[b] for him, and lie in your bosom,[c] so that my lord, the king, shall be warm." 3 And they sought a beautiful young woman in all the territory of Israel, and they found Abishag the Shunammite[d] and brought her to the king. 4 And the young woman was extremely beautiful, and she was an attendant for the king; she served him, but the king did not know her intimately.

5 And Adonijah ben Haggith promoted himself, saying, "I will be king!" and he provided himself with a chariot and horses with fifty men running before him. 6 Now his father had never in his life reprimanded him by saying, "Why did you do that?" He was also very handsome, and she (his mother) bore him after Absalom. 7 And he conferred with Joab ben Zeruiah and with Abiathar the priest, and they supported Adonijah. 8 But Zadok the priest, and Benaiah ben Jehoiada, and Nathan the prophet, and Shimei, and Rei,[e] and David's warriors were not with Adonijah. 9 And Adonijah sacrificed sheep and cattle and fattened lambs at the Zohelet stone,[f] which is beside Ein Rogel,[g] and he invited all his brothers, the sons of the

king, and all the men of Judah, the servants of David. 10 But he did not invite Nathan the prophet, Benaiah, the warriors, or Solomon his brother.

11 And Nathan said to Bath Sheba, the mother of Solomon, "Have you not heard that Adonijah ben Haggith has assumed kingship, and our lord David does not know about it? 12 And now, come, let me give you counsel so that you may save[h] your life and the life of your son Solomon. 13 Come now, and go to King David, and say to him, 'Did you not, my lord the king, swear to your maidservant saying, "When[i] Solomon your son becomes king after me, he shall sit upon my throne"? Then why has Adonijah become king?' 14 Then while you are still speaking with the king I will enter after you and confirm your words."

15 And Bath Sheba came to the king in his chamber, but the king was very old, and Abishag the Shunammite was serving the king. 16 And Bath Sheba bowed and prostrated herself to the king, and the king said, "What do you want?" 17 And she said to him, "My lord, you have sworn by YHWH your G-d to your maidservant that Solomon your son shall be king after me, and he shall sit upon my throne. 18 And now, behold, Adonijah has become king, but now, my lord the king, you do not know about it. 19 And he has sacrificed oxen, and fat lambs, and sheep in great quantities, and he invited all the sons of the king, and Abiathar the priest, and Joab the commander of the army, but Solomon your servant he did not invite. 20 And you, my lord the king, the eyes of all Israel are upon you to declare to them who shall sit upon the throne of my lord the king after him. 21 And when my lord the king lies with his fathers, then I and my son Solomon shall be considered as criminals."

22 And then, while she was speaking with the king, Nathan the prophet came. 23 And they announced him to the king, saying, "Behold, Nathan the prophet." And he entered before the king, and he prostrated himself to the king with his face to the ground. 24 And Nathan said, "My lord the king, have you said, 'Adonijah shall become king after me, and he shall sit upon my throne'? 25 because he has gone down today, and he has sacrificed oxen, and fat lambs, and sheep in great quantities, and he invited all the sons of the king, and the commanders of the army, and Abiathar the priest, and they are eating and drinking before him, and they said, "May the king, Adonijah, live!" 26 But me, I your servant, and Zadok the priest, and Benaiah ben Jehoiada, and Solomon your servant, he did not invite. 27 Could this thing have come from my lord the king, and you did not inform your servant[j] who shall sit upon the throne of my lord the king after him?"

28 And King David answered and said, "Summon Bath Sheba for me!" And she came and stood before the king. 29 And the king swore and said, "As YHWH lives, who has redeemed my life from every adversity, 30 just as I have sworn to you by YHWH, the G-d of Israel, saying, 'that

Solomon, your son, shall become king after me, and he shall sit upon my throne in my place,' indeed, so shall I do this day." 31 And Bath Sheba bowed to the ground and prostrated herself to the king, and she said, "May my lord, King David, live forever!"

32 And King David said, "Summon to me, Zadok the priest, and Nathan the prophet, and Benaiah ben Jehoiada!" And they came before the king. 33 And the king said to them, "Take with you the servants of your lord, mount Solomon my son upon my own mule, and take him down to Gihon,^{k} 34 and Zadok the priest and Nathan the prophet shall anoint him there as king over Israel. And you shall blow the Shofar and say, 'May King Solomon live!' 35 And you shall go up after him, and he shall enter, sit upon my throne, and be king in my place, for have I commanded him to be ruler over Israel and Judah." 36 And Benaiah ben Jehoiada answered the king and said, "So be it (Amen)! May YHWH, the G-d of my lord the king, so say! 37 Just as YHWH was with my lord the king, so shall He be^l with Solomon, and make his throne greater than the throne of my lord, King David!"

38 And Zadok the priest and Nathan the prophet, Benaiah ben Jehoiada, and the Cherethites and the Pelethites went down, mounted Solomon upon the mule of King David, and brought him to the Gihon. 39 And Zadok the priest^m took the horn of oil from the tent and anointed Solomon, and they blew the Shofar, and all the people said, "May King Solomon live!" 40 And all the people went up after him, and the people were playing pipes and rejoicing with great joy so that the land was split because of their noise.

41 And Adonijah and all the invited guests with him heard just when they had finished eating. And Joab heard the sound of the Shofar and said, "Why does the city sound so noisy?" 42 While he was speaking, behold, Jonathan ben Abiathar the priest came, and Adonijah said, "Come, for you are a man of worth, and you will announce good news." 43 And Jonathan said to Adonijah, "Indeed our lord King David has made Solomon king, 44 and the king sent with him Zadok the priest, Nathan the prophet, Benaiah ben Jehoiada, and the Cherethites, and the Pelethites, and they mounted him upon the king's mule. 45 And Zadok the priest and Nathan the prophet anointed him as king at Gihon, and they went up from there rejoicing so that the city is noisy. That is the sound that you heard. 46 And also, Solomon is seated upon the throne of the kingdom. 47 And also, the servants of the king have come to bless our lord King David saying, 'May G-d^n make the name of Solomon better than your name, and make his throne greater than your throne!' and the king prostrated himself upon the bed. 48 And also, he spoke accordingly, 'Blessed is YHWH, the G-d of Israel, who has this day granted that my eyes see one sitting upon my throne!'" 49 And all Adonijah's invited guests were afraid, and they rose, and each went on his own way.

50 And Adonijah feared Solomon, so he rose, went, and seized the horns
of the altar. 51 And it was reported to Solomon, saying, "Behold, Adonijah fears King Solomon, and behold, he has taken hold of the horns of the
altar, saying, 'Let King Solomon swear to me today that he will not kill
his servant by sword.'" 52 And Solomon said, "If he will be worthy, not
even a hair shall fall to the ground. But if evil is found in him, then he
shall die." 53 And King Solomon sent (people) who brought him down
from upon the altar, and he came and prostrated himself to King Solomon,
and Solomon said to him, "Go home."

2:1 As David's time to die drew near, he commanded Solomon his son,
saying, 2 "I am going by the way of all the earth, and you must be strong
and be a man. 3 And you shall observe the charge of YHWH, your G-d,
to walk in His ways, to observe His statutes, His commandments, and His
laws, and His precepts, as written in the Torah of Moses, in order that you
will succeed in everything that you would do °and everywhere that you
would turn,° 4 in order that YHWH will carry out His promise that He
made about me, saying, 'If your sons will watch their way, to walk before
Me in truth, in all their heart and in all their soul,' then 'there shall never
cease to be for you a man sitting upon the throne of Israel.' 5 And also you
know what Joab ben Zeruiah did to me, what he did to the two commanders of Israel's army, to Abner ben Ner and to Amasa ben Yeter, how he
killed them claiming that they were targets of war in a time of peace, how
he stained his sword belt on his loins and his shoes on his feet with the
blood of war.[p] 6 And you shall act according to your wisdom, and you
shall not allow his gray head to go down to Sheol in peace. 7 And as for
the sons of Barzillai the Gileadite, you shall show fidelity, and they shall
be among those who eat at your table, for so they stood by me when I fled
from before Absalom, your brother. 8 And behold, Shimei ben Gera the
Benjaminite from Bahurim[q] is with you, and he cursed me with a violent
curse on the day that I went to Mahanaim, then he came down to meet me
at the Jordan, and I swore to him by YHWH saying, 'I will not kill you
by sword.' 9 And now, do not hold him innocent, for you are a wise man
and you know what you should do to him so that you will bring his gray
head down to Sheol in blood."

10 And David slept with his fathers, and he was buried in the city of David.

11 And the time that David ruled over Israel was forty years: in Hebron he ruled for seven years and in Jerusalem he ruled for thirty-three years.

a. The idiom "and she shall stand before (the king)" implies that she serves in an official capacity (cf. Num 16:9; Deut 10:8; 1 Sam 16:22; 1 Kgs 17:1; 2 Kgs 3:14; Jer 15:9; Ezek 44:11, 15).

b. Hebrew *sōkenet,* "attendant, stewardess," is derived from the root *skn,* "to be of use, service" (see Job 15:3; 22:2; 34:9; 35:3). The masculine form *sōkēn,* "steward," appears in Isa 22:15 as a designation for Shebna, who is otherwise identified in his official capacity as the one who is "over the house," that is, the chief administrator of the royal palace (cf. 2 Kgs 18:18, 37; 19:2/Isa 36:3, 22; 37:2; Fox, *In the Service of the King,* 178–82, 81–96).

c. LXX eliminates any indication of a direct address to the king by reading *koimēthēsetai met' 'autou,* "and she shall go to sleep with him," which does not necessarily connote sexual relations.

d. LXX reads *Sōmanitin,* "the Somanite," by reversing the letters *nun* and *mem* from Hebrew *šûnammît,* "Shunammite." Peshitta reads, *šylwmyṱ,* "Shilomit," identifying Abishag with the Shulammite woman of Song of Songs (Song 7:1).

e. Rei is otherwise unknown. Because of the similarity of the Hebrew name *rēʿî* to the word, *rēʿeh,* "friend, companion," some have followed Lucianic LXX and Josephus (*Ant* 7.14.4) in reading the term as a noun, that is, "and Shimei and his comrades (*etairoi autou*), the warriors."

f. Hebrew, *ʾeben hazzōḥelet,* "the stone of serpents," based upon the Hebrew root, *zḥl,* "to shrink back, crawl away" (Deut 32:24; Mic 7:17). Cf. Targum Jonathan which reads, *ʾeben sākûtāʾ,* "lookout stone," or more likely "the stone of Saturn," based upon the reference to Saturn as *sikkût* in Amos 5:26 (Leivy Smolar and Moses Aberbach, *Studies in Targum Jonathan to the Prophets* [New York: KTAV; Baltimore: Baltimore Hebrew College, 1983], 112–13).

g. Hebrew, *ʿên rōgēl,* sometimes rendered as "Walker Spring" or "Fuller Spring," based upon the Hebrew root, *rgl,* "to go about (by foot), tread."

h. The use of the feminine, singular, imperative verb, *ûmallĕtî,* "and save," conveys the urgent need for Bath Sheba to act.

i. MT, *kî,* often translated as "for, because, that." The particle is inherently conjunctive, but it may be employed conditionally, temporally, causally, or emphatically (Anneli Aejmelaeus, "Function and Interpretation of *כ* in Biblical Hebrew," *JBL* 105 [1986]: 193–209, esp. 208).

j. Qere, *ʿabdĕkā,* "your servant," that is, Nathan; cf. LXX, *tōi doulō sou,* "your servant"; Vulgate, *servo tuo,* "your servant." See Ketiv, *ʿăbādêkā,* "your servants"; cf. Targum Jonathan, *ʿabdāk,* "your servants"; Peshitta, *ʿdyk,* "to your servants."

k. Cf. Targum Jonathan, *lĕšîlôḥāʾ,* "to the Shiloaḥ," and the Peshitta, *lšylwḥʾ,* "to the Shiloaḥ," which both identify the location as the Shiloaḥ pool. The pool of Shiloaḥ (Siloam in English) was formed at the southern tip of the city of David from the waters that flowed from the Giḥon spring, located outside of the walls of the city near its eastern gate in the Kidron valley, through the tunnel dug by Hezekiah in the eighth century B.C.E. (2 Chr 32:2–4).

l. Ketiv, *yĕhî,* "may He (YHWH) be"; Qere, *yihyeh,* "shall He (YHWH) be."

m. Peshitta adds, *wntn nbyʾ,* "and Nathan the prophet."

n. Qere, *ʾlhyk,* "your G-d"; Ketiv, *ʾlhym,* "G-d." Cf. LXX, *ho Theos,* "G-d"; Targum Jonathan, *ywy,* "YHWH"; Peshitta, *mryʾ ʾlhyn,* "the L-rd, G-d"; Vulgate, *Deus,* "G-d."

o–o. LXX reads, *kata panta hosa an enteilōmai soi,* "according to all that I command you" (cf. the characteristic phraseology of Deut 4:2; 6:2, 6; etc.); Peshitta reads, *dtslḥ bkl dtʿbd wlʾybʾ dtʾnl tbšr,* "that you may succeed in all that you do and you may prosper wherever you go." Both readings appear to be the results of attempts to render a stylistically difficult text.

   p. LXX, *haima athōion*, "innocent blood," apparently an attempt to clarify an enigmatic phrase.

   q. Targum Jonathan, "Almat"; Hebrew *baḥûrîm*, "young men" is ʿ*ălĕmat*, "youth," in Aramaic.

[1:1–4] This passage begins with a noun clause that signals the focus on David's old age and its implications for his ability to exercise royal authority, and continues with a sequence of *waw*-consecutive imperfect verbal formations in vv. 1b–4 that portray his inability to "warm himself" by having sexual relations with Abishag. This notice sets the stage for 1 Kgs 1:5–49, which relates Adonijah's failed attempt to succeed David as king.

   The literary context relates Adonijah's assumption that he should succeed his father immediately following the notice that David did not engage in sexual relations with Abishag. Kings in the ancient world were frequently judged as fit to rule based in part upon their virility, particularly their ability to marry the daughters (or other female relations) of foreign kings and key supporters within their own realms, thereby maintaining a network of alliances based upon family relationships. David built up his own kingdom through such marriage alliances.[3] In some cultures, the king's sexual vitality was displayed publicly. The Sumerian Akitu or New Year festival required that the king engage in sexual relations with a priestess as part of the process by which he would be authorized to exercise kingship for another year.[4]

   The question of David's relationship to the house of Saul underlies the concern for his ability to exercise kingship in this narrative. David's claim to the throne is justified in part by his marriage to Michal and the inability of Saul's sons to assume the throne due to death (see 1 Sam 31; 2 Sam 1–5 [6–7]; 21) or incapacity (see 2 Sam 9; 19:24–30). His refusal to have relations with Michal ensures that she will not have children who would then have a greater claim to the throne by virtue of their descent from Saul.[5] Abishag's hometown of Shunem is noted for its ties to the house of Saul. Shunem is identified with the modern village of Sulim, located about three miles east of Afula in the Jezreel Valley (Josh 19:18). Saul died in battle at Mount Gilboa as part of his efforts to defend the Jezreel against the Philistines, who were encamped at Shunem (1 Sam 28:4;

---

   3. Jon D. Levenson and Baruch Halpern, "The Political Import of David's Marriages," *JBL* 99 (1980): 11–28.
   4. J. Klein, "Akitu," *ABD* 1:138–40; Klein, "Sacred Marriage," *ABD* 5:866–70.
   5. The assumption of Saul's son Eshbaal to kingship (2 Sam 2–5) and the presumption that his other sons might become king demonstrates that Saul's kingship was dynastic (see Giorgio Buccellati, *Cities and Nations in Ancient Syria: An Essay on Political Institutions with Special Reference to the Israelite Kingdoms* [Studi Semitici 26; Rome: Istituto di Studi del Vicino Oriente, 1967]).

31). A union between David and Abishag, and later between Adonijah and Abishag, would tie the house of David more closely to a region known for its Saulide connections and thereby provide further support for Davidic rule in the north. Sheba's revolt against David (2 Sam 20), which encompassed the northern tribes, and the later revolt of the north against Rehoboam (1 Kgs 12) underscores David's need for such support (2 Sam 20).

[1:5–49] This unit begins with a noun clause that identifies Adonijah ben Haggith as the principal instigator of a sequence of events that results in David's declaration of Solomon as his heir. It is followed by a standard *waw*-consecutive construction to portray the events that emphasize the fear of Adonijah and his supporters as a result of David's action.[6] The narrative presents Adonijah as the self-presumed heir who acts rashly to claim his father's throne. When Adonijah's intentions become evident, Nathan takes action together with Bath Sheba, the mother of Solomon; Benaiah ben Jehoiada, the commander of David's mercenaries; and the priest Zadok, to manipulate the aged monarch into designating Solomon as his successor. The seven episodes appear in seven subunits of 1 Kgs 1:5–49. Each is identified initially by a shift in the principal character of the narrative, who then instigates the actions that define each episode—that is, vv. 5–10 (Adonijah), vv. 11–14 (Nathan), vv. 15–27 (Bath Sheba), vv. 28–31 (David), vv. 32–37 (David again), vv. 38–40 (Zadok, Nathan, and Benaiah), and vv. 41–49 (Adonijah and his supporters).

[1:5–10] Adonijah is "the son of Haggith," listed fourth among David's wives at Hebron (2 Sam 3:2–5). The text emphasizes Adonijah's presumptuous character. The first statement of his actions employs the verb *mitnaśśēʾ*, "promoted/raised himself," to portray Adonijah's claim to kingship; there is no indication that he has any specific reason to believe that he is the one to succeed David. His claim also employs an emphatic and otherwise unnecessary pronoun, *ʾănîʾemlōk*, "*I* will be king," as opposed to simply *ʾemlōk*, "I will be king," which stresses his own volition. He provides himself with a chariot, horses, and fifty men to run before him as a signal of his royal status, but this action interestingly enough mirrors those of his older brother Abimelech, who likewise had no claim to the throne as he attempted to win popular support for his abortive attempt to overthrow his own father (2 Sam 15:1). When considered in relation to Absalom's revolt, Adonijah's actions once again seem premature and threatening. Even the description of him as a handsome young man recalls the description of Absalom (2 Sam 14:25–26). The notice that David never reproved his son removes all doubt as to his character.

The notices concerning Adonijah's supporters and those whom he failed to invite to his coronation point to a very important political dimension of Adoni-

6. Burke Long, "A Darkness between Brothers: Solomon and Adonijah," *JSOT* 19 (1981): 79–94.

jah's claim to the throne. His allies are Joab, David's nephew and longtime military commander; Abiathar, the surviving Elide priest from Saul's massacre of the priests at Nob (1 Sam 22); the sons of the king (except Solomon); and the men of Judah identified as the servants of David. Those not invited to the coronation include Zadok the priest, Benaiah the military commander, Nathan the prophet, Shimei, Rei, and David's own warriors. The two groups represent two very distinct constituencies within the royal court of David: those associated with David prior to his ascent to Jerusalem and those associated with him afterward. As the son of Haggith, Adonijah is a son born to David during his days at Hebron. Joab and Abiathar were longtime supporters of David from his days as a fugitive from Saul, through his seven-year reign at Hebron and his years in Jerusalem. Likewise, the men of Judah who served the king in Jerusalem would relate to David's Judean constituency from his pre-Jerusalem days. The status of the sons of the king is less certain, as 2 Sam 5:13–16 lists sons born to David in Jerusalem; but Adonijah appears to control the sons, with the exception of Solomon. As the son of Bath Sheba, Solomon is born to David after his ascent to Jerusalem. Those not invited relate largely to David's Jerusalem days. Zadok the priest shares priestly duties with Abiathar following David's move to Jerusalem (2 Sam 8:17; 20:25), and later emerges as the sole priest following Abiathar's banishment to Anathoth (2 Kgs 2:35). Nathan does not appear until after David is ensconced in Jerusalem (2 Sam 7), and may even be a son born to David in Jerusalem (2 Sam 5:14). Shimei appears to be a member of the house of Saul who supported Absalom's revolt out of resentment for David's taking the throne of Saul (2 Sam 16:5–8; cf. 19:16–24). David was at war with the house of Saul during his years at Hebron immediately prior to his move to Jerusalem. Shimei would therefore have been associated with David's court only during his days in Jerusalem. Rei is otherwise unknown. The only parties associated with David prior to his Jerusalem days would then be Benaiah the commander of the Cherethites and Pelethites, and David's warriors. Benaiah is always listed after Joab, who is described as commander of the entire army (2 Sam 8:16–18; 20:23). When Benaiah later kills Joab on Solomon's orders, he is then appointed as commander of the entire army (2 Kgs 2:28–35). Although Benaiah is associated with David in his pre-Jerusalem days, he has something to gain by the shift in power in the royal house. Subsequent events make it clear that a coup takes place within the house of David in that a Jerusalem-based faction takes control of the throne from a Hebron-based faction.[7]

The selection of Ein Rogel, situated at the border of Judah and Benjamin (Josh 15:7; 18:16), is calculated to claim that his (and David's) kingship is based in the assent of the tribes of Benjamin, Saul's own tribe, and Judah.

7. Gwilym H. Jones, *The Nathan Narratives* (JSOTSup 80; Sheffield: Sheffield Academic Press, 1990), and the relevant portions of his commentary on 1 Kgs.

[1:11–14] The explicit identification of Bath Sheba as "the mother of Solomon" and Adonijah as "the son of Haggith" likewise makes clear her interests in overturning Adonijah's coronation in favor of her own son. Nathan's relationship with Bath Sheba has changed. Whereas he previously condemned David for his relationship with her and announced that the child born of their union would die, he now treats her as an ally. Nathan employs a combination of truth and deceit to persuade Bath Sheba to take action. His initial question, asking whether she has heard that Adonijah has declared himself king without David's knowledge, is true according to the prior statements of the narrative. But his subsequent statements move from the realm of potential supposition to blatant lies, at least in relation to information conveyed by the narrative. The suggestion that Bath Sheba needs to act in order to save herself and her son is plausible, but it is by no means clear that Adonijah intends to kill them. His failure to invite Solomon demonstrates hostile intent, but it may be designed only to ensure that Adonijah is able to present Solomon with fait accompli. Apart from the ambiguities of this statement, Nathan's instruction that she should claim that David had sworn that Solomon should succeed him is simply not true according to the information provided to the reader. Yet the ambiguities of the use of the particle *kî,* which can function emphatically—that is, "Indeed, Solomon your son shall rule after me," or conditionally, "when/if Solomon your son shall rule after me"—serve the manipulative character of the speech. A strict construction of Nathan's statement indicates that it was not false—namely, "if Solomon your son rules after me, then he shall sit on my throne." But his strategy does not allow time for David or his attendants to parse the statement, because Bath Sheba follows immediately with the rhetorical question, "why does Adonijah rule?" after which Nathan enters the king's chamber to confirm her words. The key question has been asked, and insofar as the reader and David are concerned, no one ever stated that Adonijah should be king.

[1:15–27] The accounts of the two audiences by Bath Sheba and Nathan constitute a single subunit because they are temporally coordinated by the introductory statement of v. 22.

The portrayal of Bath Sheba's audience relates two key points that provide a context for understanding her approach to the king. First, it reiterates that the king is very old (cf. v. 1), which establishes that the king is dependent upon others and that he can be manipulated. Second, it states that Abishag is there, ministering to the king (cf. vv. 3–4). The identities of the two women, Bath Sheba, the wife of David with whom he started his relationship with an adulterous sexual encounter, and Abishag, the beautiful concubine with whom he was unable to consummate a sexual relationship, make clear the tension between two women.

Bath Sheba's statements display an interesting shift in characterization. Up to this point, she has been largely silent. Apart from her message to David that she was pregnant (2 Sam 11:5), she did not speak during the entire affair with

David, the death of her first child, and the birth of Solomon, nor did she speak when Nathan advised her in the preceding pericope. After entering David's chamber, she at first continues in her passive role, repeating virtually word for word what Nathan had told her to say. But once she relates Adonijah's sacrifices and invitation list in vv. 18–19, she speaks more independently. By the time she tells the king that all Israel looks to him to designate his successor, she speaks entirely for herself.

Nathan's words lend credibility to Bath Sheba and help to remove any doubt about her claims. His language is constructed subtly to remind David of the prophet's loyalty to him. He emphatically states, "I, your servant," in v. 26 when reciting the list of those excluded from Adonijah's coronation celebration, and he again identifies Solomon as "your servant" at the end of the list. These reminders are read in relation to Nathan's earlier prophecy that a son of David would sit on the throne; Solomon, of course, would be that son. The linchpin for Nathan's argument, and for the credibility of Bath Sheba's earlier claims, appears in v. 27, where he employs a conditional statement to assert that Adonijah's accession to the throne could only have taken place if (1) David had authorized it and (2) David did not inform Nathan of this decision. He thereby informs David that Adonijah has acted without the king's authorization, but his language is framed in such a way that he does not directly challenge David's competence or authority.

[1:28–31] David's declaration signals to Adonijah and his supporters that they are in danger, yet the formulation of David's oath to declare Solomon as his heir leaves questions in the mind of the reader. The oath follows a conditional statement concerning David's prior oath to Bath Sheba, but the narrative records no such oath on David's part. This raises questions about the legitimacy of David's oath; if the condition under which it is issued is false, is the oath itself valid? When read in relation to Solomon's later executions of Adonijah, Joab, and Shimei, and his expulsion of Abiathar (1 Kgs 2), the oath also raises questions about Solomon.

[1:32–37] Zadok, Nathan, and Benaiah are, respectively, the high priest who represented the presence of the Deity in the Jerusalem sanctuary that housed the ark of the covenant, the prophet who likewise represented the Deity and had earlier announced that David's son would succeed him on the throne, and the commander of David's mercenary soldiers who guaranteed the king's protection. Together with Solomon and Bath Sheba, these figures constitute a faction of the royal house that emerged once David had established his capital in Jerusalem.

No word from YHWH appears to confirm David's command. The designation of Solomon as the next monarch is David's decision alone. The various actions associated with Solomon's designation, however, appeal to the public at large and convey the trappings of divine approval. The first is the mounting of Solomon on David's royal mule, a clear symbol of Solomon's taking the place of David insofar as the royal family oftentimes appeared mounted on mules (2 Sam 13:29; 18:9; 1 Kgs 10:25; 18:5). Although a horse or chariot might seem to be a more fitting mount for a king (2 Sam 15:1; 1 Kgs 1:5; 10:26; 2 Kgs 23:30), the hilly terrain of Judah and Jerusalem in particular would call for a more sure-footed animal.

The selection of the Gihon spring is calculated to make a public impression of Solomon's legitimacy as king. The Gihon is the major water source for Jerusalem, located on the lower slope of the eastern side of the city as it descends into the Kidron Valley (cf. 2 Kgs 18:17/Isa 36:2; 7:3).[8] Solomon's anointing at the Gihon would be held in full view of the entire city, whereas Adonijah's anointing, while visible from Jerusalem, took place at a greater distance. The anointing of Solomon by Zadok and Nathan and the blowing on the Shofar lend divine sanctity to Solomon's designation as king. The anointing of Israel's kings by prophets and priests (1 Sam 9:16; 10:1; 16:3); the people (Judg 9:15; 2 Sam 19:11); and prophets, priests, and people together (2 Kgs 9:6; 2 Kgs 11:12; 2 Kgs 23:30) is well attested. Solomon's anointing is the first to be portrayed as a public act. The blowing of the Shofar, made from a ram's horn, indicates its sanctity, as the Shofar announced cultic occasions (Pss 47:6; 81:4; 98:6; 150:3; 2 Chr 15:14), such as the celebration of the New Year (Num 29:1), the Jubilee year (Lev 25:9), and revelation of Torah at Mount Sinai (Exod 19:16).

[1:38–40] The Cherethites and Pelethites constitute David's personal guard, which served him throughout his career.[9] The gentilic names indicate that they are foreigners, which ironically may apply to the people who rejoice at Solomon's anointing. The accounts of David's capture of the city of Jerusalem include no mention of its Jebusite inhabitants being killed or driven away. Other traditions are quite explicit that Jerusalem is Jebusite (2 Sam 5:6–12; cf. Josh 15:8; 18:14; Judg 1:21; contra Judg 1:8–9). The issue is even more striking when read in the context of the DtrH and the Deuteronomic law code, which prohibits Israel from intermarrying seven Canaanite nations, the last of which is the Jebusites (Deut 7:1–5). The question of the people's identity indicates ambiguity in the presentation of Solomon's accession—that is, is he acclaimed by Jebusites and supported by Philistine mercenaries?

---

8. See Amihai Mazar, *Archaeology of the Land of the Bible, 10,000–586 B.C.E.* (New York: Doubleday, 1990), 417–19, 423; Hillel Geva, "Jerusalem," *NEAEHL* 2:715–16.

9. The Cherethites are equated with the Philistines in Zeph 2:5; Ezek 25:16. The term is often compared to Crete, which many believe to be the original home of the "Sea Peoples" who ravaged the eastern Mediterranean coastal regions in the twelfth century B.C.E. before settling down in Gaza as the ancestors of the Philistines. David served as a Philistine vassal when he was a fugitive from Saul (1 Sam 21:10–15; 27; 29) and when he became king over first Judah and then Israel (see 2 Sam 5; cf. 1 Sam 30:14, which refers to the "Negeb of the Cherethites," a region that borders Philistia). The identity of the Pelethites is not known.

[1:41–49] The immediate appearance of Jonathan ben Abiathar suggests cause for concern, because the earlier narrative concerning Absalom's revolt against David reported that Jonathan and his father remained behind when David fled Jerusalem to report to the king concerning Absalom's activities (2 Sam 15). Because of his prior role as a runner who would report trouble to David, his appearance now suggests that trouble is at hand. By stating that the news will be good, Adonijah attempts to reassure himself about the commotion in the city. Jonathan's report indicates quite the opposite: the news is disastrous for Adonijah. His report begins with statements that reiterate David's instructions to Zadok, Nathan, and Benaiah, to indicate that the three men have complied with the king's orders.

[1:50–2:10] Interpreters generally read the portrayal of Adonijah's fear in 1 Kgs 1:50–52 as a self-contained unit, but the initial noun clause of v. 50 and the *waw*-consecutive constructions that introduce the narratives concerning David's last words or testament to Solomon in 1 Kgs 2:1–9 and David's death in 1 Kgs 2:10 suggest that 1 Kgs 1:50–52 introduces these subunits. This structural division is evident on thematic grounds as well. By placing the portrayal of Adonijah's fear as the introduction to the accounts of David's last words and death, the narrative subtly demonstrates that Adonijah's fears are well-founded. Up to this point, David has threatened no one, and he appears to be a helpless old man susceptible to manipulation. But his last words to Solomon indicate that he does indeed have his wits about him and that he is capable of formulating plans and initiating action. He supplies reasons for each case—Joab committed murder, Barzillai supported him during Absalom's revolt, and Shimei cursed him—and he is willing to justify killing his enemies even when their actions do not warrant such punishment.

[1:50–53] Although no threat has been made against Adonijah, he understands his tenuous position. He now finds himself in defiance of the will of his father and his father's successor. He takes the only course available to him: refuge at the altar. According to Num 35:9–28; Deut 19:1–13; and Josh 20, six cities of refuge were set aside throughout the land, to which one who commits unintentional manslaughter might flee for protection.

Adonijah has hardly committed manslaughter, but the narrative makes it very clear that he has challenged the authority of his king in his attempt to claim the throne. Exodus 22:27 prohibits cursing G-d or the "prince" (Hebrew, *nāśîʾ,* thought by some to refer to the king; see also 1 Kgs 21:13; Isa 8:21; 2 Sam 16:5–14), and Adonijah's actions might be construed as an expression of disloyalty to the chosen monarch. His demand for Solomon's oath that he not be put to death expresses his presumption that he has committed a capital offense. Solomon's oath is noteworthy because of its conditional nature. The conditional formulation of Solomon's oath gives him the necessary basis to execute Adonijah should he prove untrustworthy.

[2:1–9] Scholars have long noted the character of David's speech in vv. 2–9 as a testament in which David gives final instructions to his son Solomon concerning the treatment of selected individuals (Long 43–45, 249). The testament genre also appears in Egypt in which various royal or wise figures provide instruction for their sons or disciples (*ANET*, 412–25).

The use of the testament genre in this instance is particularly important when considered in relation to its role in the DtrH. Deuteronomy as a whole is formulated as Moses' last words to Israel immediately prior to his death as he reiterates YHWH's Torah before the people take possession of the land of Israel. Indeed, Noth identifies major speeches or discourses, such as Joshua's last speech to Israel (Josh 23) and Samuel's last speech to Israel (1 Sam 12), as the primary structural transitions in the DtrH.[10] He also includes Joshua's initial speech to Israel (Josh 1); the discourse at the beginning of the Judges period (Judg 2); Solomon's speech at the dedication of the temple (1 Kgs 8); and the discourse concerning the fall of the northern kingdom (2 Kgs 17) among the DtrH's transition texts, and argues that all of the speeches convey the historiographical and theological viewpoints of the DtrH. David's testament to Solomon conforms to the testaments of Moses, Joshua, and Samuel, and to the others by calling upon Solomon to observe YHWH's commands as expressed in Mosaic Torah.

David's testament to Solomon presents a warped understanding of Torah observance insofar as David instructs his son to eliminate his opponents on questionable grounds. David's grounds for advising Solomon to kill Joab include Joab's killing of Abner ben Ner (2 Sam 3:6–39) and Amasa ben Yeter during a time of peace, yet Abner was the man who killed Joab's brother Abishai at Gibeon (2 Sam 2:12–32), which would give Joab the right to avenge his brother's death. Amasa had served as Absalom's army commander during the revolt against David (2 Sam 17:25), but David appointed him as his own army commander in place of Joab in an effort to entice him to desert Absalom (2 Sam 19:11–15). When Amasa later failed to act against Sheba so that Sheba's revolt proved to be a greater threat to David than Absalom's revolt, Joab killed him and assumed command of the army to put down the revolt (2 Sam 20:1–22). In both cases, Amasa was a traitor to David, and Joab was justified in killing him as a threat to the king as well as to himself. Many speculate that David sought revenge for Joab's killing of Absalom, for whom David wept loudly despite Absalom's treachery (2 Sam 18–19).

Similar considerations apply to David's instructions to Solomon that he should find a way to kill Shimei ben Gera. Shimei was a member of the house of Saul who had cursed David during Absalom's revolt (2 Sam 16:5–14), but he received David's forgiveness after David's victory (2 Sam 19:16–23). Afterward, Shimei showed no overt signs of disloyalty. Why then should David advise Solomon to kill him in violation of David's oath to spare his life?

---

10. Martin Noth, *The Deuteronomistic History* (JSOTSup 15; Sheffield: JSOT Press, 1981), 4–11.

Only David's instructions to show fidelity to the sons of Barzillai do him credit. Barzillai, after all, had shown fidelity to David during Absalom's revolt, providing the king with supplies when he crossed to Jordan to establish a base for defense in Mahanaim (2 Sam 17:27–29). David invited Barzillai to eat at his table, that is, enjoy the king's protection. When Barzillai declined due to his advanced age, he proposed that his son Chimham take his place (2 Sam 19:31–43). This act helped to cement David's relationship with the Transjordan, and thereby provided a base of support against the tribes of the northern Israelite hill country, who had supported Absalom (2 Sam 15), revolted against David under the leadership of Shebna (2 Sam 20:1–20), and later revolted against David's grandson Rehoboam (1 Kgs 12). David advises Solomon to show loyalty to the descendants of a man who helped to secure his throne, and who had the potential to do so again. Although David's advice in these instances is motivated by a desire to enable Solomon to protect his throne, the narrative already signals that Shimei's execution will be on trumped-up charges designed to negate an oath to YHWH. Such a portrayal undermines both David and Solomon and indeed the house of David as a whole. When read in the context of the entire DtrH with its portrayal of the fall of the house of David, David's testament to Solomon indicates that the dynasty was corrupt at its very foundation. It portrays a private side to David and Solomon that contrasts with the oft-stated portrayal of David's righteousness and fidelity to YHWH and Solomon's reputation for great wisdom. Such a portrayal thereby aids in justifying the DtrH presentation of Josiah's reign, in which the king corrects illicit practices and removes idolatrous installations from the time of Solomon, and its presentation of the destruction of Jerusalem and the temple together with the downfall of the house of David.

[2:10] The formulaic notice of David's death and burial corresponds to other examples throughout Kings (e.g., 1 Kgs 11:43; 14:20). The "city of David" designates the older Jebusite city of Jerusalem that David captured with his own mercenary troops (2 Sam 5:6–12).[11] Archaeologists once identified David's tomb with the so-called tombs of the Judean kings, located to the north of the Siloam pool at the southern tip of the city, but evidence of later Roman quarrying renders this hypothesis speculative.[12]

[2:11] The final summation of David's reign in 1 Kgs 2:11 returns to David once again as the major character of the text (cf. 1 Kgs 1:1). It relates to the introductory notice of his reign in 2 Sam 5:4–5, which likewise states that his reign lasted for forty years, with a seven-year-and-six-month reign over Judah in Hebron and a thirty-three-year reign over all Israel in Jerusalem.

11. For the location of Jebusite and Davidic Jerusalem, see Nahman Avigad, *Discovering Jerusalem* (Jerusalem: Shikmona and the Israel Exploration Society, 1983), 26–31.
12. See Nahman Avigad, "Jerusalem: Tombs," *NEAEHL* 2:712; Jan J. Simons, *Jerusalem in the Old Testament* (Leiden: E. J. Brill, 1952), 194–225.

II. Regnal Account of Solomon ben David
1 Kings 2:12–14:20

The account of Solomon's reign in 1 Kgs 2:12–14:20 is demarcated by the initial noun clause in 1 Kgs 2:12 which states that "Solomon sat on the throne of David his father," and that "his kingdom was very secure," and by the thematic focus throughout on Solomon's reign and its immediate aftermath.[1] Although the formal summation of Solomon's reign appears in 1 Kgs 11:41–43, the narrative in 1 Kgs 12:1–14:20 concerning Jeroboam ben Nebat's reign over the rebellious northern kingdom of Israel appears as an appendix to Solomon's reign. This is indicated by the initial *waw*-consecutive that introduces the narrative in 1 Kgs 12:1, which is unique in the Kings narratives in that the accounts of individual reigns are otherwise always introduced with a noun clause. This formation suggests a deliberate redactional association of the accounts of Solomon's and Jeroboam's reigns. Such an association serves the Josianic DtrH, which portrays Josiah as a devout adherent of YHWH in contrast to his predecessors, especially Solomon, who worshiped foreign gods.[2] The association clearly links Jeroboam's reign and the northern Israelite revolt with Solomon's tolerance of foreign deities as stated in 1 Kgs 11.

The subunits are demarcated by initial noun clauses, each of which focuses on Solomon in presenting a chronological account of the major stages of his reign, in 1 Kgs 2:12; 2:46b; 5:1; and 11:1. The subunits include 1 Kgs 2:12–46a, which recounts the initial stage of Solomon's reign when he secures his throne; 1 Kgs 2:46b-4:20, which relates Solomon's wisdom and power; 1 Kgs 5:1–10:29, the fundamental account of Solomon's activities during his reign; and 1 Kgs 11:1–14:20, which relates Solomon's apostasy and the consequent revolt of the northern tribes. This last section includes two subdivisions: the account of Solomon's apostasy and revolts against his reign in 1 Kgs 11:1–43, culminating in the summation of his reign (vv. 41–43), and the account in 1 Kgs 12:1–14:20 of the revolt of the northern tribes and the reign of Jeroboam ben Nebat, culminating in the summation of Jeroboam's reign (14:19–20).

1 Kings 2:12–46a Solomon Secures His Throne

First Kings 2:12–46a portrays Solomon's compliance with his father's instructions, although he goes well beyond David's testament. David had instructed

---

1. Lucianic LXX editions mark 1 Kgs 2:12 as the beginning of 3 Rgns. See Rahlfs's note (*Septuaginta*).

2. See Marvin A. Sweeney, "The Critique of Solomon in the Josianic Edition of the Deuteronomistic History," *JBL* 114 (1995): 607–22; Marvin A. Sweeney, *King Josiah of Judah: The Lost Messiah of Israel* (Oxford and New York: Oxford University Press, 2001), 21–177, esp. 93–109.

Solomon to kill Joab, which he orders Benaiah to do despite the fact that Joab sought sanctuary at the altar like Adonijah in 1 Kgs 1:50–53. He sets conditions by which Shimei will continue to live by requiring that he reside in Jerusalem and not cross the Wadi Kidron. But Solomon later orders Shimei's execution when he travels to Gath to recover two lost slaves, despite the fact that a strict reading of Solomon's conditions indicates that Shimei did not violate the terms of their agreement.

Solomon puts Adonijah to death for making a claim to the throne by requesting marriage to Abishag, and he expels Abiathar the priest from Jerusalem. Both cases suggest impropriety. Adonijah's request for Abishag implies intent to claim the throne, but it only comes to Solomon from his mother Bath Sheba. There are no witnesses to Adonijah's audience with Bath Sheba. The fact that both Bath Sheba and Solomon have much to gain must be considered in relation to Bath Sheba's prior conspiracy to gain the throne for her son. Adonijah appears to be completely naive, which is consistent with his prior actions, but he does not survive to present his side of the story. The expulsion of Abiathar also raises questions in that Solomon states no clear grounds for the action other than that Abiathar deserves death. The reason is not difficult to fathom: Abiathar had supported Adonijah's bid for the throne.

The placement of this narrative immediately prior to the portrayal of Solomon's wisdom and power in 1 Kgs 3–4 suggests a malicious and self-destructive side to Israel's great monarch. This subunit bolsters the later portrayals of Solomon's improprieties in relation to his treatment of the northern tribes and the worship of foreign gods. The narrative is shaped at beginning and end to suggest that Solomon's faults prompt the disintegration of the kingdom after his death.

Various scholars have argued that 1 Kgs 2:12–46a shows evidence of later redaction in which a narrative highly critical of Solomon's actions is transformed into a pro-Davidic or pro-Solomonic account by the addition of statements indicating YHWH's choice of Solomon in keeping with the promise of a royal house of David.[3] The following commentary attempts to demonstrate that statements supporting Solomon's claim to the throne ironically raise questions concerning his character, wisdom, and legitimacy. First Kings 2:12–46a appears to be the product of a Josianic DtrH that was designed to discredit Solomon in relation to Josiah.

The structure of 1 Kgs 2:12–46a falls naturally into two parts. The first is the narrative statement in 1 Kgs 2:12 that Solomon sits securely upon the throne of David. This statement provides the basic premise demonstrated in the following

3. Ernst Würthwein, *Die Erzählung von der Thronfolge Davids* (Zurich: Theologischer Verlag, 1974); cf. Stefan Seiler, *Die Geschichte von der Thronfolge Davids (2 Sam 9–20; 1 Kön 1–2)* (BZAW 267; Berlin and New York: de Gruyter, 1998); Timo Veijola, *Die ewige Dynastie* (Helsinki: Suomalainen Tiedeakatemia, 1975), 19–30 (cf. Sophia Katharina Bietenhard, *Des Königs General* [OBO 163; Freiburg: Universitäts-Verlag; Göttingen: Vandenhoeck & Ruprecht, 1998], 212–52); Langlamet, "Pour ou contre Salomon?" *RB* 83 (1976): 505–24.

verses. First Kings 2:13–46a then relates Solomon's actions to eliminate or contain potential challengers to his rule. The first component appears in vv. 13–25, which employ a *waw*-consecutive narrative construction to relate Solomon's execution of Adonijah. The second component appears in vv. 26–46a, which disrupt the *waw*-consecutive narrative construction with a noun clause that introduces the three reports concerning the disposition of Abiathar (vv. 26–27), Joab (vv. 28–35), and Shimei (vv. 36–46a).

2:12 And Solomon sat upon the throne of David his father,[a] and his kingdom was very secure.

13 And Adonijah ben Haggith came to Bath Sheba, the mother of Solomon, and she said, "Do you come in peace?" and he said, "Yes, in peace." 14 And he said, "May I have a word with you?" and she said, "Speak." 15 And he said, "You know that the kingdom was mine and that all Israel expected me to rule,[b] but the kingdom changed course and went to my brother, because it came to him from YHWH. 16 And now, one request I make of you; please do not refuse me,"[c] and she said to him, "Speak." 17 And he said, "Please say to King Solomon—he will not refuse you—that he should give to me Abishag the Shunammite as a wife." 18 And Bath Sheba said, "Good, I will speak on your behalf to the king."

19 And Bath Sheba came to King Solomon to speak to him on behalf of Adonijah, and the king rose to greet her and prostrated himself to her. And he sat upon his throne and ordered a throne for the mother of the king, so she sat to his right. 20 And she said, "One small request I would like to make of you. Please do not refuse me." And the king said to her, "Ask, my mother, for I will not refuse you." 21 And she said, "Let Abishag the Shunammite be given to Adonijah your brother as a wife." 22 And King Solomon answered his mother, "And why are you requesting Abishag the Shunammite for Adonijah? Why not request the kingdom for him, for he is my older brother, and for Abiathar the priest and Joab ben Zeruiah?"

23 And King Solomon swore by YHWH saying, "Thus shall G-d do to me and even more, for at the cost of his life has Adonijah spoken this word! 24 And now, by the life of YHWH, who has established me and seated me on the throne of David my father, and who has made for me a house just as He promised, today Adonijah shall be put to death." 25 And King Solomon sent Benaiah ben Jehoiada, who attacked him so that he died. 26 And to Abiathar the priest the King said, "Anathoth![d] Go to your fields! for you are subject to death.[e] But I will not put you to death on this day because you bore the ark of my lord G-d before David my father and because you shared all the travails of my father." 27 And Solomon expelled Abiathar from serving as priest to YHWH, to fulfill the word of YHWH which He spoke concerning the house of Eli in Shiloh.

₂₈ And the report came to Joab because Joab had followed Adonijah (although he had not followed Absalom), and Joab fled to the Tent of YHWH and seized the horns of the altar. ₂₉ And it was reported to King Solomon that Joab had fled to the Tent of YHWH, and behold, he was by the altar, and Solomon sent[f] Benaiah ben Jehoiada saying, "Go, attack him!" ₃₀ And Benaiah came to the Tent of YHWH and said to him, "Thus said the king, 'Come out!'" And he said, "No, for here will I die." And Benaiah sent word to the king, saying, "This is what Joab said to me." ₃₁ And the king said to him, "Do just as he said, and attack him and bury him, and you shall remove from me and the house of my father the innocent blood which Joab shed. ₃₂ And YHWH will repay his bloodguilt upon his own head for attacking two men more righteous and moral than him, and killing them with the sword without my father knowing: Abner ben Ner, commander of the army of Israel, and Amasa ben Yether, commander of the army of Judah. ₃₃ And their blood shall return to the head of Joab and his descendants forever, but to David, his descendants, and his throne, there shall be everlasting peace from YHWH." ₃₄ And Benaiah ben Jehoiada went up, attacked him, and killed him, and he buried him in his house in the wilderness. ₃₅ And the king appointed Benaiah ben Jehoiada in his place over the army, and the king appointed Zadok the priest in place of Abiathar.[g]

₃₆ And the king sent and summoned Shimei, and he said to him, "Build for yourself a house in Jerusalem, dwell there, and do not go out anywhere else. ₃₇ And on the day that you go out and cross the Wadi Kidron, you certainly know that you will surely die.[h] Your blood shall be on your own head." ₃₈ And Shimei said to the king, "The statement is good. Just as my lord the king has spoken, so shall your servant do." And Shimei resided in Jerusalem many days. ₃₉ And at the end of three years, two of Shimei's servants fled to Achish ben Maacah, king of Gath, and they declared to Shimei, "Behold, your servants are in Gath." ₄₀ And Shimei rose, saddled his ass, and went to Gath to Achish to seek his servants. And Shimei went and brought his servants from Gath. ₄₁ And it was told to Solomon that Shimei had gone from Jerusalem to Gath and returned. ₄₂ And Solomon summoned Shimei, and said to him, "Did I not cause you to swear by YHWH, and I witnessed it, 'On the day that you go out, and you go anywhere else, you know that you will surely die,'[h] and you said to me, 'The statement that I have heard is good'? ₄₃ And why did you not abide by the oath of YHWH and the command concerning you that I issued?" ₄₄ And the king said to Shimei, "You know in your heart all the wrong that you did to David my father, and YHWH will repay your wrongdoing upon your head. ₄₅ And King Solomon is blessed, and the throne of David will be secure before YHWH forever." ₄₆ₐ And the king commanded Benaiah ben Jehoiada, who went out, attacked him, and he died.

a. Lucianic versions add *huios etōn dōdeka,* "a son of twelve years"; cf. *Seder ʿOlam Rabbah* 14, which states that Solomon was twelve, and Josephus, *Ant.* 8.211, who states that he was fourteen.

b. MT, lit., "and upon me all Israel set their faces to rule," an idiomatic statement that expresses the people's expectation that Adonijah would become king.

c. MT, *ʾal-tāšibî ʾet-pānāy,* literally, "do not cause my face to return," or "do not turn away my face" (cf. the use of the verb *šûb* in the expression, *lōʾ ʾăšîbennû,* "I will not turn it [the punishment] aside," i.e., "I will not revoke the punishment" [Amos 1:3, 6, etc.]. Contra. LXX reads, "do not turn away your face," i.e., Bath Sheba's face.

d. Note the assonantal association between *ʿănātōt,* "Anathoth," *hitʿannîtā,* "you shared the travails, i.e., you were afflicted," and *hitʿannâ,* "(with which) he (my father) was afflicted." Solomon's statement conveys a pun that associates the place name Anathoth with the root *ʿnh,* "to afflict, oppress," so that the pun forms the rationale for sparing Abiathar's life. Cf. v. 31, where Solomon employs the technique to justify the killing of Joab, i.e., "do just as he says" (kill him).

e. MT, *ʾîš māwet,* lit., "man of death," an idiomatic expression indicating that Abiathar is subject to the death penalty, presumably for conspiring to overthrow the king (Exod 22:27; 1 Kgs 21:10).

f. LXX contains two versions of the statement, "and Solomon sent," i.e., "And King Solomon sent to Joab, saying, 'What has happened to you that you have fled to the altar?' and Joab said, 'Because I was afraid of you, and fled to the L-rd.' And Solomon sent to Benaiah son of Jehoiada, saying, 'Go and take him up and bury him.'" LXX purportedly provides Solomon with justification to kill Joab, i.e., if Joab feared Solomon, he must have done something wrong (n.b., cities of refuge are only for those who have committed manslaughter, not those guilty of deliberate killing, see Num 35:6–28; Deut 19:1–13; Josh 20:7–9). The MT simply presents Solomon's unqualified action to kill him, which suggests wrongdoing on Solomon's part.

g. LXX includes an extensive addition in v. 35, based largely on paraphrase and summation of other sections of the Solomon narrative which laud the king's wisdom and accomplishments or report David's instructions to him (Hrozný, *Die Abweichungen des Codex Vaticanus* esp. 10–21; James A. Montgomery, "The Supplement at the End of 3 Kingdoms 2 [1 Reg 2]," *ZAW* 50 [1932]: 124–29, esp. 126–27; Gooding, *Relics of Ancient Exegesis;* for recent discussion, see Schenker, *Septante* 77–82). The additions appear to be intended to justify his actions by pointing to David's instructions as a means to account for Solomon's ruthless treatment of Adonijah, Abiathar, Joab, and Shimei (see esp. Gooding, *Relics,* who emphasizes that the additions focus on Solomon's wisdom; see also, "The Shimei Duplicate and Its Satellite Miscellanies in 3 Reigns II," *JSS* 13 [1968]: 76–92; "Problems of Text and Midrash in the Third Book of Reigns," *Textus* 7 [1969]: 1–29). These additions do not indicate a witness to an earlier text tradition as Hrozný contends, but point to early "midrashic" or interpretative efforts as Gooding argues. Each statement corresponds in whole or in part to other statements in the presentation of Solomon. Thus, vv. 35ab are derived from 4:25–26 (5:9–10 Hebrew); v. 35c from 3:1 and 7:8; 6:38; v. 35d from 5:15 (5:29 Hebrew); v. 35e summarizes 7:10–50; vv. 35fg are derived from 9:24–25; 35h from 9:23 and 5:16 (Hebrew 5:30); vv. 35ik from 9:15, 17, 18; vv. 35lmno from 2 Kgs 2:8–9.

The LXX reads v. 35 as follows:

35 And the king appointed Banaiah son of Jehoiada in his place over the army, and the kingdom was established in Jerusalem. And Zadok, the priest, the king appointed as high/first priest in place of Abiathar. And Solomon son of David ruled over Israel and Judah in Jerusalem. 35a And the L-rd gave understanding to Solomon, and very much wisdom, and largeness of heart as the sands by the sea. 35b And the wisdom of Solomon was more abundant than the wisdom of all the ancient ones and than all the wise men of Egypt. 35c And he took the daughter of Pharaoh, and brought her into the city of David until he had finished building his house and the house of the L-rd first, and the surrounding wall of Jerusalem; in seven years he made and finished them. 35d And Solomon had seventy thousand bearers and eighty thousand cutters of stone in the mountain. 35e And Solomon made the sea, and the bases, and the pillars, and the fountain of the court, and the bronze sea. 35f And he built the fortress as a defense for it. He made a breach in the wall of the city of David, so the daughter of Pharaoh went up out of the city of David to her house which he built for her. Then he built the fortress. 35g And Solomon offered three whole burnt offerings in the year, and peace offerings on the altar which he built for the L-rd, and he burned incense before the L-rd, and finished the house. 35h And these are the chiefs who supervised over the works of Solomon, three thousand and six hundred masters of the people that did the work. 35i And he built Hazor, Megiddo, Gezer, upper Beth-Horon, and Baalath; 35k only after he built the house of the L-rd and the surrounding wall of Jerusalem, then he built these cities. 35l And when David was still alive, he charged Solomon, "Behold, with you is Shimei the son of Gera of the seed of Benjamin from Hebron (LXX reverses the letters Beth and Ḥeth from Bahurim to read Hebron). 35m He cursed me with a terrible curse in the day that I went into the camp. 35n And he came down to meet me at the Jordan, and I swore to him by the L-rd, 'If he shall (i.e., he shall not) be killed with the sword.' 35o But now, do not acquit him, for you are a man of understanding; you shall know what you will do with him, and you shall bring down his gray hair to the grave with blood."

h. Solomon employs the death sentence formula, *môt tāmût*, "you shall surely die" (cf. Exod 21:12, 15; Lev 20:2, 9; 1 Sam 14:39, 44; 22:16).

[12] This brief notice provides the basic premise for the following material.
[13–46a] First Kings 2:13–46a illustrates how Solomon secured his king-dom. The sequence of action includes four basic episodes, each of which is defined by its focus on the major characters who carry out the action. The first relates Adonijah's audience with Bath Sheba, in which he asks her to approach Solomon on his behalf to request that Abishag be given to him as a wife (vv. 13–18). The second is Bath Sheba's audience with Solomon, who understands Adonijah's request, in league with Abiathar and Joab, as a challenge to his rule (vv. 19–22). The third portrays Solomon's actions that follow from his audience with Bath Sheba, including the killing of Adonijah, the expulsion of Abiathar, and the killing of Joab (vv. 23–35). The fourth presents Solomon's execution

of Shimei (vv. 36–46a). By the end of this sequence, every major personality who might constitute a threat to Solomon's rule is eliminated.

[13–18] Readers of 2 Samuel already know that Adonijah's request for Abishag is loaded with political significance because it constitutes a claim to the throne. It may be compared to Abner's relations with Saul's former concubine Ritzpah, which threatened his son Ish-Boshet's (Esh-Baal's) throne (2 Sam 3:6–11), and Absalom's relations with David's concubines, which symbolized Absalom's assumption of kingship (2 Sam 16:15–23; cf. 20:3). Nathan's statement that YHWH had given Saul's house and wives to David suggests that David's inheritance of Saul's wives aids in legitimizing his claim to the throne (2 Sam 12:8).[4]

The narrative highlights the distinctions between Adonijah and Bath Sheba. Adonijah is "the son of Haggith," *not* the son of Bath Sheba. Bath Sheba is "the mother of Solomon," *not* the mother of Adonijah. The distinction, crucial in the context of the competing claims to the throne, is highlighted by Bath Sheba's initial question, "Do you come in peace?" Tension is conveyed by the very abrupt answers, generally one word in Hebrew, that each gives to the other. It is also conveyed by Adonijah's first statements in v. 15, "You know that the kingdom was mine and that all Israel expected me to rule, but the kingdom changed course and went to my brother." The tension is only partially resolved by his next statement, in which he seems to accept the outcome as divinely ordained. Tension also appears in Bath Sheba's reaction to his question. She agrees to do what he asks without further comment. She never says a word about the possible consequences, although readers of Samuel know very well what such a request entails.

[19–22] Tension in 1 Kgs 2:19–22 prompts the reader to question the basis by which Solomon acts against his brother. The first major point involves Bath Sheba's entrance into the royal court. Solomon clearly treats her with great respect. Many note that Bath Sheba must have assumed the role of *gĕbîrâ*, "queen" or "queen mother," a powerful role in the royal court insofar as the term designates Tahpenes the wife of the Egyptian Pharaoh (1 Kgs 11:19), Maacah the mother of King Asa (1 Kgs 15:13; 2 Chr 15:16), and other royal ladies (Jer 13:18; 29:2).[5] Solomon bows to Bath Sheba when she enters the court. By contrast, Bath Sheba bows to David when she enters his chamber (1 Kgs 1:31). Given the suspicious circumstances by which Solomon comes to power, Bath Sheba's power over Solomon suggests that something is amiss.

---

4. E.g., Jon D. Levenson, "1 Samuel 25 as Literature and as History," *CBQ* 40 (1978): 11–28, esp. 27–28; Jon D. Levenson and Baruch Halpern, "The Political Import of David's Marriages," *JBL* 99 (1980): 11–28; Matitiahu Tzevat, "Marriage and Monarchical Legitimacy in Ugarit and Israel," *JSS* 3 (1958): 237–43.

5. See esp. Niels-Erik A. Andreasen, "The Role of the Queen Mother in Israelite Society," *CBQ* 45 (1983): 179–94, esp. 188–90; cf. L. S. Schearing, "Queen," *ABD* 5:583–86.

Second, Bath Sheba's statement that she has only a "small request" to make of the king is deceptive; it is not small at all. Solomon clearly understands that the request for Abishag is a request for the throne. Bath Sheba's statement contradicts the reality of the situation and raises questions concerning the integrity of the interchange between her and her son.

The third source of tension involves the repeated assertions that Solomon will not refuse the request of his mother by Adonijah (v. 17 above), Bath Sheba (v. 20), and even Solomon himself (v. 20). Despite these claims, that is precisely what he does. Having just made a public statement concerning his intended action, he flatly contradicts what he has just said. Such a reversal suggests that Solomon lacks credibility; if he can break his own word to his mother, what can one conclude concerning his wisdom or his royal and legal judgments?

Fourth, other elements of Solomon's response to his mother's request also raise questions. He cites the fact that Adonijah is his older brother as a reason that the kingdom might be given to him. Many interpreters speculate that the relative age of the sons determines the right to succession (e.g., Noth, *Könige* 34; DeVries 38; Jones 113). The laws of inheritance state that the firstborn son receives a double share of the father's estate, and the father may not refuse that right to the firstborn son of a wife that he does not love in favor of the son of a wife that he does love (Deut 22:15–17). Indeed, that principle is in play here as Adonijah is the firstborn of Haggith, a wife married to David prior to his marriage to Bath Sheba.

[23–35] Solomon's oath emphasizes the life of YHWH and a self-imprecation that punishment should fall upon Solomon if he does not carry out his punishment of his brother and his supporters. Such motifs are normally part of biblical and ancient Near Eastern oaths and treaty making,[6] but they take on special significance when read in the overall context of the DtrH presentation of Solomon and the history of Israel and Judah in general. Solomon suffers punishment, although it is for allowing himself to engage in apostasy as a result of the religious practices of his many foreign wives and concubines. Furthermore, Solomon's statements emphasize the security of his hold on the throne of David and his house at large, but the reader of the DtrH knows that the Davidic dynasty loses the throne by the end of 2 Kings.

Tensions remain. Adonijah's death marks the end of the Hebron-based faction of the Davidic house; Solomon, born in Jerusalem, represents a different branch of the family. The account of Abiathar's expulsion to Anathoth likewise

---

6. Moshe Weinfeld, "Covenant Terminology in the Ancient Near East and Its Influence on the West," *JAOS* 93 (1973): 190–99; D. J. Wiseman, *The Vassal Treaties of Esarhaddon* (*Iraq* 20 [1958]; London: British School of Archaeology in Iraq, 1958); Simo Parpola and K. Watanabe, *Neo-Assyrian Treaties and Loyalty Oaths* (SAS 2; Helsinki: University of Helsinki, 1988).

conveys tension.[7] Readers of 1–2 Samuel know that the house of Eli already backed one dynastic house, which turned against it when Saul ordered the slaughter of the (Elide) priests at Nob (1 Sam 22:6–23). Abiathar was the only Elide to escape. He served David for the rest of his life, including Absalom's revolt (2 Sam 15:24–29). Nevertheless, David's son turns against him for supporting Adonijah, and the narrative justifies his fall by citing the prophetic oracle that calls for the deaths of the Elide priests and the replacement of the surviving member by "a faithful priest" (1 Sam 2:22–36). Finally, the account of Joab's death continues a major source of narrative tension.[8] Joab was David's "hatchet man," and ironically falls at the hand of Benaiah ben Jehoiada, who fills the same role for Solomon. The narrative begins with a notice that Joab hears a report of what transpires and immediately understands his vulnerability. Joab's loyalty to David is never in question, even when he kills David's son Absalom and upbraids the king for grieving before his troops (2 Sam 18–19). Instead, David's loyalty to Joab comes into question, when he plans to replace Joab with Abner (2 Sam 3:6–39), when he replaces Joab with Amasa (2 Sam 30), and when he instructs Solomon to kill him (1 Kgs 2:1–9). Solomon's order to kill Joab is the final expression of duplicity. Although Solomon cites Joab's killing of Abner and Amasa as the reason for Joab's guilt (v. 31), the narrative makes it clear that his support of Adonijah is the cause (v. 28).

[36–46a] Solomon's quotation of Shimei demonstrates that he agreed to the terms. David had earlier counseled Solomon to put Shimei to death (1 Kgs 2:1–9). The reasons for David's advice are not hard to fathom. Shimei ben Gera is identified as a member of the house of Saul, who cursed David when the king was forced to flee Jerusalem during Absalom's revolt (2 Sam 16:5–14). Although David later pardoned Shimei when he begged forgiveness following Absalom's defeat (2 Sam 19:16–23), his initial treachery against David could hardly be forgotten.

Shimei appears to be the last member of the house of Saul who might claim his kinsman's throne. David's ascent to the throne was justified in part on the basis of his marriage to Michal, the daughter of Saul. Saul's sons had perished by one means or another (1 Sam 31; 2 Sam 21). It is noteworthy that David handed the seven sons of Saul's concubine, Ritzpah, and his daughter, Michal (or Merab), to the Gibeonites, since their deaths would also eliminate them as claimants to the throne. He allowed Jonathan's son Mephibosheth to live, out of consideration for his deep friendship with Jonathan, but Mephibosheth's eating at the king's table ensured that David kept him under control (2 Sam 9).

---

7. Anathoth is identified either with Ras el-Kharrubeh immediately south of the modern village of Anata or in the valley next to Anata, about two and three-quarters miles northeast of Jerusalem. See J. L. Peterson, "Anathoth," *ABD* 1:227–28; "Anathoth," *EncJud* 1:927.

8. Cf. Bietenhard, *Des Königs General,* 196–206, who ascribes the tension to later redaction.

Although Ziba attempted to claim that his master had revolted against the king (2 Sam 16:1–4), Mephibosheth remained loyal to David throughout the revolt, and renounced his claim to his property in favor of Ziba (2 Sam 19:24–30).

Shimei's actions resemble those of a king, or at least a royal aspirant who conspires to seize power. After Solomon restricted him to Jerusalem, he departs some three years later to claim two runaway slaves from King Achish of Gath. The right to reclaim slaves appears regularly in ancient Near Eastern treaty texts between the kings of two states.[9] Achish of Gath was once David's suzerain (1 Sam 21:11–16; 27:1–28:2; 29). David had subjugated the Philistines after his removal to Jerusalem (2 Sam 5:17–25), but it could hardly be expected that Achish or his successors would ever balk at an opportunity to bring the Davidic kingdom back under their control. Shimei's journey to visit Achish under the pretext of recovering lost slaves could well be interpreted as an attempt to join forces in an attempt to overpower their overlord.

Although there are grounds to suspect Shimei, it seems unlikely also that he would return to Jerusalem if he was indeed guilty of conspiring with Achish to overthrow Solomon. It seems unlikely that his return indicated that he had forgotten his oath to Solomon; a death penalty is not the sort of thing that one forgets. Instead, Shimei's actions suggest that he is not aware of any wrongdoing. He had not violated his oath to the king. This is especially noteworthy when one considers the terms of his agreement with the king. Shimei lived in Baḥurim, which is located on the northeastern slope of the Mount of Olives at a site now known as Ras et-Tmin or Khirbet Ibqe'dan.[10] The location is across the Wadi Kidron, which defines the eastern border of the city of David. Solomon's instructions to Shimei to build his house in Jerusalem, not to leave the city, and not to cross the Wadi Kidron, appear designed to ensure that Shimei will not return to his own city, where he would escape the scrutiny of the king and plan a revolt. Solomon's statement that Shimei would suffer death specifically mentions the condition that he not cross the Wadi Kidron (v. 37). But a journey from Jerusalem to Gath requires no need to cross the Wadi Kidron. One might read Solomon's statements in vv. 36–37 broadly so that Shimei was forbidden from going anywhere, but the death penalty is applied only on the condition that he cross the Kidron.

Solomon's reiteration of the stipulation that Shimei go nowhere (v. 42) suggests some misunderstanding on Shimei's part. It might also be interpreted as outright trickery by Solomon insofar as he employed his wisdom to set a verbal trap for a man who intended to commit no wrong. The careful recording of the words of Shimei's oath, especially his statements that he accepted Solomon's

---

9. See the treaty between Hattusilis of Hatti and Rameses II of Egypt (thirteenth century B.C.E.; *ANET* 203); cf. Moshe Weinfeld, *Deuteronomy and Deuteronomic Law* (Winona Lake, Ind.: Eisenbrauns, 1992), 272.

10. See "Baḥurim," *EncJud* 2:102.

statement, point to a writer who wants to be sure that the execution of Shimei was justified by his own acceptance of Solomon's terms.

1 Kings 2:46b–4:19 Solomon's Subsequent Rule: Power and Wisdom

The syntactical structure of 1 Kgs 2:46b-4:19 and its basic concern with the security of Solomon's kingdom identifies it as a coherent, self-contained literary unit. The introductory noun clause in 1 Kgs 2:46b, *wĕhammamlākâ nākônâ bĕyad šĕlōmōh,* "and the kingdom was secure in the hand of Solomon," demarcates the unit. It comprises three subunits, each linked by a *waw*-consecutive verbal construction, including (1) the introductory statements in 1 Kgs 2:46b–3:2, which focus on Solomon's control of the kingdom and the character of his reign; (2) the portrayal of Solomon's wisdom in 1 Kgs 3:3–28, which depicts YHWH's grant of wisdom to Solomon and his application of that wisdom; and (3) 1 Kgs 4:1–19, which returns to the theme of the initial statement by describing Solomon's administrative officers.

Interpreters generally read chs. 3–4 as laudatory accounts of Solomon's wisdom and power. They point to various ancient Near Eastern parallels to the account of Solomon's dream at Gibeon in 1 Kgs 3:4–15 to indicate an interest in legitimizing Solomon's rule by emphasizing his wisdom from YHWH. Comparisons include the Egyptian *Königsnovelle,* which justifies the rule of the Pharaoh;[11] the dream of Pharaoh Thut-Mose IV, who was promised kingship while sleeping in the shadow of the Sphinx (*ANET* 449); and the dreams and sacrifices of King Keret and Danel in Ugaritic literature.[12] But close attention to the present form of the narrative, particularly its initial elements and its literary context in the DtrH, points to an effort to critique Solomon's adherence to YHWH and his fitness to rule.[13] The first item is the notice that he married the daughter of the Egyptian pharaoh (1 Kgs 3:1). Although this notice may reflect Solomon's high standing in the ancient Near Eastern world,[14] it implicitly criticizes Solomon for marrying the daughter of Israel's oppressor in the Exodus traditions. The cri-

---

11. Siegfried Hermann, "Die Königsnovelle in Ägypten und Israel," *Wissenschaftliche Zeitschrift der Karl Marx Universität Leipzig* 3 (1953–54): 51–62; cf. Manfred Görg, *G-tt-König-Reden in Israel und Ägypten* (BWANT 105; Stuttgart: W. Kohlhammer, 1975), 16–115; and Burke O. Long, *1 Kings, with an Introduction to Historical Literature* (FOTL 9; Grand Rapids: William B. Eerdmans, 1984), 64–66, who notes challenges to this hypothesis.

12. C. L. Seow, "The Syro-Palestinian Context of Solomon's Dream," *HTR* 77 (1984): 141–52.

13. See also Sweeney, "Critique of Solomon"; Sweeney, *King Josiah,* 93–109.

14. Abraham Malamat, "Aspects of the Foreign Policies of David and Solomon," *JNES* 22 (1963): 1–17, esp. 8–17; Malamat, "A Political Look at the Kingdom of David and Solomon and Its Relations with Egypt," in *Studies in the Period of David and Solomon and Other Essays* (ed. T. Ishida; Winona Lake, Ind.: Eisenbrauns, 1982), 189–204.

tique is even more telling when one reads that Solomon—like Pharaoh—imposes state slavery on his own people (1 Kgs 5:27–30), that the revolt of the northern tribes against his son Rehoboam was prompted by his harsh treatment of his subjects (1 Kgs 12), and that the DtrH identifies Solomon's penchant for foreign women (and their gods) as a major cause of the revolt (1 Kgs 11).

Immediately following the notice of Solomon's marriage to the daughter of Pharaoh is a notice that the people were worshiping at the high places (1 Kgs 3:2), which the DtrH identifies as a problem throughout Israel's history.[15] The following verse (1 Kgs 3:3) explicitly states that Solomon engaged in such practice. This statement follows assertions of Solomon's love for YHWH, but his love for YHWH is challenged by his apostasy.

Other features of the Gibeon narrative suggest a critique of Solomon. First, Gibeon is identified as a Canaanite city in Josh 9–10. Although Gibeon concluded a treaty with Israel, which allowed the Gibeonites to remain in Israel, its Canaanite identity raises questions: why would Solomon worship at a Canaanite city, particularly when the ark was already located in Jerusalem? When viewed in relation to his subsequent tolerance for foreign gods, such an observation suggests that Solomon was already prone to apostasy.

Even the narrative concerning Solomon's resolution of the dispute between the two prostitutes presents an implicit critique of the monarch when read in the larger context of the DtrH. According to Deut 16:18–17:13, the Levitical priests —*not* the king—are the chief judges of the land. Much like his father David (2 Sam 12:1–15), Solomon exercises judicial authority without authorization. An implicit critique of Solomon's rule appears even in the narrative concerning Solomon's administration of the land (1 Kgs 4:1–20), which portrays the twelve administrative districts of Solomon's kingdom, each of which is obligated to support the king's court for a month. It is clear that the system is heavily weighted in favor of Solomon's own tribe of Judah, which is responsible for only one month of royal support each year in contrast to the eleven months for which the rest of the kingdom is responsible. This is particularly noteworthy in relation to the charges by the northern tribes of Solomon's harsh treatment (1 Kgs 12).

Altogether, these features show an interest in portraying Solomon as an unsatisfactory ruler, who did not adhere to YHWH's expectations. The narrative framework of the DtrH deliberately undermines the positive portrayal of Solomon that underlies 1 Kgs 2:46b-4:20. Interpreters have long recognized that the present form of this unit, particularly 1 Kgs 3, is the product of redactional activity in which earlier traditions that lauded Solomon's wisdom and power were reread

---

15. W. Boyd Barrick, "On the Meaning of בית-ה/במות and בתי-הבמות and the Composition of the Kings History," *JBL* 115 (1996): 621–22.

and rewritten to provide a critique of the king's actions consistent with the goals of the various editions posited for the Deuteronomistic History.[16]

2:46b ᵃAnd the kingdom was secure in the hand of Solomon.ᵇ 3:1 And Solomon became the son-in-law of Pharaoh, King of Egypt, and he took the daughter of Pharaoh in marriage and brought her into the city of David until he completed building his house, the house of YHWH, and the surrounding wall of Jerusalem.ᵃ 2 But the people were sacrificing at the high places because the house to the Name of YHWH was not (yet) built during those days.

3 And Solomon loved YHWH, walking in the statutes of David his father; only he was sacrificing and burning incense at the high places. 4 And the king went to Gibeon to sacrifice there because it was the great high place. Solomon offered a thousand whole burnt offerings at that altar. 5 At Gibeon YHWH appeared to Solomon in a dream of the night, and G-d said, "Ask what I shall give to you." 6 And Solomon said, "You have kept great fidelity with your servant, David my father, just as he walked before you in truth, righteousness, and integrity of heart with you, you kept this great fidelity with him and gave him a son sitting on his throne this day. 7 And now, YHWH my G-d, you have made your servant rule in place of David my father. But I am a mere youth; I have no experience.ᶜ 8 And your servant is in the midst of your people which you have chosen, a great people which may not be measured or counted because of their great number. 9 And you should give to your servant a listening heart to judge your people, to understand between right and wrong, for who is able to judge this great people of yours?" 10 And the matter was good in the eyes of the L-rd because Solomon asked this thing. 11 And G-d said to him, "Because you have asked this thing, and did not ask for yourself long life and did not ask for yourself wealth and did not ask for yourself the life of your enemies, but asked for yourself understanding to hear justice, 12 behold, I have done according to your words. Behold, I have given you a wise and discerning heart so that no one has been like you before, and no one like you shall arise afterward. 13 And also, that which you did not ask, I have given to you, wealth and honor, so that no one has been like you, a man among the kings, all your days. 14 And if you walk in my ways, to observe my statutes and my commandments just as David your father walked, then I will lengthen your days." 15 And Solomon awoke,

16. Cf. Stefan Wächli, *Der weise König Salomo* (BWANT 141; Stuttgart: W. Kohlhammer, 1999), 28–67, 108–28, who identifies DtrN as the primary redactor of an earlier tradition concerning Solomon's dream at Gibeon; David McLain Carr, *From D to Q: A Study of Early Jewish Interpretations of Solomon's Dream at Gibeon* (SBLMS 44; Atlanta: Scholars, 1991), 7–87, who identifies three levels of redaction of an early story concerning Solomon at Gibeon.

and behold, it was a dream. And he came to Jerusalem, and he stood before the ark of the covenant of the L-rd, and he offered whole burnt offerings, made peace offerings, and made a feast for all his servants.

16 Then two women who were prostitutes came to the king and stood before him. 17 And the first woman said, "Please, my lord, this woman and I live in the same house, and I gave birth together with her in the house. 18 And on the third day after I gave birth, this woman also gave birth, and we were together—there was no stranger with us—in the house, except the two of us in the house. 19 And the son of this woman died one night when she lay upon it. 20 And she rose in the middle of the night, took my son from beside me while your maidservant was asleep, laid it in her bosom, and her dead son she laid in my bosom. 21 And I arose in the morning to nurse my son, and behold, he was dead. And I examined him in the morning, and behold, he was not my son whom I had born."
22 And the other woman said, "No, for my son is the live one, and your son is the dead one. But this one says, 'No, your son is the dead one, and my son is the live one.'" And they spoke before the king. 23 And the king said, "This one says, 'This is my son, the live one, and your son is the dead one,' and this one says, 'No, your son is the dead one, and my son is the live one.'" 24 And the king said, "Get me a sword!" and they brought a sword before the king. 25 And the king said, "Saw[d] the live boy in two, and give half to one and half to the other." 26 And the woman whose son was alive said to the king because her compassion was stirred for her son, and she said, "Please, my lord, give the living newborn[e] to her, and do not indeed put it to death." And the other one said, "Neither for me nor for you shall it be. Saw!"[d] 27 And the king answered and said, "Give the living newborn[e] to her, and do not indeed put it to death. She is his mother." 28 And all Israel heard the judgment which the king made and feared the king because they saw that the wisdom of G-d was within him to carry out justice.

4:1 And King Solomon was king over all Israel.

2 [f]And these are his officers: Azariah ben Zadok, the priest; 3 Elihoreph and Ahijah, sons of Shisha', scribes; Jehoshaphat ben Ahilud, the recorder; 4 and Benaiah ben Jehoiada over the army; and Zadok and Abiathar, priests; 5 and Azariah ben Nathan over the prefects; and Zabud ben Nathan, priest, companion of the king; 6 and Ahishur over the house;[g] and Adoniram ben 'Abda' over the corvée.[f]

7 And Solomon had twelve prefects over all Israel, and they provisioned the king and his house; each[h] would be obligated to provision for one month in the year. 8 And these are their names: Ben-Hur, in the hill country of Ephraim; 9 Ben-Deqer in Maqatz and in Sha'albim, and Beth Shemesh, and Eylon Beth Hanan; 10 Ben-Hesed in Aruboth (Sokoh and

all the land of Hepher were his); 11 Ben Abinadab, all Naphat-Dor (Taphat bat Solomon was his wife); 12 Ba'ana' ben Ahilud, Taanak and Megiddo and all Beth Shean which by Zaretan below the Jezreel from Beth Shean until Abel Meholah across from Jokmeam; 13 Ben-Geber in Ramoth Gilead (the villages of Jair ben Manasseh which were in Gilead were his; the district of Argov which is in Bashan, sixty great walled cities with bronze bars, were his); 14 Ahinadab ben Iddo', Mahanaim; 15 Ahimaaz in Naphtali (he also to Basmat bat Solomon for a wife); 16 Ba'ana' ben Hushai in Asher and Aloth;[i] 17 [j]Jehoshaphat ben Paruah in Issachar;[j] 18 Shimei ben Ela' in Benjamin; 19 Geber ben Uri in the land of Gilead, the land of Sihon, the Amorite king,[k] and Og, the king of Bashan. And each garrison[l] which was in the land.[m]

a–a. LXX does not read the text of 1 Kgs 2:46b-3:1 at this point. Verses 2:46b–3:1a are entirely absent, and v. 1b appears as part of v. 35d in the midrashic addition to 2 Kgs 2:35 noted above. LXX instead includes another lengthy addition drawn largely from the accounts of Solomon's administration and the provisions of his court in 1 Kgs 4:2–6; 4:20–5:6; 9:18. The hypotheses that LXX represents an earlier text form or a textual corruption (Schenker, *Septante* esp. 17–35, 38–44) must be rejected in favor of the hypothesis that the LXX tradent deliberately employed material from other portions of Kings to provide an account of Solomon's greatness (Gooding, *Relics of Ancient Exegesis*). The motivation for such work would be discomfort with the portrayal of Solomon in relation to his execution of Shimei in 1 Kgs 2:46a and his marriage to the daughter of Pharaoh in 1 Kgs 3:2. By rewriting the text, the LXX emphasizes Solomon's power and greatness in an attempt to alleviate any doubts about him. Elements of the addition are drawn from other texts in Kings: v. 46a is derived in part from 4:20 and perhaps 10:23; v. 46b from 5:1; v. 46c perhaps from 9:19; v. 46d from the Qere reading in 9:18; v. 46e from 5:2–3; v. 46f from 5:4; v. 46g from 5:5 and 4:20; v. 46h is derived with extensive modification from 4:2–6; v. 46i from 5:6; v. 46k from 5:1; and v. 46l has no parallel in the MT, but appears to presuppose 2:46b. The LXX text of v. 46a–k reads as follows:

46a And King Solomon was very prudent and wise, and Judah and Israel were very numerous as the sand which by the sea for a multitude, eating, drinking, and rejoicing. 46b And Solomon was chief among all the kingdoms, and they brought gifts and they served Solomon all the days of their lives. 46c And Solomon began to open the domains of Lebanon, 46d and he built Thermai in the wilderness. 46e And this was the provision for Solomon: thirty measures of flour, and sixty measures of ground meal, ten choice calves, and twenty oxen from the pastures, and a hundred sheep, stags and does, and choice fed birds, 46f for he ruled everything beyond the River from Raphi until Gaza, over all the kings beyond the river. 46g And he was at peace on all sides around him, and Judah and Israel dwelled in confidence, everyone under his vine and under his fig tree, eating and drinking, from Dan until Beer Sheba, all the days of Solomon. 46h And these were the princes of Solomon: Azariah son of Zadok the priest, and Orniou son of Nathan chief of the officers, and Edram over his house, and Suba the scribe, and Basa son of Ahitalam recorder, and Abi son of Joab military commander, and Achire son of Edrei over the levies, and Banaiah son of Jodae over the house and over the brick-work, and Zachur son of Nathan counselor. **46i** And Solomon had forty thousand brood mares for his chariots and twelve thousand horses. **46k** And he reigned over all the kings from the river until the land of the Philistines and until the borders of Egypt. **46l** Solomon the son of David ruled over Israel and Judah in Jerusalem.

b. Vulgate considers v. 2:46b as part of the introduction to the following material in 3:1.

c. Lit., "I do not know coming and going."

d. The Hebrew text employs the verb *gzr*, "to cut, divide, saw," rather than the usual *krt*, "to cut." The verb *gzr* may be used in reference to dividing the Red Sea (Ps 136:13), the felling of trees (2 Kgs 6:4), or the extermination of enemies (Hab 3:17).

e. Hebrew, *hayyālûd*, a passive participle form of *yld*, "to bear," i.e., "that which was born." *BHS* notes that some manuscripts read the term as *hayyeled*, "boy."

f–f. An alternative version of this passage appears in LXX 3 Rgns 2:46h.

g. LXX adds *kai Eliab huios Saph epi tēs patrias*, "and Eliab son of Saph was over the guard" (cf. 1 Chr 11:25, where LXX reads *patria* for *mišmaʿtô*, "his bodyguard"; Mulder 167). The source of this comment is unknown, although critics concede that it is not an original text (e.g., Montgomery and Gehman 119; Noth, *Könige* 57).

h. Read with Qere, *hāʾeḥād*, "the one (each)"; cf. Ketiv, *ʾeḥād*, "one."

i. There is some confusion in reading the letter *beth* in *ûbĕʿālôt*, which can function either as the preposition *bĕ-*, "in," or as the initial letter of the city name. It may also be emended to *ûbaʿālôt*, "and Baalot." LXX reads *en tēi Maalath* (and in Maaloth); Peshitta as *wbbʿlwt* (and in Baʿalot); Targum Jonathan as *ûbʿālôt* (and in ʿAlot); and Vulgate as *in Balod* (in Baalot).

j–j. LXX places v. 17 after v. 19.

k. LXX reads *basileōs tou Esebōn*, "the king of Heshbon," in place of Hebrew "the Amorite king," apparently to specify the location of Sihon's kingdom in Moab and its capital Heshbon.

l. The Hebrew term *nĕṣîb* means "garrison," although it is often understood as a variant of *niṣṣāb*, "prefect," under the influence of the appearance of the term in vv. 5 and 7. LXX has difficulty with the term, and simply transliterates it as *nasiph*, "and one prefect in the land of Judah"; Peshitta reads it as *wqywmʾ*, "and one prefect in the land"; Targum Jonathan reads, *wĕʾistartĕgāʾ had dimmûnaʾ bĕʾarʿāʾ*, "and one garrison which was appointed in the land" (n.b., the word for prefect would have been *ʾistartĕgôs*); and Vulgate reads *super omnia quae erant in illa terra*, "besides the superiors who were in that land" (n.b., Vulgate uses neither *praefectus*, "prefect," nor *praesidium*, "garrison," which suggests uncertainty concerning the meaning of the term).

m. LXX reads *en gēi Iouda*, "in the land of Judah," drawing "Judah" from the beginning of v. 20 so that it will be represented among Solomon's twelve prefectures. Verse 17 follows v. 19. LXX continues with the statement in 1 Kgs 5:7–8, which repeats the responsibility of the prefects to provision Solomon's house, followed by the MT sequence in 1 Kgs 5:2–4, 9–32 (with additions). Verse 20 appears only in LXX at 3 Kgdms 2:46g, where it is combined with 1 Kgs 5:5. The addition of "Judah" to v. 19 specifies LXX's interpretation of the verse (Gooding, *Relics* 40–43).

[2:46b–3:2] The notice of Solomon's marriage to the daughter of Pharaoh in 3:1 builds upon the portrayal of national security since the marriage entails Solomon's alliance with Egypt. The qualification in v. 2 concerning the people's worship at the high places notes the religious situation in the kingdom at the outset of Solomon's reign, and thereby points forward to Solomon's role as temple builder. Verse 3 notes Solomon's worship at the high places, and thereby introduces the narrative concerning Solomon's dream at Gibeon.

Scholars generally assume a favorable presentation of Solomon in these verses, and therefore maintain that v. 2, which charges that the people are worshiping at the high places, is out of place.[17] This conclusion is supported by the critique of Israel for worshiping at the high places throughout the DtrH and the lack of antecedent for the particle *raq*, "only, but, except," at the beginning of the verse. Verse 2 is viewed as a redactional addition that justifies the Babylonian exile or the destruction of northern Israel. But several considerations suggest that the verse is neither critical of Israel nor redactional. First, it provides a reason that the people are worshiping at the high places—that is, the Jerusalem temple is not yet built. Although the ark is present in Jerusalem, it is not yet clear that Jerusalem functions as YHWH's selected sanctuary. Second, the particle *raq* does have an antecedent in v. 2:46b—that is, Solomon holds the kingdom, but the people are worshiping at the high places because the temple is not yet built. Insofar as the temple symbolizes YHWH's promise of security for Israel and the Davidic house, Solomon's hold on the kingdom is not yet complete. Verse 2:46b therefore introduces ch. 3.

But this raises questions concerning the role and character of 3:1. Solomon's marriage to the daughter of Pharaoh signals Solomon's secure hold on the throne. This is an odd way to laud Solomon in the context of the DtrH, which portrays Egypt as Israel's oppressor and forbids the king to engage in trade relations with the Egyptians (Deut 17:14–20, esp. v. 16). This statement is closely related to four other references to Pharaoh's daughter: 7:8, which repeats the notice that Solomon married while reporting the construction of her house; 9:16, which relates Pharaoh's gift of Gezer to Solomon as a wedding present; 9:24, which relates the move of the daughter of Pharaoh into her new house; and 11:1, which places the daughter of Pharaoh first in the list of foreign women that Solomon loved, thereby turning his heart from YHWH. These notices are intrusive in their respective contexts, and 3:1 is dependent upon them. Indeed, 3:1 is also intrusive. It suggests that Solomon holds the kingdom with Egyptian support, an ominous claim in relation to the notice that Pharaoh conquered

17. See Erik Eynikel, *The Reform of King Josiah and the Composition of the Deuteronomistic History* (OTS 33; Leiden: Brill, 1996), 50–60, esp. 53 n. 35; Helga Weippert, "Die 'deuteronomistschen' Beurteilungen der Könige von Israel und Juda und das Problem der Redaktion der Königsbücher," *Bib* 53 (1972): 301–39, esp. 314–315; Iain W. Provan, *Hezekiah and the Books of Kings* (BZAW 172; Berlin and New York: Walter de Gruyter, 1988), 68–69, esp. 68 n. 30.

Gezer and gave it as a wedding present to Solomon (9:16). This is a stunning role reversal in the DtrH—that is, an Israelite king who depends upon the Egyptian pharaoh to complete the conquest of the land of Israel![18]

These considerations suggest that 1 Kgs 3:1, not 3:2, is a redactional work, which raises questions concerning Solomon and undermines an otherwise positive notice concerning his control of the kingdom. Such a rereading would serve the exilic DtrH insofar as Solomon's alliance with Pharaoh would help to bring about the downfall of Israel. But it corresponds much more closely to the Josianic DtrH. Solomon's alliance with Egypt would help to explain his penchant for foreign wives, his tolerance for their religious practices, and his very pharaohlike actions in imposing state slavery on the Israelite population. Insofar as Josiah later corrects many of Solomon's faults—and those of other kings[19]—Solomon sets into motion a pattern of misbehavior on the part of Israel's and Judah's kings that Josiah attempts to reform. The underlying positive portrayal of Solomon would best serve the interests of the Hezekian edition of the DtrH. Hezekiah is the monarch who finally puts an end to the use of the high places (18:4) that were in use during Solomon's time. Although Solomon is portrayed worshiping at the high place at Gibeon, readers must recall that it was a dream and that Solomon received wisdom as a result of his dream. When he awoke, he worshiped at Jerusalem.

[3:3–15] The historical dimensions of the narrative must be addressed first. Solomon's dream is set at the high place at Gibeon, identified with modern El-Jib, five and a half miles north/northwest of Iron Age Jerusalem.[20] No sanctuary has been found, prompting many to speculate that the Gibeonite sanctuary lay outside the city at al-Nabi-Samwel, traditionally identified as the "tomb of Samuel," about one and a quarter miles south of El-Jib.[21] As the highest hill overlooking ancient Jerusalem, it would explain Solomon's offerings at this site.

Biblical tradition provides several accounts concerning Gibeon that may have some bearing in understanding Solomon's presence at the city's high place.[22] According to Josh 9:1–10:27 (cf. Josh 18:11–28), Gibeon was a Hivite city that headed a coalition including Chephirah, Beeroth, and Kireath-Jearim, located in Benjaminite territory north and west of Jerusalem. Fearing Israel, the men of Gibeon disguised themselves as travelers from a distant land to conclude a treaty. Although their Hivvite identity was later discovered, Joshua defended Gibeon

---

18. See Amos Frisch, "The Exodus Motif in 1 Kings 1–14," *JSOT* 87 (2000): 3–21.

19. See Sweeney, "Critique of Solomon"; *King Josiah,* 33–177, esp. 40–51.

20. See James B. Pritchard, "Gibeon," *NEAEHL* 2:511–14.

21. See "Samuel; Tomb of Samuel," *EncJud* 14:785–86.

22. See Joseph Blenkinsopp, *Gibeon and Israel: The Role of Gibeon and the Gibeonites in the Political and Religious History of Early Israel* (SOTSMS 2; Cambridge: Cambridge University Press, 1972).

against a Jerusalem-led Canaanite coalition, and the Gibeonites were allowed to live in the land.

Several traditions illustrate aspects of Gibeon's relations with the houses of Saul and David. Second Samuel 2:12–32 (cf. 1 Chr 14:8–17) narrates the battle at Gibeon between the forces of David, led by Joab, and the forces of Saul's son Ish-bosheth/Eshbaal, led by Abner. Second Samuel 21:1–14 relates the Gibeonites' demand that David turn over the sons of Saul to avenge Gibeonite deaths when Saul broke the treaty with Gibeon. Biblical tradition does not relate the incident in which the Gibeonites were killed, although it could be associated with Abner's battle against David's men at Gibeon or Saul's killing of the priests at Nob (1 Sam 22:6–23) who may have had some association with Gibeon or its ally Kiriath Jearim, which housed the ark. Kiriath Jearim is also called Kiriath Baal (Josh 15:60; 18:14) or Baalah (Josh 15:9).

Biblical sources suggest that Gibeon is key to David's assumption of kingship in Israel. David was still a Philistine vassal, and Ish-bosheth's confrontation with him at Gibeon suggests an attempt to protect his territory against further Philistine encroachment. David later turned against his Philistine overlords upon moving to Jerusalem to become king over all Israel and Judah, and Gibeon remained loyal to him. The deaths of Saul's seven sons ensure that loyalty, and they remove the major Saulide claimants to the throne. Only Mephibosheth, whom David controls, and Shimei, who supported Absalom's revolt against David, remain as possible Saulide contenders. The presence of Kiriath Jearim in the Gibeonite-led coalition is noteworthy because it housed the ark for a period of time between the Philistine defeat of Israel at Aphek and David's ascension to the throne of all Israel at Jerusalem (1 Sam 4–6; 2 Sam 6). The account of David's relocation of the ark from Kiriath Jearim to Jerusalem and his refusal to have further relations with Michal bat Saul immediately precedes Nathan's oracle promising David a lasting dynasty. Saul's killing of the priests at Nob likewise indicates a shift in allegiance from Saul to David on the part of the Elide priesthood, which was responsible for the ark. Baanah and Rechab, the men who killed Ish-bosheth/Eshbaal, were from Beeroth, one of Gibeon's allies (2 Sam 4:1–12). Solomon's presence at Gibeon presupposes Gibeonite support.

Solomon's worship at Gibeon presages his tolerance of foreign religious practice. YHWH's promises to Solomon are conditioned on his adherence to YHWH's commands (v. 14), but Solomon does not adhere to these conditions. Consequently, he does not attain old age, virtually bankrupts his kingdom, and finds himself surrounded by enemies at the end of his reign.

These observations are based upon a reading of the Gibeon narrative in relation to the larger literary context of the DtrH; the narrative in and of itself is not overtly or inherently critical of Solomon. It is only when the narrative context is considered that the critique against Solomon becomes clear. When considered as a self-contained narrative, 1 Kgs 3:3–15 presents quite a positive portrayal of Solomon as a pious and righteous young king to whom YHWH grants wisdom. Verse 2 provides a reason that Solomon worships at the Gibeonite high place: the temple is not yet built. The reader can hardly escape the significance of such a statement when it is considered that Solomon is the one who will carry out the task of constructing the temple.[23] The promises of a dynasty are made in the expectation that Solomon will meet the conditions, and thereby ensure the future of his kingdom. The portrayal of the young king's character—he is an inexperienced boy (v. 7), he desires "a listening heart" to judge his people responsibly, and he lacks interest in personal advancement—presents a monarch who thinks only of doing what is right for his people while continuing in his love for YHWH.

Insofar as the critique is established only in relation to the literary context of the DtrH, redactional work in the DtrH is responsible for the critical presentation of Solomon. Solomon's actions are relevant to the Josianic redaction of the DtrH, particularly because Solomon appears as one of the royal foils for King Josiah's reforms. Second Kings 23:13 cites Josiah's destruction of the high places to the east and south of Jerusalem that were erected by Solomon for the gods Astarte, Chemosh, and Milcom on behalf of his foreign wives (1 Kgs 11:5–7). Josiah's reforms also include the destruction of the Beth El altar (2 Kgs 23:15–20). Although Solomon is not directly responsible for building the altar, 1 Kgs 11 makes it clear that Solomon's apostasy was the cause for YHWH's grant of kingship to Jeroboam ben Nebat, who in turn established Beth El as an illegitimate worship site (1 Kgs 12–13). Josiah was the first to observe Passover since Joshua (2 Kgs 23:21–24). Such a claim entails that Solomon did not observe Passover, the first of the three major temple festivals, despite the fact that he built the temple. Indeed, the Josian redaction of the DtrH has a great deal of interest in presenting a critical portrayal of Solomon because it aids in building up the righteous character of Josiah, who must correct the wrongs created by his predecessors. The claims in 2 Kgs 23:25 of Josiah's incomparability in observing Mosaic Torah undermine the claims of Solomon's incomparability in 1 Kgs 3:12–13.

[3:16–28] First Kings 3:16–28 is demarcated at the outset by the particle *ʾāz*, "then," followed by the imperfect verb *tābōʾnâ*, "they (the two prostitutes) come," which indicates a redactional attempt to correlate a past event with the preceding material concerning Solomon's dream.[24]

The narrative presents a legal dispute between two women, who both claim to be the mother of a living baby rather than one that died. The understanding

23. Cf. Moshe Weinfeld, *Deuteronomy and the Deuteronomic School* (Winona Lake, Ind.: Eisenbrauns, 1992), 244–54, who argues that YHWH's granting wisdom to Solomon at Gibeon enables him to build the temple.

24. Isaac Rabinowitz, "*ʾĀZ* followed by Imperfect Verb-Form in Preterite Contexts: A Redactional Device in Biblical Hebrew," *VT* 34 (1984): 53–62.

of the women as "prostitutes" is essential to the narrative. It explains why the women are living alone in the same house, why they are both pregnant when no men are living with them, and why there are no witnesses available to establish their claims. The narrative passes no moral judgment on the women, but their designation as prostitutes trivializes Solomon as a monarch who spends his time resolving quarrels between prostitutes. The wearisome nature of the women's presentations and the striking contrast of their perspectives highlight the impossible nature of the decision for the young monarch.[25] There are no witnesses, the women cannot establish credibility, and their claims are diametrically opposed and in need of immediate resolution because the life of a newborn baby is at stake. Even the aggrieved party claims to have been asleep at the time that the purported switch was made! The narrator has gone to great lengths to present a classic case of one party's word contradicting the other's, with no apparent criteria to decide between them.

The concluding statement in v. 28 confirms the narrative interest in demonstrating Solomon's wisdom, and it further confirms that he is indeed ready to serve as king. And yet, there are also critical dimensions to the portrayal of Solomon, although they are not inherent to the narrative itself. One must ask why Solomon serves as the chief magistrate. Examples of the king acting in this capacity present models for the abuse of power, such as Saul, who condemns the priests at Nob (1 Sam 22:6–30); David, who sits in judgment of himself for his adultery with Bath Sheba and murder of Uriah (2 Sam 11–12); and Absalom, who employs the exercise of judicial authority to build support for his revolt against his own father. Although the king is responsible for the maintenance of justice in the land (Deut 32:41–42; Isa 11:1–5; Jer 21:11–12), the Deuteronomic law code presents a very different view of judicial power in which the Levitical priests, not the king, serve as the chief magistrates of the land (Deut 17:8–13). From the perspective of Deuteronomy and the DtrH, Solomon's assumption of judicial power is illegal.

The critique of Solomon is accomplished through redactional framing of an earlier narrative, which presents Josiah as a foil to Solomon. First Kings 3:16–28 is not written by the Josianic redaction, but it is read in the context of that redaction, and becomes a part of the basis by which the redaction charges Solomon with misconduct. Insofar as 1 Kgs 3:16–28 lauds Solomon for his wisdom, it functions in relation to the Hezekian DtrH, which honors Solomon and presents him as a model for Hezekiah.

[4:1–19] First Kings 4:1–19 presents a register (see Long 71) of Solomon's administrative officers over all Israel. This register lauds Solomon for his wisdom in organizing this large and complex empire and in delegating responsibil-

25. Long, 1 Kings, 69; Ellen Van Wolde, "Who Guides Whom? Embeddedness and Perspective in Biblical Hebrew and in 1 Kings 3:16–28," JBL 114 (1995): 623–42.

ity for the various tasks that ensure its viability (cf. 2 Sam 8:15–18; 20:23–26). A critical perspective appears only when this chapter is read in relation to the account of the revolt of the northern tribes that emphasizes Solomon's oppressive treatment of them. The laudatory portrayal of Solomon suggests that the chapter forms part of the Hezekian edition of the account of Solomon's reign, and that it was later incorporated into the Josianic DtrH that portrayed Solomon critically as a foil to the righteous Josiah. The unit begins in v. 1 with a *waw*-consecutive form, *wayĕhî,* "and it came to pass," to introduce a new concern with Solomon's administration. The pericope falls into three basic subunits: v. 1 introduces the chapter by identifying Solomon as king over all Israel; vv. 2–6 identify the officers of Solomon's central administration; and vv. 7–19 identify Solomon's prefects who preside over the administrative districts of "all Israel."

[4:1] "All Israel" includes Judah. Although the central officers could have served for both Judah and Israel, the prefects preside only over the districts that comprise northern Israel.

[4:2–6] First Kings 4:2–6 is demarcated in v. 2a with the formula, "and these are his officers." Its subsequent structure is determined in part by a series of nine statements which list the names of Solomon's officers followed by the title for their respective offices. The statements pertaining to the first three lack a conjunction, but those pertaining to the remaining six each begin with a conjunctive *waw,* "and." The "priest," "scribes," and "recorder" have the greatest overall power and continuous presence in the king's court, whereas the latter six require their respective officers to function at some distance from the king or to oversee functions less central to state authority.

The register begins with v. 2a, which identifies Azariah ben Zadok as "the priest." Although he is identified as the son of Zadok, the genealogy of the Levites in 1 Chr 5:27–41 specifies the line of descent as Zadok, Ahimaaz, Azariah, Johanan, and Azariah, noting that Azariah ben Johanan served as priest in Solomon's temple (vv. 34–36). This expanded genealogy accounts for Zadok's earlier service together with Abiathar as priest to David (2 Sam 8:17; 15:24–29; 20:25) and the length of time that would have passed from David's forty-year reign to the completion of the temple in Solomon's eleventh year (1 Kgs 6:38). The genealogy also accounts for the identification of Ahimaaz as the son of Zadok, who carried reports to David concerning Absalom's activities and his death (2 Sam 15:27; 17:17, 20; 18:19–32).

Azariah's designation as "the priest" indicates that he functions as the "high priest" (cf. 1 Chr 5:36). The priest is later designated as *hakkōhēn haggādôl,* "the great priest" (2 Kgs 12:11), or *kōhēn hārō'š,* "the head priest" (2 Kgs 25:18). As "the priest" or "the high priest" of the temple, Azariah ben Zadok was the chief representative of the people before YHWH and the chief representative of YHWH to the people. Given the close interrelationship between king and temple in ancient Israel, in which the king builds the temple for YHWH and YHWH guarantees the security of the king (see 2 Sam 7; 1 Kgs 8; Pss 2; 89; 110; 132),[26] the high priest is one of the chief officers in Solomon's administration.

The second listing includes Elihoreph and Ahijah, the sons of Shisha', designated as scribes. These men are otherwise unknown, although the name *šîšā'*, "Shisha'," is often viewed as a corrupted form of the names given for David's scribe, respectively *šĕrāyâ*, "Seraiah," in 2 Sam 8:17 and *šĕwā'*, "Sheya'," in 2 Sam 20:25 (cf. 1 Chr 18:16). The name *šîšā'* frequently plays a role in assertions that Solomon's bureaucracy is modeled on that of Egypt, since it is similar to the Egypt term *ss šᶜ.t* or *sh šᶜ.t*, "scribe of letters, secretary."[27] The name *šîšā'* might designate a professional class or a personal name based upon a term for a professional scribe. The city states of Israel and Judah had a long history of Egyptian rule that dates back to the Amarna Age (fourteenth century B.C.E.), but there would be no need to borrow models from Egypt as pre-Israelite Canaanite models would be readily at hand for David and Solomon.[28]

The scribes were in charge of all functions that required written records, announcements, messages, and so on.[29] Various narratives indicate that scribes served more generally in administrative and advisory capacities within the royal court. Only two individuals are listed as scribes in 1 Kgs 4:3, but evidence for a larger scribal body in later periods, the portrayal of Solomon's extensive empire, and the supervisory capacities of many of the offices in this register suggest that these men were the chief scribes who supervised an unknown number of subordinates.[30]

Jehoshaphat ben Ahilud is listed as David's secretary in 2 Sam 8:16; 20:24; and 1 Chr 18:15. The term *mazkîr*, "recorder," a *hiphil* participle form of the verb *zkr*, "to remember," suggests a scribal function that calls for the recording of information.[31] The term *mazkîr*, however, is never associated with writing activities until later versions such as the LXX render it as *hupomnēmatograpos*, a title for Ptolemaic period annalists.[32] The only other occurrences of the term in biblical literature refer to Joah ben Asaph, who was part of a delegation sent

26. See G. W. Ahlström, *Royal Administration and National Religion in Ancient Palestine* (SHANE 1; Leiden: Brill, 1982), 1–9; Ahlström, *CANE*, 2:590–98.

27. T. N. D. Mettinger, *Solomonic State Officials* (Lund: Gleerup, 1971), 27–29; cf. Nili Sacher Fox, *In the Service of the King: Officaldom in Ancient Israel and Judah* (Monographs of the Hebrew Union College 23; Cincinnati: Hebrew Union College, 2000), 99–101.

28. See esp. Ahlström, *Royal Administration,* 27–43.

29. For a full discussion of scribal functions, see Fox, *In the Service,* 96–99, 101–10.

30. E. W. Heaton, *Solomon's New Men: The Emergence of Ancient Israel as a National State* (New York: Pica, 1974); cf. David W. Jamieson-Drake, *Scribes and Schools in Monarchic Judah: A Socio-Archaeological Approach* (JSOTSup 109; Sheffield: Sheffield Academic Press, 1991).

31. See Fox, *In the Service,* 110–14, for discussion.

32. See Mettinger, *Solomonic,* 19–24.

by King Hezekiah to hear the demands of the Assyrian Rab-Shakeh during Sennacherib's siege of Jerusalem (2 Kgs 18:18, 37; Isa 36:3, 22), and Joah ben Joahaz, who served King Josiah (2 Chr 34:8), but this reference provides little information concerning the function of the office. Foreign models from Ugarit, Mesopotamia, and Egypt refer to a "herald" or major domo of the royal court.[33]

Benaiah ben Jehoiada, the army commander, is the man ordered by Solomon to kill Joab (1 Kgs 2:28–35). The registers of David's officers in 2 Sam 8:18; 20:23; and 1 Chr 18:17 list him as the commander of the Cherethites and the Pelethites, who function as David's mercenary bodyguard. He was from Kabzeel, a southern Judean village near the border with Edom (Josh 15:21), and won his position for great deeds in battle (2 Sam 23:20–23).

The priest Abiathar was the sole member of the house of Eli to escape Saul's massacre of the priests at Nob (1 Sam 22:6–23). He fled to David and served him for the rest of his life (1 Sam 23:6–14; 30:7–10), remaining behind in Jerusalem with Zadok during Absalom's revolt to provide information to David through his son Jonathan (2 Sam 15:13–29, 35–36; 17:15–22; 19:12–15). He was expelled from Jerusalem by Solomon to Anathoth. Zadok likewise serves David together with Abiathar during Absalom's revolt, sending his own son Ahimaaz as a messenger to David (e.g., 2 Sam 18:19–32; cf. 2 Sam 8:17; 20:25). Second Samuel 8:17 and 1 Chr 5:34 list Zadok as the son of Ahitub. Because Ahitub was the father of Ahimelech who headed the priests at Nob (2 Sam 22:11–12, 20), he would then be the uncle of Abiathar ben Ahimelech and a member of the Elide line. Following Abiathar's expulsion to Anathoth, Zadok was the head of the sole priestly line under Solomon.

Azariah ben Nathan is otherwise unknown, although there is a great deal of speculation that his father is Nathan the Prophet. Alternatively, he could be a grandson of David as 2 Sam 5:14 and 1 Chr 3:5; 14:4 (see also Zech 12:12) list a Nathan as a son born to David in Jerusalem. Azariah's status as head of the prefects anticipates the following register of prefects in vv. 7–19. The term *niṣṣāb*, "prefect," a *niphal* participle from the root *nṣb*, "to take a stand," or "to be stationed/appointed" (see Gen 45:1; 1 Sam 4:20; 19:20; 22:6; 2 Sam 13:31; Isa 21:8; Ps 45:10; Ruth 2:5), is employed for the officers of Solomon's administration who govern the provinces or territories that constitute Israel (1 Kgs 4:7; 5:7, 30; cf. Jehoshaphat's governor of Edom in 1 Kgs 22:48). The term may also be employed for Solomon's officers in charge of forced labor (1 Kgs 9:23; 2 Chr 8:10, read Qere, *niṣṣābîm* instead of Ketiv form *nĕṣîbîm*). Although the Qetil form *nĕṣîb* is sometimes confused with *niṣṣāb* (see 2 Chr 8:10; 1 Kgs 4:19), *nĕṣîb* is a term for a garrison (see 1 Sam 10:5; 13:3; 8:6, 14; 1 Chr 11:16; 17:2), which is commanded by a *niṣṣāb*.

---

33. Fox, *In the Service,* 114; Mettinger, *Solomonic,* 57–60.

The appointment of prefects is a new element in Israelite administration.[34] David appointed garrisons in subject countries, such as Aram (2 Sam 8:6), Edom (2 Sam 8:14), and Philistia (2 Sam 23:14), but there is no indication of a chief administrator for these garrisons other than the king himself or that such prefects were appointed over the people of Israel. Solomon's appointment of prefects provides efficient governance for an expanded empire. The prefect acted on behalf of the king to collect revenues due and to provide defense and other services of the central government. The appointment of a chief over the prefects recognizes the need for oversight of the officers appointed over the districts of Israel and subject territories.

Zabud ben Nathan, identified as priest and friend of the king, is unknown. Some speculate that he is the son of the prophet Nathan or the son of David's own son Nathan (see 2 Sam 5:14; 1 Chr 3:5; 14:4; see also Zech 12:12). Far more problematic is Zabud's designation as *rēʿeh hammelek*, "the friend of the king." Although the term *rēʿeh* and its variations refers generally to a friend, the expression connotes an official capacity. Thus, the title "friend of the king" or its equivalent applies to Hushai the Archite, the "friend" of David who remained behind in Jerusalem to serve as David's agent in Absalom's court (2 Sam 15:37; 16:16; cf. 1 Chr 27:33, which employs the term *rēʿa*, "friend") and unnamed friends of King Baasha of Israel (1 Kgs 16:11). Genesis 26:26 indicates that the Philistine king Abimelek came to meet Isaac together with Ahuzzath, his "friend" (*mērēʿ*), and Phicol, his military commander. Some point to the designation of Jonadab ben Shimah as Amnon ben David's "friend" (*rēʿa*), who counseled the young prince on how to seduce his half-sister Tamar. Others point to Samson's "friends" (*mērēʿ*; Judg 14:11–20; 15:2), who accompanied him to his wedding (ultimately, one married the bride!). Many conclude that the role is that of a counselor (*yôʿeṣ*), although the various roles described here hardly convey the image of a good counselor. First Chronicles 27:33 carefully distinguishes between Ahitophel the counselor and Hushai the friend of David.

The absence of clear criteria by which to define the role of the "friend" of the king has prompted interpreters to look to sources from Mesopotamia, Egypt, and Canaan, but none has garnered support.[35] Given the distinction between "counselor" and "friend" in biblical sources, it seems best to conclude that "the friend of the king" is a sort of royal agent, who is delegated with special tasks. Hushai serves as a mole in Absalom's court due to his ability to convince Absalom that he turned against the king (2 Sam 15:32–37; 17). Ahuzzath's role is unclear, although he accompanies Abimelek at a time when the Philistine king must negotiate to resolve tensions with Isaac. Each of these men would have served their respective kings by keeping them informed and carrying out nec-

34. See Mettinger, *Solomonic*, 111–27; Fox, *In the Service*, 141–49.
35. Mettinger, *Solomonic*, 66–69; Fox, *In the Service*, 124–26.

essary tasks. The Babylonian and Persian kings employed special emissaries to inform them of events within their empires.[36] As for Zabud's role as a priest, Jonathan ben Abiathar and Ahimaaz ben Zadok, both of whom were priests, kept David informed of Absalom's intentions by bringing him reports from their fathers (2 Sam 15:23–31; 17–18).

Ahishar, who is "over the house," is unknown, and the issue is complicated by the absence of his father's name. The LXX likewise lacks the father's name, although it adds, "and Eliab the son of Saph was over the guard." Given the careful recording of the patronymics throughout this register, most scholars claim that the absence of the name is the result of some omission or textual corruption. A comparison of the names of the other persons who hold this office, however, indicates that the patronymic is missing in most of these cases, including Arza, who was over the house of Elah in Tirzah (1 Kgs 16:9); Obadiah, who was over the house of Ahab (1 Kgs 18:3); an unnamed figure who was over the house of Jehoram (2 Kgs 15:5); and Shebna, who is listed as over the house of Hezekiah (Isa 22:15). Other instances indicate some ambiguity. Jothan, who is over the house of Uzziah, is designated as "the son of the king," which may indicate some official appointed status, special status as a member of the royal family, or both. Eliakim ben Hilkiah is designated as "over the house" of Hezekiah in 2 Kgs 18:18, 37; 19:2/Isa 36:3, 22; 37:2. This appears to be an exceptional case, however, since Eliakim ben Hilkiah would have replaced Shebna in this role (see Isa 22:15–25). The lack of a patronymic in biblical sources is bolstered by the recently discovered inscription over the tomb of the royal steward in the Silwan village, located across the Wadi Kidron from biblical Jerusalem;[37] a seal discovered at Lachish;[38] and a collection of seals and bullae, each of which lacks a patronymic for the personal name.[39] The reason for the lack of a patronymic is unknown.

Ahishar's office, *ʿal habbāyit,* "over the house," indicates that he supervises activities in the king's palace and properties, much like Joseph, who is appointed over the house of Potiphar to oversee everything in the house and fields (Gen 39:4–6), and Joseph's own steward, who supervises the preparation of food and the baggage of guests (Gen 43:16, 19; 44:1, 4).[40]

Adoniram ben Abda' appears in 2 Sam 20:24; 1 Kgs 5:28; 12:18; and 2 Chr 10:18 as Solomon's supervisor of forced state labor. He is called Adoram in

---

36. A. L. Oppenheim, "The Eyes of the L-rd," *JAOS* 88 (1968): 173–80.

37. Nahman Avigad, "The Epitaph of a Royal Steward," *IEJ* 3 (1953): 137–52, 143; cf. David Ussishkin, *The Village of Silwan* (Jerusalem: Israel Exploration Society, 1993), 247–50.

38. See Mettinger, *Solomonic,* 70–71; Fox, *In the Service,* 82.

39. Nahman Avigad, *Hebrew Bullae from the Time of Jeremiah: Remnants of a Burnt Archive* (Jerusalem: Israel Exploration Society, 1986), 21–23; Fox, *In the Service,* 82, 304–5 (Table A2).

40. See esp. Mettinger, *Solomonic,* 80–110; Scott C. Layton, "The Steward in Ancient Israel: A Study of the Hebrew (ʾăšer) ʿal-habbayit in Its Near Eastern Setting," *JBL* 109 (1990): 633–49; Fox, *In the Service,* 81–96.

1 Kgs 12:18 and Hadoram in 2 Chr 10:18, which are variants of the same name. The differences in the names lie in the fact that Adoram and Hadoram are theophoric names based on variations of the Aramean storm god, Hadad/Adad, whereas Adoniram removes the pagan associations by replacing Hadad/Adad with Adoni, "my lord (is exalted)."[41] He supervised Israelite work crews sent to Lebanon to cut trees for Solomon's palace and the temple, and he was stoned to death by the northern Israelites when Rehoboam sent him to impose control in the aftermath of the northern revolt.

The Hebrew term *mas* appears some twenty-three times in the Bible, always in reference to labor imposed by the state (e.g., Gen 49:15; Exod 1:11; Isa 31:8; Prov 12:24; and Esth 10:1). References to Solomon's imposition of forced labor on the Canaanites appear in 1 Kgs 9:15, 21; 2 Chr 8:8, and his imposition of forced labor on Israel appears in 1 Kgs 5:27. The remaining references appear in the above-mentioned references to Adoniram/Adoram/Hadoram (2 Sam 20:24; 1 Kgs 4:6; 5:28; 12:18; 2 Chr 10:18). The term originates in Canaan, as indicated by its appearance in various Akkadian texts from Alalakh and an Amarna letter from Megiddo.[42] State imposition of forced labor was a common means throughout the ancient world to accomplish major projects, such as the building of temples and palaces and the digging and maintenance of canals. The practice employed subject populations, although indigenous populations could also be tapped for such service. Biblical sources indicate that ancient Israel required such labor from the various foreign populations that were incorporated into the Davidic state. First Kings 9:15–23 indicates that Solomon employed the foreign populations under his rule to perform the necessary labor for the building of cities and fortifications under the supervision of Israelite officers.[43] First Kings 5:15–32 indicates that Solomon also imposed forced labor on Israelites in order to carry out the building of the temple. This text speaks only of Israelite—and not Judean—laborers. Likewise, the following references in 1 Kgs 4:7–19 to Solomon's prefectures responsible for the provision of the royal court include only Israelite territories. Solomon imposed forced labor only on northern Israel, which would explain the demands of the northern tribes that Solomon's son, Rehoboam, lift the heavy yoke imposed on them by his father.

[4:7–19] First Kings 4:7–19 is demarcated initially by the noun clause in v. 7 that introduces the register of prefects, *wĕšlōmōh šĕnêm-ʿāśār niṣṣābîm ʿal-kol-yiśrāʾēl*, "And Solomon had twelve prefects over all Israel . . ." The internal structure in vv. 7–19 falls into two basic parts: vv. 7–19ab provides the

---

41. See Mettinger, *Solomonic,* 133.

42. Mettinger, *Solomonic,* 129–32; Anson Rainey, "Compulsory Labor Gangs in Ancient Israel," *IEJ* 20 (1970): 191–202.

43. Amihai Mazar, *Archaeology of the Land of the Bible, 10,000–586 B.C.E.* (New York: Doubleday, 1990), 368–402.

register of Solomon's twelve prefects and v. 19bß follows with a statement concerning the one garrison that Solomon maintained in the land.

Several observations must be made concerning this register. First, it contains a list of prefects who preside only over the territories of the northern tribes of Israel. Judah appears only in v. 20, which introduces the next textual unit. Consequently, the initial statement in v. 7 that Solomon's twelve prefects presided over their respective districts in "all Israel" refers to northern Israel alone. Although many interpreters follow the LXX's rendition of v. 19b to account for a prefect over Judah as well, the LXX's reading appears to be part of a larger reorganization of this text that was designed to resolve its various interpretative problems. One of the key issues was the absence of Judah in the register of prefects. The other versions reflect the MT.

This differentiation has important consequences for understanding Solomon's state administration. Solomon treated the northern tribes differently than Judah. Whereas he apparently ruled Judah directly as his home tribe, he ruled Israel through administrators much as one would rule a foreign or subject state. This observation is supported by his imposition of the corvée upon "all Israel" (1 Kgs 5:27–32) and his use of "officers of the prefects" (*śārê hanniṣṣābîm*) to supervise the work just as they supervised the forced labor of the Canaanites. Judah is not mentioned in relation to this work at all. This observation is also supported by the statement that there was "one garrison (*něṣîb*) in the land" (v. 19bß) since such garrisons were otherwise posted only in foreign territories (e.g., Aram, 2 Sam 8:6, and Edom, 2 Sam 8:14). Judah's privileged status undoubtedly played a role in the revolt of the northern tribes against Rehoboam, particularly in relation to their demand that he lighten their burden (1 Kgs 12).

Second, although the definitions of Solomon's twelve administrative districts bear a close relationship to the tribal boundaries of the northern tribes as delineated in Joshua, they do not always correspond to those boundaries. Various theories have been put forward to explain this anomaly—for example, Solomon attempted to maintain the tribal boundaries in keeping with past tradition, Solomon reorganized the tribes to establish districts of approximately equivalent economic capacity, or this list reflects adjustments to the tribal boundaries as Israel occupied all of Canaan and conceded some territory to the Phoenicians.[44]

An examination of the changes in tribal boundaries, however, indicates that the system is designed to weaken or contain major elements within the northern kingdom, particularly the two central Joseph tribes of Manasseh and Ephraim. Solomon's district 1 (v. 8b) constitutes the hill country of Ephraim, but its territory is defined only in relation to its neighbors. It differs markedly

---

44. Albrecht Alt, "Menschen ohne Namen," *Kleine Schriften* 3:198–213; George Ernest Wright, "The Provinces of Solomon," *ErIsr* 8 (1967): 58*–68*.

from the territory delineated for Ephraim in Josh 16.[45] Whereas Ephraim's territory extended from Lower Beth-Horon and Gezer through the coastal plain and to the sea in Josh 16, these areas have been given over in the southwest to Solomon's district 2 (v. 9) and in the west to district 3 (v. 10). District 1 therefore appears to have lost its access to the coastal plain and the sea, which provide access to the major trade routes that run through the land of Israel. The prefect, identified only by patronymic as ben Hur, is otherwise unknown.

District 2 (v. 9) includes the cities of Makaz, Shaalbim, Beth Shemesh, and Elon Beth Hanan. This territory includes some portions of southwestern Ephraim as well as territory originally assigned to Dan in Josh 19:40–48.[46] The site of Makaz is uncertain, although it may be identified with two possible sites in the Judean Shephelah, either Khirbet el-Mukheisin, about four miles south of Ekron, or another site between Gezer and Timnah.[47] Shaalbim appears as an Amorite city in the tribal territory of Dan (Josh 19:42 [as Shaalabin]; Judg 1:35), and is identified with Selbit, three miles northwest of Aijalon.[48] Beth Shemesh is a well-known city in the northeastern Shephelah. It is identified as Ir-shemesh in the tribal territory of Dan (Josh 19:41) and later given by Judah to the Kohathite sons of Aaron (Josh 21:16). The site is identified with Tel Rumeilah near modern Beth Shemesh, about twelve and a half miles west of Jerusalem in the Sorek valley.[49] Elon Beth Hanan presents problems as many scholars emend "Elon" (ʾêlôn) to "Aijalon" (ʾayyālôn) with Josh 19:42, although Josh 19:43 indicates that the territory of Dan also includes a city called Elon. Elon Beth Hanan or Beth Hanan is uncertain, although it seems clear that it was located in the original tribal territory of Dan. District 2 includes Gezer, a Canaanite city conquered by Pharaoh as a wedding gift for Solomon and his daughter (1 Kgs 9:16). The district defines the boundary between Philistia and Israel. Its prefect, ben Deqer, is unknown.

District 3 (v. 10) includes the cities of Aruboth, Sokoh, and all the land of Hepher. Aruboth is now identified with Khirbet el-Hamam, located in the northwestern Samarian hills about three miles west of the Arab village of Arabeh.[50] The site would then be situated within the western territory of Manasseh, although it is not mentioned by name (Josh 17:1–13). Sokoh is identified with

45. Cf. Zechariah Kallai, *Historical Geography of the Bible* (Jerusalem: Magnes; Leiden: Brill, 1986), 47–49, who notes this loss, although he maintains that Ephraim had an expanded border to the north based upon his reading of Josh 16.

46. Cf. Kallai, *Geography,* 49.

47. G. A. Herion, "Makaz," *ABD* 4:477.

48. W. I. Toews, "Shaalbim," *ABD* 5:1147; Dan Barag, "Shaalbim," *NEAEHL* 4:1338.

49. Shlomo Bunimovitz and Zvi Lederman, "Beth-Shemesh," *NEAEHL* 1:249–53; F. Brandfon, "Beth-Shemesh," *ABD* 1:696–98.

50. Adam Zertal, "Hammam, Khirbet el-," *NEAEHL* 2:563–65; Zertal, "Arubboth," *ABD* 1:465–67.

Shuweiket er-Ras, located in the territory of western Manasseh about one and three-quarter miles north of modern Tulkarm near the pass leading to Shechem.[51] It is not mentioned in Josh 17:1–13. The decisive identification of the district is the mention of the land of Hepher, which comprises part of the western territory of Manasseh (Josh 17:2, 3; cf. Josh 12:17). This territory constitutes part of western Manasseh located in the northwestern hill country of Samaria with possible access to the sea.[52] Insofar as it constitutes only a portion of western Manasseh's territory, it points to an interest in dividing and weakening Manasseh further and controlling access to the coastal plain and the sea north of Philistia. The prefect, ben Hesed, is unknown.

District 4 (v. 11) includes Nephat Dor. The city of Dor was a well-known Phoenician port that was associated with a broader area known as Nephat Dor (Josh 12:23; cf. Josh 11:2).[53] The term Nephat might be derived from either of the two forms of the root *nwp*. If it is derived from *nwp* I, "to swing, wave," it refers to the forested hills overlooking Dor. If it is derived from *nwp* II, it refers to elevation of height, which would again refer to the hills overlooking Dor. It might constitute a loan word from the language of the Sea Peoples insofar as Greek *napē*, "wooded vale, glen," corresponds to Hebrew *šārôn*, "plain, woodland," which is the name of the Sharon plain to the south of Dor.[54] Dor itself is identified with Khirbet el-Burj on the Mediterranean seacoast south of Kibbutz Nahsholim and north of Tantura. Nephat Dor would then encompass the hills separating Dor from the Jezreel Valley, Megiddo, and Taanach (district 5).[55] Because the definition of district 3 is not entirely certain, it might also include the Plain of Sharon to the south with its access to the sea. It is identified with the territory of Manasseh (but see Josh 17:11–13; Judg 1:27–28). Again, the definition of this district shows an interest in dividing Manasseh and in controlling access to the sea. Given Solomon's interest in sea trade in conjunction with the Phoenicians (1 Kgs 5; cf. 1 Kgs 9:26–28), the port of Dor would provide a key point for importing raw materials from Lebanon into Israel. Although ben Abinadab is unknown, his marriage to Solomon's daughter Taphat reflects the importance of this district.

District 5 (v. 12) includes most of the Jezreel Valley and the key cities of Megiddo, Taanach, Beth Shean, Zarethanah, and Ebel Meholah. The fertile Jezreel Valley is one of the breadbaskets of ancient Israel, and it defines the major east-west trade route that runs between the Galilee and the hill country of Samaria, allowing access from Damascus to Egypt.[56] Megiddo guards the

---

51. H. D. Lance, "Sokoh," *ABD* 6:99.
52. Cf. Kallai's extensive discussion, *Geography,* 50–60, which also allows for access to the sea.
53. E. Stern, "Dor," *ABD* 2:223–25; Stern, "Dor," *NEAEHL* 1:357–68.
54. Kallai, *Geography,* 61; cf. H. R. Weeks, "Sharon," *ABD* 5:1161–63.
55. Cf. Kallai, *Geography,* 60–61.
56. Cf. ibid., 61–64, who also includes the hills to the south of the Jezreel.

western approach into the Jezreel Valley through the Carmel range from the coastal plain.[57] Taanach, identified with Tell Ti'innik some five miles southeast of Megiddo, also guards the approaches to the western Jezreel.[58] Beth Shean, situated at the conjunction of the eastern Jezreel Valley and the northern Jordan Valley, guards the eastern approaches to the Jezreel.[59] The locations of Zarethan, Abel Meholah, and Jokmeam are heavily disputed, and have been located in the regions of the eastern Jezreel, the Jordan Valley, and the Transjordan.[60] Although they are identified as Canaanite cities, Taanach, Megiddo, and Beth Shean fall within the territory of Manasseh together with the Jezreel (Josh 17:11–13; Judg 1:27–28). Abel Meholah and Zarethan would likewise fall within Manasseh's territory whether they were located to the west or the east of the Jordan. Judges 7:22 suggests that Zarethan and Abel Meholah controlled the fords over the Jordan that would allow access from the Transjordan to the Jezreel. Jokmeam is generally placed at the northeast corner of Ephraim, either in the hills or the Jordan Valley.[61] First Kings 19:16 identifies Abel Meholah as the home of the prophet Elisha, who is associated with the Transjordan. Again, the definition of this district suggests an interest in breaking up the territory of Manasseh, in this case with a focus on the strategic Jezreel Valley. The prefect, Baana ben Ahilud, may be the brother of Jehoshaphat ben Ahilud the herald (1 Kgs 4:3).

District 6 (v. 13) includes Ramoth Gilead, the villages of Jair ben Manasseh in Gilead, and the region of Argob in the Bashan. All of these locations are identified with the territories of Gad and Manasseh in the Transjordan (Josh 13:24–28, 29–31; 20:8). The site of Ramoth Gilead is uncertain, although it is generally situated in the eastern region of Manasseh or Gad somewhere south of the Yarmuk River and north of the Jabbok, perhaps at Tell Ramith.[62] Gilead, the location of the villages of Jair ben Manasseh, generally encompasses the Transjordanian region from the Wadi Arnon in the south to perhaps the Jabbok or beyond in the north, although this would also include the territory of district 12 (see below). The villages of Jair ben Manasseh would be located in the northern region of Gilead (Num 32:41; Judg 10:3–5).[63] The Bashan region, which includes Argob, is situated in the high ground east of the Kinneret/Sea of Galilee north of the Yarmuk.[64] In this case, the territory of eastern Manasseh has been

57. Yigal Shiloh, "Megiddo," *NEAEHL* 3:1003–22; D. Ussishkin, "Megiddo," *ABD* 4:666–79.

58. A. E. Glock, "Taanach," *ABD* 6:287–90; Glock, "Taanach," *NEAEHL* 4:1428–33.

59. Amihai Mazar, "Beth Shean: Tel Beth Shean and the Northern Cemetery," *NEAEHL* 1:214–23; P. E. McGovern, "Beth Shan," *ABD* 1:692–96.

60. For discussion, see H. Thompson, "Zarethan," *ABD* 6:1041–43; D. V. Edelman, "Abel Meholah," *ABD* 1:11–12; W. Toews, "Jokmeam," *ABD* 3:933.

61. Kallai, *Geography*, 63.

62. P. M. Arnold, "Ramoth Gilead," *ABD* 5:620–21.

63. M. Ottosson, "Gilead," *ABD* 2:1020–22.

64. J. C. Slayton, "Bashan," *ABD* 1:623–24; H. O. Thompson, "Argob," *ABD* 1:376.

combined with parts of Gad,[65] although this association is already suggested in the sources from Joshua. Again, it shows an interest in splitting up Manasseh into its geographic subregions. The prefect, ben Geber, is unknown, although he may be the son of Geber ben Uri, the prefect of district 12.

District 7 (v. 14) is centered on the city of Mahanaim, identified with Telul ed-Dhahab el-Garbi on the north bank of Jabbok in the Transjordan.[66] The site is also identified as the southern boundary of Manasseh (Josh 13:30) or the southern boundary of Gad (Josh 13:26). It served as Saul's and Eshbaal's administrative capital for the Gilead (2 Sam 2:9) and David's headquarters during Absalom's revolt (2 Sam 17:24–19:8). Although the extent of the district's territory is uncertain, it comprises elements claimed by both Gad and Manasseh, again showing an interest in dividing Manasseh's former holdings.[67] Ahinadab ben Iddo the prefect is unknown.

District 8 (v. 15) comprises the territory of Naphtali (Josh 19:32–39), situated in the northern Galilee to the south of the Lebanon mountains and to the west of the Kinneret/Sea of Galilee.[68] The prefect, Ahimaaz, is probably Ahimaaz ben Zadok, the son of the high priest who provided David with information during Absalom's revolt. The appointment suggests a measure of trust since Naphtali defines Israel's northern border with Aram.

District 9 (v. 16) comprises the territory of Asher (Josh 19:24–31) and an unknown location called Alot, Beʿalot, or Baalot (see the textual note).[69] The territory is not defined, although 1 Kgs 9:10–14 notes that Solomon ceded twenty cities to Hiram king of Tyre in order to pay his debts for Hiram's assistance in his building projects. The twenty cities are collectively known as the land of Cabul, and they would have been taken from the territory of Asher and perhaps Zebulun, which bordered Phoenicia. Solomon's districts lack an equivalent to the tribal territory of Zebulun, and it may be that Asher and Zebulun were consolidated perhaps as a consequence of this loss. The interpretation of *ûbĕʿālôt* is uncertain, insofar as it may read, "and in ʿAlot," "and Beʿalot," "and in Baʿalot," or "and in Beʿalot." None of these names corresponds to any known city or region in or near the territory of Asher, although a town named Beʿalot appears in Josh 15:24 as a city in southern Judah, and a town named Baʿalat appears in Josh 19:44 (cf. 1 Kgs 9:18) as a city in Dan. Baana ben Hushai is unknown.

District 10 (v. 17) comprises the territory of Issachar (Josh 19:17–23), situated in the southern Galilee and portions of the northern Jezreel Valley.[70] It

65. Cf. Kallai, *Geography,* 64–65.
66. D. V. Edelman, "Mahanaim," *ABD* 4:472–73.
67. Cf. Kallai, *Geography,* 65, who associates it with Gad.
68. Cf. ibid., 65.
69. See ibid., 66.
70. See ibid., 67–69.

borders the northern portion of the Jordan River south of the Kinneret/Sea of Galilee. Jehoshaphat ben Paruah is unknown.

District 11 (v. 18) is the territory of Benjamin (Josh 18:11–28),[71] sandwiched between Ephraim to the north, Judah to the south, Dan to the west, and the Jordan River to the east. Shimei ben Ela' is unknown, although some speculate that he is the Shimei mentioned in 1 Kgs 1:8 who remained loyal to David and Solomon when Adonijah attempted to claim the throne.

District 12 (v. 19ab) comprises the land of Gilead, including the former territories of Sihon king of the Amorites and Og king of the Bashan (Num 21:21–35; Deut 2:24–3:7). Sihon is associated with the city of Heshbon in what later became the territory of Reuben (Josh 13:15–23). The inclusion of Og, however, presents a problem in that he is consistently identified with the Bashan, which is already included in the territory of district 6 together with portions of Gilead (v. 13).[72] Many note that Gilead is a rather fluid term in the Bible that can designate a great deal of territory east of the Jordan, but the Bashan is generally located to the east of the Kinneret in the modern Golan Heights and the northern portions of Jordan. One may note, however, that the prefect of district 6 is ben Geber, and that the prefect of district 12 is Geber ben Uri. Neither of these men is mentioned elsewhere, but it is entirely possible that the prefect of district 6 is the son of the prefect of district 12, suggesting that some relationship existed between the two districts and their respective prefects in which the territory of the father is presumed to include that of the son. Likewise, one may note the rather consistent association between Sihon and Og in biblical tradition, which might also carry over in the definition of the territory of district 12. Given the boundaries of district 6 and the location of district 7 around Mahanaim, it seems likely that the territory of district 12 comprises the former territory of Reuben from the Wadi Arnon in the south to the region just to the north of Heshbon.

A number of tribes remained unaccounted for. The tribal territory of Zebulun is likely combined with that of Asher. Dan's original territory appears to comprise Solomon's district 2 with additions from Ephraim and access to the sea, but its later territory (Josh 19:47–48) appears to be combined with Naphtali in Solomon's district 8. Simeon and Judah are not listed at all, Judah because it was not administered by a prefect and Simeon because it lay to the southwest of Judah (Josh 19:1–10) and likely was absorbed by Judah.

Altogether, Solomon's district boundaries accomplish several ends that make it easier for him to control the tribes and territories that comprise northern Israel: (1) they contain Ephraim, the dominant tribe of northern Israel, and deny it access to the major trade routes through the Jezreel, the coastal plain, and the

71. Ibid., 69.
72. See ibid., 69–72, for a summary of the discussion.

sea; (2) they break up and contain Manasseh, the second most powerful tribe of the north that controlled the trade route through the Jezreel from the Transjordan to the sea (n.b., Manasseh was also known in tradition for revolt, see Josh 22); (3) they contain Asher and eliminate Zebulun, perhaps as a result of pressure from the Phoenicians to whom Solomon was in debt for their assistance with his building activities (1 Kgs 5; 9:10–28); (4) they appear to constrict Gad, perhaps to bolster Ramoth Gilead/Bashan (district 6) and Gilead/Reuben (district 12), which faced potentially hostile territories in Aram (cf. 1 Kgs 11:23–25) and Moab or Edom (1 Kgs 11:14–22); (5) they give Solomon full access to the sea, although they divide the seacoast into three districts, which would prevent them from uniting against him; and (6) they do not account for Simeon at all, which suggests that Simeon was already under Judean control. Solomon's administrative districts indicate an interest in placing Judah at an advantage within the federation so that Solomon would be able to control and exploit the northern tribes.

1 Kings 4:20–14:20 Solomon's Reign and Its Consequences

First Kings 4:20–14:20 comprises a lengthy and complex account of Solomon's reign in 1 Kgs 4:20–11:40 and its consequences in the revolt of the northern tribes of Israel against Solomon's son Rehoboam and the establishment of the northern kingdom of Israel in 1 Kgs 11:41–14:20. The basic account of Solomon's reign appears in 1 Kgs 4:20–11:40. It includes accounts of Solomon's wealth and power in 1 Kgs 4:20–5:32, Solomon's construction of the temple complex and royal palace in 1 Kgs 6:1–9:9, and Solomon's final years in 1 Kgs 9:10–11:40. An appendix in 1 Kgs 12:1–14:20 relates the revolt of the northern tribes against Rehoboam and the reign of Jeroboam ben Nebat as consequences of Solomon's reign.

1 Kings 4:20–5:32 Solomon's Wealth and Power

20 ᵃJudah and Israel were as numerous as the sand by the sea; they were eating, drinking, and happy.

5:1 And Solomon was ruling over all the kingdoms, ᵇfrom the Euphrates Riverᶜ to the land of the Philistines and up to the border of Egypt,ᵇ that were bringing tribute and serving Solomon all the days of his life.ᵃ 2 ᵈAnd Solomon's food provisions for one day included thirty kors of fine flour and sixty kors of meal; 3 ten fattened cattle, twenty range cattle, and one hundred sheep, apart from rams, gazelles, deer, and geese of the crib. 4 For he controlled all the region west of the Euphrates from Tipsah to Gaza, all the kings of the region west of the Euphrates, and he had peace from all who passed by around him. 5 And Judah and Israel lived in safety, each under his vine and under his fig tree, from Dan to Beer Sheba, all the days of Solomon.[d] 6 [e]And Solomon had forty thousand stalls of horses for his chariots and twelve thousand horses for his cavalry.[e] 7 [f]And these prefects supplied King Solomon and all who drew near to the table of King Solomon, each for his month; they did not leave anything lacking. 8 And the barley and the straw for the horses and for the cavalry mounts they brought to the place where each was supposed to be according to his assignment.[f]

9 And G-d gave wisdom to Solomon, very great understanding and breadth of mind like the sand which is upon the shore of the sea. 10 And Solomon's wisdom was greater than the wisdom of all the easterners and all the wisdom of Egypt.[g] 11 And he was the wisest of all humanity, including Ethan the Ezrahite, Heman, Kalkol, and Darda', the sons of Mahol, and his name was known among all the nations around him. 12 And Solomon composed three thousand proverbs, and his poetry numbered one thousand and five. 13 And Solomon spoke about the trees, from the cedar which is in Lebanon to the cypress which grows out from the wall, and he spoke about animals, birds, insects, and fish. 14 And they came from all the peoples to hear the wisdom of Solomon, from all the kings of the earth who heard his wisdom.

15 [h]And Hiram, the King of Tyre,[h] sent his servants to Solomon because he heard that they anointed him as king in place of his father, for Hiram had always loved David. 16 And Solomon sent to Hiram, saying, 17 "You know that David my father was not able to build a house for the name of YHWH his G-d because of the warfare that preoccupied him until YHWH placed them under the soles of my feet.[i] 18 And now, YHWH my G-d has given me rest all around; there is no opponent and there is no disturbance. 19 And behold, I intend to build a house for the name of YHWH my G-d just as YHWH said to David my father, saying, 'Your son whom I shall appoint in your place upon your throne; he shall build the house for my name.' 20 And now, give orders, and let them cut for me cedars from Lebanon, and my servants shall be with your servants, and I will pay to you the wages of your servants according to whatever you say, for you know that there is no one among us who knows how to cut trees like the Sidonians." 21 And when Hiram heard the words of Solomon, he was very happy and said, "Blessed is YHWH today who has given to David a wise son over this numerous people!" 22 And Hiram sent to Solomon, saying, "I have heard what you sent to me. I will do all that you desire with the trees of cedar and the trees of cypress. 23 My servants shall bring them down to the sea, and I will make them into rafts in the sea at the place that you send me, and I will disassemble them there, so that you can carry them off. And you will do what I desire by giving food to my house." 24 And Hiram was giving to Solomon

cedar wood and cypress wood, all his desire. 25 And Solomon paid to Hiram twenty thousand kors of edible wheat for his house and twenty thousand kors of beaten oil. Thus Solomon paid to Hiram every year.

26 And YHWH gave wisdom to Solomon just as he told him, and there was peace between Hiram and Solomon, and the two of them made a treaty. 27 And Solomon raised a corvée from all Israel, and the corvée was thirty thousand men. 28 And he sent them to Lebanon, ten thousand per month in shifts. One month they would be in Lebanon, two months at home, and Adoniram was in charge of the corvée. 29 ʲAnd Solomon had seventy thousand porters and eighty thousand stonecutters in the hills,ʲ 30 apart from the officers of Solomon's prefects who were in charge of the work: three thousand, three hundred, who were supervising the people doing the work. 31 ᵏAnd the king commanded, and they quarried great stones, expensive stones, for the foundation of the house, dressed stones. 32 And the builders of Solomon and the builders of Hiram and the Gebalites/metal workersˡ cut,ᵏ and they prepared the trees and the stones to build the house.

a–a. 1 Kgs 4:20–5:1 has been transposed to 3 Kgdms 2:46a²–b in the LXX.

b–b. The "brook (wadi) of Egypt" marks the southern boundary of the land of Israel/Canaan (see Num 34:5; Josh 15:47; 1 Kgs 8:65; 2 Chr 7:8; Ezek 47:19; 48:28).[73]

c. MT, *min-hannāhār,* lit., "from the river," i.e., the Euphrates River.

d–d. 1 Kgs 5:2–5 appears as 3 Kgdms 2:46e–g; an abbreviated form appears in 3 Kgdms 5:2–4.

e–e. 1 Kgs 5:6 appears in LXX as 3 Kgdms 2:46i.

f–f. 1 Kgs 5:7–8 appear in LXX 3 Kgdms 5:1, immediately following the reference to the prefect Josaphat son of Phuasud in Issachar (4:17), which concludes the LXX list of Solomon's prefects.

g. 1 Kgs 3:10 appears in LXX as 3 Kgdms 2:35a and 5:9.

h–h. LXX adds material derived from 1 Kgs 3:1; 9:16–17 concerning Solomon's marriage to the daughter of Pharaoh, and Pharaoh's conquest of Gezer as a wedding present.

i. Qere, *raglāy,* "my feet"; Ketiv, *raglāw,* "his feet."

j–j. 1 Kgs 5:29 appears in LXX as 3 Kgdms 2:35d and 5:29.

k–k. 1 Kgs 5:31–32a appears as LXX 3 Kgdms 6:1ab.

l. Cf. Targum Jonathan, *wĕ'ārgôbĕlayā',* "and the master masons"; Peshitta, *w'rgg-wbl',* "and the master masons." Both terms are based on the root *gbl,* which appears in Hebrew, *giblîm,* "Gebalites." Although the root *gbl* generally refers to "boundaries" or "limits," the basic meaning refers to "twisting," "winding," or other actions that connote metal working; see Exod 28:22; 39:15, where *šaršōt gablut* refers to the chains of the high priest's breastplate.

First Kings 4:20–5:32 commences with the notice that Solomon's kingdom included both Israel and Judah, which marks him as the monarch who succeeded

73. M. Görg, "Egypt, Brook of," *ABD* 2:321; L. F. DeVries, "Besor, the Brook," *ABD* 1:679–80.

in fulfilling the divine promises to Abraham and Jacob that Israel would become a great and numerous nation (Gen 22:17; 32:12). It highlights Solomon's role as the ruler of many kingdoms and his worldwide reputation for wisdom. Solomon's attributes point to his ability to enlist the support and cooperation of Hiram king of Tyre as part of his overall effort to organize and carry out the work of building the temple in Jerusalem as the capstone of YHWH's created world order.[74] The portrayal of Solomon recalls that of the Mesopotamian and Syro-Canaanite kings who likewise complete creation by building temples for their respective national deities.[75]

This unit is demarcated by the syntactically independent noun clause of 1 Kgs 4:20, "Judah and Israel were as numerous as the sands which are by the sea. . . ." The focus on Judah and Israel both distinguishes v. 20 from the preceding material concerning Solomon's administration, and builds upon that material by emphasizing the role played by Solomon's administration in providing for the unity and security of his people and in building the temple. The reference to "the sands which are by the sea" likewise points forward to the use of the same metaphor in 1 Kgs 5:9 to portray Solomon's wisdom. First Kings 4:20 thereby constitutes the first subunit of the passage and sets the stage for the second subunit in 1 Kgs 5:1–25, which portrays Solomon's vast wealth and power that extended from Mesopotamia to Egypt. This subunit likewise begins with a noun clause in 1 Kgs 5:1, although it includes an initial conjunctive, "and Solomon (*ûšĕlōmōh*) was ruling all the kingdoms . . ." The subunit then employs a *waw*-consecutive narrative sequence to relate a series of topics, including the provisions to support Solomon's house (vv. 2–5), the provisions to support Solomon's chariots and cavalry (vv. 6–8), Solomon's worldwide reputation for wisdom (vv. 9–14), and the relationship between Hiram and Solomon that provided Solomon with the raw materials to build the temple. This sequence prepares for the third subunit in 1 Kgs 5:26–32, which relates the covenant between Hiram and Solomon that allows Solomon to raise a corvée in Israel to gather the building materials for the temple. This third subunit begins with a noun clause syntactically joined to the preceding material by a conjunctive *waw*, "And YHWH (*wayhwh*) gave wisdom to Solomon . . ."

74. Jon D. Levenson, "The Temple and the World," *JR* 64 (1984): 275–98; Moshe Weinfeld, "Zion and Jerusalem as Religious and Political Capital: Ideology and Utopia," in *The Poet and the Historian: Essays in Literary and Historical Biblical Criticism* (HSS 26; Chico, Calif.: Scholars Press, 1983), 75–115.

75. Arvid S. Kapelrud, "Temple Building, a Task for Gods and Kings," *Orientalia* 32 (1963): 56–62; Victor (Avigdor) Hurowitz, *I Have Built You an Exalted House* (JSOTSup 115; Sheffield: Sheffield Academic Press, 1992); cf. Michael Fishbane, *Text and Texture: Close Readings of Selected Biblical Texts* (New York: Schocken, 1979), 3–16, who points to the associations between Gen 2:1–3 and Exod 35–40 to establish the role of the wilderness tabernacle or sanctuary as the completion of creation.

[4:20] The reference to Judah and Israel indicates the basic structural composition of the united kingdom of Israel. It is not fundamentally a federation of twelve tribes, but a federation of the southern tribe of Judah and the northern tribes of Israel.[76] This division is evident in the early years of David's reign, when he ruled Judah as a vassal of the Philistines and fought Eshbaal ben Saul, who ruled the northern tribes following the death of his father (2 Sam 2–5). It is also evident in the revolt of the northern tribes against the house of David following Solomon's death. The metaphor that the people were as numerous as the sands of the sea (cf. Josh 11:4; Judg 7:12; 1 Sam 13:5; 2 Sam 17:11; Isa 10:22; Jer 33:22; Hos 2:1) is an especially noteworthy feature of the divine promises to Abraham (Gen 22:17) and Jacob (Exod 32:13) that Israel would become a great nation in the so-called JE tradition of the Pentateuch. Overall, the portrayal of Judah's and Israel's unity, prosperity, and happiness under the rule of the Davidic monarch Solomon supports later claims for the reunification of Israel and Judah under a Davidic monarch.

[5:1] The geographic range of Solomon's rule is defined as the entire Syro-Israelite region west of the Euphrates River and south to Philistia and the border of Egypt. The term *hannāhār,* literally, "the river," frequently appears in the Bible as a reference to the Euphrates (e.g., Gen 31:21; Exod 23:31; Num 22:5; Josh 22:2; 2 Sam 8:3; Isa 7:20; Jer 2:18; Mic 7:12; Zech 9:10; Ps 72:8), and presupposes Davidic control of Aram and the Transjordan (2 Sam 8:2–14; cf. 1 Kgs 11:14–25). Second Samuel 5:17–25 and 8:1 indicate that David had defeated and subdued the Philistines early in his reign. The border of Egypt is identified with the so-called *naḥal miṣrayim,* "brook of Egypt," in both biblical and Akkadian sources (Num 34:5; Josh 15:4, 47; 1 Kgs 8:65; Ezek 47:19; 48:28; 2 Chr 7:8; cf. Akkadian *naḥal Muṣur*).[77]

[2–5] Verses 2–5 enumerate the daily provisions for Solomon's court. The *kōr* is a dry or liquid measure of volume that generally equates to 6.5 to 14 bushels. Thirty kors of fine flour would therefore range from 195 to 420 bushels, and sixty kors of meal would range from 390 to 840 bushels. When taken together with the numbers of animals mentioned, this amount would obviously support a very large number of people, namely, from three thousand to four thousand heads of families to some thirty-two thousand people (Montgomery-Gehman 127–28; Kittel 38; Šanda 1:93). Insofar as ancient Jerusalem's population probably numbered no more that five thousand, it seems likely that these provisions were intended to support Solomon's administrative and military establishment throughout the land, to pay state debts (see below, vv. 23, 25), and to supply goods for international trade.

76. See Albrecht Alt, "The Monarchy in the Kingdoms of Israel and Judah," in *Essays on Old Testament History and Religion* (Garden City, N.Y.: Doubleday, 1967), 311–35.
77. Anson F. Rainey, "Toponymic Problems (cont.): The Brook of Egypt," *TA* 9 (1982): 131–32; Nadav Na'aman, "The Brook of Egypt and Assyrian Policy on the Border of Egypt," *TA* 6 (1979): 68–90.

The reference to Solomon's rule over all the region west of the Euphrates has prompted some scholars to claim that this is a very late text because the expression ʿēber hannāhār, literally, "across the river," functions as the Persian provincial designation for this region in the early Second Temple period. Nevertheless, the term first appears in Neo-Assyrian texts from the late eighth and seventh centuries B.C.E.[78] Tipsah is located along the banks of the Euphrates River some seventy-five miles south of Carchemesh.[79] Gaza is the southernmost of the five Philistine cities, identified with the site of the modern city located on the Mediterranean seacoast in the Gaza Strip. Finally, the reference to the extent of the land of Israel from Dan to Beer Sheba is a commonly employed means to designate all Israel (Judg 20:1; 1 Sam 3:20; 2 Sam 3:10; 17:11; 24:2, 15). Dan, identified with Tel Dan or Tel el-Qadi, is the northernmost major city of ancient Israel located at the foot of Mount Hermon.[80] Beer Sheba, identified with Tel Beer Sheba in the northern Negeb east of modern Beersheba, is the southernmost major city of Judah/Israel.[81]

[6–8] Verses 6–8 enumerate the horses maintained by Solomon for his chariot corps and his cavalry together with the grain and straw provided by the prefects to support them. The chariots and cavalry would have been necessary to protect the trade routes through the Jezreel Valley and the coastal plain, as mounted forces require relatively flat terrain in which to operate effectively. The reference to forty thousand (ʾarbāʿîm ʾelep) teams/stalls of horses appears to be exaggerated (cf. 2 Chr 9:25, which corrects this to four thousand [ʾarbaʿat ʾălāpîm]). Solomon's fourteen hundred chariots in 1 Kgs 10:26 and 2 Chr 1:14 would require some four thousand horses, as ancient chariots generally required anywhere from two to four horses each.[82]

The question of the number of horses is compounded by uncertainties concerning the meaning of the term ʾurwôt, here translated as "teams" or "stalls." The basic meaning of the term is "manger" or "crib," which connotes the "stalls, stables" where the horses were housed and fed or the "teams" of horses that would have been housed in the same stable to serve with a single chariot.[83] The twelve thousand pārāšîm refer to Solomon's cavalry forces.

[9–14] The passage claims Solomon's greatness in relation to the great sages of the east and Egypt, apparently the two regions known for wisdom in antiq-

---

78. See M. W. Stolper, "The Governor of Babylon and Across-the-River in 486 B.C.," *JNES* 48 (1989): 283–305.

79. J. H. Hull Jr., "Tiphsah," *ABD* 6:571.

80. Avraham Biran, "Dan," *NEAEHL* 1:323–32; Biran, "Dan," *ABD* 2:12–17.

81. Z. Herzog, "Tel Beersheba," *NEAEHL* 1:167–73; D. W. Manor, "Beer Sheba," *ABD* 1:641–45.

82. M. A. Littauer and J. H. Crouwel, "Chariots," *ABD* 1:888–92.

83. See G. I. Davies, "ʾUrwōt in 1 Kings 5:6 (EVV, 4:26) and the Assyrian Horse Lists," *JSS* 34 (1989): 25–38.

uity. The expression *bĕnê qedem* may refer to "the sons of the east," where the sun rises, or "the sons of antiquity." The term *qedem* means literally "what is in front, before," which may refer either spatially to the direction of worship in the east or temporally to time that has already passed. Wisdom is frequently ascribed to eastern desert tribes (Judg 6:3, 33; 7:12; Isa 2:6; 11:14; Jer 49:28), who were claimed as ancestors or distant cousins of Israel, since Abraham and Israel at large also came from the east. Even Job was associated with the east and antiquity (Job 1:3). The major wisdom figures cited in this passage were apparently well known to the intended readers of Solomon's history; unfortunately, modern scholars know virtually nothing about them. Ethan the Ezrahite must have been a Canaanite or native sage because his gentilic name, *hāʾezrāḥî*, means "the indigenous." He is otherwise mentioned as the author of Ps 89 (Ps 89:1). Heman, Kalkol, and Dardaʿ are all listed as the sons of Mahol, but 1 Chr 2:6 lists them as the sons of Zerah,[84] apparently a variant of Ezrahite, and thus as grandsons of Judah. Psalm 88 is ascribed to Heman the Ezrahite (Ps 88:1). The reference to the father of these three men as Mahol employs the term *māḥôl*, derived from the root *ḥwl*, which means "to writhe" or "to dance." The name may indicate some sort of professional status of those who were associated with music and dancing, e.g., Miriam's role in leading the Israelite women in singing and dancing (*mĕḥōlōt*) at the Red Sea in Exod 15:20–21; the women who dance at the Shiloh sanctuary at Sukkot in Judg 21:21; and the women who came to celebrate David's victories in 1 Sam 18:6. Psalm 9:6 associates such writhing or dancing with worship of YHWH, and Ps 87:7 likewise associates cultic singers and dancers. The name Kalkol is sometimes associated with the Egyptian name. Kulkul or Kurkur, a thirteenth-century female singer for the god Ptah, ruler of Ashkelon, which may also suggest a Canaanite background for the figures mentioned here.[85]

[15–25] Verses 15–25 relate the establishment of formal relations between King Hiram of Tyre and King Solomon of Israel, which continues the alliance originally established between David and Hiram (2 Sam 5:11–12). Tyre and the other Phoenician cities, such as Sidon, Byblos, Akko, and so on, were long known as the major maritime powers of the ancient Near Eastern world from the early years of the second millennium B.C.E.[86] By the mid-tenth century B.C.E., Tyre had emerged as the dominant Phoenician city under King Hiram I (reigned ca. 970–936 B.C.E.), the son of Abibaal.[87] Although the present narrative emphasizes

---

84. N.b., Dardaʿ is called Daraʿ in 1 Chr 2:6, apparently omitting the second daleth.
85. W. F. Albright, *Archaeology and the Religion of Israel* (Garden City, N.Y.: Doubleday, 1969), 127 n. 96.
86. See H. Jacob Katzenstein, *The History of Tyre: From the Beginning of the Second Millennium B.C.E. until the Fall of the Neo-Babylonian Empire in 538 B.C.E.* (Jerusalem: Schocken Institute, 1973).
87. Ibid., 77–115.

Hiram's role in supplying Solomon with the raw materials necessary to build the temple in Jerusalem, the establishment of such a relationship has far wider implications. The relationship between Hiram and Solomon appears to be a parity treaty relationship.[88] The two monarchs struck a deal by which Hiram would exchange wood and stone to build the temple for food. This relationship established the basis for important trade relations, insofar as Hiram assists Solomon in establishing a fleet of trading ships at Ezion Geber, which enables him to open maritime trade relations with African and Arabian kingdoms such as Sheba situated along the Red Sea (1 Kgs 9:26–10:22). The relationship enabled Solomon to play a role in trade along the eastern Mediterranean (1 Kgs 10:26–29). The combination of Israel, Tyre/Phoenicia, and Egypt would have completely dominated trade in the eastern Mediterranean and western Asia, which would explain Solomon's wealth and control of the region west of the Euphrates.

The narrative makes it clear that Hiram initiated relations with Solomon, much as he had initiated relations with David (2 Sam 5:11–12), apparently in keeping with his efforts to expand his influence and trade relations throughout the eastern Mediterranean and western Asia. This contrasts with 2 Chr 2:2, which claims that Solomon initiated the relationship, apparently to emphasize further Solomon's role in building the temple. The notice that Hiram "loved" (*ʾōhēb*) David employs standard ancient Near Eastern terminology for allies in treaty relationships.[89]

Solomon's response to Hiram, however, shifts the initiative to Solomon, in keeping with the narrative's interest in lauding Solomon as the ideal monarch and builder of YHWH's temple. Solomon, too, employs standard language from ancient Near Eastern treaties insofar as the verb *yādaʿ*, "to know," expresses treaty relationships between monarchs: "you knew (*ʾattâ yādāʿ*) David my father."[90] Solomon's message to Hiram explains his interest in building the temple to YHWH that David had envisioned, although many of the details of Solomon's statements do not conform to the earlier accounts of David's plans to build the temple and the founding of the Davidic house in 2 Sam 7. Nevertheless, Solomon emphasizes YHWH's promise that David's son would build the temple, and his characterization of the temple as the place

88. F. C. Fensham, "The Treaty between the Israelites and Tyrians," *VTSup* 17 (1969): 71–87; H. Donner, "Israel und Tyrus im Zeitalter Davids und Salomos. Zur Gegenseitigen Abhängigkeit von Innen- und Aussenpolitik," *JNSL* 10 (1982): 43–52.

89. W. L. Moran, "The Ancient Near Eastern Background of the Love of G-d in Deuteronomy," *CBQ* 25 (1963): 77–87.

90. H. B. Huffmon, "The Treaty Background of Hebrew Yāda'," *BASOR* 181 (1966): 31–37; H. B. Huffmon and S. B. Parker, "A Further Note on the Treaty Background of Hebrew Yāda'," *BASOR* 184 (1966): 36–38.

for the name of YHWH is characteristically Deuteronomistic (cf. 1 Kgs 8:15–21, 27–30).[91]

Solomon proposes that Hiram cut cedars of Lebanon, known throughout the ancient world for their beauty, strength, and height, and thus for their value as a highly prized building material. Later Assyrian and Babylonian monarchs would routinely bring their armies to Phoenicia to cut such trees so that they might be used in building projects at home (*ANET* 291, 307). Solomon offers to pay for the wages of Hiram's workmen at whatever rate that Hiram might ask. Although such an offer seems a bit naive, it highlights the high esteem in which the Lebanese cedars were held. Solomon spares no expense to get the best.

Hiram's response to Solomon's request indicates full agreement as well as an interest in magnifying the characters of both Solomon and YHWH. His blessing of YHWH is particularly noteworthy insofar as Hiram is supposed to be a pagan foreigner. Such praise of a foreign partner's deity would be expected in the context of international relations in the ancient world. When considered in relation to biblical literature, however, Hiram resembles Moses' father-in-law Jethro, the priest of Midian, who likewise blesses YHWH upon hearing about the deliverance of Israel from Egypt (Exod 18:10). First Kings 7:14 later states that Hiram was the son of a Tyrian artisan and a widow from the tribe of Naphtali.

[26–32] The narrative introduces the account of Solomon's corvée imposed upon Israel by reiterating YHWH's grant of wisdom (cf. v. 9) and by stating that Solomon and Hiram had concluded a treaty that guaranteed peace between them. The present context indicates that the imposition of the corvée was prudently conceived to provide the labor necessary for acquiring the wood and stones necessary for building the temple without overly burdening the Israelite population. It further emphasizes that Israelite, not pagan, labor contributed to the building of the temple. Nevertheless, the later narrative concerning the revolt of the northern tribes against Solomon's son Rehoboam (1 Kgs 12) is quite explicit in expressing Israelite dissatisfaction at the burdens carried for Solomon as a cause for the revolt (1 Kgs 12:11).

The use of forced labor in service of the state is well known in Solomon's kingdom and throughout the ancient Near Eastern world.[92] It must be considered as a form of taxation that appears alongside requirements to present a certain percentage of one's crops and other goods to the state. The numbers and

---

91. Gerhard von Rad, *Studies in Deuteronomy* (SBT 9; London: SCM, 1953), 37–44; T. N. D. Mettinger, *The Dethronement of Sebaoth: Studies in the Shem and Kabod Theologies* (ConBOT 18; Lund: Gleerup, 1982).

92. See Rainey, "Compulsory Labor Gangs"; I. Mendelsohn, "State Slavery in Ancient Palestine," *BASOR* 85 (1942): 14–17; Mendelsohn, "On Corvée Labor in Ancient Canaan and Israel," *BASOR* 167 (1962): 31–35; David Jobling, "'Forced Labor': Solomon's Golden Age and the Question of Literary Representation," *Semeia* 54 (1991): 57–76.

organization of the corvée are designed so that they will not impose an excessively heavy burden on the population. When compared to the census totals presented in 2 Sam 24:9—that is, that there were eight hundred thousand men in Israel and five hundred thousand men in Judah—the thirty thousand men employed in the corvée does not seem to be excessive. The use of shifts of ten thousand men per month with a three-month rotation ameliorates the service imposed on the work crews so that any given man would be absent for only one month. As in 1 Kgs 4:6b (cf. 2 Sam 20:24), Adoniram is placed in charge of the corvée. In addition to the previously mentioned thirty thousand men, seventy thousand labor as porters and eighty thousand labor as stone cutters. Curiously, the terms of the agreement mention nothing about the stones, although they are absolutely essential to the construction of the temple. The role of the prefects in assigning officers to supervise the workmen is made very clear, which would likely help to fuel the resentment against the Davidic state.

1 Kings 6:1–9:9 Solomon's Construction of the Temple Complex and Royal Palace

1 Kings 6:1–7:12 Palace and Temple Complex

6:1 [a]And in the four hundred and eightieth year[b] from the Exodus of the people of Israel from the land of Egypt, in the fourth year, in the month of Ziv, which is the second month,[a] [c]of the reign of King Solomon over Israel, he built the house for YHWH.[c]

2 And the house which King Solomon built for YHWH was sixty[d] cubits long, twenty cubits wide, and thirty[e] cubits high. **3** [f]And the foyer before the Great Hall of the house was twenty cubits long along the width of the house, and ten cubits deep before the house.[f] **4** And he made enclosed observation windows for the house. **5** And he built an enclosure[g] around the wall of the house, the walls of the house around the Great Hall and the Inner Sanctuary, and he made (side) levels all around. **6** The lower (level of the) enclosure was five cubits wide and the middle (level) was six cubits wide and the third (story) was seven cubits wide, for he placed supporting ledges for the house around the outside so as not to attach the walls of the house. **7** And the house was built of whole (unfinished) quarry stone during its construction, and no hammers, chisel, or any iron tool were heard in the house during its construction. **8** The door of the middle level was on the right wing of the house, and spiral stairs went up upon the middle level, and from the middle (level) to the third (levels). **9** And he built the house, completed it, and roofed the house with mortises and cedar planks. **10** And he built the enclosure against the entire house, five cubits was its height, and secured the house with beams of cedar.

11 And the word of YHWH came to Solomon, saying, 12 "Concerning this house which you are building, if you follow my statutes, carry out my laws, and carefully follow my commands, then I shall establish my word with you, which I spoke to David your father, and I will dwell in the midst of the sons of Israel, 13 and I will not abandon my people Israel." 14 And Solomon built and completed the house. 15 And he built the walls of the house from the inside with planks of cedar from the floor of the house to the walls of the roof;[h] he overlaid wood from the inside. And he overlaid the floor of the house with cypress planks. 16 And he built twenty cubits from the far end[i] of the house with cedar planks from the floors to the walls, and he built inside it the Inner Sanctuary, the Holy of Holies. 17 And the house was forty cubits, that is, the Great Hall before Me. 18 [j]And the cedar of the interior of the house was carved with gourds and flower blossoms; the whole was cedar, no stone was seen. 19 And the Inner Sanctuary,[j] twenty cubits long, twenty cubits wide, and twenty cubits high, he overlaid with fine gold, and he overlaid the cedar altar.[k] 21 And Solomon overlaid the house interior with fine gold, applied chain work[l] of gold before the Inner Sanctuary, and overlaid it with gold. 22 [m]And he completely overlaid all the house with gold, and he overlaid all the altar for the Inner Sanctuary with gold.[m]

23 And he made two cherubim of olive wood, ten cubits high, in the Inner Sanctuary. 24 And the wing of one cherub was five cubits, and the wing of the other cherub was five cubits, ten cubits from the ends of its wings to the other ends of its wings. 25 And the second cherub was ten cubits, the same measure and size for the two cherubs. 26 The height of the one cherub was ten cubits, and so was the second cherub. 27 And he placed the cherubim in the midst of the house interior, and the wings of the cherubim spread out, and the wing of the one cherub touched the wall, and the wing of the second cherub was touching the second wall, and their wings were touching in the middle of the house. 28 And he overlaid the cherubim with gold.

29 And the wall of the house throughout, he engraved with carved relief of cherubs, palm trees, and flowering blossoms inside and outside. 30 And he overlaid the floor of the house with gold inside and outside. 31 And for the entrance of the Inner Sanctuary, he made doors of olive wood; the pilaster of the doorposts was five sided.[n] 32 And he carved upon the two doors of olive wood reliefs of cherubim, palm trees, and flowering blossoms, and he overlaid them with gold and bonded them with gold. 33 And so he made four-sided doorposts for the entrance of the Great Hall. 34 And for the two doors of cypress wood, two planks of the one door could rotate and two planks of the second door could rotate. 35 And he engraved cherubim, palm trees, and flowering blossoms, and overlaid them with gold directly upon the incision.

36 And he built the inner court with three courses of dressed stone and
one course of cut cedar.[o]
37 In the fourth year, the foundation of the house of YHWH was laid
in the month of Ziv. **38** [p]And in the eleventh year in the month of Bul,[q]
which is the eighth month, he completed the house according to all its
requirements and specifications, and he built it in seven years.
7:1 [r]And Solomon built his house in thirteen years, [s]and he completed
his house.[s] **2** And he built the House of the Forest of Lebanon, one hundred cubits long, fifty cubits wide, and thirty cubits high, on four[t] rows of
cedar columns with cut beams[u] of cedar upon the columns. **3** [v]And it was
overlaid with cedar above the ribs which were upon the forty-five columns,
fifteen per row.[v] **4** And window frames, three rows, [w]each of the three facing the other.[w] **5** And all the doors and the doorposts had squared frames
opposite, [w]each of the three facing the other.[w] **6** And he made the hall of
columns, fifty cubits long and thirty[x] cubits wide, and a foyer was before
them, and columns and a canopy before them. **7** And he made the Hall of
the Throne where he would rule, that is, the Hall of Justice, and it was
overlaid with cedar from floor to floor. **8** And his living quarters, which
were in another court from the Hall, were of the same construction. And
a house that he would make for the daughter of Pharaoh whom Solomon
took in marriage was like this Hall. **9** All these buildings were made of
expensive stones, cut according to measure, shaved with a chisel inside
and out, from the foundation to the roof supports. **10** And the foundation
stones were large, expensive stones of ten and eight cubits. **11** And above
them were expensive stones, cut according to measure, and cedar. **12** And
the surrounding great court had three rows of cut stone and one row of
cut cedar beams, [y]like the inner court of the House of YHWH and the
foyer of the House.[yr]

a–a. LXX places a shortened form of 1 Kgs 6:1a immediately after 1 Kgs 5:32b and before 1 Kgs 5:31–32a to provide a more logically consistent account (Hrozný, *Abweichungen* 65–66).

b. LXX reads, “in the four hundred and fortieth year.”

c–c. Lacking in LXX, which reads 1 Kgs 6:37 here to provide a stylistically consistent narrative.

d. LXX, “forty.”

e. LXX, “twenty-five.”

f–f. LXX, “and the *ailam* (‘foyer’) in front of the temple, twenty cubits was its length according to the breadth of the house in front of the house; and he built the house and finished it.”

g. The meaning of the Hebrew word *yaṣîᶜa* (Qere; Ketiv, *yaṣûᶜa,* “bed, couch”) is uncertain. The versions tend to render it as “chambers.” The singular form of the term, however, indicates that it refers to a single gallery for each level rather than chambers.

h. LXX clarifies the enigmatic Hebrew by reading, "and on to the walls and to the beams."

i. Qere, *miyyarkĕtê*; Ketiv, *myrkwty*.

j–j. LXX omits v. 18 and rewrites vv. 17, 19, "And the temple was forty cubits in front of the Debir (transliteration of Hebrew, *dĕbîr*, 'Inner Sanctuary') in the midst of the inner house."

k. The versions have difficulty understanding how an altar is overlaid with cedar: Origen, "and he made an altar in front of the Debir, and covered it with gold" (Rahlfs's note; *Septuaginta*); Targum Jonathan, "and he covered the house with boards of cedar"; Peshitta, "and he covered the altar with gold."

l. Read Qere, *ratîqôt* (Ketiv, *ratûqôt*), "chains, twisted work." The versions have difficulties in understanding "chain work." LXX deletes the bulk of the verse, and attaches the phrase "before the Debir, and he overlaid it with gold" to v. 20: "and he made an altar before the Debir, and he overlaid it with gold"; Targum Jonathan reads, "and he stretched chains of gold in front of the house of atonements"; Peshitta reads, "and he made a doorpost in front of the sanctuary."

m–m. LXX deletes because it employed this verse to resolve the problems of v. 20.

n. Cf. Targum Jonathan, "its pilaster, its doorpost, are joined"; Peshitta, "the lintel and the doorposts were strengthened," which read Hebrew *ḥamšît*, "one fifth," in relation to Aramaic, *ḥamšîta'*, "a collection of five," to refer to joining five pieces to produce a strong door frame.

o. LXX adds, "and he made the curtain of the court of the *ailam* (foyer) of the house that was before the sanctuary" (see Rahlfs's note; *Septuaginta*; Rahlfs, *Septuaginta-Studien* 1:78).

p. LXX reads v. 38 following 1 Kgs 6:1 in reference to the date of the temple's construction.

q. LXX reads "Bul" (Hebrew, *bûl*) as "Baal," due to the associations of *bûl* with *yabûl*, "produce," and *yabal*, "stream," and Baal's role in relation to fertility and rain.

r–r. 1 Kgs 7:1–12 appears after vv. 13–51 in LXX, to provide greater stylistic consistency in the portrayal of the construction of the temple and its furnishings (1 Kgs 6:1–36; 7:13–51) and Solomon's palace (1 Kgs 7:1–12; see Kittel 56; cf. Burney 78; contra Benzinger, 38).

s–s. V. 1b appears after v. 12 in the LXX for stylistic consistency.

t. LXX reads "three" to harmonize this statement with the three rows of vv. 3, 4, and 5.

u. LXX reads *omiai*, "shoulders, side pieces," which presupposes Hebrew *wĕkitpôt* in place of *ûkerūtôt*, "and cut beams of (cedar)." The LXX translator apparently does not understand the architectural role of the *kĕrutôt*, which are placed atop the four rows of columns to support the roof. They are distinguished from the *ṣĕlā'ōt*, "ribs," in v. 3 which refer to the forty-five crossbeams placed between the four rows of columns to form the three major spaces presupposed throughout vv. 3–5. LXX understands the *kĕrutôt* as "side pieces" that form the basis for small chambers constructed within the supposed three (not four) rows of columns.

v–v. LXX reads v. 3, "And he overlaid the house above upon the ribs of one of the columns, and the number of columns was forty-five per row." Thus, LXX maintains that there are only three rows of forty-five columns with only two (royal) cubits (ca. forty inches) between each column. Such a construction is architecturally impractical, but literarily consistent.

w–w. Hebrew, *měḥezâ ʾel měḥezâ*, lit., "view unto view."

x. LXX, "fifty," in keeping with width measurement in v. 2.

y–y. LXX omits (but see 3 Kgdms 6:36), and reads v. 1b at this point.

This unit begins with the introductory chronological notice in 1 Kgs 6:1. The temple construction account follows in 1 Kgs 6:2–38, and palace construction follows in 1 Kgs 7:1–12.

[6:1] The month of Ziv, the second month, occurs in April–May (see 1 Kgs 6:37). The later Jewish calendar identifies the second month as Iyyar, which indicates that Ziv may be a Canaanite name, like Ethanim (1 Kgs 8:2) and Bul (1 Kgs 6:38).[93] Some contend that 480 years represents an attempt to periodize history, based on its rough correspondence to the period from the conclusion of Solomon's reign (920 B.C.E.) to the year when Cyrus of Persia authorized construction of the second temple (539 B.C.E.), but this chronology is not secure (see Jones 1:162–63; Mulder 231; Burney 59–61). Others contend that the figure results from calculating twelve generations (one from each tribe) of 40 years each, but there is no convincing basis for this proposal (Mulder 231). It is possible to reconstruct such a chronology based on the presentation of Israel's early history in the DtrH. Deuteronomy 2:7; 8:2, 4; 29:4; and Josh 5:6 maintain that Moses led Israel for 40 years in the wilderness. Judges lists 296 years for the rule of individual judges, including 40 years for Othniel (Judg 3:11); 80 for Ehud (Judg 3:30); 40 for Deborah (Judg 5:31); 40 for Gideon (Judg 8:28); 23 for Tola (Judg 10:2); 22 for Jair (Judg 10:3); 6 for Jephthah (Judg 12:7); 7 for Ibzan (Judg 12:9); 10 for Elon (Judg 12:11); 8 for Abdon (Judg 12:14); and 20 for Samson (Judg 16:31). First Samuel 4:18 states that Eli ruled for 40 years, and 1 Kgs 2:11 states that David ruled for 40 years. First Kings 6:1 maintains that Solomon commenced construction in his fourth year. These figures produce a total of 420 years. The remaining 60 years are accounted for by the 20 years that the ark resided in Kiriath Jearim (1 Sam 7:2) and a presumed 40 years for Joshua's rule following the death of Moses. The absence of a definitive figure for Joshua's rule accounts for the LXX's 440 years.

[6:2–38] First Kings 6:2–38 begins with a noun clause that states the basic dimensions of the structure. The account continues through vv. 37–38, which provide dates for both the foundation of the temple in the fourth year of Solomon's reign and its completion in his eleventh year.

Although 1 Kgs 6:2–38 appears to be a simple account of the construction of the temple, vv. 11–13 give this narrative a very different character by presenting YHWH's statement to Solomon in the form of a prophetic word. In classic Dtr form,[94] YHWH's statement exhorts Solomon to abide by YHWH's

---

93. J. C. Vanderkam, "Calendars, Ancient Israelite and Early Jewish," *ABD* 1:814–20.

94. Cf. von Rad, *Studies in Deuteronomy,* 11–24.

expectations in building the temple in order to ensure YHWH's promise to David and presence among the people of Israel. Although the narrative presumes Solomon's observance, a different perspective emerges in the larger literary context. YHWH's earlier communication to Solomon by dream (1 Kgs 3:1–15) promises long life if he observes YHWH's requirements, and the following dream communication by YHWH to Solomon likewise calls for Solomon to observe YHWH's requirements in order to prevent the exile of the people and destruction of the temple (1 Kgs 9:1–19). This element of threat is highlighted in the larger DtrH context; 2 Sam 7 indicates that YHWH does not want a temple, and 2 Kgs 25 concludes the history with an account of the temple's destruction. First Kings 6:2–38 therefore functions as a warning of impending disaster within the overall context of the DtrH.

Verses 11–14 mold the text into an account of YHWH's exhortation to Solomon to observe YHWH's commands. In and of themselves, these verses do not suggest that Solomon will fail; the narrative assumes Solomon's observance, suggesting that the Dtr redaction of this chapter is not to be identified with either the Josianic or exilic editions of the work, both of which employ critiques of Solomon to serve their respective ends. Rather, they build up the character of the righteous Solomon, which serves the interests of the Hezekian DtrH by supporting Hezekiah's efforts to renovate and purify the temple for the worship of a reunited Israel. When read in relation to the Josianic edition, the narrative reminds the reader of Solomon's shortcomings in observing YHWH's will. When read in relation to the exilic DtrH, Solomon becomes a fitting ancestor of Manasseh (2 Kgs 21:1–20), whose actions lead to exile.

This reconstruction of the redaction history of 1 Kgs 6:2–38 suggests that the building account stems from an earlier narrative concerning the construction of the temple. Many note that it provides insufficient detail to constitute a blueprint for the temple, since it lacks essential technical points for construction, and suggest instead that this is a postexilic remembrance of the Solomonic temple written by parties dependent on the oral or written accounts of others. Some argue that this is a plan for the second temple read back into the time of Solomon.[95] But such contentions overlook the fundamental point that this narrative is not written to provide a blueprint for the temple;[96] rather, it is written to impress the reader with the glory of the Solomonic temple and the care taken during construction to ensure its sacred character.

The temple mount is situated immediately to the north of the biblical city of David on a site now occupied by the Dome of the Rock, a Muslim edifice built

95. E.g., John Van Seters, "Solomon's Temple: Fact and Ideology in Biblical and Near Eastern Historiography," *CBQ* 59 (1997): 45–57; cf. Roger Tomes, "'Our Holy and Beautiful House': When and Why Was 1 Kings 6–8 Written?" *JSOT* 70 (1996): 33–50.

96. See Noth, *Könige,* 102–6, who emphasizes the reporting character of the narrative.

to cover the site of the Jewish temple and overshadow the Church of the Holy Sepulchre.[97] The presence of the Muslim structure and Orthodox Jewish concerns for the sanctity of the site make any meaningful excavation impossible. In any case, the site has been stripped and rebuilt sufficiently to eliminate the likelihood of recovering major remains of Solomon's temple. Nevertheless, the account points to a historical basis. The basic three-part structure of the temple, with its interior *děbîr* (inner sanctuary) to house the ark; the *hêkāl* (great hall) set before the *děbîr*; and the *ʾûlām* (foyer) that provides an entryway into the holy structure is typical of Phoenician, Canaanite, Aramean, and even Israelite sanctuaries of the late Bronze and Iron Ages.[98] Indeed, the structure of temples is based upon the structure of a royal palace in which the throne room is set in the place of the inner sanctuary, apparently to emphasize the close relationship between ancient monarchs and their national deities for whom they built temples.[99]

[6:2–10] Verses 2–10 focus on construction of the shell of the temple structure, including the three-part temple building and the three-storied structure built around its three sides.[100]

Verse 2 begins with the dimensions of the basic temple structure. The cubit is the standard measure of the ancient world,[101] equivalent to the length of a man's forearm from the elbow to the tip of the fingers. Alternative measures are twenty-four fingers or six handbreadths. It is about eighteen inches, although a long cubit of seven handbreadths is also known. Based on the standard cubit, the sixty-cubit length of the building would be ninety feet, the twenty-cubit width would be thirty-feet, and the thirty cubit height would be forty-five feet. The variant measures in the LXX represent a very strict reading of vv. 10, 16, 17, and 19. The five cubits of v. 10 indicate a loft to the LXX translator, which is taken as a reference to height and added to the twenty cubits at the rear of the house to produce a height of twenty-five cubits. The forty cubits of the Heikhal in v. 17 then becomes the measure of temple length.[102]

Verse 3 provides the dimensions of the *ʾûlām* or foyer of the temple. It is situated at the entrance of the temple building, and functions as a reception area

---

97. See Rivka Gonen, *Contested Holiness: Jewish, Muslim and Christian Perspectives on the Temple Mount in Jerusalem* (Jersey City, N.J.: KTAV, 2003); Th. A. Busink, *Der Tempel von Jerusalem von Salomo bis Herodes* (2 vols.; Leiden: Brill, 1970–80), 1:77–111.

98. See esp. Jean Oullette, "The Basic Structure of Solomon's Temple and Archaeological Research," in *The Temple of Solomon: Archaeological and Medieval Tradition in Christian, Islamic and Jewish Art* (ed. J. Guttmann; AAR/SBL Religion and the Arts 3; Missoula, Mont.: Scholars Press, 1976), 1–20; Busink, *Der Tempel* 1:162–565.

99. Baruch Halpern, *The First Historians: The Hebrew Bible and History* (San Francisco: Harper and Row, 1988), 46–54; cf. Weinfeld, "Zion and Jerusalem."

100. See esp. Busink, *Der Tempel,* 1:162–218.

101. M. A. Powell, "Weights and Measures," *ABD* 6:897–908, esp. 899–901.

102. D. W. Gooding, "Temple Specifications: A Dispute in Logical Arrangement between the MT and the LXX," *VT* 17 (1967): 143–72.

for the main temple building. Only priests are allowed into the temple. Even the king did not enter the temple, but stood by the pillar (2 Kgs 11:14; 23:3), situated on either side of the *ʾûlām* (1 Kgs 7:21). The eastern orientation of the *ʾûlām* allowed light from the rising sun to illuminate the interior of the temple at morning services to symbolize the daily reenactment of creation.

Verse 4 notes the construction of the temple windows. The term *ḥallônê šĕqūpîm ʾăṭūmîm* refers to a closed or recessed lattice window that permits looking out but prevents looking in (n.b., the meaning of the roots *šqp*, "to look down, out," and *ʾṭm*, "to shut"). Burney (62) maintains that the expression refers to "'windows with narrowed frames,' i.e., wide on the inner side of the thick wall, and gradually sloping so as to form a mere slit on the outer side."

Verses 5–6 describe the exterior structure built around the sides of the temple. The term *yāṣîᶜa* is not well understood. The basic meaning of the root *yṣᶜ*, "to lay, spread out," indicates a structure laid out from the three sides of the temple building (the *ʾûlām* would be open). Although *ṣēlāᶜ ôt* is often understood as a reference to chambers, *ṣēlāᶜ* means "rib, side," which suggests three levels for the *yāṣîᶜa* structure. The text provides no indication that the *ṣĕlāᶜ ôt* are placed upright. Furthermore, their attachment to the *migrāᶜ ôt* that are not themselves attached to the temple precludes a roof structure that would facilitate upright placement. The root *grᶜ*, "to diminish, restrain, withdraw," suggests that *migrāᶜ ôt* refers to retaining walls built along the outside of the temple structure to provide support for both the temple and the *yāṣîᶜa* structure as well as a basis for attaching exterior structures that would not require compromising the stone of the temple itself. The *migrāᶜ ôt* thus constitute outer support structures that are thicker on the bottom and progressively thinner for each of its upper stories (to account for progressively smaller *yāṣîᶜa* from top to bottom). The *ṣĕlāᶜ ôt* are placed horizontally so that they emerge from the *migrāᶜ ôt* that line the outer walls of the temple, enabling the *ṣĕlāᶜ ôt*, "ribs," to form the bases for the three floors of the *yāṣîᶜa* structure. The result would be a three-storied structure in which each story is constructed as an arcade that can be divided into rooms for living, storage, and so on.

Verse 7 adds a note concerning the use of undressed stones, cut only in the quarry, for the construction of the temple. Because this verse appears to interrupt the discussion of the *yāṣîᶜa* structure, many consider it to be a secondary addition to the text. But this overlooks the logic of the placement of the verse directly following the notice concerning the *migrāᶜ ôt* in v. 7, which stipulates that they were placed outside the walls of the temple in part to prevent any attachment to the temple walls. The *migrāᶜ ôt* then play a role in preventing the use of iron to cut into the quarried stone of the temple walls. The present verse describes the stones employed in the construction of the temple as *ʾeben-šĕlēmâ-massaᶜ*, "whole quarry stone"—that is, stones cut from the quarry, but not dressed or trimmed to size at the construction site. This would preclude the use of iron tools (cf. Deut 27:6; Josh 8:31; Exod 20:25). The prohibition may reflect an ideal, remote past, since the introduction of iron in the ancient Near East only took place about the time of the formation of Israel at the beginning of the Iron Age (ca. 1200 B.C.E.). Alternatively, it preserves the pristine quality of the temple as the center of YHWH's creation.

Verse 8 describes the construction of a staircase that provides access to the upper stories of the *yaṣîʿa* structure. The term *ṣēlāʿ* refers to a story or level of the *yaṣîʿa* structure. The reference to the middle story (*haṣṣelaʿ hattîkkonâ*) is correct and should not be emended to the lower story (*haṣṣēlāʿ hattaḥtonâ*) since the verse describes a staircase that goes up *upon* (*ʿal*) the middle story beginning at the bottom level in order to reach up to the middle and upper stories. The term *lûllîm* is a hapax that refers to a winding staircase based upon the use of the term *lûlay*, "loop," to describe the means by which curtains are fastened to the tabernacle. Its placement at the entrance to the middle story on the right wing of the structure is on the south side, facing the royal palace, with the temple oriented to the east. This location allows access to the galleries of the *yāṣîʿa* structure directly from the royal palace.

Verses 9–10 conclude with statements concerning the completion of the basic structure of the temple, its roof, and the height of the *yāṣîʿa* structure. Some interpreters regard v. 9a as a gloss due to its similarity to v. 14, but it introduces the discussion of roofing just as v. 14 introduces discussion of the interior. The use of the verb *spn*, "to cover (with panels)," describes the roofing, especially since *sippūn* appears in v. 15 as a designation for the roof and *sĕpînâ* appears in Jonah 1:5 as a term for a ship. Insofar as ships are constructed of paneled boards laid over a frame and sealed with pitch or bitumen (Gen 6:14), the term describes the roofing of the temple, which is built of wooden panels that would be sealed to protect the structure from the elements. The term *śedērōt*, "rows," refers to the planks set on top of the roof to constitute the roof surface. The term *gēb* (pl., *gēbîm*) presents problems, since it normally refers to pits, ditches, cisterns, and so forth (2 Kgs 3:16; Jer 14:3; 39:10) rather than to the crossbeams that one would expect for a roof (see *HALOT*, 1:170; Noth, *Könige*, 96, 99, 117), but crossbeams presuppose the term *gab*, "back," which does not appear in the text. The most cogent explanation for *gēb* presupposes shipbuilding, for which the Phoenicians were well known. Ships are built of wooden planks attached together and sealed over a wooden frame. Such construction requires the use of mortises and tenons, which are holes bored into the planks for the insertion of the wooden dowels that secure them together. The term *gēbîm* refers to the holes and grooves that are bored into the planks to facilitate bonding with tenons and the lips of the next plank.[103]

Verse 10 then indicates that the height of the *yāṣîʿa* structure is five cubits, which refers to the height of each story, for a total of fifteen cubits, half the

103. See L. Casson, "Ships and Shipbuilding," *IDBSup* 823–24; Casson, *Ships and Seamanship in the Ancient World* (Princeton, N.J.: Princeton University Press, 1971), 201–16.

height of the temple building. Verse 10b employs the verb *ʾḥz,* "to attach, grasp, hold firm," to indicate that the *yaṣîʿa* structure supports the temple with the aid of wooden beams, which support the *yaṣîʿa* structure roof.

[6:11–13] Verses 11–13 interrupt the building account to relate YHWH's statement to Solomon, calling upon him to observe YHWH's requirements in building the temple. It employs a typical example of the prophetic word formula, "and the word of YHWH came to Solomon, saying . . ."[104] Most interpreters maintain that the Dtr language indicates that these verses constitute a Dtr redactional insertion designed to tie the building account of the temple into the larger framework of the Josianic or exilic DtrH. When read in relation to the present context, the statement presumes that Solomon observes YHWH's commands and that YHWH will uphold the promise for security to the house of David and the city of Jerusalem. As noted above, the larger DtrH literary context points to more ominous understandings.

[6:14–36] Verses 14–36 present the details of the construction of the temple interior, including an introductory statement in v. 14, the *dĕbîr* (inner sanctuary) and *hêkāl* (great hall) in vv. 15–22, the cherubim in vv. 23–28, the carvings and gold overlays in vv. 29–32, the doors of the temple in vv. 33–35, and the inner court in v. 36.[105]

The introductory statement in v. 14 repeats language from v. 9 to signal the completion of the temple interior. The account of the construction of the *dĕbîr* and *hêkāl* begins in v. 15 with the interior frame of the building. It employs *ṣĕlāʿôt,* "ribs (of cedar)," to refer to the major wooden beams extending along the walls from the floor to the ceiling. The term *qarqaʿ* indicates the floor of the wilderness tabernacle in Num 5:17 and the floor of the sea in Amos 9:13. The term *sippūn* refers to the ceiling. There is no provision for an attic or other undercover. The basic dimensions and layout of the *dĕbîr* and *hêkāl* appear in vv. 16–17. The area of the *dĕbîr* is measured twenty cubits from the innermost wall of the temple. The designation "*dĕbîr*" is derived from the root *dbr,* "to speak," which suggests a linguistic origin in relation to oracle divination. The root may also mean "to lead, guide," which would presuppose the leadership role of YHWH and the priests. Because the *dĕbîr* is the location of the ark, the expression *qōdeš qōdāšîm,* "the Holy of Holies," appears frequently as an alternate designation. The remaining forty cubits of the temple interior form the *hêkal,* Hebrew *hêkal,* a term ultimately derived from Sumerian E-GAL, "great house, palace." The *dĕbîr* and *hêkāl* together emphasize the analogy of the throne room and great hall of a royal palace.

---

104. Marvin A. Sweeney, *Isaiah 1–39* (FOTL 16; Grand Rapids and Cambridge: Eerdmans, 1998), 546–47; Samuel Meier, *Speaking of Speaking: Marking Direct Discourse in the Bible* (VTSup 46; Leiden: Brill, 1992), 314–19.

105. For a detailed discussion, see Busink, *Der Tempel,* 1:257–75.

The decorations, measurements, and gold overlay for the temple interior appear in vv. 18–22. The cedar lining of the temple is decorated with carvings of gourds and blossoming flowers. The term *pĕqāʿîm* is a reference to cucumbers or gourds to indicate the fertility of the natural world. The *pĕṭûrê ṣiṣṣîm,* "blossoming flowers," likewise symbolize fecundity. Both images suggest the garden of Eden to symbolize the role of the temple as the center of creation.

Verses 19–20 return to the *dĕbîr,* where the ark of the covenant is placed. The ark symbolizes the presence of YHWH in the wilderness (Num 10:35–36), and is conceived as a throne (see "YHWH who is enthroned above the cherubim" in 1 Sam 4:4; 2 Sam 6:2; 2 Kgs 19:5; Isa 37:16; Pss 80:2; 99:1; cf. 2 Sam 22:11; Ezek 10; Ps 18:1). It functions as a place for revelation in early traditions, where YHWH speaks (Exod 25:22; Num 7:89), where the two tablets of the Torah reside (Deut 10:2, 5; 1 Kgs 8:9), and where the testimony that constitutes the covenant between YHWH and Israel resides (Exod 25:22; Num 4:5; 7:89; Josh 4:16). Variants of *ʾarôn bĕrît yhwh,* "the ark of the covenant of YHWH," appear throughout the DtrH as a characteristic designation (e.g., Deut 10:8; 31:9; Josh 3:6; Judg 20:27; 1 Sam 4:4; 2 Sam 15:24).

Because the ark is housed in the *dĕbîr,* the *dĕbîr* (and the temple) symbolizes the relationship between YHWH and Israel/Judah. The dimensions of the *dĕbîr* are twenty cubits long, twenty cubits wide, and twenty cubits high. Because the height of the temple is thirty cubits, the *dĕbîr* is built on a platform some ten cubits high, much like the platforms or upper rooms employed in royal palaces for the king's throne.[106] The gold employed to decorate the temple, *zāhāb sāgûr,* literally, "hidden gold," indicates fine gold that was hammered into the engravings of gourds and blossoms. The gold chains, *rattûqôt* (Qere), refers to a partition or a curtain that employs interlooped designs overlaid or embroidered with gold. Its placement before the *dĕbîr* marks a boundary beyond which only the high priest would walk.

Verses 23–28 describe the cherubim placed within the *dĕbîr* where the ark resides. The present text provides little detail concerning their appearance, but Ezek 1; 10 indicate that cherubim are composite creatures, with a combination of human and animal features that are typical of the ancient Near Eastern world.[107] Cherubim relate to the mythological world, and represent the manifestation of the divine on earth as guardians of sacred sites, kings, cities, and so forth. They are constructed on top of the "mercy seat" of the ark (Exod 25:18–22; 37:7–9), and were woven into the curtains and veil that shielded the inner sanctuary of the wilderness tabernacle (Exod 26:1, 31; 36:8, 35). Within the temple,

106. Halpern, *First Historians,* 50–51.

107. See T. N. D. Mettinger, "Cherubim," *DDD²,* 189–92; Othmar Keel, *JHWH-visionen und Siegelkunst* (SBS 84–85; Stuttgart: Katholisches Bibelwerk, 1977), 15–45; *ANEP* 534, 537, 617, 644–53, 666–68, 761, 765.

they stand guard over the ark. They are carved into the walls and doors of the *děbîr,* together with palm trees, flowers, and so on (see vv. 29, 32, below, Ezek 41:15–26), which calls to mind the cherub that guards the garden of Eden and its tree of life. The cherubim thereby symbolize the roles of YHWH as king and creator and the temple as representative of the garden of Eden.

The cherubim are constructed of ʿ*eṣ šemen,* "tree/wood of oil," which refers to olive wood. At a height of ten cubits (fifteen feet), the two cherubim fill half the height of the *děbîr.* The five-cubit wingspan would total twenty cubits for both cherubim and would fill the *děbîr* to overshadow the ark as a protective and intimidating presence. Insofar as pentateuchal traditions call for two (probably smaller) cherubim atop the ark (Exod 25:10–22; 37:1–9; cf. 1 Sam 4:4; 2 Sam 6:2), a total of four cherubim would be present in the *děbîr* (cf. Ezek 1; 10).

The carvings that decorate the interior walls in v. 29 refer to the *děbîr* since they differ from those of v. 18. They include images of cherubim and palm trees as well as blossoming flowers to recall the role of the *děbîr* as a symbol of the garden of Eden. The floor of the temple is overlaid with gold (v. 30), which may indicate gold trim or flourishes rather than the entire floor surface. Overlaying both the inside and outside suggests that the undersides of the planks would include gold not visible to the onlooker, again indicating the importance of this sacred area that is visible to divine eyes as well as human.

Verses 31–32 describe the two doors of the *děbîr,* constructed of "olive wood" to symbolize fecundity. The "pilaster of the doorpost" employs the term *ʾayil,* "ram, pilaster," to signify the strength inherent in a structure that supports the doors of the *děbîr.* It is described as five-sided, one more than the four-sided pilaster of the sanctuary doorposts (v. 33). Engravings of blossoming flowers, cherubim, and palm trees overlaid in gold signify the garden of Eden.

Verses 33–35 describe the main doors of the temple. The four-sided doorposts are constructed of olive wood, whereas the doors themselves are constructed of cypress, which provides even greater strength. The *ṣělāʿîm,* "ribs," are the support beams placed on jambs or pivots (Hebrew, *gělîlîm,* lit., "rollers") that allow them to open. Such door jambs are well known from archaeological contexts where they appear as hollowed stones or a larger stone mantel into which the main beams of a heavy wooden door are inserted.[108] Engraved images of blossoming flowers, cherubim, and palm trees overlaid in gold symbolize Eden. The concluding phrase, *měyuššar ʿal-hamměḥuqqeh,* "directly on the engraving," indicates that the gold leaf was applied to the engravings and not to the entire surface of the door.

Verse 36 concludes the account of the construction of the temple interior with a notice concerning the walls of the inner court. It encloses the area where

108. M. G. Hasel, "Door," *EDB* 353.

the altar and the molten sea are placed before the entrance to the temple. A later reference to an "other court" in 1 Kgs 7:18 may indicate a court connected to the royal palace, but not necessarily the temple. The "great court" in 1 Kgs 7:12 may enclose the entire temple and palace complex. The walls of the court include three courses of dressed stone and one course of cut cedar (cf. Ezra 6:4).

[6:37–38] These verses conclude the account of the construction of the temple with dates specifying the beginning and conclusion of the building activity. The foundation of the temple was laid in the month of Ziv during the fourth year of Solomon's reign (see v. 1). The temple was completed in the eighth month of Solomon's eleventh year. This month is designated as Bul, which is known from Canaanite sources. The month is now designated Heshvan in the Jewish calendar. The term *bûl* is associated with *yĕbûl,* "produce," and *yabal,* "watercourse," which is appropriate for the period immediately following Sukkot in the seventh month when the harvest is gathered and the rainy season in Israel begins. The temple is built in seven years, whereas Solomon's palace, a much larger structure, takes thirteen years (1 Kgs 7:1).

[7:1–12] The proximity of the temple and royal palace reflects the intimate association between the Davidic king and YHWH, who is consistently portrayed with royal imagery in the ideology of the Judean state. The Davidic king is authorized to rule by the creator G-d, YHWH (2 Sam 7; Pss 89; 110; 132; cf. Ps 2), and the worship of YHWH is authorized by the Davidic king, who erects the sanctuary for YHWH's honor.[109] Verse 1 discusses the time taken to build the temple complex. The complex includes five buildings: the house of the forest of Lebanon (vv. 2–5), the hall of columns (v. 6), the hall of the throne or the hall of justice (v. 7), and the private quarters of Solomon and the daughter of Pharaoh (v. 8). Verses 9–11 discuss construction details common to these buildings, and v. 12 discusses the surrounding courtyard.

[7:1] The palace takes thirteen years to build as opposed to seven years for the temple. The larger palace structure is placed to the south of the temple building overlooking the city of David to shield the temple from view and to present the public face of the temple complex.

[7:2–5] The house of the forest of Lebanon is the largest structure of the palace complex. The name derives from the use of the cedar columns that form the basis for its structure. Cedars of Lebanon were highly prized in the ancient Near East for their strength, size, and beauty, and were frequently employed in Mesopotamian palaces. The size of this structure indicates that it functions as the major gathering area for public events, and the size and construction of the

---

109. Weinfeld, "Zion and Jerusalem"; Elizabeth Bloch Smith, "'Who Is the King of Glory? Solomon's Temple and Its Symbolism," in *Scripture and Other Artifacts: Essays on the Bible and Archaeology in Honor of Philip J. King,* ed. M. D. Coogan et al. (Louisville, Ky.: Westminster John Knox, 1994), 18–31.

house of the forest of Lebanon are intended to impress the visitor or onlooker with the power and wealth of the Davidic king. It is a typical Bit-Hilani structure found throughout Mesopotamia, Phoenicia, Syria, and Israel—that is, a large public structure, either palace or temple, based on rows of columns that support a large roof.[110] The four rows of cedar columns define three major elongated spaces within. The *kĕrutôt ʾărāzîm,* "cuttings of cedar," refer to the heavy beams that sit astride the columns to provide the main supports for the roof. Insofar as v. 3 mentions the *ṣĕlāʿôt,* "ribs," that support the roof, the *kĕrutôt ʾarazîm* would be placed lengthwise along the four rows of columns to provide the primary roof support. The *ṣĕlāʿôt* would then be smaller crossbeams placed between the *kĕrutôt ʾărāzîm.* The roof (presumably cedar planks) is placed atop the *ṣĕlāʿôt.* Although the specification of forty-five, fifteen per row, is sometimes understood as a reference to the cedar columns (LXX), this is impossible since forty-five columns can hardly be divided into the four rows of columns mentioned in v. 2. Rather, this specification refers to the *ṣĕlāʿôt* that are placed between the four rows of columns. Sixty columns constitute the four rows of columns employed in the house of the forest of Lebanon.

Such an arrangement explains the three rows of facing windows and squared doors. The four rows of main support beams (*kĕrutôt ʾărāzîm*) define space for three elongated rooms into which the *šĕqupîm,* "window frames," are built. In order for the windows to be placed so that "view" (*meḥĕzeh*) faces "view" (*meḥĕzeh*), the roof structure atop the four rows of columns would comprise three separate but parallel segments into which the windows were built as paired sunlights. The three pairs of squared door frames likewise face each other from opposite ends of the three elongated rooms defined by the four rows of columns, thus providing access to the building through its smaller fifty-cubit-wide ends.

[7:6] The hall of the columns is a separate structure from the house of the forest of Lebanon. Its placement relative to the house of the forest is uncertain, but the fifty-cubit length suggests that it abutted one of the fifty-cubit sides of the house with its three doors. The hall of the columns would serve as a foyer for the house, much like the *ʾûlām* of the temple.

[7:7] The hall of the throne is the royal throne room or hall of justice from which the king rules the kingdom. The text provides few details concerning its construction, except that it is overlaid with cedar "from floor to floor." This causes some consternation among the versions, which eliminate it altogether (LXX) or understand it as "from floor to ceiling" (Peshitta; Vulgate). The phrase instead refers to the flooring at the base of the walls and support columns that define the structure of the building. The dimensions and orientation of the building are not provided, but it is possible that the hall of the throne is constructed

110. See Busink, *Der Tempel,* 1:129–61; Halpern, *First Historians,* 46–54.

to abut the other end of the house of the forest of Lebanon, much like the hall of columns. One would enter the hall of the throne after passing first through the hall of columns and then the house of the forest of Lebanon. The three-part structure of the throne complex resembles that of the temple.

[7:8] Verse 8 describes the private quarters of Solomon and his most prominent wife, the daughter of Pharaoh. These buildings are separate from the throne complex as indicated by their location in "the other court." The house of the daughter of Pharaoh is separate from that of Solomon, and is built to the same specifications. Such parallel structures indicate the importance of the daughter of Pharaoh as Solomon's primary wife and his alliance with Egypt. These structures would likely be placed behind or on the flanks of the throne complex. Living quarters for Solomon's other wives are not mentioned.

[7:9–11] The outer walls of the five palace buildings are constructed of dressed stone. Dressed stone differentiates the royal palace complex from the pristine temple that reflects the holiness of YHWH and the natural state of the created world. The reference to the "great court" indicates a courtyard wall that surrounds the entire palace complex. The ten-cubit stones constitute the base of the outer walls, with eight-cubit stones and a cedar layer at the top.

[7:12] The walls of the great court are constructed similarly to the outer walls of the palace complex, with three dressed courses of stone and a course of cut cedar atop the stones.

1 Kings 7:13–51 The Construction of the Temple Implements

7:13 And Solomon sent for Hiram from Tyre. 14 He was a son of a widow from the tribe of Naphtali, and his father was a Tyrian bronze smith. He came to Solomon, and did all his work. 15 And he fashioned two bronze columns, each was eighteen cubits high with a circumference of twelve cubits. 16 And he made two capitals to place upon the tops of the columns, cast in bronze, each five cubits high. 17 Lattices with twisted and chain patterns were made for the capitals on top of the columns, seven[a] for each capital. 18 [b]And he made the columns and two rows around each lattice to cover the capitals which were on top of the pomegranates, and he did the same for the second capital.[b] 19 [c]And the capitals which were on top of the columns in the hall were of lily work, four cubits high. 20 And the capitals upon the two columns were also above the bulge which was next to the lattice, and the pomegranates were in rows of two hundred around the second capital.[c] 21 And he set up the columns for the hall of the palace, and he set up the right column, and called it Yachin, and he set up the left column and called it Boaz. 22 [d]And upon the top of the columns was lily work, and the work of the columns was complete.[d] 23 And he made the cast sea ten cubits from lip to lip, rounded all about, and five cubits high with a circumference of thirty cubits. 24 ^eAnd gourds were below its lip all around it, ten cubits encircling the sea, with two rows of gourds cast with it.^e 25 It was standing upon twelve oxen, three facing north, three facing west, three facing south, and three facing east, and the sea was above them, and all their backsides were inside. 26 ^fAnd its thickness was a handbreadth, and its lip was like the lip of a cup, a blossom of a lily; two thousand baths was its capacity.^f

27 And he made ten bronze stands, each four cubits long, four cubits wide, and three cubits high. 28 This was the work of the stand; they had framed insets between the connecting pieces. 29 And upon the framed insets which were between the connecting pieces were lions, cattle, and cherubim, and upon the connecting pieces, both above and below the lions and cattle were sloping wreaths. 30 And four wheels of bronze were for each stand, with axles of bronze and four feet at their sides. Below the basin ^gthe sides were cast beneath each wreath. 31 And its mouth inside the capital was a cubit above. Its mouth was rounded; it was a pedestal work of a cubit and a half, also upon its mouth were carvings, and their frame was squared, not rounded. 32 And four wheels were below the framed insets,^g and the brackets of the wheels were in the stand, and the height of each wheel was a cubit and a half. 33 And the work of the wheels was like the work of a chariot wheel; their brackets, their rims, their spokes, and their hubs were all cast. 34 And there were four supports at the four corners of each stand; the supports were of one piece with the stands. 35 And at the top of the stand, half a cubit high, was a round band around it, and upon the top of the stand, its brackets, and its framed insets were of one piece from it. 36 And he engraved upon the surfaces of its brackets and upon its framed insets, cherubim, lion, and palm trees, ^hlike the pubic place of a man,^h and wreaths all about. 37 Accordingly, he made the ten stands, each of them cast in the same measure and shape. 38 And he made ten basins of bronze, with forty baths capacity for each basin; each basin was forty cubits, and each of the ten basins was on a stand. 39 And he placed five stands upon the right side of the house and five upon the left side of the house, and he placed the sea by the right side of the house at the southeast. 40a And Hiram made the basins, shovels, and libation bowls.

40b And Hiram completed all the work on the House of YHWH which he did for King Solomon: 41 two columns, the two globes of its capitals which were on top of the columns, and the two lattices to cover the two globes of the capitals which were on top of the columns, 42 and the four hundred pomegranates for the two lattices, two rows of pomegranates for each lattice to cover the two globes of the capitals which were upon the columns, 43 and ten stands, and the ten basins upon the stands, 44 and the one sea, and the twelve cattle below the sea, 45 and the pans, shovels, and libation bowls, and all these[i] vessels of polished bronze which Hiram made for King Solomon for the House of YHWH.

46 [j]The King cast them in the thick clay of the earth in the plain of the Jordan between Sukkot and Zarethan.[j] 47 [k]And Solomon let all the very, very many implements remain without calculating their weight in bronze.[k]

48 And Solomon made all of the implements which were for the house of YHWH: the gold altar and the gold table upon which was the bread of the presence, 49 and the lampstands, five to the right and five to the left before the Debir, of fine gold, and the blossom, the lamps, and the tongs were gold, 50 and the basins, the snuffers, the libation bowls, the ladles, and the incense pans were fine gold, and the inner door sockets of the House for the Holy of Holies, for the doors of the house for the Heikhal, were gold.

51 And the work which King Solomon did for the house of YHWH was complete, and Solomon brought the holy things of David, his father, the silver, the gold, and the implements he placed in the treasuries of the house of YHWH.

a. LXX reads, *diktuon*, "a net," from Hebrew, *śĕbākâ*, "network," for Hebrew, *šibʿâ*, "seven."

b–b. LXX simplifies the statement, "and hanging work, two rows of bronze netted pomegranates, hanging work, row upon row, and thus he made the second capital."

c–c. LXX reads a modified version of vv. 19–21 after v. 21, "and on the tops of the pillars, lily work against the *Ailam*/Hall, four cubits, and a roof upon both of the columns, and upon the capital sides, a roof equal in thickness," to produce a logically consistent text.

d–d. LXX omits v. 22 and replaces it with a modified version of vv. 19–20.

e–e. LXX contains a combined and modified version of vv. 24 and 26, "and supports below its rim round about encompassed it ten cubits around, and its rim was the work of a rim of a cup, a lily flower, and its thickness, the palm of a hand," for logical consistency.

f–f. LXX combines a modified version of this verse with v. 24.

g–g. LXX omits vv. 30ba[3–4]-32aa.

h–h. Hebrew, *kĕmaʿar ʾîš*, lit., "like the naked place of a man," apparently comparing the sculpted engravings metaphorically to the protrusion of pubic hair and genitalia on the otherwise smooth body of a man. LXX and Peshitta omit, perhaps for reasons of modesty.

i. Read Qere, *hāʾēlleh*, "these (implements)," in place of Ketiv, *hāʾōhel*, "the tent," i.e., the wilderness tabernacle that sets the pattern for the temple.

j–j. LXX places v. 46 after v. 47 for logical consistency.

k–k. LXX rewrites v. 47, "there was weighing of the bronze of which he made all these works; from the great abundance, there was no end of weight of the bronze."

First Kings 7:13–50 emphasizes Solomon's role in overseeing the manufacture of the temple's metal installations and implements. The account begins in vv. 13–14 with a brief notice concerning Solomon's appointment of Hiram of Tyre as the metalsmith responsible for the work. It then provides accounts concerning the manufacture of the two bronze columns before the temple (vv. 15–22), the cast sea or water tank (vv. 23–26), the ten basin stands within the temple (vv. 27–40a), a summation of Hiram's work (vv. 40b–45), a notice concerning Solomon's role in casting these items and his decision not to calculate the value of the bronze employed (vv. 46–47), and a summation of Solomon's work (vv. 48–50).

[7:13–14] There has been a great deal of speculation concerning the identity of the metalsmith Hiram of Tyre, since the Phoenician king who provided raw materials to Solomon bears the same name (1 Kgs 5:15–32). Based upon the identification of his mother as a widow from the tribe of Naphtali, many argue that the man is not to be identified with the Phoenician king (e.g., DeVries 110; Fritz 80–81; Würthwein 75). The role of a foreigner in the construction of the temple is noteworthy, especially because the DtrH is so adamant about Israel's need to separate itself from foreigners who lead it into apostasy (Deut 7:1–6; Judg 2; 1 Kgs 11; 12–13; 2 Kgs 17). The text takes special care to identify Hiram as the son of a woman from Naphtali. Perhaps the notice was included to establish a semi-Israelite identity for the key figure in the construction of the central religious shrine of Israel?

[15–22] The two columns that stand at the entrance to the temple, Yachin and Boaz, are constructed by segments that are bound and pressed together to create a massive eighteen-cubit (twenty-seven-feet)-high structure.[111] The two "crowns" or "capitals" cast in bronze are typical features at the tops of columns in the ancient world, although they have no practical function to support a roof structure. They are intended for symbolic and decorative purposes. Each capital is five cubits high. When added to the eighteen cubits of the columns, the total is only twenty-three cubits, well short of the thirty-cubit height of the temple building.

The decorative work presents problems due to the obscurity of its language. The initial reference to *śĕbākîm,* based on the root *śbk,* "to interweave," refers to lattice work. The adjective *gĕdilîm,* "twisted work," is otherwise employed in reference to the twisted fringes of the Tzittzit or fringed garment that evolved into the Jewish prayer shawl (Deut 22:12; Num 15:38, 39). The term *śĕbākîm* is appositionally defined as *ma'ăśeh šarśĕrôt,* "chain work, mesh," which depict the interwoven strands that shape the seven twisted lattice designs on each capital.

The lattice work provides the background for fruit and flower images that are placed on the capitals. The first are two rows of one hundred pomegranates each that are placed around the two capitals. The pomegranate is one of the staple

---

111. Carol L. Meyers, "Jachin and Boaz in Religious and Political Perspective," *CBQ* 45 (1983): 167–78.

fruits grown in the land of Israel together with grapes, figs, and others (Num 13:23; 20:5; Deut 8:8) that symbolize the fertility of the land. Its use as a motif in the temple (and in the tabernacle on the priests' robes: Exod 28:33, 34; 39:24–26) symbolizes YHWH's role as creator and the temple's role as the center of creation. The lily work, placed between the two rows of pomegranates, likewise symbolizes natural fecundity (see Hos 14:7; Song 2:2, 16; cf. Pss 45:1; 60:1; 69:1; 80:1).

The two columns are placed at either side of the entrance to the *ʾûlām*. Yachin (*yākîn*), the name of the right column, means "he establishes," and Boaz (*bōʿaz*), the name of the left column, is of uncertain meaning although it is interpreted in relation to *bĕʿōz,* "in strength." When read from right (north) to left (south), the names produce the phrase "in strength he establishes," which suggests that the columns symbolize the foundations of the earth and the stability of creation (Mic 6:2; Isa 24:18; Jer 31:37; Ps 82:5; Prov 8:29; cf. "foundations of the world" in Ps 18:16; 2 Sam 22:16; "foundations of the mountains" in Deut 32:22; Ps 18:8; "foundation of heaven" in 2 Sam 22:8; "foundations of generation and generation" in Isa 58:12; "pillars of the earth" in Job 9:5; Ps 75:4; and "pillars of heaven" in Job 26:11).

[23–26] The sea is a large cast bronze water tank that most likely served for the purification of priests prior to their service at the temple (cf. Lev 8:6). It might provide water for washing the entrails of sacrificial animals (see Lev 8:21; 9:14). It might also serve a symbolic function, perhaps to depict the sea from which creation emerged (Gen 1) or the sea through which Israel passed on the way from Egypt to the land of Israel (Exod 14–15).

The sea is described as *mûṣāq,* "a molten casting," formed by pouring molten bronze into clay or earthen molds. The lip or rim of the tank is described as *ʿagol,* "rounded, rolled," which is compared to the rim of a cup (v. 26). Two rows of gourds are molded into the tank below the rim to serve as decoration and to symbolize the fertility of the created world. The tank is mounted on the backs of twelve cast oxen or bulls, which stand in a square three to each cardinal point of the compass, with their heads facing out. Perhaps the bulls symbolize the twelve tribes, but this is uncertain. The four cardinal points of the compass symbolize all creation, and the bulls symbolize strength and virility. The expression "petal of lily" likely serves as a metaphorical expression for the rolled edge of the rim. The tank's capacity is two thousand baths. The Hebrew term *bat* also means "daughter." Some speculate that it refers to the amount of water carried by one girl (cf. Exod 2:16; Gen 29:1–12). It is calculated at ten gallons.[112]

[27–40a] The function of the ten bronze basin stands is uncertain, although they likely contain water for purification or libations. The basic construction of the body of the stand includes *misgĕrôt,* "enclosures, frames," which designate

112. Powell, "Weights and Measures," 904.

the panels fitted within the framework pieces or *šĕlabbîm*, "joinings," to form the surfaces of the stands. The *misgĕrôt* are decorated with images of lions, cattle, and cherubim that were molded, hammered, or inscribed into the surfaces. The *šĕlabbîm* are decorated with *loyôt*, wreath work that is attached to the framework (the root *lwh* means "to attach, join"). The expression *maʿăśeh môrād*, "applied work," suggests that they were hammered or welded, since *môrād* is derived from *yrd*, "to go down."

The bronze wheels and axles at the sides of the basin stands in v. 30 are held in place by four *paʿămôt*, "steps, feet" or "brackets." The stands are constructed with an opening, "mouth," inside a pedestal or crown structure to accommodate the basin. The *yĕdôt haʾôpannîm* (lit., "the hands of the wheels") refer to the clasps that grasp the wheel axles from inside the stand. The clasps, the rims (*gabbîm*), the spokes (*ḥiššûqîm*), and the hubs (*ḥiššûrîm*) are all cast from bronze. The four sides where the supports for the axles are located form one piece with the stands. The rounded rim and its "hands" clasp the pedestal structure atop the stand. The surface of its clasps and panels includes engravings of cherubim, lions, and palm trees that are described like the nakedness of a man to portray the way in which the engravings stand out against a smooth surface. The ten basins atop the stands are molded from bronze and have a capacity of forty baths—that is, ninety-six liters or forty-three and a half gallons. They are placed along right and left sides of the temple *hêkāl*.

Verse 40a completes the notice of Hiram's work with a listing of basins, scrapers or shovels, and sprinkling or pouring bowls. The basins (*kîyorôt*) may be pots (*sîrôt*) used for cooking or incense (cf. v. 45). The shovels are to remove residue from sacrifices and incense, and the sprinkling or pouring bowls are for libations and purification (Num 19:13; Ezek 36:25), or to sprinkle blood on the altar (Exod 24:6; 29:16; Lev 1:5) or the people (Exod 24:8; Lev 7:14).

[40b–45] This section presents a summation of the various fixtures and implements manufactured by Hiram. Although it repeats items previously discussed in detail, it adds some more information. The statement concerning the columns in v. 41 includes the *gullôt*, "basins, bowls," which refer to a bowl-like feature of the columns that might be identical to the *beṭen*, "belly" or "bulge," mentioned in v. 20. Verse 45 lists the *sîrôt*, "pots," whereas v. 40a mentions *kîyorôt*, "basins." The term *sîrôt* appears in priestly literature concerning the construction of the tabernacle, where they are employed to boil sacrificial meat (Exod 27:3; 38:3; Zech 14:20–21). Due to similarity in spelling and meaning of *sîrôt* and *kîyorôt*, it may be that *sîrôt* was inadvertently read in place of an original *kîyorôt*. The Qere reading of *hāʾēlleh*, "these," in place of Ketiv *hāʾōhel*, "the tent," supports this suggestion since the reading of *hāʾōhel* in place of an original *hāʾēlleh* would likewise be influenced by a scribe familiar with Exod 38:3 and other priestly pentateuchal texts who would have inadvertently transposed *lamadh* and *he* of *hāʾēlleh* to produce *hāʾōhel*. The Qere reading corrects the transposition.

[46–47] The narrative legitimately credits Solomon for carrying out the work since he commissioned Hiram to perform the work on his behalf. Molded bronze requires a foundry in which bronze can be melted and poured into preformed earthen or clay molds. Modern foundries employ specially treated casting sand that can be pressed into forms to shape the molds,[113] but such techniques were not available to the ancients. Rather, models of the implements were made and pressed into large quantities of clay to produce objects of the size discussed here. Suitable clay is found en masse in low-lying areas near water, such as the Jordan River, which would allow the molds to be formed in deep pits of clay, so that the molten bronze could be poured and dug out after it had hardened. The location in the Jordan River plain between Zarethan, an uncertain site located south of Beth Shean along either bank of the Jordan, and Sukkot, likely identified with Deir 'Alla along the east bank of the Jordan, makes sense, since extensive clay deposits are found in this region.[114] The notice that Solomon was unable to weigh the vast quantity of bronze impresses the reader with his wealth and efforts on behalf of the temple.

[48–50] The various fixtures and implements of gold manufactured by Solomon for the temple appear in vv. 48–50. The list includes the altar of gold and the table for the bread of the presence that are placed before the holy of holies (1 Kgs 6:20, 22). The altar was employed for incense (Exod 30:1–10; 40:5), which would fill the temple with smoke to symbolize the divine presence (Exod 40:34–38). The bread of the presence is placed upon the table to symbolize the grain offerings brought by the people to the temple (Exod 25:23–30; 37:10–16; cf. Exod 40:23; 1 Sam 21:2–7). The ten *měnōrôt,* "lampstands,"[115] placed five to each side of the *hêkāl,* provide light within the temple to symbolize the first of YHWH's creative acts (Gen 1:3–5). The seven lamps of the menorah symbolize the seven days of creation and the week (Exod 25:31–40; 37:17–24; Zech 4; Gen 1:1–2:3). The petals of the lamp refer to the various lips that contain the oil and the wicks of the lamps. The tongs were used for the incense altars (see Isa 6:6) or perhaps the *měnōrôt.* The other basins, snuffers, libation bowls, and ladles would be used in relation to the basin stands, the incense altars, menorahs, and so on. The gold inner door sockets for the holy of holies and *hêkāl* correspond to the gold overlay noted in 1 Kgs 6:20–22, 30, 32.

[51] The temple serves as a national treasury where Solomon places the holy things, that is, wealth acquired by David and dedicated to YHWH (cf. 2 Sam 8:10–12; Josh 6:19; 7:1–26).

---

113. These observations are informed by my experience as a foundry man at the Wagner Castings Company, Decatur, Illinois.

114. See H. O. Thompson, "Zarethan," *ABD* 6:1041–43; J. H. Seely, "Sukkot," *ABD* 6:217–18; G. Van der Kooij, "Deir 'Alla, Tell," *NEAEHL* 1:338–42; Jonathan N. Tubb, "Sa'idiyeh, Tell-es," *NEAEHL* 4:1295–1300.

115. See Carol L. Meyers, *The Tabernacle Menorah: A Synthetic Study of a Symbol from the Biblical Cult* (ASORDS 2; Missoula, Mont.: Scholars Press, 1976).

1 Kings 8:1–66 Solomon's Dedication of the Temple

8:1 ªThen Solomon assembled the elders of Israel, all the heads of the tribes, the ancestral leaders of the sons of Israel, to King Solomon in Jerusalem to bring up the ark of the covenant of YHWH from the City of David, which is Zion.

2 And every man of Israel was assembled to King Solomon in the month of Ethnanim at the Festival, which is the seventh month. **3** And all the elders of Israel came,ª and the priests carried the ark. **4** And they brought the ark of YHWH, the Tent of Meeting, and all the holy vessels which were in the Tent; and the priests and the Levites brought them up. **5** And King Solomon and all the congregation of Israel, which had been summoned to him, was with him before the ark sacrificing sheep and cattle, which were neither numbered nor counted because of their quantity. **6** And the priests brought the ark of the covenant of YHWH to its place at the Debir of the Temple, the Holy of Holies, under the wings of the Cherubim, **7** for the Cherubim spread wings to the place of the ark, and the Cherubim covered the ark and its poles from above. **8** And the poles extended so that the ends of the poles were seen from the sanctuary before the Debir, but they were not seen outside, ᵇand they are there to this day.ᵇ **9** There was nothing in the ark except the two tablets of stone which Moses placed there at Horeb when YHWH concluded a (covenant) with the sons of Israel when they went out from the land of Egypt.

10 And when the priests had gone out from the sanctuary, the cloud filled the house of YHWH, **11** so that the priests were not able to stand to serve before the cloud because the glory of YHWH filled the house of YHWH.

12 ᶜThen Solomon said, "YHWH has decided to live in deep darkness! **13** I have surely built an exalted house for you, an eternal place for your dwelling!"ᶜ

14 And Solomon turned his face, and he blessed all the assembly of Israel, and all the assembly of Israel was standing. **15** And he said, "Blessed is YHWH, G-d of Israel, who spoke by his mouth with David my father and by his hand he has fulfilled (his word), saying, **16** 'From the day that I brought my people Israel from Egypt, I have not chosen a city from all the tribes of Israel to build there a house for my name, but I chose David to be over my people Israel.' **17** And it was the will of my father David to build a house for the name of YHWH, G-d of Israel. **18** And YHWH said to my father, 'Because it is your will to build a house for my name, you have done well, because it is your will. **19** But you will not build the house; your son who comes out from your loins, he will build the house for my name.' **20** And YHWH established his word which he had spoken. I rose in place of David my father; I sat upon the throne of Israel just as YHWH promised; I built the house for the name of YHWH, G-d of Israel; 21 and I provided there a place for the ark which houses the covenant of YHWH which he made with our ancestors when he brought them out of the land of Egypt."

22 And Solomon stood before the altar of YHWH in front of all the assembly of Israel, and he spread his hands to the heavens, 23 and he said, "O YHWH, G-d of Israel, there are no gods like you in the heavens above or upon the earth below, keeping covenant and fidelity to your servants who walk before you with all their heart, 24 who kept for your servant David my father that which you promised to him—and which you promised by your mouth and by your hand—you have fulfilled this day. 25 And now, O YHWH, G-d of Israel, keep for your servant David my father that which you promised to him, saying 'No one of your line shall be denied from sitting before me on the throne of Israel, if only your sons watch their way to walk before me just as you have walked before me.' 26 And now, O G-d of Israel, let your words[d] which you have promised to your servant David my father be confirmed. 27 For does G-d truly dwell upon the earth? Behold, the heavens and the heavens of the heavens cannot contain you, much less so this house which I have built. 28 And you shall turn to the prayer of your servant and to his supplication, O YHWH my G-d, to listen to the outcry and to the prayer which your servant prays before you today. 29 May your eyes be open to this house night and day, to this place of which you have said, 'My name shall be here,' to listen to the prayer which your servant will pray unto this place. 30 And you shall listen to the appeal of your servant and your people Israel which prays to this place, and you shall listen in the place of your heavenly dwelling, and you shall listen, and you shall pardon.

31 "When[e] a man sins against his neighbor, and he utters a curse to curse him, and a curse comes before your altar in this house, 32 then you shall listen in the heavens, and act, and judge your servants to condemn the guilty, to place his way upon his head, to absolve the innocent, to treat him according to his innocence.

33 "When your people Israel is smitten before an enemy when they sin against you, and they turn to you, praise your name, pray, and make supplication to you in this house, 34 then you shall listen in the heavens, pardon the sin of your people Israel, and restore them to the land which you have given to their fathers.

35 "When the heavens are stopped up and there is no rain because they sin against you, and they pray unto this place, praise your name, and return from their sin because you would answer them,[f] 36 then you shall listen in the heavens, pardon the sin of your servants and your people

Israel, for you shall teach them the good path on which they should walk, and you shall give rain upon your land which you have given to your people for an inheritance.

37 "When famine is in the land, plague, blight, withering, locust, grasshopper or when his enemy afflicts him in the land at his gates with any blow, any sickness; 38 when any prayer, any supplication which any person makes for all your people Israel—each of whom knows the affliction of his heart—and he spreads his hands out to this house, 39 then you shall listen in the heavens at the place of your dwelling, and you shall pardon, and act, and treat each according to all his ways because you know his heart—for you yourself know the heart of every human being— 40 so that they will revere you all the days that they are alive upon the face of the land that you have given to their fathers.

41 "And also to the foreigner who is not from your people Israel, who comes from a far land for the sake of your name— 42 for they shall hear about your great name and your strong hand and your outstretched arm, and they shall come and pray unto this house— 43 you shall listen in the heavens in the place of your dwelling, and you shall act according to all that the foreigner asks of you so that all the peoples of the land shall know your name, to revere you like your people Israel and to know that your name is called upon this house that I have built.

44 "When your people goes out to war against its enemy on the path that you send them, and they pray to YHWH toward the city that you have chosen and the house that I have built for your name, 45 then you shall hear in the heavens their prayer and their supplication, and you shall carry out their cause.

46 "When they sin against you—because there is no one who does not sin—and you become incensed against them, and you deliver them up before an enemy, and their captors take them captive to the land of the enemy, far or near, 47 and they return to their senses in the land where they are held captive, and they repent and make supplication to you in the land of their captors saying, 'We have sinned, we have transgressed, we have done wrong,' 48 and they return to you with all their heart and with all their being in the land of their enemies who have taken them captive, and they pray to you in the direction of their land which you have given to their fathers, to the city which you have chosen and to the house that I have builtᵍ for your name, 49 then you shall hear in the heavens in the place of your dwelling their prayer and their supplication and you shall carry out their cause, 50 and you shall pardon your people who have sinned against you and all their crimes that they have committed against you, and you shall give them mercy before their captors so they will be merciful to them.

51 Because they are your people and your inheritance, whom you brought out of the land of Egypt, from the midst of the iron furnace, 52 may your eyes be open to the supplication of your servant and to the supplication of your people Israel, to listen to them in all their calling out to you. 53 For you have set them apart for yourself as an inheritance from all the peoples of the earth just as you said through Moses, your servant, by whom you brought our ancestors out from Egypt, O YHWH, G-d."

54 And when Solomon finished praying to YHWH all this prayer and supplication, he arose from before the altar of YHWH, from bowing down upon his knees with his hands spread out to the heavens, 55 and he stood and blessed all the assembly of Israel in a loud voice, saying, 56 "Blessed is YHWH who has given rest to his people Israel according to all that he promised. Not one word has failed from all his good word that he spoke through Moses his servant. 57 And YHWH, our G-d, is with us just as he was with our fathers. He will not abandon us, and he will not forsake us. 58 May our hearts incline to him, may we walk in all his paths, and may we observe his commandments, his statues, and his laws which he commanded our ancestors. 59 And may these my words, by which I have made supplication before YHWH, be near unto YHWH, our G-d, day and night, to do justice for his servant and justice for his people Israel each and every day, 60 so that all the peoples of the earth will know that YHWH is G-d, there is no other. 61 And your heart will be completely with YHWH our G-d to walk in his statutes and to observe his commandments as on this day."

62 And the king and all Israel with him were making sacrifice before YHWH. 63 And Solomon made an offering of well-being, when he sacrificed to YHWH twenty-two thousand cattle, one hundred twenty thousand sheep; and the king and all the sons of Israel dedicated the house of YHWH.

64 On that day, the king sanctified the inner court before the house of YHWH, because he made there the whole burnt offering, the grain offering, and the fat of the offering of well-being, because the bronze altar which is before YHWH was too small to complete the whole burnt offering, the grain offering, and the fat of the offering of well-being. 65 And Solomon celebrated the festival at that time, together with the people of Israel, a great assembly, from Lebo Hamath to the Wadi of Egypt, before YHWH our G-d, ʰtwo full weeks, fourteen days.ʰ 66 On the eighth day, he sent the people home, and they blessed the king and they went to their tents rejoicing and good of heart concerning all the good that YHWH did for David his servant and for Israel his people.

a. The LXX shortens vv. 1–3a and combines its reading with elements from 1 Kgs 7:1 to present a stylistically and chronologically consistent text, "And it came to pass when

Solomon had finished building the house of the L-rd and his own house after twenty years, then king Solomon assembled all the elders of Israel in Zion to bring the ark of the covenant of the L-rd out of the city of David, which is Zion, in the month of Athanin. And the priests carried the ark . . ."

b–b. Lacking in LXX because the ark had already disappeared by the late second century B.C.E.

c–c. LXX places vv. 12–13 immediately after v. 53, "Then Solomon spoke concerning the house when he had finished building it, 'He made the sun known in heaven. The L-rd said that he would dwell in darkness. "Build my house, a beautiful house, for yourself to dwell in newness."' Behold, is this not written in the book of Song?"

d. Read with Qere, *dĕbārĕkā*, "your word," in place of Ketiv, *dĕbārêkā*, "your words."

e. MT combines the Hebrew direct object marker and relative pronoun, *ʾet ʾăšer*, to indicate an unspecified action as the object of the verbal clause. This requires that the initial statements of v. 31a be read as the object of the last verb of v. 30—that is, "and you shall forgive whoever sins, each against his neighbor, . . ." The general protasis/apodosis structure of the following cases suggests a conditional understanding of this statement: "when/if a man sins against his neighbor" cf. MT 2 Chr 6:22, *ʾim*, "if"; Peshitta, *ʾn*, "if"; Vulgate, *si*, "if."

f. MT reads, *taʿănēm*, a Hiphil form of the root, *ʿnh*, "(because) you would/will answer them." Cf. LXX, "you shall humble them"; Peshitta, "you afflict them," which presuppose *tĕʿannēm*, a Piel form of the root *ʿnh*, "you shall oppress/humble them."

g. Read with Qere, *bānîtî*, "I have built"; cf. Ketiv, *bānîtā*, "you have built."

h–h. Cf. LXX, which draws on v. 66 and 1 Kgs 4:20, "before the L-rd our G-d in the house which he built, eating and drinking and rejoicing before the L-rd our G-d seven days."

First Kings 8:1–66 is clearly demarcated in v. 1 by the use of a temporal verbal clause to depict Solomon's assembly of Israel's leadership to commence the temple dedication. It concludes in 1 Kgs 8:66 with a notice of Solomon's dismissal of the people at the conclusion of the festivities. The structure of the unit is determined by the narrative framework for Solomon's speeches. The syntactical and thematic features point to three major subunits. The combination of the temporal particle *ʾaz*, "then," followed by the imperfect verb, *yaqhēl*, "he assembled," marks the beginning of the text as a whole and its first subunit in vv. 1–11, which relates Solomon's assembly of Israel to bring the ark to the temple. A similar combination of the temporal particle *ʾaz* followed by the perfect verb *ʾāmar*, "(Solomon) said," introduces the second subunit of the text in vv. 12–61, which presents Solomon's three speeches, including his initial statement concerning the construction of the temple in vv. 12–13, his two-part prayer to YHWH in vv. 14–21, 22–53, and his blessing of the people in vv. 54–61. First Kings 8:62, introduced by the combination of a conjunctive *waw* and the noun *hammelek*, "and the king," marks the beginning of the third and final subunit of this text which recounts the dedicatory sacrifices and the celebration of "the festival" of the seventh month.

Solomon's temple dedication speech is particularly important to understanding Dtr theology and historiographical perspectives.[116] This narrative stresses the importance of the Jerusalem temple as the central focal point for the worship of YHWH, and it emphasizes YHWH's promise to secure the rule of the house of David in Jerusalem provided that the Davidic kings adhere to YHWH's commandments. The text conveys the expectation that YHWH will protect Israel, but it also anticipates punishment, particularly exile, if the people do not abide by YHWH's expectations. It further anticipates restoration of the people to the land once they repent, suggesting that the narrative does not simply chronicle the causes of the destruction of Israel, Jerusalem, and Judah, but also laying the theological foundations for the return of the people and the restoration of Jerusalem, Judah, and Israel in the aftermath of exile.

Tensions in the portrayal of the temple, the house of David, and the potential exile and restoration of the people suggest that this text was not originally written to address the problems posed by the Babylonian exile. First, the notice in v. 8 that the poles of the ark remain visible within the temple building "until this day" indicate that the temple and the ark remain intact from the perspective of the writer of this text. Such a statement would be impossible when the temple was destroyed. Although the text anticipates exile, it does not anticipate the Babylonian exile. Second, the statements concerning YHWH's promises to ensure the continuity of the house of David if the Davidic monarchs observe YHWH's expectations (e.g., v. 25) do not focus on any particular fate for the monarch, nor do they anticipate his return. Solomon's petitions address the fate of the people quite clearly; they may be exiled and they may return to a temple that remains standing. The king is not exiled, nor does he return; he only loses his right to rule.

These observations suggest that the account of Solomon's dedication of the temple was not originally written to address the problems of the Babylonian exile, although the literary context of the final form of the DtrH requires that it be read with the Babylonian exile in mind. The text presupposes the Assyrian exile of the northern tribes of Israel, insofar as the people were removed from the land, the temple still stood, and the Davidic monarch might qualify to rule if he abides by YHWH's expectations. Such a scenario expresses the interests of the Josianic redaction of the DtrH in the centrality of the Jerusalem temple and the rule of a Davidic monarch over a restored people of Israel. It also expresses the interests of the Hezekian reaction.

---

116. Martin Noth, *The Deuteronomistic History* (JSOTSup 15; Sheffield: JSOT Press, 1981), 6–9; E. Talstra, *Solomon's Prayer* (CBET 3; Kampen: Kok Pharos, 1993); Jon D. Levenson, "From Temple to Synagogue: 1 Kings 8" in *Traditions in Transformation: Turning Points in Biblical Faith* (ed. B. Halpern and J. D. Levenson; Winona Lake, Ind.: Eisenbrauns, 1981), 143–66; J. G. McConville, "1 Kings viii 46–53 and the Deuteronomic Hope," *VT* 42 (1992): 67–79; and Gary N. Knoppers, "Prayer and Propaganda: Solomon's Dedication of the Temple and the Deuteronomistic Program," *CBQ* 57 (1995): 229–54.

[1–11] This subunit plays an important role in tying the present narrative into the overall framework of the DtrH account of the origins of Israel's kingship, particularly the rise of David. David's rise is linked to the history of the ark from the time of the high priest Eli when the ark resided at Shiloh (1 Sam 1–3) through the time of its transfer to Jerusalem by David (2 Sam 6). The transfer of the ark to Jerusalem must also be read in relation to the period of Moses and Joshua since it represents YHWH's protection at that time as well. The ark houses the tablets of the covenant placed there by Moses at Mount Horeb (1 Kgs 8:9; Deut 9:1–10:5), and it accompanied the people through the conquest of the land of Israel (e.g., Josh 3; 6; 8:30–35).

Although this passage has clear links to the overall DtrH, many observe that it has affinities with priestly literature as well.[117] This connection suggests that the passage has been retouched by a priestly editor (Würthwein 86–89) interested in establishing links between the DtrH presentation of the movement of the ark into the temple and an early pentateuchal narrative concerning the construction of the ark and its role in symbolizing YHWH's presence in the wilderness.

The "festival" in the seventh month—that is, Ethnaim, now known in the Jewish calendar as Tishri—is noteworthy. The term "Ethnaim" appears in Phoenician inscriptions as the name for the seventh month,[118] which indicates that it was a Canaanite name employed in Israel much like the names Ziv and Bul (1 Kgs 6:1, 37–38) prior to the introduction of the Babylonian calendar. The seventh month marks the beginning of the rainy season in Israel and the conclusion of the harvest. The festival of Sukkot celebrates this season, beginning on the fifteenth of the seventh month, with sacrifices and libations to highlight the fecundity of creation (see Lev 23:33–43; Num 29:12–38; cf. Exod 23:16; 34:22; Deut 16:13–15). Because Sukkot follows Rosh ha-Shanah (New Year) and Yom Kippur (Day of Atonement), it is sometimes considered to be the preeminent of the three major temple festivals so that it is designated simply as *heḥāg,* "the festival" (1 Kgs 8:65; Ezek 45:23; Neh 8:14; 2 Chr 7:8; cf. 1 Kgs 12:32). Ezra 3:1–7 associates Sukkot with the dedication of the temple altar.

[12–13] Some scholars maintain that vv. 12–13 are a late addition to this text.[119] The reasons include its placement following v. 53 in the LXX, its position

117. C. F. Burney, *The Book of Judges and Notes on the Hebrew Text of the Books of Kings* (New York: KTAV, 1970), 104–12; I. Benzinger, *Die Bücher der Könige* (Kurzer Hand-Commentar zum Alten Testament 9; Tübingen: Mohr Siebeck, 1899), 56–59; Antony F. Campbell and Mark A. O'Brien, *Unfolding the Deuteronomistic History: Origins, Upgrades, Present Text* (Minneapolis: Fortress, 2000), 349–50.

118. H. Donner and W. Röllig, *Kanaanäische und aramäische Inschriften* (Wiesbaden: Harrassowitz, 1966–69), 37:1–2; 41:4.

119. E.g., Wellhausen, 271; G. H. Jones, *1 and 2 Kings* (2 vols.; New Century Bible Commentary; Grand Rapids: William B. Eerdmans; London: Marshall, Morgan and Scott, 1984), 196; Ernst Würthwein, *Die Bücher der Könige* (Das Alte Testament Deutsch 11/2–2; Göttingen: Vandenhoeck & Ruprecht, 1977), 88–9; James A. Montgomery and Henry Snyder Gehman, *The Books of Kings* (International Critical Commentary; Edinburgh: T & T Clark, 1951), 189–92.

prior to and apart from Solomon's prayer in vv. 14–53, and the general obscurity of Solomon's statement. This contention is unwarranted. The obscurity of
the MT suggests that it is the original text, which the LXX attempts to clarify.
First, LXX expands the initial notice of Solomon's speech, "then Solomon spoke
concerning the house when he had finished building it," in order to specify that
the king's reference to YHWH dwelling in deep darkness must refer to the temple and its darkened holy of holies where the ark resides. Second, LXX begins
Solomon's statement by noting YHWH's role as creator, beginning with the
sun, "He manifested the sun in the heavens, but the L-rd said he would dwell
in darkness." The statement thereby explains the obscure MT reference to the
darkness of the holy of holies by contrasting it with YHWH's creative acts.
Third, Solomon's first-person statement in MT that he built a stately house for
YHWH now becomes in LXX YHWH's command to Solomon to build the temple: "Build my house, a beautiful house, for you to dwell in anew." Solomon's
statement thereby becomes YHWH's authorization to build the temple, which
overcomes YHWH's reservations as expressed in 2 Sam 7. It also protects
YHWH's holiness by indicating that the temple satisfies a human need for a
dwelling place rather than a need by YHWH. Finally, LXX adds a notice concerning the citation of this oracle, "Behold, is this not written in the book of the
Song?" The Greek term *oidos*, "song," likely presupposes Hebrew *šîr*, "song,"
but scholars argue that the term should be emended to *yašar*, that is, "the book
of Yashar," which is cited elsewhere as a source for the other poetic statements
presented in the DtrH (Josh 10:13; 2 Sam 1:18).[120] This emendation is unnecessary, because the statement very likely refers to a psalm that authorizes the
building of the temple (Ps 132; cf. 2 Sam 7), presents YHWH's dwelling in deep
darkness (Ps 97; 2 Sam 22/Ps 18), or rehearses YHWH's creation of the sun
(Hab 3). The placement of vv. 12–13 after v. 53 in the LXX indicates an effort
to provide a suitable conclusion to Solomon's prayer.

Although the LXX reading is interpretative, it clarifies the function of
vv. 12–13. The statement addresses a central feature of the temple, the darkened
holy of holies in which the ark resides, which receives the light of the
sun as it rises in the east each morning. The Hebrew statement, "YHWH has
decided to reside in deep darkness," employs the Hebrew term *ʿărāpel*, "deep
darkness," literally, "dark cloud." Insofar as darkness precedes the first act of creation, the temple symbolizes the center of the cosmos created by YHWH, but the
darkened state of the holy of holies indicates that YHWH remains separate from
the created world. Indeed, various images of darkness and cloud convey divine
presence—for example, the pillar of fire and cloud in the wilderness (Exod
13:17–22; 14:19–20), the darkness atop Mount Sinai (Exod 20:18; Deut 5:19;
2 Sam 22:10/Ps 18:12; Ps 97:2; Zeph 1:15; Joel 2:2; Isa 8:21–23), and the image
of the "glory of YHWH" descending upon the tabernacle (Exod 40:34–38).

120. Julius Wellhausen, *Die Composition des Hexateuch* (Berlin: de Gruyter, 1963), 271.

Solomon's statement in v. 13, "I have indeed built a stately house for you, a place of dwelling forever," indicates Solomon's compliance with YHWH's wishes. The term *zĕbul,* "lofty, stately," has royal connotations in Ugaritic (Mulder 398–99), and it conveys the sense of holiness and sovereignty suitable to YHWH's temple at the center of creation (cf. Isa 63:15).

[14–21] The first segment of Solomon's speech rehearses the basic principles of the relationship between YHWH and the house of David as the ideological basis for the construction of the temple. His speech reflects a common ancient Near Eastern pattern in which a monarch builds, refurbishes, or supports a temple to honor the deity credited with bringing him to power, and the temple provides theological justification for his rule (2 Sam 7; Pss 2; 89; 132).[121]

Several features of Solomon's statements convey this understanding. First is the effort to tie the choice of David into the exodus, the foundational tradition of ancient Israel. Insofar as the exodus tradition is especially rooted in the north and the house of David is a Judean dynasty, Solomon's speech aims to unite the two major segments of his kingdom, which had fought each other during David's early reign (2 Sam 1–5). Second, Solomon addresses the question of YHWH's lack of desire for a temple. Such a strategy undercuts the claims of other cities that had once housed the ark or served as a sanctuary site for the people of Israel, and instead builds a basis for popular support of David and his house by portraying him as righteous and altruistically interested in honoring YHWH. Third, the speech builds a basis for ensuring the continuity of the house of David. David had built his support in both Judah and northern Israel by delivering the people from their enemies, but major threats to Israel are no longer evident at the beginning of Solomon's reign. The speech thereby draws on David's popularity to build a foundation of support for Solomon by (1) pointing to Solomon as the son who builds the temple and fulfills the desires of the ever-popular David, (2) pointing to Solomon as the realization of YHWH's dynastic promise to David, and (3) portraying Solomon as the protector of the ark. Solomon emerges as the heir to David and the ancestors: Abraham, Isaac, Jacob, Joseph, Moses, and Joshua.

[22–53] Solomon's prayer of petition (Long, *1 Kings* 101–4) draws heavily on Dtr terminology and concepts, especially in the seven petitions that reflect the language of blessing and curse in Deut 28–30.[122] Solomon begins with statements concerning YHWH's incomparability (cf. Exod 15:11; Deut 4:39; Ps 86:8, 10) and fidelity to those loyal to the covenant (cf. Exod 15:13; Deut 7:9, 12; Ps 86:13). Such statements motivate his audience (and readers of the text) to adhere to YHWH, and they motivate YHWH to act on behalf of the petitioner.

121. Weinfeld, *Deuteronomy and the Deuteronomic School,* 36–37, 247–51.
122. See Levenson, "From Temple to Synagogue," 160–64; Burney, *Book of Judges,* 112–29.

Solomon's petition mentions YHWH's promise to the royal house of David, but it qualifies the terms on which the promise is made—that is, if the Davidic king suffers misfortune, it must be because he failed to adhere to YHWH's expectations. Several observations follow. First, this statement specifies that a son of David shall sit on the throne of Israel, which may refer to all Israel or only to northern Israel. Second, this statement corresponds to Dtr statements concerning the royal house of David in 1 Kgs 2:4; 9:4–5, but it differs markedly from the dynastic promise in 2 Sam 7, which does not envision the removal of the dynasty. Insofar as Solomon's conduct later leads to the revolt of the northern tribes against the house of David, this statement explains the loss of northern Israel to the house of David. In later times it would have been read in relation to the Babylonian exile. The petitions presuppose that the people pray toward the temple while in exile, although there is no suggestion that the temple is destroyed.

Verses 27–30 call on YHWH to hear the prayers, petitions, and so on of the Davidic king and the people of Israel. The passage employs a rhetorical question to assert that YHWH does not dwell on earth and thereby avoids the theological problem inherent in the standard Dtr statements that the temple is the place chosen by YHWH for the divine name (v. 29; cf. Deut 12:5; 14:23; 16:2; 26:2). The temple then is the place where the people assemble to address YHWH. The speech presupposes the DtrH view that YHWH demands adherence to divine expectations, punishes those who fail to abide by those expectations, and restores those who repent.

Verses 31–53 relate Solomon's seven petitions on behalf of his people. Each petition is formulated casuistically, much like standard forms of case law, so that the circumstances of the petition are followed by a statement of the recommended course of action.[123] The petitions present a standard Dtr theological portrayal of YHWH as a G-d of justice and mercy who punishes the wicked and restores those who repent (cf. Deut 28–30).

The first petition in vv. 31–32 takes up a person who curses another. The petition presupposes that it is frequently impossible to determine which party is right. Solomon asks that YHWH judge these cases individually to ensure that justice is done (Deut 17:18–13).

The second petition in vv. 33–34 takes up Israel's repentance following defeat by an enemy. Such a petition presupposes the Dtr conceptualization of punishment for wrongdoing and restoration for repentance, but Solomon's petition adds a reference to YHWH's promises to the ancestors as motivation to accept the appeal of the people.

The third petition in vv. 35–36 calls upon YHWH to restore the natural fecundity of the land when the people repent. This presupposes the Dtr view that nat-

---

123. See Albrecht Alt, "The Origins of Israelite Law," *Essays on Old Testament History and Religion* (Garden City, N.Y.: Doubleday, 1967), 101–71.

ural calamity, such as drought, results from human wrongdoing (Deut 28:23, 24). YHWH takes on the role of the Canaanite storm god, Baal, or the Aramean storm god, Hadad, but the passage ties this role to YHWH's moral order. The passage outlines YHWH's responsibility to teach the people, which points to the teaching role of the priests (see Moses in Deut 6:1–3; cf. Lev 10:10–11).

The fourth petition in vv. 37–40 takes up the natural calamities, such as famine, plague, crop failure, and locusts (Deut 28:21, 22, 27), that result from enemy invasion. The passage points to YHWH's all-encompassing power to know the heart of those afflicted and thereby prompts the audience to accept the claims of YHWH's power, justice, and mercy.

The fifth petition in vv. 41–43 focuses on the prayers and petitions of a foreigner who comes to the land of Israel to revere YHWH (Deut 29:21). Concern with the foreigner or resident alien (*gēr*) is a common theme in Deuteronomy (see Deut 1:16; 5:4; 10:18; 14:21; 16:11; etc.). The term *gēr* refers to a convert to Judaism in rabbinic Hebrew. Many argue that concern with foreigners stems from the exilic or postexilic eras, but concern with this issue throughout Exodus and Deuteronomy points to earlier periods, such as the Hezekian and Josian periods, in which the return of exiles was already anticipated.[124] Such concern builds the case that YHWH is sovereign over all creation, and that the temple symbolizes that sovereignty.

The sixth petition in vv. 44–45 addresses Israel's petitions to YHWH while engaged in war authorized by YHWH outside the land of Israel (cf. Deut 20; 28:25). The people should pray in the direction of the city chosen by YHWH for the temple. The use of legal language—"you shall do justice"—presupposes that they have suffered some setback due to lack of righteousness. The petition builds upon the earlier concerns with YHWH's power over nature and all humanity. The issue of offensive war precludes an exilic or postexilic date.

The seventh petition in vv. 46–53 is a subcase of the sixth, which presupposes that the people have been defeated and taken captive because they have failed to abide by YHWH's expectations (cf. Deut 28:36, 37, 64–68). The contrasting uses of the verb roots *šbh*, "to take captive," and *šûb*, "to return, repent," reinforce the Dtr association of misfortune, here portrayed as captivity, and repentance, here portrayed as a necessary result of the people's misfortune.[125] This petition functions as a conclusion for the seven petitions as a whole, insofar as it presents the themes of justice and mercy, YHWH's sovereignty over all nations, and YHWH's deliverance of Israel at the exodus, in an effort to persuade its audience that such mercy is possible once again in a time of distress.

124. See Christiana van Houten, *The Alien in Israelite Law: A Study of the Changing Status of Strangers in Ancient Israel* (JSOTSup 107; Sheffield: JSOT Press, 1991).
125. Jon D. Levenson, "The Paranomasia of Solomon's Seventh Petition," *HAR* 6 (1982): 135–38.

[54–61] Solomon's blessing rehearses the major themes of his prayer, which correspond to the major tenets of Dtr theology. He blesses YHWH for having given *mĕnûḥâ,* "rest," to the people as promised (cf. Deut 12:9; 25:19; Josh 21:41–43; 23:1; 2 Sam 7:1). This theme points to YHWH's fidelity to the covenant, symbolized by Israel's security in the land under David and Solomon and the building of the temple. Second, Solomon's blessing emphasizes that YHWH's promises were made through Moses, which ensures that temple is tied directly to Mosaic tradition. Third, Solomon's blessing also ties YHWH's promise to the ancestors, again establishing a link with past tradition. Fourth, it incorporates exhortations to observe YHWH's commandments, one of Dtr's fundamental concerns. Fifth, it expresses once again the hope and expectation that YHWH will heed Solomon's prayers and petitions on behalf of Israel, which cements the relationship between YHWH and Israel, insofar as Solomon states that YHWH's justice and mercy provide the means by which the people will know that YHWH is G-d.

[62–66] The sacrifices made by Solomon are described as *zebaḥ haššĕlāmîm,* "the offering of well-being/peace."[126] Well-being offerings do not have an expiatory function like the whole burnt offering, the guilt offering, and the sin offerings, but tend to be made for celebration, thanksgiving, fulfillment of a vow, a free will offering, and so on (see Lev 3; 7:11–16; Deut 27:7). The meat of the well-being offering is eaten by the priests and people near the altar (1 Sam 2:13; 9:24), but the fat of the well-being offering is devoted entirely to YHWH and burned on the altar (Lev 3:3–5, 9–11, 14–16). Verse 64 indicates that the daily whole burnt offering (*ʿolâ;* see Lev 1) and the grain offering (*minḥâ;* see Lev 2) are also made. Both atone for the guilt of the sanctuary and the priesthood (Num 18:1), and thereby play a role in symbolizing the maintenance of cosmic order. The quantity of sacrifices made over a fourteen-day period would feed some one hundred thousand to two hundred thousand people. Estimates of Jerusalem's population range from one hundred thousand to four hundred thousand by the eighth century B.C.E.[127]

Verse 65 states that Solomon and all Israel celebrated *heḥāg,* "the Festival," throughout the land of Israel. The boundaries of the land are defined as Lebo-Hamath, "the Entrance to Hamath," identified with modern Lebweh, located to the south of modern Hama/ancient Hamath in northern Syria (cf. Num 34:8; Josh 13:15; 2 Kgs 14:25; Ezek 47:15). Naḥal Mitzraim, "the Wadi of Egypt," is generally identified with Naḥal Bezor, which runs into the Mediterranean south of Gaza and north of Raphia, although some identify it with Wadi el-Arish to the south of Raphia (Num 34:5; Josh 15:4; 2 Kgs 24:7; Isa 27:12; Ezek 48:28).[128] The "festival" refers to Sukkot, "Tabernacles, Booths," in the sev-

---

126. See esp. Jacob Milgrom, "Sacrifices and Offerings, OT," *IDBSup* 763–71.

127. Magen Broshi and Israel Finkelstein, "The Population of Palestine in Iron Age II," *BASOR* 287 (1992): 47–60.

128. M. Görg, "Egypt, Brook of," *ABD* 2:321.

enth month as the festival par excellence (1 Kgs 12:32, 33). Sukkot is normally a seven-day holiday, but the doubling of the celebration to fourteen days was a one-time act that would convey the importance of the temple dedication. Second Chronicles 7:9 explains this period by stating that the first seven days were for the celebration of Sukkot and the second seven days were for the dedication of the altar. The reference to Solomon's dismissal of the people on the eighth day marks Shemini Atzeret, the holiday immediately following the conclusion of Sukkot (Lev 23:36; Num 29:35–38). The concluding portrayal of the people rejoicing as they return to their "tents" recalls the portrayal of Israel's and Judah's happiness in 1 Kgs 4:20, but it contrasts markedly with the call of the people of northern Israel to return to their tents when they revolt against the house of David (1 Kgs 12:16; cf. 2 Sam 20:1).

1 Kings 9:1–9 Solomon's Second Encounter with YHWH

9:1 And when Solomon had finished building the House of YHWH, the house of the King, and every desire of Solomon that he wished to do, 2 YHWH appeared to Solomon a second time just as He appeared to him at Gibeon. 3 And YHWH said to him, "I have heard your prayer and your petition which you made before Me. I have sanctified this house, which you have built to place My Name there forever, and My eyes and heart are there always. 4 And you, if you walk before Me just as David your father walked, with a complete heart and in righteousness to do all that I have commanded you, observing My statutes and My laws, 5 then I shall establish the throne of your kingdom over Israel forever just as I promised David your father saying, 'You shall never lack a successor on the throne of Israel.' 6 If you or your sons indeed turn from Me and do not observe My commandments or My statutes which I have placed before you, and you go and serve other gods and worship them, 7 then I will cut Israel off from upon the land that I gave to them. And I will dismiss from My presence the house where I have sanctified My Name, and Israel shall become a proverb and a mockery among all the peoples. 8 And this house shall be exalted.[a] All passing by it shall gasp and whistle, and they will say, 'Why did YHWH do this to this land and to this house?' 9 And they will say, 'Because they abandoned YHWH their G-d, who brought their ancestors out from Egypt, and they took other gods, and they worshiped them and served them. Therefore, YHWH has brought upon them all this evil.'"[b]

a. Hebrew, *ʿelyôn,* "exalted, high," makes little sense here. Cf. Targum Jonathan, "and this house which has been high shall become ruins"; Peshitta, "and this house shall become ruins." Although LXX supports the Hebrew, Targum and Peshitta read *ʿelyôn* as

ʿîyîn, "ruins" (see *BHS* note). The Hebrew text expunges a statement that would compromise the temple's sanctity. Targum and Peshitta likely reflect the original text.

b. LXX reads v. 24 at this point, perhaps to emphasize Solomon's association with Egypt as the initial cause for Israel's later problems (cf. 1 Kgs 3:1; Deut 17:14–20).

First Kings 9:1–9 prepares the reader first for the upcoming revolt of the northern tribes and even later for the destruction of the temple.[129] Verse 2 signals the relationship between this passage and the dream report of 1 Kgs 3:3–15 by referring to YHWH's second appearance to Solomon. Verse 3 signals that YHWH's statements to Solomon are formulated as a response to his petitionary prayer in 1 Kgs 8:14–53. YHWH's statements take up the primary concerns expressed in both 1 Kgs 3:3–15 and 1 Kgs 8—that is, the continuity of the Davidic line, the temple, and the people of Israel—in relation to YHWH's expectations that the terms of the covenant be fulfilled. Insofar as YHWH's statements in 1 Kgs 8:14–53 threaten each of these elements if divine expectations are not met, the second vision undermines the previous laudatory accounts of Solomon's reign and thereby establishes the basis for the upcoming punishments.

The passage first states the basic postulates concerning the representation of YHWH's presence in the temple and commitment to both the house of David and Israel, and then it undermines these postulates point by point. Thus, v. 3 presents YHWH's first-person statement that YHWH has sanctified the temple, that YHWH's name will be there "forever," and that YHWH's eyes and heart will be there for all days. Verse 4 then states YHWH's expectations that Solomon will walk before YHWH wholeheartedly and righteously like his father David to carry out YHWH's statutes and laws. When such a statement is read in the larger context of the DtrH, problems emerge. David has committed adultery and murder in relation to his affair with Solomon's mother, Bath Sheba (2 Sam 10–12). David advised Solomon to eliminate his enemies, some on very questionable grounds, as he prepared to ascend the throne (1 Kgs 2). When Solomon is compared to David, the reader senses that the relationship is in trouble.

The threat to the dynasty emerges in vv. 5–6. YHWH reiterates the promise to David, "You shall never lack a successor on the throne of Israel." A variation of this formula appears already as part of Solomon's reiteration of YHWH's promise to David during his temple dedication prayer, and other expressions of

129. Cf. K. I. Parker, "Solomon as Philosopher King? The Nexus of Law and Wisdom in 1 Kings 1-11," *JSOT* 53 (1992): 75–91, esp. 83; contra Marc Z. Brettler, "The Structure of 1 Kings 1–11," *JSOT* 49 (1991): 87–97, who places the beginning of the critique of Solomon at 1 Kgs 9:26, based on perceived relations with the Torah of the king in Deut 17:14–20 (see also David Glatt-Gilad, "The Deuteronomic Critique of Solomon: A Response to Marvin A. Sweeney," *JBL* 116 [1997]: 700–703, who follows Brettler, but offers little critical discussion. For response, see Sweeney, *King Josiah*, 93–94 n. 1; Sweeney, "Synchronic and Diachronic Considerations in the Portrayal of the Demise of Solomon's Kingdom," forthcoming in the untitled Shalom Paul Festschrift, ed. Baruch J. Schwartz et al.; Winona Lake, Ind.: Eisenbrauns).

YHWH's commitment to David appear at the conclusion of the narrative concerning Solomon's securing the throne (1 Kgs 2:45) and in the Gibeon vision report (1 Kgs 3:14). Verse 6 expresses the qualification of this promise that the monarch will lose YHWH's support if he fails to abide by YHWH's commands. Although such a condition is not expressed in 2 Sam 7, it appears repeatedly in the Kings texts.[130] The generally positive context of these earlier expressions suggests that the king will do precisely as required. But the following narratives concerning Solomon's decline indicate that the stated conditions will not be fulfilled and that the resulting punishments are therefore justified.

Verses 7–9 indicate that this threat encompasses Israel and the Jerusalem temple as well. The verb *wĕhikrāttî,* "and I will cut off (Israel)," contrasts markedly with the earlier statement of promise to David, that is, *lō' yikkārēt-lĕkā,* "there shall not be cut off to you," to emphasize the reversal of the earlier implied promise. The term "Israel" at this point may be read with two different connotations: in relation to all Israel, which would encompass the twelve tribes ruled by Solomon, or in relation to the northern tribes of Israel. With regard to the latter option, the narrative concerning Solomon's reign has already distinguished Israel and Judah as the two major constituents of Solomon's empire (see 1 Kgs 4:20; contra 4:1). The threat against the temple, "and this house which I have sanctified for My Name, I will expel (*ʔăšalaḥ*) from My presence," reverses YHWH's statement in v. 3, "I have sanctified this house which you have built for My Name forever." Many take this statement as evidence that the passage was composed in exilic or postexilic times in reference to the Babylonian destruction of the temple,[131] but the use of the piel form of the verb *šlḥ* indicates situations in which the people are dismissed from a public assembly with no expectation that they will be destroyed (Josh 22:7); a bird is shooed away without killing it (Deut 22:7); or a woman is divorced but not killed (Deut 24:1–4). The term does not entail the destruction of the temple as *ʔašlîk,* "I will cast off," does in 2 Chr 7:20. The dismissal of the temple from YHWH's presence indicates an act that can be reversed, much like the dismissal of the house of David from ruling the northern tribes. Such an understanding fits easily into the perspective of either the Hezekian or Josianic DtrH editions, which anticipate northern Israel's return to Davidic rule and the Jerusalem temple. Only later is YHWH's statement understood in reference to the destruction of the temple, as in 2 Chr 7:20.

---

130. Richard D. Nelson, "Dynastic Oracle in Dtr: A Workshop in Recent Trends," *SBL 1976 Seminar Papers* (ed. G. MacRae; Missoula, Mont.: Scholars Press, 1976), 1–14.

131. See Richard D. Nelson, *The Double Redaction of the Deuteronomistic History* (JSOTSup 18; Sheffield: JSOT Press, 1981), 73–77, who also argues that vv. 7–9 are dependent on supposedly post-Dtr traditions in Deut 29:24–25; Jer 22:8–9. His argument presupposes that references to the destruction of the temple can only function retrospectively rather than as warnings to Judah after the fall of northern Israel.

Verses 8–9 more likely presuppose the actual destruction of the temple, but evidence is not conclusive. The first element involves the text-critical problem of v. 8aa, "and this house shall be exalted (ʿelyôn; cf. 2 Chr 7:21)." Most interpreters agree that the statement is a textual corruption (e.g., Burney 132–33; Noth 195; Mulder 468–69). The argument for emendation depends on the readings of the Targum and Peshitta, which substitute ʿîyîn, "ruins," in place of ʿelyôn, "exalted." Neither 2 Chr 7:21 nor LXX read "ruins," but instead presuppose ʿelyôn, which suggests that ʿelyôn must be retained as a secondary reading that attempts to protect the temple's sanctity. The subsequent claims of gasping, whistling, and questions of those who pass by can easily function as a threat well before the actual destruction of the temple. Having witnessed the destruction of Samaria and the deportation of much of the northern Israelite population, the portrayal of the temple's potential destruction and the removal of the people would have been quite conceivable to the Hezekian and Josian DtrH editions, which portray a succession of Israelite sanctuaries that were no longer functioning (e.g., Gilgal, Shiloh, Dan, and Beth El). The statement that YHWH will bring evil upon the nation reflects language that anticipates both the Babylonian exile (2 Kgs 21:12; 22:16) and the punishment of northern Israel (1 Kgs 14:10; 21:21; 22:23).

1 Kings 9:10–11:40 The Rise of Solomon's Adversaries

First Kings 9:10–11:40 presents a full account of the decline of Solomon's kingdom following the completion of the temple. This unit begins with the temporal formula in v. 10, which introduces the account of the final years of Solomon in 1 Kgs 9:11–11:40. These narratives demonstrate how Solomon's actions, particularly his involvement with foreign monarchs and women, characterize him as a monarch like the pharaoh of the exodus and lead directly to the revolt of the northern tribes following his death.[132]

First Kings 9:11–11:40 indicates its structural divisions with noun clauses that introduce each subunit. First Kings 9:11–28 names Hiram of Tyre to emphasize Solomon's collaboration with him on building projects reminiscent of Pharaoh; 1 Kgs 10:1–29 names the queen of Sheba to recall Solomon's trade across the Red Sea with Egypt; 1 Kgs 11:1–25 identifies Solomon's love for foreign women as a cause for challenges to his rule; and 1 Kgs 11:26–40 names Jeroboam ben Nebat, in charge of forced labor under Solomon, to recount his dynastic oracle from YHWH.

132. Cf. Pekka Särkiö, *Die Weisheit und Macht Salomos in der Israelitischen Historiographie* (Schriften der Finnischen Exegetischen Gesellschaft 60; Helsinki: Finnische Exegetische Gesellschaft; Göttingen: Vandenhoeck & Ruprecht, 1994), who argues for a redactional reworking of the Solomonic traditions to present him as a monarch like Pharaoh.

Although Noth (208) correctly notes little evidence of explicit DtrH composition, the arrangement of this material points to an editorial interest in portraying Solomon in a very negative light. The topical arrangement, beginning with notices concerning Solomon's use of forced labor and the strategic placement of otherwise unnecessary statements concerning Pharaoh and Pharaoh's daughter, highlights an interest in drawing an analogy between Solomon and the pharaoh of the exodus. Such an interest would hardly come from the Hezekian account of Solomon's reign, which is interested in lauding the true founder of the house of David and the builder of the Jerusalem temple. This material explains the withdrawal of the northern tribes from Davidic rule and the exile of the northern Israel as a result of both Solomon's (and Jeroboam's) actions. Insofar as 2 Kgs 22–23 present Josiah as the monarch who corrected the problems initiated by Solomon and Jeroboam,[133] this material represents the Josianic DtrH.

1 Kings 9:10 Introduction

9:10 And at the end of twenty years, Solomon had built the houses, the house of YHWH and the house of the King.

The temporal formula in 1 Kgs 9:10 introduces the subunits that treat each element of concern during Solomon's final years, including his relationship with Hiram of Tyre (1 Kgs 9:11–28), his relationship with the queen of Sheba (1 Kgs 10:1–29), his love for foreign women which leads to the dissolution of his kingdom (1 Kgs 11:1–25), and the rise of Jeroboam ben Nebat, who will become the first king of northern Israel (1 Kgs 11:26–40).

1 Kings 9:11–28 Solomon's Association with Hiram of Tyre

9:11 Hiram, King of Tyre, had supplied Solomon with as much cedar, cypress, and gold as he wished. Then King Solomon gave twenty cities in the land of Galilee to Hiram. **12** And Hiram went out from Tyre to see the cities which Solomon had given to him, and he did not think that they were very good. **13** And he said, "What are these cities that you have given to me, my brother?" and he called them the land of Kabul[a] to this day. **14** And Hiram sent one hundred twenty talents of gold to the king.

15 [b]And this is the matter of the corvée which Solomon raised to build the House of YHWH, his house, the Millo,[c] and the wall of Jerusalem, Hazor,[d] Megiddo, and Gezer. **16** [e]Pharaoh, King of Egypt, had gone up, captured Gezer, and burnt it with fire, and he killed the Canaanites who

133. Sweeney, "Critique of Solomon"; Sweeney, *King Josiah,* 93–109.

were living in the city, and he gave it as dowry for his daughter, the wife of Solomon.[e] 17 And Solomon built Gezer, Lower Beth Horon, 18 Baalat,[f] Tadmor[g] in the wilderness in the land, 19 [h]and all of Solomon's store cities,[h] chariot cities, cavalry cities, and all that Solomon desired to build in Jerusalem, [i]in Lebanon, and in all the land of his rule. 20 All the people who were left from the Amorites, the Hittites, the Perizzites, the Hivvites, and the Jebusites, who were not from the sons of Israel,[i] 21 and their children who were left after them in the land whom the sons of Israel were not able to wipe out, Solomon brought them up for a labor corvée until this day. 22 But Solomon did not assign the people of Israel as slaves. Instead, they were men of war, his servants, his commanders, his chariot crews, his chariot officers, and his cavalrymen. 23 These are the officers of the prefects who were in charge of labor for Solomon, [j]fifty-five hundred,[j] who were supervising the people doing the work. 24 [k]As soon as the daughter of Pharaoh went up from the City of David to her house which he had built for her, then he built the Millo.[k] 25 [l]And Solomon three times each year presented whole burnt offerings and well-being offerings upon the altar that he built for YHWH, and he burned incense [m]with it, which was[m] before YHWH, and he completed the house.[bl] 26 And Solomon built ships at Ezion Geber, which is Elat, by the shore of the Reed Sea[n] in the land of Edom. 27 And Hiram sent on the ships his servants, sailors who knew the sea, with the servants of Solomon. 28 And they came to Ophir, took from there four hundred and twenty talents of gold, and brought it to King Solomon.

a. LXX, *Horion,* "boundary," which presupposes Hebrew, *gĕbûl.*

b–b. LXX lacks vv. 15–25 here, but a modified version of vv. 15–25 appears as 3 Kgdms 10:22a–c. Verse 16 appears after v. 9 as 3 Kgdms 9:9a. Another modified version of vv. 15a, 16, 24–25, 15b, and 17 appears as 3 Kgdms 2:35f–k, and a modified form of v. 18 appears in 3 Kgdms 2:46d.

c. Hebrew, *hammillô*, "filling," perhaps in reference to a depression that was filled in and fortified for defensive purposes; cf. LXX, *ten akran,* "the citadel."

d. LXX reads *ḥāṣōr,* "Hazor," as *Assour,* "Assur/Assyria," apparently based in part on assonance.

e–e. LXX lacks v. 16, apparently because it is parenthetical.

f. Baalat is lacking in 3 Kgdms 10:22, but it appears with Tamar/Tadmor in 3 Kgdms 2:35.

g. Ketiv, *tāmār,* "Tamar/Palm Tree"; read with Qere, *tadmōr,* "Tadmor" (cf. 2 Chr 8:24; Targum Jonathan; Peshitta). The term is lacking in 3 Kgdms 2:35, but it appears as *Iethermath,* "Yethermath," in 3 Kgdms 10:22 and in 3 Kgdms 5:14d as "and he built Thermai (*thermai*) in the wilderness."

h–h. Lacking in 3 Kgdms 10:22 (there is no corresponding text in 3 Kgdms 2:35).

i–i. Cf. 3 Kgdms 10:22, "the work of Solomon which he determined to build in

Jerusalem and in all the land so that none of the people should rule over those left of the Hittite, the Amorite, the Perizzite, the Canaanite, the Hivvite, the Jebusite, and the Gergeshite who were not of the children of Israel . . ." There is no corresponding text in 3 Kgdms 2:35.

j–j. 3 Kgdms 2:35 reads, three thousand six hundred; cf. 1 Kgs 5:30; see also 2 Chr 8:10, "two hundred fifty."

k–k. LXX places v. 24 after 3 Kgdms 9:9, reading, "then Solomon brought up the daughter of Pharaoh out of the City of David to his house which he built for himself in those days." The version of this verse in 3 Kgdms 2:35 corresponds more closely to the Hebrew.

l–l. Verse 25 appears in 3 Kgdms 2:35, after the reading of v. 24 as follows, "and Solomon offered up three whole burnt offerings in the year, and peace offerings on the altar which he built to the L-rd, and he burned incense before the L-rd, and finished the house."

m–m. Hebrew, ʾittô ʾăšer, "with it, which," is very awkward insofar as hammizbēaḥ, "the altar," is the only possible antecedent to the pronoun and the relative particle ("and he burned incense with it [the altar], which was before YHWH").

n. Hebrew, yam-sûp, "sea of reeds (Reed/Red Sea)"; cf. LXX, Ailath epi tou cheilous tes eschates thalasses en gei Edom, "Elath upon the shore of the end of the sea in the land of Edom," which presupposes Hebrew, yam-sôp, "sea of the end."

The initial reference to Hiram of Tyre introduces the primary character of 1 Kgs 9:11–28. Although Pharaoh and his daughter appear (vv. 16, 24), the reference to each parenthetically demonstrates that Solomon's association with foreign monarchs prompts him to become more like the Egyptian pharaoh who enslaved Israel in the exodus traditions.[134] Solomon thereby represents the antithesis to ideal Israelite kingship.

[11–15] The first subunit portrays Solomon's relationship with Hiram of Tyre. The present text differs markedly from its counterpart in 1 Kgs 4:20–5:32 because it emphasizes the problems that arise as a result of Solomon's association with the Tyrian monarch (cf. Ahab ben Omri, married to the Sidonian princess Jezebel, in 1 Kgs 16–2 Kgs 13). The subunit begins by noting Hiram's support of Solomon, supplying him with raw materials and gold necessary to construct the temple and royal palace. The notice that Solomon ceded twenty Galilean cities to Hiram indicates Solomon's attempt to pay Hiram, but it contrasts with 1 Kgs 5:20, 21–25, which note that Solomon was to repay Hiram with food supplies.

Solomon's ceding twenty Galilean cities is striking. Having been granted the land of Israel by YHWH in the DtrH Joshua traditions, Solomon gives part of the land to Hiram, a Phoenician/Canaanite monarch. The cities would presumably have come from Solomon's ninth district, which included the tribal territory of Asher and the enigmatic Bealoth (1 Kgs 14:16). In contrast to Joshua,

134. See Särkiö, *Weisheit und Macht Salomos,* esp. 103–81.

Solomon spurns the land of Israel granted by YHWH by giving it back to the Canaanites. The narrative continues by portraying Hiram's dissatisfaction. His name for the region, Kabul, may indicate the name by which it was known in antiquity, but later readers speculate that the term represents a pun that combines the preposition kĕ-, "like," with the particle of negation, bal, "not," to produce a term that means "like nothing" (Mulder 477; Thenius 145; Burney 135). Others follow the LXX in noting the onomatopoeic relation to the Hebrew word gĕbûl, "border" (Mulder 477). Hiram nevertheless sends Solomon 120 talents of gold; Hiram meets his obligations and Solomon needs the cash.

Solomon's imposition of the mas, "tax, corvée," in v. 15 indicates that Solomon can only build up the land with foreign support. The building projects demonstrate Solomon's supposed wealth and power. The Millo likely refers to a fortified stepped structure uncovered by archaeological excavation between the lower city of David and the upper temple and royal palace complex.[135] The cities Hazor, Megiddo, and Gezer each occupy strategic positions in tenth-century Israel, north of the Galilee by the border with Aram, at the western entrance to the Jezreel Valley, and in the coastal plain along the southwestern borders of Judah, respectively.[136]

[16–19] The second major subunit of the passage is demarcated by the syntactically independent reference to Pharaoh in v. 16 and by the waw-consecutive chain that runs through v. 19. The initial statement concerning Pharaoh interrupts the account of Solomon's building activities and thereby indicates crucial interpretative implications. First, it calls to mind Solomon's relationship with Pharaoh, which reminds the reader of Solomon's marriage to Pharaoh's daughter (1 Kgs 3:1) and Pharaoh's role as oppressor in the Exodus. Second, it builds upon the role reversal of Solomon's giving land to Hiram by noting that Solomon receives land (Gezer) from Pharaoh as dowry for Pharaoh's daughter. Third, the association with Pharaoh in the midst of an account of Solomon's imposition of forced labor to carry out his building projects reinforces the portrayal of Solomon as a monarch like the oppressive pharaoh of the exodus.

This characterization of Solomon then informs the reading of vv. 17–19, which further discuss Solomon's building projects. Beth Horon the Lower is one of two Ephraimite cities named Beth Horon that faced each other near the border of Ephraim and Benjamin, eleven miles northwest of Jerusalem, where they protect access to Ephraim, Benjamin, and Jerusalem and enable Israel to project power into the coastal plain (Josh 16:3, 5; 18:13–14).[137] Baalath appar-

---

135. Mazar, Archaeology, 379–80, cf. 374; Yigal Shiloh and Hillel Geva, "Jerusalem," NEAEHL 2:698–716, esp. 704, 716.

136. Yigal Yadin and Amnon Ben Tor, "Hazor," NEAEHL 2:594–606; Yigal Yadin and Yigal Shiloh, "Megiddo," NEAEHL 3:1003–24; William G. Dever, "Gezer," NEAEHL 2:496–506; see also Mazar, Archaeology, 375–402, for a survey of Solomonic building features.

137. J. L. Peterson, "Beth Horon," ABD 1:688–89.

ently refers to Kiriath Jearim (Josh 15:9; 1 Chr 13:6) eight miles west of Jerusalem along the Judean-Benjaminite border where it controls access to and from the coastal plain.[138] Tamar is frequently read as Tadmor in keeping with the Qere tradition, but Tadmor is located in Aram some 140 miles northeast of Damascus. Tamar likely refers to a town mentioned in Ezek 47:19; 48:28, located south of the Dead Sea, that will mark the border of the restored land of Israel, perhaps Hazazon-tamar (Gen 14:7), which protects the Negev from Edomite incursion.[139] The subunit concludes with reference to Solomon's store cities along the coastal plain.

[20–28] The third subunit takes up seemingly unrelated topics, including the continued presence of Canaanites in the land, the labor corvée imposed upon them, the role of Israelites as soldiers and taskmasters, the move of the daughter of Pharaoh to the Temple Mount, and Solomon's joint trading ventures along the Red Sea with Hiram. The subunit is constructed so that the reader may conclude that Solomon has become a monarch like Pharaoh.

Verses 20–22 relate Solomon's imposition of forced labor on the Canaanites who had not been killed or driven away. Because 1 Kgs 5:27–32 indicates that Solomon imposed the corvée on Israel, some have attempted to distinguish the *mas,* "tax, corvée," of 1 Kgs 5:27–32 from the *mas-ʿōbēd* or state labor in the present passage.[140] Such efforts to distinguish the terminology miss the fundamental point, however, that the Israelites perform the labor to build the holy temple in 1 Kgs 5:27–32 whereas Canaanites work on "secular" projects. Notably, our passage states that this practice continues "until this day," which indicates a preexilic setting.

The second portion of this subunit in vv. 23–28 contains the most disparate elements of the passage. The initial statement in v. 23 appears at first sight to function as a conclusion to the statements concerning Solomon's imposition of forced labor in vv. 20–22. But the initial third-masculine-plural pronoun, *ʾelleh,* "these," is ambiguous since it is uncertain whether it refers to the Israelites in 22 who supervise the Canaanite laborers or to the following total of fifty-five hundred who are assigned such functions. Nevertheless, the introductory particle *ʾak,* "but, indeed," in v. 24 must be considered, because it typically relates the following statement to what precedes. In the present case, the move of the daughter of Pharaoh from the city of David to the Temple Mount and Solomon's completion of the Millo function as means to characterize Solomon's use of prefect officers to supervise Canaanite labor. First, Solomon's use of such labor

138. C. S. Ehrlich, "Baalah," *ABD* 1:555; R. Greenberg, "Baalath," *ABD* 1:555.

139. S. A. White, "Tadmor," *ABD* 6:307; J. K. Lott, "Tamar," *ABD* 6:315–16; contra Yohanan Aharoni, "Tamar and the Roads to Elath," *IEJ* 13 (1963): 30–42; Aharoni, *The Land of the Bible: A Historical Geography* (2d ed.; London: Burns and Oates, 1979), 55, 70, 140, 142, who identifies it with 'Ain Husb, ca. twenty miles southwest of the Dead Sea.

140. See esp. Rainey, "Compulsory Labor Gangs."

again associates him with Pharaoh. Second, Solomon's completion of the Millo precedes the move of Pharaoh's daughter to the Temple Mount and palace complex. The move takes place in full view of the city of David, and the Millo then protects the complex from the lower city, thereby separating the city's inhabitants from their king and his Egyptian wife. The reference to Solomon's sacrifices three times a year must refer to his observance of the three major temple festivals, namely, Pesach (Passover), Shavuoth (Weeks), and Sukkoth (Tabernacles), required of every male (Deut 16:1–17; cf. Exod 23:14–19; 34:18–26). It is ironic that Canaanites, who are supposed to be removed from the land according to Dtr tradition, aid in completing the building of the temple and palace complex that enables Solomon to offer these sacrifices.

Verses 26–28 then complete the subunit with an account of Solomon's partnership with Hiram to engage in maritime trade along the Red Sea. When read in the context of 1 Kgs 9:11–28, these statements suggest that Solomon is compelled to engage in such trade to compensate Hiram for the unsatisfactory cities ceded to the Phoenician. They also demonstrate Hiram's ability to take charge of the relationship by providing Solomon with the naval expertise that enables them both to become rich. Such cooperation with a Phoenician and the accumulation of wealth are matters of Dtr concern (see Deut 7:1–6; 17:14–20). Ezion Geber/Elath is located along the shore of the Red Sea, or *yam-sûp,* "Reed Sea," the same body of water that Israel crossed to escape from Egypt. Crossing the Red Sea to return to Egypt for wealth is expressly forbidden in Deut 17:16–17. Ezion-Geber/Elath may refer to two sites that stand in close proximity (Deut 2:8; 2 Chr 8:17), but the exact location of either remains uncertain.[141] The site of Ophir is uncertain, although biblical tradition notes it as a source for gold (Josh 22:24; 28:16; Ps 45:9; Isa 13:12). It is variously identified with the general region of modern Yemen along the south Arabian peninsula, the Egyptian site of Punt in what is now Somalia, Ethiopia due to claims by the now-deposed Ethiopian dynasty to be descended from Solomon and the queen of Sheba, or even (S)upara, around forty miles north of Bombay based on Josephus's identification in *Ant* 8:164.[142]

First Kings 9:11–28 clearly indicates redactional activity. The present form of the text indicates a deliberate effort to critique Solomon by the overall arrangement of this text, particularly the strategic placement of statements concerning Solomon's relationship with Egypt and his marriage to the daughter of Pharaoh. The result is a portrayal of Solomon as a king who has transformed Israel into a nation like Egypt of the exodus tradition, who allows the Canaanites to remain in the land, who turns Israelite cities over to a Phoenician/Canaan-

---

141. M. Lubetzki, "Ezion Geber," *ABD* 2:723–26; J. Zorn, "Elath," *ABD* 2:429–30; Nelson Glueck and Gary Pratico, "Kheleifah, Tel el-," *NEAEHL* 3:867–70.
142. D. W. Baker, "Ophir," *ABD* 5:26–27.

ite king, and who sends his people back across the Red Sea to amass wealth from Egypt contrary to Dtr law. Most of the statements in this passage would be understood as praise of Solomon if read apart from their present literary framework, suggesting that laudatory traditions concerning Solomon have been reworked into a context that presents Solomon as failing to meet the Dtr ideal. Such interests are represented in the Josianic DtrH, which emphasizes the celebration of Passover with its focus on the exodus from Egypt as a foundational event in Israelite identity.

1 Kings 10:1–29 Solomon's Association with the Queen of Sheba

10:1 And the Queen of Sheba heard Solomon's reputation for the name of YHWH, and she came to test him with riddles. 2 And she came to Jerusalem with a very great retinue: camels bearing spices, a vast quantity of gold, and precious stones. And she came to Solomon, and she said to him all that was on her mind. 3 And Solomon told her all that she wanted to know—there was not one thing hidden to the king that he did not tell her. 4 And the Queen of Sheba saw all the wisdom of Solomon, the house that he built, 5 the food of his table, the seating of his servants, the standing of his ministers[a] and their attire, his cupbearers, and his whole burnt offering, and she was left breathless. 6 And she said to the king, "The report that I heard in my land was true concerning your words and your wisdom! 7 I did not believe the reports until I came so that I could see for myself, and behold, the half of it was not told to me! You have even more wisdom and goodness than the report that I heard! 8 Happy are your men; happy are your servants who stand before you always, hearing your wisdom! 9 May YHWH your G-d who chooses you be blessed, to place you on the throne of Israel. Because YHWH loves Israel forever, He appoints you king to do justice and righteousness!" 10 And she gave to the king one hundred twenty talents of gold, very many spices, and precious stones. And there has not come since such a quantity of spice, which the Queen of Sheba gave to King Solomon. 11 And also the ships of Hiram, which carried gold from Ophir, brought from Ophir a great quantity of almug wood and precious stones. 12 And the king used almug wood as decoration for the house of YHWH and the house of the king, and for harps and lyres for the singers, and almug wood has never again come like this, nor has it been seen until this day. 13 And Solomon gave to the Queen of Sheba all her desire that she asked, besides that which he gave her of King Solomon's own accord, and she turned and went back to her own land, she and her servants.

14 And the weight of gold that came to Solomon in one year was six hundred sixty-six talents of gold, 15 besides what came from the caravaneers,

from the trade of the merchants, the kings of Arabia, and the governors of the land. 16 And Solomon made two hundred shields of beaten gold with six hundred shekels of gold on each shield, 17 and six hundred bucklers of beaten gold with three minas of gold on each buckler, and the king placed them in the house of the forest of Lebanon.

18 And Solomon made a great throne of ivory, and he overlaid it with refined gold. 19 There were six steps to the throne, and the top of the throne was rounded behind him, and there were arms on either side of the seat, and two lions were standing beside the arms, 20 and twelve lions were standing there by each of the six steps. Such was not done for any other kingdom.

21 And all the drinking vessels of King Solomon were gold, and all the vessels of the house of forest of Lebanon were fine gold. There was no silver. It was not reckoned for anything in the days of Solomon. 22 For the king had a ship of Tarshish at sea with the ship of Hiram. Once every three years the ship of Tarshish came bearing gold and silver, [b]elephants and monkeys and peacocks.[b]

23 And King Solomon was greater than all the kings of the land in wealth and wisdom. 24 And all the land was seeking the face of Solomon to hear his wisdom which G-d placed in his heart. 25 And they were each bringing his gift, vessels of silver and vessels of gold, robes, weapons, spices, horses and mules, an annual amount each year.

26 And Solomon assembled chariots and horses, and he placed them in the chariot cities and with the king in Jerusalem.[c]

27 And the king made silver in Jerusalem as plentiful as stones, and cedar as sycamore which is so numerous in the Shephelah. 28 And Solomon exported horses from Egypt, and traders of the king from Que would buy horses from Que for a price. 29 And a chariot from Egypt would sell for six hundred shekels of silver, and a horse for one hundred fifty shekels, and so it was for all the kings of the Hittites and the kings of Aram who export by their own hand.[d]

a. Ketiv, *měšārtô*, "his minister": read with Qere, *měšārtāyw*, "his ministers."
b–b. Cf. LXX, which refers to the types of building stones brought by the ships together with a modified version of 1 Kgs 9:15, 17b–22.
c. LXX adds a version of 1 Kgs 5:1, which relates the extent of Solomon's rule from the Euphrates to Philistia and Egypt.
d. MT, *běyādām*, "by their hand"; cf. LXX, *kata thalassan*, "by sea," presupposes Hebrew, *běyam.*

The initial noun clause, "and the Queen of Sheba heard the report of Solomon . . . ," demarcates the beginning of the new unit in 1 Kgs 10:1–29. The emphasis on the queen of Sheba marks a shift from a focus on Solomon's trade relations per se to his passion for foreign women, which ultimately prompts his apostasy and his punishment by YHWH. By emphasizing his trade with the queen of Sheba, located along the Red Sea, the narrative critiques Solomon by portraying him as a monarch who leads his people back across the Red Sea (cf. 1 Kgs 9:26) so that he might trade horses and chariots with Egypt and Que, multiply gold for himself, and engage in relations with foreign women, contrary to Dtr teachings (see Deut 17:14–20).

This unit contains no explicit critique of Solomon; the critique is realized by means of the larger DtrH literary context in 1 Kgs 9 and 11. The account of the visit of the queen and the accounts of Solomon's wisdom, wealth, and trade relations were originally written to laud Solomon.[143] Such an effort serves well the Hezekian DtrH, which portrayed Solomon as the ideal monarch of all Israel and model for Hezekiah's rule. The redactional reworking and critique of Solomon serves the interests of the Josianic DtrH, which portrayed Solomon as an errant monarch whose misdeeds were set right by Josiah. The exilic DtrH treats Solomon as a link in a long chain of miscreants that ultimately brought down the Israelite and Judean kingdoms.

[1–13] Interpreters have been unable to establish definitively the queen's identity or the location of her kingdom. Past scholarship identified Sheba with Ethiopia, based in part on the tradition that the Ethiopian ruling dynasty, which ended with the overthrow of Haile Selassie in 1974, was descended from King Menelik, the son of Solomon and the queen of Sheba.[144] Supporters of an Ethiopian identification point to Egyptian traditions concerning trade with the kingdom of Punt, located along the Red Sea in modern Eritrea, from 2500 B.C.E. through 1170 B.C.E., particularly during the rule of Queen Hapshetsut (ca. 1490–1469 B.C.E.), whose funerary temple at Dei el-Bahri includes a portrayal of the queen of Punt.[145] Many prefer identification of Sheba with the south Arabian

143. Cf. Wächli, *Der weise König Salomo*, 92–102.
144. See Josephus, *Ant.* 8.6.5–6, who refers to her as "the Queen of Egypt and Ethiopia" and the Ethiopian narrative Kebra Nagast, "Glory of the Kings," which presents the traditional account of the origins of the Ethiopian dynasty (E. A. Budge, *The Queen of Sheba and Her Only Son Menyelek, Also Known As Kebra Nagast [The Glory of the Kings]* [Cambridge: Cambridge University Press, 1922]). See also Edward Ullendorff, *Ethiopia and the Bible: The Schweich Lectures 1967* (London: Oxford University Press, 1968), 131–45; Ullendorff, "The Queen of Sheba in Ethiopian Tradition," in *Solomon and Sheba* (ed. J. Pritchard; London: Paidon, 1974), 104–14. For discussion of the Jewish, Muslim, and Christian traditions concerning the queen, see Jacob Lassner, *Demonizing the Queen of Sheba: Boundaries of Gender and Culture in Postbiblical Judaism and Medieval Islam* (Chicago and London: University of Chicago, 1993); Lou H. Silberman, "The Queen of Sheba in Jewish Tradition," in *Solomon and Sheba*, 65–84; W. Montgomery Watt, "The Queen of Sheba in Islamic Tradition," in *Solomon and Sheba*, 85–103; and Paul F. Watson, "The Queen of Sheba in Christian Tradition," in *Solomon and Sheba*, 115–45.
145. K. A. Kitchen, "Egypt and East Africa," in *The Age of Solomon: Scholarship at the Turn of the Millennium* (ed. L. Handy; Leiden: Brill, 1997), 106–25; cf. Gus van Beek, "The Land of Sheba," in *Solomon and Sheba*, 40–63; Amélie Kuhrt, *The Ancient Near East*, 191–93.

kingdom of Saba, located along the coast of the Red Sea south of Medina into modern Yemen.[146] Excavations at Sabean sites indicate a well-developed civilization from the eleventh–tenth centuries B.C.E. through the third century C.E. Saba was especially well known for its trade in spices, frankincense, and myrrh, and for its wealth in gold. Assyrian texts from the eighth and seventh centuries make frequent mention of queens from Arabia.[147]

The initial statement of the narrative clearly magnifies Solomon's reputation, since the queen would hear about Solomon from a location considered to lie at the ends of the earth in ancient Israelite/Judean perspective. Her purpose, to test him with riddles or hard questions, is a typical means by which wisdom might be expressed or assessed in the ancient world. Such interchanges are part of the process by which the two monarchs would define their relationship.

The portrayal of the queen's retinue in v. 2 magnifies Solomon's reputation and reflects the type of camel caravans employed by Arab traders in the ancient Near East during the Iron Age. The notice that the queen told Solomon all that was on her mind likely refers to trade relations, although later tradition reads it as an expression of love. The queen's observations in vv. 3–5 of Solomon's wisdom and power contribute to the laudatory portrayal of Solomon. Solomon's wisdom is linked to the construction of the temple, which is conceived as the holy center of creation in Judean thought. Her observations of Solomon's table, the seating and placement of his servants, and so on, all attest to his power. Such concerns are typical of wisdom literature, which frequently focuses on the proper means to conduct oneself before the king or other superiors (e.g., Prov 23:1–2; 25:1–7). The queen's statements to Solomon in vv. 6–9 likewise magnify the king and YHWH, who stands behind him. The first reiterates Solomon's worldwide renown; the second adds superlative; and the third employs the beatitude, a typical wisdom formulation, "happy are . . . ," associated with blessings or praise (Long 119–20). Her concluding blessing of YHWH for placing Solomon on the throne lauds Solomon as a king whose greatness is recognized to the very ends of the known world.

Verses 10–13 turn to trade relations, the primary purpose of the queen's visit. The queen's gifts to Solomon include a standard list of items that one would expect from trade with Saba during the Iron Age. The amount of gold corresponds precisely to the amount of gold that Hiram gave to Solomon after expressing his disdain for the twenty cities ceded him in 1 Kgs 9:10–14. The especially large quantities of gold, spices, and precious stones aid in portraying Solomon's reign as an ideal period in Israel's history. Verses 11–12 note imports

146. Kitchen, "Sheba and Arabia," in *Age of Solomon c. 3000–330 BC* (London and New York: Routledge, 1995), 126–53; van Beek, "The Land of Sheba."

147. *ANET* 283, 286; Nabia Abbot, "Pre-Islamic Arab Queens," *AJSL* 58 (1941): 1–22; Israel Ephal, *The Ancient Arabs* (Jerusalem: Magnes, 1984), passim.

brought to Israel by Hiram's fleet, which ties Solomon's relationship with the queen to his overall relationship with Hiram. Such an association suggests that Hiram's payment of 120 talents of gold was an investment in the partnership with Solomon that would realize greater rewards when trade with the south commenced. Almug wood is a rare import item. Scholars are not certain of its identity, although most suggest it is a form of red sandalwood (see *HALOT* 57–58; Mulder 520–21). Finally, v. 13 indicates that Solomon gave to the queen all that she desired. The noun, *ḥepeṣ*, "desire," does not always convey sexual desire, but it prompts an extensive tradition that Solomon and the queen engaged in sexual relations that produced a son, Menelik, founder of the Ethiopian dynasty.

[14–29] This subunit emphasizes Solomon's immense wealth. The quantity of gold received by Solomon, 666 talents, approximates the gold received from Hiram (120 talents, 1 Kgs 9:14), the ships from Ophir (420 talents, 1 Kgs 9:28), and the queen of Sheba (1 Kgs 10:10)—660 talents total.

Verses 16–17 describe the gold shields manufactured for ceremonial use in the royal court.[148] The first is the *ṣînâ*, a relatively large shield that covers most of a man's trunk. The exact weight of the six hundred shekels of gold is uncertain, although it approximates thirteen and one-third pounds. The smaller shield is the *māgēn*, "buckler," which weighs some three and one-third pounds. Verses 18–20 describe Solomon's throne. The use of ivory (from Africa or India) and gold (from Ophir) indicates materials acquired by Solomon's Red Sea trading fleet.[149] The portrayal of Solomon's throne is analogous with Phoenician and Egyptian models from the late Bronze and early Iron Ages. The tenth-century sarcophagus of King Ahiram (Hiram) of Byblos portrays him seated on a throne flanked by winged lions with human heads, arms, and a rounded headrest on the back (*ANEP* 456, 458; cf. the twelfth-century throne of Rameses III).

Verses 21–25 summarize Solomon's great wealth, power, wisdom, and prestige resulting from his trade relations. "Ships of Tarshish" indicates seagoing ships, and may be based on a reference to the Phoenician trading colony at Tartessos in southwestern Spain; the Greek term, *tarsos*, "oar"; or other explanations.[150] The translations of *šenhabbîm*, "tusked elephants," *qōpîm*, "monkeys," and *tukkîyîm*, "peacocks," are uncertain, but they suggest trade with Africa or India.[151] Verse 24 lauds Solomon as the greatest monarch in the world. The

148. Alan Millard, "Solomon's Shields," *Scripture and Other Artifacts: Essays on Bible and Archaeology in Honor of Philip J. King* (ed. M. D. Coogan et al.; Louisville, Ky.: Westminster John Knox, 1994), 286–95.

149. Philip J. King, *Amos, Hosea, Micah: An Archaeological Commentary* (Philadelphia: Westminster, 1988), 139–49; F. Caniani and G. Pettinato, "Salomos Thron. Philologische und archäologische Erwägungen," *ZDPV* 8 (1965): 88–108.

150. D. W. Baker, "Tarshish (Place)," *ABD* 6:331–33.

151. See, respectively, *HALOT* 1602, 1089, and 1731.

reference to gifts, *minḥâ,* in v. 25 refers to an offering at the temple (Gen 4:3; Num 16:15; 1 Sam 2:17) or to tribute from a vassal to a suzerain (Judg 3:15; 2 Sam 8:2; 2 Kgs 17:3).

Verses 26–29, which relate Solomon's trade in horses and chariots, appear in vv. 21–25 in the LXX. Egypt was well known for the production of chariots. Que, located in the Cilician plain, south of the Taurus Mountains in Asia Minor, is an ideal place for breeding horses.[152] Although these verses emphasize his wisdom, shrewdness, and wealth, they also point to the fact that Solomon is engaged in trade with Egypt, which is strictly forbidden to the Israelite king in Deut 17:14–20. Placement of this notice deliberately raises questions about the king immediately prior to the account in 1 Kgs 11 of his love of foreign women and his apostasy.

1 Kings 11:1–25 Solomon's Apostasy

11:1 [a]And King Solomon loved many foreign women, including the daughter of Pharaoh, Moabites, Ammonites,[b] Edomites, Sidonians, Hittites,[c] 2 from the nations that YHWH said to the people of Israel, "You shall not marry them, and they shall not marry you, lest they turn your heart after their gods." To them, Solomon clung for love. 3 And he had seven hundred royal wives and three hundred concubines, and his wives turned his heart.[a] 4 And in Solomon's old age his wives turned his heart after other gods, and so his heart was not fully dedicated to YHWH, his G-d, like the heart of David his father. 5 [d]And Solomon followed Ashtoret, god of the Sidonians, and Milcom, the abomination of the Ammonites.[d] 6 And Solomon did wrong in the eyes of YHWH, and he did not fulfill his obligations to YHWH like David his father. 7 [d]Then Solomon built a high place to Chemosh, the abomination of Moab, on the mountain before Jerusalem and to Molek,[e] the abomination of the sons of Ammon. 8 And so he did for all his foreign wives who were burning incense and offering sacrifices to their gods.[e] 9 And YHWH became incensed against Solomon because he turned his heart from YHWH, the G-d of Israel, who appeared to him two times. 10 And He commanded him concerning this matter not to follow other gods, but he did not observe what YHWH commanded.

11 And YHWH said to Solomon, "Because this is what you have done, that you have not observed my covenant and my statutes which I commanded you, I will indeed tear the kingdom from you, and I will give it

152. Yutaka Ikeda, "Solomon's Trade in Horses and Chariots in Its International Setting," *Studies in the Period of David and Solomon and Other Essays* (ed. T. Ishida; Winona Lake, Ind.: Eisenbrauns, 1982), 215–38.

to your servant. 12 But I will not do it in your days for the sake of David your father; I will tear it from the hand of your son. 13 Only I will not tear away all the kingdom; one tribe I will give your son for the sake of David My servant and for the sake of Jerusalem, which I have chosen.

14 [f]And YHWH raised an adversary against Solomon, Hadad the Edomite from the royal family in Edom.[f] 15 When David took control of Edom, at the time that Joab went up to bury the dead bodies when he killed every male in Edom, 16 for six months Joab and all Israel remained there until he cut off every male in Edom. 17 And Adad[g] fled, he and his Edomite men from the servants of his father with him, to go to Egypt. And Hadad was a small boy. 18 And they arose from Midian, and came to Paran, and took men with them from Paran, and came to Egypt, to Pharaoh, King of Egypt, and he gave him a house, and authorized food for him, and gave him much land. 19 And Hadad found much favor in the eyes of Pharaoh, and he gave him a wife, the sister of his own wife, the sister of Tahpenhes the Queen. 20 And the sister of Tahpenhes bore to him Genubat his son, and Tahpenhes weaned him within the house of Pharaoh, and Genubat was in the house of Pharaoh among the sons of Pharaoh. 21 And Hadad heard in Egypt that David slept with his fathers and that Joab, the commander of the army, was dead, and Hadad said to Pharaoh, "Send me, and I will go to my land." 22 And Pharaoh said to him, "For what do you lack with me that, behold, you wish to return to your land?" And said, "No, but you should send me."

23 [h]And G-d raised an adversary for him, Rezon ben Elyada, who fled from Hadadezer, King of Zobah, his master. 24 And he gathered men about him, and he became the commander of a raiding band when David was killing them, and they went to Damascus, settled there, and ruled in Damascus. 25 And he was an adversary to Israel all the days of Solomon, and together with the evil that Hadad did, he became odious in Israel and ruled over Aram.[h]

a–a. Cf. LXX, which rearranges vv. 1–3 to emphasize Solomon's many wives followed by his love for foreign women and his apostasy: "And King Solomon was a lover of women. And he had seven hundred royal wives and three hundred concubines. And he took Gentile women, and the daughter of Pharaoh, Moabites, Ammonites, Syrians, and Idumeans, Hittites and Amorites, of the nations concerning which the L-rd said to the sons of Israel, 'You shall not go in to them, and they shall not come in to you, lest they turn away your hearts after their idols.' To them, Solomon clung in love" (see Hrozný, *Abweichungen* 70–72; Vanoni 24–57).

b. LXX adds "Syrians," apparently reading the letter *dalet* in [ʾ]*ădōmîyōt*, "Edomites," as the very similar *resh*, namely, [ʾ]*ărāmîyōt*, "Arameans/Syrians." The reference to "Idumeans" is derived from *ṣēdeniyōt*, "Sidonians," insofar as the term is based upon the root *ṣwd*, "to hunt." The noun *ṣayid*, "hunter/hunting," characterizes Esau, the ancestor of the Edomites, in Gen 25:27, 28; 27:3. With the addition of Amorites, this reading results in a total of seven nations in keeping with Deut 7:1–6, which forbids intermarriage with seven foreign nations.

c. LXX adds "Amorites."

d–d. LXX presents here a reworked version of vv. 7, 5, and 8, which takes up Solomon's building of high places for Chemosh, their king (Milcom), and Astarte (Ashtoreth) on behalf of his wives: "Then Solomon built a high place to Chemosh, the idol of Moab, and to their king the idol of the sons of Ammon, and to Astarte, the abomination of the Sidonians, and thus he acted towards all his Gentile wives who burnt incense and sacrificed to their idols."

e. LXX and Peshitta read names based on Milcom in both instances.

f–f. LXX reworks v. 14 by adding elements from vv. 23–25 to give a complete listing of Solomon's adversaries: "And the L-rd raised an adversary to Solomon, Ader the Idumean, and Esrom son of Eliadae who was in Raamath, and Adadezer king of Souba his master. And men gathered to him and he was head of the conspiracy, and seized Damascus, and they were adversaries to Israel all the days of Solomon. And Ader the Idumean was of the royal seed in Edumea." The reference to Esrom's location in Raamath is based on a reading of Hebrew, *bāraḥ mēʾēt,* "(who) fled from (Hadadezer)," as one word, *běraḥmaʾat,* here construed as *en Raemmath.* LXX v. 14 thereby anticipates later reverses against the Israelite kingdoms, including Ahaz's death in battle against the Arameans at Ramaath Galaad (3 Kgdms/1 Kgs 22) and Edom's revolt against Judah during the reign of Jehoram (4 Kgdms/2 Kgs 8:20–24).

g. Adad is a variant of Hadad.

h–h. Having moved much of vv. 23–25 to v. 14, LXX reads a shortened version of v. 25, "this is the evil which Ader did, and he was a bitter enemy of Israel, and he ruled in the land of Edom."

First Kings 11:1–25 is demarcated initially by the noun clause in v. 1, which introduces the theme of Solomon's love for many foreign women. It comprises two major subunits, vv. 1–6, which relate Solomon's adherence to the gods of his foreign wives, and vv. 7–25, which relate YHWH's establishment of adversaries against Solomon as a punishment for his apostasy. First Kings 11:1–25 points to Solomon's apostasy as the primary cause of the division of Israel.

[1–6] The initial reference to the daughter of Pharaoh appears intrusive because the initial combination of a conjunctive *waw* and the indirect object particle, *wěʾet,* disrupts the syntax by introducing an unnecessary conjunction. Likewise, the identification of the daughter of Pharaoh contrasts markedly with the gentilic identifications of the other women in Solomon's harem. The notice thereby calls attention to other intrusive references to the daughter of Pharaoh in 1 Kgs 3:1; 9:16, 24, and aids in emphasizing the primary role played by Egypt in undermining Israel through the marriage to Solomon; the sanctuary given to Jeroboam ben Nebat (1 Kgs 11:26–40; 12–13); the invasion of Israel and Judah in the aftermath of the northern revolt (1 Kgs 14:25–28); and the killing of King Josiah much later in Judean history (2 Kgs 23:28–30).

The identification of the nationalities of Solomon's wives is particularly note-worthy, especially in relation to the portrayal in v. 2 of his marriages as a viola-tion of the Dtr prohibition against marriage to foreigners. In addition to the awkward reference to the daughter of Pharaoh, v. 1 lists six nations, namely, Egypt, Moabites, Ammonites, Edomites, Sidonians, and Hittites. By contrast, Deut 7:1–6 lists seven Canaanite nations with which Israel was not to marry: Hittites, Girgashites, Amorites, Canaanites, Perizzites, Hivites, and Jebusites. The lists do not coincide, and their differences indicate a secondary redactional effort to apply the Dtr injunction to Solomon rather than an original author's effort to demonstrate Solomon's violation of this command. Indeed, the nations listed for Solomon's wives presuppose David's own alliances and conquests, including the Moabites (2 Sam 8:2), the Ammonites (2 Sam 10:1–19; 12:26–31), the Edomites (2 Sam 8:13–14), the Philistines (2 Sam 5:17–25), and the Arameans (2 Sam 8:3–12; 10:1–19). Sidon is closely associated with Hiram of Tyre, who was allied with David at the outset of his reign in Jerusalem (2 Sam 5:11–12). Insofar as relations between nations were generally cemented by mar-riage between the royal families of each nation, the enumeration of the nation-alities of Solomon's wives and the large numbers of wives and concubines noted in v. 3 portray his power and status as a major ruler among the nations.

The gods worshiped by Solomon include Ashtoreth of the Sidonians, a vari-ation of Astarte, the Ugaritic and Phoenician goddess of war and love.[153] Mil-com, whose name is sometimes vocalized as Molech, "Ruler," or Malkam, "their king" (2 Sam 12:30; Zeph 1:5), is the patron god of Ammon known for child sacrifice (2 Kgs 23:10; Lev 18:21).[154]

[7–25] Although vv. 7–8 appear to continue vv. 1–6, the conjunctive parti-cle, *ʾaz,* "then," disrupts the *waw*-consecutive sequence that governs vv. 1–2, 3–6, and introduces the following *waw*-consecutive sequence in vv. 9–25. By distinguishing vv. 7–8 from the preceding material, the text makes it clear that Solomon's *actions* in building the high places for the gods of his wives are the cause of YHWH's actions against Solomon. Each of the four basic subunits in vv. 7–10, 11–13, 14–22, and 23–25 focuses on YHWH's actions concerning Solomon's apostasy.

Verses 7–10 begin the sequence with an account of YHWH's angry reaction to Solomon's construction of high places for the worship of his wives' foreign gods. Verse 7 notes high places for Chemosh of Moab[155] and Molech of the Ammonites. The high place to Molech is located on the Mount of Olives, the large hill that stands immediately to the east of the city of David across the Kidron Val-ley. Although v. 5 identifies the Ammonite god as Milcom, v. 7 identifies him as

153. See N. Wyatt, "Astarte," *DDD*² 109–14.
154. See E. Puech, "Milcom," *DDD*² 575–76; G. C. Heider, "Molech," *DDD*² 581–85.
155. See H.-P. Müller, "Chemosh," *DDD*² 186–89.

Molech. Second Kings 23:10 and Jer 32:35 indicate that child sacrifice to Molech took place in the Hinnom Valley, situated along the southwestern edges of eighth-century Jerusalem, but 2 Kgs 23:13 notes a shrine dedicated to Milcom on the Mount of Olives.

YHWH's oracle of judgment against Solomon in vv. 11–13 is a classic example of the prophetic judgment speech.[156] The grounds for judgment appear first with the introductory formulation, *ya'an 'ăšer,* "because . . . ," followed by the announcement of punishment. The violation of YHWH's commands is a matter of Dtr theology and therefore plays an important role in justifying the qualification of the divine promise to David. The abrogation of YHWH's unconditional promise to David (2 Sam 7) is a major theological problem in the DtrH—that is, why did YHWH abrogate the divine word to David? The text addresses this problem by supplying two qualifications for Solomon's punishment in vv. 12–13. The first is that the punishment will take place after Solomon's death, which follows from the statements in 2 Sam 7:12–16 that David's sons will suffer if they do wrong, but it creates a theological problem by ensuring that the guilty party does not suffer the consequences for his own actions; YHWH's statements call for punishment of an innocent man. An attempt to address this problem follows in v. 13, which adds that Solomon's son and the house of David will retain one tribe. In this manner, the text can maintain that YHWH will keep the promise of eternal rule to the house of David even as it loses control of the other tribes, but the problem of punishment applied to an innocent man remains. This may be explained only by the DtrH view of collective punishment applied to a corporate entity, whether that might be Israel, which suffers for the sins of Jeroboam and the other northern kings; Judah, which suffers for the sins of Manasseh; or the house of Ahab, that is, Ahab's sons, who suffer for the sins of their father.

Verses 14–22 continue with an account of the activities of Hadad the Edomite, the first adversary raised against Solomon. The Hebrew term *śāṭān,* "opponent, adversary," later becomes the basis for the name Satan (Job 1–2; Zech 3:1; 1 Chr 21:1), but its basic usage is much more mundane (Num 22:22; 1 Sam 29:4; 2 Sam 19:23). Edom is located to the south and east of the Dead Sea, and borders Israel along the Aravah rift that extends south from the Dead Sea to the Gulf of Aqaba. Although biblical tradition maintains that Edom is descended from Jacob's brother Esau, there is little evidence of settlement in Edom until ninth–eighth centuries B.C.E.[157] Hadad the Edomite is unknown, although he is identified as a member of the Edomite royal line (cf. Gen 36:31–43, which includes two Edomite kings named Hadad).

---

156. See Sweeney, *Isaiah 1–39,* 533–34; Claus Westermann, *Basic Forms of Prophetic Speech* (Cambridge: Lutterworth; Louisville, Ky.: Westminster/John Knox, 1991) 129–89; Klaus Koch, *The Growth of the Biblical Tradition* (New York: Charles Scribner's, 1969), 210–13.

157. J. R. Bartlett and B. MacDonald, "Edom; Archaeology of Edom," *ABD* 2:287–301.

Although little is known about tenth-century Edom, 2 Sam 8:13–14 reports David's conquest and slaughter of Edomites in the Valley of Salt. This is particularly important because the present narrative links Hadad's flight to Egypt to this event. Solomon's problems with Hadad and Edom are actually rooted in David's earlier actions. Nevertheless, the theological dimensions of this narrative must be considered, especially since it employs motifs from the Exodus tradition to portray Hadad as a figure who resembles Moses. Solomon plays the role of Pharaoh in the exodus tradition. Thus, Hadad flees to Egypt on account of Joab's slaughter of Edomite males (cf. Exod 1:15–2:10). At the time of his flight, Hadad was a small boy, much as Moses was an infant when set adrift by his mother. Moses also fled Pharaoh's court by way of the Sinai wilderness after killing an Egyptian taskmaster (Exod 2:11–15). Hadad escapes to Midian and Paran, sites of Israel's wilderness encampment (Num 10:11–12), before going on to Egypt.

Once Hadad is in Egypt, the narrative adopts motifs from the Joseph story. Hadad found favor in the eyes of Pharaoh in a manner analogous to Joseph (Gen 41:37–45). Hadad's marriage to Pharaoh's sister recalls Joseph's marriage to Asenath, the daughter of Potiphera. The name of Pharaoh's wife, Tahpenhes, is unknown, although it represents an Egyptian title, *t.hmt.nsw,* "the wife of the king" (Jones 239). The name of the son born to them, Genubat, may be based on an Egyptian name, but its present form is derived from the root *gnb,* "to steal," which suggests derision. Like Joseph's sons, Hadad's son is half-Egyptian.

The use of motifs from the Exodus and Joseph traditions makes a point about Hadad and Solomon—that is, Hadad appears as a second Moses and Solomon appears as Pharaoh in a reversal of roles that raises critical questions about Solomon and his rule.

Verses 23–25 present a brief account of G-d's raising Rezon ben Elyada of Aram as an opponent to Solomon. Rezon is otherwise unknown, although the root, *rzn,* "to be weighty, judicious," may reflect a royal title (see Judg 5:3; Hab 1:10; Ps 2:2; Prov 14:28).

1 Kings 11:26–40 The Rise of Jeroboam ben Nebat

11:26 And Jeroboam ben Nebat, an Ephraimite from Zaredah ªwhose mother's name was Zeruah, a widow woman,ª a servant to Solomon, rebelled against the king.

27 And this is the cause of his rebellion against the king. Solomon built the Millo. He enclosed the breach of the City of David his father. **28** And the man Jeroboam was a powerful warrior. And Solomon saw that the boy carried out his work, and he appointed him over all the forced labor of the house of Joseph.

29 And at that time Jeroboam went out from Jerusalem, and Ahijah the Shilonite, the prophet, found him on the road wearing a new tunic, and the two of them were alone in the field. 30 And Ahijah grabbed the new tunic which was on him, and tore it into twelve pieces. 31 And he said to Jeroboam, "Take for yourself ten pieces, for thus says YHWH, the G-d of Israel, 'Behold, I am tearing the kingdom from the hand of Solomon, and I will give it to you, ten pieces. 32 And the one tribe will be for him for the sake of my servant David and for the sake of Jerusalem, the city which I have chosen from all the tribes of Israel. 33 Because they abandoned me, and bowed down to Ashtoreth, the god of the Sidonians, and Chemosh, the god of Moab, and to Milcom, the god of the sons of Ammon, and they did not walk in My way to do what is right in My eyes, and My statutes and My laws like David his father. 34 But I will not take the whole kingdom from his hand, ᵇfor I will appoint him ruler all the days of his lifeᵇ for the sake of David, My servant, whom I have chosen, who observed My commands and My statutes. 35 And I will take the kingdom from the hand of his son, and I will give it to you, ten tribes. 36 And to his son I will give one tribe in order that there will be a dominionᶜ for David, My servant, all the days before Me in Jerusalem, the city which I chose for Myself to place My name. 37 And you I will take, and you shall rule over all that you desire, and you shall be king over Israel. 38 And if you observe all that I command you, walk in My way, and do what is right in My eyes to observe My statutes and My commands just as David My servant did, then I will be with you, and I will build for you a secure house just as I built for David, and I will give Israel to you. 39 And I will afflict the line of David because of this, but not for all days."

40 And Solomon sought to kill Jeroboam, and Jeroboam arose and fled to Egypt, to Shishaq, King of Egypt, and he was in Egypt until the death of Solomon.

a–a. LXX omits the mother's name, and reads simply, "the son of a widow woman."
b–b. Cf. LXX, "for I will certainly oppress him all the days of his life," reading *nāśîʾ ʾăśîtennû,* "(a) ruler I will appoint him," as *nāśôʾ ʾaśśitennû,* "I will surely oppress him." The reading is influenced by v. 39, which is otherwise lacking in LXX. Cf. the similar phrase in Hos 1:6.
c. Hebrew, *nîr* is frequently read as *nēr,* "lamp," and taken as a metaphorical reference to the performance of the Davidic dynasty; cf. LXX, *thesis,* "a position"; Peshitta, *šrgʾ,* "lamp"; Targum Jonathan, *bĕdîl lĕqāmāʾ malkô,* "in order to establish his kingdom"; Vulgate, *lucerna,* "lamp." The Semitic term *nîr,* "yoke," refers metaphorically to "dominion."[158]

158. Paul Hanson, "The Song of Heshbon and David's *NîR," HTR* 61 (1968): 297–320; cf. Ehud Ben Zvi, "Once the Lamp Has been Kindled . . . A Reconsideration of MT Nîr in 1 Kgs 11:36; 15:4; 2 Kgs 8:19 and 2 Chr 21:7," *Australian Biblical Review* 39 (1991): 19–26.

First Kings 11:26–40 is distinguished from the preceding material by its initial noun clause, which identifies Jeroboam ben Nebat. It highlights Jeroboam as a principal character—and later monarch of Israel—within the overall Kings narrative even though it includes his narrative as part of the account of Solomon's reign. Such an interrelationship emphasizes Solomon's responsibility for enabling Jeroboam to ascend the throne of northern Israel. First Kings 11:26–40 presents Ahijah's oracle justifying Jeroboam's kingship as an act of YHWH, and it defends YHWH's integrity by demonstrating that such an act does not entail YHWH's abrogation of the previous promise to David that his sons would rule after him forever (2 Sam 7).

Narrative tension emerges, however, since YHWH's promise presupposes divine support for the soon-to-be-crowned king, but his subsequent apostasy earns him the harshest condemnation in the DtrH as the monarch who set in motion the pattern of evil behavior on the part of all northern kings. Such apostasy ultimately caused the destruction of northern Israel according to the DtrH theological schema (see esp. 2 Kgs 17).[159] This narrative represents an early Israelite tradition concerning YHWH's dynastic promise to Jeroboam that has been reworked for placement within the larger DtrH. The tension in the portrayal of the dynastic promise addresses the question of theodicy by blaming Solomon's violation of YHWH's commands for the decision to qualify the eternal Davidic promise and make Jeroboam king.

Verse 26 identifies Jeroboam as an Ephraimite, which justifies his assumption of kingship as a member of the principal tribe that dominated northern Israel. His home city of Zeredah is identified with 'Ain Seriday near Deir Ghassaneh, about fifteen miles southwest of Shechem.[160] The identification of his widowed mother as Zeruah represents Judean polemic, insofar as her name, *ṣĕrûʿâ*, means "leprous." Her name was likely Zeruiah (*zĕrûyâ*), "fruitful" (BDB 863). Jeroboam is identified as an officer of Solomon, who revolted against his master.

Verse 27 serves as a second introductory statement, which explains the circumstances of Jeroboam's revolt. It notes the building of the Millo and repair of the wall of the city as stimuli for Jeroboam's revolt. Such notices recall 1 Kgs 9:16, 24, which mention both Solomon's imposition of forced labor and his marriage to the daughter of Pharaoh, which highlights the portrayal of Solomon as a monarch like Pharaoh. The motif continues in v. 28, which notes that Jeroboam is placed in charge of the forced labor of the house of Joseph.

[28–40] This subunit builds on the previous material by noting that Jeroboam's capabilities came to the attention of the king, which in turn led to his

---

159. See esp. Frank M. Cross Jr., "The Themes of the Books of Kings and the Structure of the Deuteronomistic History," in *Canaanite Myth and Hebrew Epic* (Cambridge: Harvard University Press, 1973), 278–85.

160. H. O. Thompson, "Zaredah," *ABD* 6:1082.

appointment as taskmaster over Joseph. The narrative weaves in references to the Joseph tradition as well, insofar as Joseph brought Israel down to Egypt in the first place, thereby setting the stage for Egyptian slavery. It presages Jeroboam's own flight to Egypt and the resulting consequences.

The account of Ahijah's oracle to Jeroboam in vv. 29–39 is formulated as a typical prophetic legend.[161] There are no witnesses to the event in the open country. Ahijah functions like Nathan in 2 Sam 7, insofar as he delivers the dynastic promise to Jeroboam, but he also delivers the judgment oracle against the house of Jeroboam in 1 Kgs 14:1–18. Ahijah's designation as a Shilonite ties him to the city of Shiloh, which had been the site of Israel's earlier temple where the ark was housed under the control of the priestly house of Eli. Shiloh is the sanctuary of Samuel, who anointed both Saul and David (1 Sam 1–3; 7; 8–12; 16). Ahijah therefore appears as a figure like Samuel; the symbolic action of the torn garment recalls the symbolism employed to express Samuel's tearing the kingdom away from Saul (1 Sam 15:27–28).

Ahijah's oracle employs a typical prophetic symbolic action in which a physical act both symbolizes and effectuates the prophet's oracular statements (cf. 1 Kgs 22; Isa 27–28).[162] Ahijah also employs an expanded version of the typical prophetic messenger formula, *kōh ʾāmar yhwh ʾlhy yiśrāʾēl*, "thus says YHWH, the G-d of Israel,"[163] to introduce the balance of his speech as a presentation of YHWH's own words. There is a discrepancy in the number of pieces since the total of eleven does not account for all twelve tribes. The twelfth tribe would likely be the priestly tribe of Levi, which holds no land of its own. The Chronicler accounts for the difference by noting that the house of David retains Benjamin as well. The grounds for the punishment are specified in v. 33 with the typical formulation, "because (*yaʿan kî*) they abandoned me . . ." Ironically, the plural formulation indicates the DtrH view that all Israel is responsible, even though Solomon committed the apostasy.

Verses 34–36 elaborate on the announcement of punishment by carefully noting that YHWH will tear the entire kingdom from Solomon because of his appointment as *nāśîʾ* for "all the days of his life," the earlier promise to David, and David's observance of YHWH's commands. Whereas 2 Sam 7 promises David eternal rule over *Israel*, the present statement promises rule in *Jerusalem*. Verses 37–39 emphasize YHWH's expectations of Jeroboam as the condition for the promise of "a sure house (*bayit neʾĕmān*) just as I built for David," which in turn reflects the language of 2 Sam 7:16, "and your house shall be secure (*wĕneʾman bêtkā*) . . . forever." The qualification that YHWH's affliction will not

161. Alexander Rofé, *The Prophetical Stories* (Jerusalem: Magnes, 1988), 13–22.

162. W. D. Stacey, *Prophetic Drama in the Old Testament* (London: Epworth, 1990), esp. 79–82; Georg Fohrer, *Die symbolischen Handlungen der Propheten* (Zurich: Zwingli, 1968).

163. Sweeney, *Isaiah 1–39*, 546; Westermann, *Basic Forms*, 98–115.

last forever keeps to the terms of the Davidic promise (2 Sam 7:14), and points to the possibility that the house of David will some day regain control of the north. Verse 40 notes that Solomon sought to kill Jeroboam, forcing him to flee to Egypt. This statement reiterates the reversal of the exodus and Joseph motifs. Pharaoh Shishak is identified as Sheshonq 1, the founder of the twenty-second Libyan dynasty (940–919 B.C.E.).[164] First Kings 14:25–28 notes that Shishak invaded Israel following the death of Solomon, which suggests an Egyptian interest in encouraging revolt in order to divide and conquer the Solomonic kingdom.

1 Kings 11:41–14:20 Solomon's Death and the Consequences of His Reign: The Establishment of Northern Israel

First Kings 11:41–14:20 presents an account of the establishment of the northern kingdom of Israel as a consequence of Solomon's apostasy following his death. This unit begins with the concluding regnal formula in 1 Kgs 11:41–43, which employs the standard form to report the great monarch's death, burial, and successor, but this form serves as an introduction to the following account of the revolt of the northern tribes and the establishment of the northern kingdom of Israel under the rule of Jeroboam ben Nebat in 1 Kgs 12:1–14:20. A combination of thematic and syntactical features justifies this demarcation.

The rise of Jeroboam and the concluding years of Solomon are closely intertwined so that the revolt of the northern tribes appears as a direct consequence of Solomon's apostasy and abuse of his royal office. First Kings 11:26–40 identifies Jeroboam as an adversary of Solomon's adversaries, who began his career as an officer of the king but revolted as a result of Solomon's imposition of forced labor upon his people. The account of Jeroboam's reign in 1 Kgs 12:1–14:19 is tied syntactically to Solomon's regnal résumé by a *waw*-consecutive verbal formulation in 1 Kgs 12:1, *wayyēlek rĕhabʿām šĕkem,* "and Rehoboam went to Shechem." This stands in striking contrast to the accounts of nearly all subsequent monarchs in the DtrH, which focus directly upon the king in question with a noun clause that states his age or the year in which his reign began (n.b., the account of Jehu's reign in 2 Kgs 9–10 is an exception). By focusing initially on Rehoboam ben Solomon, who has his own discrete regnal account in 1 Kgs 14:21–31, the narrative recounts the failure of Rehoboam to obtain the Israelite throne as a prelude to the return and accession of Jeroboam. But by tying the account of Jeroboam's reign so closely to that of Solomon, the narrative also signals its interest in the question of the continuity of the Davidic line (cf. 1 Kgs 9:1–9; see also 1 Kgs 8:22–26; 3:10–14; 2:4).

---

164. See Siegfried Horn, "Who Was Solomon's Egyptian Father-in-Law?" *BR* 12 (1967): 3–17, who identifies Siamon as Solomon's father-in-law and Sheshonq as the usurper of the throne from Siamon's successor, Psusennes II.

Insofar as Jeroboam is ultimately condemned, it also addresses the related question of the continuity of Israel in the land (see 1 Kgs 9:1–9; cf. 8:27–53) and dominates the balance of the DtrH (see the subsequent notices concerning the sins of Jeroboam for the Israelite kings; cf. 2 Kgs 17; 21–25).[165]

The account of Jeroboam's accession to kingship and his reign begins in 1 Kgs 12:1–33 with an account of the northern tribes' revolt against Rehoboam ben Solomon. The introductory noun clause in 1 Kgs 13:1 signals the beginning of the second major subunit in 1 Kgs 13:1–34 concerning the condemnation of the Beth El altar and Jeroboam by an unnamed man of G-d. The temporal clause in 1 Kgs 14:1 introduces the third subunit in 1 Kgs 14:1–18 concerning Ahijah the Shilonite's condemnation of the house of Jeroboam. The regnal summation for Jeroboam in 1 Kgs 14:19–20 concludes the unit.

1 Kings 11:41–43 Solomon's Death: Regnal Résumé

11:41 And the rest of the chronicles of Solomon and all that he did and his wisdom, are they not written in the book of the chronicles of Solomon? **42** And the days that Solomon ruled in Jerusalem over all Israel were forty years. **43** And Solomon slept with his fathers, and he was buried in the city of David his father,[a] and Rehoboam his son ruled in his place.[a]

a–a. LXX inserts material from 1 Kgs 12:2 before this notice: "and it came to pass when Jeroboam son of Nebat heard, while he was still in Egypt as he fled from before Solomon and lived in Egypt, he directly came to his own city in the land of Sarira in the hill country of Ephraim. And King Solomon slept with his fathers, and Rehoboam his son ruled in his place." The LXX notice thereby points to Jeroboam as the instigator of the revolt, whereas MT notes that he returned to Israel only after the revolt had begun.

A typical form of the regnal résumé (Long 259) concludes the account of Solomon's reign in 1 Kgs 11:41–43. The "book of the chronicles of Solomon" is otherwise unknown, and it is impossible to verify the validity of Solomon's forty-year reign in the absence of attestations from extrabiblical sources. The site of the royal tombs in the city of David has not been firmly established.

1 Kings 12:1–24 The Establishment of the Northern Kingdom of Israel: Israel's Revolt against Rehoboam

12:1 And Rehoboam went to Shechem because all Israel came to Shechem to make him king. **2** [a]And Jeroboam ben Nebat heard—he was still in Egypt where he had fled from King Solomon, and Jeroboam had settled[b]

---

165. Cross, "Themes of the Books of Kings," 78–85.

in Egypt—3 ᶜand they summoned him, and Jeroboam and all the congregation of Israel came,ᵈᵃ and spoke to Rehoboam, saying, 4 "Your father made our yoke hard. But you, now, ease up from the hard service of your father and from the heavy yoke which he placed upon us, and we will serve you." 5 And he said to them, "Go away for three days, and then return to me." And the people went. 6 And King Rehoboam took counsel with the elders who were standing before Solomon his father when he was alive, saying, "How do you advise (me) to answer this people?" 7 And they spokeᵉ to him, saying, "If today you will be a servant to this people, and you serve them, answer them, and say good things to them, then they will be servants to you always." 8 And he abandoned the counsel of the elders who would advise him, and he took counsel with the boys who grew up with him who were standing before him. 9 And he said to them, "What do you advise that we should answer this people, who spoke to me, saying, 'Ease up from the yoke which your father placed upon us!'" 10 And the boys who had grown up with him spoke to him, saying, "Thus you shall speak to this people, who spoke to you saying, 'Your father made our yoke heavy, but you, ease up from us,' thus you shall say to them, 'My little thingieᶠ is thicker than my father's loins! 11 And now, my father imposed on you a heavy yoke, but I will add to your yoke! My father chastised you with whips, but I will chastise you with scorpions!'"

12 And Jeroboam and all the people cameᵍ to Rehoboam on the third day, just as the king had spoken, saying, "Return to me on the third day." 13 And the King answered the people harshly, and he abandoned the counsel of the elders who would advise him. 14 And he spoke with them according to the advice of the boys, saying, "My father made your yoke heavy, but I will add to your yoke! My father chastised you with whips, but I will chastise you with scorpions!" 15 And the King did not listen to the people because ʰYHWH took charge of the actionʰ in order to establish His word which YHWH spoke by the hand of Ahijah the Shilonite to Jeroboam ben Nebat. 16 And all the people of Israel saw that the King did not listen to them, and the people answered the King, saying, "What portion do we have with David? There is no inheritance with ben-Jesse! To your tents, O Israel! Look after your house, David!" And Israel went to its tents. 17 And the people of Israel dwelled in the cities of Judah, and Rehoboam ruled over them. 18 And King Rehoboam sent Adoram who was over the corvée, and all Israel stoned him with stones so that he died. And King Rehoboam hurriedly mounted his chariot to flee to Jerusalem. 19 And Israel rebelled against the house of David to this day.

20 And when all Israel heard that Jeroboam had returned, they summoned him to the assembly and made him king over all Israel. None followed the house of David except for the tribe of Judah.ᶜ

21 ⁱAnd Rehoboam cameʲ to Jerusalem, and he assembled all the house
of Judah and the tribe of Benjamin, one hundred eighty thousand young
men ready for war, to fight with the house of Israel to restore the kingdom to Rehoboam ben Solomon. 22 And the word of G-d came to Shemaiah, the man of G-d, saying, 23 "Say to Rehoboam ben Solomon, king
of Judah, and to all the house of Judah and Benjamin and the rest of the
people, saying, 24 'Thus says YHWH, "Do not go up and do not fight with
your brothers, the people of Israel. Return, each to his house, because on
account of me has this thing happened."'" And they turned back according to the word of YHWH.ⁱᵏ

a–a. Lacking in LXX, although a modified form of this statement appears in 3 Rgns
11:43. LXX notes that Jeroboam returned to Sarira on hearing of Solomon's death, and
thereby places him in Israel prior to Rehoboam's meeting with Israel. By contrast, the
MT places Jeroboam in Egypt at the outset of the meeting (cf. the alternative version in
3 Rgns 12:24–25). 3 Rgns 11:43 accounts for the statement, "and Jeroboam
dwelled/remained (*wayyēšeb*) in Egypt" from v. 2b (see n. b below) and the reading of
2 Chr 10:2, "and Jeroboam returned (*wayyāšāb*) from Egypt." LXX thereby charges that
Jeroboam was an instigator of the revolt since he had already returned to Israel.

b. Hebrew, *wayyēšeb běmiṣrāyim*, "and he stayed in Egypt"; contra. 2 Chr 10:2,
which rereads the consonantal Hebrew text as *wayyāšob mimmiṣrāyim*, "and he returned
from Egypt."

c–c. An alternative version of vv. 3–20 appears in 3 Rgns 12:24p–u.

d. Read with Qere, *wayyābōʾ*, "and he came," instead of Ketiv, *wayyābōʾû*, "and they
came."

e. Read with Qere, *wayědabběrû*, "and they said," rather than Ketiv, *wayědabber*,
"and he said."

f. Hebrew, *qāṭonnî*, literally, "my littleness"; cf. LXX, *hē mikrotēs mou*, "my littleness"; Targum Jonathan, *halšôtî*, "my weakness"; Peshitta, *hysry*, "my little finger"; Vulgate, *minimus digitus meus*, "my little finger." The renditions of the Targum, Peshitta,
and Vulgate are interpretative.

g. Read with Qere, *wayyābōʾ*, "and he came," rather than the defective Ketiv,
wayyābô.

h–h. Hebrew, *kî-hāytâ sibbâ mēʿim yhwh*, lit., "because there was a change from
YHWH"; cf. 2 Chr 10:15, which reads the noun, *něsibbâ*, lit., "a being turned," in place
of *sibbâ*, "a turn."

i–i. An alternative version of vv. 21–24 appears in 3 Rgns 12:24x–z.

j. Read with Qere, *wayyābōʾ*, "and he came," instead of Ketiv, *wayyābōʾû*, "and they
came."

k. LXX adds an alternative account of Jeroboam's revolt against Solomon, his sojourn
in Egypt, his rise to power, the condemnation of his house by Ahijah, and his role in
northern Israel's revolt against Rehoboam in 3 Rgns 12:24a–z (for discussion of the
alternative LXX accounts, see Montgomery and Gehman 251–54; Gooding, "The Septuagint's Rival Versions"; Gooding, "Jeroboam's Rise to Power: A Rejoinder," *JBL* 91

(1972): 529–33; Debus, *Die Sünde Jerobeams*; Gordon, "The Second Septuagint Account of Jeroboam: History or Midrash?"; Trebolle Barrera, *Salomón y Jeroboán*; Ralph W. Klein, "Jeroboam's Rise to Power," *JBL* 89 (1970): 217–18; Klein, "Once More: 'Jeroboam's Rise to Power,'" *JBL* 92 (1973): 582–84; McKenzie, *The Trouble with Kings*, esp. 21–80; Talshir, *The Alternative Story*; Schenker, "Jéroboam et la division du royaume"; Marvin A. Sweeney, "A Reassessment of the Masoretic and Septuagint Versions of the Jeroboam Narratives in 1 Kings/3 Kingdoms 11–14," *JSJ* 38 [2007]: 165–95):

24a And King Solomon sleeps with his fathers and he is buried in the city of David. And Rehoboam his son reigned instead of him in Jerusalem. He was sixteen years old when he became king, and he ruled twelve years in Jerusalem. And the name of his mother was Naamah the daughter of Anan, the son of Naas, the king of Ammon. And he did evil before the L-rd, and he did not walk in the ways of David his father. 24b And there was a man from the hills of Ephraim, a servant of Solomon, and his name was Jeroboam. And the name of his mother was Sarira, a harlot. And Solomon appointed him as head of staff over all the men of the house of Joseph. And he built for Solomon Sarira in the hills of Ephraim, and he had three hundred chariots of horse. He built the citadel with the men of the house of Ephraim. He enclosed the city of David, and he was exalted over the kingdom. 24c And Solomon sought to kill him, and he was afraid, and he escaped to Sausakim, king of Egypt, and he was with him until Solomon died. 24d And Jeroboam heard in Egypt that Solomon had died, and he spoke into the ears of Sausakim, king of Egypt, saying, "Send me away, so that I will go unto my land." And Sausakim said to him, "Ask any request, and I will grant it to you." 24e And Sausakim gave to Jeroboam Ano, the oldest sister of Thekeminas, his own wife, to him as a wife. She was great in the midst of the daughters of the king, and she bore to Jeroboam Abijah his son. 24f And Jeroboam said to Sausakim, "Indeed, send me away, so that I may go." And Jeroboam went out of Egypt, and he came to the land of Sarira which was in the hills of Ephraim. And he gathered there all the tribe of Ephraim, and Jeroboam built there fortifications. 24g And his child was sick with a strong, vehement sickness. And Jeroboam went to inquire concerning the child. And he said to Ano, his wife, "Rise, and go to inquire of G-d concerning the child, if he will live from his sickness." 24h And there was a man in Shiloh, and his name was Ahijah, and he was sixty years old, and the oracle of the L-rd was with him. And Jeroboam said to his wife, "Arise, and take in your hand to the man of G-d loaves of bread and cakes for his children and a bunch of grapes and a jar of honey." 24i And the woman arose, and she took in her hand loaves of bread and two cakes and a bunch of grapes and a jar of honey to Ahijah. And the man was old and his eyes were dim. 24k And she arose from Sarira, and she went, and it came to pass that she came into the city of Ahijah the Shilonite. And Ahijah said to his boy, "Go out, indeed, to meet Ano, the wife of Jeroboam. And you shall say to her, 'Come in, and do not stand, because thus the L-rd has spoken, "I have sent harsh news upon you."'" 24l And Ano came into the man of G-d, and Ahijah said to her, "Why to me have you brought loaves of bread and bunches of grapes and cakes and a jar of honey? Thus says the L-rd, 'Behold, you shall depart from me, and it shall be that when you enter the gate unto Sarira, then your maidens shall come out to meet you and they shall say to you, "The child is dead."' 24m For thus says the L-rd, 'Behold, I will destroy of Jeroboam those who piss on the wall, and the dead of Jeroboam that shall be in the city the dogs shall eat, and those that die in the field the birds of the heaven shall eat, and for the child he shall mourn, "Woe, O L-rd," for a moral fault concerning the L-rd is found in him.'" 24n And the woman left when she heard, and it came to pass when she came to Sarira that the child died, and the crying came out to meet her. 24o And Jeroboam went to Shechem, which was in the hills of Ephraim, and he assembled there all the tribes of Israel. And Rehoboam the son of Solomon went up there. And the word of the L-rd came to Shamaiah the Elamite saying, "Take for yourself a new cloak which has not gone into water, and tear it into twelve pieces, and give to Jeroboam, and you shall say to him, 'Thus says the L-rd, "Take for yourself ten pieces to cover yourself."'" And Jeroboam took. And Shamaiah said, "Thus says the L-rd, 'Concerning the ten tribes of Israel.'" 24p And the people said to Rehoboam the son of Solomon, "Your father made heavy his yoke upon us, and he made heavy the food of his table. And now, if you ease up upon us, then we shall serve you." And Rehoboam spoke to the people, "Yet three days, and I will return to you an answer." 24q And Rehoboam said, "Bring in to me the elders, and I will take counsel with them what I will answer to the people on the third day." And Rehoboam spoke into their ears how the people sent to him. And the elders of the people said, "Thus have the people spoken to you." 24r And Rehoboam rejected their counsel, as it did please before him. And he sent, and he brought in those who grew up with him, and he said to them, "Thus and thus have the people sent to me saying." And those who were brought up with him (said), "Thus you shall speak to this people saying, 'My littleness is thicker than my father's loins. My father whipped you with whips, and I will begin with scorpions!'" 24s And the statement pleased Rehoboam, and he answered the people as those who were brought up with him, that is, the children, counseled him. 24t And all the people said as one man, each to his neighbor, and they cried out together, "There is no portion for us in

David, and no inheritance in the son of David! To your dwellings, O Israel, for this man is not (fit) for a ruler nor leading!" 24u And all the people dispersed out of Shechem, and they departed, each to his dwelling. And Rehoboam strengthened himself, and he went and he mounted upon his chariot, and he went into Jerusalem, and there went behind him all the tribe of Judah and all the tribe of Benjamin. 24x And it came to pass at the beginning of the year that Rehoboam assembled all the men of Judah and Benjamin, and he went up to fight Jeroboam at Shechem. 24y And the word of the L-rd came to Shamaiah, the man of G-d, saying, "Speak to Rehoboam, king of Judah, and to all the house of Judah and Benjamin, and to the remnant of the people, saying, 'Thus says the L-rd, "Do not go up, do not fight against your brothers, the sons of Israel. Return, each to his house, because from me this thing comes." ' " 24z And they listened to the word of the L-rd, and they ceased to go up according to the oracle of the L-rd.

Shifts of scene in the plot sequence determine the basic structure of 1 Kgs 12:1–24.[166] The first major subunit in vv. 1–2 sets the theme for the whole by relating the circumstances of the two major characters: Rehoboam's journey to Shechem to become king of all Israel and Jeroboam's remaining in Egypt on hearing of Rehoboam's journey. The second major subunit in vv. 3–17 relates the circumstances of northern Israel's revolt against Rehoboam. The third major subunit in vv. 18–20 relates Rehoboam's failed attempt to put down the revolt and the crowning of Jeroboam ben Nebat as king by the people of northern Israel. Finally, the fourth subunit in vv. 21–24 relates Rehoboam's return to Jerusalem to gather his forces and the oracle of YHWH from the prophet Shemaiah that prompted Rehoboam and the tribes of Judah and Benjamin to desist from any attempt to force the return of the northern tribes to Davidic rule.

[1–2] Whereas Rehoboam journeyed to Shechem, apparently unaware of any potential challenge to his claims to the throne, Jeroboam remained in Egypt. The narrative emphasizes that Jeroboam played no direct role in fomenting revolt against the house of David and instead points to Rehoboam's own failings as the cause of the revolt. Rehoboam had the opportunity to convince the people of northern Israel to accept him as king. Had he followed the advice of the elders who served his father, the people would have accepted his rule. By following the advice of the young men with whom he grew up, Rehoboam squandered his chance to rule the northern tribes. By contrast, the LXX versions modify vv. 2–3a and shift them to another location in the narrative so that they might portray Jeroboam's return to Israel prior to the revolt. Thus, 3 Rgns 11:43 indicates that

---

166. See esp. Long, *1 Kings,* 131–40; Vanoni, *Literarkritik und Grammatik;* Ina Plein, "Erwägungen zur Überlieferung von 1 Reg 11 26–14 20," *ZAW* 78 (1966): 8–24, who considers the subunit to be 1 Kgs 12:1–19.

Jeroboam returned to his home city of Sarira in the hill country of Ephraim to gather the men of Ephraim and fortify the city immediately after hearing of the death of Solomon. Third Reigns 12:24d–f makes the case clearer by noting that when Jeroboam heard of Solomon's death, he requested that Pharaoh Susakim allow him to return to his home. Susakim granted the request after giving Jeroboam the sister of his own wife in marriage, which then ties Jeroboam to the pharaoh who later invaded Judah in 1 Kgs 12:25–28/3 Rgns 12:25–28.

First Kings 11:43b indicates that Rehoboam had already assumed the throne following the death of Solomon, but he must travel to Shechem to be accepted as king by the northern tribes of Israel. This procedure points to the federated nature of the Davidic monarchy, not as a combination of twelve individual tribes, but as a combination of two major components: the southern tribe of Judah and the ten northern tribes of Israel.[167] When considered in relation to the federated Davidic state, the choice of Shechem as the site where Rehoboam's kingship would be confirmed makes great sense. Ancient Shechem is identified with Tel Balata, located along the southern outskirts of modern Nablus, in the pass between Mount Ebal and Mount Gerizim.[168] The site commands the major north-south and east-west mountain passes and roads through the central hill country of Israel that provide access to the coastal plain, the Jezreel Valley, and the Jordan Valley.

Biblical tradition points to Shechem as an early political center of Israel. Joseph's bones were buried at Shechem (Gen 50:25, 26; Exod 13:19; Josh 24:32). Deuteronomy 27 portrays Israel's ratification of the covenant at the site of Shechem. Joshua 24 portrays Shechem as the site of the renewal of the covenant at the end of Joshua's lifetime. Joshua 20:7 and 1 Chr 6:67 identify it as a city of refuge, and Josh 21:21 identifies it as a Levitical city. Abimelek, the son of the judge Gideon, established Shechem as his capital in his abortive attempt to assert kingship over Israel. The assembly of northern Israel at Shechem to confirm Rehoboam's kingship marks a return to the ancient political center following years of political stability under the reigns of David and Solomon. Such a move signals northern Israel's rising power within the federation. The active role of Ephraim in this council recalls earlier traditions in which Ephraim sought to assert itself over the other northern tribes in the period of the Judges (see Judg 8:1–3; 12:1–6), as well as Sheba ben Bichri's revolt against David among the northern tribes (2 Sam 20:1–22).

[3–17] Jeroboam ben Nebat is present at the Shechem assembly, but he plays a minor role in the revolt. He may have functioned as an instigator of the revolt,

---

167. See esp. Albrecht Alt, "The Formation of the Israelite State in Palestine" in *Essays on Old Testament and Religion* (Garden City, N.Y.: Doubleday, 1967), 223–310; Alt, "The Monarchy in the Kingdoms of Israel and Judah" in *Essays,* 311–35; cf. Marvin A. Sweeney, "The Origins of Kingship in Israel and Japan: A Comparative Analysis," *OPIAC* 33 (1995).

168. For discussion of Shechem, see esp. E. F. Campbell, "Shechem," *NEAEHL* 4:1345–54.

but the present form of the MT indicates little interest in focusing on the character of Jeroboam. The two LXX narratives present differing accounts. Both emphatically state in 3 Rgns 11:43 and 12:24d–f that Jeroboam had returned to his home city of Sarira immediately upon hearing the news of Solomon's death. Third Reigns 12:20, however, states that Jeroboam joined the assembly only after the northern tribes had successfully revolted against Rehoboam and then heard that he had returned from Egypt. Such a notice suggests a distant role as an instigator prior to his flight to Egypt that only resumed upon his return to the assembly. The second account in 3 Rgns 12:24f emphasizes that, prior to the revolt, Jeroboam gathered the people of Ephraim at Sarira and built fortifications there following his return from Egypt. This notice points clearly to Jeroboam as the leader of the revolt.

The narrative identifies the underlying causes for the revolt. A fundamental issue is the unfair treatment of the northern tribes, insofar as Solomon imposed upon them far greater responsibility for the support of the royal court and military establishment (1 Kgs 4:7–19), the labor corvée that built the temple and royal palace complex (1 Kgs 5:26–32), and the ceding of territory to Hiram of Tyre (1 Kgs 9:10–14). Another issue, not explicitly raised in the present narrative but evident in the overall presentation of the DtrH, is the character of the northern tribes, particularly Ephraim. The larger DtrH narrative, particularly Judges, presents the northern tribes as lacking in the qualities of leadership needed within Israel.[169] The juxtaposition of northern Israel's complaints with the glorious portrayal of Solomon's reign implies that the northern tribes did not appreciate the greater good of wisdom, wealth, and power represented by Solomon's reign.

First Kings 12:3–17 points to the flawed character of Rehoboam as a basic factor in Israel's revolt. The narrative makes it clear that the northern Israelites were ready to accept Rehoboam's reign if only he would treat them properly by lightening the heavy load of responsibility that they had borne under Solomon. Although his father's mature advisors prudently counseled him to take such action, his reliance on the "boys" with whom he had grown up prompted him to respond harshly in a manner that speaks more to the character of an immature adolescent rather than to a wise king. Although 2 Kgs 14:21 (see also 3 Rgns 14:21) indicates that Rehoboam began his reign at the age of forty-one, 3 Rgns 12:24a states that he was only sixteen years old.

The narrative begins in vv. 3–5 with an account of the initial stage of the audience between Rehoboam and the people of Israel. The summons of Jeroboam in v. 3a builds upon the earlier statement in v. 2 that Jeroboam remained in Egypt. This notice is missing in LXX 3 Rgns 12:3, which only refers to the

---

169. Marvin A. Sweeney, "Davidic Polemics in the Book of Judges," *VT* 47 (1997): 517–29; Sweeney, *King Josiah*, 110–24.

people of Israel who spoke to King Rehoboam. The MT places him at the assembly but gives him no evident speaking or leadership roles. Although the LXX notes that he had already returned to Israel in 3 Rgns 11:43, 3 Rgns 12:20 indicates that he joined the people of Israel only after they had successfully rebelled against Rehoboam. The question posed to Rehoboam speaks directly to the people's dissatisfaction with the burdens imposed upon them during Solomon's reign. After having served David and Solomon, the northern tribes concluded that the time was now ripe for a shift in power within the federation, especially since Solomon's kingdom was so dependent upon the taxes, manpower, and strategic position of northern Israel.

Verses 6–7 relate Rehoboam's counsel with his father's older advisors. Their statements are revealing insofar as they correctly recognize Rehoboam's weak position. Lacking sufficient power to subdue the northern tribes, Rehoboam will have to convince the northerners that it is in their best interests to serve him. The advice that he present himself as a servant to them would hardly provide a lasting basis for his rule; he would become a very weak ruler, and power within the coalition would clearly shift to the north. Such a response would allow Rehoboam time to consolidate his position, and perhaps to turn key elements of the northern tribes into his supporters.

Verses 8–11 portray Rehoboam as an immature boy, unfit to rule. The narrative emphasizes Rehoboam's immaturity by referring to his comrades as the *yĕlādîm,* "children" or "boys," with whom he had grown up. This label is striking for the comrades of a forty-one-year-old man! They advise that he demonstrate strength rather than accommodation in responding to the demands of the northern tribes. The crude reference to Rehoboam's *qāṭonnî,* literally, "my littleness," which "is thicker than my father's loins," is a reference to his penis. Such a reference highlights the immaturity of Rehoboam's comrades, and could only be understood by the Israelites as a display of contempt. Rehoboam's answer that he will employ "whips" and "scorpions" to subdue Israel displays a certain logic, since he is clearly in a weakened position, and must act to consolidate his power. He might bluff his way into forcing the northern tribes to submit to his rule, but the younger men fail to recognize that the question posed to Rehoboam by the northern tribes reveals the futility of such bravado. The long period of peace during Solomon's reign suggests that the younger men had little practical experience in facing a determined enemy.

The audience between Rehoboam and the northern tribes appears in vv. 12–15. Verse 15 explains the reason for Rehoboam's ill-considered response as divine intervention—that is, YHWH had caused a *sibbâ,* literally "a turning (of events)," so that Rehoboam would follow the advice of his comrades and confirm Ahijah's prophetic word concerning Jeroboam's kingship (1 Kgs 11:26–40). Such a statement is particularly controversial because it indicates divine intervention to ensure the downfall of an otherwise innocent man. Some might understand it as a reference to absolute divine power and freedom, but it points to YHWH as a trickster who works to undermine the human protagonists (cf. 1 Kgs 22). Such a statement raises once again the question of YHWH's fidelity to the covenant with David (see the discussion of 1 Kgs 11:26–40). YHWH's action might be justified in relation to Solomon on account of his apostasy (1 Kgs 11:1–13), but this is a case of the sins of the father visited on the son (cf. Deut 5:9–10; Exod 20:5–6; contra Ezek 18; Jer 31:29–30). Rehoboam has done nothing to justify divine punishment (contra Walsh, *1 Kings* 165).

The anticipated results—that is, the northern tribes reject Rehoboam as king—follow in vv. 16–17. The formulaic statement, "what is our portion in David? There is no inheritance with the son of Jesse!" clearly indicates the northern tribes' view that they have nothing to gain by continuing to accept Davidic rule. The statement, "To your tents, O Israel! Now, look to your (own) house, O David!" indicates the rejection of Davidic rule. Similar formulations appear in the narrative concerning the unsuccessful revolt of the Benjaminite Sheba against David in 2 Sam 20:1. Verse 17 describes the situation that resulted from the revolt: Rehoboam was able to rule only the people of Israel who were dwelling in the cities of Judah. The use of the participle *hayyōšbîm,* "those who were dwelling," suggests a continuing situation that persisted through the time of the writer of this narrative, either in the time of Hezekiah or Josiah.

[18–19] Adoniram ben Abda' is identified in 1 Kgs 5:6, 28 as Solomon's officer in charge of the corvée. Second Samuel 20:24 identifies him as Adoram, but this is a variation of the same name. The reaction of the people aptly demonstrates Rehoboam's egregious miscalculation in sending Adoniram to enforce Rehoboam's authority; Adoniram is stoned to death, and Rehoboam is forced to flee for his life to Jerusalem. The concluding notice that Israel rebelled against the house of David "until this day" indicates that this narrative dates to the reign of Hezekiah, since northern Israel did not exist following its destruction by the Assyrians in 722/721 B.C.E.

[20] The notice that Judah alone followed Rehoboam contradicts the claim in vv. 21–24 that Rehoboam ruled over both Judah and Benjamin and the account of the prophecy of Ahijah the Shilonite in 1 Kgs 11:26–39 that awarded ten tribes to Jeroboam.

[21–24] The inclusion of a prophetic oracle advising Rehoboam against any attempt to reassert control over the north provides a link to the earlier narrative concerning Ahijah's prophecy to Jeroboam (1 Kgs 11:26–39) and thus the means for the narrator to assert that the division of the kingdom was the result of divine action. This segment begins with the notice in v. 21 that Rehoboam assembled Judah and Benjamin to fight against Israel to restore his authority. One hundred eighty thousand men correspond to the total number of men employed in the corvée in 1 Kgs 5:27–29 (e.g., Walsh, *1 Kings* 169). Verses 22–24a comprise the report of a prophetic oracle by the prophet Shemaiah to

Rehoboam and the people. The oracle report begins with a standard example of the prophetic word transmission formula, "and the word of G-d came to Shemaiah, a man of G-d, saying."[170] The reference to him as "man of G-d" rather than "man of YHWH" is characteristic of northern prophets, for example, Moses (Deut 33:1; Josh 14:6), Samuel (1 Sam 9:6–10), and Elijah and Elisha (1 Kgs 13; 17:18–24; 20:28; 2 Kgs 1:9–13; 4:7–42; 5:8–20; 6:6–15; 7:2, 17; 8:2–11; 13:19; 23:16–17). Such usage undermines attempts to claim that this passage is a late insertion. The appearance of this designation establishes literary continuity with Samuel, who legitimized Saul and David as earlier kings of Israel. It thereby aids in demonstrating the oracle's central premise that the revolt against Rehoboam is an act of G-d/YHWH.[171] Shemaiah's oracle begins in v. 23 with G-d's instruction to speak to Rehoboam ben Solomon, king of Judah. The title "king of Judah" very pointedly highlights Rehoboam's new status as the monarch of a much more limited territory. The oracle to Rehoboam and the people in v. 24a employs the typical messenger formula,[172] and it employs the name YHWH rather than G-d. The oracle constitutes a divine instruction to Rehoboam and the people that prohibits them from going to war with Israel and demands that they return to their homes. The nature of the instruction is consistent with earlier oracular inquiries (2 Sam 2:1–4). The concluding statement of the oracle certifies that the oracular answer—and thus the revolt of the northern tribes—is indeed an act of YHWH, which raises questions concerning YHWH's role in punishing Rehoboam for his father's actions. The concluding statement of the narrative in v. 24b depicts the revolt as the product of the divine will.

1 Kings 12:25–13:34 Jeroboam's Apostasy

12:25 And Jeroboam built Shechem in the hills of Ephraim, dwelt in it, and went out from there and built Penuel.

26 And Jeroboam said in his heart, "Now, the kingdom will return to the house of David. 27 If this people goes up to make sacrifices in the house of YHWH in Jerusalem, this people will change (its) heart to their master, to Rehoboam, king of Judah, and they will return to Rehoboam, king of Judah." 28 And the king took council, made two calves of gold, and said unto them, "You have gone up to Jerusalem too much! Behold your gods, O Israel, who brought you up from the land of Egypt!" 29 And

---

170. Sweeney, *Isaiah 1–39,* 546–47; Meier, *Speaking of Speaking,* 314–19.

171. Cf. Amos Frisch, "Shemaiah the Prophet versus King Rehoboam: Two Opposed Interpretations of the Schism (1 Kings XX 21-4)," *VT* 38 (1988): 466–68, who distinguishes the political understanding of the revolt on the part of Rehoboam and the religious assessment of the revolt on the part of Shemaiah.

172. Sweeney, *Isaiah 1–39,* 546; Meier, *Speaking of Speaking,* 273–98.

he placed the one in Beth El, and the other in Dan. 30 And this thing was a sin, and the people went before the one as far as Dan. 31 And he made temples of high places, and priests from throughout the people who were not from the sons of Levi.

32 And Jeroboam held a festival in the eighth month, on the fifteenth day of the month, like the festival in Judah, and he went up on the altar— so he did in Beth El—to sacrifice to the calves which he made, and he stationed at Beth El the priests of the high places that he had made. 33 And he went up on the altar which he had made at Beth El on the fifteenth day of the eighth month, in the month^a which he had devised from his heart,^b and he held a festival for the children of Israel, and went up upon the altar to burn incense. 13:1 And behold, a man of G-d came from Jerusalem by the word of YHWH to Beth El, and Jeroboam was standing on the altar to burn incense. 2 And he called out against the altar by the word of YHWH, and said, "O altar, altar, thus says YHWH, 'Behold, a son is born to the house of David, Josiah is his name, and he shall sacrifice upon you the priests of the high places who burn incense upon you, and human bones shall burn upon you.'" 3 And he gave a sign on that day, saying, "This is the sign that YHWH spoke, "Behold, the altar is broken down, and the ash that is upon it is poured out." 4 And it came to pass when the king heard the word of the man of G-d that he called out against the altar in Beth El, Jeroboam stretched out his hand from upon the altar, saying, "Seize him!" but his hand that he had stretched out against him withered, and he was not able to bring it back to himself. 5 And the altar broke down, and the ash upon the altar poured out according to the sign that the man of G-d gave by the word of YHWH. 6 And the king answered and said to the man of G-d, "Please entreat the presence of YHWH your G-d, and pray on my behalf that my hand may be restored to me," and the man of G-d entreated the presence of YHWH, and the hand of the king was restored to him, and it was as before. 7 And the king spoke to the man of G-d, "Come with me to the house, and dine, and I will give to you a gift." 8 And the man of G-d said to the king, "If you give to me half of your house, I will not come with you, and I will not eat bread, and I will not drink water in this place. 9 Because thus he commanded me by the word of YHWH, saying, 'You shall not eat bread, and you shall not drink water, and you shall not return by the road by which you came.'" 10 And he left by another road, and he did not return by the road by which he came to Beth El.

11 And one old prophet was living in Beth El, and his son came and related to him everything that the man of G-d did that day in Beth El with the words that he spoke unto the king, ^cand they related them to their father.^c 12 And their father spoke to them, "By which road did he go?" and his sons showed (him) the road by which the man of G-d went when he

came from Judah. 13 And he said to his sons, "Saddle for me the ass," and they saddled for him the ass, and he rode it. 14 And he went after the man of G-d, and he found him sitting under the oak, and said to him, "Are you the man of G-d who came from Judah?" and he said, "I am." 15 And he said to him, "Come home with me, and eat bread." 16 And he said to him, "I am not able to return with you or to come with you, and I will not eat bread, and I will not drink water with you in this place, 17 ᵈbecause a word came to me by the word of YHWH,ᵈ 'You shall not eat bread, and you shall not drink there water. You shall not return to walk on the path by which you came.'" 18 And he said to him, "I, too, am a prophet like you, and an angel spoke to me by the word of YHWH, saying, 'Return him with you to your house, and he shall eat bread and drink water.'" He lied to him. 19 ᵉAnd he returned with him,ᵉ ate bread in his house, and drank water. 20 And they were sitting at the table, and the word of YHWH came to the prophet who returned him. 21 And he called out to the man of G-d who came from Judah, saying, "Thus says YHWH, 'Because you have rejected YHWH's instruction, and did not observe the command that YHWH your G-d commanded you, 22 and you returned, ate bread, and drank water in the place that He said to you, "Do not eat bread, and do not drink water," your corpse will not enter the tomb of your fathers.'" 23 And after he ate bread and drank, he saddled for him the ass of the prophet who returned him. 24 And he went, and a lion found him on the road and killed him, and his corpse was cast out on the road, and the ass was standing beside it, and the lion was standing beside the corpse. 25 And behold, people were passing by, and they saw the corpse cast out on the road, and the lion standing beside the corpse, and they came and reported it in the city in which the old prophet was dwelling. 26 And the prophet who returned him from the road heard, and said, "He was a man of G-d who rejected YHWH's instruction, and YHWH gave him to the lion, and it tore him up and killed him according the word of YHWH which He spoke to him." 27 And he spoke to his sons, "Saddle for me the ass," and they saddled (it), 28 and he went and found his corpse cast out in the road, and the ass and the lion were standing beside the corpse. The lion did not eat the corpse, and it did not tear apart the ass. 29 And the prophet lifted the corpse of the man of G-d, and he set it upon the ass and returned it, and he came to the city of the old prophet to mourn and to bury it. 30 And he set his corpse in his own tomb and mourned over it, "Woe, my brother!" 31 And after he buried it, he said to his sons, "When I die, you shall bury me in the tomb in which the man of G-d is buried; set my bones by his bones, 32 for the word that he called out by the word of YHWH against the altar in Beth El and against all the temples of the high places in the cities of Samaria shall surely happen."

33 After this, Jeroboam did not return from his evil way, and he again made priests for the high places from among the people; whoever desired ᶠhe ordainedᶠ so that he became a priest of the high places. 34 And this thing was a sin of the house of Jeroboam, which would eradicate (it) and destroy (it) from upon the face of the earth.

a. Hebrew, *baḥōdeš*, "in the month"; cf. LXX, *en tēi heortēi*, "in the festival," which presupposes Hebrew, *beḥāg*.

b. Ketiv, *millibbād*, "alone"; read with Qere, *millibbô*, "from his heart." Cf. Targum Jonathan, "from his own will."

c–c. Cf. LXX, *kai epestrepsan to prosōpon tou patros autōn*, "and they turned the face of their father." LXX presupposes Hebrew, *wayyassēbbû ʾet pĕnê ʾăbîhem*, apparently based upon a misunderstanding of the oral reading of Hebrew, *wayyĕsappĕrûm laʾăbîhem*.

d–d. Cf. LXX, *Oti outōs entetaltai moi en logōi Kurios*, "for thus the L-rd commanded me by (His) word," apparently reading the initial *kî*, "because," both as *kî* and as *kēn*, "thus" (cf. the appearance of *kēn* in place of the expected *kî* in 1 Kgs 12:32). LXX takes *yhwh* as the subject of the verb rather than as the second element of a construct relationship with *bidbar* (cf. v. 9).

e–e. Hebrew, *wayyāšāb ʾittô*, "and he returned with him"; cf. LXX, *kai epestrepsen auton*, "and he returned him," which presupposes Hebrew, *wayyāšēb ʾōtô*, in keeping with vv. 20, 23, 26, 29.

f–f. Hebrew, *yĕmallēʾ ʾet yādô*, literally, "he would fill his hand," a technical expression for the ordination of priests (see, e.g., Exod 28:41; 29:9; Lev 8:33; Num 3:3; Judg 17:5; Ezek 43:26; 1 Chr 29:5); cf. Peshitta, "he offered a sacrifice"; Targum Jonathan, "he was offering his sacrifice."

First Kings 12:25–13:34 lacks an initial formal demarcation, since 1 Kgs 12:25 continues the *waw*-consecutive narrative formulation that governs 1 Kgs 12:1–24. Thematic shifts mark the beginning of the unit, which focuses on Jeroboam instead of Rehoboam. Because 1 Kgs 12:25–13:34 is formulated throughout with *waw*-consecutive verbs, the internal structure must be determined on other grounds. The initial statement in 1 Kgs 12:25 relates Jeroboam's building of Shechem, which functioned as his administrative capital for ruling the central hill country of Ephraim and associated territories of Israel west of the Jordan River, and Penuel, which functioned as his secondary capital for ruling Israelite territory east of the Jordan. Beginning in v. 26, the focus shifts to his interests in establishing cultic centers at Beth El and Dan and the narrator's accusation that he sinned for having done so (see 1 Kgs 12:30 and 13:34). The narrative distinguishes two sins committed by Jeroboam: the first is his establishment of golden calves for worship by Israel at Beth El and Dan (1 Kgs 12:30) and the second is his ordination of priests from throughout the people of Israel rather than from the priestly tribe of Levi (1 Kgs 13:34). The deliberate mention of Jeroboam's name in 1 Kgs 12:25; 12:26; and 12:32 marks the beginning of three subunits that treat three primary concerns: Jeroboam's building of administrative centers in 1 Kgs 12:25, Jeroboam's apostasy in establishing golden calves in Beth El and Dan in 1 Kgs 12:26–31, and Jeroboam's appointment of non-Levitical priests in 1 Kgs 12:32–13:34. The narrative depicts Jeroboam's attempt to offer incense at the Beth El altar, a prerogative reserved only for the high priest (Exod 30:1–10; see also Num 16; 17:5; 2 Chr 26:16–21; Lev 10:1–3).

[12:25] The site of Shechem is Tel Balatah, located in the central hill country of northern Israel to the east of modern Nablus.[173] The site of Penuel is unknown, although it is sometimes identified with Tell edh-Dhahab on the banks of the Wadi Jabbok, east of the Jordan River.[174] Biblical tradition identifies Penuel as the site where Jacob wrestled with the man of G-d (Gen 32:24–32; cf. Hos 12:4) and the site of the tower destroyed by Gideon when its inhabitants refused to supply his men during his war against the Midianites (Judg 8:8–9, 17). Shechem is the logical choice for rule of the central hill country, based on its strategic location at the intersection of the road system in the northern Israelite hills that provides access to Judah to the south, the Jordan Valley to the east, the coastal plain to the west, and the Jezreel Valley to the north. Penuel, Sukkoth, and Mahanaim are located along the Wadi Jabbok. Located farther to the east than Sukkoth, Penuel is especially useful for projecting Israelite power into the Transjordan.

[12:26–31] The narrative charges that Jeroboam inaugurates the worship of the golden calves to protect himself from assassination or overthrow by his own people. If the people continue to bring their sacrifices to Jerusalem, they will inevitably come under the influence of Rehoboam, pointedly called "the king of Judah" and not "the king of Israel." Such a motivation demonstrates that this text is composed to serve Judean interests by portraying Jeroboam as a cynical monarch interested in his own hold on power.

The statement in v. 28 that Jeroboam took counsel with his subjects hardly inspires confidence insofar as the book of Judges points to Ephraim as an abusive tribe that will provoke civil war to advance its own power and to the northern tribes in general as subject to Canaanite religious influence. Exodus 32–34 depicts Israel's apostasy in the wilderness in similar terms, insofar as the people make a golden calf to worship while Moses is on Mount Sinai.[175] The relationship is reinforced by Jeroboam's statement, "Behold your gods, O Israel,

---

173. See Edward F. Campbell, "Shechem, " *NEAEHL* 4:134–35; George Ernest Wright, *Shechem: The Biography of a Biblical City* (New York: McGraw-Hill, 1965).

174. See J. C. Slayton, "Penuel," *ABD* 5:223.

175. Moses Aberbach and Leivy Smolar, "Aaron, Jeroboam, and the Golden Calves," *JBL* 86 (1967): 129–40; Marvin A. Sweeney, "The Wilderness Traditions of the Pentateuch: A Reassessment of Their Function and Intent in Relation to Exodus 32–34," *SBLSP* (1989): 291–99.

who brought you up from the land of Egypt," which corresponds to Aaron's statement in Exod 32:4 (see also Neh 9:18).

Calf or bull images are frequently associated with Baal in Canaanite religion as a means to depict strength, virility, or fertility.[176] Similar images are attributed to YHWH, who is described as *ʾābîr yaʿăqōb,* "the mighty one/bull of Jacob," in Gen 49:24; Isa 49:26; 60:16; Ps 132:2, 5, or *ʾābîr yiśrāʾēl,* "the mighty one/bull of Israel," in Isa 1:24. The charge of Jeroboam's apostasy serves Judean polemical interests. His use of the golden calves did not depict YHWH or any other god per se, but the mount on which YHWH rides. In similar fashion, the ark in the Jerusalem temple symbolized YHWH's throne or footstool on which YHWH was seated (1 Sam 4:4; 2 Sam 6:2; Isa 66:1; see Jones 258). The sites of Beth El and Dan are both well known. Beth El, identified with the modern village of Beitin, approximately 10.5 miles north of Jerusalem to the northeast of Ramallah, saw continuous occupation at the beginning of the Middle Bronze Age (ca. 1800 B.C.E.).[177] Much of the early remains were discovered at a Middle Bronze I sanctuary on the site, although the site of the Israelite sanctuary has not yet been located. Originally known as Luz (Judg 1:22–25), Beth El has a sordid reputation in the Hebrew Bible associated with deception and remorse. The Israelites take Ai (Beth El?) only after splitting their forces to deceive Ai's inhabitants into coming out into the open (Josh 8). A similar act of deception ensures the conquest of Beth El in Judg 1:22–25. Judges 2:1–5 refers to Beth El as a site of Israel's weeping (Hebrew, Bochim), and Judg 20:18 identifies it as the site where Israel decides to wage war against Benjamin. Second Kings 17:28 identifies Beth El as the site of worship for gentiles brought to the northern kingdom by the Assyrians, and 2 Kgs 23:15–20 relates Josiah's destruction of the Beth El altar as part of his reforms.

Dan is identified with Tell el-Qadi or Tel Dan, located at the sources of the Jordan River north of the Kinneret at the foot of Mount Hermon.[178] Dan was a flourishing city from the Early Bronze Age through Greco-Roman times. The site of the Iron Age altar is located on the northwestern portion of the mound, and it included a large high place, a four-horned altar, *pithoi* with figures of writhing snakes, an Astarte figure, and other artifacts. The altar was destroyed in the ninth century by the Arameans who fought against Ahab and Jehu, but it was rebuilt and served through the Assyrian destruction of the city. The Tel Dan inscription in which the ninth-century Aramean king, ben Hazael, claims to

176. Ora Negbi, *Canaanite Gods in Metal* (Jerusalem: Israel Exploration Society, 1976).

177. James Leon Kelso, "Bethel," *NEAEHL* 192–94; W. F. Albright and J. L. Kelso, *The Excavation of Bethel 1934–1960* (AASOR 39; New Haven, Conn.: American School of Oriental Research, 1968).

178. Avraham Biran, "Dan," *NEAEHL* 1:323–32; Biran, *Biblical Dan* (Jerusalem: Israel Exploration Society and Hebrew Union College—Jewish Institute of Religion, 1994).

have defeated "the house of David" was also discovered at the site.[179] Jeroboam's decision to place temples at Beth El and Dan ensures that the people will bring their prescribed offerings to support the royal establishment and the priesthood of the temples (see 1 Sam 8:11–18). Two sanctuaries were necessary due to the size and geographical divisions of the land. Beth El served the central hill country, and Dan served the Galilee.

The text labels Jeroboam's establishment of cultic centers in Beth El and Dan as a sin that led the people astray from their obligation to observe the covenant with YHWH (Deut 5:8–10; 12:29–13:19), who may be worshiped only at the one place in the land that YHWH designates (Deut 12:2–28). Jeroboam violates the covenant as stipulated in Deuteronomy and presupposed throughout the DtrH. Such a characterization of Jeroboam's actions hardly constitutes the work of northern circles who sought to bring Israel into conformity with its covenant traditions; after all, there is never an attempt to close the temples at Dan or Beth El in the northern kingdom. Such polemics represent Judean interests that sought to justify the belief that YHWH had chosen Jerusalem as the true worship site and the house of David as the true monarchs of Israel.

Jeroboam's appointment of priests from among all the people of Israel anticipates the specific identification in 1 Kgs 13:33–34 of this act as another of Jeroboam's fundamental sins. Although early Israelite tradition indicates that the firstborn sons of Israel were originally consecrated to YHWH, the Levites were designated to serve as priests in place of the consecrated firstborn sons of Israel (see Num 3, esp. vv. 11–13, 40–51; 8; cf. Exod 12–13; 22:28–30; 34:19–20; 1 Sam 1–3; Exod 32). The text charges Jeroboam with violating this norm of holiness, and thereby allowing the sanctuaries to become defiled by the presence of priests who were not properly consecrated to YHWH. It seems likely that Jeroboam acted in accordance with earlier Israelite tradition by consecrating the firstborn to serve as priests, much as Samuel, the firstborn of Hannah, was dedicated to serve as a priest in the Shiloh temple.

[12:32–13:34] The initial notices in vv. 32–33 concerning Jeroboam's sins introduce a two-part narrative in 1 Kgs 13:1–32 that discredits the Beth El sanctuary, first by portraying the condemnation of the Beth El altar by an unnamed man of G-d from Judah (vv. 1–10) and then by portraying the death of the Judean man of G-d as a result of lies told to him by an old prophet who resided in the city (vv. 11–32). The concluding statements in 1 Kgs 13:33–34 reiterate Jeroboam's sin in establishing illegitimate priests, and condemn his dynasty to extinction. Although the narrative may be based on an older tradition concern-

179. Avraham Biran and Joseph Naveh, "An Aramaic Stele Fragment from Tel Dan," *IEJ* 43 (1993): 81–98; Biran and Naveh, "The Tel Dan Inscription: A New Fragment," *IEJ* 45 (1995): 1–18; Steven L. McKenzie, *King David: A Biography* (Oxford and New York: Oxford University Press, 2000), 11–13.

ing the tomb of the two prophets in Beth El, the present narrative serves the interests of the Josianic DtrH, insofar as the anonymous man of G-d states that Josiah will ultimately destroy the Beth El altar (see esp. 13:2; cf. 2 Kgs 23:15–20).[180]

Jeroboam's illegitimate actions at the Beth El temple begin with his institution of a festival on the fifteenth day of the *eighth* month, apparently modeled on the similar festival observed in Judah. This would be Sukkot, "booths," observed for seven days beginning on the fifteenth day of the *seventh* month (Lev 23:33–43; cf. Exod 23:16; 34:22; Num 29:12–38; Deut 16:13–15). Sukkot concludes the fruit and olive harvest and inaugurates the rainy season in Israel. Some argue that Jeroboam's action reflects the legitimate religious practice of the northern kingdom of Israel based on a different system of calendar reckoning.[181] Nevertheless, the text represents Jeroboam's act as an abrogation of the holiness required of YHWH's temple, particularly since the reckoning of time and the holidays are sacred. Jeroboam's ascent on the altar to offer sacrifice is sinful, since service on the altar is the sole prerogative of the priests (Exod 29; Lev 1–16; Num 8; 18).

The narrative concerning the anonymous man of G-d from Judah and the old prophet from Beth El clearly serves the agenda of the DtrH, insofar as it condemns Jeroboam, the altar at Beth El, and even the city itself as the home of a lying prophet. The present narrative serves the Josianic DtrH by pointing to Josiah as the figure who will eventually destroy the Beth El altar, ridding the land of Jeroboam's sins. The concern with Josiah and Jeroboam appears only in the first episode in vv. 1–10, which prompts suggestions that these verses are a secondary addition to an earlier tradition concerning the two prophets (e.g., Würthwein 168). Others observe, however, that the narrative concerning the Judean man of G-d and the old prophet from Beth El in vv. 11–32 is dependent on the earlier portion of the narrative insofar as it explains the presence of the Judean man of G-d in Beth El and states the conditions by which he is to appear there—that he eat no food, drink no water, and depart by a different path—that then play an essential role in the second narrative concerning his demise (see now Noth *Könige* 291–95; Gray 320–23).[182] Despite their dependence on vv. 1–10, vv. 11–32 show no awareness of Josiah, Jeroboam, or even the altar at Beth El, but they are very much concerned with explaining the origins of the

180. See esp. Werner Lemke, "The Way of Obedience: 1 Kings 13 and the Structure of the Deuteronomistic History," in *Magnalia Dei/The Mighty Acts of G-d* (ed. F. M. Cross Jr. et al.; Garden City, N.Y.: Doubleday, 1976), 301–26; E. Theodore Mullen Jr., "The Sins of Jeroboam: A Redactional Assessment," *CBQ* 49 (1987): 212–32.

181. E.g., Shemaryahu Talmon, "Discrepancies in Calendar Reckoning in Ephraim and Judah," *VT* 8 (1958): 48–74.

182. For literary studies of 1 Kgs 13, see also Rofé, *Prophetical Stories,* 170–82; Robert L. Cohn, "Literary Techniques in the Jeroboam Narrative," *ZAW* 97 (1985): 23–35; J. T. Walsh, "The Contexts of 1 Kings xiii," *VT* 39 (1989): 355–70.

tomb of the prophets which Josiah observes at the time of his destruction of the Beth El altar (2 Kgs 23:15–20). Furthermore, this portion of the narrative is very much concerned with portraying the old prophet from Beth El as a liar who tricks the Judean man of G-d into violating his divine commission. This suggests that the present narrative is based on an older tradition concerning the etiology of the tomb of the prophets in the vicinity of Beth El that has been reworked to address Josianic concerns.

The first part of the narrative in vv. 1–10 focuses on the condemnation of Jeroboam and the altar at Beth El. The fundamental conflict between Judah and northern Israel is signaled at the outset when the narrative introduces the major protagonist as "a man of G-d from Judah," who appears at the Beth El altar while Jeroboam stands on it to offer incense. The anonymity of the prophet is inherent to the narrative, insofar as it reflects a local tradition concerning two prophets who were buried in the same tomb near Beth El. The prophet's origins in Judah are essential to highlight the tension between Judah and Israel concerning the legitimacy of the Beth El altar.

The condemnation of the Beth El altar by the man of G-d employs classic prophetic forms, including the reference to "the word of YHWH" (*bidbar yhwh*) and the messenger formula, "thus says YHWH" (*kōh ʾāmar yhwh*).[183] The address to the altar employs the typical prophetic announcement of punishment, but it lacks any statement of the grounds for the punishment. The grounds for the announcement have already been laid out in 1 Kgs 12:32–33, which notes Jeroboam's illegitimate actions in establishing a Sukkot festival in the eighth month, illegitimate priests, and illegitimate offerings on the altar. Instead, the man of G-d's announcement emphasizes the role that Josiah will play in carrying out the judgment (see 2 Kgs 23:15–20).

A concern with symbolic actions appears in the withering of Jeroboam's hand when he attempts to order the seizure of the man of G-d. In contrast to Moses, who extends his hand at the time that YHWH performs the signs and wonders of the exodus tradition, Jeroboam's extended hand only represents his impotence in relation to YHWH. The withering of Jeroboam's hand is also noteworthy in relation to the account of the challenge of Moses' leadership by Aaron and Miriam in which Miriam was turned into a leper for daring to question Moses' prophetic authority on the basis of his marriage to a Cushite woman (Num 12). Again, this points to tensions between Judah and northern Israel insofar as the northern king challenges the Judean prophet. The northern king must beg the Judean prophet for assistance in restoring his arm. The power of the prophet is confirmed when he prays to YHWH on Jeroboam's behalf so that his arm is restored.

The restoration of Jeroboam's hand introduces the final element of the narrative in vv. 1–10 in which the man of G-d turns down Jeroboam's invitation to

183. Sweeney, *Isaiah 1–39,* 546.

dine with him. The man of G-d cites G-d's instructions that he is not to eat bread in Beth El, drink water in Beth El, nor return by the road on which he entered the city. This episode constitutes a transition to vv. 11–32 insofar as G-d's stipulations become the basis upon which the man of G-d ultimately dies. But these stipulations also point to the evaluation of Beth El as unfit for Judean worship. Eating and drinking are characteristic activities of Israelite worship, insofar as the sacrifices of meat, grain, and fruit, and the libations of water and wine accompany festival meals (see 1 Sam 9:11–26; cf. Deut 12; 1 Sam 2:27–29). The significance of the command that he not return by the same road is less certain; perhaps it presupposes that he would bring a curse back to Judah.

The second part of the narrative in vv. 11–32 focuses on the deception of the Judean man of G-d by the old prophet from Beth El. The issue of true and false prophecy is secondary to the larger concern with discrediting Beth El. Tensions between Judah and northern Israel come clearly to the forefront when the narrative depicts the old prophet from Beth El as a liar who deceives the Judean man of G-d into violating G-d's commission.

The north-south tensions are further highlighted by the repeated references to the ass and the lion. The narrative mentions the ass repeatedly (see. vv. 13, 23, 24, 27, 28, 29). It also repeatedly mentions the lion that kills the man of G-d (see vv. 24, 25, 26, 27, 28). Although these images seem relatively innocuous, the focus on them calls for reflection. Each of the animals has symbolic significance. The ass, Hebrew, *ḥămôr*, is associated with the city of Shechem insofar as Hamor is the father of Shechem, who raped Jacob's daughter Dinah in Gen 34. Jacob purchased land from Shechem ben Hamor in Gen 33:19, and Jacob's son Joseph was later buried on this plot of ground (Josh 24:32). The name may be related to the practice of slaughtering an ass as part of a treaty or covenant ceremony, which suggests that the name may signify Shechem's role as a site where treaties were ratified in ancient Israel or Canaan. Stratum XIV excavations (Late Bronze) at Shechem have uncovered the ceremonial burial of an ass with its head severed, which suggests that it may have been killed as part of such a treaty ratification ceremony.[184] In any case, the tradition associates the name Hamor with Shechem, the capital of Jeroboam.

The lion is the symbol of the tribe of Judah. Genesis 49:9 identifies Judah as a lion cub (*gûr ʾaryēh*). The lion is a typical motif in the depiction of kings throughout the ancient Near East, and it is associated with David, who first appears as a shepherd boy who protects his flocks from lions (1 Sam 16:31–37). The name Ariel, "lion of G-d," is associated with Jerusalem (Isa 29:1, 2, 7) as a designation for the hearth of the temple altar. The lion kills the man of G-d who betrayed his G-d—even if he was deceived—but it does not molest the ass or any passersby.

184. L. Toombs, "Shechem," *ABD* 1174–86, 1182; see also Wright, *Shechem,* 130–32.

These associations suggest that the image of the ass and the lion standing by the body of the man of G-d is an important element in the interpretation of this narrative. These symbols reinforce the point that the northern kingdom, with its capital in Shechem and its sanctuary in Beth El, is a place of deception and lies. Jerusalem, Judah, and the house of David, by contrast, are identified with YHWH, who will act against those corrupted by their association with Beth El and the north.

The narrative concludes with the portrayal of the burial of the Judean man of G-d by the old prophet of Beth El and his instructions to his sons that his bones should also be placed in the tomb after he dies. This notice establishes the etiology of the tomb that Josiah observes in 2 Kgs 23:15–20. It notes that the initial prophetic word directed against the altar by the Judean man of G-d will ultimately be fulfilled, both against the Beth El altar and the high places established throughout Samaria. The concluding reference to Samaria indicates the late date of this story, given that Samaria is not established as the capital of northern Israel until the reign of Omri (1 Kgs 16:24).

1 Kings 14:1–18 Ahijah's Oracle against the House of Jeroboam

14:1 [a]At that time, Abijah ben Jeroboam became ill. 2 So Jeroboam said to his wife, "Rise, please, and disguise yourself so that nobody will know that you[b] are the wife of Jeroboam, and go to Shiloh. Behold, Ahijah the prophet is there. He declared me as king over this people. 3 And you shall take in your hand ten (loaves of) bread, and cakes, and a jar of honey, and you shall come to him. He shall tell you what will happen to the boy."

4 And the wife of Jeroboam did so, and she arose, went to Shiloh, and came to the house of Ahijah, but Ahijah was not able to see because his eyes were dim[c] due to his age.

5 And YHWH said to Ahijah, "Behold, the wife of Jeroboam has come to request a word from you concerning her son because he is ill. You will speak to her like this and that, and when she comes she will be disguised."
6 When Ahijah heard the sound of her feet coming to the door, he said, "Come in, wife of Jeroboam. Why are you disguised? I am sent to you with bad news. 7 Go, tell Jeroboam, 'Thus says YHWH, G-d of Israel, "Because I raised you from the midst of the people, and I appointed you as ruler over my people Israel, 8 and tore the kingdom from the house of David, and gave it to you, but you have not been like my servant, David, who observed my commands, and walked after me with all his heart to do only what is right in my eyes, 9 and you have done more evil than all who were before you, and you went and you made for yourself other molten gods to provoke me, and you cast me behind your back, 10 therefore, behold, I am bringing evil to the house of Jeroboam; I will cut off

to Jeroboam everyone who pisses against the wall, [d]bond and free,[d] in Israel, and I will burn the house of Jeroboam just as dung burns until it is consumed. 11 The dogs shall eat the dead of Jeroboam in the city, and the birds of the heavens will eat the dead in the field, because YHWH has spoken. 12 And you, arise, go to your house. When your feet come to the city, the child shall be dead. 13 And all Israel shall mourn for him, and shall bury him, for this one alone of Jeroboam shall come to the grave because YHWH the G-d of Israel found in him something good in the house of Jeroboam. 14 And YHWH shall establish for Himself a king over Israel who will cut off the house of Jeroboam, this day, even now! 15 And YHWH shall strike Israel, just as a reed sways in the water, and He shall uproot Israel from upon this good land which He has given to their fathers, and He shall scatter them from across the river because they made their asherim, provoking YHWH. 16 And He shall appoint (this for) Israel because of the sins which Jeroboam committed and which he caused Israel to commit.'" 17 And the wife of Jeroboam arose, went, and came to Tirzah. She came to the threshold of the house, and the boy was dead. 18 And they buried him, and all Israel mourned for him according to the word of YHWH which He spoke by the hand of His servant Ahijah the prophet.[a]

a–a. 1 Kgs 14:1–18 appears in a heavily modified form in 3 Rgns 12:24g–n.

b. Hebrew Ketiv, *ʾaittî,* "with me"; read with Qere, *ʾatt,* "you" (feminine singular).

c. Hebrew, *qāmû,* literally, "(his eyes) rose (from his age)."

d–d. Hebrew, *ʿāṣûr wĕʾāzûb,* literally, "bound and released," is a reference to those who have become slaves to repay a debt (see Exod 21:1–11; Deut 15:12–18; 32:36; 1 Kgs 21:21; 2 Kgs 9:8; 14:26).

The introductory temporal formula *bāʿēt hahîʾ,* "at that time," marks the beginning of 1 Kgs 14:1–18, and correlates it with the preceding narrative. The structure of the text moves easily through a sequence of subjects and actions, including the notice of Abijah's illness in v. 1, Jeroboam's instructions to his wife in vv. 2–3, her compliance with Jeroboam's instructions including the account of the oracle delivered to her by the prophet in vv. 4–16, and her return to Tirzah in vv. 17–18, where she found that her son was dead. The concluding regnal formula in vv. 19–20 indicates that the present subunit concludes with v. 18. First Kings 14:1–18 builds upon the accounts of Jeroboam's sins in 1 Kgs 12:25–13:34 by presenting a prophetic oracle that condemns him for his actions. It counters Ahijah's oracle in 1 Kgs 11:29–39 by indicating that Jeroboam's line will be eradicated as a result of his failure to abide by YHWH's expectations. This passage thereby anticipates the reign of Nadab ben Jeroboam and his overthrow in 1 Kgs 15:25–32.

[14:1] The timing of this episode is crucial within the MT framework because it points to Jeroboam's culpability in establishing the worship of the golden calves at Dan and Beth El as the basic cause for his dynasty's downfall. It is also crucial because Ahijah's prior oracle in 1 Kgs 11:29–39 made it clear that YHWH's promise of kingship to Jeroboam depended entirely on Jeroboam's compliance with YHWH's commands, especially the prohibition against other gods.

The identity of Jeroboam's sons as Abijah and Nadab (see 1 Kgs 15:25) is noteworthy. Aaron's sons, Abihu and Nadab, accompanied Aaron, Moses, and the seventy elders to dine in the presence of YHWH at Mount Sinai (Exod 24:1, 9–11), but they were later consumed for offering unholy fire (Lev 10:1–2). Insofar as Aaron allowed the golden calf to be built at Sinai, Exod 32 depicts Aaron and his sons at Sinai in terms similar to Jeroboam and his sons.[185]

The temporal framework differs markedly from the LXXB account of events in 3 Rgns 12:24g–n, which eliminates the phrase "in that time." LXXB instead places a shortened version of this narrative immediately following the account of Jeroboam's sojourn in Egypt and return to Israel in 3 Rgns 12:24a–f, prior to the oracular promise of kingship to Jeroboam in 3 Rgns 12:24o. The LXXB narrative is concerned with theodicy and true and false prophecy, insofar as the order of the text in the MT indicates that Ahijah's prior oracle to Jeroboam is now undermined. By placing Ahijah's condemnation of the house of Jeroboam prior to the dynastic oracle and the account of the events at Shechem, LXXB signals that Jeroboam's dynasty is destined to fail from the outset. The identification of Shemaiah rather than Ahijah as the prophet who delivered the dynastic oracle in 3 Rgns 12:24o speaks to such a concern. Insofar as Shemaiah is identified in Greek as *Samaion ton Elami/Enlamei*,[186] "Shemaiah the Elamite/Enlamite," he is identified with Shemaiah the Nehelemite (*šĕmaʿyāhû hannehĕlāmî*), to whom Jeremiah refers as a false prophet in Jer 29:24, 31, 32. LXXB thereby signals that the dynastic oracle to Jeroboam is false to begin with and avoids questions concerning the integrity of YHWH's original oracle through Ahijah. By contrast in the MT, the oracle condemning Jeroboam by the same prophet who authorized his reign provides ample justification for the demise of his dynasty.

[2–3] Prophets were often consulted in cases of illness (e.g., 1 Kgs 17:17–24; 2 Kgs 5:1–19a; 8:7–15; 2 Kgs 20:1–11/Isa 38). The narrative highlights the prophet's powers, insofar as he recognizes Jeroboam's wife despite her disguise and his own blindness. The foodstuffs brought by Jeroboam's wife are payment

185. See Moses Aberbach and Leivy Smolar, "Aaron, Jeroboam, and the Golden Calves," *JBL* 86 (1967): 129–40; Sweeney, "Wilderness Traditions."
186. Note the confusion concerning Shemiah's identification as *Elami, Elamitēn,* and *Enlamei* in the LXX manuscripts (see Rahlfs's note, ad loc). The original *Enlamei* (Hebrew, *hannehĕlāmî*) was misunderstood because it does not appear in association with Shemaiah's name in 1 Kgs 12:22, which prompted the elision of the term to the more familiar *Elami* or *Elamitēn,* "the Elamite."

for the prophet's oracle (cf. 1 Sam 9:6–8; 2 Kgs 8:8). Shiloh is identified with modern Khirbet Seilun, located south of Tirzah, about ten miles north of Beth El and east of the Jerusalem-Shechem road.[187] The priestly house of Eli presided over the sanctuary at Shiloh, and the ark resided there until its capture by the Philistines at Aphek (1 Sam 4). The site was destroyed in the mid-eleventh century, perhaps by the Philistines (see also Jer 7:12–15; 26:6–9).

[4–16] Ahijah's origins in Shiloh play an important role within the DtrH since Samuel, also based at Shiloh, authorized the establishment of the house of Saul (1 Sam 8–12) and the house of David (1 Sam 16:1–13). Ahijah's blindness and the disguise of Jeroboam's wife recall Isaac's blindness and Jacob's disguise in the blessing of Jacob (Gen 27).

Ahijah employs classical prophetic language. The initial messenger formula, *kōh ʾāmar yhwh ʾĕlōqê yiśrāʾēl*, "thus says YHWH, G-d of Israel," represents the typical prophetic messenger formula and identifies YHWH as the deity of the northern kingdom of Israel. The content of YHWH's message is formulated as a typical prophetic judgment speech.[188] The accusation, which establishes the grounds for Jeroboam's punishment, appears in vv. 7aβ–9, beginning with the typical introduction, *yaʿan ʾăšer*, "because." The accusation rehearses YHWH's actions on behalf of Jeroboam, which highlights the gravity of Jeroboam's failure to keep YHWH's commandments.

The formal announcement of punishment against the house of Jeroboam follows in vv. 10–16, beginning with the typical particle, *lāqēn*, "therefore," which identifies the following punishment as a consequence of Jeroboam's purported wrongdoing. The announcement of punishment begins with the formulaic statement, *hinĕnî mēbîʾ rāʿâ ʾel bêt yārobʿām*, "behold, I am bringing evil to the house of Jeroboam," which appears elsewhere in 1 Kgs 21:21 (Qere) as part of Elijah's condemnation of Ahab and the house of Omri, in 2 Kgs 21:12 as part of YHWH's oracle concerning Manasseh in which YHWH announces the intention to destroy Jerusalem, and in 2 Kgs 22:16, 20 (cf. 2 Chr 34:24, 28) as part of Huldah's oracle during the reign of Josiah concerning the punishment of Judah and Jerusalem (see also Jer 4:6; 6:19; 11:11; 19:3; 42:17; 45:5; and 51:64).

Insofar as the Kings texts pertain to the Josianic DtrH and the Jeremian texts appear in the context of a prophet who began his career during the reign of Josiah, the phrase indicates a Josian setting for the present formulation of Ahijah's oracle. Other language suggests relationships with other textual traditions. The use of the term *maštîn bĕqîr*, "those who piss against the wall," which suggests an element of contempt for the house of Jeroboam, also appears to be a characteristic phrase of the Jehu history (see 1 Kgs 16:11; 1 Kgs 21:21; and

---

187. A. Kempinski and I. Finkelstein, "Shiloh," *NEAEHL* 4:1364–70.
188. Westermann, *Basic Forms,* 98–115, 129–209; Meier, *Speaking,* 273–98.

2 Kgs 9:8; cf. 1 Sam 25:22, 34). The reference to the men of Jeroboam's house as ʿāṣûr wĕʿāzûb, a formulaic statement generally understood as "bond and free," appears elsewhere, in Deut 32:36, where it signifies the totality of the people who have suffered oppression; 1 Kgs 21:21 and 2 Kgs 9:8, where it again refers to the totality of the house of Omri; and 2 Kgs 14:26, where it refers to the destitute state of the people of Israel. Finally, the reference to the dogs eating the dead of Jeroboam left in the city and the birds eating the dead of Jeroboam left in the field corresponds to similar statements applied to the demise of the house of Baasha in 1 Kgs 16:4 and the demise of the house of Omri, particularly King Ahab and his wife Jezebel, in 1 Kgs 21:19, 23, 24; 22:38; 2 Kgs 9:10, 36. Although the bulk of the language appears to be rooted in the Jehu history concerning the revolt of Jehu against the house of Omri, the use of the formula "behold, I am bringing evil . . ." in Josian texts indicates that the earlier Elijah/Elisha cycle concerned with the rise of Jehu has been worked into the Josian DtrH.[189]

The return of Jeroboam's wife to Tirzah and the immediate death and burial of her son confirms Ahijah's prophetic oracle. It is not clear why she returned to Tirzah, since Jeroboam's home city is Zaredah (1 Kgs 11:26) and his capitals are Shechem and Mahanaim (1 Kgs 12:25). Tirzah is identified with Tel el-Farah (north), seven miles northeast of Shechem at the head of the Wadi Farah.[190] It later served as the capital of northern Israel during the reigns of Baasha (1 Kgs 15:21, 33; 16:6), Zimri (1 Kgs 16:8–9), and Omri (1 Kgs 16:15–23).

1 Kings 14:19–20 Regnal Summary for the Reign of Jeroboam

19 ᵃAnd the rest of the affairs of Jeroboam, when he fought and when he ruled, are they not written in the book of the Chronicles of the Kings of Israel? **20** And the time that Jeroboam ruled was twenty-two years, and he slept with his fathers, and Nadab his son ruled in his place.ᵃ

a–a. LXX omits 1 Kgs 14:19–20.

The concluding regnal formula in 1 Kgs 14:19–20 is a distinct structural element within the larger Jeroboam narrative in 1 Kgs 12:1–14:20. It is joined to the preceding material by a conjunctive *waw,* and includes a citation formula in v. 19 that alerts the reader to the Chronicles of the Kings of Israel where more information might be found.

---

189. See Antony F. Campbell, S.J., *Of Prophets and Kings. A Late Ninth-Century Document (1 Samuel 1–2 Kings 10)* (CBQMS 17; Washington, D.C.: The Catholic Biblical Association, 1986), who assigns this material to the Prophetic Record.

190. R. de Vaux and P. de Miroschedji, "Farʿah, Tell el- (North)," *NEAEHL* 2:433–38.

III. Regnal Account of Rehoboam ben Solomon of Judah
1 Kings 14:21–31

14:21 ªAnd Rehoboam ben Solomon ruled in Judah. Rehoboam was forty-one years old when he began to rule, and he ruled for seventeen years in Jerusalem, the city from all the tribes of Israel where YHWH chose to place His name. And the name of his mother was Naamah the Ammonite.ª 22 Judahᵇ did evil in the eyes of YHWH, and they prompted Him to jealousy more than their fathers did in their sins which they committed. 23 And they even built for themselves high places, stelae, and asherim upon every high hill and under every green tree. 24 And cultic prostitutionᶜ was also in the land. They did according to all the abominations of the nations which YHWH drove out from before the people of Israel.

25 And in the fifth year of King Rehoboam, Shishaq,ᵈ King of Egypt, came up against Jerusalem. 26 He took the treasuries of the house of YHWH and the treasuries of the house of the king, and he took everything, and he took all the golden shields that Solomon made. 27 And King Rehoboam made in their place bronze shields, and he assigned them to the officers of the guards who watched the door of the house of the king. 28 And whenever the king went to the house of YHWH, the guards took them up, and they returned them to the chamber of the guards.

29 And the rest of the affairs of Rehoboam and all that he did, are they not written in the book of the Chronicles of the Kings of Judah? 30 And there was war between Rehoboam and Jeroboam all the time. 31 And Rehoboam slept with his fathers, and he was buried with his fathers in the city of David. And the name of his mother was Naamah the Ammonite, and Abijam his son ruled in his place.

a–a. An alternative version of 1 Kgs 14:21 appears in 3 Rgns 12:24a.
b. Cf. LXX, "Rehoboam." See also 2 Chr 12:14.
c. Hebrew, *qādēš*, literally, "a (cultic) prostitute"; cf. LXX, *sundesmos*, "conspiracy," which presupposes Hebrew, *qešer*, an interpretative rendition of the problematic *qādēš*.
d. Ketiv, *šôšaq*, "Shoshenq" (cf. LXX, *Sousakim*); read with Qere, *šîšaq*, "Shishaq."

First Kings 14:21–31 is easily demarcated by the introductory regnal résumé in vv. 21–24 and by the concluding regnal résumé in vv. 29–31. The account in vv. 25–28 of Pharaoh Shishaq's invasion during the fifth year of Rehoboam's reign is joined structurally to the introductory regnal résumé by the initial *waw*-consecutive construction *wayěhî,* "and it came to pass." The introductory regnal résumé lacks the typical synchronistic accession formula, since Jeroboam's reign does not commence until after that of Rehoboam.

[21–28] The combination of subunits reinforces the notion that Shishaq's invasion is conceived as a divine punishment for the sins with which Rehoboam is charged. Insofar as the Egyptian pharaoh stripped the treasuries of the temple and the royal palace, including the golden shields manufactured by Solomon (cf. 1 Kgs 10:17), the punishment is portrayed as retribution for Solomon's pharaohlike actions in constructing the temple and palace.

Verse 21 gives Rehoboam's age as forty-one, which means that he was born a year prior to Solomon's accession to the throne. Rehoboam was likely his firstborn son. The LXXB account in 3 Rgns 12:24a states that Rehoboam was only sixteen, but this age reflects the characterization of his childhood companions as "children" (1 Kgs 12:8, 10, 14; 3 Rgns 12:24s; cf. the LXXA account, 3 Rgns 12:8, 10, 14). The reference to Jerusalem as the city where Rehoboam ruled employs typical DtrH language to emphasize YHWH's choice of the city as the place where the divine name would be manifested and YHWH's promise of eternal kingship to David (see 2 Sam 7; 1 Kgs 11:32). It also identifies Jerusalem as the place where YHWH manifests the divine name (cf. Deut 12:4–7, which authorizes only one worship site in Israel but does not disclose its location). The identification of Rehoboam's mother as Naamah the Ammonite recalls Solomon's marriages in 1 Kgs 11:1–2 to foreign women, who were forbidden by the DtrH (Deut 7:1–6). It also reflects David's suzerain/vassal alliance with King Shobi ben Nahash of Ammon who supported him during Absalom's revolt (2 Sam 17:27–29; cf. 2 Sam 8:12; 10:1–19; 12:26–31).[1]

The theological assessment of Rehoboam's reign employs stereotypical language that ties his actions to the portrayal of Israel's sins in the days of the Judges and the other monarchs of Judah and Israel. The statement *wayyaʿaś yěhûdâ hāraʿ běʿênê yhwh,* "and Judah did evil in the eyes of YHWH," represents the typical assessment of all the kings of Israel as well as the kings of Judah judged to be evil in Kings (see 1 Kgs 11:6; 15:26, 34; 16:25, 30; 22:53; 2 Kgs 3:2; 8:18, 27; 13:2, 11; 14:24; 15:9, 18, 24, 28; 17:2; 21:2, 20; 23:32, 37; 24:9, 19; cf. 1 Kgs 16:19; 21:20, 25; 2 Kgs 17:17; 21:6, 9, 15, 16). The statement is unique, however, in that Judah rather than one of the kings is the subject of the statement. The following statement concerning Judah's provoking YHWH more than their ancestors can hardly be read in relation to the kings of Israel or Judah, since Rehoboam is only the third monarch of the Davidic line. It therefore

---

1. Baruch Halpern, *David's Secret Demons: Messiah, Murderer, Traitor, King* (Grand Rapids and Cambridge: Eerdmans, 2001), 235–37, 345–53.

points to earlier usage of the expression "to do evil in the eyes of YHWH" in Deuteronomy and the DtrH (see Deut 4:25; 9:18; 17:2; 31:29; Judg 2:11; 3:7, 12; 4:1; 6:1; 10:6; 13:1; 1 Sam 15:19; 29:7; 2 Sam 12:9). The following statements in vv. 23–24 concerning the construction of high places, pillars, and asherim on every high hill and under every leafy tree point to Judah's failure to take action against the religious practices of the Canaanite as stipulated in YHWH's fundamental command to establish only one worship place in Deut 12:2–7. Insofar as these cultic installations are prominently mentioned in 2 Kgs 17:10 as part of the DtrH treatise on the fall of northern Israel and in 2 Kgs 18:4; 23:6, 14, 15, these statements presuppose the interests of the Josian edition of the DtrH. The reference to every high hill and leafy tree is characteristic of Jeremiah (Jer 2:10; 3:6, 13; 11:16; 17:2, 8).[2] Although cultic prostitution is rarely mentioned in Kings (see 1 Kgs 15:12; 22:47; 2 Kgs 23:7) and Deuteronomy (see Deut 23:18), it becomes emblematic of the *tôʿēbôt*, "abominations," of the nations who were driven out by YHWH (see Deut 18:9; 2 Kgs 16:3; 21:2; 23:13).

The account of Pharaoh Shishaq's (Sheshonq) advance against Jerusalem in vv. 25–28 demonstrates YHWH's punishment against Rehoboam and Judah within the larger DtrH theological scheme (cf. 2 Chr 12:1–12). The notice is based on a historical event, Pharaoh Sheshonq's (Libyan, *ššnq*) invasion of Israel in the late tenth century.[3] Sheshonq, the founder of the twenty-second Libyan dynasty (ca. 931–910 B.C.E.), came to the throne after Pharaoh Psusennes II died without a male heir and invaded Israel to reassert Egyptian hegemony in the region. It appears that Sheshonq is the pharaoh who gave refuge to Jeroboam, apparently to undermine Solomon's united kingdom as part of a larger strategy to advance Egypt's interests.[4] The account of his campaign appears in a relief at Karnak in which he claims to have destroyed 154 towns and cities throughout the Negeb, coastal plain, northern hill country, and the Transjordan (see *ANET* 242–43, 263–64). Jerusalem is not included in the list.

[29–31] The concluding regnal résumé notes continuous warfare between Rehoboam and Jeroboam. The Chronicler's account of Rehoboam's extensive fortification of the cities of Judah (2 Chr 11:5–12) indicates an interest in defending Judah from attack by the north.[5]

---

2. Susan Ackerman, *Under Every Green Tree: Popular Religion in Sixth-Century Judah* (HSM 46; Atlanta: Scholars Press, 1992).

3. See Donald Redford, *Egypt, Canaan, and Israel in Ancient Times* (Princeton: Princeton University Press, 1992), 312–18; Kevin A. Wilson, *The Campaign of Pharaoh Shosthenq I into Palestine* (FAT 2/9; Tübingen: Mohr Siebeck, 2005); Lowell Handy, "On the Dating and Dates of Solomon's Reign," in *Age of Solomon*, 96–105, esp. 99–101.

4. Cf. Malamat, "Political Look at the Kingdom of David and Solomon."

5. Mazar, *Archaeology*, 429.

IV. Regnal Account of Abijam ben Rehoboam of Judah 1 Kings 15:1–8

15:1 And in the eighteenth year of King Jeroboam ben Nebat, Abijam ruled over Judah.

2 Three years he ruled in Jerusalem, and the name of his mother was Maacah bat Abishalom. 3 And he followed in all the sins of his father, which he did before him, and his heart was not true to YHWH his G-d, like the heart of David his father, 4 but for the sake of David, YHWH his G-d gave to him dominion[a] in Jerusalem to establish his son after him and to uphold Jerusalem 5 because David did what was right in the eyes of YHWH, and he did not turn from all that He commanded him all the days of his life, except in the matter of Uriah the Hittite. 6 And there was war between Rehoboam and Jeroboam all the days of his life.

7 And the rest of the affairs of Abijam and all that he did, are they not written in the books of the Chronicles of the Kings of Judah? And there was war between Abijam and Jeroboam. 8 Abijam slept with his fathers, and they buried him in the city of David, and Asa his son ruled in his place.

a. Hebrew, *nîr*, "dominion"; cf. LXX, *kataleimma*, "a remnant"; TJ, *malkô*, "his kingdom"; Peshitta, *šrgʾ*, "a lamp," which presupposes Hebrew, *nēr*, "lamp."

In contrast to the extensive account in 2 Chr 13 of Abijam's/Abihu's wars with Jeroboam, 1 Kgs 15:1–8 includes only the reference in v. 6 to war between Rehoboam and Jeroboam and a similar reference in v. 7b to war between Abijam and Jeroboam. The Chronicler's account is likely based in part on authentic historical tradition.[1] This suggests that DtrH downplays these events to present Abijam's reign as a paradigm for the condemnation of subsequent Judean monarchs, much as the account of Othniel in Judg 3:7–11 serves as a paradigm for the accounts of the judges in Judg 3–16. Abijam's regnal account explains the continuity of the house of David and the city of Jerusalem as the result of YHWH's promise to grant dominion to the house of David due to his righteousness. The account stresses that Abijam followed the sins of his ancestors, presumably in neglecting to observe YHWH's commandments (cf. v. 5).

1. See Sara Japhet, *I & II Chronicles: A Commentary* (OTL; Louisville, Ky.: Westminster John Knox, 1993), 686–88.

Such emphases suggest the interests of both the Hezekian and the Josian DtrH editions. The awkward reference to David's murder of Uriah the Hittite indicates that the narrative has been editorially retouched.

Second Kings 15:10 identifies Abijam's mother, Maacah bat Abishalom, as the mother of his son Asa. Some maintain that Abijam and Asa are brothers, but two factors suggest that this is not the case, including the identification in 2 Chr 13:2 of Mikayahu bat Uriel from Gibeah as the mother of Abijah/Abijam and the emphasis placed in 1 Kgs 15:13/2 Chr 15:16 on Asa's removal of his mother Maacah from her role as queen. Nevertheless, 2 Chr 13:2 contradicts 2 Chr 11:18–23, which notes that Maacah bat Absalom was Rehoboam's favorite wife and the mother of Abihu. There is confusion in the Chronicler's account. One might speculate that Abijam's mother actually was Mikayahu bat Uriel; Rehoboam's marriage to a woman from Gibeah, the home of Saul, would have cemented both Solomon's and Rehoboam's hold over this potential center of resistance to Davidic rule. Her early death, however, would have led to the elevation of another of Rehoboam's wives, Maacah bat Abishalom, as the Gebirah or Queen Mother and thus facilitate the identification of her as the mother of Abijah/Abijam. Rehoboam's marriage to the daughter—or more likely the granddaughter[2]—of Absalom makes great sense since her family lineage traces back to King Talmai of Geshur (2 Sam 3:3). Such a marriage would enable Rehoboam to attempt an overture to the Aramean kingdom situated on northern Israel's borders. If Maacah is neither the mother of Abijam nor Asa, but another wife of Rehoboam who assumed the role of Gebirah, such an explanation provides a reason that Asa was willing to take action against her.

V. Regnal Account of Asa ben Abijam of Judah 1 Kings 15:9–24

15:9 And in the twentieth year of Jeroboam, King of Israel, Asa, King of Judah, ruled. 10 Forty-one years he ruled in Jerusalem, and the name of his mother was Maacah bat Absalom. 11 Asa did what was right in the eyes of YHWH like David his father. 12 He expelled the cultic prostitutes[a]

---

2. 2 Sam 14:27 identifies Absalom's only daughter as Tamar. Following the genealogy given by Josephus, *Ant.* 8.10.1, many identify Maacah as the daughter of Tamar, which would mean that she was named for her great-grandmother, Maacah bat Talmai, the mother of Absalom. One must proceed with caution, however, in that it is not entirely certain that Absalom is necessarily to be identified with Absalom ben David.

from the land, removed all the idols that his fathers had made, 13 and also, Maacah his mother, he removed from (the position of) queen mother because she made a monstrosity for Asherah. Asa cut down her monstrosity, and he burned (it) in the Wadi Kidron. 14 But the high places did not cease. Nevertheless, the heart of Asa was true to YHWH all his days, 15 and he brought the sacred objects of his father ᵇand his own sacred objectsᵇ (to) the house of YHWH, silver, and gold, and implements.

16 And there was war between Asa and Baasha, King of Israel, all their days. 17 Baasha, King of Israel, went up against Judah, and he built up Ramah so as not allow passage to Asa, King of Judah. 18 Asa took all the silver and the gold that was left in the treasuries of the house of YHWH and the treasuries of the house of the king,ᶜ and gave it to his servants, and King Asa sent them to Ben-Hadad ben Tabrimon ben Hezyon, King of Aram, who ruled in Damascus, saying, 19 "(Let us make) a treaty, (like that) between my father and your father. Behold, I have sent to you a gift of silver and gold. Go, break your treaty with Baasha, King of Israel, so he will withdraw from me." 20 And Ben Hadad listened to King Asa, sent his army commanders against the cities of Israel, and struck 'Iyyon and Dan and Abel Beth-Maacah and all the Kinneretᵈ beside all the land of Naphtali. 21 And when Baasha heard, he stopped building up Ramah, and stayedᵉ in Tirzah. 22 King Asa called up all Judah—no one was exempt—and they carried the stones and timbers of Ramah, which Baasha had built, and King Asa built with them Geba of Benjamin and the Mitzpah.

23 And all the rest of the affairs of Asa and all his power and all that he did and the cities that he built, are they not written in the book of the Chronicles of the Kings of Judah? But in his old age, he became ill in his feet. 24 Asa slept with his fathers. He was buried with his fathers in the city of David his father, and Jehoshaphat his son ruled in his place.

a. Hebrew, *qĕdēšîm*, generally understood as a reference to "sacred (male) prostitutes," based upon the use of the root, *qdš*, "to be holy." Cf. LXX, *tas teletas*, "the mystic rites"; TJ, *palî nāpĕqāt*, "old (female) prostitutes"; Peshitta, *zny'*, "(male) prostitutes."

b–b. Ketiv, *wqdšw*; Qere, *wĕqodšê*, "and the holy things of (the house of) YHWH"; read, *wĕqodšāyw*, "and his (own) holy things," with 2 Chr 15:18. The *yod* was lost due to similarity to the following *waw*.

c. Read with Qere, *hammelek*, "the king"; cf. Ketiv, *mlk*.

d. Hebrew, *kinrôt*, a variation of the term *kineret*, the Hebrew name for the sea of Galilee. The variation in the name prompts some difficulties in the versions, i.e., LXX, *tēn chezrath*, "Chezrath"; Targum Jonathan, *ginêsar*, "Ginesar"; Peshitta, *qwry'*, "territories."

e. Hebrew, *wayyēšeb*, "and he stayed"; cf. LXX, "and he returned (to Tirzah)," which presupposes Hebrew, *wayyāšāb*, "and he returned."

First Kings 15:9–24 comprises three sections, each introduced by a conjunctive *waw*: the initial regnal account in vv. 9–15, the account of Asa's war with Baasha of Israel in vv. 16–22, and the concluding regnal account in vv. 23–24. The positive evaluation of Asa serves the Hezekian and Josian DtrH editions, since Asa burns the "monstrosity" of Maacah in the Wadi Kidron, much as Josiah burned the Asherah in the Kidron (2 Kgs 23:6).

[9–15] Asa is credited with an exceptionally long reign of forty-one years, one year longer than both David and Solomon. The problems of the identification of his mother as Maacah bat Abishalom are noted in the regnal account of Abijam (1 Kgs 15:1–8) above. Asa's willingness to remove her as *gĕbîrâ* lends credence to the supposition that she is not actually his mother. She may not even be Asa's grandmother, but a wife of Rehoboam who assumed the role of *gĕbîrâ* after the death of Abihu's/Abijam's actual mother, Mikayahu bat Uriel (see 2 Chr 13:2).[1] Asa's removal of Maacah as *gĕbîrâ* occurs in the context of his own religious reforms, including the removal of (male) cultic prostitutes, idols, and a particularly odious cultic item belonging to Maacah. All appear to be associated with Asherah, the Canaanite goddess of fertility,[2] and their removal anticipates actions later undertaken by King Josiah (2 Kgs 23:4–7). Alternatively, the term *qĕdēšîm*, "cultic prostitutes," is derived from the root *qdš*, "holy," and may be a derisive pun employed for the priests of Asherah. The term *mipleset*, "monstrosity," based upon the root *pls*, "to shudder," refers to a sacred tree or pole associated with the worship of Asherah that Asa cuts down and burns. The failure to remove the high places is not presented as a major failing, and it anticipates the later actions of Hezekiah (2 Kgs 18:4) and Josiah (2 Kgs 23:5, 9, 15, 19–20).

[16–22] The account of Asa's war against Baasha of Israel provides reasons for his religious reforms, particularly his displacement of Maacah. Baasha was a usurper from Issachar, located in the southern Galilee to the west of the Kinneret (1 Kgs 15:27). His revolt is an attempt to capitalize on a potentially unstable situation in which Nadab, the Ephraimite king of Israel, was occupied in the Philistine coastal plain with a siege against Gibbethon. Such an operation suggests that northern Israel was relatively secure insofar as Nadab was able to mount an offensive operation against the Philistines without fear of attack from the north, east, or south. Nadab's short two-year reign suggests that Baasha attempted to assert his interests or those of his Galilean-based tribe over against the authority of the centrally located tribes of Ephraim and Manasseh. His advance into the Benjaminite city of Ramah, modern er-Ram located five miles

---

1. See Zafira Ben-Barak, "The Status and Right of the *gĕbîrâ*," *JBL* 110 (1991): 23–34; Susan Ackerman, "The Queen Mother and the Cult in Ancient Israel," *JBL* 112 (1993): 385–401.
2. N. Wyatt, "Asherah," *DDD*[2] 99–105; Linda Day, "Asherah," *ABD* 1:483–87.

north of Jerusalem,[3] intimidated Judah by invading territory that would have remained under Davidic control.

By making overtures to the Damascus-based Aramean monarch Ben-Hadad ben Tabrimon ben Hezyon, Asa created an enemy for Baasha who would threaten Israel's northern borders in the upper Galilee. The move is especially clever because it reestablished the former alliance between the house of David under David and Solomon with the Arameans, including Hadadezer of Zobah, the Arameans of Damascus, Toi of Hamath, and others (2 Sam 8:3–12; 10:6–19). Damascus remained under Davidic control until the revolt of Rezon ben Eliada (1 Kgs 11:23–25). Asa's proposed alliance also gave Ben-Hadad carte blanche to invade northern Israel and to claim territory for Aram, which would alleviate Israelite pressure against Judah.

The cities taken by Ben-Hadad are all located in the northern Galilean territory of Naphtali to the north of Baasha's home tribe of Issachar. Iyyon is identified with Merj 'Ayyun, to the north of modern Metulla, along the Israelite-Aramean border.[4] Dan, identified with Tel Dan in the Huleh Valley, is the major temple city of Jeroboam located along the north-south road connecting Aramean Qatna with Israelite Hazor.[5] Abel Beth Maacah is identified with Tell Abil al-Qamh, located near Metulla at the junction of the Huleh and Beqa valleys at the tributaries of the Jordan. It is situated to the south and west of Iyyon and Dan, where it functioned as the "gateway" between Israel and Aram.[6] The reference to the Kinneret along the land of Naphtali refers to the northern Galilean territory of Naphtali situated along the northern and western shores of the Sea of Galilee.[7]

Such a plan had internal political ramifications for Judah. Whereas David and Solomon had defeated the Arameans, Asa clearly approached them as an ally in need of their support. His removal of Maacah bat Abishalom as *gĕbîrâ* or queen mother is therefore noteworthy. David had been allied with King Talmai of Geshur, an Aramean ruler whose territory was located along the northern shores of the Kinneret, perhaps at the site of et-Tell, known in Greco-Roman times as Beth Saida.[8] David's marriage to Maacah, the daughter of King Talmai, produced their son Absalom. David successfully put down Absalom's revolt, which meant that Geshur would have remained firmly under Davidic control until the late reign of Solomon or perhaps the revolt of the northern

3. P. M. Arnold, "Ramah," *ABD* 5:613–14.

4. R. A. Mullins, "Ijon," *ABD* 3:387–88.

5. Avraham Biran, "Dan," *NEAEHL* 1:323–32.

6. W. G. Dever, "Abel-Beth-Maacah," *EDB* 3–4.

7. Some identify *kinrôt* with Tel-Chinnereth along the north shore of the Kinneret, but Volkmar Fritz, "Tel-Chinnereth," *NEAEHL* 1:299–301, notes that 1 Kgs 15:20 refers to the region.

8. See Rami Arav and Richard Freund, eds., *Bethsaida: A City by the North Shore of the Sea of Galilee* (Kirksville, Mo.: Thomas Jefferson University Press, 1995).

tribes. Insofar as Rehoboam was married to Maacah bat Abishalom, perhaps the great-granddaughter of Maacah bat Talmai, it appears that Solomon attempted to shore up his relationship with Geshur as Aram continued to threaten his borders. Asa's removal of Maacah bat Abishalom, however, marks an important reversal in the relationship between the house of David and Geshur. Whereas Geshur had been a Davidic ally, Asa was now prepared to allow Ben Hadad of Damascus free rein to take control of territory in the northern Galilee, including Geshur.

Asa's ploy worked. Baasha was forced to abandon Ramah and return to Tirzah to secure his northern borders against Aramean incursions. Asa's fortification of Geba and Mitzpah, both located in Benjamin north of Ramah, defended the northern border of Benjamin against Israelite attack. Geba is identified with modern Jeba, six miles north/northeast of Jerusalem along the northern Benjaminite border.[9] Mitzpah is identified with Tell en-Nasbeh eight miles north/northwest of Jerusalem, although some identify it with the less suitable Nebi Samwil five miles north of the city.[10] Mitzpah means "watchtower," which signifies its role as a border post.

[23–24] The concluding regnal résumé highlights Asa's building activities. The notice that he became ill "in his feet" is a euphemism for some sort of genital ailment, perhaps prostate cancer.

VI. Regnal Account of Nadab ben Jeroboam of Israel
1 Kings 15:25–32

15:25 And Nadab ben Jeroboam ruled over Israel in the second year of Asa, King of Judah, and he ruled over Israel two years. 26 He did evil in the eyes of YHWH, and he followed in the path of his father and in his sin which he caused Israel to commit. 27 Baasha ben Ahijah of the house of Issachar conspired against him, and Baasha struck him down in Gibbeton of the Philistines while Baasha and all Israel were besieging Gibbeton. 28 Baasha killed him in the third year of Asa, King of Judah, and ruled in his place. 29 When he came to rule, he struck down all the house of Jeroboam; he did not allow a soul to remain to Jeroboam until he exterminated him according to the word of YHWH which He spoke by the hand

9. P. M. Arnold, "Geba," *ABD* 2:921–22.
10. Jeffrey R. Zorn, "Tell en-Nasbeh," *NEAEHL* 3:1098–1102; P. M. Arnold, "Mizpah," *ABD* 4:879–81.

of his servant Ahijah the Shilonite 30 concerning the sins of Jeroboam which he sinned and which he caused Israel to commit, thereby provoking YHWH, the G-d of Israel.

31 And the rest of the affairs of Nadab and all that he did, are they not written in the book of the Chronicles of the Kings of Israel? 32 And there was war between Asa and Baasha, King of Israel, all their days.

The syntax indicates that 1 Kgs 15:25–32 comprises three basic parts. First is the account of his reign per se in vv. 25–30, which includes both the regnal résumé and the account of Nadab's assassination by Baasha ben Ahijah. The introductory *waw*-conjunctive formulation of the concluding regnal résumé in v. 31 marks the second subunit. Another *waw*-conjunctive formulation marks the notice in v. 32 concerning war between Asa and Baasha as the concluding statement. The passage notes the fulfillment of Ahijah the Shilonite's oracle concerning the extermination of the house of Jeroboam in 1 Kgs 14:1–20.

[25–30] The introductory regnal résumé initiates the DtrH practice of condemning all of the northern monarchs for prompting Israel to sin. Such an agenda clearly serves the Josian DtrH, which emphasizes the condemnation of northern Israel for following in the sins of Jeroboam. It also serves the Hezekian DtrH by pointing to the instability of the northern tribes.

The assassination of Nadab reflects a power struggle within the newly formed northern Israelite state. Nadab's campaign against Philistine Gibbethon suggests that northern Israel was not threatened by its neighbors to the north, east, and south—that is, Aram, Ammon, Moab, Edom, and Judah. This is due to a treaty with the Arameans, indicated by Asa's overtures to Ben-Hadad in 1 Kgs 15:17–22, Israel's dominance of the Transjordan as a result of its treaty with Aram, and Israel's superiority over Judah in the aftermath of the division of the kingdom. The campaign against Philistine Gibbethon, identified with Tell Malat about three miles southeast of Ramla near the eastern boundary of the coastal plain,[1] is an attempt to extend Israel's power into the coastal plain, perhaps by recovering territory that once belonged to Dan (see Josh 19:44; 21:23). The proximity of the site to Gezer suggests that Nadab intended to check Judean advances into the coastal plain or even to threaten Judean holdings. In such circumstances, Baasha's revolt is an attempt by the Galilean-based tribe of Issachar to tip the balance of power within the northern kingdom away from the tribes of Ephraim and Manasseh in the central hill country. Such a move would give the Galilean-based tribes—Issachar, Naphtali, Zebulun, Asher, and perhaps Dan—greater control over the Jezreel Valley and access to the coastal plain.

The DtrH emphasizes theological considerations in that Nadab's death and the extermination of his entire family was in keeping with the earlier oracle of

1. J. L. Peterson, "Gibbethon," *ABD* 2:1006–7.

Ahijah the Shilonite prophet, who condemned the entire house of Jeroboam in 1 Kgs 14:1–20 for rejecting YHWH.

VII. Regnal Account of Baasha ben Ahijah of Israel
1 Kings 15:33–16:7

15:33 In the third year of Asa, king of Judah, Baasha ben Ahijah ruled over all Israel in Tirzah for twenty-four years. 34 And he did evil in the eyes of YHWH, and he walked in the way of Jeroboam and in his sin which he caused Israel to commit.

16:1 And the word of YHWH came to Jehu ben Hanani concerning Baasha, saying, 2 "Because I raised you from the dust and appointed you leader over my people Israel, and you walked in the way of Jeroboam and you caused my people Israel to provoke me with their sins, 3 behold, I am consuming[a] Baasha and his house, and I will make your house like the house of Jeroboam ben Nebat. 4 Whoever of Baasha dies in the city the dogs shall eat, and whoever dies in the open country the birds of the heavens shall eat."

5 And the rest of the affairs of Baasha, that which he did, and his power, are they not written in the book of the Chronicles of the Kings of Israel? 6 And Baasha slept with his fathers and was buried in Tirzah, and Elah his son ruled in his place.[b]

7 And also by the hand of Jehu ben Hanani the prophet the word of YHWH came to Baasha and to his house, concerning all the evil that he did in the eyes of YHWH to provoke Him with the work of his hands, to be like the house of Jeroboam, and because he struck him down.

a. Hebrew, *mab'îr,* literally, "burning (after)" or "grazing (after)," hence "consume." LXX reads *exegeirō,* "I will arouse (after)," presupposing Hebrew, *mē'îr,* and eliminating the awkwardness of MT. Cf. Targum Jonathan, *mĕpalê,* "searching after, gleaning, removing."

b. LXX adds "in the twentieth year of king Asa."

The introductory regnal formula for Baasha ben Ahijah in 1 Kgs 15:33–34 is joined syntactically to the basic presentation of the events of his reign in 1 Kgs 16:1–4. Verses 1–4 include only an account of YHWH's oracle against Baasha communicated to the prophet Jehu ben Hanani. Although the concluding regnal formula appears in 1 Kgs 16:5–6, an appendix in v. 7 concerning the transmission of YHWH's oracle to Baasha by the prophet Jehu appears together with the formula. Many note problems with v. 7b in that it presents Baasha's destruction of the house of Jeroboam as an additional motivation for his condemnation (e.g., Montgomery and Gehman 282). Such a reading conflicts with vv. 1–4 (cf. 1 Kgs 14:1–18; 15:25–32), which indicates that YHWH authorized the destruction of Jeroboam's house. Baasha is guilty of murdering the king of Israel in DtrH perspective (see 1 Sam 24:6; 26:9; 31:4; 2 Sam 1:1–16; 4:1–12), and 1 Kgs 16:7 suggests that all later royal assassins, such as Zimri (1 Kgs 16:10), Jehu (2 Kgs 9:14–26), Shallum (2 Kgs 15:10), Menahem (2 Kgs 15:14), Pekah (2 Kgs 15:25), and Hoshea (2 Kgs 15:30) are culpable.

This narrative serves both the exilic and Josian DtrH editions. The affinities between the prophetic oracle against Baasha in 1 Kgs 16:1–4 and those against Jeroboam in 1 Kgs 14:1–18 and Ahab in 1 Kgs 21:21–24 and 2 Kgs 9:8–10 indicate that this account of Baasha's reign was composed to link the accounts of Solomon's reign and Jehu's revolt against the house of Omri as part of the larger history of Israel and Judah presented in the Jehu history and the Hezekian DtrH.

[15:33–34] The introductory regnal formula in 15:33–34 is a standard introduction for the kings of northern Israel from Nadab through Ahaziah who ruled up to the time of Jehu's revolt.[1]

[16:1–4] The account of Baasha's reign includes only a notice concerning YHWH's oracle to Jehu ben Hanani condemning Baasha and his house. The other major events of Baasha's reign, including his assassination of Nadab ben Jeroboam and his unsuccessful advance against Judah during the reign of Asa, appear in the respective accounts of the reign of each of these monarchs (see 1 Kgs 15:25–32; 15:9–24). The focus on the major activities of a northern king in relation to his Judean counterpart demonstrates the Judean perspective of the DtrH. The prophet Jehu ben Hanani appears elsewhere in relation to the reigns of Baasha (see vv. 1–4, 7) and his son Elah (1 Kgs 16:12; but see 2 Chr 19:2–3; 2 Chr 20:34).

The focus on the oracle concerning Baasha indicates that this passage functions as a link between two larger bodies of material within the larger DtrH— that is, the account of Solomon's reign in 1 Kgs 1–14 and the account of Jehu's overthrow of the house of Omri in 1 Kgs 17–2 Kgs 13. The passage shares much of its language with the accounts of prophetic oracles condemning Jeroboam in ·1 Kgs 14:10–11 and Ahab in 1 Kgs 21:21–24; 2 Kgs 9:8–10. Thus, the language of v. 2 reflects that employed in relation to Jeroboam. The designation of Baasha as YHWH's designated "leader" or *nāgîd* appears in Ahijah's oracle to Jeroboam in 1 Kgs 14:7. The language of vv. 3–4, however, reflects that employed

---

1. Cf. Helga Weippert, "Die 'deuteronomistischen' Beurteilungen der Könige von Israel und Juda und das Problem der Redaktion der Königsbücher," *Bib* 53 (1972): 335.

in relation to Jeroboam and Ahab. The use of the verbal expression *mabʿîr ʾahărê,* "consume," to describe YHWH's destruction of the monarch and his house recalls the similar expression in the oracles condemning Jeroboam (1 Kgs 14:10) and Ahab (1 Kgs 21:21). The reference in v. 4 to the dogs that will eat the dead of Baasha in the city and the birds of the heavens that will eat the dead of Baasha in the open field corresponds to the oracles condemning Jeroboam (1 Kgs 14:11) and Ahab (1 Kgs 21:19–24; 2 Kgs 9:10, 36).

[**16:5–7**] The introductory conjunctive particle *wĕgam,* "and also," marks the notice concerning Jehu's oracle in v. 7 as an appendix to the preceding regnal account in 1 Kgs 15:33–16:6. Insofar as the presentation of Asa's reign also contains an account of his defeat of Baasha's incursions in 1 Kgs 15:17–22, the report of Jehu's oracle against Baasha in 1 Kgs 16:7 may originally have appeared as a conclusion to that account. The relationship between 1 Kgs 16:1–4 and the oracles concerning Jeroboam in 1 Kgs 14:10–11 and Ahab in 1 Kgs 21:21–24; 2 Kgs 9:8–10 suggests that 1 Kgs 16:1–4 was also composed in part on the basis of the statement in 1 Kgs 16:7 as a link between the accounts concerning the reigns and downfalls of both Jeroboam and Ahab.

VIII. Regnal Account of Elah ben Baasha of Israel
1 Kings 16:8–14

16:8 In the twenty-sixth year of Asa, king of Judah, Elah ben Baasha ruled over Israel in Tirzah for two years.

9 And his servant Zimri, commander of half of the chariotry, conspired against him. He was in Tirzah drinking himself drunk[a] in the house of Arza, who was over the house[b] in Tirzah. 10 And Zimri came and struck him down so that he died in the twenty-seventh year of Asa, king of Judah, and he ruled in his place. 11 And when he sat on his throne to rule, he struck down all the house of Baasha; he did not leave to him anyone pissing against the wall, his kinspeople, or his supporters. 12 So Zimri destroyed all the house of Baasha according to the word of YHWH which He spoke to Baasha by the hand of Jehu the prophet 13 concerning all the sins of Baasha and the sins of Elah his son, which they sinned and which they caused Israel to commit, provoking YHWH, the G-d of Israel, with their empty gods.

14 And the rest of the affairs of Elah and all that he did, are they not written in the book of the Chronicles of the Kings of Israel?

a. Hebrew, *šikkôr*, is an adverb that refers to "drunkenness"; cf. Peshitta, *ʿtyqʾ*, "old (wine)," apparently reading *šikkôr* as a noun.

b. The expression *ʾăšer ʿal habbayit*, "who is over the house," is a technical term for "the royal steward" or chief administrator of the king. Cf. Peshitta, "in the house of Arʿa (Hebrew, Arza), which he built in Tirzah," and Targum Jonathan, which understands Zimri's drunkenness as religious idolatry, "and he was in Tirzah, drinking himself drunk at the house of Arza, the idol which was in the house in Tirzah."

First Kings 16:8–14 takes its lead from the preceding account of Baasha's condemnation as indicated by the reference to the fulfillment of Jehu ben Hanani's prophetic oracle in v. 12. The present account is the product of the Jehu History. Its focus on Zimri's assassination of Elah serves the Jehu History's agenda by portraying unchecked violence throughout the history of the northern kingdom of Israel. The narrative also serves the agendas of the Hezekian, Josian, and exilic DtrH editions, insofar as it notes that Elah follows in the sins of Jeroboam.

[8] The typically formulated evaluation of Elah's reign is lacking here. It appears instead at the conclusion of Elah's reign as part of the justification for his overthrow.

[9–13] The account of Elah's reign focuses exclusively on his assassination and the extermination of his house by Zimri. The text provides little information concerning Zimri other than that he was commander of half of the Israelite chariot corps. This lack of information should not be surprising, insofar as he ruled only for seven days and had little impact other than the removal of the house of Baasha (see 1 Kgs 16:15–22). The motives for the coup are readily intelligible on the basis of Asa's reign in 1 Kgs 15:17–22; Baasha's moves against Judah had been effectively countered by King Asa, who forged a new alliance with the Arameans. The result was a military and political disaster for northern Israel insofar as it opened the northernmost territories of Israel to invasion by the Arameans and forced Baasha to abandon his forward position in Ramah that threatened Judah. The Judeans capitalized on this reversal to build their own forward positions in Benjamin. The narrative provides no information concerning Arza other than his office as royal steward, "he who is over the house" (*ʾăšer ʿal habbayit*; cf. 1 Kgs 4:6; 18:3; 2 Kgs 10:5; 15:5; 18:18).

Following the assassination of Elah, Zimri took the throne and exterminated the entire royal house in keeping with the oracle of Jehu ben Hanani. The use of the term *maštîn běqîr*, "he who pisses against the wall," in reference to the males of the house of Baasha/Elah indicates the relationship between this passage and the oracles condemning Jeroboam (1 Kgs 14:10) and Ahab (1 Kgs 21:21; 2 Kgs 9:8), much like that noted above in the discussion of Jehu's oracle against Baasha in 1 Kgs 16:1–4. The account of Elah's reign functions together with the account of Baasha's reign in 1 Kgs 15:33–16:7 as a means to link the narrative complexes concerning Solomon and Jeroboam and Ahab and Jehu within the larger framework of the Jehu History and the Hezekian, Josian, and Exilic DtrH. The concluding assessment of Elah's reign, which notes that he followed in the sins of Jeroboam, cements the account into the DtrH framework. The reference to the "empty gods" (Hebrew, *hablêhem*, lit., "their vanities") indicates that the king's emulation of the sins of Jeroboam entailed the worship of foreign gods (cf. 1 Kgs 16:26; 2 Kgs 17:15).

[14] The concluding regnal résumé omits reference to his burial with his fathers, no doubt due to the circumstances of his death and the statement in 1 Kgs 16:4 that the dogs and the birds of the heavens would eat the dead of the house of Baasha.

IX. Regnal Account of Zimri of Israel
1 Kings 16:15–22

16:15 In the twenty-seventh year of Asa, king of Judah, Zimri ruled for seven days in Tirzah. The people were encamped against Gibbethon of the Philistines. 16 The people who were encamped heard that "Zimri has conspired, and also he has struck down the king," ᵃand all Israel made Omri, commander of the army, king over Israelᵃ on that day in the camp. 17 And Omri and all Israel went up with him from Gibbethon, and besieged Tirzah. 18 When Zimri saw that the city was captured, he went to the palaceᵇ of the house of the king, and burned the house of the king upon him with fire, so that he died 19 because of his sinsᶜ which he committed, to do evil in the eyes of YHWH, to walk in the path of Jeroboam and in his sin which he caused Israel to commit.

20 And the rest of the affairs of Zimri and his conspiracy which he carried out, are they not written in the book of the Chronicles of the Kings of Israel? 21 Then the people of Israel were divided in half; half of the people went behind Tibni ben Ginat to make him king, and half were behind Omri. 22 And the people who were behind Omri overpowered the half of the people who were behind Tibni ben Ginat, and Tibni died, and Omri ruled.

a–a. Cf. LXX, "and they made Omri, commander of the army, king in Israel in that day," which calls for reading Greek *ev* (Hebrew, *bĕ*), "in (Israel)," in place of Hebrew, *kol*, "all Israel."

b. Hebrew, *ʾarmôn*, "palace, citadel"; cf. LXX, *antron*, "cave, inner chamber"; Targum Jonathan, *ʾidrôn*, "inner chamber"; Peshitta, *nwsʾ*, "shrine, inner sanctuary."

c. Ketiv, *ḥaṭṭaʾtô*, "his sin"; read with Qere, *ḥaṭṭōʾtâw*, "his sins."

The introductory regnal account of Zimri of Israel in 1 Kgs 15:15a is joined syntactically to the presentation of the events of Zimri's reign in vv. 15b-19. The concluding regnal résumé follows in v. 20, but it is joined to an appendix in vv. 21–22 that briefly relates the civil war between Omri and Tibni ben Ginat. Like the accounts of Baasha and Elah, the account of Zimri's reign serves the agendas of all editions of the DtrH. The focus once again on the outbreak of violence in Israel indicates that it is the product of the Jehu History. Nevertheless, the focus on the sins of Jeroboam and Israel also serves the Hezekian, Josian, and Exilic DtrH editions.

[15–19] Zimri's coup takes place in a manner reminiscent of Baasha's coup against Nadab ben Jeroboam during the Israelite siege of Gibbethon (1 Kgs 15:27). The continued assault against Gibbethon some twenty-four years later points once again to the military reverses suffered by the house of Baasha. The placement of the Israelite army at such a distant location helps to explain the circumstances under which Zimri, apparently subordinate to Omri (v. 16), would attempt to carry out his coup. The location of the army at Gibbethon gave Zimri more freedom to act; perhaps his plan depended on his ability to consolidate his position before the army had the time to react. The narrative indicates that Omri quickly garnered the army's support and moved against Zimri in Tirzah. The portrayal of Zimri's suicide indicates that he did not anticipate such a rapid military response. The concluding statement that he followed in the path of Jeroboam to cause Israel to sin ties the account into the larger DtrH framework.

[20–22] The appendix relates the civil war between Omri and Tibni ben Ginat. Tibni was likely a supporter of Zimri, although it is possible that he was simply an opportunist who attempted to capitalize on Israel's instability following the deaths of Baasha, Elah, and Zimri.

X. Regnal Account of Omri of Israel
1 Kings 16:23–28

16:23 In the thirty-first year of Asa, king of Judah, Omri ruled over Israel twelve years; in Tirzah he ruled for six years.

24 He acquired the hill of Samaria from Shemer with two talents of silver, built up the hill, and called the name of the city which he had built after the name of Shemer, the owner of the hill, Samaria. 25 Omri did evil in the eyes of YHWH, and he was worse than all who were before him. 26 He walked in all the way of Jeroboam ben Nebat and in his sin[a] which he caused Israel to commit to provoke YHWH, G-d of Israel, with their empty gods.[b]

27 And the rest of the affairs of Omri which he did and his power, are they not written in the book of the Chronicles of the Kings of Israel? 28 Omri slept with his fathers and was buried in Samaria, and Ahab his son ruled in his place.

a. Ketiv, *ûběḥaṭṭōʾtâw,* "and in all his sins"; read with Qere, *ûběḥaṭṭāʾtô,* "and in all his sin."

b. LXX adds a lengthy addition (3 Rgns 16:28a–h), which constitutes an introductory regnal account of the reign of Jehoshaphat ben Asa. The text is based upon 1 Kgs 22:41–51, and it is included here to anticipate Jehoshaphat's appearance in the account of Ahab's death in 1 Kgs 22 (see Hrozný, 42–44). The translation of the Greek text is as follows:

16:28a And in the eleventh year of Omri, Jehoshaphat son of Asa ruled Judah; (he was) thirty-five years (old) at the beginning of his reign, and he ruled for twenty-five years in Jerusalem, and the name of his mother was Gezouba daughter of Selei.

28b And he walked in the path of Asa his father and did not turn from it to do what is right before the L-rd; only the high places they did not remove. They sacrificed in the high places and burned incense. 28c And the agreements of Jehoshaphat and all his power and those whom he fought, behold, are they not written in the book of the Chronicles of the Kings of Judah?

28d And the rest of the installations which they made in the days of Asa his father he removed from the land. 28e And there was no king in Syria, only a prefect. 28f And King Jehoshaphat made a ship at Tarshish to go to Sophir for gold, but it did not go because the ship was crushed at Ezion Geber. 28g Then the king of Israel said to Jehoshaphat, "I will send out your servants and my servants in the ship," but Jehoshaphat would not.

28h And Jehoshaphat slept with his fathers, and he was buried with his fathers in the city of David, and Joram his son ruled in his place.

The regnal account of Omri constitutes the next link in the sequence of regnal accounts leading to the establishment of the Omride dynasty and the reign of Omri's son Ahab. Omri is mentioned in the Mesha stone as a powerful king who took possession of Moabite territory in the mid-ninth century (*ANET* 320–21), and later Assyrian records refer to Israel as "the house of Omri" even after the Omride dynasty was overthrown by Jehu.[1] Considering the importance of Omri as the founder of the first major dynasty of northern Israel and its capital city of Samaria, the present report seems somewhat nondescript. This is due to the DtrH interest in theological evaluation of Israel's history and the key role of Ahab—and not Omri—as the worst of Israel's monarchs.

---

1. E.g., Shalmaneser III (853–824 B.C.E.) refers to Jehu as "the son of Omri" (*ANET* 282), and a century later Tiglath-pileser III (744–727 B.C.E.) refers to northern Israel as "the land of Omri" (*ANET* 284). See also Tammi Schneider, "Rethinking Jehu," *Bib* 77 (1996): 100–107.

The account displays a typical structure beginning with the introductory regnal formula in v. 23, which is joined with the summation of the events of Omri's reign in vv. 24–26. The concluding regnal formula appears in vv. 27–28. The account functions integrally as a part of the Jehu History and all three major DtrH editions; Omri's evil deeds aid in explaining the ultimate exiles of Israel and Judah in the exilic DtrH. They form a suitable basis for contrasting the apostasy of the northern monarchs with Josiah's righteousness, and they demonstrate within the Hezekian DtrH and the Jehu History the problems of violence and instability in the northern monarchy.

[23] The introductory regnal formula places the beginning of Omri's reign in the thirty-first year of Asa and states that he ruled for twelve years. By contrast, Zimri's death takes place in the twenty-seventh year of Asa (1 Kgs 16:15–22), which indicates that Omri's war with Tibni lasted for some four years before Omri was fully acknowledged as king.

[24–26] The presentation of the events of Omri's reign focuses exclusively on his foundation of Samaria as the new capital of northern Israel. Samaria is identified with the modern village of Sebaste, about six and one-half miles northwest of Shechem. It was situated on top of a small hill, and its position in the northwestern hill country of northern Israel along the road running north from Shechem gave it greater access than Tirzah afforded to both the Jezreel Valley and the coastal plain. The position enabled the Omrides to cooperate more fully with the Phoenicians in controlling the trade of the western Mediterranean and western Asia. The move from Tirzah left the eastern Jezreel and the Transjordan exposed, as illustrated by the death of Omri's son Ahab while defending Ramoth Gilead in the Transjordan from Aramean incursions. Excavations at the site of Samaria confirm that it was founded in the mid-ninth century B.C.E., that a well-built royal acropolis stood atop the hill, and that its fortifications were among the most impressive in Israel.[2]

Omri's purchase of the hill of Samaria from Shemer, who is otherwise unknown, indicates an interest in establishing a capital for the Omride dynasty on much the same basis as Jerusalem—that is, Omri acquired Samaria as a personal possession, much as David acquired Jerusalem.[3] Although Samaria was located in the territory of Manasseh, Omri would not be dependent on the northern tribes, giving him greater flexibility and power in ruling over the northern coalition.

[27–28] Omri was the first northern monarch buried in Samaria. Iron Age burial chambers have been found north of the city, but the location of the royal tombs remains uncertain.[4]

---

2. N. Avigad, "Samaria (City)," *NEAEHL* 4:1300–1310; Amihai Mazar, *Archaeology of the Land of the Bible, 10,000–586 B.C.E.* (New York: Doubleday, 1990), 406–10.

3. See Albrecht Alt, "The Monarchy in the Kingdoms of Israel and Judah," in *Essays on Old Testament History and Religion* (Garden City, N.Y.: Doubleday, 1967), esp. 321–24.

4. Avigad, *NEAEHL* 4:1306.

XI. Regnal Account of Ahab
ben Omri of Israel
1 Kings 16:29–22:40

The regnal account of Ahab ben Omri in 1 Kgs 16:29–22:40 includes the initial regnal account in 1 Kgs 16:29–34, the introductory legends concerning Elijah in 1 Kgs 17:1–24, YHWH's role as G-d of creation and Israel in 1 Kings 18–19, the condemnation of Ahab in 1 Kgs 20, the condemnation of the house of Ahab for the murder of Naboth in 1 Kgs 21, the death of Ahab in 1 Kgs 22:1–38, and the concluding regnal account in 1 Kgs 22:39–40.

1 Kings 16:29–34 The Initial Regnal Account of Ahab

16:29 Ahab ben Omri ruled over Israel [a]in the thirty-eighth year of Asa, king of Judah, and[a] Ahab ben Omri ruled over Israel in Samaria for twenty-two years.

30 Ahab ben Omri did more evil in the eyes of YHWH than all who were before him. 31 Walking in the sins of Jeroboam ben Nebat wasn't enough for him,[b] so he took as wife Jezebel bat Ethbaal, king of the Sidonians, and he went and he served Baal, and he worshiped him. 32 He erected an altar to Baal in the house of Baal which he built in Samaria. 33 Ahab made the Asherah and did more to provoke YHWH, the G-d of Israel, than all the kings of Israel before him.

34 In his days, Hiel the Beth Elite built Jericho; with Abiram his firstborn he founded it, and with Segub[c] his younger son he set up its gates according to the word of YHWH which He spoke by the hand of Joshua ben Nun.

a–a. LXX reads, "in the second year of Jehoshaphat," to account for 3 Rgns 16:28a–h.

b. Hebrew, *hănāqēl,* inexplicably begins with a *he*-interrogative, but most interpreters read the initial *he* as the definite article with the niphal infinitive *hannāqēl,* "that which is light." The interrogative form may stand, i.e., "and it came to pass—was it a light thing his walking in the sins of Jeroboam?—and (that) he took, etc." (cf. Ezek 8:17; Burney 206; Montgomery-Gehman 291).

c. Ketiv, *ûbiśgîb,* "and with Segib"; read with Qere, *ûbiśgûb,* "and with Segub."

The regnal résumé in v. 29 is joined to an evaluation of Ahab's reign in vv. 30–33. An appendix in v. 34 concerning the reestablishment of Jericho by Hiel of Beth El closes the subunit.

[29–33] The evaluation of Ahab's reign serves the theological interests of the DtrH insofar as it emphasizes that he committed more evil than all who were before him. Although the narrative makes a similar statement concerning Omri (see 1 Kgs 16:25), v. 31 ensures that the reader grasps the point by stating that it was not sufficient for him to follow in the path of Jeroboam, so he also married the Sidonian princess Jezebel bat Ethbaal, who prompted him to worship Baal and Asherah. This runs counter to the Dtr prohibition against intermarriage with the seven Canaanite peoples in Deut 7:1–6 (cf. 1 Kgs 11:1–8), and illustrates the concern articulated there that such intermarriages would lead Israelites to the worship of their pagan gods. No clear pagan temple complex has been found in Samaria, but the so-called ivory house includes great quantities of inlaid ivory carvings characteristic of Phoenician art.[1] Jezebel's name, *ʾîzebel, "where* is honor/exaltation?" is a polemical parody of a fuller name that was designed to honor the Phoenician gods Baal or Asherah (cf. the name Ichabod, *"where* is glory?" in 1 Sam 4:21).

From a political and economic standpoint, Ahab's marriage to Jezebel makes perfect sense. She is identified as the daughter of Ethbaal, king of Sidon, a priest of Astarte, who overthrew the ruling house of Hiram in Tyre and ruled Phoenicia during 887–856 B.C.E.[2] He was known for his unification of the major Phoenician cities and his aggressive expansion of Phoenician trade opportunities, which an alliance with Israel would well serve. From Israel's standpoint, alliance with the Phoenicians also enhanced trade, and it is possible that the alliance served as a countermeasure against the Arameans who had invaded northern Israel and the Transjordan following their alliance with Asa of Judah. The ninth-century Melqart stela, however, indicates that relations between the Phoenicians and the Arameans were cordial,[3] but this relationship may have been motivated by a common fear of the Assyrians that would have prompted the Phoenicians and Arameans to put aside their differences to meet a common enemy. Ahab, who ultimately died fighting the Arameans, joined the Arameans to fight the Assyrians in 853 B.C.E.

[34] The appended notice concerning the reestablishment of Jericho by Hiel of Beth El fulfills the curse uttered by Joshua in Josh 6:26 that the one who would reestablish the city would do so at the cost of his firstborn and younger sons. Such an act points to the growing influence of Canaanite idolatry in Israel as a result of Ahab's marriage to Jezebel. The mention of Jericho is no accident at this point, insofar as it points to a reversal of Israel's control of land acquired

1. Avigad, *NEAEHL* 4:1304–6; Amihai Mazar, *Archaeology of the Land of the Bible, 10,000–586 B.C.E.* (New York: Doubleday, 1990), 409–10.
2. For full discussion of Ethbaal and his reign, see H. Jacob Katzenstein, *The History of Tyre: From the Beginning of the Second Millennium B.C.E. until the Fall of the Neo-Babylonian Empire in 538 B.C.E.* (Jerusalem: Schocken Institute, 1973), 129–66.
3. *KAI* 201; *ANET* 655; see Katzenstein, *History,* 137–41.

with Joshua's conquest. It likewise points forward to the Babylonian destruction of Jerusalem and capture of King Zedekiah at Jericho (2 Kgs 25:1–7).[4] The association of Hiel with Beth El points to the northern Israelite sanctuary as a source of religious corruption in northern Israel.

1 Kings 17:1–24 Introductory Legends concerning Elijah

17:1 [a]Elijah the Tishbite from the settlers of Gilead[a] said to Ahab, "By the life of YHWH, G-d of Israel, before whom I stand, there will be neither dew nor rain during these years except by my word."

2 The word of YHWH came to him, saying, 3 "Go from this place, and turn eastward, and hide in the Wadi Cherith, which is by the Jordan. 4 And you will drink from the wadi, and I have commanded the ravens to support you there." 5 And he went, and he did according to the word of YHWH. And he went and he stayed in the Wadi Cherith, which is by the Jordan. 6 And the ravens would bring him bread and meat in the morning and the evening, and from the wadi he would drink. 7 But after some time the wadi dried up because there was no rain upon the land. 8 And the word of YHWH came to him, saying, 9 "Arise, go to Zarephath, which belongs to Sidon, and stay there. Behold, I have commanded there a widow to support you." 10 And he arose and went to Zarephath, and he came to the gate of the city, and behold, there was a widow gathering sticks. And he called to her, and said, "Bring me, please, a little water in a vessel that I may drink." 11 She went to bring it, and he called to her and said, "Bring me, please, a piece of bread in your hand." 12 And she said, "By the life of YHWH, your G-d, I have nothing baked, only a handful of meal in a jar and a little oil in a jug. And behold, I am gathering two sticks, and I shall go and make it for myself and my son, and we shall eat it and die." 13 And Elijah said to her, "Do not fear! Go, do as you have said, but make for me a little cake first and bring it out to me, and for yourself and for your son you shall make something afterwards, 14 for thus says YHWH, G-d of Israel, 'The jar of meal shall not empty, and the jug of oil shall not run out until the day that YHWH gives[b] showers upon the face of the land.'" 15 And she went and she did as Elijah said, and she ate—[c]she and he[c] and her house—many days. 16 The jar of meal did not empty, and the jug of oil did not run out as YHWH said when He spoke by the agency of Elijah.

4. See Marvin A. Sweeney, "On the Literary Function of the Notice concerning Hiel's Reestablishment of Jericho in 1 Kings 16.34," in *Seeing Signals, Reading Signs: The Art of Exegesis* (ed. M. A. O'Brien and H. N. Wallace; JSOTSup 415; Sheffield: Sheffield Academic Press, 2004), 104–15.

17 And after these things the son of the woman, the mistress of the house, became sick, and his sickness was very severe until there was no breath left in him. 18 And she said to Elijah, "What do you have against me, O man of G-d? Have you come to me to punish my sins and to kill my son?" 19 He said to her, "Give me your son." And he took him from her breast, and brought him up into the upper level where he was staying, and laid him upon his bed. 20 And he called to YHWH, and said, "O YHWH, my G-d, have you also brought evil upon this woman with whom I am staying to kill her son?" 21 ᵈAnd he stretched himself outᵈ over the boy three times, and he called unto YHWH, and he said, "O YHWH, my G-d, restore, please, the life of this boy within." 22 YHWH listened to the voice of Elijah, and the life of the boy returned within him, and he lived. 23 Elijah took the boy, brought him down from the upper level of the house, and gave him to his mother, and Elijah said, "See, your son is alive." 24 And the woman said to Elijah, "Now I know this, that you are a man of G-d, and the word of YHWH in your mouth is true."

a–a. Note the variations in LXX and Targum, prompted by problems in understanding the references to Elijah as "the Tishbite (*hattišbî*)" and to his provenance "from the settlers of Gilead (*mittōšābê gilʿād*)," i.e., LXX, "And Elihu the prophet, the Thesbite, who is from Thesbon of Galaad"; Targum Jonathan, "And Elijah, who was from Teshub from the settlers of Gilead."

b. Read with Qere, *tēt,* "gives" (infinitive construct); cf. Ketiv, *tittēn,* "she shall give," which does not correspond with the masculine construction of the subject, *yhwh,* "YHWH." See also Targum Jonathan, *dĕyitēn,* "who shall give (masculine)"; Peshitta, *dntl,* "who gave (masculine)."

c–c. Qere, *hîʾ wāhûʾ,* "she and he"; Ketiv, *hûʾ wāhîʾ,* "he and she."

d–d. Cf. LXX, *kai enephusēsen,* "and he breathed," which attempts to explain Elijah's stretching out upon the boy.

Although 1 Kgs 17:1–24 contains three discrete narratives, they constitute episodes of a single block of material that functions as the introduction to the narratives concerning Elijah and his opposition to the rule of King Ahab of Israel in 1 Kgs 17–22.⁵ The text is demarcated by the notice of Elijah's statement in v. 1 concerning YHWH's vow that no rain would fall upon the land. The only formal indicator is the *waw*-consecutive phrase, *wayyōʾmer ʾēlîyāhû hattišbî mittōšābê gilʿād ʾel-ʾaḥʾāb,* "and Elijah the Tishbite from the settlers of Gilead said to Ahab," which shifts the focus of the narrative from Ahab to the prophet. The full details of the prophet's identity introduce him as a major protagonist. The reference to Ahab indicates the other major protagonist. The citation of Eli-

5. Cf. Herbert Chanan Brichto, *Toward a Grammar of Biblical Poetics: Tales of the Prophets* (New York and Oxford: Oxford University Press, 1992), 122–30.

jah's statement concerning YHWH's vow signals the major concerns of both the immediate context and the Elijah/Elisha cycle at large—that is, opposition to the influence of Baal, the Canaanite/Phoenician god of rain, storm, and fertility, and the house of Omri, which was allied with the Phoenicians by Ahab's marriage to Jezebel. The emphasis on YHWH's withholding of rain indicates the general intent to target Baal, the deity who brought rain to the land in order to ensure its fertility and productivity.[6] The following narratives emphasize various aspects of the polemic against Baal—that is, Elijah is supported by YHWH and not Baal insofar as YHWH provides the Wadi Cherith for water and the ravens are sent by YHWH to support the prophet. YHWH also sends Elijah to Zarephath of the Sidonians, the homeland of Baal, and provides a widow to support him; and YHWH enables Elijah to restore the widow's son to life when he nearly dies as the result of the drought. Each of these episodes claims a different aspect of Baal's power for YHWH: control of nature, location in Phoenicia/Canaan, and the ability to sustain life.[7]

The primary characters, Elijah and Ahab, point to YHWH and Baal as the underlying protagonists. The narrative asserts YHWH's control over the rain, nature, Phoenicia, and life itself to demonstrate YHWH's efficacy over against Baal. It also emphasizes the power of YHWH's word as the means by which YHWH's power will be realized. Such an emphasis points to the role of Elijah as the representative of YHWH and the agent by which YHWH's words and power are manifested. Following the introductory statement by Elijah of YHWH's vow in v. 1, the successive subunits address each concern. Verses 2–7 begin with the prophetic word transmission formula *wayĕhî dĕbar-yhwh ʾēlāyw lēʾmōr*, "and the word of YHWH came to him, saying," which emphasizes the importance of YHWH's word and the prophet's role in communicating it.[8] YHWH instructs the prophet to live in the Wadi Cherith where he will be supported by creation itself. Verses 8–16 begin with another example of the prophetic word transmission formula, which introduces YHWH's instructions to the prophet to travel to Zarephath where he will be supported by the widow, who is bereft of food due to the drought. YHWH—and not the Phoenician god Baal—will provide her with meal and oil. Finally, vv. 17–24 begins with a temporal statement, "and after these things," to introduce the prophet's revival of the widow's son. The disruption of the prior emphasis on the introductory prophetic word transmission formula emphasizes Elijah's ability to call on YHWH and YHWH's power to grant life.

---

6. Cf. Leah Bronner, *The Stories of Elijah and Elisha: As Polemics against Baal Worship* (POS 6; Leiden: Brill, 1968); Alan J. Hauser, "YHWH versus Death—The Real Struggle in 1 Kings 17–19," in *From Carmel to Horeb: Elijah in Crisis* (JSOTSup 85; Sheffield: Almond Press, 1990), 9–89.

7. See W. Herrmann, "Baal," *DDD²* 132–39.

8. Sweeney, *Isaiah 1–39*, 546–47; Meier, *Speaking*, 314–19.

The emphasis on the power of the prophet as YHWH's representative is characteristic of the prophetic legends.[9] Both legends support the polemical intent to assert YHWH's power over that of Baal and to point to YHWH's role in the eventual death of Ahab. Although the narratives of 1 Kgs 17 currently function at the synchronic level within the regnal account of Ahab's reign (1 Kgs 16:29–22:40) as an introduction to Elijah's role as the major opponent of Ahab, this material also functions diachronically in relation to the larger Elijah/Elisha cycle that has been taken up by the DtrH and worked into presentation of the reigns of Israel's and Judah's kings.[10] The narrative easily serves the interests of the Jehu History and all three editions of the DtrH, insofar as the conflict between Elijah and Ahab or YHWH and Baal points to sins of the northern kingdom of Israel. The polemical portrayal of Baal and the house of Omri also points to the eventual overthrow of the house of Omri by Jehu of Israel, supported by Elijah's successor, Elisha. Second Kings 10, for example, relates Jehu's killing of Ahab's descendants and the worshipers of Baal as the culmination of the revolt that brought the house of Jehu to power. These narratives ultimately indicate the establishment of an empire extending from Lebo-Hamath to the Sea of the Arabah under the reign of Jeroboam ben Joash, the great-grandson of Jehu (2 Kgs 14:23–29).[11]

[1] The name Elijah, Hebrew *ʾēlîyāhû*, testifies to the religious dimensions of this conflict insofar as it combines the Hebrew expressions *ʾēlî*, "my god," and *yāhû*, a variation of the divine name, YHWH: "YHWH is my god."[12] He is identified as *hattišbî*, "the Tishbite," a gentilic attribution applied to Elijah (see also 1 Kgs 21:17, 28; 2 Kgs 1:3, 8; 9:36) that suggests that he comes from a town, village, or region called Tishbe. No such name is otherwise attested in biblical literature or ancient Near Eastern records, apart from the reference to Tobit's home in Tob 1:2, a Galilean town called Thisbe (Greek, *thisbēs*), located in the territory of Naphtali. This site can hardly be associated with the present reference to Tishbe, however, because of its location and the relatively late date (fourth–third century B.C.E.) for the composition of Tobit. Early Christian tradition identifies Tishbe with the site of el-Ishtib, located some eight miles north of the Wadi Jabbok near the monastery of Mar Elias, but this site was founded

9. Sweeney, *Isaiah 1–39*, 534; Alexander Rofé, *The Prophetical Stories* (Jerusalem: Magnes, 1988); cf. Georg Fohrer, *Elia* (2d ed.; AThANT 53; Zurich: Zwingli, 1968), who treats the individual narratives as originally independent legends.

10. See esp. Georg Hentschel, *Die Elija-erzählungen* (Erfurter Theologische Studien 33; Leipzig: St. Benno, 1977).

11. Cf. Odil Hannes Steck, *Überlieferung und Zeitgeschichte in den Elia-Erzählungen* (WMANT 26; Neukirchen-Vluyn: Neukirchener, 1968); Marsha C. White, *The Elijah Legends and Jehu's Coup* (BJS 311; Atlanta: Scholars, 1997).

12. Cf. Martin Noth, *Die israelitische Personennamen im Rahmen der gemeinsemitischen Namengebung* (BWANT 3/10; Hildesheim: Georg Olms, 1966), 140–42.

in Roman times.[13] Otherwise, scholars emend the term Tishbite, but none proves satisfactory.[14] The issue is complicated by the specification, *mittōšābê-gilʿād,* "from the settlers of Gilead." Gilead refers to Israelite territory located across the Jordan River in the present-day Golan Heights and western Jordan. The Hebrew term *tôšāb* is a relatively late term that appears in priestly literature (see Exod 12:45; Lev 22:10; 25:6; Num 35:15; 1 Chr 29:15) as a parallel to *gēr,* "resident alien" (Gen 23:4). Consequently many interpreters follow the LXX in rejecting the term *tôšāb,* "settler," reading instead *Thesbōn tēs Galaad,* "of the Teshbites of Gilead," insofar as the consonants of *mittōšābê* suggest an association with the term *hattišbî.* The term is well-attested in Aramaic as a reference to a foreigner who settles among an indigenous people. This has fueled speculation that Elijah is a foreigner who identified with Israel (e.g., Walsh, *1 Kings* 226). The Transjordanian territories of Gilead were frequently under threat by foreign powers, including Aram, Ammon, and Moab—indeed, the Mesha inscription indicates that the territory of Gad and Reuben was conquered by the Moabites in the mid-ninth century B.C.E. (*ANET* 320–21). Likewise, Josh 22 indicates that there were questions within Israel as to whether these territories were fully loyal. From the perspective of Ephraimite hill country, the people of the Transjordan might very well be viewed as foreigners.

Elijah's initial statement employs the oath formula *ḥay-yhwh,* "by the life of YHWH," which typically serves as a form of self-curse to bind the party taking the oath to a specific course of action.[15] Elijah speaks on behalf of YHWH, who is bound not to provide rain until the prophet states otherwise. Such an oath reinforces the contention that YHWH controls the elements of creation, including the rains attributed to the rain god Baal in Canaanite/Phoenician culture.

[2–7] The first narrative in the sequence constitutes an account of Elijah's compliance with YHWH's instructions to hide in the Wadi Cherith. The prophetic word transmission formula portrays the following statement as a quotation of YHWH's instructions to the prophet. Because YHWH instructs Elijah to travel eastward, it presupposes that Elijah is located initially in the land of Israel west of the Jordan. The location of the Wadi Cherith is unknown. The term "Cherith" (Hebrew, *kĕrît*) means "that which is cut," and could refer to any natural wadi that is formed by water that erodes or cuts through the surrounding landscape. Many identify it as the Wadi Qelt, which extends from the Benjaminite hill country north of Jerusalem eastward into the Jordan Valley in the vicinity of Jericho.[16] The claim is not decisive, however, because it is not

---

13. J. T. Walsh, "Tishbe," *ABD* 6:577–78.

14. See ibid.; cf. Nelson Glueck, *The River Jordan* (Philadelphia: Jewish Publication Society, 1946), 170, who emends the text to refer to Jabesh Gilead.

15. See Sweeney, *Isaiah 1–39,* 525–26, 546.

16. See R. W. Younker, "Cherith, Brook of," *ABD* 1:899.

clear that Elijah crosses the Jordan. Verse 5 locates the Wadi Cherith "before (by) the Jordan" (ʿal-pĕnê hayyardēn), without specifying whether it lies to the east or the west. Because of the prevailing view that the Wadi Cherith lies to the east of the Jordan, other scholars identify the Wadi Cherith with the Wadi Jabesh, which flows into the Jordan from the east opposite the southern boundaries of the Jezreel Valley.[17] Indeed, the association with the Wadi Jabesh is highlighted by the notice in v. 7 that the wadi "dried up" (Hebrew, wayîbaš). No one knows if this wadi was called the Jabesh in antiquity, although interpreters associate it with the site of Jabesh Gilead (see Judg 21; 1 Sam 11). A location to the east of the Jordan would presumably return Elijah to his home territory in the Gilead. The eastern location is useful in associating Elijah with the Arameans, whose interests Elijah served, whether intentionally or not, by playing a role in the overthrow of the houses of Omri of Israel and Ben-Hadad of Aram, which cleared the way for Aramean domination of Israel during the early reign of Jehu.

YHWH's statements that the prophet will drink the water of the Wadi Cherith and eat the food brought to him by the ravens highlight the contention that YHWH controls nature to support the prophet. The reference to ravens presupposes their ability to scavenge for food (cf. Prov 30:17), to live in inhospitable environments (cf. Isa 34:11), and to find their way generally (cf. Noah's use of ravens in Gen 8:7). Job 38:41 indicates that YHWH cares for the ravens, which is analogous to the use of the raven to care for Elijah in the present context. This motif suggests associations with the wilderness tradition of the Pentateuch in which YHWH sustained the people by providing water, manna, and quails (see Exod 16:1–17:7; Num 11; 20:1–13; cf. Jer 35, which refers to the Rechabites, who live in the desert in keeping with the traditions of their ancestors). The use of the expression lĕkalkelĕkā, "to support/sustain you," in vv. 4 and 9 aids in establishing a relationship between this narrative and the following material concerning the widow of Zarephath. Both narratives emphasize YHWH's power over creation and the human world well outside the usual boundaries of the Ephraimite hill country.

The concluding notice that the wadi dried up confirms YHWH's intention to demonstrate mastery of nature by bringing drought on the land. Because the wadi runs dry, Elijah must move—to Zarephath.

[8–16] Elijah's residence with the widow of Zarephath emphasizes Elijah's status as a foreigner—that is, an Israelite living in a Phoenician city. This episode serves the larger purpose of demonstrating YHWH's power over against Baal even in a Phoenician city. Zarephath is located eight miles south of Sidon and fourteen miles north of Tyre at the site of modern Sarafand.[18]

---

17. Glueck, *River Jordan,* 170, 172, although he notes that the identification cannot be proved.
18. R. L. Roth, "Zarephath," *ABD* 6:1041.

Archaeological investigation indicates that it was founded in the Late Bronze Age (ca. 1500 B.C.E.), and functioned as a commercial port and industrial center for the production of textiles, pottery, agricultural produce, and the purple dye for which Phoenicia was famous.

Elijah takes up residence in the "upper chamber" of the widow's house (cf. vv. 19, 23 below). Many houses in ancient Israel and Phoenicia were constructed with two levels, the lower level being used for storage, cooking, and the housing of livestock and the upper level being used for living and sleeping quarters.[19] The woman is described as a widow, which subtly raises questions concerning her god Baal, who is responsible for the maintenance of life in Phoenician religion. Lacking a husband or other family for support, the woman is compelled to support herself and her son by whatever means are available, including the lodging of boarders, the gleaning of fields, and so on. Israelite law allows widows, orphans, and resident aliens to glean from the fields in order to support themselves (Deut 14:28–29; cf. Exod 23:10–11; Lev 19:10–11; 23:22; Ruth 2). Despite rampant speculation, the text contains no intimation that Elijah had any relationship with her other than as her tenant.

The prophet's demand that the woman bring water and food for him seems entirely impertinent given the drought, but it highlights the lack of food and water and the capacity of Baal or YHWH to provide both. In keeping with the portrayal of YHWH as the one who has made arrangements for the widow to support Elijah, she employs the oath formula *ḥay yhwh*, "by the life of YHWH," to respond to the prophet. Her use of the oath formula emphasizes her relationship with the Israelite deity, despite her identity as a Phoenician woman, and indicates YHWH's role as master of creation outside of the land of Israel. It also provides a link with the previous narrative context in v. 1, in which Elijah employs the oath formula to announce the drought to Ahab.

The prophet's demand emphasizes the miraculous nature of the narrative and its testimony to YHWH's power to provide. Elijah employs the technical language of prophecy, including the reassurance formula *ʾal-tîrēʾî*, "fear not" (v. 13),[20] and the so-called prophetic messenger formula (v. 14)[21] to indicate that YHWH, the G-d of Israel, is the source of his statements and the actions that are to follow. The promise that neither the meal nor the oil will run out coupled with the promise that YHWH will no longer withhold rain emphasizes once again that YHWH controls the rains and the capacity of creation to provide food. The prophet's role in making the announcement emphasizes his role as YHWH's authoritative spokesperson. The narrative carefully emphasizes

19. J. S. Holladay Jr., "House, Israelite," *ABD* 3:308–18.

20. Sweeney, *Isaiah 1–39*, 547; Edgar W. Conrad, *Fear Not Warrior: A Study of ʾal tîrāʾ Pericopes in the Hebrew Scriptures* (BJS 75; Chico, Calif.: Scholars Press, 1985).

21. Sweeney, *Isaiah 1–39*, 547; Meier, *Speaking*, 273–98.

that the woman, Elijah, and her house eat as a result of the prophet's actions. The Masoretic Text repoints the consonants so that she eats before the prophet.

The miraculous provision of meal and oil echoes a similar tradition concerning the prophet Elisha in 2 Kgs 4:1–7, in which Elisha likewise miraculously provides oil for a widow and her children. The parallel with this tradition (see also 2 Kgs 4:38–44 concerning Elisha's purifying food and providing for one hundred men) and the corresponding parallels between the narratives concerning Elijah's revival of the widow's son (vv. 17–24) and Elisha's revival of the Shunammite woman's son (2 Kgs 4:37) have fed persistent claims that the Elijah narratives are modeled on those of Elisha.[22] Indeed, the Elijah narratives function as an introduction to the longer narratives concerning Elisha and the successful revolt against the house of Omri.

[17–24] Elijah's revival of the widow's son continues the narrative assertion of YHWH's power over Baal by emphasizing that YHWH, acting through the prophet Elijah, restores the life of the Phoenician boy. Many have argued that vv. 17–24 constitute an originally independent narrative because of its distinctive features.[23] It lacks the introductory prophetic word transmission formula that introduces the narratives in vv. 2–7 and 8–16; the woman is initially identified in v. 17 as "mistress of the house," although she is later identified in v. 20 as "the widow"; and Elijah is identified in vv. 18 and 24 as "man of G-d" rather than as "the Tishbite." Nevertheless, the narrative is tied into the preceding narrative context, in which the characters of the widow and her son are introduced, by the introductory formula, "and after these things."

The narrative actually focuses on two fundamental themes: YHWH's power to grant life over against that of Baal and the role of Elijah as a man of G-d. The first is the question of the life or death of the boy, which serves as part of the larger narrative polemic. As god of rain and fertility, Baal is ultimately responsible for the life or death of the land; it is presumed that all life is the result of Baal's capacity to bring rain. Indeed, the mythologies of Canaan and the larger Mesopotamian world indicate that the restoration of life plays an important role in ancient theology concerning the fertility deity. Ugaritic myths concerning Baal and Aqhat and Mesopotamian myths concerning the descent of Inanna or Ishtar to the underworld point to a pattern in which the male fertility figure— Baal or Aqhat in Canaanite literature, Dumuzi in Sumerian literature, and Tammuz in Babylonian literature—dies and descends into the netherworld for a

---

22. E.g., White, *Elijah Legends,* 11–17.

23. E.g., Otto Thenius, *Die Bücher der Könige* (Kurzgefasstes exegetisches Handbuch zum Alten Testament 9; Leipzig: Weidmann, 1849), 220; G. H. Jones, *1 and 2 Kings* (2 vols.; New Century Bible Commentary; Grand Rapids: William B. Eerdmans; London: Marshall, Morgan, and Scott, 1984), 307; Stefan Timm, *Die Dynastie Omri* (FRLANT 124; Göttingen: Vandenhoeck & Ruprecht, 1982), 58–59.

period of time.[24] In each case, the figure is mourned, and ultimately, a feminine figure—Baal's consort Anath, Aqhat's sister Paqhat, Dumuzi's consort Inanna, and Tammuz's consort Ishtar—descends into the netherworld to rescue the male figure, restore him to life, and return him to the world of creation. The mythic pattern explains the seasonal cycle of rainy winters and dry summers in which the world blooms with life as a result of the rains while the male figure lives, dies for lack of rain while the male figure is in the netherworld, and blooms once again when the male is rescued and the rains return. The contention that YHWH restores the lifeless boy plays upon this mythic pattern, and undermines contentions that Baal or his consort Astarte, Asherah, or Anath plays a role in granting life/rain to the land.

The second fundamental theme is the assertion of Elijah's role as the man of G-d. This validates YHWH's role as the efficacious deity over against Baal or Astarte, but it introduces a separate concern with the identity of YHWH's representative as well. This motif functions as a means within the narrative to establish Elijah's authority as a prophet of YHWH who may speak for and act on YHWH's behalf. Such a contention prepares the reader for the following narrative in 1 Kgs 18 for Elijah's confrontation with the 400 prophets of Baal and the 450 prophets of Asherah. The motif also plays a role in tying the narrative into the larger narrative framework of 1 Kgs 17, insofar as the concluding assertion by the widow that Elijah is a man of G-d is accompanied by her statement that the word of YHWH in his mouth is true.

Although some view this narrative as a depiction of the boy's resurrection,[25] it is never clear that he is actually dead. Rather, the narrative portrays the boy as gravely ill and near death, with no breath left within him. Elijah's action therefore is one of healing (cf. Isa 38). The mother's rhetorical question to the prophet functions as an assertion that he has come to punish her for some sin that she has committed. It expresses a very commonly held view in the ancient world that death and disease are visited upon human beings by the gods because of some wrongdoing or divine capriciousness. Such an assertion emphasizes YHWH's beneficent role in relation to the widow. The exact nature of the prophet's action in stretching himself out over the boy three times is a symbolic action of sympathetic magic in which the prophet takes the illness of the boy into himself. By placing himself face-to-face with the boy, the prophet provides a means by which the illness is transferred from the body of the boy into his own.[26] The prophet's

24. The Baal myth appears in *ANET* 129–42; Aqhat, in *ANET* 149–55; the Descent of Inanna to the Netherworld, in *ANET* 52–57; and the Descent of Ishtar to the Netherworld, in *ANET* 106–9.

25..E.g., Rofé, *Prophetical Stories,* 132–35.

26. John Gray, *I & II Kings: A Commentary* (2d ed.; OTL; Philadelphia: Westminster, 1970), 382–83; Jones, *1 and 2 Kings,* 308; cf. Hentschel, *Elia-erzählungen,* 193–94 n. 550, who notes Mesopotamian parallels.

prayer to YHWH in v. 20 signals this concern, insofar as it emphasizes YHWH's action in healing the boy as a response to the prophet's petition. It also prepares the reader for the following narrative in which Elijah calls upon YHWH to light the fire on the altar and thereby to counter the claims of the prophets of Baal.

1 Kings 18:1–19:21 YHWH's Role as G-d of Creation and Israel

18:1 After many days the word of YHWH came to Elijah in the third year, saying, "Go, appear before Ahab, and I will give rain on the earth." 2 And Elijah went to appear before Ahab; and the famine was severe in Samaria.

3 Ahab summoned Obadiah, who was in charge of the palace. Now Obadiah revered YHWH greatly. 4 When Jezebel cut off the prophets of YHWH, Obadiah took one hundred prophets of YHWH, hid them, fifty each, in the cave, and supported them with bread and water. 5 And Ahab said to Obadiah, "Go about the land to all the springs of water and to all the wadis. Perhaps some grass will be found so that we may keep alive horse and mule ᵃand not lose any animals."ᵃ 6 And they divided the land between themselves to pass through it. Ahab went in one direction by himself, and Obadiah went in one direction by himself.

7 Obadiah was on the road, and behold, Elijah (was there) to meet him. He recognized him, and fell on his face, and said, "Is it you, my lord, Elijah?" 8 And he said to him, "It is me. Go, say to your lord, 'Elijah is here.'" 9 And he said, "How have I sinned that you give your servant into the hand of Ahab to kill him? 10 By the life of YHWH your G-d, there is no nation or kingdom where my lord has not sent me to seek you, and they say, 'he's not here,' and he makes the kingdom or nation swear, but he does not find you. 11 And now you say, 'Go, say to your lord, "Elijah is here."' 12 And when I go from you, a wind from YHWH will carry you off—where, I do not know—and I will come to tell Ahab, and when he does not find you, he shall kill me. Your servant has revered YHWH since my youth. 13 Has it not been told to my lord what I did when Jezebel killed the prophets of YHWH, that I hid one hundred of the prophets of YHWH, fifty in each cave, and I supported them with bread and water? 14 And now you say, 'Go, say to your lord, "Elijah is here."' Now he will kill me!" 15 And Elijah said, "By the life of YHWH of Hosts before whom I stand, indeed today I will appear before him." 16 And Obadiah went to meet Ahab, and he told him, and Ahab went to meet Elijah.

17 When Ahab saw Elijah, Ahab said to him, "Is it you, O troubler of Israel?" 18 And he said, "I have not troubled Israel, but you and your father did when you abandoned the commandments of YHWH and followed the Baals. 19 And now, send, gather to me all Israel at Mount Carmel, and the

four hundred fifty prophets of Baal and the four hundred prophets of Asherah who eat at the table of Jezebel.

20 Ahab sent among all the people of Israel, and gathered the prophets at Mount Carmel. 21 And Elijah drew near to all the people, and said, "How long have you been hopping on two opinions?[b] If YHWH is G-d, follow him, and if Baal is G-d, follow him." But the people did not answer him a word. 22 And Elijah said to the people, "I alone am left as a prophet for YHWH, and the prophets of Baal are four hundred fifty men.[c] 23 Let them give to us two bulls, and they will choose for themselves one bull, cut it up, and place it on wood, but they shall not light a fire. And I will prepare one[d] bull, and place it on wood, but I will not light a fire. 24 You shall call upon the name of your god. I will call upon the name of YHWH, and the god who answers with fire is G-d." And all the people answered, and said, "That's fine."[e]

25 Elijah said to the prophets of Baal, "Choose for yourselves one bull, and prepare it first, for you are many, and call upon the name of your god, but do not light a fire." 26 And they took the bull which he gave to them, and prepared it, and called upon the name of Baal from morning until noon, saying, "O Baal, answer us!" but there was no sound and there was no one answering, and they hopped[f] about the altar which he had made. 27 At noon Elijah mocked them, and said, "Call out in a loud voice, for he is G-d! [g]Maybe he is in conversation, or occupied, or on the road! Perhaps he is asleep, and must awaken!"[g] 28 And they called out in a loud voice, and gashed themselves with knives and lances according to their custom until blood poured out upon them. 29 When noon passed, they prophesied until the time for offering the afternoon sacrifice, but there was no sound, and there was no one answering, and there was no one listening.

30 And Elijah said to all the people, "Draw near to me," and all the people drew near to him, [h]and he repaired the damaged altar of YHWH.[h] 31 Elijah took twelve stones according to the number of the tribes of the sons of Jacob, to whom the word of YHWH had come, saying, "Israel shall be your name," 32 and he built with the stones an altar in the name of YHWH,[i] and made a trench that would enclose an area of two seahs of seed around the altar. 33 He arranged the wood, and cut up the bull, and placed it on the wood. 34 And he said, "Fill four jugs of water, and pour it on the whole burnt offering and on the wood!" And he said, "Do it again!" and they did it again, and he said, "Do it a third time!" and they did it a third time. 35 And the water went around the altar, and also the trench filled with water. 36 At the offering of the afternoon sacrifice Elijah the prophet drew near, and said, "O YHWH, G-d of Abraham, Isaac, and Israel, today let it be known that you are G-d in Israel and I am your servant, and by your words I have done all these things. 37 Answer me, O

YHWH, answer me, that this people may know that you, YHWH, are G-d, and you have turned their heart back." 38 And the fire of YHWH fell, and consumed the whole burnt offering and the wood and the stones and the dirt, and the water that was in the trench it licked up. 39 All the people saw, and they fell on their faces, and said, "YHWH is G-d! YHWH is G-d!" 40 And Elijah said to them, "Seize the prophets of Baal; let not a man escape from them!" and they seized them, and Elijah brought them down to the Wadi Kishon, and slaughtered them there.

41 And Elijah said to Ahab, "Go up, eat, and drink, for the sound of rushing is rain!" 42 And Ahab went up to eat and to drink. And Elijah went up to the top of the Carmel, crouched down on the earth, placed his face between his knees,[j] 43 and said to his attendant, "Go up now, gaze in the direction of the sea!" And he went up, gazed, and said, "There is nothing," and he said, "Do it again seven times." 44 At the seventh (time), he said, "Behold, a small cloud like the palm of man [k]is going up from the sea,"[k] And he said, "Go up, say to Ahab, 'harness (your mule), and get down before the rain stops you!'"

45 After a while, the heavens darkened with clouds and wind, and there was much rain, and Ahab rode,[l] and went to Jezreel. 46 And the hand of YHWH was with Elijah, and he girded his loins, and ran before Ahab until your coming to Jezreel.

19:1 Ahab told Jezebel all that Elijah had done and how[m] he killed all the prophets with the sword. 2 And Jezebel sent a messenger to Elijah, saying, "May the gods do even more, for by this time tomorrow I will make your life like the life of each of them."

3 And he saw,[n] rose, and ran for his life, and he came to Beer Sheba, which is in Judah, and he left his servant there. 4 He went in the wilderness a day's journey, came, sat under a certain[o] broom tree, and asked to die, and he said, "It's too much, now, O YHWH! Take my life, for I am no better than my fathers." 5 And he lay down, and slept under a certain broom tree, and behold, there was an angel touching him, and he said to him, "Arise! Eat!" 6 He looked, and behold, by his head was a cake cooked on hot stone and a jug of water. He ate, drank, sat, and lay down. 7 And the angel of YHWH returned a second time, touched him, and said, "Arise! Eat! lest the journey will be too great for you." 8 And he arose, ate, and drank, and went with the strength of that food forty days and forty nights, to the Mountain of G-d, Horeb.

9 He came there to a cave, and stayed there, and behold, the word of YHWH came to him, and said to him, "What are you doing here, Elijah?" 10 And he said, "I am very zealous for YHWH, the G-d of Hosts, because the people of Israel have abandoned your covenant. Your altars they have pulled down, and your prophets they have killed with the sword, and I

alone am left, and they intend to take my life." 11 And he said, "Go out, and stand on the mountain before YHWH," Pand behold, YHWH was passing by, and there was a great and strong wind breaking mountains to pieces and shattering rocks before YHWH. (But) YHWH was not in the wind. After the wind was earthquake, but YHWH was not in the earthquake. 12 After the earthquake was fire, but YHWH was not in the fire, and after the fire was a sound of faint silence.pq 13 When Elijah heard, he covered his face with his mantle, went out, and stood at the entrance of the cave, and behold, the sound came to him, and said, "What are you doing here, Elijah?" 14 And he said, "I am very zealous for YHWH, G-d of Hosts, for the sons of Israel have abandoned your covenant. Your altars they have pulled down, and your prophets they have killed with the sword, and I alone am left, and they intend to take my life." 15 And YHWH said to him, "Go, return by the road to the wilderness to Damascus, and come and anoint Hazael as king over Aram. 16 And Jehu ben Nimshi you shall anoint as king over Israel, and Elisha ben Shaphat from Abel Meholah you shall anoint as a prophet in your place. 17 He who escapes from the sword of Hazael Jehu shall kill, and he who escapes from the sword of Jehu Elisha shall kill. 18 And I will leave in Israel seven thousand, all the knees that did not bend to Baal and every mouth that did not kiss him."

19 He went from there and found Elisha ben Shaphat. He was plowing with twelve pairs (of oxen) before him, and he was with the twelfth. Elijah passed over to him, and threw his mantle to him. 20 He abandoned the cattle, ran after Elijah, and said, "Please, let me kiss my father and my mother, and I will go after you." But he said to him, "Go, return, for what have I done to you?" 21 He came back, took the pair of cattle, and sacrificed them. With the gear of the cattle he boiled them, i.e., the meat, and gave it to the people, and they ate. And he arose, went after Elijah, and served him.

a–a. MT, *wĕlôʾ nakrît mēhabbĕhēmâ*, lit., "and we will not cut off from the animal"; cf. LXX, *kai ouk exolothreuthēsontai apo tōn ktēnōn*, "and they shall not be destroyed from the herd," which presupposes the niphal Hebrew verb *nikrat*, "there shall not be cut off."

b. N.b., Hebrew *hassĕ'ippîm* constitutes a pun in that the term means both "branches" and "opinions." Cf. LXX, "how long will you go about lame on both thighs?" which passes over the pun for a rendition that understands *hassĕ'ippîm* in relation to the verb *psh*, "to hop, limp."

c. LXX adds "and the prophets of the groves (Asherah) are four hundred."

d. LXX reads *ton allon*, "the other," presupposing Hebrew, *haʾaḥēr*, "the other," in place of *hāʾeḥād*, "the one."

e. Lit., "Good is the word"; cf. LXX, "Good is the word which you have spoken"; Peshitta, "Good you have spoken."

f. Hebrew, *wayĕpassĕḥû,* literally, "and they limped"; cf. LXX, *kai dietrechon,* "and (they were) running back and forth"; Peshitta, *wᵓtktšw,* "and they strove hard, painfully"; Targum Jonathan, *ûmištatan,* "and (they were) moving back and forth."

g–g. Cf. LXX, "for he is meditating, or perhaps he is transacting business, or perhaps he is asleep and will awaken"; Targum Jonathan, "perhaps he is having a conversation, or he is indeed easing (i.e., relieving) himself, or he is on a journey, or perhaps he is asleep and will be awakened."

h–h. LXX places v. 30b immediately after v. 32a, to reconcile Elijah's "repair" of the altar with the statement that he "built" the altar in v. 32a.

i. LXX places v. 30b immediately after v. 32a.

j. Read with Qere, *birkāyw,* "his knees," instead of Ketiv, *birkô,* "his knee."

k–k. Hebrew, *ʿōlâ miyyām,* "going up from the sea"; cf. LXX, *anagousa hudōr,* "bringing up water," which presupposes the consonantally similar Hebrew, *maʿăleh mayim.*

l. Cf. LXX, "and (Ahab) wept," which presupposes Hebrew, *wayyibk,* in place of *wayyirkab.*

m. N.b., the stylistically awkward Hebrew, *wĕʾēt kol ʾăšer,* "and all that (he killed all the prophets with the sword)"; cf. LXX, *kai hōs,* "and how . . ."

n. Hebrew, *wayyarʾ,* "and he saw"; cf. LXX and Peshitta, "and he was afraid," which presupposes Hebrew, *wayyirāʾ,* "and he was afraid."

o. Read with Qere, lit., *ʾeḥād,* "one (masc.)," rather than Ketiv, *ʾeḥāt,* "one (fem.)."

p–p. Targum Jonathan reads, "And behold, YHWH was revealing himself, and before him were armies of angels of the wind breaking apart the mountains and shattering the rocks before YHWH; not in the army of the angels of the wind was the presence of YHWH. And after the army of the angels of the wind was the army of the angels of the earthquake; not in the army of the angels of the earthquake was the presence of YHWH. And after the army of the angels of the earthquake was the army of the angels of fire; not in the army of the angels of fire was the presence of YHWH; and after the army of the angels of the fire was the voice of those who were praising softly."

q. LXX reads *phōnē auras leptēs kakei kurios,* "(the) sound of a delicate breeze, and there was the L-rd"; for Targum Jonathan, see note p.

First Kings 18:1–19:21 builds upon the previously expressed concerns with the drought and the questions of life and death in an effort to demonstrate YHWH's roles as the G-d of Israel and the natural world of creation.[27] Although the narrative focuses on Elijah's demonstration of YHWH's power over against the Phoenician deities, Baal and Asherah, and YHWH's revelation to Elijah at Mount Horeb, it ultimately has larger concerns with the overthrow of the house of Omri and Ben Hadad of Aram through the efforts of the prophet Elisha ben Shaphat.[28] These concerns are expressed toward the end of the narrative by the divine voice that instructs Elijah to anoint Hazael as king of Aram and Jehu ben Nimshi as king of Israel and to designate Elisha as his successor.

27. Hauser, "YHWH versus Death"; cf. Robert L. Cohn, "The Literary Logic of 1 Kings 17-19," *JBL* 101 (1982): 333–50.
28. White, *Elijah Legends.*

First Kings 18:1–19:21 is demarcated by the introductory temporal formulation "and after many days the word of YHWH came to Elijah in the third year, saying . . ." Verse 1 introduces the themes of 1 Kgs 18—Elijah's appearance to Ahab and YHWH's capacity to provide rain for the land—but it does not explicitly address YHWH's revelation to Elijah in 1 Kgs 19. The introductory statements of 1 Kgs 19 relate Jezebel's efforts to kill Elijah to the preceding material in ch. 18 and thereby make it clear that chs. 18 and 19 must be considered together. The unit lacks clear formal markers of its subunits, which indicates that character and plot movement provide the criteria for defining its literary structure. The series of encounters between the various protagonists point to seven basic episodes:

1. YHWH's instructions to Elijah to appear before Ahab in 1 Kgs 18:1–2.
2. Ahab's instructions to Obadiah concerning his attempt find water in 1 Kgs 18:3–4.
3. Obadiah's encounter with Elijah in 1 Kgs 18:5–16.
4. Elijah's encounter with Ahab, including Elijah's demonstration of YHWH's power at Carmel, in 1 Kgs 18:17–46.
5. Jezebel's message to Elijah following Ahab's report to her, which prompts Elijah to flee to Mount Horeb in 1 Kgs 19:1–8.
6. YHWH's revelation to Elijah at Horeb in 1 Kgs 19:9–18.
7. Elijah's compliance with YHWH's instructions to designate Elisha as his successor in 1 Kgs 19:19–21.

First Kings 18:1–19:21 is a composite unit insofar as its constituent narrative subunits have little inherent relationship with each other.[29] The narratives concerning Elijah's confrontation with the prophets of Baal and Asherah at Carmel and YHWH's revelation to Elijah each constitute potentially independent traditions that have been incorporated into the present literary context. Each is a self-contained narrative that does not require the surrounding literary context to make its respective point. The Carmel narrative pits a lone prophet of YHWH against some 850 prophets of Baal and Asherah before the eyes of all Israel. It does not require reference to actions of Ahab and Jezebel—or any other parties for that matter—to make the point that YHWH controls creation, and that Baal and Asherah do not.[30] Apart from the identification of Elijah as the protagonist, this narrative could be set in any number of different periods in Israelite history. When read in relation to the present literary context, it provides a major basis for the condemnation of Ahab, namely, he has abandoned YHWH by virtue of his marriage to Jezebel and his support of the Phoenician gods, and here he witnesses YHWH's power over these gods.

---

29. Fohrer, *Elia*, 33–58.
30. Bronner, *Stories of Elijah and Elisha*.

Much the same may be said for the Horeb narrative, which makes its point without reference to the larger literary context, namely, YHWH is revealed to the prophet at Mount Horeb. Only through YHWH's specific instructions to Elijah to anoint Hazael and Jehu and to designate Elisha as his successor does any major link to the larger literary context appear. Many contend that the Horeb narrative is dependent upon Mosaic traditions concerning the incident of the golden calf at Sinai and YHWH's revelation to Moses in Exod 32–34.[31] Such a position holds that Moses would represent an earlier foundational figure in the historical consciousness of Israel (cf. Hos 12:13; 11:1). Other Exodus motifs, such as Elijah's sojourn in the wilderness, his association with the Jordan Valley, and the mysterious way in which his life concludes, leaving him without a known gravesite, are frequently cited as evidence of an attempt to portray Elijah as a prophet like Moses. Quite the opposite is the case.[32] Exodus 32–34 is secondary because it brings together several widely separated literary traditions, including Jeroboam's golden calves (1 Kgs 12:25–33), the law code of Exod 23:1–19; the Deuteronomic prohibition against intermarriage with the Canaanites (Deut 7:1–6), and YHWH's revelation to Elijah at Horeb (1 Kgs 19).

It is difficult to understand how the Obadiah narrative could have been an independent tradition. The narrative points to the threats posed to the prophets and Obadiah's attempts to hide them, but it does not provide any resolution or conclusion to this theme, other than to serve as a counterpoint to Elijah's execution of the prophets of Baal and Asherah. Moreover, the narrative does not develop the character of Obadiah in any meaningful way, other than to use him as a vehicle to point to the dangers faced by the prophets of YHWH during the reign of Ahab and Jezebel. Although the name "Obadiah" is attested elsewhere in the Bible, it simply means "servant of YHWH," which suggests that he plays a secondary role in the narrative. The Obadiah narrative functions as an introduction to the encounter at Carmel by defining the situation that leads to the confrontation. The threat to the prophets of YHWH is ironically reversed by Elijah's slaughter of the prophets of Baal and Asherah in an act of retributive justice. The Obadiah narrative likewise anticipates the account in 1 Kgs 19 concerning Elijah's flight from Jezebel and his experience of YHWH's presence at Horeb. Although Obadiah plays no role in the Horeb narrative, the general threat against the prophets of YHWH articulated in 1 Kgs 18:2–16 is now explicitly directed against Elijah.

This point raises the question as to when and why 1 Kgs 18:1–19:21 was assembled into the present configuration. The concluding focus on the anoint-

31. White, *Elijah Legends*, 2–11; Steck, *Überlieferung und Zeitgeschichte*, 109–25.

32. Sweeney, "The Wilderness Traditions of the Pentateuch: A Reassessment of Their Function and Intent in Relation to Exodus 32–34," *Society of Biblical Literature 1989 Seminar Papers* (ed. David J. Lull; Atlanta: Scholars Press, 1989), 291–299.

ing of Hazael and Jehu and the designation of Elisha as Elijah's successor provides the basic criteria for answering such a question: this material points forward to the conflicts between Israel and Aram and the overthrow of the Omride dynasty by Jehu during the course of Elisha's lifetime. Such a concern is facilitated by the narrative framework, which employs the Obadiah narratives to introduce the basic sequence of narrative action and the concluding Elisha episode to point to the ultimate realization of YHWH's instructions to overthrow Ahab and Ben Hadad. Both of these narratives share certain basic motifs with the narratives concerning the designation of Saul as king of Israel in 1 Sam 8–12, namely, the search by Saul and his servant for his father's lost asses, which results in Samuel's anointing of Saul at Ramah in 1 Sam 9:1–10:16, and Saul's deliverance of the city of Jabesh Gilead in 1 Sam 11, in which Saul summons the tribes to action with portions of the oxen that he had been using to plow his fields. Obadiah's and Ahab's search through the land resembles that of Saul and his servant, and Elisha's sacrifice of the oxen that he used to plow his fields resembles that of Saul. Although the motifs are similar, their functions differ: whereas Saul finds the prophet Samuel, who anoints him king, Ahab finds the prophet Elijah, who initiates the process by which the house of Omri will fall; whereas the sacrifice of Saul's oxen plays a role in his heroic deliverance of Jabesh Gilead which secures his kingship, the sacrifice of Elisha's oxen sets him on his task to overthrow the Omride dynasty. By employing these allusions to Saul traditions, the narrator signals an interest in kingship. By placing them in relation to Elijah's confrontation with the prophets of Baal and Asherah at Carmel and YHWH's revelation to Elijah at Horeb, the narrator employs irony in that these traditions do not facilitate the dynasty of Omri, but play a role in bringing it down.

Some suggest that such a scenario calls for a ninth-century edition of this narrative that would point to the inauguration of Jehu's rule,[33] but Jehu's ascension to the throne hardly resolves Israel's problems; Aram harasses and subjugates Israel well beyond the life of Jehu. The northern kingdom of Israel achieves security from its enemies only during the reign of Jehu's great-grandson, Jeroboam ben Joash (r. 786–746 B.C.E.). Insofar as the Elijah-Elisha narrative complex is constructed to point to the reign of Jehu as a means by which Israel's problems came to an end, the narrative would not have been composed during the reign of Jehu, but during the reign of his successors, most likely Jeroboam ben Joash. In this manner, the Jehu dynasty could point to the overthrow of the house of Omri through the agency of the prophets Elijah and Elisha as

---

33. E.g., Antony F. Campbell and Mark A. O'Brien, *Unfolding the Deuteronomistic History: Origins, Upgrades, Present Text* (Minneapolis: Fortress, 2000); Antony F. Campbell, S.J., *Of Prophets and Kings. A Late Ninth-Century Document (1 Samuel 1–2 Kings 10)* (CBQMS 17; Washington, D.C.: The Catholic Biblical Association, 1986).

the beginning of the process by which Israel achieved security in the first part of the eighth century B.C.E. Following the dissolution of the Jehu dynasty in the mid-eighth century and the destruction of the northern kingdom in the latter part of the eighth century, the tradition would have been taken up in the Hezekian DtrH as a means to demonstrate that the religious corruption of the northern kingdom during Omride rule provided some basis for Israel's punishment by YHWH at the hands of the Assyrians. It serves a similar function in relation to the Josian and exilic DtrH editions.

[18:1–2] This subunit is demarcated formally by the temporal formula "and after many days," which establishes a new temporal context for the following events, and by the concluding notice concerning the famine, which constitutes the basic premise for the following narrative. By relating Elijah's compliance with YHWH's instruction, the subunit identifies one set of protagonists, YHWH and Elijah, and sets the narrative sequence of action into motion.

[18:3–6] The fundamental demarcation of this subunit is determined by the interaction of the two characters, Ahab and Obadiah. The narrator takes care to provide background information that establishes Obadiah's role as an agent of YHWH and ally of Elijah. His name, ʿōbadyāhû, means "he who serves YHWH." Obadiah is otherwise unknown in the Bible, but it is possible that the prophetic book of Obadiah is constructed as the work of the present ninth-century figure.[34] He functions as an intermediary who facilitates the meeting between Ahab and Elijah that provides the context for Elijah's confrontation with the prophets of Baal and Asherah. Obadiah is identified as "(the one) who is over the house" (Hebrew, ʾăšer ʿal-habbāyit), a term employed as an official title for the chief palace administrator in both the Israelite and Judean monarchies as well as in relation to Egyptian contexts (cf. 1 Kgs 4:5; 16:9; 18:3; 2 Kgs 10:5; 15:5; 20:1; Isa 22:15; 36:3; 38:1; see also Gen 39:4; 44:1, 4).[35] Although Obadiah is one of Ahab's chief administrators, v. 3b emphasizes that he reveres YHWH greatly, and v. 4 states that he hid one hundred prophets of YHWH in caves when Jezebel attempted to kill them. The narrative thereby serves several purposes. First, it explains how Obadiah can serve as the intermediary who brings Ahab and Elijah together. Second, the narrative indicates that there is support for YHWH within the royal administration, but that supporters of YHWH are threatened by the presence of the Phoenician Queen Jezebel. Third, it signals the threat of death against YHWH's prophets, which provides a basic premise for both Elijah's confrontation with the prophets of Baal and Asherah at Carmel and Elijah's flight to Horeb. Fourth, the subunit indicates its relationship to the

34. Marvin A. Sweeney, *The Twelve Prophets* (Berit Olam; Collegeville, Minn.: Liturgical, 2000), 1:280.

35. Nili Sacher Fox, *In the Service of the King: Officialdom in Ancient Israel and Judah* (Monographs of the Hebrew Union College 23; Cincinnati: Hebrew Union College, 2000), 81–96, and the literature cited there.

larger narrative context by noting that Obadiah hid the prophets in caves, just as Elijah would hide in a cave at Horeb (1 Kgs 19:9), and that he supported the prophets with bread and water, just as YHWH supported Elijah in the Wadi Cherith (1 Kgs 17:5–6).

The narrative then turns to Ahab's instructions that Obadiah should assist him in searching the land for water. The motif of the search throughout the land reflects the earlier tradition of Saul's search through the land for his father's lost asses in 1 Sam 9:1–10:16. Indeed, Obadiah's identity as Ahab's officer reflects the relationship between Saul and his servant, and the reason for the search— to provide water for the horses and mules—recalls the lost asses of the Saulide narrative. The use of the motif differs markedly, however, from its use in 1 Sam 9:1–10:16. Whereas Saul and his servant remain together through the Saulide narrative, Obadiah and Ahab search separately, indicating in part their desperation and need to cover as much ground as soon as possible. It also accentuates the fundamental difference between the two men insofar as Ahab allows Jezebel a free hand in establishing foreign religious practice and the suppression of YHWH's supporters. Whereas Saul found the prophet Samuel, who in turn anointed him as king, Ahab's encounter with Elijah initiates the process by which Ahab will ultimately lose his life and dynasty by the agency of Elijah and other prophets working on behalf of YHWH.

[18:7–16] This subunit is demarcated by the interaction of the characters Obadiah and Elijah. The episode builds upon Obadiah's role as the intermediary between Ahab and Elijah, but it also highlights two additional motifs: the threat posed to the lives of the prophets and supporters of YHWH and the hidden nature of Elijah. Although some suggest that Obadiah had not met Elijah previously, the use of the verb *wayyakkirēhû*, "and he recognized him," indicates that Obadiah knew who Elijah was. The recognition is reinforced by Obadiah's reaction insofar as he fell on his face to do obeisance to the prophet and addressed him both by name and by the title *ʾădōnî*, "my lord." Elijah's instruction to Obadiah to go to Ahab causes great consternation in Obadiah, which highlights once again the dangers to the supporters of YHWH. Obadiah's opening statement employs an element of sarcasm insofar as he suggests that he must have committed some sin since Elijah sends him on a mission that will surely cost him his life. He reinforces the sarcasm by repeating Elijah's instruction twice while stating his objections. Obadiah employs the oath formula *ḥay yhwh ʾlhyk ʾim . . .*, "by the life of YHWH, your G-d, if . . ."[36] to emphasize the certainty of death if he carries out the prophet's request, and he reinforces this statement by referring to the oaths that kings take when they make treaties.[37] Such

---

36. For discussion of the oath and the oath formula, see Burke O. Long, *1 Kings, with an Introduction to Historical Literature* (FOTL 9; Grand Rapids: William B. Eerdmans, 1984), 253.

37. *ANET* 199–206, 529–41; M. L. Barré, "Treaties in the ANE," *ABD* 6:653–56.

oaths include providing troops and support to allies in time of war, paying tribute to a suzerain ally, turning over any enemies who flee from the ally, and so on. Obadiah's statement alludes to the last stipulation insofar as Ahab's allies would swear to turn Elijah over to Ahab as an enemy of the Israelite state. The treaty context is particularly important because an ally who refused to abide by the treaty would be subject to punishment. Obadiah personalizes the matter by indicating that he would face death for failing to turn Elijah over to the king. He emphasizes the danger by alluding to Elijah's known tendency to disappear—that is, if he were to announce Elijah's presence to the king, he would still be subject to death if Elijah failed to show. He emphasizes his own actions and the danger that he has already faced on YHWH's behalf.

[**18:17–46**] This subunit is demarcated by the interrelationship between the two principal protagonists of the narrative from the point at which they first meet in v. 17 until the point at which they last appear together in v. 46. Elijah's interaction with Ahab in vv. 17–19, 20, and 41–46 stands in contrast with the Carmel narrative in vv. 21–40 in which Ahab does not appear at all. The encounter with Ahab forms a literary framework that incorporates a much earlier tradition concerning Elijah's confrontation at Carmel into the larger narrative.[38]

First Kings 18:17–46 demonstrates YHWH's efficacy as master of creation and Israel over that of the Phoenician deities Baal and Asherah. The passage is an example of the prophetic confrontation story in which a prophet or other figure identified with YHWH is pitted against false prophets or opponents in an effort to demonstrate the credibility of the prophet and his message (cf. Amos 7:10–17; Jer 27–28; Isa 36–37/2 Kgs 18–19).[39] The terms of the confrontation are based in a demonstration of the respective deities' capacity to bring rain and thereby to relieve the drought that has afflicted the land since the first verse of ch. 17. Drought is a particularly crucial issue in relation to the Phoenician deities because they are the gods of fertility in the land; Baal is god of the storm and heavens, and is responsible for bringing rain so that the natural world may flourish at the onset of the rainy season in the land of Israel in late September or early October.[40] Because Baal is considered to be dead during the dry summer season, he must be ritually brought back to life at the onset of the rainy season to symbolize the return of rain, fertility, and life. As goddess of the earth, Asherah is portrayed as the wife of Baal, who receives the rain brought by her husband.

[**17–19**] Ahab's charge that Elijah is the "troubler," *ʿōkēr*, of Israel is noteworthy, because the Hebrew root *ʿkr*, "to trouble," also underlies the name of the "Valley of Achor," located in the Jordan Valley in the broad plain along the

38. Susanne Otto, *Jehu, Elia und Elisa* (BWANT 152; Stuttgart: W. Kohlhammer, 2001), 171–78, with bibliography.

39. Sweeney, *Isaiah 1–39*, 518.

40. W. Herrmann, "Baal," *DDD*[2] 132–39; N. Wyatt, "Asherah," *DDD*[2] 99–105.

northwestern shores of the Dead Sea (see Josh 7:26; cf. Hos 2:17). The use of this term for Elijah recalls the traditions concerning his residence in the Wadi Cherith in the Jordan Valley (1 Kgs 17:1–7). Elijah's reference to the prophets who eat at Jezebel's table indicates that they are supported by the queen, much . as Mephibosheth was supported by David (2 Sam 9:13; 19:28) and Jehoiachin by Evil Merodach (2 Kgs 25:29). Jezebel's support contrasts with the support provided by YHWH to Elijah in the Wadi Cherith (1 Kgs 17:5–6) and the support provided by Obadiah to the prophets of YHWH (1 Kgs 18:4, 13).

Mount Carmel refers to a fifteen-mile range of fertile, heavily forested hills that runs south along the Mediterranean coast from the region of Acre or modern Haifa to the region of Dor and Megiddo at the western entrance to the Jezreel Valley.[41] The largest mountain in the range, Mount Carmel, Jebel Kurmul, or Jebel Mar Elyas, juts out into the Mediterranean where it forms the cape that marks the southern boundary of Haifa Bay. The range is filled with caves, which may indicate the area where Obadiah hid the prophets of YHWH.[42] The Carmel range forms a natural boundary that allows it to serve as a border area between Israel and Phoenicia. The presence of prophets of Baal and Asherah at the site is hardly surprising given the portrayal of Phoenician influence in Israel as a result of Jezebel's marriage to Ahab. The exact site of Elijah's confrontation with the Phoenician prophets is unknown. Various religious installations have been located in the Carmel range through the centuries. A temple to Zeus is mentioned by Pseudo-Skylax in the fourth century B.C.E. Tacitus reports that the priests of the Carmel oracle promised Vespasian mastery of the world. A stone foot with the inscription "To Heliopoleitan Zeus Carmel from Gaius Julius Eutychas, citizen of Caesarea" was discovered at the monastery of Elijah in 1952.

[20–24] Elijah proposed the terms by which each party would have the opportunity to demonstrate the power of its respective god(s). Elijah's initial statement employs elements of metaphor and sarcasm, insofar as his language mocks the religious practice of the Phoenicians from the outside. His question, "How long will you hop/limp (*pōsĕḥîm*) between two opinions (*hassĕʿippîm*)?" is clearly rhetorical; indeed, it points to the futility of attempting to accommodate both sets of gods and demands that the people make a decision. The use of the verb *psḥ*, "to spring over, to limp," clearly plays a role in relation to the religious observance of ancient Israel and Judah. It stands behind the Hebrew word *pesaḥ*, "Passover," one of the three major festivals of Jewish tradition, and *pesaḥ* also refers to the main sacrifice of the festival. The verbal form is employed to describe YHWH's "passing over" the Israelite houses marked with lamb's blood at the time of the exodus from Egypt (Exod 12:13, 27). The use

41. H. O. Thompson, "Carmel, Mount," *ABD* 1:874–75.
42. A. Ronen, "Carmel Caves," *ABD* 1:873–74.

of this verb to describe the dancing of the prophets of Baal and Asherah around the altar (see v. 26 below) suggests that it was employed—or at least under-stood—in relation to Canaanite/Phoenician practice as well. The Philistine practice of jumping over the threshold of the temple of Dagon in Ashdod (see 1 Sam 5:5; cf. Zeph 1:9) may provide some analogy, although the significance of this practice is not well understood. Likewise, Jacob's limping as a result of his struggle with the (angelic) man at Jabbok may be considered because the incident provides an etiology for the Israelite practice of refraining from eating the hind quarters of an animal so that they might be offered exclusively to YHWH (see Gen 32:22–32).

[25–29] Elijah's instruction to the Baal prophets emphasizes their advan-tages: they choose their bull first, call upon their god first, and are far more numerous. The narrative likewise emphasizes the futility of their actions by indicating that they danced and cried out from morning until noon without an answer, which would indicate that their efforts extended beyond the time of the daily morning sacrifice (see Lev 6:1–6; Exod 29:38–42; Num 28:3–8). Elijah then ridiculed the Baal prophets with his suggestions as to why Baal has not responded. Perhaps he is in conversation; perhaps he is engaged; perhaps he is on a journey; perhaps he is asleep! Although many interpreters follow Targum Jonathan in presupposing that *śîg,* "engaged," refers to Baal's need to relieve himself, this is only an inference, as the term means simply "to move away." The renewed efforts of the Baal prophets include gashing themselves until their blood flowed. Such practice is attested in an Akkadian text from Ugarit for ecstatic *muḫḫu* prophets, "who drench themselves in their own blood," and in Hellenistic contexts (Cogan *1 Kings* 441). The practice reflects ancient mythol-ogy concerning the death of the fertility god, whether Baal, Tammuz, Dumuzi, or others, who descends into the netherworld during the dry season and must be brought back to life in order for the rains to come in the fall.[43] By gashing themselves, the Baal prophets ritually identify with the dead in an act that reverses the normal course of the created world. Such identification with the dead Baal plays a role in stimulating his revival; perhaps it motivates his con-sort, Asherah, Anat, Ishtar, Inanna, and so on, to descend to the netherworld in order to bring him back to life. Such practice is forbidden for Israelites (see Lev 19:28; 21:5; Deut 14:1). The efforts of the Baal prophets extend to the time of the afternoon or Minha offering without result. Having missed the times for the two daily sacrifices, the narrative emphasizes that the Baal priests have failed. Some maintain that the reference to the Minha offering indicates a later com-position,[44] but such a position ignores the fact that sacrifice constituted the core of ancient Israelite worship.

43. *ANET* 138–41, 106–9, 52–59, 149–55.
44. Timm, *Die Dynastie Omri,* 77.

[30–40] Interpreters have puzzled over the reference to Elijah's repair of the damaged altar of YHWH, speculating that the Baal prophets had somehow damaged the altar. It seems more likely that he repaired an Israelite altar that had been previously destroyed as Baal worship became prevalent in the region. Elijah sets up twelve stones to represent the twelve tribes of Israel in an action reminiscent of Moses' erection of twelve stones by the altar at Sinai (Exod 24:4) and Joshua's erection of twelve stones in the middle of the Jordan River at Gilgal (Josh 4).

Elijah's trench marks the sacred boundaries of the holy altar and conveys blood into the ground (see Deut 12:16, 23–24; 15:23; Lev 17:12–13; cf. 1 Sam 14:31–35). The area marked by the trench is defined as two seahs. The seah is a unit of dry volume measure equivalent to about one-third of a bushel or 7.3 litres. The expression indicates that the trench encloses an area that would be planted by two seahs of seed. Suggestions that Elijah actually filled the trench with naphtha to ensure that the sacrifice would burn (F. Hitzig, cited in Gray 401) indicate a fundamental misunderstanding of the narrative's attempt to portray Elijah's actions as divine action. Water libations were a characteristic part of temple worship and sacrifice at Sukkot to symbolize the onset of the rains (*m. Sukkah* 4:9; 5:1–3).[45] Insofar as Elijah's sacrifice brings about rain to end the drought, it constitutes a Sukkot ritual to mark the change of season.

Elijah's invocation to YHWH recalls the relationship between YHWH and Israel from the time of the ancestors. Such a formulation appeals to the history of the covenant between YHWH and Israel as motivation for both YHWH and the reader to respond to Elijah's appeal (cf. 1 Chr 29:18; 2 Chr 30:6). The miraculous response to Elijah's prayer, in which fire consumes the bull, the altar, the water, and everything associated with the altar, provides stunning confirmation that YHWH is G-d. Elijah's order to seize the prophets of Baal is an ironic reversal of the theme of Jezebel's threats against the lives of the prophets of YHWH. Although some decry Elijah's violent act (Montgomery and Gehman 406; Fritz 194), it demonstrates the prophet's actions to remove a threat to his life, the lives of the prophets of YHWH, and the integrity of the nation Israel. The reference to the Wadi Kishon reinforces this perspective insofar as it recalls the victory by Deborah and Barak over the forces of Jabin and Sisera (Judg 4:7; 5:21; Ps 83:9). The Kishon flows from the western entrance to the Jezreel Valley by Megiddo through the valley that cuts between the hills of the Galil and the Carmel range, and empties into the Mediterranean south of Akko.[46]

[41–46] Elijah bids Ahab to go up, eat, and drink, which were characteristic activities at the festival sacrifices in Israel's temples. Elijah goes to the top of Carmel and prostrates himself, with his head between his knees, in a position

45. "Sukkot," *EncJud*, 495–502.
46. R. Frankel, "Kishon," *ABD* 4:88–89.

of prayer. The purpose of this action becomes evident as he bids his servant seven times to look out to the sea. When the boy observes at his seventh attempt a small rain cloud forming over the Mediterranean, it is evident that the drought is about to come to an end. Elijah's warning to Ahab that he should saddle up and get down off of the mountain before the rain comes highlights YHWH's power as the drought will end not simply with rain, but with a downpour and raging torrents that are characteristic of the rainy season in the land of Israel (cf. Judg 5:21, which relates the role of the Kishon in Deborah and Barak's defeat of Sisera).

Ahab's flight to Jezreel highlights the site where Jehu will overthrow the house of Omri (2 Kgs 9). Elijah's action in running before the chariot of Ahab is an ecstatic act, particularly because of the use of the formula "and the hand of YHWH was upon him" (e.g., Ezek 1:5). Elijah deliberately shows respect for the king by joining the escort that normally accompanies a king's chariot (see 2 Sam 15:1; 1 Kgs 1:5). The confrontation at Carmel demonstrated YHWH's power to the king and the people so that they might turn their hearts back to YHWH (see v. 37 above). Ahab still has the possibility to repent, but his later treaty with Aram (1 Kgs 20) and his murder of Naboth (1 Kgs 21) earn him condemnation.

[19:1–8] Although Elijah and Jezebel never met, they interacted through intermediaries. Ahab and Jezebel appear only at the outset of the subunit, and play no further role in the accounts of Elijah's flight to the wilderness, his vision of YHWH, and his designation of Elisha as his successor. This suggests that vv. 1–2 at the very least provide the narrative framework that incorporates an older tradition concerning Elijah's vision of YHWH in the wilderness into the larger narrative concerning Elijah and his relationship to Ahab and the house of Omri. The framework is clearly redactional,[47] and represents early-eighth-century redaction from the time of Jeroboam ben Joash.

[1–3] Ahab's report to Jezebel dispels any notions of Ahab's repentance. It indicates that she is in charge of the kingdom, and will continue in her attempts to replace YHWH as G-d of Israel by killing off YHWH's prophets. Ahab incurs guilt because of his failure to act as a responsible monarch. The fundamental issues are religious apostasy and murder, since the king stands by while Jezebel kills the prophets of YHWH. Jezebel's message to Elijah employs the oath formula. It cannot employ the classic version, *ḥay yhwh,* "by the life of YHWH," because she is not a follower of YHWH. Instead, it states that she should suffer death or worse if she does not have Elijah killed by the same time tomorrow. LXX addresses this absence by adding variations of the oath formula, i.e., "if you are Elijah and I am Jezebel . . . ,' to point to a known reality that provides the basis for projected action in the oath formulas. Elijah understands

---

47. Hentschel, *Elija-erzählungen,* 65–69.

the message. His flight to Beer Sheba took him to the southernmost boundary of Judah at the edge of the Negeb wilderness and the Sinai wilderness beyond the Negeb.

[4–8] Elijah's journey to Horeb draws heavily upon the wilderness traditions. The narrative also includes elements that frequently appear in visionary accounts, such as Elijah's sleeping under the broom tree (cf. Gen 15:12–21; 28:10–22; 1 Sam 3; Jer 31:26), the presence of the angel (Ezek 40–48; Zech 1–6; Dan 10), and the special food and drink that enables him to make the forty-day journey (Num 11; fasting also facilitates visionary experience—see Dan 10). Although many see these features as a sign of late composition, ecstatic visionary experience is well attested throughout the ancient Near East from the early second millennium B.C.E.[48]

The "broom tree," Hebrew *rōtem,* is well known in the Sinai, Dead Sea, and Petra regions as the Retama roetam or the Genista roetam (Jones 329–30). Elijah's desire for death is linked to his sense of failure in the aftermath of the Carmel narrative, but it also portends visionary experience beyond the normal experience of the living. The narrative shows affinities with Jonah 4, in which the prophet sat under a "qiqayon" plant and expressed his desire to die after YHWH declined to punish Nineveh, but the fact that Jonah ben Amitai is drawn from 2 Kgs 14:25 indicates that the Jonah narrative is dependent upon the Elijah narrative. Elijah's comment that he is no better than his fathers expresses his sense of failure, perhaps in relation to the wilderness tradition in which the entire exodus generation perished during forty years of wandering as a result of its resistance to YHWH. When Elijah fell asleep under the broom tree, the stage was set for his visionary experience. The angel bid him to eat in order to prepare himself for the visionary journey through the wilderness. Just as YHWH had to call Samuel three times (1 Sam 3), the angel had to repeat his attempt to set Elijah on his way. The provision of food by the angel recalls YHWH's support of Elijah in the Wadi Cherith (1 Kgs 17:1–6) and YHWH's provision of food and water in the wilderness (Exod 16–17; Num 11; 20). The cake baked on hot stones is a form of unleavened bread like that eaten by the Israelites in the exodus from Egypt and journey in the wilderness. The journey of forty days and forty nights recalls the time spent by Moses at Mount Sinai receiving the revelation of YHWH's Torah (Exod 24:18; 34:28). The mountain of G-d at Horeb appears as part of the E (Exod 3:1; 33:6) and D (Deut 1:6; 4:10) traditions of the Pentateuch. It is called Mount Sinai in the J (Exod 19:11, 20) and P (Lev 25:1) traditions. Mount Sinai/Horeb is traditionally identified since Byzantine times with Jebel Musa in the southern Sinai peninsula.

---

48. R. P. Gordon, "From Mari to Moses: Prophecy at Mari and in Ancient Israel," in *Of Prophets' Visions and the Wisdom of Sages* (Fest. R. N. Whybray; ed. H. A. McKay and D. J. A. Clines; JSOTSup 162; Sheffield: Sheffield Academic Press, 1993), 63–79.

[19:9–19] Elijah's vision of YHWH at Horeb has clear parallels to Moses' vision of YHWH at Sinai in Exod 32–34.[49]

[9–10] Elijah stays in a cave at Mount Horeb, much as Moses hid in a cleft of rock at Sinai (Exod 33:22). The narrative employs the prophetic word formula "and behold, the word of YHWH came to him," to portray the encounter as a prophetic experience. YHWH questions Elijah twice as to why he is there, first upon his arrival and later following the manifestation of the divine voice. The repetition of YHWH's question reflects the repeated calls of the prophet's name during visionary experience, for example, Moses (Exod 3:4) and Samuel (1 Sam 3:4). Elijah's repeated answer emphasizes the major themes of 1 Kgs 18–19: Elijah's zealousness for YHWH, Israel's abandonment of its covenant with YHWH, Israel's tearing down of YHWH's altars, the slaying of YHWH's prophets, Elijah as the last remaining prophet of YHWH, and the attempts to kill him.

[11–14] The initial manifestation of YHWH's self-revelation emphasizes YHWH's holy, incorporeal character. YHWH's command that Elijah should stand outside the cave while YHWH "passes by," Hebrew ʿōbēr, employs the same verb as Exod 33:22, although the Moses narrative emphasizes that Moses must remain inside the cleft of rock since human beings cannot see the face of YHWH. Whereas the Exodus narrative expresses YHWH's holiness by referring to "the glory of YHWH," the Elijah narrative employs a series of metaphors, all of which typically appear in theophanic texts, to demonstrate the impossibility of describing YHWH's presence. Each represents a manifestation of power in the natural world, and yet each represents power that is impossible to define as tangible objects. The first is the wind, which breaks down mountains and rocks despite the fact that it remains unseen and unformed. YHWH is not to be equated with wind. Next is earthquake, which again unleashes its destructive force while remaining unseen and unformed. YHWH is not to be equated with earthquake. Third is fire, a powerful destructive force in nature that may be seen but remains unformed while emitting intangible heat and light. YHWH is not to be equated with fire. Finally, Elijah hears a faint sound of silence. The terms qôl, "sound," and dĕmāmâ, "silence," contradict each other in a metaphorical presentation of power through a combination of presence and absence. The term daqqâ, "crushed, thin, fine," is an attempt to minimize the presence of the sound as much as possible through the use of language to emphasize its holy character as the voice of G-d. Elijah covers his own face with his mantle much as YHWH places a hand over the cleft of rock so that Moses cannot see the divine face (Exod 33:21–23). Elijah's vision may be compared to the high priest's vision of YHWH each Yom Kippur when he enters the Holy of Holies and utters YHWH's name (see Lev 16:1–3; *m. Yoma* 3:8).

---

49. Steck, *Überlieferung und Zeitgeschichte,* 109–25; Sweeney, "Wilderness Tradition."

[15–18] YHWH's instructions to Elijah serve as an introduction to the Elisha traditions, which focus on the overthrow of the houses of Omri of Israel (2 Kgs 9–10) and Ben Hadad of Aram (2 Kgs 8:7–15). YHWH told Elijah that he is to anoint Hazael as king of Aram in place of Ben Hadad and Jehu ben Nimshi as king of Israel in place of the house of Omri. He is also to designate Elisha ben Shaphat of Abel Meholah as his successor. The location of Abel Meholah is disputed, although it appears to be located in the Jordan Valley, south or southeast of Beth Shean. The Midianites fled to Abel Meholah when Gideon defeated them (Judg 7:22), and 1 Kgs 4:12 places it on the boundary of Solomon's fifth district. The narrative serves the interests of the house of Jehu, which overthrew the Omride dynasty with Elisha's support (2 Kgs 9–10). Jehu's grandson, Jehoash ben Jehoahaz, was able to defeat Hazael's son Ben Hadad (2 Kgs 13:22–25), which paved the way for peace during the reign of Jeroboam ben Joash/Jehoash (2 Kgs 14:23–29).

[19:19–21] This subunit relates Elijah's designation of Elisha ben Shaphat as his servant and successor. Elisha's twelve pairs of oxen indicate that he was a man of wealth who gave up a very stable and secure life to serve Elijah. The twelve teams recall the twelve tribes of Israel like the twelve stones that Elijah erected at Carmel (1 Kgs 18:31) and the portrayal of Saul, who cut up his own twelve oxen to summon the twelve tribes of Israel to rescue the beleaguered city of Jabesh Gilead (1 Sam 11). Without speaking, Elijah threw his mantle to Elisha. Although scholars know of no distinctive prophetic dress, garments oftentimes signify an official role, such as the royal garments worn by Tamar bat David (2 Sam 13:18; cf. Gen 37:3), kings Ahab and Jehoshaphat (1 Kgs 22:10), and Mordecai (Esth 6:8–9), or the priestly garments (see Exod 28). Numbers 20:25–28 indicates that Eleazar's wearing of Aaron's garments signifies the transfer of the high priesthood at Aaron's death, and the dressing of Joshua ben Jehozadak in pure garments signifies his consecration to serve at the altar (Zech 3). Elijah's mantle, which he used to cover his face at YHWH's revelation (1 Kgs 19:13), apparently carries special powers, which are transferred to Elisha at Elijah's death (see 2 Kgs 2:8, 13–14). Although Elijah's response to Elisha's request to kiss his parents goodbye is sometimes viewed as a rebuke, the statement merely means, "For what have I done to you?" The question is a rhetorical statement that Elijah has indeed done something momentous to Elisha and that he should return to do as he proposed. Elisha's sacrifice of the oxen to feed the people represents a spontaneous thanksgiving sacrifice that signifies his entry into holy service. The verb *wayĕšārĕtēhû,* "and he served him," is typically employed in relation to priestly service (e.g., Exod 28:35; Num 3:6; 1 Kgs 8:11), although it may also be used in relation to royal officers (1 Chr 27:1; Esth 1:10), royal domestic service (Gen 39:4; 2 Sam 13:7), the service of angels to YHWH (Ps 103), and Joshua's service to Moses (Exod 24:13; 33:11; Num 11:28). Just as Moses has Joshua as his assistant and successor, Elijah has

Elisha as his assistant and successor (cf. 1 Kgs 19:3, where Elijah leaves his servant behind as he flees to the wilderness).

1 Kings 20:1–43 Prophetic Condemnation
of Ahab for Releasing Ben-Hadad

20:1 [a]Ben-Hadad, King of Aram, gathered all his army, and thirty-two kings, horses, and chariots were with him, and he went up, besieged Samaria, and fought against it. 2 He sent messengers to Ahab, King of Israel, in the city, 3 and said to him, "Thus says Ben-Hadad, 'Your silver and your gold are mine, and your good wives and children are mine.'" 4 And the King of Israel answered and said, "According to your word, my lord the king, am I and all that is mine." 5 And the messengers returned and said, "Thus says Ben-Hadad, saying, 'Because I sent to you saying "Your silver and your gold and your wives and your sons you shall give to me," 6 indeed, tomorrow I will send my servants to you, and they will search your house and the houses of your servants, and they will seize all the delight of your eyes.'" 7 And the King of Israel called to all the elders of the land, and he said, "Know, now, and see that this one seeks evil, because he has sent for my wives and for my sons and for my silver and for my gold, and I have not refused him." 8 And all the elders and all the people said to him, "Do not listen, and do not comply." 9 And he said to the messengers of Ben-Hadad, "Say to my lord, the king, 'All that you have sent to your servant in the beginning I will do, but this thing I am not able to do,'" and the messengers went and gave him the answer. 10 And Ben-Hadad sent to him and said, "[b]Thus shall the gods do to me and even more if the dust of Samaria suffices for handfuls for all the people who are at my feet."[b] 11 And the King of Israel answered and said, "Tell him, 'Let not one who buckles his weapons boast like one who unbuckles them.'" 12 When (he) heard this answer, he was drinking, he and the kings, in pavilions, and he said to his servants, "Proceed!" and they proceeded against the city.

13 And behold, one prophet drew near to Ahab, King of Israel, and said, "Thus says YHWH, 'Have you seen all this great crowd? Behold, I am giving it into your hand, and you will know that I am YHWH.'" 14 And Ahab said, "By whom?" And he said, "Thus says YHWH, 'By the young men of the provincial commanders.'" And he said, "Who will begin the battle?" And he said, "You." 15 And he mustered the young men of the provincial commanders, and they were two hundred and thirty-two, and after them he mustered all the people, all the people of Israel, seven thousand. 16 And they went out at noon, and Ben-Hadad was getting drunk in the pavilions,[c] he and the thirty-two kings who were helping him. 17 And

the young men of the provincial commanders went out first. ᵈBen-Hadad sent (scouts), and they declared to him,ᵈ saying, "Men have gone out from Samaria." 18 And he said, "If they have come out for peace, take them alive, and if they have come out for war, take them alive." 19 ᵉAnd these went out from the city, the young men of the provincial commandersᵉ ᶠand the army that was behind them. 20 And each killed his man,ᶠ and Aram fled, and Israel pursued them, and Ben-Hadad, King of Aram, escaped ᵍby horse and cavalry.ᵍ 21 And the King of Israel went out, and he struck the horses and chariots, and he struck Aram a great blow. 22 And the prophet drew near to the King of Israel and said to him, "Go, strengthen yourself, and know and see what you should do, because at the turn of the year, the King of Aram is going up against you."

23 And the servants of the King of Aram said to him, "Their G-d is a god of the mountains. Therefore they overpowered us. But perhaps we should fight with them in the plain. Maybe we will overpower them. 24 And do this thing: remove the kings, each from his position, and appoint governors in their places. 25 And you conscript for yourself an army like the army that is fallen from you, and horses like the horses and chariots like the chariots, and we shall fight them in the plain. Perhaps we shall overpower them." And he listened to their voice, and he did accordingly. 26 And at the turn of the year, Ben-Hadad mustered Aram, and went up to Aphek for war with Israel. 27 And the people of Israel mustered and equipped themselves and went to meet them. The people of Israel encamped opposite them like two small flocks of goats, but Aram filled the land. 28 And a man of G-d drew near, and said to the King of Israel, "Thus says YHWH, 'Because Aram has said, "YHWH is a G-d of the mountains and not a G-d of the valleys," so I shall give all this great crowd into your hand, and you will know that I am YHWH.'" 29 And they were encamped opposite each other for seven days, and on the seventh day the battle commenced, and the people of Israel struck Aram, one hundred thousand foot soldiers in one day. 30 And those who were left fled to Aphek into the city, and the wall fell upon twenty-seven thousand men who were left. And Ben-Hadad fled, and he came into the city, to a room within a room. 31 And his servants said to him, "Behold now, we have heard that the kings of the house of Israel are trustworthy kings. Let us place sack-cloth on our loins and cords on our heads, and we shall go out to the King of Israel. Perhaps he will spare your life." 32 And they bound sackcloth on their loins and cords on their heads, and they came to the King of Israel, and they said, "Your servant, Ben-Hadad, has said, 'Please, spare my life.'" And he said, "Is he still alive? He is my brother." 33 And the men considered, quickly determined what he meant, and said, "Ben-Hadad is your brother." And he said, "Go, bring him." And Ben-Hadad came out to

him and brought him up on his chariot, 34 and said to him, "The cities which my father took from your father, I will return, and markets you shall set up for yourself in Damascus just as my father did in Samaria." "And I by treaty will send you home," and he made a treaty with him, and he sent him home.

35 And one man from the sons of the prophets said to his neighbor, "By the word of YHWH, strike me, please," but the man refused to strike him. 36 And he said to him, "Because you have not listened to the word of YHWH, behold, when you go from me, the lion will strike you." And he went from him, and the lion found him and struck him. 37 And he found another man and said, "Strike me please," and the man struck him a blow and wounded him. 38 And the prophet went, stood before the king on the road, and he was concealed with a bandage[h] over his eyes. 39 And when the King was passing by, he cried out to the King and said, "Your servant went out in the midst of the battle, and behold, a man turned aside, and brought to me a man, and he said, 'Watch this man! If he is indeed missing, then your life shall be in place of his life, or a square of silver you shall pay.' 40 And your servant was doing this and that, and he was gone!" And the King of Israel said to him, [i]"So you have decided your sentence."[i] 41 And he hurriedly [j]removed the bandage from over his eyes,[j] and the King of Israel recognized him because he was from the prophets. 42 And he said to him, "Thus says YHWH, 'Because you have set free from custody a condemned man, then your life shall be in place of his life and your people in place of his people." 43 And the King of Israel went to his house, angry and sullen, and he came to Samaria.[a]

a–a. LXX places chs. 20 and 22 together (because Elijah does not appear in either chapter) after 17–19; 21 (in which Elijah does appear).

b–b. LXX, "So may G-d do to me and more if the dust of Samaria will suffice for foxes to all the people, my foot soldiers." LXX reads Hebrew, *lišʿolîm,* "for handfuls," as *lěšûʿālîm,* "for foxes," which presupposes that there will not be enough left of Samaria for foxes to burrow in (Montgomery and Gehman 321; Klostermann 375). Targum Jonathan explains the reference to "handfuls" and "feet": "So may the gods do to me and more if the dust of Samaria is sufficient for carrying in the hollows of the soles of the feet of the people who are with me."

c. LXX reads *ev Sokchōth,* "in Sukkot," reading *bassukkôt* as a reference to the Transjordanian city of Sukkot, in contrast with the LXX reading of *bassukkôt* as *en skēnais,* "in tents," in v. 12.

d–d. LXX, "and they sent and reported to the King of Syria (Aram)," is an attempt to resolve the somewhat awkward formulation of the Hebrew.

e–e. LXX, "and let not the young men of the provincial commanders go out from the city." LXX clearly understands this statement to be part of Ben-Hadad's instructions. It also rereads the somewhat enigmatic Hebrew *ʾēlleh,* "these," as *ʾal,* "(let) not."

f–f. LXX reads v. 19b as the subject of v. 20a, viz., "And the army that was behind them smote each man the man next to him, and each man a second time smote the man next to him." The addition of the statement concerning the second smiting of opponents accounts for the plural formulation of the verb *wayyakkû*, "and they struck," with a singular subject, *ʾîš*, "man," at the beginning of v. 20. This interpretation contrasts with the singular formulations of the verb, *wayyak/wĕhikkâ*, "and he struck," both with "the king of Israel" as subject, in v. 21.

g–g. The Hebrew is somewhat awkward here. Cf. LXX, "the horse of a horseman"; Targum Jonathan, "upon horses and two horsemen were with them"; Peshitta, "in chariots with horsemen."

h. Hebrew, *ʾăpēr*, is a hapax legomenon related to Assyria *ipru*, "covering," and *êpartu*, "garment" (*BHS* 68); cf. Targum Jonathan, *maʿpĕrāʾ*, "a cloak with a hood"; LXX, *telamōni*, "a broad linen bandage." Peshitta reads the term as *ʾōper*, "ashes," viz., "and disguised his face with ashes (*qtmʾ*)."

i–i. LXX, "and behold, (one setting) snares for me, you have slain/destroyed," reading *mišpātekā*, "your sentence/judgment," as a hiphil form of *tps*, "to seize, take hold," i.e., *matpîs*, "one who takes hold," and *hārāṣtā*, "you have determined," as *rāhaṣtā*, "you have slain." This rendering enhances Ahab's gullibility by suggesting that he views the man as more concerned with defending his king than with watching his charge.

j–j. Peshitta, "wiped off the ashes from his face."

First Kings 20:1–43 prepares for 1 Kgs 22, where Ahab is killed in battle at Ramoth Gilead. It also prepares for the accounts in 2 Kgs 1–10 of Aramean harassment of Israel during the reigns of Ahab's sons, Ahaziah and Jehoram, and the demise of the house of Ahab. The narrative begins in v. 1 with a finite verbal sentence introduced by a conjunctive *waw* and a proper name—"And Ben-Hadad (*ûben-hădad*) gathered all his army . . ."—that joins the present narrative to the preceding chapter and distinguishes it syntactically as a discrete unit. Verse 1 introduces a self-contained narrative that relates Ahab's defeat of Ben-Hadad and the condemnation of Ahab for releasing Ben-Hadad and concluding a treaty with him. Primary characters include Ben-Hadad, Ahab, the servants of Ben-Hadad, and several anonymous prophets of YHWH.

Commentators (e.g., Benzinger, Gray, Würthwein, Long, Fritz, Buis) argue that the literary structure of the narrative comprises two or three basic components, based on the two accounts of Ben-Hadad's attempts to attack Israel at Samaria and Aphek (vv. 1–25 and vv. 26–34) and the prophetic condemnation of Ahab (vv. 35–43). Such a view confuses a diachronic model for the composition of the narrative with a synchronic model for the organization of the present text. They are correct to point out that the change of location, Samaria in vv. 1–25 and Aphek in vv. 26–43, and the change in characters, "the prophet" (*hannābîʾ*) in vv. 13–14, 22, and "the man of G-d" (*ʾîš hʾlqym*) in v. 28, point to the independent origins of the two accounts. But such a view overlooks the crucial role played by the anonymous prophets in the synchronic form of the

narrative.[50] These prophets are hardly the same man, but their interaction with
Ahab aids in uniting the elements of the narrative and in advancing its plot to
the climactic condemnation of Ahab in vv. 35–43.

Such a diachronically based view overlooks the syntactical organization of
the narrative in which the conjunctive *waw* coupled with a proper name or a
reference to a major character introduces a narrative subunit based in *waw*-
consecutive verbs that relates a successive step in the overall plot sequence.
Thus, *ûben-hădad,* "and Ben-Hadad," in v. 1 introduces vv. 1–12, which relate
Ahab's refusal of Ben-Hadad's initial terms for surrender. The phrase *wĕhinnēh
nābî' 'ehād,* "and behold, one prophet," in v. 13 introduces vv. 13–22, in which
the prophet informs Ahab that YHWH will give him victory and then warns
Ahab that Ben-Hadad will attack him again. When read apart from the narrative context, this warning is enigmatic, but when read in relation to vv. 35–43,
it suggests to Ahab that he should eliminate Ben-Hadad immediately. The
phrase *wĕ'abdê melek-'ărām,* "and the servants of the king of Aram," in v. 23
introduces vv. 23–34, in which they advise Ben-Hadad to mount a second attack
against Israel in the plains by Aphek, located to the east of the Sea of Galilee.
After the battle is lost, the Aramean servants play an important role in prompting Ahab to spare Ben-Hadad's life. Again, a prophet, here called "a man of
G-d" in v. 28, informs Ahab that YHWH will give him the victory. Finally, *wĕ'îš
'ehād mibbĕnê hannĕbî'îm,* "and one of the sons of the prophets," introduces
vv. 35–43, which presents the prophet's condemnation of Ahab for releasing
Ben-Hadad and making a treaty with him. These verses constitute the climactic subunit of the chapter, which demonstrates Ahab's failure to grasp the opportunity presented to him by YHWH. Ironically, his failure contrasts with the
recognition by the servants of Ben-Hadad of the opportunity to save their king
in vv. 32–33.

The historical setting presupposed by this narrative has been the subject of
considerable debate.[51] Elijah plays no role in this chapter, and apart from vv. 2,
13, 14, Ahab is identified throughout simply as "the king of Israel" (vv. 4, 7, 11,
21, 22, 28, 31, 40, 41, 43; cf. vv. 38, 39), which is typical of the narratives concerning the prophet Elisha. The events portrayed in the narrative, in which Israel
is oppressed by the Arameans during the reigns of Ahab and his father Omri (see
v. 34), appear to be unlikely insofar as ancient Near Eastern documents portray
the Omrides as powerful monarchs. The Assyrian King Shalmaneser III, for
example, lists the considerable forces of Ahab of Israel, two thousand chariots

50. Julius Wellhausen, *Die Composition des Hexateuch* (Berlin: de Gruyter, 1963), 285, maintains that the references to the prophets are secondary.
51. See Steven L. McKenzie, *The Trouble with Kings: The Composition of the Books of
Kings in the Deuteronomistic History* (VTSup 42; Leiden: Brill, 1991), 88–93, for an overview of
the discussion.

and ten thousand foot soldiers, as part of the coalition led by Adad-idri (Hada-dezer) of Damascus that fought him at Qarqar in 553 B.C.E. (*ANET* 278–79), and in the Moabite Stone, King Mesha of Moab speaks of Israel's domination of Moab during the reigns of Omri and his son (*ANET* 320). The biblical accounts suggest Omride power by emphasizing Omri's building of the city of Samaria (1 Kgs 16:24), Ahab's ivory house and the cities that he built (1 Kgs 22:39), Omride control over the Jezreel (1 Kgs 21; 2 Kgs 8–9) and Transjordan (1 Kgs 22), and the Omride alliance with Phoenicia (1 Kgs 16:31–34). Additional com-plicating factors include Ahab's death notice in 1 Kgs 22:40, which appears else-where only in 1–2 Kings in relation to the peaceful deaths of kings, and Shalmaneser III's identification of the Aramean king as Adad-idri (Hadadezer) rather than as Bar(Ben)-Hadad.

These factors suggest to some that the present narrative and that concerning Ahab's death at the hands of the Arameans at Ramoth Gilead in 1 Kgs 22 relate not to Ahab, but to some other Israelite king, such as Joash ben Jehoahaz (2 Kgs 13:14–25; see also 2 Kgs 10:32–33)[52] or Jehoahaz ben Jehu, since 2 Kgs 13:3 suggests that Ben-Hadad succeeded his father during Jehoahaz's reign.[53] The Ben-Hadad of the present narrative would then be identified as the Ben-Hadad son of Hazael of the Elisha narratives. The king of Israel was originally anony-mous in these narratives, which enabled later tradents to employ them in order to strengthen the condemnation of Ahab.

Such argumentation may be questioned on a number of grounds.[54] First, the mid-ninth-century Melqart inscription, which was discovered in Aleppo, men-tions a certain Bar-Hadad by name as king of Aram (*ANET* 655). Earlier schol-ars identify him as Ben-Hadad son of Tabrimmon, mentioned in 1 Kgs 15:16–22 as the king who allied with Asa of Judah and attacked the Galilee region during the reign of Baasha. Recent studies argue, however, that Bar-Hadad's father's name should be read as 'Attar-hamek, which differentiates this Bar-Hadad from the Ben-Hadad son of Hazael mentioned throughout the Elisha tradition.[55]

Second, the portrayal of Israel's oppression by Aram in 1 Kgs 20; 22 need not contradict our understandings of Omride power during this period. The bor-der between Israel and Aram was frequently a flashpoint of conflict, even when Israel was strong. Biblical sources indicate that conflicts between Israel and

52. A. Jepsen, "Israel und Damaskus," *AfO* 14 (1941–45): 153–72; C. F. Whitley, "The Deutero-nomic Presentation of the House of Omri," *VT* 2 (1952): 137–52.

53. J. Maxwell Miller, "The Elisha Cycle and the Accounts of the Omride Wars," *JBL* 85 (1966): 441–54; Miller, "The Rest of the Acts of Jehoahaz (1 Kings 20. 22, 1–38)," *ZAW* 80 (1968): 337–42.

54. See Cogan, *1 Kings,* 471–72, who argues that Jehoshaphat's presence together with the Israelite king in 1 Kgs 20 and 22 requires that the Israelite king must be Ahab, since Joash and the contemporary Judean monarch, Ahaziah, did not have a cooperative relationship.

55. Wayne Pitard, "The Identity of the Bir Hadad of the Melqart Stele," *BASOR* 272 (1988): 3–21.

Aram broke out during the reigns of David (2 Sam 8:3–12; 10), Solomon (1 Kgs 11:23–25), and after the fall of the house of Jehu, when Israel saw four of its next six kings assassinated as pro-Aramean and pro-Assyrian interests struggled for control of the throne (see 2 Kgs 15–16; Hos 1; 12). The Syro-Ephraimitic War was fought after Aram succeeded in placing the pro-Aramean Pekah on the throne, thereby paving the way for Aram and Israel to invade Judah with the intent to overthrow Jotham and Ahaz of the house of David and to bring Judah into its anti-Assyrian coalition (Isa 7). The strength of the house of Omri would hardly protect it from challenges by the Arameans. The portrayal of Ahab's defeat of Ben-Hadad and his treaty with him testifies to the power of the house of Omri during the mid-ninth century.

Third, the portrayal of conflict between Israel and Aram does not necessarily conflict with the portrayal of the alliance between Israel and Aram against Shalmaneser III at Qarqar. Interpreters cannot assume that Aram was reluctant to employ force in order to compel another state to join an alliance against the Assyrians. Given the history of conflict between Israel and Aram, one cannot assume that Israel would join Aram to oppose the Assyrians. The history of the Jehu dynasty's alliance with Assyria indicates that Israel had much to gain by allying with Assyria to contain Aram. Ben-Hadad's failed attempts to force Israel into an anti-Assyrian alliance would have demonstrated Aram's relative weakness to Ahab, prompting him to conclude that he had much to gain by using Aram as a buffer against an emerging Assyria. First Kings 20 portrays a situation in which Ahab capitalized on Aram's weakness by defining a treaty with Ben-Hadad along lines that served his interests rather than Aram's. Such an alliance would explain Ahab's very powerful presence as part of the Aramean-led coalition against Shalmaneser III in 853 B.C.E. The heavy losses suffered by the coalition—particularly among the chariots—in its successful attempt to repulse the Assyrian advance shifted the balance of power between Aram and Israel once again.[56]

The history of this particular composition remains clouded. The differentiation in the prophetic figures suggests that it is based on two originally separate accounts of Israel's battles with Aram at Samaria and Aphek in vv. 1–25 and 26–43. The narrative is placed together with the accounts of Ahab's relationship with Jezebel and the supporters of Baal (1 Kgs 18–19) and the murder of Naboth (1 Kgs 21) to discredit the king and to prepare the reader for his death in 1 Kgs 22 and the collapse of his dynasty in 2 Kgs 1–10. Such a composition serves the interests of the Jehu dynasty, insofar as it justifies Jehu's overthrow of the house of Omri. In relation to the Hezekian, Josian, and exilic DtrH editions, it justifies the downfall of northern Israel.

---

56. Shalmaneser claims to have killed either fourteen thousand or twenty-five thousand soldiers of Adad-idri's coalition in addition to taking chariots, horses, and equipment (*ANET* 279, 281). Ahab's two thousand chariots would have suffered considerable losses.

[1–12] The initial subunit demonstrates the nature of Ben-Hadad's threat—that is, he will never be placated, but will demand more and more of Ahab even when he submits. Consequently, the text demonstrates the reasons that Ahab should seize the opportunity presented to him by YHWH to eliminate Ben-Hadad. Insofar as the Arameans later kill Ahab in battle at Ramoth Gilead (1 Kgs 22), the passage points to Ahab's fatal error in concluding a treaty with such a man.

The thirty-two kings in v. 1a are Ben-Hadad's allies, who would be called out to support his campaigns. Such an obligation is typical of ancient Near Eastern treaties. The narrative action is conveyed by the following sequence of *waw*-consecutive verbs. Verse 1b states the purpose for the gathering of Ben-Hadad's army: launching an attack against Samaria. The laying of siege to a city was a typical means employed by ancient Near Eastern kings to force the payment of tribute, the signing of treaties, participation in military campaigns against another state, and so on.[57]

Ahab's initial acceptance of Ben-Hadad's terms appears in vv. 3–4. The demands for silver and gold and for Ahab's best wives and sons are typical demands for tribute and hostages. The messenger formula *kōh ʾāmar ben-hădad,* "thus says Ben-Hadad," is typically employed in diplomatic exchange.[58] Ahab's easy submission illustrates his character; he quickly accepts an alliance with Ben-Hadad just as he accepted an alliance with Ethbaal of Sidon (1 Kgs 16:31).

Ben-Hadad reiterates his initial demands for silver, gold, wives, and sons in vv. 5–6, and stipulates that Ben-Hadad's "servants" will arrive the next day to search Ahab's palace and the houses of his "servants" to ensure compliance with the initial demand. Ben-Hadad's stipulations are designed to humiliate Ahab. The term *maḥmad ʿênêkā,* "delight of your eyes," is undefined, although it refers to Ezekiel's wife in Ezek 24:16 and to silver in Hos 9:6.

Ahab's response to Ben-Hadad's increased demands appears in vv. 7–9. He first consults with the elders to ensure their support in a negotiation that will likely lead to war.[59] Ahab emphasizes that he did not refuse Ben-Hadad's initial demands, which presents him in a favorable light in that he was initially unwilling to risk the lives and property of his subjects.

The monarchs posturing in vv. 10–12 precedes battle. Ben-Hadad's response to Ahab includes a proverbial saying that expresses his contempt for Samaria's ability to defend itself. It begins with an oath (Long 253), "may the gods do to me and more . . . ," that is, he should suffer the fate he proposes for Samaria if he does not carry out his threats. The following statement, "if the dust of

---

57. H. Tadmor, "The Campaigns of Sargon II of Assur: A Chronological-Historical Study," *JCS* 12 (1958): 22–40, 77–100.

58. See Isa 36–37/2 Kgs 18–19; Meier, *Speaking,* 273–98.

59. For discussion of the elders, see Fox, *In the Service,* 63–72.

Samaria suffices for handfuls for all the people that are at my feet," indicates
that Samaria is less than dirt compared to Ben-Hadad's powerful army. Ahab's
proverbial response, "let not the one who buckles (his weapons) boast like one
who unbuckles (them)," is clear: Ben-Hadad should not presume that he has
won the battle. Ben-Hadad's command to engage battle is telling; he and his
allies are drunk, overconfident, rash, and therefore easy targets for Ahab.

[13–22] The subunit begins in v. 13 with a conjunctive-*waw* formulation that
introduces a statement based on a perfect verb, "And behold, one prophet
(*wĕhinnēh nābîʾ ʾeḥād*) drew near (*niggaš*) to Ahab, King of Israel. . . ." The
balance of the action is conveyed by *waw*-consecutive verbs. Emphasizing the
prophet, the narrative focuses on YHWH's statements to Ahab. YHWH thereby
warns Ahab that Ben-Hadad will be a continuing threat if Ahab does not eliminate him now.

The anonymous prophet's interaction with Ahab appears in vv. 13–14. The
prophet's initial statement employs the messenger formula *kōh ʾāmar yhwh*,
"Thus says YHWH," which identifies him as a spokesperson for YHWH. The
prophet states that YHWH will grant Ahab victory over the powerful Aramean
forces. The concluding prophetic proof saying, "and you shall know that I am
YHWH," indicates that Ahab's victory over Ben-Hadad must be construed as
a revelation of YHWH's power (cf. Ezek 12:19–20; 25:2–3; Isa 41:17–20;
49:22–26).[60] Ahab's question, "by whom?" presupposes oracular inquiry (see
also 2 Sam 2:1). The answer identifies the young men of the provincial commanders—that is, Ahab will call for support from his own officers (cf.
Solomon's district rulers in 1 Kgs 4:7–19).[61] The "young men" (*nĕʿārîm*) are
the squires of the established warriors who would form mobile light forces to
attack Ben-Hadad's army prior to the main engagement. Ahab's second inquiry
informs him that he should not wait for Ben-Hadad to attack, but that he should
seize the advantage by engaging his light forces first.

Ahab's resounding victory appears in vv. 15–21. The decision to attack at
noon gave the Arameans plenty of time to drink; by noon they would be wasted.
This strategy is evident in the report to Ben-Hadad that Israelite forces had come
out. His response to take them alive whether they came out to surrender or to
fight indicates drunken lack of judgment. The battle proceeds much differently,
as the young men and the main force are able to route the Aramean army.

The subunit concludes in v. 22 by returning to the prophet who had initiated
the action in vv. 13–14. The warning that the king of Aram will "go up" (attack)
again at the turn of the year informs Ahab that he had better prepare now to protect himself and his people.

60. W. Zimmerli, "The Word of Divine Self-Manifestation (Proof-saying): A Prophetic Genre,"
I am YHWH (trans. D. W. Stott; Atlanta: John Knox, 1982), 99–110.
61. For discussion of the *śārîm* and *nĕʿārîm,* see Fox, *In the Service,* 150–63, 182–91; John
MacDonald, "The Status and Role of the Naʿar in Israelite Society," *JNES* 35 (1976): 147–70.

[23–34] The third subunit emphasizes the role of "the servants of the king of Aram"[62] in instigating Ben-Hadad's second attack and in the negotiations with Ahab that save Ben-Hadad's life and result in a treaty with Israel. Their ability to see an opportunity—in contrast to Ahab, who is informed of his opportunities by YHWH—saves Ben-Hadad so that he will later kill Ahab.

The subunit begins in v. 23 with a *waw*-conjunctive formulation followed by a perfect verbal statement, "And the servants of the King of Aram (*wĕʿabdê melek-ʾărām*) said (*ʾāmĕrû*) to him . . . ," which introduces the primary characters. The balance of the action is carried by *waw*-consecutive verbs. The servants' proposal to Ben-Hadad to resume hostilities against Israel caricaturizes pagan perspective insofar as they propose that Israel's victory must be due to the fact that YHWH is a god of the mountains. This assumption contradicts the Israelite understanding that YHWH is the G-d of all creation (see 1 Kgs 17–19) and that YHWH will grant Ahab victory. The proposal to fight Israel in the plain attempts to draw Ahab out from the protective cover of the Samarian hills into the open plains by the Golan Heights that provide access to the Jezreel Valley. By targeting the plains, the Arameans aim for the trade routes in the valleys.

The account of the battle between Aram and Israel at Aphek appears in vv. 26–30. The site of Aphek remains uncertain. A likely location is at Ein Gev on the eastern shore of the Sea of Galilee (M. Kochavi, "ʿEn Gev," *NEAEHL* 2:409–12). The narrative portrays the battle itself as an unequal contest. The "man of G-d" appears in v. 28, however, to emphasize divine intervention. The concluding prophetic proof saying, "and you shall know that I am YHWH," reinforces the revelatory character of the victory. Ben-Hadad flees and hides like a coward in an inner room.

Ben-Hadad's servants were able to act upon the opportunity provided by the heedless Ahab to spare their king's life in vv. 31–34. The servants are aware of the Israelite king's capacity for fidelity, and act accordingly. The term "fidelity," *ḥesed,* refers to loyalty within a covenant or treaty relationship, and it connotes mercy and compassion.[63] The Arameans manipulate Ahab by appearing before him in customary mourning attire to plead for Ben-Hadad's life. Ahab responds with compassion by employing a rhetorical question to express surprise that he is still alive and then by stating, "he is my brother." The term "brother" is a characteristic term for allies in ancient parity treaties (cf. 1 Kgs 9:13; Amos 1:9). Ahab thereby declares his willingness to recognize Ben-Hadad as an ally (and spare his life). Ahab states terms that give him considerable advantage: the return of cities taken by the Arameans from his father and the ability to establish markets in Damascus much as the Arameans had previously established

---

62. For discussion of the *ʿebed hammelek,* see Fox, *In the Service,* 53–63.
63. Nelson Glueck, *Hesed in the Bible* (Cincinnati: Hebrew Union College, 1967).

markets in Samaria. He then concludes a new treaty with Ben-Hadad and sends him home. Although the treaty is favorable to Ahab, he missed the point of YHWH's statements: the man is a threat.

[35–43] The concluding subunit emphasizes the consequences of Ahab's failure to eliminate Ben-Hadad, that is, he is condemned to death by a prophet from YHWH. The subunit begins with a sentence formed by a combination of a *waw*-conjunctive formulation and a perfect verb, "And one of the sons of the prophets (*wĕʾîš eḥād mibbĕnê hannĕbîʾîm*) said (*ʾāmar*) to his neighbor . . . ," which emphasizes the importance of the prophet as a primary character who conveys YHWH's statements to Ahab. The balance of the action is conveyed with *waw*-consecutive verbs. The narrative has links to the prophetic legends, particularly since it emphasizes the lion that kills the prophet who refuses to wound his colleague (cf.1 Kgs 13:11–32).

The preparations made by one of the "sons of the prophets" appear in vv. 35–36. The term *bĕnê hannĕbîʾîm*, "sons of the prophets," refers to prophetic guilds in ancient Israel (viz., the groups of prophets hidden from Ahab in 1 Kgs 18:4; cf. 2 Kgs 2:3; 5:22; 6:1; 9:1).[64] The term *ben-nābîʾ*, "son of a prophet," designates a professional prophet (see Amos 7:14). The prophet's request that his colleague wound him facilitates his attempt to disguise himself for his encounter with Ahab. The disguise ironically enables the prophet to prompt Ahab to condemn himself.

The encounter between the prophet and Ahab appears in vv. 38–42. The prophet presupposes the role of the king as judge (cf. 2 Sam 12:1–15; 1 Kgs 3:16–28). The prophet states that he was asked to guard a prisoner during a battle and that he would be subject to death or a fine if the man escaped (cf. Exod 22:6–7). A "talent" of silver is a considerable amount of money, equivalent to anywhere from fifty to thirty-six hundred shekels (W. Dever, "Weights and Measures," *HBD* 1206–11), presumably beyond his capacity to pay. When the man escapes, the king responds as expected by declaring that the man has decided his own sentence. The prophet then reveals himself to deliver an oracle of judgment against Ahab. The oracle employs typical prophetic language, including the messenger formula "thus says YHWH," and a prophetic oracle of judgment.[65] It states the grounds for punishment, beginning with the particle *yaʿan*, "because (you released a condemned man)." The term *ḥermî* is an adjective that means "banned" to indicate the condemned man. The penalty reiterates the *lex talionis* (see Exod 21:23–25; Lev 24:19–21; Deut 19:21), which states that punishment be commensurate with the crime. Ahab's crime affects his people; all Israel will suffer for Ahab's irresponsibility in letting Ben-Hadad go.

---

64. A. Haldar, *Associations of Cult Prophets among the Ancient Semites* (Uppsala: Almqvist & Wiksell, 1945), 90–160.

65. Sweeney, *Isaiah 1–39*, 533–34.

The narrative concludes in v. 43 with an angry and sullen Ahab returning to Samaria, which points to Ahab's anger and sullenness when Naboth refuses to sell him his vineyard (1 Kgs 21:4).

1 Kings 21:1–29 Elijah's Condemnation of the House of Ahab

21:1 [a]And after these things Naboth the Jezreelite had a vineyard, which was in Jezreel beside the palace of Ahab, King of Samaria. 2 And Ahab spoke to Naboth, saying, "Give me your vineyard so that it may be a vegetable garden for me because it is near my house, and I will give to you in its place a better vineyard. (Or) if it is preferable to you, I will pay you its price in cash." 3 And Naboth said to Ahab, "YHWH forbid that I give the inheritance of my ancestors to you!" 4 And Ahab went to his house, angry and sullen concerning the answer that Naboth the Jezreelite gave to him when he said, "I will not give to you the inheritance of my ancestors." And he lay upon his bed, turned his face, and did not eat food.

5 And Jezebel, his wife, came to him, and said to him, "What is this? Your spirit is gone and you are not eating food?" 6 And he said to her, "Because I spoke to Naboth the Jezreelite, and said to him, 'Give me your vineyard for cash, or, if it is preferable to you, I will give you a vineyard in its place,' and he said, 'I will not give to you my vineyard.'" 7 And Jezebel his wife said to him, "You, now, exercise sovereignty over Israel. Rise, eat food, and let your heart be good. I will give to you the vineyard of Naboth the Jezreelite." 8 And she wrote letters in the name of Ahab, sealed them with his seal, and sent letters[b] to the elders and to the nobles who were in his city, those who sat with Naboth. 9 And she wrote in the letters, saying, "Proclaim a fast, and seat Naboth at the head of the people! 10 And seat two scoundrels before him, so that they will witness against him, saying, 'You have cursed[c] G-d and King!' then bring him out and stone him so that he dies." 11 And the men of his city, the elders and the nobles who were sitting in his city, did just as Jezebel sent unto them, just as (what) was written in the letters which she sent to them. 12 They proclaimed a fast and sat Naboth at the head of the people. 13 And twelve scoundrels came and sat before him, and the scoundrels testified against Naboth before the people, saying, "Naboth has cursed[d] G-d and King," and they brought him outside the city and stoned him with stones, and he died. 14 And they sent to Jezebel, saying, "Naboth has been stoned, and he died." 15 And when Jezebel heard that Naboth was stoned and died, that Jezebel said to Ahab, "Arise, take possession of the vineyard of Naboth the Jezreelite that he refused to give to you for cash, for Naboth is not living for he is dead." 16 When Ahab heard that Naboth was dead, [e]Ahab rose to go down to the vineyard of Naboth the Jezreelite to take possession of it.[e]

17 And the word of YHWH came to Elijah the Tishbite, saying, 18 "Arise, go down to meet Ahab, King of Israel, who is in Samaria, behold, by the vineyard of Naboth where he has gone down to take possession of it. 19 ᶠAnd you shall speak to him, saying, 'Thus says YHWH, "Have you committed murder and dispossessed?"' and you shall speak to him saying, 'Thus says YHWH, "In the place where the dogs lick the blood of Naboth, the dogs will lick your blood, yes, yours."'"ᶠ 20 And Ahab said to Elijah, "Have you found me, my enemy?" And he said, "I have found, because you have sold yourself to evil in the eyes of YHWH. 21 Behold, I am bringing evil to you, and I will burn you, and I will cut off to Ahab ᵍhe who pisses against the wall,ᵍ bond and free, in Israel. 22 I will make your house like the house of Jeroboam ben Nabat and like the house of Baasha ben Ahiyah concerning the provocation that you made so that you caused Israel to sin." 23 And also to Jezebel YHWH spoke, saying, "The dogs will eat Jezebel at the outer wall of Jezreel. 24 The dogs will eat the dead to Ahab in the city, and the birds of the heavens will eat the dead to Ahab in the field." 25 Indeed there was no one like Ahab who sold himself to do evil in the eyes of YHWH whom Jezebel his wife instigated. 26 And he committed a grave abomination going after the idols according to all that the Amorites, whom YHWH dispossessed from before the sons of Israel, had done. 27 When Ahab heard these words, he tore his garments, placed sackcloth upon his flesh, fasted, sat in sackcloth, and went about subdued. 28 And the word of YHWH came to Elijah the Tishbite, saying, 29 "Have you seen that Ahab has humbled himself before me? Because he has humbled himself before me, I will not bring the evil in his days. In the days of his son I will bring the evil upon his house."ᵃ

a–a. 1 Kgs 21 appears between 1 Kgs 19 and 1 Kgs 20 in the LXX. LXX groups together the Elijah narratives in 1 Kgs 17–19; 21 and the anonymous prophets narratives in 1 Kgs 20; 22.

b. Read with Qere, *sĕpārîm,* "letters," in place of Ketiv, *hassĕpārîm,* "the letters"; cf. LXX, Targum Jonathan, and Peshitta, "a letter."

c. MT employs the verb *bēraktā,* literally, "you have blessed," but the verb is sometimes employed in the antithetical sense, "you have cursed" (Job 1:5, 11; 2:5, 9; Ps 10:3; see BDB 139); cf. LXX, "he has blessed"; Peshitta, "Naboth has cursed."

d. LXX, "blessed" (see n. c above).

e–e. LXX expands the statement to portray Ahab's show of grief at Naboth's death, "and he tore his garments and put on sackcloth, and after this Ahab arose and went down to the vineyard of Naboth the Jezreelite to inherit it."

f–f. Cf. LXX, "And you shall speak to him, saying, 'Thus says the L-rd, "Because you have killed and taken possession,"' therefore thus says the L-rd, 'In every place where the pigs and the dogs licked the blood of Naboth, there shall the dogs lick your blood, and the prostitutes shall bathe in your blood,'" which simplifies the grammatical structure and highlights Ahab's degrading judgment.

g–g. Hebrew, *maštîn běqîr,* "he who pisses against the wall," a derogatory reference to the males of the house of Ahab; cf. LXX, *ourounta pros toichov,* "he who makes water against the wall"; Targum Jonathan, *yadāᶜ mādāᶜ,* "everyone knowing knowledge"; Peshitta, *dt'n b'st',* "he who makes water against the wall."

First Kings 21:1–29 relates Elijah's condemnation of Ahab for the murder of Naboth the Jezreelite. Ahab's repentance wins him a reprieve from seeing the collapse of his dynasty, but it nevertheless informs the reader that Ahab's entire house is subject to punishment for his crime.

The unit begins in v. 1a with the temporal formula, "and after these things . . ." The structure of the narrative is based on a presentation of the major characters who interact with Ahab. Thus, the first subunit in vv. 1–4 names Naboth in v. 1aß, who declines Ahab's offer to purchase his vineyard. The second in vv. 5–16 names Jezebel, who first inquires as to the cause of Ahab's ill temper and then takes action to acquire the vineyard by framing Naboth. The third in vv. 17–29 names Elijah, speaking on behalf of YHWH, who condemns Ahab and his house for the murder.

The site of Jezreel is identified with Zerin/Tel Yizra'al, located fifteen kilometers east of Megiddo at the eastern entrance to the main Jezreel Valley between Mount Gilboa to the south and Givat ha-Moreh to the north. This location is strategic, both because the rich farmland of the Jezreel constitutes the breadbasket of ancient Israel and because its low-lying plains form the highway that links the Transjordan with the coastal plain. The site protects the Jezreel Valley from any incursion from the east that would pass through the low-lying areas south of the Kinneret. Excavation points to extensive building and fortification in the mid-ninth century B.C.E., which indicates that it was built up by the Omride dynasty as a second capital to protect Israel from the Arameans.[66] Ahab's attempt to take control of Naboth's land is consistent with the portrayal of a powerful, centralized Omride monarchy, and it recalls later prophetic criticism of the monarchy in the eighth century (e.g., Isa 5:8–10; Mic 2:1–5, 8–9; cf. Amos 2:6–8; 8:4–6).

The narrative discredits Ahab and the Omride dynasty as a justification for the revolt of Jehu. Jehu cites Naboth's murder by Ahab when he kills Joram/Jehoram ben Ahab at Jezreel and throws his body on the plot of land

---

66. See M. Hunt, "Jezreel (Place)," *ABD* 3:850; David Ussishkin and John Woodhead, "Excavations at Tel Jezreel 1990–1991: First Preliminary Report," *TA* 19 (1992): 3–70; Ussishkin and Woodhead, "Excavations at Tel Jezreel 1992–1993: Second Preliminary Report," *Levant* 26 (1994): 171; "Excavations at Tel Jezreel 1994–1996: Third Preliminary Report," *TA* 24 (1997): 6–72; H. G. M. Williamson, "Jezreel in the Biblical Texts," *TA* 18 (1991): 72–92.

taken by Ahab after Naboth's death (2 Kgs 9:24–26).[67] Several other motifs also point to Jehu interests: the dogs that will lick the blood of Naboth, Jezebel, and Ahab (see v. 19; cf. 1 Kgs 22:38; 2 Kgs 9:26); the dogs and the birds that will eat the corpses of Jezebel and Ahab's house (see vv. 23–24; cf. 2 Kgs 9:30–37); and the death of all who piss on the wall, bond and free, of the house of Ahab (see v. 21; cf. 2 Kgs 9:8). These references also point to the larger narrative framework in Kings, particularly with regard to the elimination of all who piss against the wall, bond and free, of the house of Ahab in v. 21, explicitly mentioned with reference to the condemnation of the house of Jeroboam ben Nebat (1 Kgs 14:10) and the house of Baasha ben Ahijah (1 Kgs 16:11), and to the dogs who will eat the corpses left by the house of Jeroboam (1 Kgs 14:10) and Baasha (1 Kgs 16:4). The reference to Israelite men as "bond and free" also appears in 2 Kgs 14:26 as part of the explanation for YHWH's granting a great kingdom to Jeroboam ben Joash. These references suggest composition as part of an early-eighth-century narrative that was designed to justify the rule of the Jehu dynasty in Israel.[68]

The narrative also plays a role in relation to the later Hezekian, Josian, and exilic DtrH editions, where it justifies the downfall of the northern kingdom of Israel and ultimately Jerusalem and Judah as well. The formula in v. 21, *hinĕnî mēbîʾ ʾēlêkā rāʿâ*, "behold, I am bringing unto you evil," appears in relation to the condemnation of Jeroboam ben Nebat (1 Kgs 14:10; *hinĕnî mēbîʾ rāʿâ ʾel bêt-yārobʿām*, "behold, I am bringing evil to the house of Jeroboam") and Jerusalem (this place) in the account of Josiah's reign (2 Kgs 22:16, *hinĕnî mēbîʾ rāʿâ ʾel hammāqôm hazzeh*, "behold, I am bringing evil unto this place"; cf. 2 Kgs 22:20). The formula appears in a slightly different form in 2 Kgs 21:12, where it is directed against Jerusalem as a result of the sins of Manasseh (*hinĕnî mēbîʾ rāʿâ ʿal yĕrûšālim*, "behold, I am bringing evil against Jerusalem"; cf. 2 Kgs 22:20). Insofar as the Josian narrative forms the culmination of the Josian DtrH, in which the condemnation of Jeroboam figures prominently, and the Manasseh narrative provides a major element of the exilic DtrH, the presence of this phrase in 1 Kgs 21:21 indicates a direct link into both the Josian and exilic DtrH editions. With regard to the exilic edition, which announces the destruction of Jerusalem from Manasseh's time on (see 2 Kgs 21:10–15; 22:14–20; 23:26–27; 24:3–4), Elijah's leniency toward Ahab in vv. 27–29 provides the model for Huldah's declaration that the punishment ordained for Jerusalem will not be realized in Josiah's lifetime (2 Kgs 22:18–20). Ahab is also cited in the catalog of crimes committed by Manasseh (2 Kgs 21:3).

---

67. Most scholars correctly maintain that the Naboth narrative is intended to point to the overthrow of the house of Omri by Jehu in 2 Kgs 9–10 (see esp. Hentschel, *Elija-erzählungen*, 14–43, 107–12, 148–56, 208–16; Otto, *Jehu, Elia und Elisa*, 199–243; Steck, *Überlieferung und Zeitgeschichte*, 32–77; Marsha C. White, "Naboth's Vineyard and Jehu's Coup," *VT* 44 (1994): 66–76; White, *Elijah Legends*, 17–24, 33–36).

68. Cf. Campbell, *Of Prophets and Kings*, who argues for a ninth-century prophetic history.

[1–4] Ahab's offer seems innocuous; he proposes a fair transaction in which he will trade a better vineyard for Naboth's property or pay him a fair price in cash. The statements concerning the homes of Naboth and Ahab point to the crucial issue of the proposed transaction: the transference of property from one tribe to another. Naboth is described in v. 1 as "the Jezreelite" and Ahab as "the king of Samaria." Jezreel is located in the tribal territory of Issachar (Josh 19:17–23, esp. v. 18), and Samaria is located in the tribal territory of Manasseh (Josh 17:1–13, but Samaria is not listed here because it was built in the time of Omri). The distribution of the land among the tribes of Israel in general and the question of the inheritance of the daughters of Zelophehad in particular (see Num 27:1–11; 36:1–12; Josh 17:3–46) indicate that Israelite society took special care to ensure that property remained within its original family or tribal unit (see also Lev 25:8–31; Deut 25:5–10; Jer 32:6–12; Ruth). Omri's purchase of the hill of Shemer in the territory of Manasseh as the site for the capital city of Samaria (1 Kgs 16:24) suggests that Ahab is a member of the tribe of Manasseh. His establishment of a home in Jezreel is problematic because the king has used his power as monarch to acquire property outside his own tribal territory.

Ahab's attempt to acquire land entails the displacement of members of the tribe of Issachar, as the king—and thus Manasseh and perhaps Ephraim—extend their power beyond their own tribal boundaries. Such a move threatens the tribal structure that constituted ancient Israel. Even if he gives Naboth a better vineyard, there is no guarantee that it will be in the territory of Issachar. Ahab's reaction to Naboth's refusal displays his flawed character. Verse 4 employs the same language as 1 Kgs 20:43, *sar wĕzāʿēp,* "angry and sullen," to describe his mood. Ahab's actions are hardly fitting for a powerful monarch who takes seriously his responsibility to see to the proper administration, protection, and advancement of his kingdom.

[5–16] Ahab's account of Naboth's refusal to sell or trade his vineyard to Ahab omits various details of the conversation, most notably the basis for Naboth's refusal—that is, that it would be forbidden before YHWH for him to sell the inheritance of his ancestors. Such an omission suggests that the reason for Naboth's rejection is irrelevant to either Ahab or Jezebel. His omission subtly points to the rejection of Mosaic torah as the basis for Israelite social life. Jezebel's response emphasizes that rejection, "You now will exercise kingship over Israel," that is, she emphasizes Ahab's right as king to act with impunity against his subjects. Such a view contradicts Deut 17:14–20, which places certain limitations on the power of the king, most notably requiring him to study YHWH's torah under the supervision of the Levitical priests. Her emphasis on the term *ʾattâ,* "you," is ironic because she will actually exercise power rather than Ahab.

Jezebel takes action in vv. 8–14 to frame Naboth and to have him executed for sedition against the state. Her actions emphasize Ahab's refusal to act as a responsible king in that she writes a fraudulent letter in his name to commit murder. The use of the seal to fix a signature to a document is one of the most common means of identification in the ancient Near East. Cylinder seals with pictographic signatures were employed throughout Mesopotamian history from the fourth millennium through the Roman period to sign clay tablets by rolling the seal on the wet clay before it dried.[69] Judean seals are also well known as stamps that were pressed into jar handles to identify the property of the king and clay bullae that were pressed into the wet clay that sealed a papyrus document in order to fix the sender's name to the document.[70] Jezebel directs the message to the "elders," *zĕqēnîm*, and the "nobles," *hōrîm*. The elders are a council of senior figures who exercised authority within tribal groups or urban settings (Exod 24:1–11; Num 11:16–30; Judg 21:16–24; 1 Sam 8:1–9; 2 Sam 5:3). The role of the nobles is less clear, although the term emerges in later contexts (see Jer 27:20; 39:6; Qoh 10:17; Neh 2:16; 4:8, 13; 5:7; 6:17; 7:5; 13:17; Isa 34:12). The term *zĕqēnîm*, "elders," is associated with northern Israelite settings, and *hōrîm*, "nobles," is associated largely with Judean settings. Jezebel's message is ironic in that it blatantly calls upon the elders and the nobles of Jezreel to deliberately frame Naboth. They do not object.

The order to proclaim a fast, seat Naboth at the head of the people, and to seat two "scoundrels" to testify against him is oddly reminiscent of the traditions concerning the selection of Saul as king. A feast is proclaimed in the city of Ramah, and the unwitting Saul is seated as the guest of honor (1 Sam 9:1–10:16). Afterward, the newly selected Saul is denounced by two "scoundrels" (1 Sam 10:17–27). The term *bĕnê bĕlîyaʿal*, "scoundrels" (lit., "sons of Belial"), is often understood in later tradition as a personification of evil in the form of a Satan figure,[71] but the term itself is derived from a combination of the terms *bĕlî*, "without," and *yaʿal*, "profit, worth," so that the expression refers basically to "worthless men."[72] The charge brought against Naboth, "you have cursed (literally, 'blessed'; see text n. c above) G-d and king," presupposes the prohibition in Exod 22:27, "G-d you shall not curse (*lōʾ tĕqalēl*) and the prince (*nāśîʾ*) among your people you shall not revile (*lōʾ tāʾōr*)."[73] Two or more witnesses are required in Israelite law for a conviction in the case of murder or other serious crime; no one can be put to death on the testimony of one witness (Deut 17:6; 19:15). Stoning is a common means to carry out a death sentence in ancient Israel (see Exod 19:13; Deut 13:11; 17:5; 22:21, 24; Josh 7:25). The concluding report to Jezebel by the elders and nobles in v. 14 highlights their own acquiescence to the crime. The complete lack of responsibility in the exercise of royal authority

69. B. S. Magness-Gardiner, "Seals, Mesopotamian," *ABD* 5:1062–64.

70. H. D. Lance, "Stamps, Royal Jar Handle," *ABD* 6:184–85; N. Avigad, *Hebrew Bullae from the Time of Jeremiah: Remnants of a Burnt Archive* (Jerusalem: Israel Exploration Society, 1986).

71. T. H. Gastor, "Belial," *EnJud* 4:428–29; Gastor, "Belial," *IDB* 1:357.

72. B. Otzen, "בליעל," *TDOT* 2:131–36.

73. For discussion of the legal background, see Timm, *Die Dynastie Omri*, 121–26.

continues in vv. 15–16 when Jezebel tells Ahab that he can take possession of Naboth's field—because he is now dead. Ahab asks no questions.

[17–29] The third subunit takes the reader to the main point: Elijah's condemnation of Ahab and his dynasty for the murder of Naboth. The narrative thereby prepares the reader for Ahab's death in 1 Kgs 22:1–40 and Jehu's overthrow of the house of Omri in 2 Kgs 9–10.

The subunit begins with the prophetic word transmission formula ("and the word of YHWH came to Elijah the Tishbite, saying . . .") to emphasize the oracular character of YHWH's communication to Elijah and Elijah's communication to Ahab. Elijah is introduced once again as Elijah the Tishbite (cf. 1 Kgs 17:1). Each character in the narrative is similarly identified as "Naboth the Jezreelite" and "Ahab, the King of Israel who is in Samaria." Such identification again emphasizes Ahab's attempt to reach for land and power beyond his own tribal holdings in Manasseh. YHWH's instructions include two oracles, each introduced by the prophetic messenger formula "Thus says YHWH," to indicate the source for the prophet's oracles. Together, the two statements form a prophetic judgment speech. The first employs a rhetorical question to state the grounds for Ahab's punishment, "Have you murdered and also taken possession?" The second conveys the announcement of Ahab's punishment by employing the imagery of dogs that will lick up his blood. Not only does Ahab receive a death sentence from YHWH, but the image of dogs licking his blood conveys an especially humiliating and violent death in which Ahab would be killed out in the open with no one to see to his proper burial.[74]

Although the previous verses presuppose YHWH's instructions to Elijah, Ahab's statement to Elijah in v. 20a presupposes that Elijah has already begun to comply with YHWH's instructions (cf. Isa 7:3–25; Jer 7:1–8:3, which employ a similar technique). Unlike Ugaritic epic, in which a messenger repeats verbatim the message that he has been sent to deliver,[75] Elijah does not repeat YHWH's message to Ahab. Elijah's words to Ahab in vv. 20b–26 actually differ from YHWH's instructions and expand considerably upon the scenario of judgment. Following the speech formula in v. 20b, Elijah's statement to Ahab includes both a prophetic judgment speech in vv. 20b–24 and a reaffirmation of the seriousness of Ahab's crime in vv. 25–26. The judgment speech begins with a statement of the grounds for Ahab's punishment in v. 20b: Ahab has "sold himself to do evil in the eyes of YHWH."

The punishments for this crime appear in vv. 21–24 in a manner that ties the anticipated demise of the house of Ahab into the larger narrative framework of

---

74. Cf. the death of the oppressive king in Isaiah 14, probably the Assyrian monarch, Sargon II, whose body was left on the battlefield following an Assyrian defeat in southeastern Turkey (Sweeney, *Isaiah 1–39*, 218–39).

75. See, e.g., the account of Baal's message to Anath in the Baal cycle (*ANET* 136–37).

Kings. The relationship between the language employed in these verses and the Kings framework points to the successive editorial reworking of this passage in relation to the various Kings editions (see above).

Elijah's concluding statements in vv. 25–26 reiterate Jezebel's role in instigating Ahab, and tie the crime to the actions of Amorites whom YHWH displaced from the land (cf. Deut 7:1; 20:17; Josh 11:3; 12:8; Judg 3:5; 1 Kgs 9:20). Although the reference does not appear in the discourse concerning northern Israel's destruction in 2 Kgs 17, it does appear as part of the condemnation of Manasseh, which justifies YHWH's decision to destroy Jerusalem (2 Kgs 21:3, 11).

Finally, vv. 27–29 relate YHWH's decision to spare Ahab the overthrow of his dynasty. YHWH's decision demonstrates mercy and accounts for the fact that the dynasty was overthrown only during the reign of his son Jehoram/Joram ben Ahab (2 Kgs 9–10). The language of this passage is typically Deuteronomistic.[76] The exilic DtrH employs this episode as a model for Huldah's statement that Josiah will be spared the destruction of Jerusalem (2 Kgs 22:18–20).

1 Kings 22:1–38 Ahab's Death at Ramoth Gilead

22:1 Three years passed without war between Aram and Israel. 2 And in the third year Jehoshaphat, King of Judah, came down to the King of Israel. 3 The King of Israel said to his servants, "Do you know that Ramoth Gilead is ours, but we are prevented from taking it by the King of Aram?" 4 And he said to Jehoshaphat, "Will you go with me to war at Ramoth Gilead?" And Jehoshaphat said to the King of Israel, "I am with you; my people are with your people; my horses are with your horses." 5 And Jehoshaphat said to the King of Israel, "Inquire, please, today the word of YHWH." 6 And the King of Israel gathered the prophets, some four hundred men, and said to them, "Shall I go against Ramoth Gilead for war or shall I desist?" And they said, "Go up! And the L-rd will give (it) into the hand of the king." 7 And Jehoshaphat said, "Is there not here another prophet of YHWH that we may inquire of him?" 8 And the King of Israel said to Jehoshaphat, "There is yet one man from whom to inquire the word of the YHWH, but I hate him because he does not prophesy anything good concerning me, but only evil, Micaiah ben Imlah." And Jehoshaphat said, "Let not the king say that!" 9 And the King of Israel called to one eunuch, and he said, "Summon Micaiah ben Imlah at once!"

10 And the King of Israel and Jehoshaphat, the King of Judah, were sitting, each upon his throne ᵃdressed in royal regalia, at the threshing floorᵃ

---

76. Contra McKenzie, *Trouble,* 69; Reinhold Bohlen, *Der Fall Nabot* (Trierer Theologische Studien 35; Trier: Paulinus, 1978), 318–19. See Jones, *1 and 2 Kings,* 360; Weinfeld, *Deuteronomy and the Deuteronomic School,* 24.

by the door of the gate of Samaria, and all the prophets were prophesying before them. 11 And Zedekiah ben Canaaniah made for himself horns
of iron and said, "Thus says YHWH, 'With these you shall gore Aram
until they are finished.'" 12 And all the prophets were prophesying likewise, saying, "Go up to Ramoth Gilead, and succeed, and YHWH will
give (it) into the hand of the King."

13 And the messenger who went to call Micaiah spoke to him, saying,
"Behold now, the words of the prophets are unanimously good for the king.
Let your word,[b] please, be like theirs so that you will speak favorably."
14 And Micaiah said, "By the life of YHWH, for that which YHWH has
spoken to me will I speak." 15 And he came to the king, and the king said
to him, "Micaiah, shall we go to Ramoth Gilead for war or shall we desist?"
And he said to him, "Go up and succeed, and YHWH will give (it) into the
hand of the king!" 16 And the king said to him, "How many times have I
made you swear that you would not speak to me anything but the truth in
the name of YHWH?" 17 And he said, "I saw all Israel scattered unto the
mountains like sheep which have no shepherd. And YHWH said, 'There
is no master for these. Let each return to his house in peace.'" 18 And the
King of Israel said to Jehoshaphat, "Didn't I tell you that he would not
prophesy anything good about me but only evil?" 19 And he said, "Therefore[c] hear the word of YHWH! I saw YHWH sitting upon his throne, and
all the host of heaven standing before him to the right and to the left. 20 And
YHWH said, 'Who will deceive Ahab, so that he will go up and fall at
Ramoth Gilead?' And this one said this, and that one said that, 21 and the
spirit went out, and stood before YHWH, and said, 'I will deceive him!'
And YHWH said to him, 'How?' 22 And he said, 'I will go out, and I will
be a lying spirit in the mouth of all his prophets.' And he said, 'You will
deceive, and you will also prevail. Go out and do so.' 23 And now, behold,
YHWH has placed a lying spirit in the mouth of all these, your prophets.
And YHWH has spoken evil concerning you." 24 And Zedekiah ben
Canaaniah drew near, and he struck Micaiah on the cheek and said, [d]"How
is it that the spirit of YHWH has passed from me to speak through you?"[d]
25 And Micaiah said, "Behold, you will see on that day that you enter an
inner room to conceal yourself." 26 And the King of Israel said, "Take
Micaiah and turn him over to Amon, commander of the city, and to Joash,
son of the king. 27 And you shall say, 'Thus says the king, "Place this one
in the prison house, and feed him slave food and slave water until I return
in peace."'" 28 And Micaiah said, "If you indeed return in peace, YHWH
did not speak through me." And he said, "Hear, O peoples, all of you!"

29 And the King of Israel and Jehoshaphat went up to Ramoth Gilead.
30 And the King of Israel said to Jehoshaphat, "(I am) going to the battle
disguised, but you, wear your own garments." And the King of Israel

disguised himself and went to the battle. 31 And the King of Aram commanded his thirty-two chariot commanders, saying, "Do not fight the small or the large, but only the King of Israel himself." 32 And when the chariot commanders saw Jehoshaphat, they said, "Indeed, he is the King of Israel!" ᵉAnd they turned against himᵉ to fight, and Jehoshaphat cried out. 33 And when the chariot commanders saw that he was not the King of Israel, they turned from after him. 34 And one man drew his bow to full extent and struck the King of Israel between the clasps and the armor. And he said to his chariot driver, "Change direction, and get me out from the camp, for I am wounded." 35 And the battle raged on that day, and the king was stood up in his chariot before Aram and died in the evening, and the blood from the wound flowed into the inside of the chariot. 36 And a shout passed through the camp when the sun set, saying, "Each man to his city, and each to his land!" 37 And the King died, and he came to Samaria, and they buried the king in Samaria, 38 and they washed the chariot by the pool of Samaria, and the dogs licked his blood, and the prostitutes washed according to the word of YHWH which he spoke.

a–a. MT, *mĕlubbāšîm bĕgādîm bĕgōren,* lit., "dressed in garments at the threshing floor . . ."; cf. LXX, *enoploi,* "armed, in arms"; Peshitta, *wlbyšyn lbwš⁾ brd⁾,* "and dressed in colorful garments."

b. Read with Qere, *dĕbārĕkā,* "your word," and 2 Chr 18:12 instead of Ketiv, *dĕbārêkā,* "your words"; cf. LXX, *logous sou,* "your words."

c. MT, *lākēn,* "therefore"; cf. LXX, *ouch houtōs ouch egō,* "not so, not I" (n.b., *ouch houtōs* presupposes Hebrew, *lō⁾ kēn,* "not so," which appears to be a rereading of *lākēn*).

d–d. MT, "Where is this (*⁾ê-zeh*) that the spirit of YHWH has passed from me to speak (through) you?"; LXX, "What sort of (*poion*) spirit of the L-rd has spoken in you?"; Targum Jonathan, "At what time (*⁾êdā⁾ šā⁽ā⁾*) did the spirit of prophecy from before YHWH go up from me to speak with you?"; Peshitta, "How (*⁾yk⁾*) did the spirit of the L-rd pass from me so that it would speak in you?"

e–e. MT, *wayyāsurû⁽ālāyw,* "and they turned against him"; cf. 2 Chr 18:31, *wayyāsōbbû ⁽ālāyw,* "and they surrounded him."

First Kings 22:1–38 raises important historical questions concerning its portrayal of Ahab's death at Ramoth Gilead. It also raises substantive theological issues concerning YHWH's power and righteousness that have implications for reading the Ahab narratives and the DtrH.[77]

The introductory statement in v. 1 concerning the three-year lapse in warfare between Israel and Aram constitutes the first subunit of the chapter. The two-part

77. See esp. Wolfgang Roth, "The Story of the Prophet Micaiah (1 Kings 22) in Historical-Critical Interpretation," in *The Biblica Mosaic: Changing Perspectives* (ed. Robert M. Polzin and Eugene Rothman; Semeia Studies; Philadelphia: Fortress; Chico: Scholars Press, 1982), 105–37.

structure of the following narrative is based primarily on plot sequence, insofar as there are no major syntactical or other formal indicators of the remaining subunits in the narrative. The basic criteria are the interaction of the primary characters and the setting in which they interrelate. Verses 2–28 relate Ahab's consultation with both Jehoshaphat and the prophets, including Micaiah ben Imlah, concerning his plans to go to war against the Arameans at Ramoth Gilead. This subunit in turn comprises two major portions of its own: Ahab's initial consultation with his servants, including Jehoshaphat and the prophets in vv. 2–12, and his consultation with Micaiah ben Imlah in vv. 13–28. Indeed, the consultation with Micaiah, which breaks the overarching *waw*-consecutive syntactical structure with the initial conjunctive *waw* joined to the noun *hammalʾāk*, conveys the primary concerns of the narrative, including YHWH's decision to see to Ahab's death and the theological implications concerning the means by which that decision is carried out. Verses 29–38 then narrate Ahab's death at Ramoth Gilead, which demonstrates the realization of YHWH's intentions to kill Ahab.

Ahab's death at Ramoth Gilead presents two historical issues. The first is identification of the site. Ramoth Gilead, located in the territory of Gad, is set aside by Moses as a place of refuge for those who commit unintentional homicide (Deut 4:43; Josh 20:8; 21:38), and it later serves as Solomon's capital in Gilead and the Bashan (1 Kgs 4:13). Most interpreters identify the site with Tell Er-Rumeith located in the north Transjordan by the modern town of Ramtha. Others identify it with Tell el-Husn, 13.5 miles north of Gerasa, but the site has not been adequately excavated.[78] Control of Ramoth Gilead secures the Transjordan and the King's Highway that provides access to the Gulf of Aqaba, the Red Sea, the Arabian peninsula, and east Africa.

The second is far more problematic in that interpreters are reluctant to accept the historicity of the account as it currently stands for a number of reasons.[79] First, the inscriptions of Shalmaneser III indicate that he fought a coalition led by the Aramean king Hadadezer at Qarqar in his sixth year (853 B.C.E.; *ANET* 278–79). Included among the coalition was an Israelite force of two thousand chariots and ten thousand foot soldiers led by Ahab of Israel. Most interpreters find it difficult to accept that Ahab would have died in battle fighting the Arameans when Shalmaneser's inscriptions point to a close parity alliance between Ahab and Aram. Second, the notice that Ahab "slept with his fathers" in the concluding regnal formula for the account of his reign in 1 Kgs 22:40 appears only for kings who died peacefully. Third, 2 Kgs 9:14–26 reports that

78. N. L. Lapp, "Tell Er-Rumeith," *NEAEHL* 4:1291–93; M. Kochavi, "El-Husn," *NEAEHL* 2:638–39.

79. C. F. Whitley, "The Deuteronomic Presentation of the House of Omri," *VT* 2 (1952): 137–152; J. M. Miller, "The Elisha Cycle and the Accounts of the Omride Wars," *JBL* 85 (1966): 441–54; Miller, "The Rest of the Acts of Jehoahaz" (1 Kings 20. 22, 1–38)," *ZAW* 80 (1968): 337–342; Pitard, *Ancient Damascus*, 114–44.

Joram ben Ahab was wounded while fighting Hazael of Aram at Ramoth Gilead, but Jehu assassinated him at Jezreel where he had gone to recover from his wounds, which suggests that the account of Joram's wounds may provide the basis for the account of Ahab's death. Fourth, the narrative refers to Ahab primarily as "the King of Israel," much like the narratives concerning Joram ben Ahab. Fifth is the lack of any identification of the Aramean king in the narrative, which leaves open the possibility that he is to be identified with Hazael rather than as Ben Hadad. Sixth is the absence of Elijah in the narrative and the focus on Micaiah ben Imlah. Seventh are the questions concerning the identity of Ben-Hadad (see 1 Kgs 20), who is said to have succeeded Hazael in 2 Kgs 13:24–25. Insofar as this pericope indicates that Jehoash ben Jehoahaz would defeat the Arameans three times (cf. 2 Kgs 13:14–21), many interpreters maintain that the two defeats of Aram in 1 Kgs 20 and the presumed defeat of Aram in 1 Kgs 22 must constitute the defeats called for by the prophet Elisha. Eighth is the literary character of the Ahab narratives, which seems to be a redactional unit constructed from an Elijah collection in 1 Kgs 17–19; 21 and materials that take up other prophets in 1 Kgs 20; 22 to serve as a theologically oriented introduction to the narratives concerning Jehu's revolt.

Many of these questions can be answered (see 1 Kgs 20). A breakdown in the alliance between Aram and Ahab is possible, because of the potential for heavy losses among Ahab's chariot corps and the relentless efforts of Shalmaneser III to attack Aram throughout his reign (858–824 B.C.E.; *ANET* 276–81). Shalmaneser lists Jehu son of Omri as one of his tributaries (*ANET* 281), which indicates that his efforts continued after the fall of Ahab and his sons. Interpreters may only speculate as to what actually took place in relations between Israel and Aram at this time, but the prospect of such protracted warfare may have prompted Ahab and his sons to rethink their alliance with Aram.[80] Jehu's submission to the Assyrians suggests that such a strategy could serve Israel's interests. An alliance between Assyria and Israel would stop Aramean attacks against Israel by forcing Aram to contend with both Israel and Assyria on opposite borders.

Affinities with Joram ben Ahab's wars with Aram, including his wound at Ramoth Gilead, are understandable in the context of a protracted conflict with Aram. Ramoth Gilead is a strategic site situated in the Transjordan at the border of Israel and Aram; control of Ramoth Gilead is key to control of the Transjordan. The Zakkir stela demonstrates that Ben/Bar Hadad ruled Aram in the mid-ninth century (*ANET* 655–66), and Shalmaneser's inscriptions note that Hazael seized the throne of Aram following the death of Hadadezer (*ANET* 280). The change in the identities of the prophets must be attributed to the fact that the literary character of the text is not an Elijah cycle, as generally alleged,

---

80. E.g., White, *Elijah Legends,* 61–62.

but an account of Ahab's reign. An underlying Elijah cycle was employed in the construction of the account of Ahab's reign, but it does not constitute the entire text.

As for the argument that the phrase "and PN slept with his ancestors" precludes a violent death, the phrase is lacking for those kings of northern Israel who were assassinated while on the throne and left no heirs to continue their lines (Nadab, 1 Kgs 15:31–32; Elah, 1 Kgs 16:14; Zimri, 1 Kgs 16:20; Joram, 2 Kgs 9:21–26; Zechariah, 2 Kgs 15:11–12; Shallum, 2 Kgs 15:15–16; Pekahiah, 2 Kgs 15:26; Pekah, 2 Kgs 15:31; and Hoshea, 2 Kgs 17:4). Ahaziah (2 Kgs 1:18) died in an accident and left no son, so that he was succeeded by his brother Jehoram/Joram. Ahab is the only Israelite king who died in battle, but he left a son to continue the line. The operative principle here is not a violent death, but a death that ends the dynastic line. The use of the phrase "and he slept with his fathers" for Ahab does not demonstrate that Ahab died peacefully, nor does it demonstrate that the narrative concerning his death in 1 Kgs 22:1–38 originally referred to his son or to anyone else.

The objections raised thus far against the historicity of 1 Kgs 22:1–38 are not decisive. First Kings 22:1–38 clearly presents a theological agenda, but it remains the only account of Ahab's death. The narrative was composed, at least in part, as a means to present a theological interpretation of the king's death at Ramoth Gilead. It is formulated to point to the irony of Ahab's death—that is, despite all of his efforts to disguise himself, he ultimately dies at the hands of an archer who drew his bow to its full length and shot an arrow without aiming at any particular target. The fact that the arrow hit the king between the clasps that buckled his body armor was clearly a lucky shot, and in the present context becomes evidence of divine guidance in seeing to the fulfillment of the death sentence announced by Elijah in 1 Kgs 21 and by Micaiah in the present narrative.

Yet the narrator is hardly content to leave the issue to pure irony and divine intention. The narrative demonstrates that Ahab's death is indeed the result of a divine decision that will see the king die even if YHWH has to lie (through a lying spirit) to entice him to his death. The conflict between Zedekiah ben Canaaniah and Micaiah ben Imlah serves as the theological and literary highlight of this narrative, in which the two prophets are pitted against each other with conflicting opinions concerning Ahab's success in the battle.[81] Zedekiah, ironically named "the son of Canaan," tells him that YHWH has given the Arameans into his hand. After some coaxing, Micaiah finally tells him that he will die in battle. To prove his point, he recounts his experience of standing in the presence of YHWH's royal court or divine council when YHWH calls for

---

81. See Simon J. De Vries, *Prophet against Prophet* (Grand Rapids: Eerdmans, 1978); James Crenshaw, *Prophetic Conflict* (BZAW 124; Berlin and New York: Walter de Gruyter, 1971).

a spirit to "seduce" Ahab—that is, to lie to him so that he will go to Ramoth Gilead and get himself killed. The narrative takes pains to point to YHWH's control of Ahab's death; just as 1 Kgs 17–19 took pains to point to YHWH's role as the master of creation over against Baal and 1 Kgs 21 took pains to show YHWH's justice in condemning Ahab and Jezebel for murder, 1 Kgs 22:1–38 emphasizes that Ahab's death is the result of YHWH's decision to kill him.

The presentation of Ahab ensures that the reader will understand that Ahab is guilty and deserves the death sentence imposed upon him, yet the narrative has affinities with other elements of the DtrH that raise disturbing questions concerning YHWH's complicity in death. Ahab's role in the murder of Naboth has clear relations to the narrative concerning David's role in the murder of Uriah the Hittite (2 Sam 10–12), namely, both point to the king's involvement in murder, both take place in the context of war with Aram, and both point to the monarch's role in the judicial process. Yet it is striking that Ahab is condemned, and David ultimately suffers only the death of the first infant born to him and Bath Sheba. Apart from 1 Kgs 15:5, David is lauded throughout the DtrH, whereas Ahab is a model of sin. Likewise, Ahab's repentance in the Naboth narrative has affinities with Josiah's repentance and its results when he hears Huldah's oracle concerning YHWH's decision to punish Jerusalem (2 Kgs 22:14–20). Because of their repentance, Ahab and Josiah are spared the demise of their respective kingdoms during their lifetimes, but Ahab is guilty whereas Josiah is innocent, which raises questions concerning YHWH's justice in relation to Josiah and Jerusalem/Judah from his time through the destruction of 587–586 B.C.E.

The present Ahab narrative raises the issue of theodicy in the DtrH. Such a portrayal of Ahab serves the interests of the house of Jehu in the early eighth century, and the portrayal of northern sin would be adapted to serve the interests of the Hezekian, Josian, and exilic editions. Although these later DtrH texts would have used the Ahab narratives as a model, the issue is not so clear cut when it comes to the question of YHWH's righteousness in relation to Judah. YHWH's justice comes into question at both diachronic and synchronic levels. In the former, David goes free, but Manasseh's actions condemn an entire nation and its righteous king Josiah. At the synchronic level, David's actions result in the demise of his house, although it takes some four centuries for the punishment to be realized. But such a portrayal is just as problematic as the diachronic reading of the text—that is, why should the house of David (and Jerusalem and Judah) suffer for the sins of a man who committed his crimes and died some four hundred years earlier?

[1] Verse 1 establishes a link with 1 Kgs 20 so that the battle for Ramoth Gilead constitutes the third of three battles between Aram and Syria. From a narrative standpoint, it indicates that the murder of Naboth in 1 Kgs 21 took place during a period of peace. Insofar as 1 Kgs 20 ended with a treaty between

Ahab and Ben-Hadad, Naboth's murder serves as a catalyst for the renewed outbreak of war so that the divinely decreed punishment of Ahab could commence.

[2–28] These verses tie the narrative into the temporal context established by v. 1 and introduce King Jehoshaphat of Judah in v. 2. (Jehoshaphat's own regnal account appears in 2 Kgs 22:41–51.) Because one always "goes up" to Jerusalem during the course of festival pilgrimage to the temple, Jehoshaphat "goes down" upon leaving the city. Jehoshaphat is a secondary figure as a vassal to Ahab (1 Kgs 22:45),[82] and he later appears in a similar role in relation to Jehoram ben Ahab during his war with Moab (2 Kgs 3). Nevertheless, Jehoshaphat plays a key role in the present narrative in that he serves as the catalyst for the introduction of Micaiah ben Imlah, who announces YHWH's decision to deceive Ahab so that he will die. Jehoshaphat plays such a role because he is a righteous figure (1 Kgs 22:43), who serves as a foil to the wicked Ahab.

Such a role is evident in vv. 3–4 when Ahab consults with his servants concerning plans to fight the Arameans at Ramoth Gilead. The king of Israel announces that the Arameans claim Ramoth Gilead as their own, clearly an incursion into Israelite territory since the city is located in the territory of Gad (Josh 20:8; 21:38). Aram's action highlights Ahab's foolishness in concluding a treaty with Ben-Hadad of Aram following his defeat of the Arameans at Aphek (1 Kgs 20:23–43). Ahab's condemnation by the anonymous prophet in 1 Kgs 20:35–43 is now coming to realization.

In an obvious dig against Ahab, vv. 5–8 portray Jehoshaphat as the one who calls for oracular inquiry concerning the word of YHWH. Such an inquiry was a typical practice prior to a battle (cf. 1 Sam 23:1–2; 2 Sam 2:1; see also Num 22–24). Ahab's gathering of four hundred prophets calls to mind the four hundred prophets of Baal who appeared in 1 Kgs 18. Although these prophets were killed at Carmel, their presence here suggests that they were somehow replaced or that they represent an established body in the court of King Ahab. The identification of Zedekiah ben Canaanah as the son of Canaan suggests Canaanite or Phoenician associations.

Ahab sends a "eunuch" for Micaiah in vv. 9–12. Although the Aramaic word *sārîs* means "eunuch," its reference to married men (e.g., Gen 39:1) indicates that it refers simply to an officer of the king. The kings are dressed in their royal attire, because the consultation of the prophets prior to the war is an affair of state. Threshing floors are commonly associated with temples in the ancient world because of the need to process grain brought to the temple as offerings. A temple setting lends legitimacy to the event. Zedekiah ben Canaanah's symbolic act is a typical means by which ancient prophets dramatized and lent credence to their messages.[83]

---

82. Jehoshaphat married his son, Joram, to Athaliah bat Ahab (2 Kgs 8:18, 26), a typical means to establish an alliance between two kings.

83. W. D. Stacey, *Prophetic Drama in the Old Testament* (London: Epworth, 1990), esp. 87–90.

Verses 13–28 demonstrate that YHWH is responsible for Ahab's death. The account of the messenger's words to Micaiah ben Imlah in vv. 13–14 is a classic example of the application of pressure by a governmental representative; the messenger tells Micaiah that all the prophets have spoken unanimously in favor of the king and that Micaiah had better do the same. Micaiah's response begins with the oath formula *ḥāy yhwh,* "as YHWH lives," to emphasize that he is an authentic prophet who speaks only what YHWH tells him to speak (cf. Num 23:12, 26; 24:13).

Micaiah depicts a vision of judgment in which Israel is metaphorically portrayed as sheep scattered on a mountain without a shepherd (cf. Ezek 34:1–34; Zech 13:7). The call-to-attention formula in v. 19 (cf. Jer 7:2; Hos 4:1; Amos 3:1; 4:1; 5:1) directs his audience's attention to the following statements. The vision builds upon the earlier depiction of Ahab and Jehoshaphat, dressed in royal regalia and seated on their thrones (v. 10), by portraying YHWH sitting upon the divine throne before the host of heaven (cf. Isa 6; Ps 82; Jer 23:18–22; cf. Job 15:8). The analogy with the enthroned Ahab and Jehoshaphat demonstrates that both kings actually stand under the authority of YHWH. YHWH opens the discussion by asking who will "deceive" Ahab so that he will die at Ramoth Gilead. The verb *ptḥ,* "to deceive," refers to a woman seduced by a man (Exod 22:15; Hos 2:16) or a man seduced by a woman (Judg 14:15; 16:5), although it also describes a prophet deceived by YHWH (Jer 20:7; Ezek 14:9). YHWH's own involvement in deception adds to the ironic character of the narrative in which Ahab will be killed by a lucky arrow shot despite his efforts at disguise. Biblical literature presumes that false prophecy comes from a source other than YHWH (Deut 18:9–22; Jer 23:9–22; 27–28), but works such as Job suggest that YHWH has a treacherous side (cf. 1 Sam 16:14–23). Micaiah's visionary assertion that YHWH has sent a lying spirit to Ahab challenges the prevailing view that YHWH's words are true.

Zedekiah sees himself as an authentic prophet of YHWH. Although readers are informed that he is a false prophet, a canonized Bible shapes our perceptions. Ancient Israelites had to hear the competing claims of prophets, but with only the criterion that a true word of YHWH is the one that ultimately comes true. They were left to decide only on the merits of the cases presented by the prophets in question (see esp. Jer 27–28). Micaiah's response in v. 25 is scathingly crude; what Zedekiah takes to be the spirit (lit., "wind") of YHWH is actually something quite different.

The concluding segment in vv. 26–28 reinforces the portrayal of Micaiah as a true prophet. The designation of Joash as the son of the king has prompted many claims that the narrative relates an event that took place during the reign of the Jehu monarch Jehoahaz ben Jehu, the father of Joash/Jehoash. Most interpreters recognize the title *ben-hammelek,* "son of the king," as an official designation of an officer of the king (cf. Zeph 1:8; Judg 9; 2 Kgs 10:1–11).[84] The reference to Micaiah's statement, "hear, O peoples, all of them," is a gloss from Mic 1:2aa, which identifies Micaiah ben Imlah with Micah of Moresheth.

[29–38] This passage prepares for the ironic realization of Ahab's death by emphasizing that he disguised himself in order to avoid being targeted by the Arameans. Jehoshaphat serves as a decoy. Verses 31–33, set off by the introductory conjunctive *waw* joined to the noun phrase *melek ʾărām*, "and the King of Aram," relate the Aramean king's orders that his chariot commanders should concentrate only on killing the king of Israel. The emphasis on the thirty-two chariot commanders suggests narrative continuity with the previous account of war with Aram (1 Kgs 20), insofar as they are identified with the governors appointed by Ben-Hadad to replace the thirty-two kings who accompanied him in battle against Israel at Samaria (see 1 Kgs 20:1, 24).

Verses 34–38 begin with a *waw*-conjunctive joined to a noun, *ʾîš*, "and a man." The random shot of a bowman strikes the disguised Ahab at just the right point between the clasps that buckle his armor onto his body. Despite his wound, Ahab conducts himself heroically. After he commands his driver to turn aside, the wounded king is stood up in his chariot as the battle rages in order to avoid panicking his soldiers. Ahab's wound is left untreated so that he bleeds to death in his chariot by sundown when the cry goes out through the camp that everyone should return to his city and land. The cry suggests that the Israelites won the battle. The irony continues after the dead king is brought to Samaria for burial; his chariot is washed at the pool of Samaria where the dogs lap the water and the prostitutes bathe, thereby fulfilling Elijah's prophecy in 1 Kgs 21:19.

1 Kings 22:39–40 Concluding Regnal Account for Ahab

22:39 And the rest of the affairs of Ahab and all that he did, and the house of ivory that he built, and all the cities that he built, are they not written in the book of the Chronicles of the Kings of Israel? 40 And Ahab slept with his fathers, and Ahaziah his son ruled in his place.

Excavations at Samaria uncovered numerous carved ivory figures in the courtyard of a large building that presumably forms part of the royal complex along the northern wall of the Iron Age city (cf. Amos 3:15; 6:4). A jar incised with the name of Pharaoh Osorkon II (914–874 B.C.E.), found with the ivories, establishes their date in the ninth century.[85] The Bible only mentions Jericho as

84. See Gershon Brin, "The Title בן המלך and Its Parallels," *AION* 29 (1969): 433–65; contra Fox, *In the Service*, 43–53.
85. See N. Avigad, "Samaria [City]," *NEAEHL* 4:1304–6; Eleanor Ferris Beach, "The Samaria Ivories, Marzeah, and Biblical Text," *BA* 56 (1993): 94–104.

a city built during the reign of Ahab (1 Kgs 16:34), but archaeologists attribute extensive building throughout northern Israel (e.g., Samaria, Dan, Hazor, Megiddo, and Tirzah) to the ninth-century reign of the Omrides.[86] The notice that Ahab slept with his ancestors does not indicate that he died peacefully, but that he was succeeded by his son, Ahaziah, following his death.

XII. Regnal Account of Jehoshaphat ben Asa of Judah
1 Kings 22:41–51

22:41 Jehoshaphat ben Asa ruled over Judah in the fourth year of Ahab, King of Israel. 42 Jehoshaphat was thirty-five years old when he ruled, and he ruled in Jerusalem for twenty-five years. The name of his mother was Azubah bat Shilhi. 43 He walked in the way of Asa, his father—he did not turn from it—to do what is right in the eyes of YHWH. 44 Except the high places did not disappear.[a] The people continued sacrificing and burning incense at the high places.

45 And Jehoshaphat made peace with the King of Israel.

46 The rest of the affairs of Jehoshaphat and his power that he exercised, and that which he fought; are they not written in the book of the Chronicles of the Kings of Judah? 47 [b]And the rest of the male cult prostitutes who were left in the days of Asa, his father, he destroyed from the land. 48 There was no king in Edom, (only) a prefect of the king. 49 Jehoshaphat made[c] ships of Tarshish to go to Ophir for gold, but they did not go because [d]the ships of Tarshish were broken up[d] in Ezion Geber. 50 Then Ahaziah ben Ahab said to Jehoshaphat, "Let my servants go with your servants in the ships," but Jehoshaphat was not willing.[b] 51 And Jehoshaphat slept with his fathers, and he was buried with his fathers in the city of David, his father, and Jehoram his son ruled in his place.

a. MT, *lōʾ-sārû*, lit., "did not turn aside"; cf. LXX and Peshitta, "he did not remove."
b–b. LXX lacks vv. 47–50.
c. Read with Qere, *ʿāśâ*, "(he) made," instead of Ketiv, *ʿāśār*, "ten."
d–d. MT, *kî nišběrû ʾănîyôt*, "because the ships were broken," reading Qere, *nišběrû*, "they were broken," instead of Ketiv, *nišběrâ*, "it was broken."

Although the account of Jehoshaphat's actions appears only in v. 45, the regnal résumé in vv. 47–50 contains important information. It is the work of the

86. Mazar, *Archaeology,* 406–15.

Hezekian DtrH, which placed it in the midst of the earlier eighth-century account of the rise of the Jehu dynasty.

[41–44] The chronology is problematic. The fourth year of Ahab's reign would be 865 B.C.E. A twenty-five-year reign would place Jehoshaphat's death in 840 B.C.E., but LXX 3 Rgns 16:28 places his reign in the eleventh year of Omri. The LXX addresses a chronological discrepancy in the ascension of Jehoram ben Ahab to the throne, which is dated in 2 Kgs 1:17 to the second year of Jehoram ben Jehoshaphat and in 2 Kgs 3:1 to the eighteenth year of Jehoshaphat ben Asa.[1] Jehoshaphat's mother, Azubah bat Shilhi, is otherwise unknown.

[45] The account of Jehoshaphat's reign is limited to the notice that he "made peace" with the king of Israel. He is a vassal to Ahab (cf. 1 Kgs 22:1–38), and joins Jehoram ben Ahab in war against Edom (2 Kgs 3). Verses 47–50 suggest that Jehoshaphat exercised great independence in relation to the northern monarchy due to his role in controlling the Transjordanian trade routes and the increasingly weak position of the house of Omri vis-à-vis Aram.

[46–51] Jehoshaphat's power and wars refer in part to his role in the battles against Aram at Ramoth Gilead (1 Kgs 22:1–38) and against Moab in 2 Kgs 3. Verse 48 indicates that Edom was subject to Jehoshaphat, who would have established a prefect (*nissāb*) in Edom like David and Solomon (see 2 Sam 8:13–14; cf. 1 Kgs 11:14–22). Second Kings 3:8–9 suggests that Edom was a vassal of Jehoshaphat since the king of Edom accompanies Jehoshaphat and Jehoram to war against Moab. Second Kings 8:20–22 indicate that Edom revolted against Judah during the reign of Jehoram ben Jehoshaphat. Jehoshaphat's attempt to establish a fleet of ships to sail to Ophir for gold would revive Solomon's Red Sea trade (1 Kgs 9:26–28). Jehoshaphat's refusal of Ahaziah's assistance is a sign of his growing independence from a weakened house of Omri.

XIII. Regnal Account of Ahaziah ben Ahab of Israel
1 Kings 22:52–2 Kings 2:25

1 Kgs 22:52 Ahaziah ben Ahab ruled over Israel in Samaria in the seventeenth year of Jehoshaphat, King of Judah, and he ruled over Israel two years. **53** He did evil in the eyes of YHWH and walked in the path of his

---

1. Contra James Donald Shenkel, *Chronology and Rescensional Development in the Greek Text of Kings* (HSM 1; Cambridge: Harvard University Press, 1968), 43–60.

father and in the path of his mother and in the path of Jeroboam ben Nebat, who caused Israel to sin. 54 He served Baal and worshiped him, and he provoked YHWH, the G-d of Israel, just as his father did.

2 Kgs 1:1 And Moab rebelled against Israel after the death of Ahab.

2 Ahaziah fell through the lattice in his upper room, which was in Samaria, and he was hurt. He sent messengers and said to them, "Go, inquire of Baal Zebub, god of Ekron, whether I will survive this injury."

3 And an angel of YHWH spoke to Elijah the Tishbite, "Arise, go up to meet the messengers of the King of Samaria, and say to them, 'Is there no G-d in Israel that you go to inquire of Baal Zebub, god of Ekron? 4 ªTherefore,ª thus says YHWH, "(From) the bed where you have gone up, you will not come down, for you will surely die."'" And Elijah left.

5 The messengers returned to him, and he said to them, "Why have you returned?" 6 And they said to him, "A man came up to meet us and said to us, 'Go, return to the king who sent you and say to him, "Thus says YHWH, 'Is there no G-d in Israel that you send to inquire of Baal Zebub, god of Ekron? Therefore,ᵇ from the bed where you have gone up, you will not come down, for you will surely die.'"'" 7 And he said to them, "What is the manner of the man who went up to meet you and spoke to you these things?" 8 And they said to him, "A man with hair and a leather belt girded upon his loins." And he said, "He is Elijah the Tishbite."

9 He sent to him a commander of fifty and his fifty men, and he went up to him, and behold, he was sitting on top of the mountain, and he spoke to him, "Man of G-d, the king has spoken, 'Come down!'" 10 Elijah answered and said to the commander of fifty, "And if I am a man of G-d, fire from the heavens will come down, and it will consume you and your fifty men." And fire from the heavens came down and consumed him and his fifty men. 11 He again sent to him another captain of fifty and his fifty men, and he answered and spoke to him, "Man of G-d, Thus says the King, 'Come down at once!'" 12 And Elijah answered and said to them, "If I am a man of G-d, fire from the heavens will come down, and it will consume you and your fifty men," and the fire of G-d came down from the heavens, and it consumed him and his fifty men. 13 And he again sent a third commander of fifty and his fifty men, and the third commander of fifty went up, came, kneeled down on his knees before Elijah, implored him, and spoke to him, "Man of G-d, please consider my life and the life of these your fifty servants as precious in your eyes. 14 Behold, fire from heaven came down and consumed the two previous commanders of fifty and their fifty men, but now consider my life as precious in your eyes." 15 And the angel of YHWH spoke to Elijah, "Go down with him. Do not

fear him." And he arose, and he went down with him to the king. 16 And he spoke to him, "Thus says YHWH, 'Because you sent messenger to inquire of Baal Zebub, god of Ekron—is there no G-d in Israel to inquire of his word?—therefore,ᶜ from the bed where you have gone up, you will not come down, for you will surely die.'" 17 And he died according to the word which Elijah the Tishbite spoke, and Jehoram ruled in his place in the second year of Jehoram ben Jehoshaphat, King of Judah, because he had no son.

18 And the rest of the affairs of Ahaziah (and) what he did, are they not written in the book of the Chronicles of the Kings of Israel?ᵈ

2:1 When YHWH took Elijah up to heaven in the tempest, Elijah and Elisha left Gilgal. 2 And Elijah said to Elisha, "Stay here, please, because YHWH has sent me to Beth El." And Elisha said to him, "As YHWH lives and as you live, I will not abandon you." They went down to Beth El 3 and the sons of the prophets who were in Beth El came out to Elisha and said to him, "Do you know that today YHWH takes your master from you?" And he said, "Indeed I know. Be silent!" 4 ᵉAnd Elijah said to him, "Elisha,ᵉ stay here, please, because YHWH has sent me to Jericho." And he said, "As YHWH lives and as you live, I will not abandon you." They came to Jericho 5 and the sons of the prophets who were in Jericho drew near to Elisha and said to him, "Do you know that today YHWH takes your master from you?" And he said, "Indeed I know. Be silent!" 6 And Elijah said to him, "Stay here, please, because YHWH has sent me to the Jordan." And he said, "As YHWH lives and as you live, I will not abandon you." The two of them went. 7 And fifty men from the sons of the prophets went and stood before (them) from afar, and the two of them stood by the Jordan. 8 And Elijah took his mantle, rolled it up, and struck the waters, and they divided in two, and the two of them crossed on dry land.ᶠ 9 When they had crossed, Elijah said to Elisha, "Ask what shall I do for you before I am taken from you." And Elisha said, "Let there be a double portion of your spirit for me." 10 And he said, "You have made a difficult request. If you see me taken from you, it shall be so for you, but if not, it shall not be." 11 While they were walking and talking, behold, a chariot of fire and horses of fire (appeared), and they separated between the two of them, and Elijah went up in the tempest to heaven. 12 Elisha was looking and crying out, "My father! My father! The chariot of Israel and its horsemen!" and he did not see him again, and he seized his garments and tore them into two pieces. 13 He picked up the mantle of Elijah which had fallen from him, and he again stood on the bank of the Jordan. 14 He took the mantle of Elijah which had fallen from him, struck the waters, and said, ᵍ"Where is YHWH, the G-d of Elijah? Indeed, where is he?"ᵍ And he struck the waters, and they divided in two, and Elisha crossed. 15 The sons of the prophets who were before him in Jericho saw him and said, "The spirit of Elijah rests upon Elisha," and they came to meet him and bowed down to him on the ground. 16 And they said to him, "Behold, now, here are your servants, fifty capable men. Let them go now and search for your master lest the wind of YHWH carried him off and dropped him on one of the mountains or on one of the valleys." And he said to them, "Do not send (them)." 17 But they persisted with him until the point of embarrassment, and he said, "Send (them)." So they sent fifty men, and they searched thirty days, but they did not find him. 18 They returned to him, and he was staying in Jericho and said to them, "Did I not tell you, 'Do not go'?"

19 And the men of the city said to Elisha, "Behold, now, the city is a good settlement, just as my lord sees, but the water is bad and the land causes stillbirth." 20 And he said, "Bring me a new jar, and put salt there," and they brought (them) to him. 21 He went out to the source of the waters, cast salt there, and said, "Thus says YHWH, 'I have healed these waters. There shall be no more death and stillbirth from them.'" 22 And the waters were healed until this day according to the word of Elisha which he spoke.

23 He went up from there to Beth El, and he was going up on the road, and small boys came out from the city, mocked him, and said to him, "Go up baldy! Go up baldy!" 24 And he turned around, saw them, and cursed them in the name of YHWH. Two female bears came out from the woods and mangled forty-two boys from among them.

25 He went from there to Mount Carmel, and from there he returned to Samaria.

a–a. MT, *wĕlākēn,* "and therefore"; cf. LXX, *kai ouch houtōs,* "and it is not so," which presupposes Hebrew, *wĕlōʾ kēn.*

b. See n. a.

c. See n. a.

d. LXX adds 4 Rgns 1:18a–d to provide an introduction for the reign of Jehoram ben Ahab immediately after the concluding regnal résumé for Ahaziah and to resolve chronological inconsistencies between 1 Kgs 22:51–53; 2 Kgs 3:1–3; and 2 Kgs 8:16–19 (see Hrozný 45–46; Shenkel 68–86):

18a Joram the son of Ahab ruled over Israel in Samaria twelve years in the eighteenth year of Jehoshaphat, King of Judah. 18b He did evil before the L-rd, only not like his brothers nor like his mother. 18c He removed the pillars of Baal which his father made, and he broke them in pieces. Only he was joined to the sins of the house of Jeroboam, who caused Israel to sin; he did not depart from them. 18d He provoked the anger of the L-rd against the house of Ahab.

e–e. Cf. LXX; Peshitta; Vulgate, "And Elijah said to Elisha," which presupposes the omission of Hebrew, *lô*, "to him," immediately following the verb *wayyōᵓmer,* "and he said."

f. MT, *behārābâ*, "on dry land," although Hebrew, *hārābâ*, can also refer to "desert"; cf. LXX, *en erēmōi*, "in/on the desert."

g–g. MT, "where (ᵓ*ayyēh*) is YHWH, the G-d of Elijah, even he (ᵓ*ap-hûᵓ*)?" The versions have struggled with interpreting the meaning and interrelationship of ᵓ*ayyēh* and ᵓ*ap-hûᵓ*. Targum Jonathan, "Accept my petition, O L-rd, G-d of Elijah, and he also (struck the waters)," reinterprets the initial ᵓ*ayyēh* as "accept my petition," and reads ᵓ*ap-hûᵓ*, "also he," as the beginning of the following statement; Peshitta, "O L-rd, the G-d of Elijah, and he also (struck the waters)," simply eliminates ᵓ*ayyēh* and likewise reads ᵓ*ap-hûᵓ* as the beginning of the following statement; cf. LXX, "Where is the L-rd G-d of Elijah?" which elides the two phrases by eliminating ᵓ*ayyēh* and reading ᵓ*ap-huᵓ* as Hebrew, ᵓ*êpōh*, "where?" which it transliterates into Greek as *appō*.

First Kings 22:52–2 Kings 2:25 is demarcated by the introductory regnal résumé in 1 Kgs 22:52–54. The account of Ahaziah's reign proper in vv. 1–17 comprises two basic subunits. The first is the notice in v. 1 of Moab's rebellion against Israel, which looks forward to the account of Jehoram's attempt to subdue Moab in 2 Kgs 3. The second is vv. 2–17, which relates Ahaziah's inquiry of Elijah concerning his recovery. The concluding regnal résumé in 2 Kgs 1:18 introduces an appended account concerning Elijah's transfer of power to Elisha in 2 Kgs 2:1–25.[1]

Jehoshaphat refused Ahaziah's offer to assist Judah in resuming seaborne trade in the Red Sea (1 Kgs 22:50), and Moab revolted from northern Israelite rule (2 Kgs 1:2). Ahaziah was a relatively weak king because of his accident and because Israel was increasingly pressured by Aram following the death of Ahab. Although the Moabite Stone refers only to Omri and his son (*ANET* 320–21), its portrayal of Mesha's revolt against Israel in the mid-ninth century provides the historical background for the Moabite revolt and the general decline of Omride power.

The narrative hints concerning the diminution of Israel's power during the brief reign of Ahaziah provide the background for a more fundamental narrative purpose—that is, to demonstrate YHWH's power over against other gods, to demonstrate YHWH's power to carry out judgment against the house of Ahab (Omri), and to demonstrate YHWH's power manifested through the prophets Elijah and Elisha. This agenda is clear in 2 Kgs 1:2–17 in which Ahaziah is injured by accident, which suggests divine involvement, and by the condemnation of Ahaziah for attempting to inquire of the Philistine god, Baal Zebub, concerning whether or not he would recover. The repeated rhetorical question, "Is there no G-d in Israel that you go to inquire of Baal Zebub, god

---

1. Cf. J. R. Lundbom, "Elijah's Chariot Ride," *JJS* 24 (1973): 39–50.

of Ekron?" (vv. 3, 6; cf. v. 16), asserts YHWH's power. The repeated attempts of the Israelite military detachments sent to summon Elijah testify to YHWH's and the prophet's power insofar as the first two are destroyed for their arrogant treatment of the prophet, and the third succeeds only when the commander implores Elijah to spare his life and those of his men.[2] A similar agenda underlies the narrative concerning Elijah's ascent to heaven.

Such a portrayal of YHWH's and the prophet's power clearly serves the interests of the eighth-century Jehu History. It also serves the interests of the Hezekian, Josian, and exilic DtrH editions insofar as the portrayal of Omride sin and punishment lends itself to the overall portrayal of judgment against the northern kingdom of Israel.

The present narrative is a composite text. The appended narrative in 2 Kgs 2:1–25 concerning Elijah's ascent to heaven and the transfer of power to Elisha has little direct relationship to the account of Ahaziah's reign in 1 Kgs 22:52–2 Kgs 1:18 or to its underlying narrative concerning Ahaziah's illness and death in 2 Kgs 1:2–17. Indeed, 2 Kgs 2:1–25 functions as a literary bridge between 1 Kgs 17–2 Kgs 1, in which Elijah plays the dominant role, and 2 Kgs 3–13, in which Elisha serves as the dominant prophetic figure.[3] Lundbom notes an underlying concentric structure that depicts a circuitous journey that begins with Elijah in Samaria (1:2), moves to an unidentified mountain (1:9), Beth El (2:2–3), Jericho (2:4–5), the Jordan River (2:6–8), and the Transjordan, where Elijah is carried away (2:9–12).[4] The narrative then traces Elisha's movements from the Transjordan to the Jordan River (2:13–14), Jericho (2:15–22), Beth El (2:23–24), Mount Carmel (2:25), and finally to Samaria once again (2:25). Such a pattern, insofar as it is established primarily through the locations mentioned in 2 Kgs 2:1–25, suggests that the latter narrative was combined with 2 Kgs 1:1–17 to emphasize the interrelationship between Elijah and Elisha and to demonstrate that Elisha is indeed Elijah's divinely sanctioned replacement. The Elijah traditions establish the guilt of the house of Omri and the cause for punishment, whereas the Elisha traditions present the process by which that judgment is carried out. The notice of Moab's revolt in 2 Kgs 1:2 plays no role in relation to Ahaziah's injury and death, but points forward to 2 Kgs 3, in which Jehoram and Jehoshaphat attempt to suppress the Moabite revolt.

[1 Kgs 22:52–54] The introductory regnal résumé refers to Ahaziah's mother, Jezebel, who promoted the worship of foreign gods in Israel (1 Kgs 18).

---

2. See Herbert Chanan Brichto, *Toward a Grammar of Biblical Poetics: Tales of the Prophets* (New York and Oxford: Oxford University Press, 1992), 152–58, for a discussion of the role of repetition in this narrative.

3. Cf., e.g., Hermann-Josef Stipp, *Elischa—Propheten—G-ttesmänner* (ATSAT 24; St. Ottilien: EOS, 1987), 364, 442–80.

4. Lundbom, "Elijah's Chariot Ride," 41.

Indeed, v. 54 makes special mention of his worship of Baal as part of the means by which he provoked YHWH's anger.

[2 Kgs 1:1] The notice concerning Moab's revolt may be read historically in relation to the Moabite Stone, which relates Moab's successful revolt against the house of Omri in the mid-ninth century B.C.E. (*ANET* 320–21). From a literary standpoint, it points to the decline of the house of Omri and Jehoram's unsuccessful attempt to suppress the Moabite revolt (2 Kgs 3).

[2–17] Elijah's condemnation of Ahaziah following his accident emphasizes YHWH's power to punish Ahaziah for his apostasy. Although a number of interpreters argue that it is a composite narrative,[5] several factors hold this composite text together, including the messengers sent to both Baal Zebub and Elijah, the unfolding revelation of Elijah's identity, the deference shown to Elijah by the messengers, and terminology related to going up and down.[6]

The narrative begins in v. 2 with Ahaziah's fall through the lattice. The lattice is a common ornamental network of crossed wood slats employed for protection from the sun and access to free-flowing air. The lattice is in the ʿălîyâ, "upper chamber," of the king's palace in Samaria. The "upper chamber" is a typical feature of the *bit hillani,* or colonnaded house structure, where it forms a smaller, second story on top of the main structure (cf. 1 Kgs 6).[7] The emphasis on YHWH's power suggests that, like the lucky arrow that killed Ahab (1 Kgs 22:34), Ahaziah's fall was not entirely accidental. Rather than consult YHWH, Ahaziah sent messengers to Ekron to consult a Philistine god called Baal Zebub. Ekron, the northernmost of the five Philistine cities (see 1 Sam 5:10; 17:52), is identified with Tel Miqne, about twenty-two miles west of Jerusalem along the border between Philistia and Judah in the Shephelah.[8] Many interpreters consider the name Baal Zebub, "Lord of the Fly," to be a deliberate alteration of the name *baʿal zĕbûl,* "Lord of Exaltation,"

5. See e.g., G. H. Jones, *1 and 2 Kings* (2 vols.; The New Century Bible Commentary; Grand Rapids: William B. Eerdmans; London: Marshall, Morgan, and Scott, 1984), 376; Georg Fohrer, *Elia* (2d ed.; AThANT 53; Zurich: Zwingli, 1968), 43; Walter Dietrich, *Prophetie und Geschichte* (FRLANT 108; Göttingen: Vandenhoeck & Ruprecht, 1972), 125; Martin Beck, *Elia und die Monolatrie* (BZAW 281; Berlin and New York: Walter de Gruyter, 1999), 139–49; Georg Hentschel, *Die Elija-erzählungen* (Erfurter Theologische Studien 33; Leipzig: St. Benno, 1977), 9–14, 105–7, 145–48, 202–8; Susanne Otto, *Jehu, Elia und Elisa* (BWANT 152; Stuttgart: W. Kohlhammer, 2001), 144–149; and Odil Hannes Steck, "Die Erzählung von JHWH's Einschreiten gegen die Orakelbefragung Ahasjas (2 Kön 1,2-8, 17)," *EvT* 27 (1967): 546–56; cf. Alexander Rofé, *The Prophetical Stories* (Jerusalem: Magnes, 1988), 33–40, who notes late linguistic features that point to the narrative's character as a late insertion.

6. Christopher T. Begg, "Unifying Factors in 1 Kings 1.2–17a," *JSOT* 32 (1985): 75–86.

7. See the discussion of the "upper chamber" and *bit hillani* in Baruch Halpern, *The First Historians: The Hebrew Bible and History* (San Francisco: Harper & Row, 1988), 45–54.

8. T. Dothan and S. Gitin, "Miqne, Tel [Ekron]," *NEAEHL* 3:1051–9.

but many references to deities are associated with flies or plagues in classical literature.[9]

Elijah appears in vv. 3–4 in a manner reminiscent of his earlier appearances. An angel instructs him to meet Ahaziah's messengers (cf. 1 Kgs 17:3, 9; 18:1; 19:15; 21:17–18). The meeting provides the first occasion for Elijah to ask the rhetorical question, "Is there no G-d in Israel that you go to inquire of Baal Zebub, god of Ekron?" The rhetorical question asserts that there is a G-d in Israel and that Ahaziah's actions constitute rejection of the G-d of Israel. The prophet employs the messenger formula to announce that Ahaziah will never go down from the bed to which he has gone up, but he will die there. Ironically, this stands in contrast to the experience of Elijah in 2 Kgs 2, who went up to heaven in a fiery chariot and neither came down nor died.

The messengers' report of the incident to Ahaziah in vv. 5–8 repeats the rhetorical question as to whether there is a G-d in Israel. The reference to hair refers to Elijah's hairy mantle (see 1 Kgs 19:19; 2 Kgs 2:8, 13–15; cf. Zech 13:4). This statement builds dramatic effect by facilitating the revelation of Elijah to the king, and it prepares the reader to expect something noteworthy.

Ahaziah's attempts to summon Elijah in vv. 9–17 culminate in his death. This narrative emphasizes both YHWH's and the prophet's power within the larger context of Ahaziah's attempts to inquire of the Philistine god, Baal Zebub. It achieves this end by relating Ahaziah's three attempts to summon Elijah. The identification of Elijah as a "man of G-d" (ʾîš hᵉlqym) appears especially in relation to peripheral prophets (i.e., those who stand outside of normal social power structures), such as Elijah and Elisha, when they exercise special sacral power (e.g., 1 Kgs 17:17–24; 2 Kgs 4:42–44).[10] In each case, Ahaziah sends a military contingent that consists of a śar hămiššîm, "a commander of fifty," and his fifty men. Israelite military and administrative-judicial organization called for commanders of thousands, hundreds, fifties, and tens (see Exod 18:21).[11] The king's less-than-friendly attitude is conveyed by the commander's abrupt transmission of Ahaziah's one-word order, rēdâ, "come down!" The affront to a power figure such as Elijah (and YHWH) reveals his power, expressed by Elijah through the ironic rhetorical question (with its wordplay on the verb yrd, "to come down"), "If I am a man of G-d, then fire from heaven 'will come down' (tēred) and it will consume you and your fifty."

A second and a third commander of fifty return to heighten the demonstration of Elijah's power. In the second case, the commander proceeds as before,

9. E.g., W. Herrmann, "Baal Zebub," DDD² 154–56; cf. James A. Montgomery and Henry Snyder Gehman, The Books of Kings (International Critical Commentary; Edinburgh: T & T Clark, 1951), 349.

10. David L. Petersen, The Roles of Israel's Prophets (JSOTSup 17; Sheffield: JSOT Press, 1981), 40–50.

11. Roland de Vaux, Ancient Israel (New York and Toronto: McGraw-Hill, 1965), 1:214–18.

except that his order is even more demanding, "hurry, come down" or "come down at once" (*měhērâ rēdâ*). The results are identical. The third commander recognizes the danger of his situation and chooses a different course by falling on his knees and imploring Elijah to spare his life and those of his men.

Elijah's appearance before the king provides the occasion to deliver a prophetic oracle of judgment in v. 16. Following the speech formula, it begins with the prophetic messenger formula "thus says YHWH," followed by the judgment oracle itself. The grounds for judgment restate the basic formula employed in vv. 3 and 6, "because you sent messengers to inquire of Baal Zebub, the god of Ekron—is there no G-d in Israel to seek his word?" and the announcement of punishment likewise repeats the formula, "therefore from the bed where you have gone up, you will not come down, but you will surely die." The announcement emphasizes the verb *yrd*, "to go down," and employs the typical death penalty formula, *môt tāmût*.[12] Ahaziah's death in v. 17 is the direct result of his injury and the prophet's announcement of judgment in v. 16. The second part of the verse in v. 17aß–b is separated from the first part by a masoretic *pětûḥâ*, "open section," but the reason is not clear. The phrase "because he did not have a son" requires v. 17a as an antecedent.

[1 Kgs 1:18–2 Kgs 2:25] The concluding regnal résumé introduces an appended narrative concerning Elijah's ascent to heaven. This narrative is fundamentally concerned with the transfer of Elijah's prophetic powers and role to his successor Elisha. It establishes a relationship between the two prophets that builds upon the initial portrayal of Elijah's selection of Elisha as his apprentice in 1 Kgs 19, and it points to Elisha's legitimacy as a prophet of YHWH at the time when the Omride dynasty will be overthrown and replaced by the Jehide dynasty. The narrative signals the transition in prophetic leadership with its introductory notice concerning the time that YHWH took Elijah up to heaven in a whirlwind. The term *sě'ārâ*, "whirlwind, storm wind," appears frequently in depictions of YHWH's theophanies (e.g., Ezek 1:4; 13:11, 13; Zech 9:14; Job 38:1; 40:6; cf. Isa 29:6; 40:24; 41:16; Jer 23:19; 30:23) to portray YHWH's amorphous yet powerful presence. The imagery of the storm wind likely relates to YHWH's role in creation as the source of rain, wind, storm, and thus fertility, much as the Phoenician, Syrian, and Mesopotamian storm gods, such as Baal or Hadad, fill similar roles in their respective cultural contexts. The weather deities are frequently portrayed as riding chariots through the heavens. Baal is designated *rkb 'rpt*, "the rider of the clouds,"[13] and Hadad and other weather gods are likewise portrayed either

---

12. See, e.g., Exod 21:12–17; Lev 24:17; H.-J. Boecker, *Law and the Administration of Justice in the Old Testament and the Ancient East* (Minneapolis: Augsburg, 1980), 194–201.

13. See W. Herrmann, "Rider Upon the Clouds," *DDD*[2] 705–7, although he interprets the phrase as a reference to passing through the steppe/desert.

in chariots (*ANEP* 689) or in relation to winged sun disks that convey them through the heavens (*ANEP* 501, 531, 532, 534–36). Other biblical texts portray YHWH riding through the heavens in a chariot (Ps 68:5, 34; Ps 18:11/ 2 Sam 22:11; Deut 33:26; Isa 19:1; cf. Hab 3:8; Ezek 1; 8–11).

The narrative initially places Elijah and Elisha together at Gilgal. Gilgal is the site of Joshua's initial encampment in the land of Israel after crossing the Jordan River (Josh 2–5). Gilgal is identified with one of two Iron Age sites at Khirbet el-Mafjir, about one and a quarter miles north of Jericho.[14] Because Elijah and Elisha travel "downhill" from Gilgal to Beth El and Jericho (see v. 2), many interpreters maintain that Gilgal refers to another site of the same name, which is identified with modern Jiljulieh, about seven miles north of Beth El. Such a "downward" journey suggests that Gilgal is located in the hill country rather than in the Jordan Valley. Gilgal's association with the Joshua traditions establishes the analogy between the relationship of Elijah and Elisha and that of Moses and Joshua. Joshua is the successor of Moses (Num 27:12–23; Deut 31–34), whose death and burial were not witnessed by human beings, and Joshua is closely associated with Gilgal, Jericho, and the Jordan River.

The threefold, formulaic repetition of Elijah's unsuccessful attempts to convince Elisha to remain behind while the prophet proceeds respectively to Beth El (vv. 2–3), Jericho (vv. 4–5), and the Jordan River (v. 6) in vv. 2–6 heightens narrative suspense. Each instance employs the same narrative sequence: Elijah tells Elisha to remain behind, then Elisha refuses to abide by Elijah's instructions and employs an oath formula, "by the life of YHWH and by your life," to state emphatically that he will continue to travel with Elijah. Afterward, the prophets of Beth El and Jericho come out to inform Elisha that YHWH is taking his master from him on that day. In both cases Elisha states that he knows already and commands them to remain silent. Because there are no prophets living in the Jordan River region, this portion of the formulaic sequence is lacking after v. 6. Instead, the prophets of Jericho stand by the river to witness what will transpire. Overall, the repeated pattern demonstrates that Elisha is a worthy successor of Elijah.

The transference of power from Elijah to Elisha appears together with Elijah's ascent to heaven in vv. 7–18. The narrative portrays YHWH as the source of the prophets' powers, and it contrasts the efficacy of YHWH's power with that of Ahaziah and the Omride kings. Consequently, this portion of the narrative opens with a reference to the fifty "sons of the prophets" who stand from afar to witness the miraculous transfer of power and ascension of Elijah at the Jordan River. Although interpreters correctly point to this band of prophets as an example of a prophetic guild stationed respectively at Beth El (v. 3) and Jeri-

14. W. R. Kotter, "Gilgal," *ABD* 2:1022–24.

cho (v. 5), the specification of fifty prophets deliberately contrasts with the fifty-man military units sent to summon Elijah (1 Kgs 1:9–16). Just as the prophets' journey from Gilgal to the Jordan involves three stages, so three fifty-man units were sent to summon Elijah. Just as the first two references to the prophets in 2 Kgs 2:2–5 were merely stages in the journey from Gilgal to the Jordan, so the third reference to the "sons of the prophets" in v. 7 begins the sequence in which YHWH's power is made manifest in relation to the two prophets. Just as the first two units of fifty men were destroyed by fire from heaven, so a fiery chariot conveys Elijah to heaven. Just as the Omride kings have chariots (1 Kgs 18; 20; 22), so YHWH sends a chariot to bring Elijah to heaven.

The fundamental interest in the power of YHWH appears in the depiction of Elijah's division of the waters of the Jordan River. Although he is not a Levitical priest like Moses, Elijah rolls up his mantle so that he can use it to strike the waters of the Jordan, much as Moses used his Levitical rod to divide the waters of the Red (Reed) Sea in Exod 14:6, 21–29.[15] Elijah's action also recalls Joshua's parting of the waters of the Jordan, although it differs in that the waters were parted not by a staff, but by the entry of the Levites who bore the ark of the covenant into the water (Josh 3–4). Just as Israel crossed the Red Sea and the Jordan on dry ground, so Elijah and Elisha cross the Jordan on dry ground. This would place them on the east bank of the Jordan across from Jericho, the same area where Moses passed from the scene after transferring leadership of the people to Joshua (Deut 31–34). Elijah's instruction to Elisha, "ask, what shall I do for you before I am taken from you?" highlights the issue of divine power once again, in that it prompts Elisha's request for a double portion of Elijah's spirit. The spirit of YHWH generally conveys a prophetic role in the Hebrew Bible (see Num 11:24–30; 1 Sam 10:5–10; 19:18–24); indeed, it plays a primary role in the designation of Joshua as the successor of Moses in Num 27:12–23. The term *pî šĕnayim*, "double portion" (lit., "double mouth"; cf. Deut 21:17; Zech 13:8), indicates that Elisha will succeed Elijah as the head of the "sons of the prophets" or the prophetic guilds that represent YHWH (see 1 Kgs 18:4; 19:1). A double portion is the inheritance right of the firstborn son (Deut 21:17), who is recognized as the primary heir of the father and thus as the paterfamilias of the extended family. Elijah's statement that such a request is difficult provides the opportunity to state the conditions under which Elisha's request will be granted: only if he sees Elijah taken to heaven will he get his request. This condition indicates that Elisha must become a visionary prophet; if he is unable to have visions of YHWH, he can hardly function as Elijah's successor.

---

15. For the analogy between Moses and Elijah/Elisha, see esp. Robert P. Carroll, "The Elijah-Elisha Sagas: Some Remarks on Prophetic Succession in Ancient Israel," *VT* 19 (1969): 400–415.

The portrayal in v. 11 of Elijah's ascent into the heavens marks the transfer of prophetic power to Elisha. The verse emphasizes that the fiery chariot separates them as Elijah ascends to the heavens in a whirlwind to differentiate between Elijah's new place in the sacred realm of the heavens and Elisha's continued presence in the profane realm of the earth. Because the narrative includes no reference to Elijah's death,[16] he is portrayed in later tradition as an eternal figure, who will return at the time of "the Day of YHWH" (Mal 3:23–24). Elisha's outcry in v. 12, "My father, my father, the chariot of Israel and its horses!" points to 2 Kgs 6:8–23, in which Elisha reveals supernatural fiery chariots to thwart the king of Aram's chariot attack against the Israelite city of Dothan. Indeed, the king of Israel also addresses Elisha as "my father" in 2 Kgs 6:21. The motif appears in 2 Kgs 13:14, in which King Joash cries out, "my father, my father, the chariot of Israel and its horses!" at the time when Elisha falls mortally ill. The present narrative builds upon the earlier reference in 1 Kgs 18:12 to Obadiah's comment that the spirit/wind of YHWH will carry Elijah away by portraying the wind as the fiery chariot known in the Elisha tradition.

The transference of power is demonstrated beginning in v. 13 when Elisha picks up the fallen mantle of Elijah. Elisha's question, "Where is YHWH, the G-d of Elijah? Indeed, where is He?" functions as a rhetorical question which asserts that the power of YHWH exercised by Elijah has now passed to Elisha. The fifty sons of the prophets in vv. 15–18 witness Elisha's miraculous act and thereby certify Elisha as a prophet of YHWH.[17]

The narrative shifts in vv. 19–22 to Elisha's exercise of power to purify the water source of Jericho. Interpreters generally agree that the water source must be the Ein es-Sultan, identified in Christian tradition as Elisha's well, situated just to the east of Tell es-Sultan, the site of Bronze and Iron Age Jericho.[18] Some argue that geological shifts in the region have the potential to expose the spring's water to radioactive influences that would cause sterility.[19] The proximity of the Dead Sea and the location of the Jordan Valley in an area that is below sea level provides great potential for the water in the region to be

16. Cf. the portrayal of Enoch in Gen 5:21–24.

17. Cf. Hans-Christoph Schmitt, *Elischa in den Kriegen* (Gütersloh: Gerd Mohn, 1972), 106 (see also K. Galling, "Der Ehrenname Elisas und die Entrückung Elias," *ZTLK* 53 [1956]: 129–148), who argues that vv. 16–18 are secondary because they point to the fifty prophets' disbelief in the supernatural character of Elijah's departure. These verses function redactionally to tie the narrative to 1 Kgs 18:6–14, but such a contention overlooks their literary function within the present context where they emphasize Elisha's special powers to observe the divine over against those of the other prophets.

18. K. M. Kenyon, "Jericho," *NEAEHL* 2:674.

19. See John Gray, *I & II Kings: A Commentary* (2d ed.; OTL; Philadelphia: Westminster, 1970), 477–79; Jones, *1 and 2 Kings,* 388.

undrinkable, but interpreters must recognize that the point of this particular narrative is to demonstrate how the region acquired a drinkable freshwater source. The tradition concerning Moses' sweetening of the waters of Marah in Exod 15:23–25 points to the healing or sweetening of water as a traditional motif that appears in both narratives.

Interpreters treat vv. 23–24 as a typical example of a prophetic legend that relates a miraculous act by Elisha or as a grandmother's tale that promotes respect for elders.[20] Certainly, the mauling of forty-two boys for their taunts against the prophet points to him as a powerful man with whom no one should trifle. But respect for elders hardly exhausts the literary function of this brief narrative. Focus on the typical character of the pericope prompts readers to overlook its specific function in the immediate literary context: it is placed here to validate Elisha's role as Elijah's prophetic successor by demonstrating that Elijah's powers have passed to Elisha. The passage thereby functions as a part of the larger unit in 1 Kgs 1–2 to prepare the reader for Elisha's role in overthrowing the Omride dynasty and installing Jehu as an act of YHWH.

The supposition that Elisha's baldness is evidence that a tonsure or shaving of the head was practiced by Elisha's prophetic guild is intriguing (Šanda 14–15; Montgomery and Gehman 355). The shaving of the head is associated with mourning for the dead (Lev 21:5; Deut 14:1; Isa 15:2; Jer 16:6; Ezek 7:18; 27:31; Amos 8:10; Mic 1:16), and is likely associated with pagan rituals for mourning the dead god—for example, Baal or Tammuz—who must rise from the underworld to inaugurate the rainy season (cf. 1 Kgs 18:28; Deut 14:1). The name Korah ("bald" in Hebrew) is applied to a class of Levitical psalms (Pss 42; 44–49; 84; 85; 87; 88), and it is the name of the patriarch of a Levitical clan who led a revolt against Moses in the wilderness (see esp. Num 16; cf. Exod 6:21, 24; Num 26:11; 1 Chr 6:7, 22; 9:19). The name also appears in Edomite genealogies (Gen 36:5, 14, 16, 18; 1 Chr 1:35). Such associations suggest that baldness may be the mark of a holy man, who perhaps is associated with the Transjordanian region. The bears' mauling of the forty-two boys recalls the account of Jehu's slaughter of forty-two kinsmen of Ahaziah at Beth Eked (2 Kgs 10:12–14).

The concluding notice that Elisha traveled from Beth El to Mount Carmel and on to Samaria completes the itinerary that takes him from Jericho to two major sites of Elijah's activity. It thereby further associates him with the activities of his master, and completes the circle of Elijah's flight from Carmel and Samaria to the wilderness as Jezebel and Ahab sought to kill him. Elisha now returns to Samaria to finish the job of overthrowing the house of Omri.

---

20. A. Rofé, "The Classification of the Prophetical Stories," *JBL* 89 (1970): 427–440, 430; Montgomery and Gehman, *Books of Kings,* 355.

XIV. Regnal Account of Jehoram ben Ahab of Israel 2 Kings 3:1–8:15

The regnal introduction in 2 Kgs 3:1–3 opens the full account of Jehoram's reign in 2 Kgs 3:1–8:15 (contra Long 36–38). Jehoram's reign does not end until his assassination in 2 Kgs 9:14–26, but this episode appears as part of the regnal account of Ahaziah ben Joram of Judah in 2 Kgs 8:25–9:29.

2 Kings 3:1–3 The Regnal Introduction for Jehoram ben Ahab

3:1 [a]Jehoram ben Ahab ruled over Israel in Samaria in the eighteenth year of Jehoshaphat, king of Judah, and he ruled for twelve years.

2 He did evil in the eyes of YHWH, but not like his father and his mother. He removed the stela of Baal that his father made, 3 but he clung to the sins of Jeroboam ben Nebat by which he caused Israel to sin; he did not turn away from it.[a]

a–a. A rendition of 2 Kgs 3:1–3 appears in LXX 4 Rgns 1:18. The LXX verses resolve the chronological contradictions between 1 Kgs 22:51–53; 2 Kgs 3:1–3; and 2 Kgs 8:16–19, and place Elisha's succession of Elijah in 2 Kgs 2 within the chronological framework of Jehoram's reign.

The introductory *waw*-conjunction followed by the personal name, Jehoram ben Ahab, marks the formal beginning of this unit. The typically formulated regnal account form states the chronology of Jehoram's reign in v. 1 and evaluates his actions in vv. 2–3.

[1] The chronology presupposes 1 Kgs 22:51–53, which states that Ahaziah began to rule in the seventeenth year of Jehoshaphat. The notice that Jehoram began to rule in Jehoshaphat's eighteenth year suggests that Ahaziah's death took place prior to the completion of his second year. The present passage contradicts 2 Kgs 1:17, which states that Jehoram ascended to the throne during the second year of Jehoram ben Jehoshaphat of Judah, but this is mistaken, since 2 Kgs 8:16 states that Jehoram ben Jehoshaphat's reign began in the fifth year of Joram ben Ahab of Israel.

[2–3] The removal of the stela for Baal presupposes 1 Kgs 16:32–33, which states that Ahab made an altar for Baal and an Asherah in Samaria, but 2 Kgs 10:26–27 indicates that the stela for Baal remained intact until Jehu destroyed it. The presupposition by Cogan and Tadmor (43) that Jehoram removed one stela but allowed others to remain is based in the differentiation between the singular reference to the stela in the present context and the plural references to stelae in 2 Kgs 10:26–27, but it is difficult to understand why he would remove one stela and allow others to stand. It is more likely that the present text adds the statement to differentiate Jehoram from his father (and his mother), who is considered more evil than any other king of Israel (1 Kgs 16:33), but failed to reconcile it with the larger literary context.

2 Kings 3:4–27 The Account of Jehoram's Attack against Mesha of Moab

3:4 Mesha, King of Moab, was a sheep broker,[a] and he delivered to the King of Israel the wool of one hundred thousand lambs and one hundred thousand rams.

5 And when Ahab died, the King of Moab rebelled against the King of Israel. 6 King Jehoram went out from Samaria at that time, and mustered all Israel. 7 He went and sent to Jehoshaphat, King of Judah, saying, "The King of Moab has rebelled against me. Will you come with me to Moab for war?" And he said, "I will go up. [b]I, my people, and my horses are at your disposal."[b] 8 And he said, "By what way shall we go up?" And he said, "By way of the wilderness of Edom."

9 And the King of Israel and the King of Judah and the King of Edom went around on a seven-day journey, and there was no water for the camp or for the animals that were with them. 10 And the King of Israel said, "Alas! for YHWH has called for these three kings to give them into the hand of Moab!" 11 Jehoshaphat said, "Is there not here a prophet of YHWH from whom we may inquire of YHWH?" One of the servants of the King of Israel answered and said, "Here is Elisha ben Shaphat, [c]who poured water on the hands of Elijah."[c] 12 Jehoshaphat said, "The word of YHWH is with him." So the King of Israel, Jehoshaphat, and the King of Edom went down to him.

13 And Elisha said to the King of Israel, [d]"Why (do you come) to me?[d] Go to the prophets of your father and to the prophets of your mother." And the King of Israel said to him, "No, for YHWH has called for these three kings to give them into the hand of Moab." 14 And Elisha said, "As YHWH Sebaoth before whom I stand lives! For if I did not favor Jehoshaphat, King of Judah, I would not look at you or see you. 15 And now, bring me a musician." While the musician played, the hand of YHWH came upon him, 16 and he said, "Thus says YHWH, 'This wadi will certainly make many pools!'[e] 17 for thus says YHWH, 'You will not see wind, and you will not see rain, but that wadi will be full of water, and you, your cattle, and your animals shall drink.' 18 This is something minor in the eyes of YHWH, and he will give Moab into your hand. 19

You shall strike every fortified city and every choice city, and every good tree you shall fell, and all the springs of water you shall stop up, and every choice plot of land you shall ruin with stones."

20 In the morning about the time of the Minha offering, behold! water was coming from the direction of Edom, and the land was filled with water.

21 All Moab heard that the kings had gone up to fight with them, and they were called out, everyone old enough to strap on armor, and they stood at the border. 22 They arose early in the morning and the sun was shining upon the water, and Moab saw opposite them water red as blood. 23 And they said, "This is blood! The kings surely[f] were destroyed when each attacked the other! And now, to the spoil, O Moab!" 24 And they came into the camp of Israel, and Israel arose and struck down Moab, and they fled from before them, [g]and they came upon them,[g] striking down Moab. 25 And the cities they uprooted, and on all the good land they each cast his stone and filled it, and every spring of water they stopped up, and every good tree they felled [h]until only its stones remained at Kir Haresheth,[h] and the slingers surrounded it and attacked it.

26 The King of Moab saw that the attack was too strong for him, and he took with him seven hundred swordsmen to break through to the King of Edom, but they were not able. 27 So he took his firstborn son who would rule after him, and he offered him up as a whole burnt offering on the wall. Great wrath came upon Israel, and they withdrew from him and returned to the land.

a. Hebrew, *nōqēd*, "sheepherder, sheep dealer." Normally, *rōʿēh* is employed for "shepherd." Because *nōqēd* refers to the king of Moab and to Amos, who brings Judean tribute to the northern Israelite sanctuary at Beth El (Amos 1:1), it refers to some official capacity (see *HALOT*, ad loc).

b–b. Lit., "Like me, like you; like my people, like your people; like my horses, like your horses," i.e., "I am like you, my people are like your people, my horses are like your horses" (cf. 1 Kgs 22:4).

c–c. Cf. Targum Jonathan, "who served Elijah," which captures the meaning of the Hebrew phrase.

d–d. Alternatively, "What do you have to do with me?" (n.b., *mâ-lî* means, literally, "what to me?").

e. Hebrew, *gēbîm*, means, literally, "pits, cisterns."

f. MT, *hāhŏrēb*, a Hophal infinitive absolute form of the root *ḥrb*, "to attack, put to the sword." The combination of this form with the Niphal verb *neḥerĕbû*, "they were attacked, put to the sword, destroyed," is unusual, but not impossible (see GKC 113w). LXX reads *hāhŏrēb* as the noun *hāhereb*, "the sword," i.e., *kai eipan haima touto tēs hromphaias*, "this is the blood of the sword."

g–g. MT, *wayyabbû bāh*, "and they came against it." The Massorah reads Ketiv, *wayyābō[ʾ]û*, as Qere, *wayyakkû*, "and they struck." Cf. LXX, *kai eisēthon*, "and they went in"; Peshitta, *wᶜlw bhwn*, "and they went up among them," which presuppose the

Ketiv text. See also Targum Jonathan, *ûmhô bĕhôn*, "and they destroyed them," which presupposes the Qere reading.

h–h. MT, *ʿad-hišʾîr ʾăbāneyhā baqqîr ḥărāśet*, lit., "until there remained its stones in Kir Hareset"; cf. Targum Jonathan, *ʿad dĕlāʾ ʾištĕʾeret ʾabnāʾ bĕkûtlāʾ dĕlāʾ pagrûtāʾ*, "until there remained stones in the wall, which was not destroyed," taking Hebrew, *qîr*, as "wall," and *ḥărāśet* from *ḥrs*, "to destroy."

Jehoram's reign combines episodes that demonstrate Israel's deteriorating military position in relation to its neighbors in the Transjordan with episodes that demonstrate Elisha's (and thus YHWH's) power. This combination prepares for the fulfillment of YHWH's earlier statements concerning the overthrow of the house of Omri (see 1 Kgs 19:15–18; 2 Kgs 9–10).

The narrative concerning Jehoram's attack against Moab begins formally with a conjunctive *waw* followed by the personal name Mesha, king of Moab. It continues with *waw*-consecutive narrative through the conclusion of the battle. Although the narrative clearly states Elisha's oracle that YHWH gave Moab into the hand of Israel (vv. 17–19), the Israelites' disgust at Mesha's sacrifice of his son prompts them to break off the battle (v. 27). This action sets in motion events that lead to Israel's loss of the Transjordan and the overthrow of the house of Omri.

The structure of the narrative comprises two basic components in vv. 4–20 and 21–27. Each begins with reference to the actions of the Moabites, which provides the impetus for Jehoram's actions and his eventual failure. Second Kings 3:4–20 relates Mesha's revolt against Israel and the beginning of Jehoram's expedition against the Moabites together with his allies, Jehoshaphat of Judah and the king of Edom. The subunit begins with the statement in v. 4 that sets the stage for the narrative action by identifying King Mesha of Moab as a sheep broker who was obligated to send large quantities of wool to the king of Israel. Such an obligation presupposes that Mesha is Jehoram's vassal and that the wool is tribute due his overlord. The narrative shifts in vv. 5–8 to a focus on Jehoram by noting Mesha's rebellion against Jehoram and Jehoram's efforts to assemble a coalition to put down the revolt. Verses 9–12 shift to the three kings of Jehoram's coalition, Jehoram, Jehoshaphat, and the unnamed king of Edom, and their unsuccessful efforts to negotiate the dry region south of the Dead Sea as they travel from the south. When they are compelled to ask for assistance from Elisha, vv. 13–19 shift attention to the prophet, who, despite his distaste for Jehoram, delivers an oracle from YHWH that promises both water and victory for the beleaguered coalition. Verse 20 concludes the first component of the narrative with a notice that the land was filled with water, thereby testifying to Elisha's and YHWH's power.

Second Kings 3:21–27 begins with a focus on the Moabites, but shifts to its primary concern with Jehoram and Israel. This component includes two basic subunits in vv. 21–25 and 26–27. Verses 21–25 focus on Moab's unsuccessful efforts to defend itself. Deceived by the appearance of the water in the land which they mistake for blood, the Moabites make an ill-advised attack into the heart of the Israelite camp, resulting in their total defeat in keeping with Elisha's earlier oracle. Verses 26–27 shift focus to the king of Moab, who sacrifices his son on the wall of Kir Haresheth after a failed attempt to break through Jehoram's overwhelming forces. The narrative concludes with Israel's withdrawal from the battle in disgust over the Moabite king's sacrifice of his own son, despite Elisha's promises that YHWH would deliver Moab into Israel's hand. Israel's failure to capitalize on its victory over Moab constitutes the first stage in its displacement from the Transjordan and the resulting overthrow of the house of Omri.

This narrative functions within the exilic DtrH as part of the portrayal of northern Israel's ultimate destruction, which in turn provides a model or prelude for the downfall of Jerusalem and Judah. Within the Josian and Hezekian DtrH editions, the narrative depicts northern Israel's wayward character and its inability to govern itself effectively due to questionable leadership. This subunit appears to have been composed as part of the Elijah/Elisha traditions in 1 Kgs 17–2 Kgs 14 that form the basis of the eighth-century B.C.E. Jehu History. Many scholars speculate that the present chapter has a compositional prehistory in which a foundational account of Israel's failed battle against Moab (see also 1 Kgs 20; 22) has been reworked by the addition of prophetic traditions concerning Elisha in vv. 10–19.[1] The addition of the prophetic material aids in demonstrating YHWH's hand in the action. This concern is evident from the introduction of water into the otherwise dry region. The introduction of water plays a role in leading the Moabites to defeat when they are convinced that the reddish cast of the water indicates blood and thus conflict between the members of the Israelite coalition. Although some argue that the absence of clear DtrH language (and throughout much of the Elijah-Elisha traditions) indicates that this material was added to the DtrH only after its initial composition,[2] it is much more likely that an earlier form of the Jehu History/Elijah-Elisha tradition was worked into the broader DtrH framework from the time of the Hezekian edition on. The DtrH hand appears in the regnal reports, e.g., 2 Kgs 3:1–3.

Mesha, king of Moab, is mentioned prominently in the Moabite Stone, in which he claims to have defeated the Omride dynasty and to have established

---

1. Hans-Christoph Schmitt, *Elisa* (Gütersloh: Gerd Mohn, 1972), 32–37; Harald Schweizer, *Elischa in den Kriegen* (Studien zum Alten und Neuen Testament 37; Munich: Kösel, 1974), 17–210; Hermann-Josef Stipp, *Elischa—Propheten— G-ttesmänner* (ATSAT 23; St. Ottilien: EOS, 1987), 63–151.

2. Steven L. McKenzie, *The Trouble with Kings: The Composition of the Books of Kings in the Deuteronomistic History* (VTSup 42; Leiden: Brill, 1991), 95–98; J. Maxwell Miller, "The Elisha Cycle and the Accounts of the Omride Wars," *JBL* 85 (1966): 441–54.

Moabite rule over Israelite territory in the Transjordan to the north of the Wadi Arnon, Moab's northern border.[3] Such a victory would give him control of the territories of Reuben and Gad. The present narrative describes an attack against Moab in which the Israelite coalition traveled around the southern portion of the Dead Sea to attack the Moabite city of Kir Haresheth. Such an action can only be understood in the aftermath of Mesha's victory, when an Israelite attack from the north would be easily repulsed at the Jordan River. The maneuver demonstrates an attempt to take the Moabites by surprise in a region where Moabite strength would be less concentrated. The fact that it failed is consistent with the depiction of Israel's loss of territory in the Transjordan to Aram and Moab during the ninth century B.C.E.. Israel's loss of nerve builds the case for Jehu's revolt in the Jehu History, and it demonstrates northern Israel's faults in the subsequent editions of the DtrH.

[4] The Moab stela was discovered intact in 1868 at the site of ancient Dibon, just north of the Wadi Arnon (the northern border of Moab), but it was subsequently blown up by Arabs, who were interested in selling the pieces for larger sums of money.[4] Mesha's victory over Israel likely occurred after the Arameans had defeated Israel and killed King Ahab at Ramoth Gilead (see 1 Kgs 22; cf. 2 Kgs 3:5 below). The text describes Mesha as *nōqēd,* "cattle broker" (cf. Amos 1:1). The term is a title (cf. Akkadian, *nāqidu*; Ugaritic, *nqd*; *HALOT* 719–21) for an official who prepares sheep for trade, export, or delivery as tribute to an overlord. Moab is well suited for raising sheep,[5] and the wool would constitute tribute to Israel (see Isa 16:1).

[5–8] The DtrH indicates that Moab had been a vassal of Israel since the time of David (2 Sam 8:2). The death of Ahab would signal an opportune time for Moab to break away since 1 Kgs 22 indicates that Ahab was killed in battle at Ramoth Gilead by the Arameans, who were attempting to encroach upon Israelite territory in the Transjordan. Jehoram's mustering of troops would counter Mesha's advances against the territories of Reuben and Gad. Ancient Near Eastern treaties typically required vassals to provide troops and other forms of support in order to assist a suzerain against enemies.[6] Jehoshaphat's response to Jehoram's summons fulfills the requirements of such a treaty. Jehoram's failure to subdue Moab would signal the Edomites that the time for revolt was at hand (n.b., 1 Kgs 11:14–22 relates the attempted revolt against Solomon by Hadad the Edomite, and 2 Kgs 8:20–22 later relates Edom's revolt against

---

3. *ANET* 320–21. For discussion of the Moabite Stone and its role in historical reconstruction, see Andrew Dearman, ed., *Studies in the Mesha Inscription and Moab* (Atlanta: Scholars Press, 1989).

4. M. Patrick Graham, "The Discovery and Reconstruction of the Mesha Inscription," *Studies in the Mesha Inscription and Moab,* 41–92.

5. J. Maxwell Miller, "Moab and the Moabites," *Studies in the Mesha Inscription and Moab,* 1–40.

6. See, e.g., the provisions of the vassal treaties of Esarhaddon, *ANET* 534–41.

Jehoram ben Jehoshaphat of Judah). The political situation in Moab during the ninth century is unclear. The king of Edom is not named. Many note that David put "prefects" (Hebrew, *nĕsîbîm*) in Edom according to 2 Sam 8:14. First Kings 22:48 states that there was no king in Edom, but that a prefect (Hebrew, *nissāb*) served as king, yet 2 Kgs 8:20 states that Edom installed its own king at the time of its revolt against Jehoram of Judah. The reasons for this discrepancy are not certain. Little material evidence exists for either nomadic or settled life in Edom until the end of the Late Bronze and Iron ages, particularly in the ninth and eighth centuries B.C.E.[7] Edom was perhaps ruled by seminomadic chieftains who were sometimes called kings by their neighbors (see Gen 36:31–39).

[9–12] This episode has remarkable similarities to the wilderness traditions of the Pentateuch, which relate the lack of water for the people and their complaints about being brought into the wilderness to die.[8] In the present case, the narrative serves as an etiological tradition for the creation of water sources in an otherwise dry and inhospitable region. This territory is an extension of the Jordan rift known as the Arabah, "dry region," that cuts through the territory of Edom around the southern and eastern regions of the Dead Sea and continues south to the Gulf of Aqaba. The region is well known for its lack of water, although springs appear periodically and wadis supply water at times of seasonal rainfall.[9] Ironically, the unnamed king of Israel expresses reservations about the journey into the wilderness. Like the murmuring of the Israelites in the wilderness, such a complaint demonstrates Jehoram's doubts about YHWH, thereby providing grounds for his failure to defeat the Moabites and the overall narrative interest in the overthrow of the Omride dynasty by Jehu. The complaint introduces Elisha into the narrative insofar as an oracular inquiry to a prophet enables the Israelite army to find water.

[13–19] By depicting Elisha's distaste for Jehoram, the narrative builds the case for the overthrow of the house of Omri. The prophet's question to Jehoram, "Why have you come to me?" and his contemptuous statement to the king that he should consult the prophets of his father and mother (see 1 Kgs 18) tie this episode into the literary framework of the Elijah-Elisha traditions that constitute the basis for the Jehu History. Elisha's curt dismissal provides Jehoram with the opportunity once again to demonstrate his lack of trust in YHWH.

7. B. MacDonald, "Edom, Archaeology of Edom," *ABD* 2:295–301.
8. See John R. Bartlett, "The 'United' Campaign against Moab in 2 Kings 3:4–27," in *Midian, Moab and Edom: The History and Archaeology of Late Bronze and Iron Age Jordan and North-West Arabia* (JSOTSup 24; ed. John F. A. Sawyer and David J. A. Clines; Sheffield: JSOT Press, 1983), 135–46, 138; Exod 17:1–7; Num 20:1–13; see also Num 20:14–19.
9. Yohanan Aharoni, *The Land of the Bible: A Historical Geography* (2d ed.; London: Burns and Oates, 1979), 40–41; MacDonald, "Edom, Archaeology of Edom." For discussion of Moab, see Miller, "Moab and the Moabites"; Miller, "Moab," *ABD* 4:882–93; J. Maxwell Miller, ed., *Archaeological Survey of the Kerak Plateau* (Atlanta: Scholars Press, 1991).

Elisha's statement that he would not even consider Jehoram's request were it not for the presence of Jehoshaphat reiterates the generally high regard for the Judean king expressed elsewhere (1 Kgs 22:41–46; 1 Kgs 22:7).

Elisha's instructions that a musician play while he receives YHWH's oracle illumine the dynamics of oracular inquiry. The well-crafted poetic forms of oracular discourse are known from the prophetic books, but musical accompaniment is rarely indicated. The Egyptian Prophecy of Neferti relates a scene in which Pharaoh Snefru summons the lector priest Nefer-Rohu to deliver choice speeches for the entertainment of the royal court (*ANET* 444–46). Music is not mentioned in this account, but the poetic speech of the lector priest points to artistic composition intended for public performance (1 Sam 10:5–6; 1 Chr 25; 2 Chr 20; 29; 34:30; 35:15).[10]

Following the speech formula, Elisha's oracle begins with a typical prophetic messenger formula, *kōh ʾāmar yhwh*, "Thus says YHWH." The wadi in question is the Wadi el-Hesa or Zered brook, which flows westward from the Transjordan into the southeastern edge of the Dead Sea. The Wadi el-Hesa forms the border between Edom and Moab, and it is known for its red sandstone features.[11] The oracle etiologically explains flash flooding during the rainy season when this normally dry region experiences cloudbursts; the oracle also portrays YHWH's role as creator of the natural world to provide the basis for the later assertion that YHWH will act in the historical world to give Moab into Jehoram's hand (see v. 18b). The prophet's further statement, introduced by another messenger formula, that the people will see neither wind nor rain presupposes that they are located in the low-lying lands to the east of the hills that form the western boundary of (Moab and) Edom along the Dead Sea and the Aravah. YHWH's commands to destroy the fortified and choice cities, to cut down the good trees, to block up the springs of water, and to ruin the land with stones contradict the prohibition in Deut 20:19–20 against cutting down trees in time of war. YHWH's command through Elisha to destroy the land, including its trees, indicates the non-Dtr early origin of this narrative, which was only later worked into the DtrH framework.

[20] Verse 20 concludes the subunit in vv. 4–20 with a notice of the fulfillment of YHWH's promises to bring water to the land. Although some see the reference to the time of the Minha offering as an indication that this narrative is late, ancient Israelite religion was centered around the institution of temples, priesthoods, and sacrificial rituals throughout the entire monarchic period (cf. 1 Kgs 18:36). The minha was a cereal offering (Lev 2) that followed the daily olah or whole burnt offering (Lev 6:7–13; Exod 29:38–42; Num 28:3–8).

---

10. See David L. Petersen, *Late Israelite Prophecy: Studies in Deutero-Prophetic Literature and in Chronicles* (SBLMS 23; Missoula, Mont.: Scholars Press, 1977), 55–87.

11. See Nelson Glueck, "The Boundaries of Edom," *HUCA* 11 (1936): 141–57.

[21–25] The narrative shifts focus to the actions of the Moabites, who rush to defend their border upon hearing of the approach of the Israelite coalition. Again, etiological concerns with the landscape of this region play a role. The presence of reddish-hued pools in this region is a natural phenomenon in the aftermath of rain and flooding in the red sandstone landscape at sunrise. Nevertheless, the narrative maintains that the Moabites were not yet familiar with this natural feature of their land and erroneously conclude that the reddish waters were colored by blood from fighting between the kings of the Israelite coalition. The result is a fiasco for Moab in fulfillment of YHWH's earlier oracle. The land is completely destroyed, which again etiologically explains the natural landscape of the region, and the Moabites are forced to take refuge in the city of Kir Haresheth. Kir Haresheth is the ancient capital of Moab (cf. Isa 16:11, 17; Jer 48:31, 36), located along the King's Highway some seventeen miles south of the Wadi Arnon, which defines the northern border of Moab, and eleven miles east of the Dead Sea.[12] The narrative emphasizes that the destruction of the land was so thorough that only stones were left in the land in the vicinity of the city (n.b., the Hebrew word *qîr* means "wall").

[26–27] The Moabite king attacked the king of Edom because he perceived the Edomites as the weak link in the forces of the Israelite coalition. When the attempt failed, the Moabite king sacrificed his own son to appease the Moabite god Chemosh.[13] Human sacrifice is attested in biblical tradition and elsewhere in the ancient world in times of emergency (Judg 11:29–40; 2 Kgs 16:3; Mic 6:7; see Montgomery and Gehman 363; Cogan and Tadmor 47). The notice, "and great wrath was upon Israel" (Hebrew, *wayĕhî qeṣep gādôl ʿal yiśrāʾēl*) is frequently understood as a reference to Chemosh's wrath that then plays a role in Israel's defeat. Although the term *qeṣep,* "wrath," generally describes YHWH's anger "against" (*ʿal*) wrongdoers (see Num 18:5; Deut 29:27; Josh 9:20; 22:20; Cogan and Tadmor 47), the phrase here can hardly refer to wrath directed "against" Israel. Such an interpretation requires that YHWH's oracle concerning the defeat of Moab would remain unfulfilled and thereby raises doubts about its legitimacy. There is otherwise no indication in this narrative that YHWH's oracle is to be considered as false. The reference to anger must be read as "upon" (*ʿal*) Israel, that is, Israel became angry at the sight of Mesha's sacrifice of his son, and consequently withdrew from Kir Haresheth. Israel/Jehoram—and not YHWH—would be responsible for the failure to achieve victory over the Moabites. The scenario provides a parallel to the wilderness tradition—for example, the Israelite spies refused to accept YHWH's guarantees of victory and suffered as a result (Num 14).

12. See G. L. Mattingly, "Kir-Hareseth," *ABD* 4:84.
13. Cf. the Mesha stone, in which Mesha claims that Moab's initial subjugation to Israel resulted from Chemosh's anger against his own people (*ANET* 320).

2 Kings 4:1–37 Elisha's Efforts to Save the Sons
of the Widow and the Shunammite Woman

4:1 ᵃOne woman from the wives of the sons of the prophets cried out to Elisha, saying, "Your servant, my husband, is dead, and you know that your servant was one who feared YHWH.ᵃ But the creditor is coming to take my two children as his slaves." 2 And Elisha said to her, "What shall I do for you?ᵇ Tell me what you have in the house." And she said, "Your maidservant has nothing at all in the house except for a flask of oil." 3 And he said, "Go, borrow vessels for yourself from outside, empty vessels from all your neighbors,ᵇ and do not ask for only a few. 4 And you shall enter (your house), close the door behind you and your children, pour (oil) into all these vessels, and set aside each that is filled." 5 And she went from him and closed the door behind her and her children. While they were bringing (vessels) to her, she was pouringᶜ (oil). 6 And when the vessels were full, she said to her son, "Bring another vessel to me," and he said to her, "There is not another vessel," and the oil stopped. 7 And she came and told the man of G-d, and he said, "Go, sell the oil, and repay your creditor,ᵇ and you and your childrenᵇ shall live on the rest."

8 And Elisha went to Shunemᵈ that day, and a rich woman was there, and she prevailed upon him to eat food. And whenever he would pass through, he would stop by there to eat food. 9 And she said to her husband, "Behold, now, I know that he is a holy man of G-d who passes by us continually. 10 Let's make a small walled roof chamber and provide for him there a bed, a table, a chair, and a lamp, and when he comes to us, he shall stop by there." 11 And that day he came by, stopped by the upper roof chamber, and slept there. 12 And he said to Gehazi, his attendant, "Call this Shunammiteᵉ woman," and he called her, and she stood before him. 13 And he said to him, "Say to her, please, 'Behold, you have shown to us all this respect. What (shall we) do for you? Shall we speak on your behalf to the king or to the commander of the army?'" And she said, ᶠ"In the midst of my people I live."ᶠ 14 And he said, "And what (shall we) do for her?" And Gehazi said, "Indeed, she has no son, and her husband is old." 15 And he said, "Call her," and he called her, and she stood at the door. 16 And he said, ᵍ"At this time next year, youᵇ will embrace a son."ᵍ And she said, "No, my lord, man of G-d, do not lie to your maidservant." 17 And the woman became pregnant and bore a son ʰat this time in the next yearʰ that Elisha said to her. 18 And the boy grew, and one day he went out to his father to the harvesters. 19 And he said to his father, "My head! My head!" And he said to the attendant, "Carry him to his mother!" 20 And he carried him and brought him to his mother, and he lay upon her knees until noon and died. 21 And she went up, laid him on the bed of the

man of G-d, closed (the door) behind him, and went out. 22 And she called
to her husband and said, "Send, please, to me one of the boys and one of
the asses, and I will run to the man of G-d and return." 23 And he said,
"Why do you^b go^b to him today? It is not the new moon and not Shabbat." ^iAnd she said, "It is all right."^i 24 And she saddled the ass and said
to her boy, "Drive on. Do not stop me from riding unless I tell you." 25
And she went and came to the man of G-d at Mount Carmel. When the
man of G-d saw her from afar, he said to Gehazi, his boy, "Behold, this
Shunammite^j woman. Now, please run to meet her, and say to her, 'Are
you all right? And your husband? And your child?'" And she said, "It's
all right." 27 And she came to the man of G-d at the mountain and seized
his feet, and Gehazi drew near to push her away, and the man of G-d said,
"Let her be, for she is bitter. YHWH has concealed (what happened) from
me and has not told me." 28 And she said, "Did I ask for a son from my
lord? Did I not say, 'Do not deceive me'?" 29 And he said to Gehazi, "Bind
up your loins, take my staff in your hand, and go. When you find a man,
you shall not greet him, and if a man greets you, you shall not answer
him. And you shall place my staff on the face of the boy." 30 And the
mother of the boy said, "As YHWH lives and as you live, I will leave
you." And he arose and went after her. 31 And Gehazi went before them
and placed the staff on the face of the boy. There was no sound and nothing to hear, so he returned to meet him and told him, saying, "The boy
has not awakened." 32 And Elisha came into the house, and behold, the
boy was dead, laid out upon his bed. 33 And he went in, closed the door
behind the two of them, and prayed to YHWH. 34 And he went up, lay
upon the boy, and placed his face on his face, and his eyes on his eyes,
and his hands on his hands,^k and he lay upon him, and the flesh of the boy
became warm. 35 And he returned, went about in the house here and there,
and he went up and lay upon him. The boy sneezed seven times and
opened his eyes. 36 And he called to Gehazi, and said, "Call ^lthis Shunammite woman,"^l and he called her, and she came to him, and he said,
"Take up your son." 37 And she came, fell about his feet, bowed down to
the ground, took her son, and went out.

a–a. Cf. Targum Jonathan, which explains Elisha's relationship with the woman by
identifying her dead husband as Obadiah (see 1 Kgs 18): "And one of the wives of the
students of the prophets was crying out before Elisha, saying, 'Your servant, Obadiah,
my husband, is dead. And you know that your servant was one who feared from before
YHWH who, when Jezebel killed the prophets of YHWH, took from them one hundred
men and hid them, fifty men each in the cave, and he was borrowing and feeding them
so that he would not feed them from the property of Ahab because of those who were
the oppressor."
b. Read with Qere, because Ketiv preserves an archaic case ending -y.

c. Read with Qere, *môṣāqet*, "pouring out," instead of Ketiv, *myṣqt*.

d. Cf. Peshitta, "to Shiloh," based on the Peshitta's reading of v. 23 below (see n. i).

e. Cf. Peshitta, *lšylwmyt²*, "to this Shilomite," based on the Peshitta's reading of v. 23 (see n. i).

f–f. Cf. Targum Jonathan, "In the midst of the affairs of my people I endure," which reads the Hebrew as an indication of the troubles she faces instead of as a polite refusal of the prophet's offer.

g–g. MT, *lammô³ēd hazzeh kā³ēt hayâ ²at/²ty hōbeqet bēn*, lit., "at this appointed time, according to the living year, you are embracing a son." The expression *kā³ēt hayâ*, "according to the year of the living," is an idiomatic expression, based on the Akkadian analogy *ana balat*, "living year," which means "next year" (cf. Gen 18:10, 14; Cogan and Tadmor 57).

h–h. See n. g above.

i–i. MT, *wattō³mer šālôm*, "and she said, 'peace [it is all right].'" Cf. Peshitta, *w³mrt šylwmyt²*, lit., "and the Shilomite said," i.e., "and the Shilomite insisted" (cf. the use of the verb *³mr* in v. 24 below), based upon the reading of Hebrew *šālôm* as the subject of the verb *wattō³mer*. This explains the earlier references to "Shunem" (v. 8) and "the Shunammite" (vv. 12, 25) as "Shiloh" and "the Shilomite." Note also the traditional identification of David's nurse, Abishag of Shunem (1 Kgs 1–2) with the beautiful Shulammite woman of the Song of Songs (Song 7:1).

j. Peshitta, *šylwmyt² ḥd²*, "this Shilomite"; cf. n. i.

k. Read with Qere, *kappāyw*, "his hands," instead of Ketiv, *kappô*, "his hand."

l–l. Cf. Peshitta, *lšylwmyt² ḥd²*, "to this Shilomite (woman)"; see n. i.

Second Kings 4:1–37 presents two narratives concerning Elisha's efforts to save the sons of women from threat. Verses 1–7 portray his efforts to assist a widow of one of the prophets whose sons will be taken as slaves when she is unable to pay her debts. Verses 8–37 portray his efforts to enable the birth of a son to a woman from the city of Shunem and to revive her son when he dies. Each constitutes a discrete unit,[14] but they are linked syntactically by the introductory *waw*-consecutive verb *wayĕhî* (lit., "and it came to pass") in v. 8, by their common interest in the prophet's relationship with women, by their interest in the prophet's efforts to save the lives of the sons of each of the women, and by their common references to the closing of doors behind a major character who carries out miraculous actions (vv. 4, 5; vv. 21, 33).

The unit is demarcated by the combination of the conjunctive *waw* and the noun *²iššâ ²aḥat minnĕšê bĕnê-hannĕbî²îm*, "and one woman from the sons of the prophets," which introduces her as a primary protagonist. It constitutes another episode in the portrayal of Elisha's (and thus YHWH's) powers in the world of creation by illustrating the power to provide food for those in need, to provide children for an otherwise barren woman, and to heal or restore the dead to life. All of these attributes are characteristic of the Canaanite fertility god,

14. Stipp, *Elischa*, 276–77.

Baal.[15] These narratives therefore constitute elements in the polemic against the house of Omri and its ties to Baal worship.

The present unit is based on originally separate narratives that were secondarily placed together within the present literary context.[16] The narrative concerning the widow and her son in vv. 1–7 is concerned with the *běnê-hannĕbî'îm*, "the sons of the prophets," and the feeding of people from meager or questionable food sources, much like the narratives concerning Elisha's purification of food (vv. 38–41) and his feeding of one hundred men (vv. 42–44). It presupposes no particular location, although vv. 38–41 and 42–44 indicate the prophet's arrival from Gilgal and a visitor's arrival from Baal Shalishah, respectively. By contrast, the narrative concerning Elisha's actions on behalf of the Shunammite woman presupposes a setting in Shunem, located in the northern portion of the Jezreel Valley opposite Jezreel,[17] and the Carmel hills, located to the west of the Jezreel Valley and Megiddo along the Mediterranean coast. Other features distinguish the narrative in vv. 8–37 from those in vv. 1–7, 38–41, and 42–44, including the identification of the Shunammite woman as a major protagonist (cf. 2 Kgs 8:1–6), the identification of Gehazi as Elisha's servant (cf. again 2 Kgs 8:1–6 and the healing of Naaman in 2 Kgs 5, esp. vv. 19b–27), and its fundamental interest in the life and death of the Shunammite woman's son. The narrative concerning the Shunammite woman appeared originally together with 2 Kgs 8:1–6, which discusses Elisha's efforts to restore her land after a period of residence in Philistia, but it has been moved to a new literary framework that stresses Elisha's miraculous acts. The narrative concerning the Shunammite woman in vv. 8–37 may stem from local traditions associated with the Jezreel and the Carmel, but the narrative concerning the widow in vv. 1–7 lacks any indication of local ties. Both narratives are instrumental in the composition of 1 Kgs 17:8–16, 17–24, which respectively portray Elijah's similar provision of food to the widow of Zarephath and his revival of her son.

[1–7] With the death of her husband, the widow would lose the primary means of support for her family, particularly since the phrase *ben-nābî'*, "son of a prophet" (plural, *běnê-hannĕbî'îm*) indicates a professional designation that would entail some form of income (see Amos 7:10–17; cf. 1 Kgs 14:1–18). Legal traditions concerning debt slavery in Exod 21:1–11 and Deut 15:12–18 explain the circumstances of the widow.[18] When a person is unable to repay a debt in ancient Israel or Judah, that person is subject to a legal form of debt slavery. A creditor may claim a person for a period of six years in the event of fail-

---

15. Cf. Leah Bronner, *The Stories of Elijah and Elisha: As Polemics against Baal Worship* (POS 6; Leiden: Brill, 1968).

16. Stipp, *Elischa,* 268–98.

17. E. F. Huwiler, "Shunem," *ABD* 5:1228–29.

18. G. C. Chirichigno, *Debt-Slavery in Israel and the Ancient Near East* (JSOTSup 141; Sheffield: JSOT Press, 1993).

ure to repay a debt. The debtor works for the creditor for the specified period of time.[19] The woman is not to be taken by the creditor as a debt slave, but her two sons would be considered economically more viable as they mature over the coming six years. Olive oil is one of the staples of the Israelite diet. By asking the widow to borrow containers, the prophet ensures that she has enough for herself and her neighbors so that she can sell the oil to them. The closed door suggests the miraculous nature of the event.

[8–37] Elijah's oracular statement facilitates the birth of a son to the barren woman, and he revives the boy after he suffers a seemingly fatal sunstroke. The narrative emphasizes the power of the prophet and YHWH to grant and save life. Within the context of the Jehu History, it points to YHWH's power over against that of Baal and the house of Omri. It likewise functions within the Hezekian, Josianic, and exilic DtrH editions to illustrate YHWH's power to intervene in the history of Israel and Judah. The structure of the narrative comprises a portrayal of the relationship between Elisha and the woman in vv. 8–11, the prophet's oracular statement that results in the birth of her son in vv. 12–17, and Elisha's actions to save the boy's life in vv. 18–37.

[8–11] Joshua 19:18 locates Shunem in the territory Issachar. It is identified with the modern site of Sulam at the foot of Mount Moreh in the northern portion of the Jezreel Valley opposite Mount Gilboa and the site of Jezreel to the south.[20] The site is strategically located as it guards the eastern approaches to the Jezreel Valley and the western approaches into the northern regions of the Jordan Valley around Beth Shean. It thereby aids in controlling the trade routes through the Jezreel that connect the Transjordan to the Mediterranean coast. Elisha's relationship with the Shunammite woman portends the growth of a base of support for the prophet, who will be instrumental in the recovery of her own property (2 Kgs 8:1–6) and in Jehu's revolt (2 Kgs 9–10).

[12–17] This segment of the narrative introduces Elisha's attendant, Gehazi (see 2 Kgs 5:19b–27; 8:4–5). Many explain his name, *gēhăzî/gêhăzî*, as a form of the phrase "valley of vision" (see BDB, ad loc; cf. *gê* *hizzāyôn* in Isa 22:1, 5; Jones 405; Gray 495). Commentators tend to understand Elisha's initial statement to the woman, *hinnēh hāradt 'ēlênû 'et-kol-haḥărādâ hazzō't*, as an indication of the trouble to which she has gone to provide for the prophet, but the root *ḥrd* means literally "to tremble, show fear, anxiety." The term indicates the proper respect that she has shown to the holy man. Elisha's offer to speak on her behalf to the king or to the commander of the army presupposes that the prophet has standing in relation to both. Her response, "I dwell among my people," is a polite refusal that suggests that she does not need the prophet's help. Many take this as an indication of her wealth or status, although it is noteworthy that Gehazi

19. Ibid., 256–301.
20. Huwiler, "Shunem," *ABD* 5:1228–29.

speaks to the king on her behalf when she attempts to reclaim her home after living for seven years among the Philistines (2 Kgs 8:1–6). The death of her husband without a male heir leaves the woman in difficulty as the husband's property—and even the woman—might be claimed by one of his male relatives.[21] In a scene reminiscent of YHWH's announcement to Sarah that she will bear a son (Gen 18:10, 14), Elisha announces that the Shunammite woman will bear a son at this time next year. The woman's demand for reassurance that Elisha not deceive her heightens the narrative tension and prepares the reader for the son's collapse from sunstroke.

[18–37] Elisha's revival of the Shunammite woman's son portrays the prophet's and YHWH's ability to overcome death. The statement that he is dead in v. 20 is crucial to the point of the story. By portraying Elisha's and YHWH's power over death, the narrative deliberately contrasts them with the Baal supporters of the house of Omri in the Jehu History. Baal is a fertility god, who comes to life in the fall when the rains come and dies at the beginning of the dry summer season. The seasonal "deaths" of ancient fertility gods are typical mythological expressions of the dying and rising god motif. The descent of Ishtar to the netherworld (see also the descent of Inanna to the underworld and the Ugaritic epic of Aqhat) explains the death of the fertility god, Tammuz, and Ishtar's efforts to travel to the world of the dead to restore him to life and thereby to bring on the rainy season.[22] The narrative polemicizes against such conceptualizations by demonstrating that YHWH (and Elisha) actually have the power to bring the dead to life.[23]

The boy apparently suffers from sunstroke when he goes out into the field with the reapers. Like Jeroboam's wife, who visited the prophet Ahijah to seek a cure for her sick son (1 Kgs 14:1–18), the Shunammite woman informs her husband that he should send for an ass and a servant so that she might travel speedily to the prophet. The husband's comment that it is neither New Moon nor Shabbat indicates the appropriate times to consult a prophet. The woman's response that it is "all right" suggests that she has not yet informed her husband of the boy's death, but her insistence on visiting the prophet immediately conveys the urgency of the situation. The prophet's reception of the woman, particularly his instructions to Gehazi to inquire concerning her welfare and that of her husband and son, indicates that he does not know of the boy's death (cf. v. 27). Her response, "It is all right," is identical to that given previously to her husband's question, and indicates her hesitancy to speak about the matter in public.

When Elisha realizes the severity of the situation, he dispatches Gehazi with instructions to hurry without stopping to give or receive greetings from pass-

---

21. Deut 25:5–10; but cf. Num 27:1–11; 36, which allow women to inherit property.
22. For translations, see respectively *ANET* 106–9; 52–57; 149–55.
23. Cf. Bronner, *Stories of Elijah and Elisha.*

ing travelers so that he might place the prophet's staff on the boy's face. The staff is an instrument or symbol of the prophet's power, much like the rods of Aaron and Moses (see Exod 7:8–13, 14–25; 17:1–7, 8–15; Num 20:1–13, etc.). In what appears to be an act of magic, the prophet lays his body down upon the boy, with his face, mouth, and hands upon those of the boy. The reader should note the analogy with YHWH's breathing life into the first human at the time of creation (see Gen 2:7). The boy's seven sneezes indicate the perceived efficacy of the number seven in ancient Israelite popular thought.

2 Kings 4:38–41 Elisha Purifies a Pan of Food

4:38 Elisha returned to Gilgal, and famine was in the land. The sons of the prophets were sitting before him, and he said to his boy, "Prepare the large pot, and cook stew for the sons of the prophets." **39** And one went out to the field to glean vegetables, found a vine of the field, gleaned from it gourds of the field, filling his garment, and he came, and cut (them) up into the pot of stew because they did not know (what they were). **40** They dished it out to the men to eat, and when they ate from the stew, they cried out and said, "(There is) death in the pot, O man of G-d," and they were not able to eat. **41** And he said, ᵃ"Take meal, and throw it into the pot."ᵃ And he said, "Dish it out to the people," and they ate, and there was nothing bad in the pot.

a–a. MT, *ûqĕḥû qemaḥ wayyašlēk ʾel-hassîr,* lit., "and take meal, and he threw it into the pot," which makes little sense. Cf. LXX, Targum Jonathan, and Peshitta, each of which renders the statement, "take meal and throw it into the pan."

The narrative concerning Elisha's purification of a pan of food likewise demonstrates the prophet's ability to overcome death. It is demarcated at the beginning by the conjunctive *waw* and the name of the prophet. The narrative begins in v. 38 with a statement that the prophet returned to the sons of the prophets at Gilgal. Although some speculate that there was a site named Gilgal in the Ephraimite hill country, Elisha's association with the Jordan Valley suggests that he has returned to his usual haunts (see 2 Kgs 2). The motif of famine in the land explains why the prophets are not overly careful about what they eat. Elisha commands his servant—Gehazi is not named, which suggests that this tradition is independent of the preceding narrative—to prepare food. The Hebrew term *nāzîd* is a mixed mess or stew (cf. Gen 25:29, 34). The servant gathers wild *paqquʿōt,* some form of gourds or cucumbers identified as *citrullus colocynthus,* "Sodom's apples," known for their pungent smell and purgative properties. The narrative presupposes that the reader knows what they are—and what to expect from them—even though neither we nor the sons of the prophets share this information. The prophet resolves the crisis by instructing the servant to throw meal into the pan. Although the narrative presents this as a magical act, the meal would absorb oil and provide some coating in the stomach that would protect those eating the food.

2 Kings 4:42–44 Elisha Feeds One Hundred Men

4:42 A man came from Baal Shalishah, brought food to the man of G-d, twenty loaves of barley and fresh ears of corn,[a] and said, "Give to the people so they may eat." 43 And his servant said, "How shall I place this before one hundred men?" And he said, "Give to the people so they may eat, for thus says YHWH, [b]'They will eat and have some left over.'"[b] 44 And he placed before them, and they ate, and there was some left over according to the word of YHWH.

a. Hebrew, *wĕkarmel bĕsiqlōnô,* "and fresh corn in its bag," presupposes *siqqālôn,* "bag" (M. Jastrow, *A Dictionary of the Targumin, the Talmud Babli and Nerushalmi, and the Midrashic Literature* [Brooklyn: P. Shalom, 1967], 1299; cf. Targum Jonathan, "and broken corn in his garment"; contra Peshitta, "wheat rubbed from the ears in a cloth"; n.b., the expression is lacking in LXX). Based on the parallel between *bsql* and *šblt,* "ear of corn" in Ugaritic (*CTA* 19:268–74), many scholars presuppose that *bĕsiqlōnô* must be a form of the corresponding term in Hebrew that refers to "cornstalk," so that the phrase would refer to "fresh grain on the stalk" (Harold R. [Chaim] Cohen, *Biblical Hapax Legomena in the Light of Akkadian and Ugaritic* [SBLDS 37; Missoula, Mont.: Scholars Press, 1978], 112–13). Given the parallel in Ugaritic and the meaning of the term *siqqālôn,* "bag," in later Hebrew, it seems likely that the expression refers to "fresh corn in its husk."

b–b. MT, *'ākōl wĕhôtēr,* lit., "eating and leaving over."

This brief narrative demonstrates the power of the prophet (man of G-d) by portraying his miraculous feeding of one hundred men from very meager supplies of food. It is polemical in that Baal, the god identified with the house of Omri, is a god of rain and fertility who provides food. Like the other units that comprise this account, 2 Kgs 4:42–44 begins with a conjunctive *waw* joined to a noun, *'îš,* that is, "and a man (came)." The plot and structure are quite simple. A man arrives from Baal Shalishah, identified with Khirbet Sirisya located some fourteen miles north of Lod overlooking the Sharon plain,[24] bearing food. The food includes some twenty pieces of bread made from barley and *karmel bĕsiqlōnô,* very likely corn or grain in its husk (see text note above). The food serves as payment for services rendered by the prophets (cf. 1 Kgs 14:3).

24. G. A. Herion, "Baal Shalishah," *ABD* 1:553.

2 Kings 5:1–6:7 Elisha's Powers of Restoration

5:1 Naaman, commander of the army of the King of Aram, was an important and well-regarded man before his master, because YHWH gave victory to Aram through him. But the man was a mighty warrior who suffered from leprosy.

2 Aram went out (in) raiding parties and captured a young girl from the land of Israel, and she served the wife of Naaman. **3** She said to her mistress, "If only my master went before the prophet who is in Samaria, he would cure him from his leprosy." **4** ᵃSo he (Naaman) went and told his master,ᵃ saying, "This is what the young girl from the land of Israel said." **5** And the King of Aram said, "Go, and I will send a letter to the King of Israel." So he went and took in his hand ten talents of silver and six thousand (shekels) of gold and ten changes of clothing. **6** He brought the letter to the King of Israel, saying, "And now, when this letter comes to you, behold, I have sent to you Naaman, my servant, and you shall cure him from his leprosy." **7** When the King of Israel read the letter, he tore his garments and said, "Am I G-d to impose death or to give life, that this one summons me to cure a man from his leprosy? ᵇJust know and seeᵇ that he is looking for a pretext against me!"

8 When Elisha, the man of G-d, heard that the King of Israel had torn his garments, he sent to the king, saying, "Why did you tear your garments? Let him come to me, and he will know that there is a prophet in Israel." **9** Naaman came with his horsesᶜ and chariot, and he stood at the door of Elisha's house. **10** And Elisha sent a messenger to him, saying, "Go and wash seven times in the Jordan, and your flesh will be restored to you, and you will be clean." **11** And Naaman was incensed, and he went and said, "Behold, I said to myself, 'He will surely come out, stand, call on the name of YHWH, his G-d, wave his hand over the spot, and cure the leprosy.' **12** Are not the Amanaᵈ and Parpar Rivers of Damascus better than all the waters of Israel? Will I not wash in them and be cleansed?" And he turned, and walked away in anger. **13** And his servants approached, spoke to him, and said, "Father!ᵉ The prophet has spoken something great to you. Will you not do it? Indeed, he only said to you, 'Wash and be clean.'" **14** And he went down and immersed himself in the Jordan seven times according to the word of the man of G-d, and his flesh was restored like the flesh of a young boy, and he was clean. **15** He returned to the man of G-d, he and all his camp, and he came, stood before him, and said, "Behold, please, I know that there is no G-d in all the earth except in Israel. And now, accept a giftᶠ from your servant." **16** And he said, "As YHWH before whom I stand lives, I will not accept." And he urged him

to accept, but he refused. 17 And Naaman said, “And if not,[g] let there be
given to your servant a two-mule load of earth, for shall your servant not
again offer whole burnt offering and sacrifice to gods other than YHWH?
18 But for this, may YHWH forgive your servant: when my master enters
the house of Rimmon, and he is supported upon my hand, and I worship
at the house of Rimmon; when I worship at the house of Rimmon, may
YHWH pardon[h] your servant for this act.” 19 And he said to him, “Go in
peace,” and went from him for some distance.

20 Gehazi, the attendant of Elisha, the man of G-d, said, “Behold, my
master has declined to accept from the hand of Naaman, this Aramean, that
which he brought. As YHWH lives, I will run after him, and I will accept
something from him!” 21 So Gehazi pursued after Naaman, and Naaman
saw (him) running after him, dismounted his chariot to meet him, and said,
“Is everything all right?” 22 And he said, “It’s all right. My master sent me,
saying, ‘Behold, now these[i] two boys have come to me from the hills of
Ephraim, from the sons of the prophets. Give please to them a talent of silver and two changes of clothing.” 23 And Naaman said, “Please accept two
talents of silver,” and he urged him, bound two talents of silver in two bags
and two changes of clothing, and gave (them) to two of his boys, and they
carried (them) before him. 24 He came to the citadel,[j] took (them) from their
hand, deposited (them) in the house, and sent the men away, and they left.
25 And he came and stood by his master, and Elisha said to him, [k]“Where
have you been,[k] Gehazi?” And he said, “Your servant has not gone anywhere.” 26 And he said to him, [l]“Don’t I know[l] when a man has gotten down
from upon his chariot to meet you? [m]Is it a time to accept[m] silver and clothing and olives and vineyards and sheep and cattle and servants and maid-
servants? 27 And the leprosy of Naaman shall cleave to you and your
descendants forever!” And he went out from before him leprous like snow.

6:1 The sons of the prophets said to Elisha, “Behold, please, the place
where we live before you is too small for us. 2 Let us go, please, to the
Jordan, and we will each take from there one timber, and we will make
for ourselves there a place to dwell.” And he said, “Go ahead.” 3 And one
said, “Will you please go with your servants?” And he said, “I will go.”
4 And he went with them, and they came to the Jordan and cut down trees.
5 While one was felling a log, the iron ax fell into the water, and he cried
out and said, “Oh no, master! It was borrowed!” 6 And the man of G-d
said, “Where did it fall?” So he showed him the place, and he cut off some
wood and threw it there, and the iron ax floated. 7 And he said, “Pick it
up for yourself.” So he reached his hand and took it.

a–a. The pronouns present problems because the context suggests that the Israelite maidservant or her mistress goes in to speak to “her” master, viz., “and she went in and told her lord" (LXX) or "and they went in and told her lord" (Peshitta). The MT presupposes that Naaman went in to tell his master the king after hearing about the matter from his wife. Targum Jonathan agrees with MT.

b-b. MT, *kî ʾak-dĕ'û-nāʾ ûrĕʾû*, lit., "for indeed, know, and see!"

c. Ketiv, *bĕsûsô*, "with his horse," but read with Qere, *bĕsûsāyw*, "with his horses." N.b., LXX reads singular, but Peshitta and Targum Jonathan read plural.

d. Ketiv, *ăbānâ*, "Abanah"; read with Qere, *ămānâ*, "Amanah." Cf. LXX, "Abana"; Targum Jonathan, "Amana"; Peshitta, "Amnan." The name "Abanah" is correct, but MT Qere apparently reads Amanah based on the reference in Song 4:8.

e. MT reads *ʾābî*, "my father!" which functions as an indication of respect for the king (cf. 1 Sam 24:12, where David addresses Saul as "my father"; cf. 2 Kgs 2:12; 6:21; 13:14).

f. MT reads *bĕrākâ*, which normally means "blessing," but may also refer to a gift (see, e.g., Gen 33:11; Josh 15:19; Judg 1:15; 1 Sam 25:27; 30:26); cf. Targum Jonathan, *tiqrûbtāʾ*, "gift, offering."

g. Hebrew, *wālōʾ*, which has conditional force, "if not"; see GKC 104g.

h. Ketiv, *nāʾ*, "please"; read with Qere, which omits the particle altogether.

i. MT reads *zeh*, "this," which conflicts with the plural reference to the two young men.

j. Hebrew, *hāʿōpel*, "the citadel," lit., "the swelling," which is generally used in reference to the citadel in the city of Jerusalem (e.g., Mic 4:8; Isa 32:14; Neh 3:26; 2 Chr 27:3). The versions had difficulties with the use of this term to designate a location in Samaria and instead read it as a form of the root *ʾpl*, "to be dark," viz., LXX, *to skoteinon*, "the dark/hidden (place)"; Targum Jonathan, *leʾătar kĕsî*, "to a covered/hidden place"; Peshitta, *lgnzʾ*, "to a hidden (place)."

k–k. Ketiv, *mēʾān*, lit., "refuses," that is, "has Gehazi refused?"; read with Qere, *mēʿayin*, "where (have you been)?"

l–l. Hebrew, *lōʾ libbî hālak*, lit., "my heart did not go/walk," which is understood to be a rhetorical question; cf. LXX, "Did not my heart go. . ."; Targum Jonathan, "In a spirit of prophecy it was revealed to me (that a man. . .)"; Peshitta, "My heart told me (when a man . . .)."

m–m. Hebrew, *haʿēt lāqaḥat*, "is it a time to take?"; cf. LXX, "and now you have taken"; Targum Jonathan, "is it a time for you that you will take?"

Second Kings 5:1–6:7 presents two prophetic legends[25] that demonstrate Elisha's divinely granted powers of restoration. The first in 2 Kgs 5:1–27 demonstrates the prophet's powers to restore good health to an individual, in this case his healing of Naaman's leprosy. The second in 2 Kgs 6:1–7 illustrates his power to recover a lost object, in this instance an iron ax head that had fallen into the Jordan River. Although the two narratives appear to have little to do

---

25. Burke O. Long, *2 Kings* (FOTL 10; Grand Rapids: Willam B. Eerdmans, 1991), 77, 80; Alexander Rofé, *The Prophetical Stories* (Jerusalem: Magnes, 1988), 13–26; cf. Ernst Würthwein, *Die Bücher der Könige* (Das Alte Testament Deutsch 11/1–2; Göttingen: Vandenhoeck & Ruprecht, 1977), 303.

with each other,[26] they are held together by a combination of formal and thematic features. They are joined syntactically by the introductory *waw*-consecutive verb *wayyōʾmĕrû*, "and they said," in 2 Kgs 6:1. Such a link presupposes the formal definition of the narrative unit, which begins with a combination of the *waw*-conjunctive and a proper name, *wĕnaʿămān*, "and Naaman," in 2 Kgs 5:1, in keeping with the typical formulation of the constitutive narrative units in the Elisha traditions. The two narratives are held together by their concern to demonstrate the prophet's ability to restore that which has been lost, whether it pertains to the health of a human being or to a simple ax head that has dropped into the water. They are also held together by their common interest in the Jordan River, either to heal Naaman's leprosy or to cough up the sunken ax head. The interest in Elisha's powers in relation to the Jordan establishes YHWH's role as G-d of all creation, and it emphasizes the centrality of the land of Israel, particularly the Jordan Valley, as the holy center of creation.

The interest in Elisha's divinely given powers of restoration is hardly limited to the issue of power per se, as both narratives introduce moral elements into their respective presentations. Whereas 2 Kgs 5:1–27 demonstrates Elisha's, or more properly YHWH's, power to heal Naaman and Naaman's recognition of that power, it also points to the prophet's and YHWH's capacity to punish a moral wrong. The presentation of Elisha's servant Gehazi serves this purpose insofar as the narrative portrays his attempt to extort silver and clothing from Naaman by deceit. The prophet's divinely ordained powers are such that he is aware of Gehazi's deception, and punishes his servant accordingly by imposing on him the very leprosy from which Naaman had just been cured. Second Kings 6:1–7 includes a moral dimension insofar as it emphasizes that the lost iron ax head was borrowed (v. 5). The man who had borrowed the ax is responsible for the loss and, according to Exod 22:13–14, is obligated to make restitution. The prophet's powers of restoration are employed to prevent the man from having to suffer loss from a simple accident. In both cases, YHWH's powers over creation enable Elisha to act justly within that created world and to serve as an agent in promoting such action by others, whether Aramean or Israelite.

The concern to demonstrate YHWH's role in relation to creation provides a basis for the claim that YHWH must be recognized as G-d throughout the entire world, although such a claim is necessarily limited to Aram in the present narrative context. Naaman's role as commander of the Aramean army points to the recognition of YHWH as G-d by the man who is the major power behind the Aramean throne. Such nascent universalism is developed more extensively in other biblical literature, such as the Pentateuch, Isaiah, Ezekiel, Psalms, and Proverbs. It functions in a much more limited fashion to point to YHWH as the

---

26. See Stipp, *Elischa*, 359; cf. Schmitt, *Elisa*, 90–91.

true power in the world, despite the reverses suffered by the Omride monarchs in their conflicts with the Arameans, but it also plays a role in providing the basis for the claim that YHWH was ultimately responsible for the overthrow of the Omrides. These traditions were not likely composed for such a purpose; rather, they appear to be local traditions of indeterminate date from the Jordan Valley—perhaps from the sanctuary at Gilgal[27]—that were taken up by the composers of the eighth-century Jehu History to justify Jehu's rule as divinely ordained. Such a setting does not limit the reading and application of the two narratives once the literary context expands. When the Jehu History is read in the context of the various editions of the DtrH, these narratives play their roles in justifying YHWH's overthrow of the northern kingdom of Israel in the Hezekian DtrH, in portraying the role of Josiah as YHWH's agent for the restoration of Israel in the Josianic DtrH, and once again in justifying YHWH's destruction of Jerusalem and the exile of Judah in the exilic DtrH. Given the positive role that restoration plays in pointing to the rise of the Jehu dynasty, the narratives subtly hold out hope for the restoration of Jerusalem and Judah/Israel in the aftermath of the Babylonian exile.

[5:1–27] This composite unit combines concerns with the healing of Naaman in vv. 1–19 and the punishment of Gehazi in vv. 20–27.[28] Each subunit presents a relatively self-contained plot sequence in which the respective narrative tension is resolved: Naaman is healed of his leprosy and recognizes YHWH, and Gehazi attempts to extort cash and goods from Naaman, but is caught and punished. Although the different emphases indicate a combination of plot elements early in the oral development of these traditions, such contentions miss the interrelated nature of the two subplots in the present form of the narrative. These narratives are designed not merely to convey a plot sequence, but to convince their audience to adopt a viewpoint and to undertake action. The contrast between the powerful Aramean commander who recognizes YHWH's power and the subservient Israelite attendant who fails to recognize either YHWH's or the prophet's power is key to the attempt to depict YHWH as the just and powerful master of creation. The Arameans must recognize YHWH's power, but the emphasis on such recognition by a powerful Aramean warrior entails recognition of YHWH within Israel. Gehazi is the means by which the narrative addresses its Israelite audience—that is, not only should this audience recognize YHWH's role in relation to the Arameans, but it must recognize that the depiction of YHWH has consequences within Israel as well. The focus on Gehazi must be read in relation to the attempt to justify the overthrow of the house of Omri in the Jehide History: YHWH is a moral G-d who will punish wrongdoing and support those who act justly. Consequently, the depiction of

27. Cf. Schmitt, *Elisa,* 156–58.
28. For an overview, see Long, *2 Kings,* 68.

Gehazi's punishment works together with Naaman's recognition of YHWH to promote recognition of YHWH and just behavior as the Israelite audience knows that YHWH requires. The contrast between the captured Israelite maid-servant and the deceitful servant of the prophet likewise serves this agenda; if an Israelite maidservant knows YHWH in a foreign land, so must those who remain in the land of Israel.

The structure of the narrative includes an introduction to Naaman in v. 1 and a sequence of episodes in which narrative tension is created and then resolved. Thus, vv. 2–7 focus on Naaman's request for a cure from the Israelite king, who claims to be unable to comply; vv. 8–19 then present the resolution to this tension insofar as Elisha cures Naaman's leprosy and overcomes Naaman's own doubts by convincing him of YHWH's power; vv. 20–27 create tension once again by depicting Gehazi's deceit of Naaman and its resolution in Elisha's punishment of Gehazi. By the end of the narrative, the king of Israel, Gehazi, and the Israelite audience should be convinced that they should adopt the position of Naaman in recognizing YHWH as G-d of all creation.

[1] Naaman's identity marks him as an ideal figure to demonstrates YHWH's power in creation, most notably in Aram. As the commander of the Aramean army, he is responsible for Aram's military successes against Israel. Highly regarded by his king, he has little reason to abandon his position to serve the G-d of his king's enemy. He suffers from leprosy, which renders him ritually unclean (see Lev 13:45–46). The leprosy mentioned in the Bible is not Hansen's disease, which disfigures victims.[29] Because it is found in clothing or in the house (Lev 13:47–59; 14:34–53), it is considered to be a skin disease that might be caused by mold, mildew, or some other growth. The Bible gives little indication of the means by which it is cured other than by bathing or waiting for the symptoms to subside, but the Bible does prescribe procedures for the ritual purification of people and houses once the disease is cured (see Lev 13–14). Because its causes were unknown to ancient Israelites and Judeans, cause and cure were ascribed to YHWH.

[2–7] A conjunctive *waw* joined to a proper noun, *waʾărām*, "and Aram," begins the plot sequence in v. 2. The first episode in vv. 2–7 lays the foundation for the narrative by relating how Naaman becomes aware of the Israelite prophet who will ultimately cure his disease. Two key characters enable the narrative to portray YHWH as the all-powerful G-d of creation and to justify the overthrow of the house of Omri. The unnamed Israelite girl, who is captured and forced to serve Naaman's wife, becomes the agent through whom Naaman learns of Elisha's power and his potential for curing Naaman's leprosy. Although she has much reason to doubt YHWH, she nevertheless demonstrates her confidence in YHWH when she informs her mistress about the prophet of

29. D. P. Wright and R. N. Jones, "Leprosy," *ABD* 4:277–84.

G-d in Samaria, which stands in striking contrast to the powerful Naaman, whose raiding parties were responsible for Israel's subjugation and her own abduction, but who is powerless to do anything about his disease. Naaman is now dependent on YHWH and the prophet.[30]

The second key figure is the Israelite king to whom the king of Aram sends a letter to request a cure for Naaman's leprosy. The narrative employs language characteristic of ancient Aramean and Israelite letters: a letter is called *seper* (lit., "scroll"), the praescriptio of the letter includes the verb *šlḥ* and the name of the recipient, there is a formal greeting and a secondary greeting, and the contents of the letter are introduced by the particle *wĕʿattâ,* "and now."[31] The king sends a considerable sum of money: ten talents of silver, equivalent to some 660 to 1,320 pounds of silver, according to common Mesopotamian measures; six thousand shekels of gold, equivalent to some 110 to 220 pounds of gold; and ten changes of royal clothing.[32] The enormous sum conveys the gravity of the situation to both the king of Aram and Naaman and builds upon the depiction of Naaman as a powerful figure. Each of the characters supports this point; the Israelite girl, Naaman's wife, Naaman, and the Aramean king recognize YHWH's power. This stands in striking contrast to the Israelite king, who tears his garments in mourning and charges that the king of Aram is seeking a pretext to attack Israel. Such a characterization of the Israelite king demonstrates his own lack of confidence in YHWH and the prophet of G-d in his own capital city.

[8–19] The narrative does not disclose how Elisha hears of the Israel king's response to the letter sent him by the Aramean monarch. The later reference to Elisha's knowledge of Gehazi's attempt at deception makes it obvious that the man of G-d knows all because of his divinely given powers. Elisha sends his own letter to the king and advises him to send Naaman to him for treatment. The emphasis on the power of YHWH and of YHWH's prophet appears in the concluding clause of Elisha's message, "and he will know that there is a prophet in Israel." This phrase is an early form of the prophetic proof saying, in which the prophet announces punishment or blessing to demonstrate YHWH's sovereign identity in the world (e.g., 1 Kgs 20:13, 28; Isa 41:17–20; Ezek 12:19–20; 25:6–7; 25:17).[33]

The portrayal of Naaman's arrival emphasizes his power, but the prophet keeps him waiting at the door. In this manner, the narrative highlights the prophet's (and YHWH's) greater power and importance. Elisha's instruction to wash seven times in the Jordan is quite simple. Naaman becomes angry at the slight and apparently expects some elaborate ritual of cleansing in keeping with

30. Cf. Robert L. Cohn, *2 Kings* (Berit Olam; Collegeville, Minn.: Liturgical, 2000), 36–37; Cohn, "Form and Perspective in 2 Kings V," *VT* 33 (1983): 171–84.

31. Dennis Pardee, "An Overview of Ancient Hebrew Epistolography," *JBL* 93 (1994): 1–46.

32. See P. A. Bird, "Weights and Measures," *HBD* 1206–11, esp. 1206.

33. Ronald Hals, *Ezekiel* (FOTL 19; Grand Rapids: Eerdmans, 1989), 353–54.

his understanding of the gravity of the matter. Naaman's angry protests provide the occasion to emphasize YHWH's importance in relation to the land of Israel and the Jordan River. By having Naaman claim that the Abana and Pharpar rivers are just as efficacious as the Jordan, the narrative sets him up for a fall. The Abana is identified with the Barada River, which has its sources in the Anti-Lebanon Range, some twenty-three miles northwest of Damascus.[34] The Pharpar is identified with the el-Awaj River, which has its sources on Mount Hermon, and runs northeast, east, and southeast to water the oasis region (Ghouta) some ten miles south of Damascus.[35] Although the Abana and Pharpar give life to Damascus and its environs, the Jordan, located in YHWH's land of Israel, is the source of Naaman's healing. By reminding him that he would have followed the prophet's instructions had he asked something greater or more elaborate, Naaman's soldiers inform him that the issue is the source of the instruction, not the nature of the act.

Some interpreters argue that the original narrative ends at v. 14, and that a new concern with Gehazi's deceit begins in v. 15 with its focus on the question of Naaman's offer of a gift to Elisha.[36] Such a contention misses the importance of the role that Naaman's recognition of YHWH plays in the narrative. By declining to accept the gift, the narrative portrays both YHWH's and Elisha's magnanimity and highlights once again the relative power of Naaman and Elisha. Naaman arrives with all of his "army," but he stands before the man of G-d and states that he now gets the point: "I know that there is no G-d in all the earth, except in Israel." His urging Elisha to accept the gift emphasizes gratitude and subservience. Realizing that he will not convince Elisha, he calls for two mule loads of Israelite soil to take back with him to Aram so that he can worship the G-d of Israel on Israel's own soil. Naaman's parting request that YHWH pardon his worship of Rimmon, an alternative name of the Aramean storm god, Hadad,[37] caricaturizes the man to the Israelite audience. He engages in such worship to support the aged king, who is no longer the true power in Aram. Naaman is the true power behind the throne, but YHWH is the true power behind Naaman.

[20–27] The point of this episode is not to condemn Israelite chauvinism against foreigners, but to emphasize the moral character of YHWH as the G-d of all creation (cf. Seow, "The First and Second Books of Kings," 197–98). Identification of Gehazi as "the attendant of Elisha, the man of G-d" suggests that this narrative once functioned outside of its present literary context in which Gehazi is first introduced, but in the present context it emphasizes Gehazi's Israelite identity and ties to the prophet. Thus, the narrative empha-

34. R. L. Roth, "Abana," *ABD* 1:6.

35. H. O. Thompson, "Pharpar," *ABD* 5:303–4.

36. E.g., Schmitt, *Elisa*, 78–80.

37. J. C. Greenfield, "The Aramean God Rammān/Rimmōn," *IEJ* 26 (1976): 195–98.

sizes that YHWH's moral character as G-d of all creation entails expectations of Israelites and Arameans. Elisha's refusal to take payment highlights the power relationship between the prophet and Naaman outlined above: Elisha doesn't need anything from Naaman, but Naaman needs Elisha. The narrative points to a similar relationship between Naaman and Gehazi. Naaman needs nothing from Gehazi, but he is willing to give Gehazi whatever he asks because of his gratitude. Naaman shows Gehazi considerable respect, by dismounting his chariot to meet this humble servant of the prophet. Gehazi begins the conversation by lying to Naaman. His statement borrows from the formal language of ancient Aramean and Hebrew letters noted above; there is an initial salutation, *šālôm*, "peace," a statement that his master has sent (*šlḥ*) him, and the particle, *ʿattâ*, "now," which introduces the content of the message. Gehazi's request for a talent of silver and two changes of clothing does not demand the entire amount of cash and goods carried by Naaman. The request is a classic model of graft. The contrast in character continues when Naaman wraps the gifts up and sends his own attendants to carry the packages before Gehazi.

The account of Gehazi's appearance before Elisha begins in v. 25 with an introductory conjunctive, *waw*, combined with the pronoun *hûʾ*, "and he," to alert the reader to the shift in scene. Elisha's interrogation of Gehazi is ironic, insofar as the following material demonstrates that Elisha already knows what Gehazi has done. Nevertheless, he asks Gehazi where he has been, which provides Gehazi with the opportunity to lie once again. The reader wonders how Gehazi ever could have believed that he could lie to Elisha, but the emphasis on Gehazi's lie to his master removes any ambiguities about Gehazi's guilt. Elisha's rhetorical question emphasizes the uses to which Gehazi would put the cash. Gehazi's attempt to take gifts from Naaman is not only dishonest, it reverses the power relationship established between Elisha and Naaman previously—that is, YHWH/Elisha give to Naaman, and Naaman is the dependent party. By taking a gift from Naaman, Gehazi has restored Naaman's standing as a power figure.

[6:1–7] Although 2 Kgs 6:1–7 constitutes an entirely different narrative, it is joined syntactically to 2 Kgs 5:1–27 by its initial *waw*-consecutive verb, *wayyōʾmĕrû*, "and they said." Both episodes are concerned with Elisha's divinely granted powers, and both portray those powers in relation to the Jordan River. The present instance begins with a change of residence for the band of prophets led by Elisha. The narrative presents two issues in the loss of the ax head: (1) the man is unable to recover it, presumably because the water is too deep, and (2) it is borrowed, which means that he is responsible for the loss of the ax head to its owner (cf. Exod 22:13–14). The first indicates a problem of power (how to recover the ax that is otherwise impossible to recover), and the second is one of morality (the man is obligated to repay the owner for the loss of the ax).

2 Kings 6:8–7:20 Elisha's Power over the King of Aram at Samaria

6:8 The King of Aram was fighting against Israel and took counsel with his servants, saying, "At such and such a place ᵃI will encamp.ᵃ" 9 And the man of G-d sent to the King of Israel, saying, "Be careful when passing by this place, because Aram ᵇis coming down there.ᵇ" 10 And the King of Israel sent ᶜa warningᶜ to the place which the man of G-d mentioned to him, and he was careful there time and again. 11 The heart of the King of Aram was upset concerning this matter, so he called to his servants and said to them, "Will you not tell me who from among us is with the King of Israel?" 12 And one of his servants said to him, "No, my lord, the King, for Elisha the prophet, who is in Israel, tells the King of Israel the words which you speak in your bed chamber." 13 And he said, "Go and see whereᵈ he is, and I will send and take him!" And it was told to him, saying, "Behold, in Dothan." 14 He sent there horses, a chariot, and a powerful army, and they came at night and surrounded the city. 15 An assistant of the man of G-d rose early and went out, and behold, an army with horse and chariot surrounded the city, and his attendant said to him, "Alas, my lord, what shall we do?" 16 And he said, "Do not fear, because many more are with us than are with them." 17 And Elisha prayed and said, "O YHWH, open please his eyes that he might see." And YHWH opened the eyes of the attendant, and he saw, and behold, the mountain was filled with horses and chariots of fire around Elisha. 18 They came down to him, and Elisha prayed to YHWH and said, "Strike, please, this nation with blindness." And he struck them with blindness according to the word of Elisha. 19 Elisha said to them, "Not this way and not this city. Follow after me, and I will lead you to the man whom you seek." And he led them to Samaria. 20 And when they came to Samaria, Elisha said, "O YHWH, open the eyes of these people, that they may see." And YHWH opened their eyes, and they saw, and behold, they were in the midst of Samaria. 21 The King of Israel said to Elisha when he saw them, "ᵉShould I strike them, should I strike them,ᵉ my father?" 22 And he said to them, "You should not strike them. Shall you strike those whom you have captured with your sword and your bow? Place food and water before them so they may eat and drink. Then send them away so they may go to their masters." 23 And he prepared for them a great banquet, and they ate and they drank, and he sent them away, and they went to their masters, and Aramean raiding parties did not come to the land of Israel again.

24 Afterwards, Ben Hadad, King of Aram, gathered all his camp, went up, and besieged Samaria. 25 And there was a great famine in Samaria, and behold, the siege continued until a head of an ass sold for eighty shekels of silver in Samaria, and a quarter qab of ᶠpigeon dungᶠ sold for five

shekels. 26 The King of Israel was passing by upon the wall when a woman cried to him, saying, "Save (me), my lord, the King!" 27 And he said, "ᵍYHWH will not save you.ᵍ How could I save you? From the threshing floor or the wine vat?" 28 And the King said to her, "What is your problem?" And she said, "This woman said to me, 'Give up your son, that we may eat him today, and my son we shall eat tomorrow.' 29 So we cooked my son and ate him, and I said to her on the following day, 'Give up your son that we may eat him,' but she hid her son." 30 When the King heard the words of the woman, he tore his garments, and as he went by on the wall, the people saw, and behold, he was wearing sackcloth on his body underneath. 31 And he said, "Thus shall G-d do to me and even more so, if the head of Elisha ben Shaphat shall stand upon him today!"

32 And Elisha was sitting in his house and the elders were sitting with him, and he (the king) sent a man before him. Before the messenger could come to him, he (Elisha) said to the elders, "Have you seen that this son of a murderer has sent for my head? Look, when the messenger comes, shut the door, and restrain him at the door. Is not the sound of his master's feet behind him?" 33 While he was speaking with them, behold, the messenger was coming down to him, and he said, "Behold, this evil is from YHWH. Why should I wait longer for YHWH?"

7:1 And Elisha said, "Hear the word of YHWH! Thus says YHWH, 'At this time tomorrow, a seah of flour will sell for a shekel and two seahs of barley will sell for a shekel in the gate of Samaria.'" 2 And the officer of the King on whose hand he was supported answered the man of G-d and said, "Behold! YHWH is making windows in the heavens! Shall such a thing come to pass?" And he said, "Behold, you will see with your eyes, but from it you shall not eat!"

3 Four leprous men at the city gate said to each other, "Why are we sitting here until we die? 4 If we say, 'let us enter the city,' then the famine is in the city, and we die there, but if we sit here, then we die. And now, come, let us fall into the camp of Aram; either they will let us live and we will live, or they will kill us and we will die." 5 And they arose at twilight to enter the camp of Aram and came to the edge of the camp of Aram, and behold, there was no one there. 6 And the L-rd had caused the camp of Aram to hear the sound of chariots, horses, and a great army, and they said to each other, "Behold, the King of Israel has hired against us the kings of the Hittites and the kings of Egypt to come against us." 7 So they arose and fled at twilight and abandoned their tents, horses, and asses. The camp was just as it was, since they fled for their lives. 8 So these lepers came to the edge of the camp, and they entered one tent, ate, and drank, and they carried off from there silver and gold and garments, and they went and hid (them), and they returned and entered another tent, and they

carried off from there, and they went and hid. 9 And they said each to the other, "It's not right what we do today! It is a day of good news, and we are silent. If we wait until the light of morning, we will incur guilt. And now, let us go and tell the house of the King." 10 And they went and called out to the gatekeeper[h] of the city, and they told them saying, "We went to the camp of Aram, and behold, no one was there nor even the sound of a man, but the horses and the asses are tethered, and the tents are just as they are." 11 So the gatekeepers called out and informed the house of the King inside. 12 And the King arose in the night and said to his servants, "I will tell you, indeed, what Aram has done to us! They know that we are starving, so they went out from the camp to hide in the field,[i] saying, 'When they come out from the city, we shall seize them alive and enter the city.'" 13 And one of his servants answered and said, "Let them take now five of the remaining horses—[j]behold they are what is left of all the multitude of Israel—behold they are what is left of all the multitude of Israel that has perished,[j] and we will send them and see." 14 So they took two chariot teams of horses, and the King sent them after the camp of Aram, saying, "Go and see!" 15 And they went after them to the Jordan, and behold, the entire road was full of garments and equipment which Aram had thrown away in their flight,[k] and the messengers returned and told the King. 16 And the people went out and plundered the camp of Aram, and a seah of flour sold for a shekel and two seahs of barley sold for a shekel according to the word of YHWH. 17 And the King assigned the officer on whose hand he was supported to the gate, and the people trampled him in the gate, and he died just as the man of G-d had spoken when the King[l] came down to him. 18 And it was in accordance with the word of the man of G-d to the King, saying, "Two seahs of barley will sell for a shekel, and a seah of flour will sell for a shekel at this time tomorrow in the gate of Samaria." 19 And the officer answered the man of G-d and said, "And behold, if YHWH is making windows in the heavens, shall such a thing take place?" And he said, "Behold, you will see with your eyes, but you will not eat from it." 20 And so it happened to him, and the people trampled him in the gate so that he died.

a–a. MT reads *taḥănōtî,* a hapax legomenon derived from the root *ḥnh,* "to encamp," which means "my encampment" (uninflected feminine noun, *taḥănōt* [HALOT 1719] or *taḥănâ* [BDB 334]). The usual Hebrew noun for "camp" is *maḥăneh,* which refers throughout the Elisha narratives to the Aramean army (e.g., 2 Kgs 3:9; 7:16). Septuagint, Peshitta, and Vulgate read the expression as a verb, i.e., LXX, *parembalō,* "(in such a place) I will lie (in wait)"; Peshitta, *wᵓttšw,* "in such and such a place, and hide"; Vulgate, *ponamus insidias,* "(in such and such a place) we lie in ambush," which suggests that the term is a corrupted form of the verb *tēḥābĕᵓû,* "you shall hide," or (more likely), *tinḥătû,* "you shall go down (to lie in wait)" (see *nĕḥittîm,* "[for there, Aram] is lying [in wait]" in v. 9 below; e.g., Thenius 292; Klostermann 408–9). Targum Jonathan reads the expression as a noun, *la'ătar kĕsî ûtmîr bêt mašranā'*, "at a hidden and concealed place is our camp." Because of the difficulty, it is best to conclude that *tahănōtî*, "my encampment," is original, and that the LXX, Peshitta, and Vulgate resolve the difficulty by reading a verb.

b–b. MT reads *nĕhittîm*, "(Aram) is descending, i.e., lying in wait." The versions read the term as an indication of ambush, viz., LXX, "(for the Syrians) are hidden (there)"; Peshitta, "(for the Arameans) are lying in wait (there)"; Targum Jonathan, "(for the men of Aram) are hiding (there)."

c–c. Ketiv, *wĕhizhîrāh*, lit., "and he warned it"; Qere, *wĕhizhîrô*, lit., "and he warned it."

d. MT, *'êkōh*, would normally be understood as *'êkâ*, "how," but it likely reflects a northern Israelite term for "where"; cf. Aramaic, *'êkā'*, "where" (cf. BDB 32).

e–e. MT, *ha'akkeh 'akkeh*, lit., "shall I strike, I strike?" Many interpreters presuppose that one of the verbal forms should be read as the infinitive absolute, *hahakkēh*, "shall I surely strike?" with LXX, *Ei pataxas pataxō*, "shall I surely strike?" but Targum Jonathan and Peshitta read with MT.

f–f. Ketiv, *hărê yônîm*, "shit of pigeons," a crude term; read with Qere, *dibyônîm*, "pigeon dung."

g–g. Many struggle with the wording and syntax of this statement to translate it as a conditional statement or as an assertion of YHWH's willingness to help, but the jussive function of *'al yôši'ek yhwh*, "let YHWH not save you," requires that it function as a curse or as a statement of YHWH's inability or unwillingness to save the woman (cf. Cogan and Tadmor 80).

h. MT reads *šō'ēr*, "gatekeeper," which conflicts with the following plural pronoun, "and they told them, saying." Targum Jonathan and Peshitta read the term as plural, "gatekeepers," but LXX reads as the noun *tēn pulēn*, "the gate," which presupposes Hebrew, *ša'ar*.

i. Ketiv, *bĕhaśśādeh*, which preserves the definite article; read with Qere, *baśśśādeh*, "in the field." GKC 35n maintains that cases in which the definite article are not elided when preceded by a preposition appear primarily in late literature (e.g., Ezek 40:25; 47:22; Qoh 8:1; Dan 8:16; Neh 9:19), but notes instances in earlier literature as well (e.g., 1 Sam 13:21; 2 Sam 21:20).

j–j. The versions take different approaches to the problem posed by the repetition of this phrase; viz., LXX eliminates the second instance, "behold, they are to all that is left of the multitude of Israel"; Peshitta both eliminates the duplication and reworks the phrase, "if they are captured, let them be considered like all the army of Israel that has perished"; Targum Jonathan preserves both phrases, but reworks them in an attempt to make sense, "the rest that remain in it, behold, they are like all the multitude of Israel that is left in it; and if they are destroyed, behold, they are like all the multitude of Israel that has perished." The second phrase may be a gloss that explains the meaning of the first by specifying that those horses that remain are all that are left after the many horses once possessed by Israel perished in the Aramean attacks and siege.

k. Ketiv, *bĕhēhāpĕzām*; read with Qere, *bĕhēhāpĕzām*, "in their flight."

l. MT, *hammelek*, "the king"; LXX and Peshitta read "messenger," Hebrew, *hammal'āk*. Cf. 6:32–33, which notes that the messenger will come, but his master (the king) will come afterward.

Second Kings 6:8–7:20 presents two interrelated episodes that demonstrate Elisha's—and therefore, YHWH's—power over the king of Aram at Samaria. Although the focus is upon the defense of the city of Samaria against the threat posed by the Arameans, the larger literary context of the traditions concerning Elisha's (and Elijah's) remarkable powers plays an important role in determining its function. When read in relation to other Elisha traditions in 2 Kgs 3:3–8:15, this pericope emerges as another element in the chain of traditions that demonstrates that Jehu's overthrow of the house of Omri is an act of YHWH. Within the broader context of the DtrH, the pericope points to YHWH as the omnipotent G-d of creation, who brings foreign nations, for example, Aram, Assyria, or Babylonia, to Israel and defeats them when it serves divine purposes.

The passage is demarcated in the typical manner of the Elisha traditions, beginning in 2 Kgs 6:8 with a conjunctive *waw* followed by a noun clause: *ûmelek ʾărām*, "and the King of Aram (was fighting)." The first episode continues through 2 Kgs 6:23 with an account of the Aramean king's attempt to capture Elisha in Dothan and Elisha's ability to blind the Arameans and to lead them into the city of Samaria. The second episode in 2 Kgs 6:24–7:20 is linked syntactically to the first by its introductory *waw*-consecutive formulation, *wayĕhî ʾaḥărê-kēn wayyiqbōṣ ben-hădad melek-ʾărām ʾet-kol-maḥănēhû*, "and afterwards, Ben-Hadad, King of Aram, gathered his camp. . . ," which introduces a new narrative sequence concerned with Elisha's ability to foresee that the famine prompted by the Aramean siege of Samaria would be relieved when YHWH would compel the Arameans to flee to Aram in fear. Although a typical introductory conjunctive *waw* formation followed by the proper name "Elisha" appears in 2 Kgs 6:32, this particular notice is subsumed under the larger concern with the prophet's role in the relief of the famine in Samaria brought on by the Aramean siege. In the present context, this notice simply directs the reader's attention to a new character, Elisha, following the portrayal of the severity of the famine in the preceding verses, which relate the complaint of the woman who gave up her son to be eaten. The plot only concludes in 2 Kgs 7:20 when the text reiterates how the king's officer died in accordance with the word of YHWH when he expressed disbelief in the prophet's ability to foresee the relief.

Literary tensions within this material indicate that it is a combination of at least two originally independent narratives.[38] The first episode concerning Elisha's deception of the Aramean army in 2 Kgs 6:8–23 identifies neither the Aramean nor the Israelite king. It initially identifies Elisha only as "the man of G-d" and increasingly employs his name only as the narrative progresses to its

---

38. Cf. Robert LaBarbera, "The Man of War and the Man of G-d: Social Satire in 2 Kings 6:8–7:20," *CBQ* 46 (1984): 637–51, who likewise maintains that 2 Kgs 6:8–7:20 comprises two interrelated stories. Contra Rofé, *Prophetical Stories*, 60–70; Schweizer, *Elischa in den Kriegen*, 211–406; Stipp, *Elischa*, 320–58, who treat the two stories separately.

culmination. Such a literary device demonstrates that Elisha is indeed "the man of G-d." By contrast, the second narrative in 2 Kgs 6:24–7:20 identifies the Aramean king as Ben-Hadad at the outset, although it refers subsequently only to "the camp of Aram" and leaves the king of Israel as an anonymous figure. The second narrative also refers to Elisha by name throughout, apart from the concluding references to him as "the man of G-d," in 2 Kgs 7:17, 18, and 19, that tie the two parts of this subunit together. Although both narratives are ultimately concerned with Samaria, the first initially places Elisha in Dothan (2 Kgs 6:13) before he leads the Aramean army to Samaria, whereas the second presupposes that his house is located in Samaria (see 2 Kgs 6:32–7:2). When read separately, the first narrative demonstrates Elisha's power to know what the Aramean king says as well as the prophet's ability to invoke YHWH to strike the Arameans blind. A key element in this narrative is the demonstration to Elisha's servant of YHWH's otherwise unseen chariots, horses, and soldiers. Although Elisha's power is clear, the narrative demonstrates his magnanimity as well when it depicts the prophet's instruction that the Israelite king should prepare food for the Arameans rather than kill them. The second narrative is likewise concerned with Elisha's ability to invoke YHWH, but it focuses instead on the disbelief of the Israelite king's officer, who suffers death because he questioned the prophet's ability to lift the famine. Although these motifs demonstrate the separate origins of the two subunits, it is striking how they appeal to the audience by presenting the contrasting fates of Elisha's faithful servant and the king's faithless officer. Such a contrasting portrayal appeals to the audience of this combined tradition to follow the example of Elisha's servant. After the house of Omri and its supporters are destroyed, it points to the Israelite king and his servants as figures who ultimately suffer for abandoning YHWH.

These considerations indicate that 2 Kgs 6:8–7:20 was composed to function as part of the eighth-century Jehu History. Second Kings 6:8–7:20 demonstrates that YHWH, working through Elisha, is the true power capable of defeating the Arameans even when they play a key, albeit secondary, role in overthrowing the house of Omri. The narrative demonstrates YHWH's decisive role in northern Israel's and Judah's history when it is successively taken up in the Hezekian, Josian, and exilic DtrH editions. The concern to demonstrate Elisha's and YHWH's power over the Arameans figures prominently in the earliest versions of these narratives as well, insofar as they indicate Israelite fear of the Arameans and hope in YHWH's power to overcome them. This consideration suggests that the narratives originated separately during the late ninth century, either at a time when Aram threatened Israel or afterward when the threat had subsided (see 2 Kgs 13:1–9).[39]

---

39. Cf. Rofé, *Prophetical Stories,* 70–74, who places the Elisha legends in the time of the Jehu dynasty.

[6:8–23] This narrative displays a concern with divine justice insofar as Elisha advises the king of Israel not to harm the Arameans when they are brought into Samaria, but to provide them with food and drink before sending them back to Aram where they will announce YHWH's/Elisha's power and mercy. The narrative alleviates concern in Israel with the threat posed by the Arameans by demonstrating that they are ultimately subject to YHWH's control.

The narrative begins with a notice that the king of Aram was fighting against Israel, but it leaves no clue as to the historical setting of the narrative other than the general background of the Aramean/Israelite wars of the ninth century B.C.E. The anonymity of the narrative contributes to its legendary character, particularly when it turns to the prophet's miraculous powers. The setting of Aram's wars against Israel provides the occasion to turn to the demonstrations of Elisha's powers when the Aramean king calls his officers together to discuss a problem experienced during the current campaign. Somehow "the man of G-d" has been able to inform the king of Israel of the sites where the Aramean army is deployed. The narrator indicates that the Israelite king was careful enough to send scouts to the sites identified by the man of G-d to confirm the danger, and having done so, was able to avoid Aramean ambushes. Such a contention presumes Aramean military superiority over the Israelites, who appear to be on the defensive throughout the narrative.

The plot advances to its concern with the prophet's power when it relates how one of the Aramean officers claims that the Israelite prophet, Elisha, tells the king of Israel everything that the Aramean king says, even in the privacy of his own bedroom. Only at this point is Elisha identified by name, occupation, and residency, which begins to lift the aura of mystery with which the episode began by referring elliptically only to "the king of Aram," "the king of Israel," and "the man of G-d." The Aramean king issues orders for the capture of Elisha, and is told that the prophet is in Dothan. Dothan is a crucial location, both for narrative purposes and for understanding the strategic issues of Aram's invasion of Israel. Ancient Dothan is identified with Tel Dothan, located near modern Jenin some twelve miles north of Samaria and thirteen and a half miles north of Shechem at the point where the Emeq Dothan (Dothan Valley) opens into the Jezreel Valley. Emeq Dothan provides access to the Jezreel from Samaria, which makes it possible to control the Jezreel. Indeed, the site of Jezreel, where the Omride dynasty maintained an estate, is located in the very center of the Jezreel Valley approximately twelve miles north of Dothan. Samaria's strategic location near the head of the Emeq Dothan was one of the major reasons to shift the capital from Tirzah. Of course, if the Emeq Dothan provides access to the Jezreel from Samaria, it also provides access to Samaria from the Jezreel. Elisha's location at Dothan would therefore place him at the very site that determines Israel's ability to control the Jezreel. Given the Jezreel's importance, both as an agricultural breadbasket and as the site of the key east-west trade route between the Mediterranean coastal plain and the Transjordanian routes to Damascus and the Gulf of Aqaba, the Jezreel emerges as the geographical key to northern Israel's military and economic power. Dothan was a fortified city with a large public building equipped with store-rooms. The site was destroyed during the ninth century B.C.E., apparently by the Arameans, and again in the eighth century B.C.E., apparently by the Assyrians.[40]

The narrative portrays an Aramean capture of Dothan in an effort to demon-strate Elisha's power over the Arameans. The servant of the prophet emerges as an important figure. When he awakens in the morning, he sees the powerful Aramean force surrounding the city and asks Elisha, "My lord, what shall we do?" The prophet's response in v. 16 employs a typical example of the prophetic reassurance formula, *'al tîrā'*, "do not fear," which is employed in prophetic lit-erature to indicate that there is no need for concern in the face of danger.[41] Elisha prays to YHWH for the first time, asking that YHWH might open the eyes of the servant so that he can see the divine army of horses and chariots arrayed upon the hill around Elisha. Such an account draws upon ancient notions of prophetic visionary experience in which such visions are apparent to prophetic figures but not to those around them.[42] By portraying Elisha's reassurance of the servant, the narrative ensures that the reader understands that YHWH will ultimately overcome the Aramean threat.

Verse 18 presents the prophet's second prayer, but in this case he asks that YHWH strike the Arameans with blindness. Most interpreters understand the Hebrew term *sanwērîm* to refer to some temporary blindness (e.g., Hobbs 78; Cogan and Tadmor 74). The term appears elsewhere only in Gen 19:11 to describe the blindness of the men of Sodom. A clinical diagnosis of the blind-ness, however, misses its ironic narrative function, insofar as Elisha is able to lead the entire Aramean army up the Emeq Dothan to Samaria. The Arameans do not know that Elisha is the man for whom they search. Upon arrival in Samaria, Elisha calls on YHWH to open their eyes, and the Arameans now real-ize their situation—and the power of Israel's prophet. The portrayal of that power is enhanced by Elisha's response to the Israelite king's excited request—he states it repeatedly, much like a child—that he be allowed to strike down the Arameans. This provides Elisha with the opportunity to remind the impetuous Israelite king that the Arameans are to be treated as prisoners of war and should not be killed (cf. Deut 20:10–15). Such a display of magnanimity is also a dis-play of confidence in one's own—and YHWH's—power.

40. David Ussishkin, "Dothan," *NEAEHL* 1:372–74; W. G. Dever, "Dothan," *ABD* 2:226–27.

41. M. A. Sweeney, *Isaiah 1–39, with an Introduction to Prophetic Literature* (FOTL 16; Grand Rapids and Cambridge: Eerdmans, 1996), 547; Edgar W. Conrad, *Fear Not Warrior: A Study of 'al tîr~' Pericopes in the Hebrew Scriptures* (BJS 75; Chico, Calif.: Scholars Press, 1985).

42. See, e.g., the satirical account of the vision of YHWH's angel by Balaam's ass in Num 22:22–35; Joshua's vision of the angelic commander of YHWH's army in Josh 5:13–15; or Samuel's visionary experience of YHWH's call while sleeping before the ark at Shiloh in 1 Sam 3:1–18.

[6:24–7:20] This subunit builds upon the first subunit by portraying the inability of the Israelite king and his officer to recognize that YHWH will ultimately act on behalf of Israel. The subunit reinforces its point by emphasizing that a group of four lepers, considered as outcasts in ancient society, were the first to recognize what the king and his officers were unable to accept: that the Arameans had fled when they heard the sounds of YHWH's chariots, horses, and army.

The literary structure of this subunit is indicated by a combination of formal-linguistic and thematic grounds, insofar as each episode of the subunit begins with a combination of a conjunctive *waw* followed by a noun or a personal name.[43] Second Kings 6:24–31 portrays the king's view that neither YHWH nor Elisha will lift the Aramean siege due to his inability to provide any assistance to the desperate woman who ate her own son. Second Kings 6:32–7:2 portrays Elisha's prophecy that food will become readily available in Samaria when YHWH lifts the siege of the city together with the condemnation of the king's officer sent to arrest him. Second Kings 7:3–16 portrays the discovery of the Aramean flight from Samaria together with the king's suspicions that the flight is an Aramean trap, which had nothing to do with YHWH's assistance to the city. Finally, 2 Kgs 7:17–20 portrays the death of the Israelite army officer in fulfillment of Elisha's earlier prophecy that he would not live to see the relief of the famine in the city caused by the Aramean siege. This narrative thereby functions as a prophetic confrontation story, in which a prophet's legitimacy is confirmed in the context of an opponent's challenge (cf. 1 Kgs 22:1–40; Isa 36–37).[44]

[6:24–31] The introductory temporal formula *wayĕhî ʾaḥărê-kēn*, "and afterwards," ties the present subunit together with 2 Kgs 6:8–23. The phrase introduces the narrative action with the notice in v. 24 that Ben Hadad, king of Aram, had gathered his army to besiege Samaria. The narrative supplies at least a minimal historical context insofar as it identifies him as the Aramean king who attacked Ahab in the days of Elijah (1 Kgs 20). Such an association also points to Ahab's role in ensuring the destruction of his house, since he failed to capitalize on the opportunity to destroy Ben Hadad. Not only did Ahab die in battle against the Arameans (1 Kgs 22), his son is now threatened by Ben Hadad. The present literary context requires that the king be identified as Jehoram ben Ahab, since this unit appears within his regnal report in 2 Kgs 3:1–8:15.

Famine provides the backdrop for the portrayal of the desperate plight of an ancient city under siege. The ability to withstand siege depends on the ability to wait longer than the attacking forces. The cost of food items otherwise considered undesirable points to a city that is running out of supplies. The head of

43. Cf. Rofé, *Prophetical Stories*, 63–64, who opts for a similar three-part structure by subsuming 2 Kgs 7:17–20 under 7:3–16.

44. Sweeney, *Isaiah 1–39*, 518.

an ass is unfit for human consumption (Deut 14; Lev 11), but siege conditions and starvation prompt people to eat just about anything. The price of eighty shekels is a considerable sum of money. Nehemiah 5:15 indicates that forty shekels is a very heavy tax burden, and Lev 27 calls for an annual temple tax of fifty shekels for each man, thirty shekels for each woman, and so on. A quarter qab of pigeon dung is a source of fuel for fire (cf. Ezek 4:12–15) or an idiomatic reference to seeds or husks that were normally not eaten. Rabbinic sources identify a qab as one-eighteenth of an ephah or about one and six-tenths of a dry quart.[45]

The portrayal of the woman's appeal to the king indicates the sheer desperation of the people in the city. As the king walks the wall, a woman cries out to him for help, and he responds that he lacks anything to give her. A monarch's responsibility includes the storage of supplies for use during siege or other emergencies.[46] The woman tells the king a chilling story of having agreed with another woman to eat their sons. The women first ate her son, but the other woman hid her son when the time came to eat him (cf. 1 Kgs 3:16–28).[47] The king's reaction indicates his own sense of despair: he tears his garments as a sign of mourning, and the people see that he was already wearing sackcloth, another sign of mourning. This is a remarkable portrayal of the king of Israel, since royal ideology indicates that monarchs ruled with the support and blessing of YHWH (see 2 Sam 7; 1 Kgs 11; Isa 7; 36–39/2 Kgs 18–20). His concluding statement, cast in the form of a vow to remove Elisha's head, indicates his outlook—that is, YHWH has abandoned Samaria to its fate, and Elisha is a traitor who failed to employ his powers to intercede with YHWH.

[6:32–7:2] The second episode begins with a characteristic conjunctive *waw* followed by the name Elisha, *weʾĕlîšāʿ*, "and Elisha," who is sitting in his house with the elders. The location of the house is not given, although it is presumably in Samaria rather than in Dothan since Samaria is under siege. The presence of the elders in Elisha's house suggests that they have gathered to consult the prophet for an oracle from YHWH (cf. Ezek 8:1). Their deliberations will be interrupted by the king's messenger sent to arrest Elisha so that he might be executed (see 2 Kgs 6:31). Of course, Elisha's divinely granted powers enable him to see the approach and purpose of the messenger prior to his arrival, much as he was able to tell the Israelite king all of the Aramean king's plans and words in 2 Kgs 6:8–23. The prophet's view of the king is well expressed when he refers

45. W. G. Dever, "Weights and Measures," *HBD* 1211.

46. Large storage pits for grain are characteristic of ancient Israelite cities, e.g., Megiddo (Yigal Shiloh, "Megiddo," *NEAEHL* 3:1023), and the administrative building excavated at Dothan includes many storage rooms. Cf. Gen 41, in which Joseph stores grain for future use in Egypt.

47. E.g., Stuart Lasine, "Jehoram and the Cannibal Mothers (2 Kings 6:24–33): Solomon's Judgment in an Inverted World," *JSOT* 50 (1991): 27–53, who observes that the narrative portrays a topsy-turvy world that Solomon's wisdom would not have been able to address.

to him as "this son of a murderer." Such an epithet would call to mind the king's present purpose, but it would more properly refer to the role played by Ahab, father of the present king Jehoram, in killing off the sons of the prophets (1 Kgs 18). Elisha's predictions are confirmed when the messenger arrives. His statements indicate his abandonment of any hope in YHWH. By claiming that "this evil comes from YHWH," he declares that YHWH has chosen to bring about the Aramean siege rather than to defend the city. The second part of his statement is even more telling. By rhetorically asking how he could hope in YHWH, he categorically states that he in fact has no hope in YHWH. Such a sentiment corresponds precisely to the viewpoint of the king.

Second Kings 7:1 employs the typical forms of the call to attention, "hear the word of YHWH," and the prophetic messenger formula, "thus says YHWH," to indicate that the anticipated word of YHWH arrives.[48] The following oracle indicates how food will become readily available once the siege is lifted. Elisha states that a seah of flour and two seahs of barley will each sell on the next day for a shekel in the gate of Samaria. A seah is a measure of uncertain size, although LXX texts suggest it is equivalent to one and one-half modii or one-third of a bushel.[49] The officer questions Elisha's statement beginning with his observation that YHWH will open the windows of heaven, which is an idiomatic statement that YHWH will bring rain and food to the land (cf. Gen 7:11; Isa 24:18; Mal 3:10). Rain is not at issue at this point, but the reference ties into the larger theme of the narrative polemics against Baal by claiming that YHWH and not Baal is G-d of creation and bringer of rain and food (1 Kgs 17–19). The question, "shall such a thing happen?" indicates the officer's doubt in the prophet. Elisha's response that his eyes will see this event but that he will not eat the food points to the coming confirmation of his prophetic statement (see vv. 17–20 below).

[**7:3–16**] The third episode begins with a conjunctive *waw* coupled with a noun phrase, *wĕʾarbāʿâ ʾănāšîm hāyû mĕṣōrāʿîm* (lit., "and four men (who) were lepers"). Persons suffering from leprosy in ancient Israel were considered to be unclean, and were required to live outside of the community until they were cured (see Lev 13:34–36; cf. Num 12:15). The lepers provide a counterpoint to the king of Israel. They are excluded from the normal life of the city and left at its gates to beg or to perform undesirable tasks to make their living. They represent the lowest stratum of Israelite society in contrast to the king, who represents the apex of that society. But the narrative portrays the lepers as the ones who finally discover that the Arameans have abandoned their siege of the city, whereas the king is completely unaware that the Arameans have fled and refuses to believe that they have left, even after he is informed of the fact by the leprous eyewitnesses.

48. Sweeney, *Isaiah 1–39*, 544, 546.
49. Dever, "Weights and Measures," *HBD* 1210.

The portrayal of the lepers' actions illustrates their plight: if they enter the city, they will die because of the famine brought about by the siege; if they stay where they are, they will die because they are exposed to Aramean attack and lack food in any case. They reason that they have nothing to lose, and they determine to surrender themselves to the Arameans. They make their move at twilight, in part so that the darkness will hide their movements as they attempt to sneak into the Aramean camp and in part because the darkness will hide their leprosy and at least give them a chance to surrender to the Arameans without being killed or driven away.

The narrative informs the reader that the Arameans had heard the sound of chariots, horses, and a great army, which would be the army of YHWH mentioned in 2 Kgs 6:8–23. Contrary to the expectation of the Israelite king, YHWH took action to protect the Israelite nation. The narrators' portrayal of the Arameans' comments that the king of Israel must have hired the kings of the Hittites and the kings of the Egyptians indicates the political possibilities of the day. The Hittites would refer to a number of Neo-Hittite kingdoms in northern Syria, such as Carchemesh, Hamath, and others.[50] Although modern interpreters think of them as Aramean kingdoms, it is best to recall that Aram was never a unified empire in this period, but was a collection of independent city-states and their dependencies that could unite to oppose the Assyrians. They could just as easily turn against each other when their interests clashed. The Egyptians had ruled Canaan until the twelfth century B.C.E., and were always looking for opportunities to reassert their hegemony in the region.

Although the lepers are outcasts in Israelite society, they are still Israelites and feel obligated to inform their king and people that the Arameans have fled. The portrayal of the king's response to this very good news is a key element in the narrative, namely, he refuses to believe it, and supposes that it is an Aramean ruse designed to lay a trap for the Israelites. This depiction puts the king on a par with his officer, who refuses to believe that YHWH will act on behalf of the people (see 2 Kgs 7:1–2 above; cf. 2 Kgs 7:17–20 below). Such a narrative strategy points to the larger concern to demonstrate that the king and indeed the entire Omride line is unfit to rule Israel. Only when one of his soldiers suggests that the last five horses be used to send out two chariots on a scouting mission does the king reluctantly relent. The suggestion highlights the desperation of the Israelites, who were down to their last five horses from the once-powerful Israelite chariot corps.

[7:17–20] The fourth episode begins in typical fashion with a conjunctive *waw* joined to a noun, but the noun is *hammelek*, "the king," and the officer appears only as the object in the introductory phrase, "and the king appointed

---

50. G. McMahon, "Hittites in the OT," *ABD* 3:231–33; J. J. M. Roberts, "Hittites," *HBD* 430–31.

the officer on whose hand he was supported. . ." The episode presents the death of the officer as a fulfillment of Elisha's earlier prophetic word that the officer would die (see 2 Kgs 17:1–2). Verse 19 quotes both the words of the officer and the words of the prophet to demonstrate the fulfillment of Elisha's word. This episode thereby functions as the concluding episode of a prophetic confrontation story, in which a prophet's legitimacy is confirmed against a challenge by an opponent who denies the validity of the prophet's message and dies as a result of his disbelief. Because the narrative points directly to the king whom the officer serves, it demonstrates the inadequacy of the king and the house of Omri.

2 Kings 8:1–15 Concluding Examples of Elisha's Power: Restoration of the Shunammite Woman's Land and Accession of Hazael

8:1 Elisha had spoken to the woman whose son he had brought back to life, saying, "Arise and go! You[a] and your house, and reside wherever you like, for YHWH has called for a famine," and it, too, came upon the land for seven years. 2 So the woman arose, and she did as the man of G-d said. She and her house went and resided in the land of the Philistines for seven years. 3 At the end of seven years, the woman returned from the land of the Philistines, and went out to petition the king concerning her house and concerning her field.

4 And the king was speaking to Gehazi, the servant of the man of G-d, saying, "Tell me, please, all the great things that Elisha has done." 5 While he was telling the king how he brought the dead to life that, behold, the woman whose son he had brought back to life was petitioning[b] the king concerning her house and her field. And Gehazi said, "My lord, the king, this is the woman and this is her son who Elisha brought back to life." 6 So the king asked the woman, and she told him, and the king appointed an official[c] for her, saying, "Return all that is hers and all the produce of the field from the day that she left the land until now."

7 Elisha went to Damascus, and Ben Hadad, the king of Aram, was sick. It was told to him, saying, "The man of G-d has come here." 8 So the king said to Hazael, "Take in your hand a minḥa offering, and go to meet the man of G-d, and you shall make an inquiry to G-d through him, saying, 'Shall I survive [d]from this sickness?'"[d] 9 Hazael went to meet him, and he took a minḥa offering in his hand, and forty camel loads of all the best goods of Damascus, and he went, stood before him, and said, "Your son, Ben Hadad, King of Aram, has sent me to you, saying, 'Shall I survive [e]from this sickness?'"[e] 10 And Elisha said to him, "Go, say [f]to him,[f] 'You shall surely survive,' but YHWH has shown me that he will surely die." 11 His face remained expressionless to the point of embarrassment, and then the man of G-d wept. 12 Hazael said, "Why does my

lord weep?" And he said, "Because I know the evil that you will do to the people of Israel, their fortresses you will set afire, their young men you will slaughter with the sword, their babies you will dash in pieces, and their pregnant women you will rip open." 13 Hazael said, "For what is your servant, but a dog, that he should do this great deed?" Elisha said, "YHWH has shown me you as king over Aram." 14 So he went from Elisha, came to his master, and said to him, "What did Elisha say to you?" And he said, "He said to me, 'You shall surely survive.'" 15 The next day he took a cloth, soaked it in water, and spread it on his face, and he died. And Hazael ruled in his place.

a. Ketiv, *ʾattî,* an archaic feminine second-person singular pronoun, "you"; read with Qere, *ʾatt,* "you."

b. MT, *šōʿeqet,* lit., "crying out."

c. MT, *sārîs,* lit., "eunuch," frequently employed as a term for an officer or official.

d–d. MT, *mēḥŏlî zeh,* lit., "this sickness." The Hebrew noun *ḥŏlî,* "sickness," employs a *yod* for the third root letter in place of the expected *he.* LXX misreads the *yod* as the first-person-singular pronoun suffix, "this my sickness."

e–e. See n. d.

f–f. Ketiv, *lōʾ,* "not"; read with Qere, *lô,* "to him"; cf. LXX, which omits the term.

Second Kings 8:1–15 presents two concluding narratives concerning the recognition of Elisha's power and authority as a prophet of YHWH. Each portrays the recognition of the prophet by the monarchs of Israel and Aram, Jehoram in 2 Kgs 8:1–6 and the dying Ben Hadad and his successor Hazael in 2 Kgs 8:7–15. Both are concerned with characters who are ill, but vv. 1–6 emphasize Elisha's ability to heal the Shunammite woman's son as a demonstration of divine power, whereas vv. 7–15 emphasize the prophet's role in the death of the ill Ben Hadad in keeping with YHWH's plans to replace him with Hazael. Together, the two narratives present the final attempt to demonstrate that the overthrow of Jehoram ben Ahab is an act of YHWH (cf. 1 Kgs 19:15–18).

The demarcation of this unit is clearly indicated at the outset by the *waw-*conjunctive joined to the proper name Elisha. It lacks the typical concluding regnal résumé since the assassination of Jehoram ben Ahab will be related in relation to the regnal account of Ahaziah ben Jehoram of Judah below. Indeed, his assassination precludes any concluding regnal résumé since the account of his death appears within a transitional unit in 2 Kgs 8:25–11:20 that begins with an introductory regnal account for Ahaziah in 2 Kgs 8:25–29, includes a concluding regnal résumé for Jehu ben Jehoshaphat ben Nimshi in 2 Kgs 10:32–36, and concludes in 2 Kgs 11:1–20 with Athaliah bat Ahab's attempted coup in Jerusalem against the house of David. Second Kings 8:1–15 easily breaks down into two subunits: 2 Kgs 8:1–6, which relates Jehoram's recognition of Elisha's acts on behalf of the Shunammite woman and his restoration of her property, and 2 Kgs 8:7–15, in which Hazael assassinates Ben Hadad after hearing the prophet's oracles concerning Ben Hadad's impending death and his own divinely ordained destiny to rule Aram.

It is unlikely that the two narratives were originally read together. Second Kings 8:1–6 presupposes a time when Jehoram ben Ahab was still alive, and functions simply to demonstrate Elisha's power. Second Kings 8:7–15 presupposes the period following Jehu's coup, insofar as it legitimates Hazael's rise to power as an act ordained by YHWH. Both narratives function within the Jehu History as demonstrations that the overthrow of the Omride house was an act of YHWH. Within the Hezekian and Josian DtrH editions, they demonstrate YHWH's involvement in Israel's and Judah's history to overthrow the purportedly corrupt Omride dynasty and ultimately the northern kingdom of Israel. Within the exilic DtrH, these narratives contribute to the argument that YHWH acted against both Israel and Judah.

[1–6] The narrative includes two basic subunits. Verses 1–3 focus on the Shunammite woman's compliance with Elisha's instructions to leave home for seven years (cf. Gen 12:10–20; 20; 26; 41), and vv. 4–6 focus on Jehoram's recognition of Elisha at the time of her return.

Verses 1–3 begin with a notice of Elisha's earlier instructions to the Shunammite woman in v. 1. The reference to her as "the woman whose son he had restored to life" reminds the reader of 2 Kgs 4:8–37, which recounts the prophet's efforts to grant the Shunammite woman a son and to revive the boy when he collapsed. The earlier narrative makes no mention of Elisha's instructions to leave her home;[51] indeed, her emphatic statement in 2 Kgs 4:13, "I live among my own people," suggests her reluctance to leave unless there is some dire emergency. The prophet's instruction to the woman in v. 1a provides the grounds for her departure, namely, that there will be a seven-year famine in the land of Israel. The famine is noted in 2 Kgs 4:38, immediately following the account of Elisha's revival of her dead son, and it is presupposed throughout 2 Kgs 4:38–41; 4:42–44; and 6:24–7:20. Insofar as the house of Omri is identified with the worship of Baal, the Canaanite/Phoenician god of fertility, the seven-year famine during the reign of Jehoram functions as part of the religious polemic against the house of Omri to justify his assassination as an act of YHWH.[52] The woman's return to the land of Israel portends the end of the famine. Indeed, the following narrative concerning the overthrow of the house of Omri and the destruction of its Baal supporters in 2 Kgs 8:25–11:20 suggests the conclusion of the famine as Jehu comes to the throne.

---

51. N.b., 2 Kgs 4:37 notes that "she took her son and left," after the prophet restored the boy's life. The narrative builds upon this statement in claiming that Elisha had instructed the woman to leave.

52. See esp. Bronner, *Stories of Elijah and Elisha.*

The woman's choice of Philistia as a place to live is curious given Elijah's objections in 2 Kgs 1:2–4 to Ahaziah ben Ahab's attempts to seek medical advice by inquiring of the Philistine god, Baal Zebub in Ekron. There is no suggestion that she has done anything wrong, but her choice to live in Philistia for seven years recognizes Elisha's authority as a prophet of YHWH. Her temporary residence in Philistia functions much like other narratives in the Elijah and Elisha traditions that point to YHWH's power over foreign nations as well as over Israel and Judah, such as Zarephath (1 Kgs 17:7–24), Mount Horeb in the wilderness (1 Kgs 19), Moab (2 Kgs 3), and Aram (2 Kgs 8:7–15). These narratives play an important polemical role since they demonstrate that YHWH— and not Baal—holds sway over the nations outside of Israel and Judah.

Verses 4–6 shift to the royal court of Jehoram ben Ahab and his conversations with Gehazi, the servant of Elisha. This shift accompanies the appearance of the conjunctive *waw* and the noun *hammelek* at the beginning of v. 4. The narrative makes no mention of Gehazi's leprosy (see 2 Kgs 5). Instead, it focuses on how Gehazi related to the king all of the great deeds of Elisha. Gehazi's accounts of how Elisha brought the Shunammite woman's dead son back to life provide the perfect narrative entrée for her well-timed return. Upon hearing her story from her own mouth, the king restores her land, property, and the income realized from her land during the period of her absence. Such a magnanimous act may once have been related to bolster the character of Jehoram, but in the present narrative context, it functions as a means by which even the Omride monarch, Jehoram ben Ahab, recognizes the power of Elisha.

[7–15] The recognition of Elisha by both the Aramean king, Ben Hadad, and his successor and assassin, Hazael, points once again to a polemical intent to demonstrate that YHWH—and not Baal—is the true G-d of creation and of the nations that surround Israel. This account also highlights the contrast between Elisha's actions on behalf of the son of the Shunammite woman and the ill Ben Hadad. Whereas Elisha brings the woman's son back to life, he will not do so for Ben Hadad, most notably because YHWH had earlier instructed Elijah to appoint Elisha as his own successor and Hazael as the new king of Aram in place of Ben Hadad (1 Kgs 19:15–18). The unit includes three episodes based on the actions of the primary characters: vv. 7–8 relate Ben Hadad's instructions to Hazael to consult the prophet Elisha on his arrival in Damascus; vv. 9–13 relate Hazael's compliance with Ben Hadad's instructions, including Elisha's oracles; and vv. 14–15 relate Hazael's assassination of Ben Hadad following his return from consultation with Elisha.

YHWH had instructed Elijah to return to the wilderness of Damascus, but Elisha actually makes the journey. Elisha's presence in Damascus provides further indication that YHWH's power extends well beyond the land of Israel into the foreign nations that surround her. The motif of an ill character likewise supports this claim. The motif of illness and the prophet's capacity to heal it—or not—plays an important role throughout these narratives in demonstrating the prophets' powers as representatives of YHWH (1 Kgs 17:7–24; 21; 22:34; 2 Kgs 1:2–4; 4:8–37; 5; and 9:14b–16).

The narrative initially portrays Hazael as a loyal servant of Ben Hadad. Because the king is ill, he requests in vv. 7–8 that Hazael consult the prophet Elisha. This testimony of the prophet's power and reputation is striking insofar as the king of Aram, who had repeatedly attacked Israel (see 1 Kgs 20; 22; 2 Kgs 6:8–7:20), recognizes the power of the prophet and YHWH. The procedure for obtaining an oracle is typical, namely, Hazael is to take a gift to pay the prophet for his professional services (cf. 1 Kgs 14:3). The term *minḥâ*, "gift, offering," is typically employed for cultic offerings, especially grain offerings, at Israelite temples (see, e.g., Lev 2:1; 6:7, 8; Num 28:5; cf. 1 Kgs 18:29), although the term sometimes indicates a simple gift devoid of cultic significance (e.g., Gen 32:14; 33:10; 43:11; Judg 6:18; 1 Sam 10:27; 1 Kgs 10:25; 2 Kgs 20:12) or even tribute (Judg 3:15; 2 Sam 8:2; 1 Kgs 5:1; 2 Kgs 17:3; Hos 10:6). The inquiry, "Shall I live from my illness?" can be answered with a simple yes or no, which suggests a divinatory procedure.

The gift of forty camel loads of all "the goodness of Damascus," a reference to agricultural produce, indicates the high regard in which Ben Hadad holds Elisha. Hazael's reference to Ben Hadad as "your son" (v. 9) again indicates Ben Hadad's respect for Elisha, who is typically addressed as "father" by his disciples or King Joash of Israel (2 Kgs 6:21; 13:14; cf. 2:12; 5:13).

Elisha's response to Hazael is curious insofar as he instructs Hazael to lie to Ben Hadad.[53] The phrase *môt yāmût*, "he will surely die," is a version of the death-sentence formula in Israelite law.[54] Elisha's instructions facilitate YHWH's intentions to replace Ben Hadad with Hazael, insofar as it will make it easier for Hazael to kill Ben Hadad. Nevertheless, Elisha's willingness to lie to Ben Hadad, even to facilitate divine purposes, raises questions as to whether or not statements made by the prophet may be taken as true (see Deut 18:9–22; 1 Kgs 13; 22). Ultimately, such a strategy suggests that even YHWH might be questioned (see 1 Kgs 22; cf. Job). Elisha pauses as the realization of what is to transpire sinks in. Although the prophet serves as the agent to communicate YHWH's intentions to Hazael, this relationship does not prevent Elisha from expressing his strong emotions concerning YHWH's judgment. He now stands before the very man who will bring disaster on Israel by attacking its cities, killing its men,

---

53. C. J. Labuschagne, "Did Elisha Deliberately Lie?—A Note on II Kings 8:10," *ZAW* 77 (1965): 327–28.

54. See the examples of the formula in Exod 19:12; 21:12, 15, 16, 17; Lev 20:2, 9, 10; Num 15:35; 35:16; Judg 21:5; 1 Sam 14:39, etc.; see Hermann Schulz, *Das Todesrecht im Alten Testament* (BZAW 114; Berlin: Töpelmann, 1969).

and committing atrocities against its population. Hazael's question is self-deprecating insofar as he refers to himself as a mere dog, but his characterization of these actions as "this great thing" suggests the importance and magnitude of such an event as seen through the eyes of an enemy of Israel. This question paves the way for Elisha's final revelation to Hazael, that he will be king of Aram, in keeping with 1 Kgs 19:15–18.

The concluding episode in vv. 14–15 presents Hazael's communication to Ben Hadad of Elisha's false statement that he would survive. This seemingly puts Ben Hadad's mind at ease, but v. 15 indicates that it facilitates Hazael's treacherous murder of his own king. Shalmaneser III's inscriptions indicate that Hazael, a commoner, seized the throne from Hadadezer (Ben Hadad) sometime between his fourteenth and eighteenth years (848–844 B.C.E.) and that Jehu ben Omri [*sic*] was also king of Israel by his eighteenth year.[55] The concluding statement of v. 15, "and Hazael ruled in his place," mimics the characteristic statement of the closing regnal formula.

XV. Regnal Account of Jehoram ben Jehoshaphat of Judah 2 Kings 8:16–24

8:16 In the fifth year of Joram ben Ahab, King of Israel—Jehoshaphat had been King of Judah—Jehoram ben Jehoshaphat ruled as King of Judah. 17 He was thirty-two years old when he began to rule, and he ruled in Jerusalem for eight years. 18 He walked in the path of the kings of Israel just as the house of Ahab had done, because the daughter of Ahab was his wife. He did evil in the eyes of YHWH, 19 but YHWH was not willing to destroy Judah for the sake of David, His servant, just as He had promised him to grant him dominion[a] for his sons forever.

20 In his days, Edom revolted from under the hand of Judah, and they set a king over themselves. 21 Joram went to Zair, and all the chariot corps was with him. And he rose at night and struck Edom all around him and the chariot commanders, and the people fled to their tents. 22 And Edom revolted from under the hand of Judah until this day. Then Libnah revolted at that time.

---

55. See *ANET* 280–1; cf. Wayne Pitard, *Ancient Damascus: An Historical Study of the Ancient City State from Earliest Times until Its Fall to the Assyrians in 732 B.C.E.* (Winona Lake, Ind.: Eisenbrauns, 1987), 132–38.

23 And the rest of the affairs of Joram and all that he did, are they not written in the book of the affairs of the kings of Judah? 24 Joram slept with his fathers, and he was buried with his fathers in the city of David. And Ahaziah his son ruled in his place.

a. MT, *nîr,* is frequently equated with Hebrew *nēr,* "lamp" (see all LXX and Targum Jonathan), but Akkadian cognates demonstrate that the term refers to political authority or dominion (Hanson, "Song of Heshbon and David's NÎR"; contra Cogan and Tadmor 95).

Second Kings 8:16–24 is demarcated by the introductory regnal account in vv. 16–19 and the concluding regnal account in vv. 23–24. Although this brief unit focuses on Edom's (and Libnah's) revolt from Judah, it is unlikely that it was composed as part of the ninth–eighth-century B.C.E. Jehu History. Its formulaic character and interest in YHWH's promise to the house of David (v. 19) indicate that was composed as part of the Hezekian DtrH to highlight the Davidic theme. It functions similarly as part of the Josianic and exilic DtrH editions.

[16–19] The regnal account of Jehoram ben Jehoshaphat prompts confusion because he shares his name with Jehoram ben Ahab of Israel. Both monarchs are frequently referred to by the shortened form of the name, Joram (see vv. 21, 23, and 24 for Joram of Judah, and 2 Kgs 8:16, 25; 9:16 for Joram of Israel). The similarity in names is likely the result of the interrelationship established between the house of Omri and the house of David when Jehoshaphat married his son to Athaliah bat Ahab/Omri (v. 18; cf. 8:26). Jehoram ben Jehoshaphat's son, Ahaziah (2 Kgs 8:25–29), shares his name with Ahaziah ben Ahab of Israel (1 Kgs 22:51–2 Kgs 1:18).

Following the typical reference to the year of the reign of Jehoram's Israelite counterpart, the text adds a reference to the reign of Jehoram's father, Jehoshaphat. Although this reference appears in the LXX and Targum, it disrupts the transition between the introductory subordinate clause of v. 16a and the main clause in v. 16b. Its formulation as a *waw*-conjunctive clause that introduces an entirely new character, Jehoshaphat, indicates that it is a gloss. The reference does not appear to have been added haphazardly since it draws the reader's attention to the very brief regnal account of Jehoshaphat's reign in 1 Kgs 22:41–50. The gloss reminds the reader that Jehoshaphat had been king of Judah throughout this time.

Jehoram died at the relatively young age of forty after having ruled for only eight years. The portrayal of the king attacking the Edomites who surrounded him and his own chariot officers in a night action suggests the circumstances of his death. The DtrH judges him as evil due to his marriage to a daughter of Ahab. Although she is not named here, 2 Kgs 8:26 identifies his wife as Athaliah bat Omri. Her designation as "daughter of Omri" in this latter text likely reflects a dynastic identification.[1] As the daughter of the Sidonian/Canaanite princess Jezebel and the Israelite king Ahab, DtrH views her as the product of an illicit marriage that would lead to the introduction of idolatry in Judah (see Deut 7:1–6). Her unsuccessful attempt to assassinate her own grandson, Joash, and to seize the throne of Judah confirms any misgivings about her character (2 Kgs 11). DtrH reiterates YHWH's commitment to secure the house of David (2 Sam 7) as the reason that YHWH did not remove Jehoram or his descendants from the throne.

[20–23] The successful revolts by Edom and Libnah against Judean rule point to the weakening of Judah during the reign of Jehoram. Little is known about Edom during this period as excavations at Edomite sites identify little building activity prior to the period of Assyrian domination in the eighth and seventh centuries B.C.E.[2] Prior to this period, Edom would have been populated by a semi-nomadic people as represented by the figure of Esau, the eponymous ancestor of the Edomites (Gen 25–28; 32–35; 36). DtrH maintains that David subjugated the Edomites (2 Sam 8:13–14), that Hadad the Edomite unsuccessfully revolted against Solomon and fled to Egypt (1 Kgs 11:14–22), and that the unnamed king of Edom joined Jehoram of Israel and Jehoshaphat of Judah in their unsuccessful campaign to subjugate Mesha (2 Kgs 3:4–27). The failure of this campaign and the considerable inscriptional evidence of Moabite and Aramean successes against Israel in the latter half of the ninth century B.C.E. would have prompted an Edomite revolt against Judah.[3] The notice that Edom set a king over itself is puzzling given the reference to the Edomite king in 2 Kgs 3:4–27, although it is consistent with the notice in 1 Kgs 22:48 that there was no king in Edom during the reign of Jehoshaphat. The appointment of a prefect (*niṣṣāb*) in Edom would have signaled Edom's vassal status to Jehoshaphat.

In order to quell the revolt, 2 Kgs 8:21 states that Joram moved his chariot corps to Zair (*ṣāʿîr*). The location is unknown, although some identify it with

1. The Assyrians refer to northern Israel as "the house/land of Omri" long after the fall of the house of Omri (see, e.g., the annals and inscriptions of Tiglath-pileser III and Sargon II in *ANET* 284–85). Shalmaneser III even refers to Jehu as the "son of Omri" (see *ANET* 280; cf. Tammi Schneider, "Rethinking Jehu," *Bib* 77 [1996]: 100–107; see also G. H. Jones, *1 and 2 Kings* [2 vols.; The New Century Bible Commentary; Grand Rapids: William B. Eerdmans; London: Marshall, Morgan, and Scott, 1984], 446–47).

2. Amihai Mazar, *Archaeology of the Land of the Bible, 10,000–586 B.C.E.* (New York: Doubleday, 1990), 544; Ephraim Stern, *Archaeology of the Land of the Bible*, vol. 2, *The Assyrian, Babylonian, and Persian Periods (732–332 B.C.)* (New York: Doubleday, 2001), 268–79.

3. See the Mesha inscription (*ANET* 320–21) in which Mesha claims to have driven Israel out of the Transjordan; the Balaam inscription (Meindert Dijkstra, "Is Balaam Also among the Prophets?" *JBL* 114 [1995]: 43–64), which portrays Balaam's prophecy against an unnamed enemy, i.e., Israel, when the Arameans had taken control of the Transjordan; and the Tel Dan inscription (Biran and Naveh, "An Aramaic Stele"; Biran and Naveh, "The Tel Dan Inscription") in which an Aramaean king claims to have killed Jehoram of Israel and Ahaziah of Judah.

Zoar (Deut 34:3) or Zior (Josh 15:54). Others suggest that the term is an alternate version of the name Seir (*śēîr*), which refers to the heights east of the Aravah that marked the boundary between Edom and Judah.[4] Jehoram's battle with the Edomites is a fiasco. He apparently attacked at night, much as Gideon attacked the Midianites (Judg 7), but Jehoram's attack was far less successful. Verse 21 indicates that the Edomites had surrounded Jehoram, and the presence of the conjunctive direct-object marker, *wĕʾet,* immediately prior to the reference to "the commanders of the chariots" indicates that Jehoram struck both at the Edomites and at his own forces. As a result, Edom was able to revolt against Judah "until this day." Although 2 Kgs 14:7 recounts Amaziah ben Joash's victory over the Edomites, there is no indication that he was able to reimpose Judean rule. The reference to "this day" therefore indicates any time from the late ninth century on.

Edom's successful revolt prompted others, such as Libnah, a Levitical city (Josh 21:13; 1 Chr 6:57) located near Lachish, Eglon, Hebron, and Debir (Josh 10:29–39) in southern Judah. Libnah is identified with Tel Bornat to the south of Tel es-Safi and closer to the cities of the Shephelah with which it is associated in Josh 15:42.[5] The report in 2 Kgs 12:17–18 that Hazael of Aram attacked the Philistine city of Gath during the reign of Joash suggests Judean weakness.

XVI. Regnal Account of Ahaziah ben Jehoram of Judah 2 Kings 8:25–11:20

The regnal account for Ahaziah ben Jehoram of Judah begins in 2 Kgs 8:25–29 with the regnal introduction. Because Ahaziah is assassinated together with Joram ben Ahab by Jehu ben Nimshi in 2 Kgs 9:1–10:36, there is no concluding regnal form for Ahaziah. Instead, the narrative shifts to the reign of Jehu. Following the concluding regnal form for Jehu ben Nimshi of Israel in 2 Kgs 10:34–36, an appendix concerning Athaliah bat Omri/Ahab of Judah closes the account.

2 Kings 8:25–29 The Introductory Regnal Account for Ahaziah

8:25 In the twelfth[a] year of Joram ben Ahab, King of Israel, Ahaziah ben Jehoram, King of Judah, ruled. **26** Ahaziah was twenty-two years old when he began to rule, and he ruled for one year in Jerusalem. The name of his mother was Athaliah bat Omri, King of Israel. **27** He walked in the

4. See the discussion of these identifications in R. Liwak, "Zair," *ABD* 6:1038–39.
5. See J. L. Peterson, "Libnah," *ABD* 4:322–23.

path of the house of Ahab, and he did evil in the eyes of YHWH like the house of Ahab, because he was the son-in-law of the house of Ahab. 28 He went with Joram ben Ahab to war with Hazael, King of Aram, at Ramoth Gilead, and the Arameans wounded Joram. 29 So Joram the King returned to Jezreel to recover from the wounds that the Arameans had inflicted on him at Ramoth when he fought Hazael, King of Aram. Ahaziah ben Jehoram, King of Judah, went down to see Joram ben Ahab in Jezreel because he was ill.

a. Peshitta, "eleventh"; cf. 2 Kgs 9:29.

The introductory regnal account for Ahaziah ben Jehoram of Judah has been modified to account for the literary context of 2 Kgs 8:25–11:20, which relates Jehu's revolt against the house of Omri, including his assassination of Ahaziah (2 Kgs 9–10, see esp. 9:27–29) and Athaliah's attempted coup against the house of David in the aftermath of the revolt (2 Kgs 11).[1] Following the presentation of the chronological details of Ahaziah's reign in vv. 25–26a, v. 26b identifies Athaliah bat Omri as his mother. The designation of Athaliah as "the daughter of Omri" rather than "the daughter of Ahab" reflects her dynastic identification. When read in relation to the immediate context of the overthrow of the house of Omri, it highlights her role as a member of a dynasty that has been condemned, and it points to the concluding episode of this unit in 2 Kgs 11, in which she is killed after her failure to overthrow the house of David.

Verses 28–29 are frequently identified as the introduction to a new unit, but the *waw*-consecutive formulation indicates that they are to be read in relation to the preceding introductory regnal account. They help to set the stage for the following subunits in 2 Kgs 9–10 and 11 by portraying Ahaziah's alliance with Jehoram ben Ahab. Like his grandfather, Jehoshaphat, Ahaziah accompanies his ally to war against the Arameans at Ramoth Gilead. Like his father, Ahab, Jehoram is wounded in battle, but the wound is not mortal. Jehoram consequently goes to Jezreel to recover from his wounds, and Ahaziah goes to Jezreel to visit his suzerain monarch and brother-in-law.

2 Kings 9:1–10:36 The Account of Jehu's Revolt against the House of Omri

9:1 Elisha the prophet summoned one of the sons of the prophets and said to him, "Gird up your loins, and take this bottle of oil in your hand, and

1. For discussion of the interrelationship of 2 Kgs 9–11, see esp. Lloyd M. Barré, *The Rhetoric of Political Persuasion* (CBQMS 20; Washington, D.C.: Catholic Biblical Association, 1988); Julio C. Trebolle-Barrera, *Jehú y Joás. Texto y composición literaria de 2 Reyes 9–11* (Institución San Jerónimo 17; Valencia: Institución San Jerónimo, 1984).

go to Ramoth Gilead. 2 You shall go there and see Jehu ben Jehoshaphat ben Nimshi. You shall go, raise him up from among his brothers, and bring him into an inner room. 3 You shall take the bottle of oil, pour on his head, and say, "Thus says YHWH, 'I have anointed you as king for Israel.' Then you shall open the door, flee, and not wait." 4 So ᵃthe boy, the young prophet,ᵃ went to Ramoth Gilead. 5 He went, and behold, the commanders of the army were meeting, and he said, "I have a message for you, commander." Jehu said, "For which one of us?" And he said, "For you, commander." 6 And he rose, went inside the building, poured the oil on his head, and said to him, "Thus says YHWH, G-d of Israel, 'I have anointed you as king for the people of YHWH, for Israel. 7 You shall strike the house of Ahab, your master, so that I will avenge the blood of My servants of the prophets and the blood of all the servants of YHWH from the hand of Jezebel. 8 All the house of Ahab will perish, and I will cut off for Ahab he who pisses against the wall, bond and free, in Israel. 9 I will make the house of Ahab like the house of Jeroboam ben Nebat and like the house of Baasha ben Ahijah. 10 The dogs shall eat Jezebel in the territory of Jezreel without burial.'" Then he opened the door and fled.

11 Jehu went out to the servants of his master, and they said to him, "Is everything okay? Why did this crazy man come to you?" And he said to them, "You know the man and his talk." 12 And they said, "Liar! Tell us!" And he said, "Such and such he said to me, saying, 'Thus says YHWH, "I have anointed you as king for Israel."'" 13 And each one of them immediately took his garment, and they placed it on the topᵇ of the steps, blew the shofar, and proclaimed, "Jehu rules!" 14 So Jehu ben Jehoshaphat ben Nimshi conspired against Joram. Joram was on guard at Ramoth Gilead, he and all Israel, against Hazael, King of Aram. 15 And King Jehoram returned to recuperate in Jezreel from the wounds that the Arameans inflicted on him when he fought Hazael, King of Aram. And Jehu said, "'As you breathe,ᶜ let no one escape from the city to go to tell in Jezreel." 16 So Jehu rode and went to Jezreel because Joram was lying there, and Ahaziah, King of Judah, had gone down to see Joram.

17 The watchman was standing on the tower in Jezreel, saw the party of Jehu as it came, and said, "A party, I see!" And Jehoram said, "Take a chariot, and send it to meet them, and it shall say, 'Is all in order?'" 18 So the horse rider went to meet him and said, "Thus says the King, 'Peace?'" And Jehu said, "What do you have to do with peace? Follow me!" And the watchman declared, saying, "The messenger comes to them, but he does not return." 19 So he sent a second horse rider, and he came to them and said, "Thus says the King, 'Peace!'" And Jehu said, "What do you have to do with peace? Follow me!" 20 And the watchman declared, saying, "He comes to them, but he does not return! The driving is like the

driving of Jehu ben Nimshi because he drives recklessly!" 21 And Jehoram said, "Harness!" And he harnessed his chariot, and Jehoram, King of Israel, went out, and Ahaziah, King of Judah, each in his chariot. They went out to meet Jehu and found him on the property of Naboth the Jezreelite. 22 When Jehoram saw Jehu, he said, "Peace, Jehu?" And he said, "How is there peace, considering the harlotries of Jezebel, your mother, and her many sorceries?" 23 So Jehoram turned his hands, fled, and said to Ahaziah, "Treachery, Ahaziah!"

24 Jehu took bow in hand and shot Jehoram between his arms so that the arrow went out from his heart, and he collapsed ᵈin his chariot.ᵈ 25 And he said to Bidqar, ᵉhis crewman,ᵉ "Lift him up and toss him out in the portion of land of Naboth the Jezreelite, for remember that you and I were riding in teams after Ahab his father, and YHWH spoke this oracle concerning him, 26 'Surely I saw the blood of Naboth and the blood of his sons yesterday, utterance of YHWH, and I will repay you on this property, utterance of YHWH.' And now, lift him up and toss him out on this property in accordance with the word of YHWH."

27 Ahaziah, King of Judah, saw, and fled in the direction of Beth ha-Gan. Jehu pursued after him and said, "Shoot him, too, in the chariot at Maaleh Gur, which is by Ibleam!" He fled to Megiddo and died there. 28 His servants transported him to Jerusalem and buried him in his tomb with his fathers in the City of David. 29 In the eleventh year of Joram ben Ahab, Ahaziah had become king over Judah. 30 Jehu came to Jezreel, and Jezebel heard, and she put eye liner on her eyes, fixed her head, and peered through the window.

31 Jehu entered the gate, and she said, "Peace, Zimri, slayer of his master?" 32 He lifted his face to the window and said, ᶠ"Who is with me?ᶠ Who?" Two or three eunuchs looked out to him. 33 And he said, "ᵍThrow her down!"ᵍ So they threw her down, and some of her blood splattered on the wall and on the horses, and they trampled her. 34 Then he went, ate, drank, and said, "Take care of this cursed woman and bury her, for she is a daughter of a king." 35 So they went to bury her, but they did not find her, because only the skull, the feet, and the palms of the hands (were left). 36 So they returned and told him, and he said, "It is the word of YHWH, which He spoke by the hand of His servant, Elijah the Tishbite, saying, 'On the property of Jezreel, the dogs shall eat the flesh of Jezebel.' 37 And the corpse of Jezebel ʰwill beʰ like dung on the face of the field in the property of Jezreel, that no one will say, 'This is Jezebel.'"

10:1 Ahab had seventy sons in Samaria, and Jehu wrote letters and sent them to Samaria to the senior commanders of Jezreel and to those loyal to Ahab, saying, 2 "And now, when this letter comes to you, and with you are the sons of your master and the chariots and the horses and fortified city and the weapons, 3 and you will see the one who is best and fitting from among the sons of your master, and you shall place him on the throne of his father, and fight for the house of your master." 4 And they were very, very afraid and said, "Behold, two kings could not stand before him. So how shall we stand? Us?" 5 And the officer in charge of the royal household and the officer in charge of the city and the elders and the loyal ones sent to Jehu, saying, "We are your servants, and all that you say to us, we will do. We will not make anyone king. Do what you think is best." 6 And he wrote to them a second letter, saying, "If you are with me and will obey me, take the heads of the men of the sons of your master, and come to me at Jezreel at this time tomorrow." And the seventy sons of the king were with the officials of the city who were raising them. 7 When the letter came to them, they took the sons of the king, slaughtered each of the seventy, placed their heads in baskets, and sent them to him at Jezreel. 8 And the messenger came, and he told him, saying, "Bring the heads of the sons of the king." And he said, "Place them in two piles at the entrance of the gate until morning." 9 When it was morning, he went out, stood, and said to all the people, "You are innocent! Behold, I have conspired against my master and killed him. So who has struck down all these? 10 Know, then, that there shall not fall to the ground any part of the word of YHWH that YHWH spoke concerning the house of Ahab. YHWH has done that which He spoke by the hand of His prophet Elijah." 11 And Jehu struck down all who were left to the house of Ahab in Jezreel, all his officials, those known to him, and his priests until not even a remnant was left. 12 He rose, went, and came to Samaria. He was on the way to ⁱBeth Eqedⁱ of the Shepherds.

13 Jehu found the brothers of Ahaziah, King of Judah, and said, "Who are you?" And they said, "We are the brothers of Ahaziah, and we are going down to visitʲ the sons of the king and the sons of the queen." 14 And he said, "Seize them alive!" So they seized them alive and slaughtered them at the pit at Beth Eqed, forty-two men, and he did not leave one of them. 15 He went from there, found Jehonadab ben Rekeb (coming) to meet him, greeted him, and said to him, "Is your heart true, as my heart is true with your heart?" And Jehonadab said, ᵏ"It certainly is. Give me your hand."ᵏ And he gave him his hand, brought him up to him in the chariot, 16 and said, "Come with me, and see my zeal for YHWH." He had him ride in his chariot. 17 And he came to Samaria and struck down all who were left to Ahab in Samaria until he destroyed him according to the word of YHWH which he spoke to Elijah. 18 Jehu gathered all the people and said to them, "Ahab served Baal a little! Jehu will serve him much! 19 And now, summon to me all the prophets of Baal, all his servants, and all his priests! No one shall be missing because I have a great sacrifice for Baal. All who are missing shall not live!" And Jehu acted with deceit in order to destroy

the servants of Baal. 20 And Jehu said, "Sanctify an observance for Baal!" and they announced it. 21 Jehu sent throughout all Israel, and all the servants of Baal—and there was not left a man who did not come—and they came to the house of Baal and filled the house of Baal from one side to the other. 22 And he said to the official in charge of the wardrobe, "Bring out a garment for all the servants of Baal!" And he brought out for them the festal garment. 23 Jehu and Jehonadab ben Rekeb came to the house of Baal, and he said to the servants of Baal," Search, and see, lest there be here anyone from the servants of YHWH, because only servants of Baal alone should be here." 24 They came to perform the sacrifices and the whole burnt offerings, and Jehu placed for himself outside eighty men and said, "The man who allows anyone to escape from the men whom I am bringing into your hands, his life shall be in place of his life." 25 When he finished performing the whole burnt offering, Jehu said to the soldiers and the officers, "Come, kill them! No one gets out!" And they struck them down by the edge of the sword, and the soldiers and the officers threw them out, and they went into the city of the house of Baal. 26 They brought out the stelae of the house of Baal and burned it. 27 They tore down the stele of Baal, and they tore down the house of Baal, and they made it into a latrine[l] until this day. 28 So Jehu destroyed Baal from Israel.

29 But the sins of Jeroboam ben Nebat which he caused Israel to commit, Jehu did not turn aside from after them, the calves of gold which were in Beth El and which were in Dan. 30 And YHWH said to Jehu, "Because you have done well to do what is right in My eyes, according to all that was in My heart you have done to the house of Ahab, the sons of the fourth generation to you shall sit upon the throne of Israel."

31 Jehu was not careful to walk in the Torah of YHWH, the G-d of Israel, with all his heart. He did not turn from the sins of Jeroboam which he caused Israel to commit.

32 In those days, YHWH began to cut off in Israel, and Hazael struck them along the entire border of Israel 33 from the Jordan to the east, all the land of Gilead, the Gadites and the Reubenites and Manassites, from Aroer which is by the Wadi Arnon, and the Gilead, and the Bashan.

34 And the rest of the affairs of Jehu and all that he did and all his power, are they not written in the book of the Chronicles of the Kings of Israel? 35 Jehu slept with his fathers, and they buried him in Samaria, and Jehoahaz his son ruled in his place.

36 And the days that Jehu ruled over Israel were twenty-eight years in Samaria.

a–a. MT, *hanna⁄ar hanna⁄ar hannābî'*, lit., "the boy, the boy, the prophet," which is difficult grammatically. The present text may be the result of a very early error (cf. LXX and Peshitta, which eliminate the initial reference to "the boy," i.e., "the young man, the prophet," or "the young prophet"), although this text underlies Targum Jonathan's reading of *hannaᶜar hannābî ʾ* as a construct phrase, *ᶜôlêmā ʾ talmîdā ʾ dinbîyā ʾ*, "the boy, the student of the prophet," which requires the Hebrew, *na ʿar hannābî ʾ*. Because both terms include the definite article, *hannābî ʾ* functions as an adjective for *hannaᶜar*, i.e., "the prophetic boy," or in more idiomatic English, "the young prophet." The phrase then serves as an appositional specification for the initial occurrence of *hannaᶜar*.

b. Hebrew, *gerem*, lit., "bone," an idiom for the top or surface of the step.

c–c. MT, *ʾim-yēš napšĕkem*, lit., "if you have life"; cf. LXX, "if your life is with me"; Targum Jonathan and Peshitta, "if your life is willing," i.e., "if you are willing."

d–d. MT, *bĕrikbô*, "in his chariot"; cf. LXX, *epi ton gonata autou*, "upon his knees," which presupposes Hebrew, *bĕbirkāyw*. The LXX transposes the final letter *beth* of *bĕrikbô* to the beginning of *bĕbirkāyw*.

e–e. Read with Qere, *šālišô*, "his officer," in place of Ketiv, *šālišōh*, which also means "his officer."

f–f. MT, *mî-ʾittî mî*, "who is with me? who?"; cf. LXX, *tis ei su; katabēthi met' emou*, "who are you? Come down with me," which presupposes Hebrew, *mî-ʾat; ʾittî mî*, lit., "who are you? With me is who," which preserves two understandings of *ʾittî*, "with me" in relation to *mî*, "who?"

g–g. Read with Qere, *šimtuhā*, "throw her down," in place of Ketiv, *šimtĕhû*, "throw it down."

h–h. Read with Qere, *wĕhāyĕtâ*, "and it/she shall be," in place of the erroneous Ketiv, *whyt*.

i–i. The versions interpret the place name, Beth Eqed, differently, depending on their reading of the term *ᶜēqed*, "binding." LXX reads Beth Eqed as "the house of sheep-shearing," based on the use of *ᶜāqōd* in relation to sheep (Gen 30:35, 39, 40; 31:8), presupposing that sheep must be bound before they are sheared. Targum Jonathan reads Beth Eqed as "the house of assembly," i.e., "the synagogue (*bêt kĕnêsat*)," reading the root *ᶜqd* in relation to its sacrificial functions derived from its use in the binding of Isaac (Gen 22:9). Because sacrifice is permitted only in the Jerusalem temple, this particular site must be a synagogue for the shepherds. Peshitta, "he tore down the high places," reading the root *ᶜqd* as the Syriac root *ᶜqr*, "to uproot," and *hārōᶜîm*, "the shepherds," together as *bêt hārāᶜîm*, "the house(s) of evil."

j. MT, *lišlôm*, "for the welfare of," i.e., "to see to the welfare of . . ."

k–k. Jonadab's initial response, *yēš wāyēš*, "it is and it is," i.e., "it certainly is," causes confusion among the versions due to the duplication of the term *yēš*. LXX reads the repetition of the term as an indication of Jehu's response, " 'It is.' And Jehu said, 'If it is, then give me your hand.' " Peshitta holds *yēš wāyēš* together, but views the next phrase as Jehu's response, " 'It is and it is.' And he (Jehu) said, 'Give me your hand.' "

l. Read with Qere, *lĕmōṣāʾôt*, "for an outhouse" (lit. "for a going out"), a more subtle expression than the Ketiv, *lĕmahărāʾôt*, "for a latrine" (lit., "for making waste").

Second Kings 9:1–10:36 constitutes the account of Jehu ben Jehoshaphat ben Nimshi's overthrow of the house of Omri. It also serves as the account of

Jehu's reign. The issue is complicated by the narrative's relationship to the earlier regnal accounts of Jehoram ben Ahab in 2 Kgs 3:1–8:15 and Ahaziah ben Jehoram in 2 Kgs 8:25–29, neither of which include a concluding regnal summary. Because the narrative relates the assassination of both monarchs by Jehu, it omits the concluding regnal accounts for their reigns. It also omits an introductory regnal account for Jehu because he is a usurper of the throne, much as 1 Kgs 12:1–14:20 omits an introductory regnal account for Jeroboam ben Nebat. Such a pattern is not consistently applied in Kings, however, as introductory regnal accounts appear for other usurpers, including Baasha (1 Kgs 15:33–34), Zimri (1 Kgs 16:15a), Omri (1 Kgs 16:21–23, but note the modification of the form), Shallum (2 Kgs 15:13), Menahem (2 Kgs 15:17–18), Pekah (2 Kgs 15:27–28), and Hoshea (2 Kgs 17:1–2). The narrative supplies a concluding regnal account for Jehu's reign in 2 Kgs 10:31–36, much as it supplies a concluding regnal account for Jeroboam ben Nebat in 1 Kgs 14:19–20.

The unit begins with *weʾĕlîšāʿ*, "and Elisha," a combination of conjunctive *waw* and the personal name, Elisha, which signals the introduction of a new plot line concerned with Jehu's overthrow of the house of Omri. The subunits of this text are likewise demarcated by similar combinations of a conjunctive *waw* and a personal name. Each introduces a new episode within the larger framework of the revolt, so that the sequence begins with the events that pave the way for the revolt, focuses on the killings of the individuals or groups that constitute the power base for the house of Omri in Israel, and then concludes with the regnal summary for Jehu's reign, as follows:

- 2 Kgs 1–10, introduced by *weʾĕlîšāʿ*, "and Elisha (the prophet called . . .)," relates Elisha's sending of a messenger to anoint Jehu as king.
- 2 Kgs 9:11–16, introduced by *wĕyēhûʾ*, "and Jehu (went out . . .)," relates Jehu's acceptance as king by the army officers under his command.
- 2 Kgs 9:17–23, introduced by *wĕhaṣṣōpeh*, "and the watchman (was standing . . .)," relates Jehoram's discovery of Jehu's treason as the latter approached Jezreel.
- 2 Kgs 9:24–26, introduced by *wĕyēhûʾ*, "and Jehu (filled his hand . . .)," summarily recounts Jehu's killing of Jehoram.
- 2 Kgs 9:27–30, introduced by *waʾăhazyâ*, "and Ahaziah, (king of Judah, saw. . .)," relates Jehu's killing of Ahaziah.
- 2 Kgs 9:31–37, once again introduced by *wĕyēhûʾ*, "and Jehu (entered the gate . . .)," relates Jehu's role in the killing of Jezebel.
- 2 Kgs 10:1–12, introduced by *ûlĕʾahʾāb*, "and Ahab had (seventy sons . . .)," relates Jehu's killing of Ahab's seventy sons.

- 2 Kgs 10:13–30, introduced again by *wĕyēhûʾ*, "and Jehu (found . . .)," relates Ahab's killing of the brothers of Ahaziah and the supporters of Baal from throughout Israel.
- 2 Kgs 10:31–36 employs *wĕyēhûʾ*, "and Jehu (did not observe . . .)," to introduce the concluding regnal account for Jehu's reign.

The combined conjunctive *waw* and the proper name "Athaliah" in 2 Kgs 11:1 introduces the account of Athaliah's failed coup in Judah as an appendix to the narrative concerning Jehu's overthrow of the house of Omri.

Scholars note the interrelationship between this narrative and the rest of the so-called Elijah and Elisha cycles.[2] First Kings 17–19 clearly indicate an anti-Baal polemic that finds its fruition in the portrayal of Jehu's eradication of the house of Omri and its Baalist supporters. The narrative concerning YHWH's revelation to Elijah in 1 Kgs 19 explicitly names Jehu as the man who is to be anointed as king of Israel. It repeatedly refers to Elijah's prophecy of judgment against Ahab and the house of Omri for his murder of Naboth the Jezreelite (1 Kgs 21) to justify Jehu's killing of Jehoram ben Ahab; his brother-in-law, Ahaziah ben Jehoram; and his mother, Jezebel (2 Kgs 9:7–10, 25–26, 36–37; 10:10–11, 17, 30).

The account of Jehu's revolt is an early narrative that has been incorporated into the larger Elijah-Elisha cycle and then worked into the DtrH narrative framework.[3] Jehu's overthrow of the house of Omri hardly constitutes the culmination of the narrative insofar as Elisha does not die until 2 Kgs 13:14–21, Hazael and the threat to Israel from Aram are not contained until 2 Kgs 13:22–25, and Israel is not secure until Jeroboam ben Joash restores the borders of Israel from Lebo-Hamath to the Sea of the Arabah in 2 Kgs 14:23–29.[4] An early form of the narrative has been taken up and combined with narratives concerning Elijah and other prophets in 1 Kgs 17–22 and 2 Kgs 1 and those concerning Elisha in 2 Kgs 2–8 to form a narrative that recounts the rise of the house of Jehu. Insofar as Israel and the house of Jehu are not fully secure until the reigns of Joash ben Jehoahaz and Jeroboam ben Joash in 2 Kgs 14, it is best

2. Susanne Otto, *Jehu, Elia und Elisa* (BWANT 152; Stuttgart: W. Kohlhammer, 2001), 29–117; Odil Hannes Steck, *Überlieferung und Zeitgeschichte in den Elia-Erzählungen* (WMANT 26; Neukirchen-Vluyn: Neukirchener, 1968); Stefan Timm, *Die Dynastie Omri* (FRLANT 124; Göttingen: Vandenhoeck & Ruprecht, 1982), 136–56; Marsha C. White, *The Elijah Legends and Jehu's Coup* (BJS 311; Atlanta: Scholars Press, 1997).

3. Martin Noth, *The Deuteronomistic History* (JSOTSup 15; Sheffield: JSOT Press, 1981), 69–73.

4. Contra Antony F. Campbell, S.J., *Of Prophets and Kings: A Late Ninth-Century Document (1 Samuel 1–2 Kings 10)* (CBQMS 17; Washington, D.C.: The Catholic Biblical Association, 1986); Antony F. Campbell and Mark A. O'Brien, *Unfolding the Deuteronomistic History: Origins, Upgrades, Present Text* (Minneapolis: Fortress, 2000), 24–34.

to date this cycle to the reign of Jeroboam ben Joash in the first half of the eighth century B.C.E. The Jehu History would then have been incorporated later into the Hezekian DtrH, where it would have functioned as a demonstration of northern Israel's inability to govern itself without constant revolt and violence and thereby pointed to the need for Hezekiah to reestablish Davidic control over the north. As part of the Josianic DtrH, the narrative points to the failed effort to eradicate idolatry from the land; although Jehu eliminated the Omride house and its Baalist supporters, he did not eliminate the sins of Jeroboam that led to northern Israel's destruction and once again demonstrated the need for Davidic control in the Josianic age. Finally, the narrative functions as part of the exilic DtrH, where it demonstrates that the house of Omri was not entirely wiped out; Athaliah, after all, is the ancestress of the entire Davidic line from Jehoash ben Ahaziah. The narrative therefore demonstrates why Manasseh would conduct himself like his infamous ancestor Ahab, and thereby bring about YHWH's decision to destroy Jerusalem and Judah as well as northern Israel.

Other sources provide little information concerning Jehu's overthrow of the house of Omri. The inscriptions of the Assyrian monarch Shalmaneser III (858–824 B.C.E.) provide a great deal of information concerning his campaigns against Aram and its allies from his sixth through his twenty-first years.[5] According to his monolith inscription (see *ANET* 278–79), Shalmaneser III crossed the Euphrates River during his sixth year (853 B.C.E.) to attack an Aramean coalition of twelve kings near the city of Karkar led by Hadadezer of Damascus, generally identified as Ben Hadad; Irhuleni of Hamath; and Ahab of Israel. Although he claims to have defeated the coalition and inflicted heavy casualties, he was forced to return to Assyria. He reports subsequent campaigns against the same coalition of twelve kings led by Hadadezer in his tenth (849 B.C.E.), eleventh (848 B.C.E.), and fourteenth years (845 B.C.E.; see *ANET* 279–80 for translation of the relevant texts). During his eighteenth year (841 B.C.E.), Shalmaneser III reports a renewed campaign against Aram, now led by Hazael. As part of the same campaign, he claims that he besieged Hazael in Damascus (but he did not take the city), and then moved westward to the mountains of Hauran and then to the mountains of Ba'li-ra'si, where he erected a stela with his royal image and received the tribute of Jehu son of Omri (*ANET* 280). The Black Obelisk, which depicts Jehu's submission to Shalmaneser, also identifies him as Jehu son of Omri (*ANEP* 351–55, esp. 351 and 355; *ANET* 281). Another inscription mentions Hadadezer's death, and identifies Hazael as "the son of a nobody"—that is, a commoner or usurper—which would seem to support the biblical account of Hazael's assassination of Ben Hadad (2 Kgs 8:7–15; *ANET* 280). A final campaign against Hazael of Aram took place in Shalmaneser's twenty-first year (838

5. See esp. CAH 3/1, 238–81, 372–409; Timm, *Die Dynastie Omri,* 57–145; Pitard, *Ancient Damascus,* 107–44.

B.C.E.). Shalmaneser's inscriptions say nothing about a revolt in Israel, however, and the identification of Jehu as the son of Omri suggests that Shalmaneser saw Jehu as a legitimate successor to the house of Omri. Indeed, the Assyrians continue to refer to Israel as the house of Omri, although not consistently, as late as the reigns of Tiglath-pileser III (744–727 B.C.E.; *ANET* 283) and Sargon II (721–705 B.C.E.; *ANET* 285). There has been some speculation that Jehu actually was a member of the house of Omri,[6] although most scholars attribute the designation to the lasting impact of the house of Omri as the dynasty that turned Israel into a powerful kingdom with its capital in Samaria.[7] Although the Assyrian records do not depict the revolt per se, they do acknowledge both the change of rulers and foreign policy, insofar as Jehu ceased to function as an Aramean ally and made peace with the Assyrians instead. Certainly, the scenario of Shalmaneser's repeated attacks against the Aramean coalition suggests that the coalition began to weaken under the unrelenting pressure, resulting in the overthrow of Hadadezer/Ben Hadad and the capitulation of Jehu, perhaps after a coup against the house of Omri, which made such a change in policy possible.

[9:1–10] The first episode relates Elisha's role in the anointing of Jehu as king of Israel. The narrative takes pains to identify its main characters as "Elisha the prophet" and "Jehu ben Jehoshaphat ben Nimshi." It does not disclose Elisha's location—perhaps he is still in Damascus—but it does identify Ramoth Gilead as the city where Jehu is stationed with the Israelite army as it defends the city, the entire Transjordan, and the approaches to the Jezreel Valley from Aramean attack. The placement of Jehu and the army at Ramoth Gilead explains how King Jehoram is wounded in battle and must therefore retire to Jezreel to recover from his wounds. The location of the text also suggests the unrelenting pressure of the Arameans, insofar as Jehoram's father, Ahab, was killed in battle at Ramoth Gilead some thirteen years before. Many suggest that the failure of the house of Omri to contain the Arameans was the primary cause of Jehu's coup. He is a high-ranking army officer who has the support of his fellow officers as he takes action against the monarch following his most recent military reverse. The later depictions of Hazael's continued assaults against Israel and Israel's capitulation to Aram during the reigns of Jehu and his son Jehoahaz (2 Kgs 10:32–33; 13:3–7) and Jehu's submission to Shalmaneser (and his grandson Jehoash's submission to Adad-nirari V) indicate that ultimately the Jehu dynasty was forced to ally with the Assyrians in order to contain the Aramean threat once and for all.

The motif of secrecy is paramount. Elisha does not anoint Jehu himself—indeed, Elisha and Jehu never meet in the biblical narratives. Instead, he sends an unidentified young man from among his prophetic followers to carry out the

---

6. Tammi Schneider, "Rethinking Jehu," *Bib* 77 (1996): 100–107.

7. E.g., Nadav Na'aman, "Jehu Son of Omri: Legitimizing a Loyal Vassal by His Overlord," *IEJ* 48 (1998): 236–38.

task. The reference to the inner room is important for two reasons. First, it reminds the reader of prior instances in which an inner room has played a role— that is, 1 Kgs 20:30; 22:25. Ahab could have killed Ben Hadad in 1 Kgs 20, but chose to accept him as an ally instead, thereby laying the groundwork for the present campaign against Israel and his son Jehoram. YHWH would take action to overthrow the house of Omri as indicated in 1 Kgs 21 and 22. Second, it points to YHWH's unseen action in employing the prophet behind the scenes, much as Samuel anointed David in secret (1 Sam 16:1–13) and Elisha has frequently served as a means to reveal YHWH's unseen actions and powers to the eyes of his followers and the Arameans (see 2 Kgs 2:1–18; 6:8–23; 6:24–7:20). It suggests that Elisha may actually have had little to do with Jehu, and that the present episode serves merely as a literary link that ties together the discrete Elisha traditions with an otherwise discrete narrative concerning Jehu's revolt.

The servant's announcement to the army officers that he has a message for one of them allows the narrative to create suspense by drawing out the encounter so that Jehu must ask which one of them is to receive the message before finally realizing that it is for him. This encounter enables Elisha's servant to anoint Jehu as king and to commission him with the charge to carry out Elijah's oracle concerning the destruction of the house of Omri. The terms of this commission rehearse the causes for Ahab's condemnation from the earlier Elijah narratives: to avenge the lives of YHWH's prophets and servants murdered by Ahab's wife, Jezebel (see 1 Kgs 18–19). The servant's words also tie the commission to earlier acts to exterminate the dynasties of Jeroboam ben Nebat and Baasha, insofar as it refers specifically in v. 8 to the extermination of all who "piss against the wall, bond and free, in Israel (*maštîn běqîr wěʿāṣûr wěʿāzûb běyiśrāʾēl*)" (cf. 1 Kgs 14:10; 16:11 [*maštîn běqîr* only]; cf. 1 Kgs 21:21, which employs this phrase in relation to Elijah's condemnation of Ahab). The reference to the dogs who will eat Jezebel on (Naboth's) tract of land in Jezreel likewise echoes earlier condemnations of the dynasties of Jeroboam (1 Kgs 14:11) and Baasha (1 Kgs 16:4) as well as that of Ahab (1 Kgs 21:19, 23, 24; 22:38). Jehu's revolt had more to do with Israel's deteriorating military position against Aram than it did with such issues of theology and justice, but the narrator ensures that the reader understands the issue precisely as a matter of theological justice by including these concerns.

[9:11–16] The second episode focuses on the support for Jehu among the officers of the Israelite army stationed at Ramoth Gilead and his departure for Jezreel to carry out the coup. The propagandistic element of this episode is marked, insofar as it portrays Jehu as a reluctant revolutionary who is urged on both by the unnamed young prophet and by his comrades in arms.[8] The characterization of the young prophet as "crazy" (*měšuggāʿ*) speaks to the unusual

8. Cf. Barré, *Rhetoric of Political Persuasion,* 64–72.

lifestyle and behavior of the prophets who are gathered around Elisha: they live together, perhaps at times in the wild like Elijah, and their prophetic vocations would call for ecstatic behavior (cf. Hos 9:7; Jer 29:26). Only after he is urged by his comrades—who prod him by calling him a liar—to reveal the young prophet's words to him does Jehu finally disclose that he has been anointed as king of Israel. The instantaneous response conveys their full support.

[9:17–23] The third episode confirms that neither Jehoram nor Ahaziah had any inkling that a revolt might materialize. The narrative action is placed in Jezreel, where the watchman on the guard tower first spots the approach of Jehu and his entourage. The narrative builds up the suspense, since the guard does not know at first who approaches or the motives for doing so. Jehoram is not so seriously wounded that he is confined to bed, which raises questions about his judgment in leaving the field and his army. The suspense builds as Jehoram orders first one chariot and then another to make inquiries. The first chariot rider employs the common use of the messenger formula "thus says the king" to ask the approaching party if it comes in peace.[9] Jehu sarcastically responds with a rhetorical question that asserts that peace is impossible. Like the army officer that he is, he commands the rider to fall in behind him. Despite the watchman's report, Jehoram fails to grasp what is taking place and orders the second chariot to meet the approaching party. Jehoram finally decides to investigate himself as Ahaziah accompanies him. Neither Jehoram nor Ahaziah senses any danger. The narrative very auspiciously notes that Jehoram met Jehu at the parcel of land once owned by Naboth the Jezreelite (1 Kgs 21).

[9:24–26] Jehu's killing of Jehoram emphasizes a combination of dramatic and propagandistic elements. On the one hand, it emphasizes Jehu's rapid action and sure aim in dispatching Jehoram with a powerful arrow shot that strikes its victim right between the shoulder blades, penetrates the body through the heart, and kills Jehoram instantly. On the other hand, it points to the justification for the assassination by referring once again to Elijah's oracle condemning the house of Ahab. The reference to Bidkar, the crew member in the chariot, is important here because it establishes him together with Jehu as a witness to Elijah's oracle against Ahab concerning the murder of Naboth the Jezreelite. First Kings 21 makes no mention of Jehu's or Bidkar's presence, but the present reference assures the reader that Jehu is not a self-appointed aspirant to power, but a man who acts with divine legitimacy. The oracle quoted here emphasizes the blood of both Naboth and his sons, who are not mentioned in 1 Kgs 21, to point to the realization of this oracle against Ahab's and Jezebel's own sons. It also emphasizes the fulfillment of the earlier oracular statement in 1 Kgs 21:21–22 that the crime would be avenged on Naboth's own

9. See Saul Olyan, "*Hăšālôm*: Some Literary Considerations of 2 Kings 9," *CBQ* 46 (1984): 652–58.

land by highlighting Jehu's command to dump Jehoram's corpse on Naboth's former property.

[9:27–30] Having disposed of Jehoram, the fifth episode now turns to Jehu's killing of Ahaziah ben Jehoram of Judah. This is not gratuitous killing, since Ahaziah is the son of Jehoram ben Jehoshaphat and Athaliah, identified both as the daughter of Omri (2 Kgs 8:26) and as the daughter of Ahab (2 Kgs 8:18; see also 11:1). It thereby fulfills Elijah's oracle concerning the destruction of the house of Omri. Jehu has more difficulty in killing Ahaziah. The Judean king initially flees toward Beth ha-Gan, identified with a tell in the center of the modern city of Jenin.[10] The site is located to the southwest of Jezreel at the entrance to the Dothan Valley that leads to Samaria. Jehu orders that Ahaziah be intercepted at Ma'aleh Gur—"the Ascent of Gur"—by Ibleam. Ibleam is identified with Khirbet Bel'ameh, located just over a mile south of Beth ha-Gan/Jenin, where it too guards the western side of the pass into the Dothan Valley.[11] The Ascent of Gur refers to a rise in the road into the valley located by a site named Gur. Khirbet en-Najjar is located nearby on the east slope of the Wadi Belameh.[12] Ahaziah's movements suggest that Jehu succeeded in cutting him off from the Dothan Valley and access to Samaria by way of Ma'aleh Gur. His turn to Megiddo indicates a bid to seek sanctuary at the strongly fortified city, which guards the strategic western pass between the Jezreel Valley and the coastal plain.

Although the notice concerning Ahaziah's ascent to the throne in v. 29 appears out of place (cf. 2 Kgs 8:25, which states that he ascended the throne in Jehoram's twelfth year rather than the eleventh year), it functions as a retrospective notice concerning the now-dead king, suggesting that the verse is a vestige from an earlier form of this narrative that was later incorporated into the DtrH.

The episode closes with a brief notice of Jezebel's preparations as Jehu approaches Jezreel. Many male scholars fantasize that Jezebel puts eye liner[13] on her eyes and fixes her hair because she intends to seduce Jehu, but she is old enough to be the mother of two adult kings. She is the queen mother, and it appears instead that she prepares herself for an official reception of a man who will kill her (see v. 31 below). The image of a woman peering out of a window is well known from the Samarian ivories, and the portrayal of Jezebel here recalls that image.[14]

---

10. A. Zertal, "Beth Haggan," *ABD* 1:687.

11. M. Hunt, "Ibleam," *ABD* 3:355; A. Zertal, "Gur," *ABD* 2:1099.

12. Zertal, "Gur."

13. Egyptian women used a black substance called "kohl" to outline the eyes, darken the eyebrows, and perhaps to protect the eyes from the glare of the sun. Although such makeup is the subject of criticism (Jer 4:30; Ezek 23:40), the reader must bear in mind that royal women would prepare themselves properly for public appearances. For full discussion of eye makeup in the ancient Near East and bibliography through the 1950s, see J. A. Thompson, "Eye Paint," *IDB* 2:202–3.

14. See Nahman Avigad, "Samaria," *NEAEHL* 4:1300–1310, esp. 1304–6.

[9:31–37] The sixth episode portrays Jehu's killing of Jezebel with a combination of contempt and irony in its efforts to demonstrate that Jehu acts with the authorization of YHWH. Jezebel's rhetorical question to Jehu, "Peace, O Zimri, killer of his master?" indicates her own contempt. Although her question echoes that of her now-dead son (vv. 17–23), her reference to him as Zimri, killer of his master, indicates that she knows his purpose. The reference calls to mind the usurper who killed King Elah ben Baasha of Israel (1 Kgs 15:15–20). Zimri reigned for only seven days before he died in a self-inflicted fire as Omri, Jezebel's own father-in-law, approached Tirzah. Jezebel's question suggests that Jehu is a flash-in-the-pan who will meet a similar fate. The gory portrayal of Jezebel's death, with her blood splattering on the wall and the horses, provides a contemptuous counterpart to the repeated references to the Omride males as those "who piss against the wall," and it provides an excuse for the horses to trample her dead body. Jehu continues to show his own contempt for Jezebel by entering the building to have lunch, which would establish his authority with those inside. His belated command to bury Jezebel's body properly because "she is the daughter of a king" displays proper form in the treatment of her corpse, but the delay again reinforces his own disdain for her. It also provides the occasion to illustrate the fulfillment of Elijah's oracle that the dogs would eat the flesh of Jezebel in the property of Naboth the Jezreelite (see 1 Kgs 21:23). The citation reminds the reader that Jehu acts on the basis of YHWH's will as communicated by Elijah. The episode ends with another contemptuous reference to Jezebel's remains as dung scattered on Naboth's property, courtesy of the dogs that devoured her.

[10:1–12] The seventh episode portrays Jehu's killing of the seventy sons of Ahab with the consent and cooperation of those charged with their care. Such a portrayal underlines the lack of support for the Omride house, and it demonstrates that Jehu acts on behalf of YHWH to fulfill Elijah's oracle. Although there is considerable evidence that the title *ben-hammelek,* "son of the king," could function as an official title in the Israelite and Judean monarchies, it refers to a child of the king in the narrative, as indicated by the references to those entrusted with the responsibility to raise them. The number seventy may be exaggerated since it is also employed in Israelite tradition to refer to the elders who governed Israel prior to or in conjunction with the monarchy.

Jehu's letter to "the rulers of Jezreel," "the elders," and "those loyal to Ahab" follows the typical form known for ancient Israelite letters; it begins with the addressees, and the body of the letter begins with the expression *wĕʿattâ,* "and now."[15] The letter is crafted to test the loyalties and intentions of those Omride officers and officials who remained in Samaria while the king was away at war.

15. See Dennis Pardee et al., *Handbook of Ancient Hebrew Letters* (SBLSBS 15; Chico, Calif.: Scholars Press, 1982), 145–52.

Key officials, including the officer in charge of the royal household (ʾăšer ʿal habbayyit, i.e., the chief administrator of the king), the governor of the city of Samaria (ʾăšer ʿal hāʿîr), the elders, and those loyal to Jehu respond to him that they will decline his challenge, that they are his servants, and that he should do whatever he thinks is best.[16] When the officers and officials of Samaria comply with Jehu's orders to bring to him the heads of the seventy sons of Ahab at Jezreel, he makes a special point of declaring them to be innocent of any crime. The statement, "you are innocent (ṣaddiqîm ʾattem)," employs a standard judicial formula employed to state innocence in a court of law.[17] Jehu declares his complete responsibility for the killing of Ahab's seventy sons by asking the rhetorical question "Who killed all of these?" The reader knows that the sons were killed by Samaria's officials acting on the orders of Jehu, but Jehu then justifies the killing by publicly stating that it was carried out in accordance with the word of YHWH as spoken by Elijah.

The episode concludes in v. 12 with a statement of Jehu's journey from Jezreel to Samaria. The reference to Beth Eqed of the Shepherds is enigmatic due to difficulties in locating the site. Many identify it with the modern site of Beit Qad, located some three miles east of Jenin at the southeastern edge of the Jezreel Valley on the ascent to Mount Gilboa to the northeast and the hill country of Ephraim to the south. Others contend that a more direct route to Samaria would call for identification with Kafr Ro'i, located on a hill above the abandoned rail tracks from Afula to Jenin, based on the similarity of the name Ro'i with Hebrew hārōʿîm, "shepherds."[18]

[10:13–30] The eighth episode takes up Jehu's slaughter of the brothers of Ahaziah and the supporters of Baal from throughout Israel. Again, there is a concerted propagandistic effort to portray these killings as fulfillment of the word of YHWH through Elijah.

The first encounter with the brothers of Ahaziah reiterates the prior theme of Ahaziah's visit to his brother-in-law at Jezreel where he was recuperating from his wounds (see 1 Kgs 9:15, 16 above). Although it is unlikely that all forty-two of Ahaziah's brothers would have been born to Athaliah, Jehoram's marriage to the Omride princess would identify them as members of the house of Ahab and therefore subject to Jehu's action. The mention of forty-two brothers who are seized and killed by Jehu at Beth Eqed suggests affinities with the narrative concerning Elisha's killing of forty-two boys while on the road from Jericho to Beth El in 2 Kgs 2:23–25.

16. See esp. Nili Sacher Fox, *In the Service of the King: Officialdom in Ancient Israel and Judah* (Monographs of the Hebrew Union College 23; Cincinnati: Hebrew Union College, 2000), 81–96, 150–58, 63–72, 196–203.

17. See H. J. Boecker, *Redeformen des Rechtslebens im Alten Testament* (WMANT 14; Neukirchen-Vluyn: Neukirchener Verlag, 1970), 122–43.

18. M. Hunt, "Beth Eked," *ABD* 1:685.

The balance of this episode focuses on Jehu's execution of the Baal supporters from throughout the country. The enigmatic Jehonadab ben Rekeb plays a key role, particularly since he is identified as a zealous supporter of YHWH. He is otherwise known from Jer 35, where he is portrayed as the founder of the Rekabite house. The Rekabite house represents an idealized form of YHWH worship based in a seminomadic lifestyle that has analogies with Israel's experience in the wilderness. Tradition links them to the line of Jethro, the priest of Midian and father-in-law of Moses. The lifestyle and loyalty to YHWH practiced by the Rekabites shows marked parallels to Elijah, who lives in the wilderness at YHWH's command (1 Kgs 17:2–6; 19:1–21), and emphasizes his zealousness for YHWH much like Jehonadab (1 Kgs 19:10, 14).

The narrative contrasts the zealous Jehonadab with the faithless Ahab. When asked by Jehu if he is loyal to YHWH, Jehonadab answers with an emphatic *yēš wāyēš*, "yes, indeed!" before calling for Jehu to give him a hand so that he might ride with Jehu in the chariot. Jehonadab's act contrasts with that of Ahab, who gave his hand to Ben Hadad in order to help him into his chariot (1 Kgs 20:33–34). Ahab's act in saving Ben Hadad's life and renewing his treaty with him is the basis for his condemnation by the anonymous prophet (1 Kgs 20:35–43).

Verse 17 emphasizes that, upon entering Samaria, Jehu wiped out the last remnants of the house of Ahab in accordance with the word of YHWH spoken by Elijah. Such a statement serves the propagandistic character of the narrative by legitimizing the bloodshed, and it prepares the reader to accept the blatantly deceptive means by which Jehu exterminates the Baalists. Jehu calls for a sacrifice to honor Baal (cf. Zeph 1:7), declaring that he will serve Baal even more than did Ahab. The ominous nature of the call to "sanctify a festival for Baal" (v. 20) is signaled by the threat to kill anyone who fails to attend (v. 19). Jehu calls on the officer in charge of the wardrobe to supply festival garments for all of the worshipers (cf. Zeph 1:8). With the temple for Baal in Samaria filled to capacity, Jehu and Jehonadab take steps to ensure that all of the Baalists are trapped and that no innocent supporters of YHWH remain inside. Such a notice once again serves the propagandistic purposes of the narrative to demonstrate that Jehu kills only those authorized by YHWH. He stations eighty men outside the temple, and charges them to let no one escape lest it cost them their own lives. Such a command recalls the similar commission to Ahab to let none of the enemy Arameans escape (see 1 Kgs 20:39–42). Ahab's failure to kill Ben Hadad ensures the destruction of his supporters and house.

The ensuing massacre ensures the destruction of Baalism in Samaria. Once the soldiers and officers had completed their grisly task, they entered "the city" of the house of Baal—the inner sanctum analogous to the holy of holies of the temple—and removed the mazzeboth or "pillars/stelae" of the temple of Baal. Such mazzeboth were typically employed to represent the presence of gods in Canaanite/Aramean temples and religious tradition, and they frequently appear in Israelite/Judean sanctuaries (e.g., Gen 28:18; Josh 4:1–14; 24:26–27). After the mazzeboth were burned, the temple to Baal was razed and turned into a latrine. Such an act desecrates the site, but it also provides the focal point for prior references to the extermination of all the males of the house of Ahab who "piss against the wall" (see 1 Kgs 21:21; 2 Kgs 9:8; cf. 1 Kgs 14:10; 1 Kgs 16:11).

The subunit concludes in vv. 28–30 with summary and evaluative notices concerning Jehu's reign. On the one hand, Jehu is credited in v. 28 with destroying the influence of Baal in Israel, but this notice is immediately qualified with the statement in v. 29, introduced by the particle *raq,* "but," that he did not turn from the sins of Jeroboam—that is, the golden calves at Beth El and Dan. A second statement in v. 30 lauds Jehu for following YHWH's instructions and indicates that his sons will rule Israel through the fourth generation. These statements indicate the basis for the destruction of the house of Jehu in the fifth generation, when Zechariah ben Jeroboam is assassinated by Shallum (2 Kgs 15:8–12, note esp. v. 12). But the criticism leveled against Jehu's dynasty is retrospectively applied from the perspective of the Hezekian and Josianic editions, which sought to justify the downfall of the north and to pave the way for the restoration of Davidic rule over the former northern territories. The unabashed praise for Jehu's acts and the promise that his house would rule through the fourth generation points to the interests of the Jehu History.

[10:31–36] The final subunit incorporates a concluding regnal summary for Jehu ben Jehoshaphat ben Nimshi into the larger narrative structure of the account of Jehu's revolt (contra Long 126–28, 142–45). It begins in v. 31 with a notice that Jehu did not observe YHWH's Torah, and it reiterates the earlier notice in v. 29 that he followed in the sins of Jeroboam ben Nebat. The regnal summary introduces the statements in vv. 32–33 that YHWH began to cut off parts of the territory of Israel as punishment for Jehu's actions. This comment is particularly striking in view of the approval for Jehu's actions stated in vv. 28 and 30 above, but they do account theologically for the historical realities of the late ninth and early eighth centuries B.C.E., when Israel lost control of the Transjordan. The territory lost includes all of the Israelite Transjordan, including the tribal territories of Manasseh, Gad, and Reuben, east of the Jordan and north of the Wadi Arnon, which was the boundary between Israel and Moab. Aroer is a city located just to the north of the Wadi Arnon,[19] Gilead is the central region of modern Jordan between the Arnon and the Yarmuk,[20] and Bashan is the region to the north of the Yarmuk extending north toward Damascus.[21] The present narrative points to Hazael of Aram as the party responsible for these reverses. Such a notice indicates that the plot begun in 1 Kgs 19,

19. G. Mattingly, "Aroer," *ABD* 1:399–400.
20. M. Ottosson, "Gilead," *ABD* 2:1020–22.
21. J. C. Slayton, "Bashan," *ABD* 1:623–24.

in which YHWH instructs Elijah to anoint Elisha, Jehu, and Hazael, has not yet come to an end. The literary presentation is supported by inscriptional evidence, such as the Tel Dan inscription, which indicates that the Arameans claimed to have defeated Jehoram and Ahaziah, although it says nothing of Jehu.[22] The Moabite Stone indicates that King Mesha of Moab also took part by invading the Transjordanian territory of Israel north of the Wadi Arnon (*ANET* 320–21). Historically speaking, the Arameans and Moabites found common cause in their efforts to eject Israel from the Transjordan. Although Jehu's revolt took place when the house of Omri was no longer able to defend Israel, the revolt would have further weakened Israel, forcing Jehu and his grandson Joash to turn to the Assyrians for support.

2 Kings 11:1–20 The Reign of Athaliah bat Ahab over Judah

11:1 Athaliah, the mother of Ahaziah, saw[a] that her son was dead, and she arose, and destroyed all the seed of the kingdom. 2 So Jehosheba, the daughter of King Joram, the sister of Ahaziah, took Joash ben Ahaziah, and stole him from the midst of the sons of the king [b]who were to be put to death,[b] him and his wet nurse, in the bedroom, and they hid him from Athaliah so that he was not put to death. 3 He was hiding with her in the House of YHWH for six years while Athaliah was ruling over the land.

4 In the seventh year, Jehoiada sent and took the captains of hundreds of the Carites and the soldiers, and he brought them to him in the House of YHWH, made a covenant with them, caused them to swear in the House of YHWH, and showed them the son of the king. 5 And he commanded them, saying, "This is what you shall do. One third of you are standing watch over the house of the king at the beginning of Shabbat, 6 and one third are at the Sur[c] Gate, and one third are at the gate behind the soldiers, and you shall stand watch at the Temple for stragglers.[d] 7 Two companies among you, all those who stand watch over the House of YHWH at the conclusion of Shabbat, are assigned to the king. 8 You shall surround the king, each with his weapons in hand, and anyone who approaches the ranks shall be killed, and stay with the king wherever he goes." 9 And the captains of hundreds did according to all that Jehoiada the priest commanded them. Each took his men on duty at the beginning of Shabbat with those on duty at the end of Shabbat, and they came to Jehoiada the priest. 10 And the priest gave to the captains of hundreds the spears and shields of King David which were in the House of YHWH. 11 And the soldiers stood, each with his weapons in hand, around from the

---

22. Avraham Biran and Joseph Naveh, "An Aramaic Stele Fragment from Tel Dan," *IEJ* 43 (1993): 81–98; Biran and Naveh, "The Tel Dan Inscription: A New Fragment," *IEJ* 45 (1995): 1–18.

right/south end of the Temple until the left/north end of the Temple by the altar and by the house of the king. 12 And he brought out the son of the king and placed on him the crown and the testimony, and they made him king, anointed him, clapped hands, and said, "May the king live!"

13 Athaliah heard the sound of ^ethe soldiers and the people,^e and she came to the people at the House of YHWH 14 and saw, and behold, the king was standing by the pillar according to law, and the commanders and the trumpets were with the king, and all the people of the land were rejoicing and blowing trumpets. Athaliah tore her garments and cried out, "Conspiracy! Conspiracy!"

15 And Jehoiada the priest commanded the captains of hundreds in charge of the army and said to them, "Bring her out into the ranks, and kill with the sword whomever comes after her," because the priest had said, "She shall not be killed in the House of YHWH." 16 So they laid hands on her, and she came to the entryway of the horses at the house of the king, and she was killed there.

17 And Jehoiada made a covenant between YHWH and the king and the people, and between the king and the people, to be YHWH's people. 18 And all the people of the land came to the house of Baal and tore it down. Its altars and its images they thoroughly destroyed, and Mattan, the priest of Baal, they killed before the altars. And the priest assigned guards over the House of YHWH. 19 He took the captains of hundreds, the Carites, the soldiers, and all the people of the land, and they brought the king down from the House of YHWH. They came to the gateway of the soldiers at the house of the king, and he sat on the throne of the kings. 20 All the people of the land rejoiced, and the city was quiet, and Athaliah they killed with the sword ^fin the house of the king.^f

---

a. Read with Qere, *rāʾătâ,* "she saw"; cf. LXX; Targum Jonathan; Peshitta; contra Ketiv, *wĕrāʾătâ,* "and she saw."

b–b. Read with Qere, *hammumātîm,* a hophal participle that means "those who were being put to death"; cf. 2 Chr 22:11, which contains the same reading; contra Ketiv, *hammĕmôttîm,* a polel participle that means "those who were putting to death."

c. The meaning of Hebrew, *sûr,* here is uncertain. Because the root means "to turn aside," it could refer to an exit gate for the temple. The versions play on such a meaning; cf. LXX, *tōn hodōn,* "(the gate of) the highway"; Targum Jonathan, *gînayāʾ,* "(the gate) of the protectors," i.e., "those who turn aside"; Peshitta, *dqrsʾ,* "(the gate) of the chariot." See also 2 Chr 23:5, which reads *hayĕsôd,* "the foundation (gate)," in an attempt to interpret the term *sûr,* based upon the resemblance of the letters *resh* and *daleth.*

d. The meaning of the Hebrew term *massah* is uncertain. Because it is derived from the root *nsh,* "to pluck away," the versions presuppose that it refers to defense against any stragglers who might escape or do harm; cf. LXX, which omits the expression; Targum

Jonathan, *midĕyiśtĕlê*, "from that which is forgotten," i.e., "from whomever gets away"; Peshitta, *swrhy*, "(from) harm."

e–e. MT, *hārāṣîn hāʿām*, lit., "the runners, the people." The first term is the Aramaic form of *hārāsîm*, "the runners," and likely is a gloss in the text that was meant to define the term *hāʿām*, "the people." Cf. LXX, "(the sound of) the people running"; Targum Jonathan, "(the sound of) those ruling [*dĕradĕnîn*] the people," apparently reading *hārāṣîn*, "the runners," as Aramaic, *hārāṣîn*, "those who decide"; Peshitta, "the people as they rejoiced (*bd hdyn*)," perhaps reading *hārāṣîn* as a reference to the running of the people (cf. LXX) during their celebration. See also 2 Chr 23:12, "the people running (*hārāsîm*) and praising the king."

f–f. Read with Qere, *hammelek*, "(in the house of) the king"; contra Ketiv, *melek*, "king."

The account of Athaliah's reign over Judah appears as the concluding sub-unit of the regnal account of Ahaziah ben Jehoram of Judah in 2 Kgs 8:25–11:20. It is an appendix, insofar as it stands outside of the formal structure of the introductory regnal account for Ahaziah in 2 Kgs 8:25–29 and the concluding regnal account of the reign of Jehu in 2 Kgs 10:31–36. Because Athaliah is a usurper, the account of her own reign and revolt against the house of David is treated structurally much like that of northern Israel's revolt against Rehoboam in 1 Kgs 12 and Jehu's revolt against Jehoram in 2 Kgs 9–10—that is, it lacks the typical introductory regnal formula. But it also lacks a concluding regnal formula, which is supplied for both Jeroboam ben Nebat (1 Kgs 14:19–20) and Jehu (2 Kgs 10:31–36). The lack of conclusion is due to the fact that Athaliah is a foreigner and the only woman to rule autonomously over either Judah or Israel in the monarchic period.[23]

The narrative is demarcated in typical fashion with an introductory combination of a conjunctive *waw* and the proper name Athaliah, that is, *waʿătalyâ*, "and Athaliah, . . ." Verses 1–20 focus on the major events of her reign, including her seizure of the throne following her unsuccessful attempt to exterminate the entire house of David in vv. 1–3 and the account of the coup led against her by the high priest Jehoiada (vv. 4–20) that restored the seven-year-old Joash ben Ahaziah to the throne.

Although many interpreters see this narrative as an attempt to depict events in Judah related to Jehu's coup against the north,[24] the account of Athaliah's reign plays a crucial role within the exilic DtrH. It portrays the influence of the north-

23. The next Jewish queen of Judea is the Hasmonean monarch Salome Alexandra (76–67 B.C.E.), who ruled in Jerusalem following the deaths of both of her husbands, Aristobulus I (104–103 B.C.E.) and his brother Alexander Janneus (103–76 B.C.E.).

24. Note esp. the attempts to argue that 2 Kgs 11 represents a propagandistic attempt to portray the Judean coup against Athaliah as far more orderly and peaceful than Jehu's bloody revolt (see Barré, *Rhetoric of Political Persuasion*, 86–99; Patricia Dutcher-Walls, *Narrative Art, Political Rhetoric: The Case of Athaliah and Joash* (JSOTSup 209; Sheffield: Sheffield Academic Press, 1996).

ern Omride dynasty in the south, and thereby notes how issues of northern apostasy could affect Judah as well. But the issue of Omride influence goes well beyond issues of religious observance. Athaliah is the mother of Ahaziah (and the grandmother of Joash), and she is therefore an ancestress of the entire house of David beginning with the reign of Ahaziah. Interpreters might overlook the significance of this role in view of her attempt to exterminate the house of David, but it has a bearing on the presentation of the house of David throughout the rest of the history. King Manasseh of Judah is explicitly compared to his ancestor, King Ahab of Israel, in erecting an Asherah (2 Kgs 23:3) prior to being held responsible for the destruction of Jerusalem and the temple and the Babylonian exile. King Josiah of Judah is promised by the prophetess, Huldah, that because of his repentance he will die early so that he will not have to witness the destruction and exile of Judah. Huldah's prophecy bears a striking resemblance to Elijah's statements to Ahab that he would not see the full destruction of his house because he repented following his condemnation for the murder of Naboth (1 Kgs 21:27–29), yet Elijah's prophecy called for the destruction of the entire house of Ahab (1 Kgs 21:20–26). Although Athaliah's death fulfills that prophecy in the immediate context, the fate of the house of David at the end of the DtrH, in which Jehoiachin is released from prison to eat at the table of the Babylonian king (2 Kgs 25:27–30), stands in partial fulfillment of Elijah's prophecy.[25] After all, Jehoiachin's fate is analogous to that of Mephibosheth ben Jonathan ben Saul, who ate at David's table and thereby brought the dynasty of the house of Saul to an end (2 Sam 9:1–13; 19:24–30). From the standpoint of the Hezekian DtrH, her attempted coup is symptomatic of the political instability, incompetence, and violence that so characterizes the north and calls for the stabilizing hand of the house of David. Although some point to the origins of this narrative in the Judean court archives, it serves the interests of the eighth-century Jehu History insofar as it constitutes an episode in the history of the primary client-state of the house of Jehu. Jeroboam ben Joash's rule from Lebo Hamath to the Sea of the Arabah inevitably includes Judah. Judah suffered from instability during this period. With the assassinations of Ahaziah, Athaliah, Joash, and Amaziah, Judah was subdued by Jehoash ben Jehoahaz of Israel and forced to remain a client of the house of Jehu. Athaliah's rule would threaten the dynasty that had overthrown her own family, but ultimately she was dispatched and Jehu interests in Judah were maintained.

The historical dimensions of this narrative must also be considered. The typical portrayal of Athaliah's revolt as an expression of her harlotry and fanatical devotion to Baal, an analogy to her mother Jezebel, hardly does justice to her motivations. It makes little sense that she would attempt to exterminate the

---

25. See also Marvin A. Sweeney, *King Josiah of Judah: The Lost Mssiah of Israel* (Oxford and New York: Oxford University Press, 2001), 49–50.

entire house of David, including her own grandson Joash, in a bid to retain power in Jerusalem. As a foreigner in Jerusalem, particularly one of Phoenician descent, her Davidic grandson provided the key to her ability to exercise power. Although her position appears to be secure while her son Ahaziah is alive, she clearly sees Joash to be a threat to her position following the death of her son. Athaliah is the queen mother—Hebrew, *gĕbîrâ*—who exercises power in the house of David while her son is on the throne.[26] This model provides some basis to understand Athaliah's attempted coup. Her grandson Joash quite obviously had a mother, Zibiah of Beer Sheba (2 Kgs 12:2), who would exercise power as *gĕbîrâ* when her own son came to the throne. This approach would challenge Athaliah's role, but such a challenge would never be forthcoming if Joash never survived to become king. For Athaliah, the death of her grandson Joash would ensure her hold on power in Judah as *gĕbîrâ*. The reader is not told if Zibiah was killed, but the fact that Ahaziah's sister Jehosheba—and not his mother— saved the infant Joash's life suggests that she was.

Other dimensions of the historical situation must be examined. Athaliah would hardly attempt to maintain relations with an Israel ruled by the very man who had killed off her family in Samaria, yet there is no indication that Judah broke free of Israelite control in this period. Amaziah later attempted to do so, but Jehoash ben Jehoahaz forced him back into submission (2 Kgs 14:8–14). Like Israel under the Jehu dynasty (2 Kgs 10:32–33; 13:22–25), Judah suffered attacks from the Arameans during this period, and Joash had to pay Hazael off to save Jerusalem from continued assault (2 Kgs 12:17–18). In order to explain this state of affairs, two observations are necessary. First, Athaliah established or maintained a temple to Baal in Jerusalem (v. 18 below), which would express her Samarian and Phoenician background. It also expressed her continued political relationship with Phoenicia. Indeed, opposition against her reign is led by the priest Jehoiada of the Jerusalem temple, who acts to restore Davidic rule. Second, Jehu is listed as a tributary together with Sidon and Tyre by Shalmaneser III in the eighteenth year of his reign (841 B.C.E.; see *ANET* 280). This listing is particularly striking, since Jehu had presumably overthrown a dynasty with close ties to the Phoenicians, and yet Jehu was attacked repeatedly by the Arameans after having carried out this act, suggesting that Jehu remained a Phoenician client even after his overthrow of the house of Omri.[27] The key to this relationship would be Athaliah, who would maintain her family's ties to the

26. See esp. Zafrira Ben-Barak, "The Status and Right of the GᴱBÎRÂ," *JBL* 110 (1991): 23–34. See also Sarah C. Melville, *The Role of Naqia/Zakutu in Sargonid Politics* (SASA 9; Helsinki: University of Helsinki, 1999), who discusses the efforts of the Assyrian queen Naqia/Zukutu, the West-Semitic wife of Sennacherib, to ensure the succession to the Assyrian throne of her son Esarhaddon and later her grandson Assurbanipal.

27. Jehu's continuation of Israel's alliance with Phoenicia might also explain why he continued to be identified by the Assyrians as the son of Omri (cf. Schneider, "Rethinking Jehu").

Phoenicians and thereby box Jehu in with Phoenician suzerains to his northwest and a pro-Phoenician Judah to his south. Rather than ally with Aram, Jehu was forced to maintain Israel's ties with the Phoenicians, and he paid a heavy price for this alignment at the hands of the Arameans. The Phoenicians were unable or unwilling to help him.[28] Only through the Assyrians to whom both Phoenicia and Israel (and Judah) submitted were the Arameans finally held in check.

[11:1–3] This subunit provides the background for the coup against Athaliah by describing the circumstances in which she came to power. Verse 1 very carefully identifies Athaliah as the mother of King Ahaziah, and states her effort to destroy the house of David upon learning of the death of her son. The conflict within the royal house is highlighted by the actions of Jehosheba, the sister of Ahaziah, who hides the infant Joash together with his wet nurse in the temple complex to save him from Athaliah's purge. By placing baby Joash and his wet nurse in one of the temple chambers, Jehosheba would be able to keep them from Athaliah's reach, since Athaliah as a foreigner would be unable to enter the holy temple premises.

[11:4–20] This subunit presents several episodes, including Jehoiada's instructions to the temple guards in vv. 4–8, the coronation of Joash by Jehoiada and the guards in vv. 9–12, Athaliah's discovery of the coup in vv. 13–14, the execution of Athaliah in vv. 15–16, and the concluding portrayals in vv. 17–20 of the new covenant between YHWH, king, and people that called for the destruction of the sanctuary to Baal and the seating of Joash on the throne.

As the priest of the temple, Jehoiada represents the primary state religious institution that owes its existence and identity to the house of David and that in turn plays the key role in legitimizing the Davidic monarchs by identifying them as YHWH's choice to rule the state. Insofar as Jehoiada shows Joash to the soldiers, he takes them into one of the chambers that line the temple structure rather than into the sacred interior of the temple itself. The identity of the Carites is not clear. Many speculate that they constitute some special body of mercenaries, and point to 2 Sam 20:23, which identifies Benaiah ben Jehoiada as commander of the Cherethites and the Pelethites to justify this conclusion.[29] Although the Ketiv form of this text is *hakkārî*, "the Carites," the Qere form is *hakkĕrētî*, "the Cherethites," which removes it from consideration. Insofar as the term *hakkārî* is derived from the noun *kar*, "ram," which suggests strength or authority, it is possible that the term designates a class of soldier between the officers and the foot soldiers, perhaps some equivalent to a noncommissioned officer. Jehoiada's instructions indicate that he will take action at the conclusion of

---

28. See Amos 1:9 (cf. Amos 1:11), which accuses Tyre of failing to honor its treaty with Israel in the late ninth and early eighth centuries B.C.E.; M. A. Sweeney, *The Twelve Prophets* (Berit Olam; Collegeville, Minn.: Liturgical, 2000), 1:208–9.

29. See C. S. Ehrlich, "Carites," *ABD* 1:872.

Shabbat, apparently at the time of the changing of the guard when a maximum number of soldiers would be available to him. The soldiers assigned to the watch for the coming week begin duty at the beginning of Shabbat, and those of the prior week go off-duty at the conclusion of Shabbat, resulting in a double guard for the temple during the Shabbat. He assigns one-third of the soldiers to the temple, one-third to the Sur gate, and one-third at the gate behind the soldiers to watch for stragglers or those who might escape from the soldiers at the Sur gate. Jehoiada thereby cuts off escape or aid from outside the temple.

Verses 9–12 then describe the actions of Jehoiada and the soldiers in carrying out the coup. The officers make sure that their soldiers appear before Jehoiada, who arms them with the spears and shields of King David from the temple storerooms. Two-hundred-year-old weapons might not be the ideal choice, but the narrative presupposes that they are adequate for the task. Perhaps the reference to David indicates their function—that is, they are the arms of the palace or temple guard rather than relics. The soldiers are positioned in an arc before the temple from the altar on the north or left side to the south or right side (cf. 1 Kgs 7:39, which places the Bronze Sea at the southeast corner before the temple, leaving the northeast for the altar; 1 Kgs 8:64 states only that the altar is located in the courtyard before the temple). Such an arrangement provides protection for the young king, who will stand in the customary place of the king by the pillar at the entrance to the temple (see v. 14; cf. 2 Kgs 23:3). The crown (*nēzer*) is a symbol of royal authority (see 2 Sam 1:10; Pss 89:40; 132:18; Zech 9:16), although crowns may also be worn by the high priests (see Exod 29:6; Lev 8:9). The testimony (*'ēdût*) refers to a tangible expression of YHWH's commandments, frequently identified with the Ten Commandments (Exod 31:18; 32:15; 34:29), placed in the ark of the covenant (Exod 25:22; 40:3; Num 4:5; Josh 4:16), or YHWH's laws in general (Pss 19:8; 119:88; 122:4). The testimony is entrusted to the king, who will see to the observance of YHWH's expectations (see 1 Kgs 2:3; 2 Kgs 23:3; cf. Ps 2:7). The crowning of the king is accompanied by anointing, the clapping of hands, and the shout, "May the king live!" (cf. 1 Kgs 1:38–40; see also 1 Sam 9:16; 10:1; 16:3, 12, 13; 1 Kgs 1:25).

Because the temple is sacred, Jehoiada takes special care to ensure that Athaliah is not killed within the temple itself. The soldiers take her to the gate of the horses at the royal palace, and kill her there. Jehoiada's initiative in concluding a covenant reestablishes the rule of the Davidic dynasty. By emphasizing the role of the people in the relationship, this enactment of the covenant reinvigorates the role of the people in the state which had eroded from the time of Solomon. Whereas David was chosen as king by the people of Judah (2 Sam 2:4) and the elders of Israel who represented the tribes of Israel (2 Sam 5:1–5), Solomon was chosen to be king by David, acting at the instigation of Bath Sheba and Nathan (1 Kgs 1). Although the people of the northern tribes retained the power to chose their own king (1 Kgs 12:1–24), no such role is evident for the people of Judah from the time of Rehoboam. By including "the people of the land" in v. 18,[30] Jehoiada makes a bid to ensure that a palace coup like that of Athaliah would not happen again. His bid is not entirely successful, as the assassinations of Joash (2 Kgs 12:20–21), Amaziah (2 Kgs 14:18–20), and Amon (2 Kgs 21:23) indicate. The people of the land play an instrumental role in seeing to the continuity of the house of David, insofar as they take action to place Azariah ben Amaziah (2 Kgs 14:21), Josiah ben Amon (2 Kgs 21:24), and Jehoahaz ben Josiah (2 Kgs 23:30) on the throne in place of their murdered fathers. The restoration of the Davidic house entails the recognition of YHWH as G-d of Judah.

XVII. Regnal Account of Jehoash ben Ahaziah of Judah 2 Kings 12:1–22

12:1 Jehoash was seven years old when he began his reign.

2 In the seventh year of Jehu, Jehoash ruled, and he ruled for forty years in Jerusalem. The name of his mother was Zibyah from Beer Sheba. 3 Jehoash did what was right in the eyes of YHWH all his days while Jehoiada the priest instructed him. 4 Only he did not remove the high places; the people continued to sacrifice and to burn incense at the high places.

5 And Jehoash said to the priests, "All of the dedicated funds which were brought to the house of YHWH, funds transferred by each man, ªfunds according to individual assessment,ª all funds that a man might be motivated to bring to the house of YHWH, 6 the priests shall take, each from his benefactor,ᵇ and they shall repair the damage of the Temple, wherever damage is found." 7 But in the twenty-third year of King Jehoash the priests had not repaired the damage of the Temple. 8 So King Jehoash summoned Jehoiada, the priest, and the other priests and said to them, "Why are you not repairing the damage of the Temple? And now you will not receive funds from your benefactors, but for the damage of the Temple you shall pay." 9 And the priests agreed not to receive funds from the people nor to repair the damage of the Temple. 10 And Jehoiada

30. For discussion of the role of "the people of the land" in Judean society, see Halpern, "Jerusalem and the Lineages"; Christopher R. Seitz, *Theology in Conflict: Reactions to the Exile in the Book of Jeremiah* (BZAW 176; Berlin and New York: Walter de Gruyter, 1989), 42–71.

the priest took a chest, bored a hole in its lid, and placed it ᶜto the right of the altar when a man enters the House of YHWH,ᶜ and the priests who guarded the threshhold deposited there all the funds that were brought to the House of YHWH. 11 When they saw that funds had accumulated in the chest, the royal scribe and the high priest came up, and they bound and counted the funds that were found in the House of YHWH. 12 They placed the funds that were accounted for in the hands of the appointed workmen of the House of YHWH. They in turn brought it out to the carpenters and to the builders who were working on the House of YHWH 13 and to the masons and to the stone carvers to buy wood and carved stone to repair the damage of the House of YHWH, and for everything that was spent on the Temple for repair. 14 However, bowls of silver, snuffers, basins, trumpets, all vessels of gold, and vessels of silver were not made at the House of YHWH from the silver that was brought to the House of YHWH. 15 They gave it instead to the workmen, and they repaired the House of YHWH. 16 They did not check the men to whom they gave the funds to give to the workmen, for they acted honestly. 17 The funds of the guilt offering, and the funds of the sin offerings were not brought to the House of YHWH; they were for the priests.

18 Then Hazael, King of Aram, came up, fought against Gath, and captured it. Then Hazael set his face to go up against Jerusalem. 19 And Jehoash, King of Judah, took all the dedicated items, which Jehoshaphat and Jehoram and Ahaziah his fathers the Kings of Judah had dedicated, all his dedicated items and all the gold that was found in the treasuries of the House of YHWH and the House of the King, and he sent them to Hazael, King of Aram, who then departed from Jerusalem.

20 The rest of the acts of Joash and all that he did, are they not written in the book of the Chronicles of the Kings of Judah? 21 And his servants arose, conspired, and struck down Joash at Beth Millo on the way down to Silla. 22 And Jozabad ben Shimath and Jehozabad ben Shomer, his servants, struck him down, and he died. They buried him with his fathers in the city of David, and Amaziah his son ruled in his place.

a–a. MT, *kesep napšôt ᶜerkô,* "the funds of the lives of his valuation," i.e., the assessment of individuals for whom a man is responsible.

b. MT, *makkārô,* "his acquaintance (one known to him)"; cf. LXX, *apo tēs praseōs autou,* "from his sale," which presupposes Hebrew, *mimĕmakrô,* "from his sale." The expression refers to the value of the funds allotted to each priest.

c–c. Cf. LXX (Codex Alexandrinus), "by the Maṣṣebah in the house of the man of the Temple of YHWH." Alexandrinus reads *'ammazeibi,* a transliteration of Hebrew, *hammaṣṣēbâ,* "the maṣṣebah (cultic pillar)," in place of Hebrew, *mîyāmîn* (Qere; Ketiv reads *bayyāmîn*), "to the right." The Alexandrinus version acknowledges the charges of idolatry in the temple during the reign of Jehoash as depicted in 2 Chr 24:18.

Second Kings 12:1–22 is demarcated by the introductory regnal form in vv. 1–4 and the concluding regnal form in vv. 20–22. The account of Jehoash's reign in vv. 5–19 includes two episodes, vv. 5–17, which discuss his fiscal reforms for financing temple repairs, and vv. 18–19, which note his payment to Hazael of funds dedicated to the temple to ward off an Aramean attack.

The placement of the notice concerning Hazael's threat to Jerusalem indicates a primary concern with the continuing Aramean threat against the land of Israel from the time of the Omride dynasty through the early years of the Jehu dynasty. Second Kings 13:22–25 indicates that the Arameans were finally defeated only in the reign of King Jehoash ben Jehoahaz of Israel, the third monarch of the Jehu line, following the death of the prophet Elisha (2 Kgs 13:14–21). Jehoash ben Ahaziah's payment of tribute to Hazael indicates that all funds collected for temple repair by Jehoash and his ancestors were lost to the Arameans.

Such a portrayal depicts the aftereffects of the corrupting influence of the house of Omri on Israel and Judah; Jehoash ben Ahaziah is, after all, the grand-son of Athaliah and the great-grandson of Ahab ben Omri. Although Jehoash ben Ahaziah is portrayed as a righteous monarch concerned with the welfare of the temple, his good intentions come to naught when he is forced to pay an indem-nity to Hazael to save Jerusalem from Aramean attack. The narrative does not make the connection explicit, but the notice concerning Jehoash's assassination in the concluding regnal account suggests that Jehoash was killed due to his fail-ure to repel the Aramean attack and the consequent loss of funds collected dur-ing the reigns of Jehoshaphat, Jehoram, Ahaziah, and Jehoash himself.

Although Jehoash's submission to the Arameans may explain the historical cause of his assassination, the reader must note the historiographical perspec-tive of the present narrative. It is likely no coincidence that Jehoshaphat was the Judean king who gave his son Jehoram in marriage to the Omride princess Athaliah. The Davidic intermarriage into the house of Omri would have con-sequences for the rest of its history in Jerusalem. Because the house of David is descended from the house of Omri, it too suffers judgment in the DtrH. The assassination of Jehoash is therefore particularly noteworthy; despite his righ-teous actions, Jehoash is assassinated by his own servants. The same fate awaits his son, Amaziah, who is assassinated following his failed attempt to revolt against his northern Israelite overlord, King Jehoash ben Jehoahaz of the house of Jehu (2 Kgs 14:19–21; cf. 14:8–14). Up to the regnal account of King Jer-oboam ben Jehoash of Israel, who restored the borders of Israel, all Davidic monarchs of Judah are also assassinated in keeping with Elijah's announcement that not one male of the house of Omri would survive.

These considerations indicate that the regnal account of King Jehoash ben Ahaziah of Judah was written as part of the Jehu history to support its polemic against the Omride dynasty and to point ultimately to the reign of Jeroboam ben Joash who restored security to Israel. It would later be incorporated into the

Hezekian DtrH, where it would support the general polemics against the northern dynasties. When the DtrH was expanded during the reign of Josiah, it would have functioned in a similar fashion in the Josianic DtrH. The later reference to King Manasseh's asherah, like that of Ahab (2 Kgs 21:3) in the exilic DtrH, indicates that the relationship between the house of David and the house of Omri from the time of Jehoshaphat on ultimately played an important role in the presentation of the fall of Jerusalem and the demise of the Davidic dynasty in the exilic DtrH. The assassination of the righteous King Jehoash—and that of his son Amaziah—presages the death of the righteous King Josiah in the exilic DtrH.

[1–4] Jehoash's introductory regnal account is unusual in that it begins with a notice of his age in v. 1. Such a notice is typical for the Judean monarchs who ruled following the demise of the northern kingdom of Israel (see 2 Kgs 21:1; 22:1; 23:31; 23:36; 24:8; 24:18). The appearance of such a notice at this point is explained by Jehoash's young age at his accession to the throne. It highlights the parallel between the seven-year-old King Jehoash and the eight-year-old King Josiah: both came to the throne at a very young age following the assassinations of their fathers; both were considered righteous, particularly on account of their respective handling of affairs pertaining to the temple; and both were killed early in life after suffering foreign invasion.

Nothing is known of Jehoash's mother, Zibiah, but the identification of her home city as Beer Sheba points to an interest in the city that defines the southern boundaries of Judah (2 Sam 17:11; 24:2; 1 Kgs 5:5). Jehoash's marriage into a Beer Sheban family points to an attempt to consolidate Davidic rule over Judah. Such a move would have been particularly important during the early eighth century B.C.E. to protect Judean interests in the Negeb region following the loss of Edom and the assassination of Ahaziah. Judah would be perceived as weak during this period, and Jehoash would need to establish control over the land by allying with local chieftains.

The notice that Jehoash was righteous and instructed by the priest Jehoiada makes great sense when one considers that Jehoash was only a boy when he came to the throne. Although the Chronicler argues that Jehoash became corrupt following the death of Jehoiada (2 Chr 24:15–22), this statement is an attempt to explain why a righteous king like Jehoash was assassinated by his own men. Jehoash is treated like Solomon, Asa, and Jehoshaphat—that is, he is a righteous king who did not remove the high places. Such an act was left to Hezekiah in the Hezekian DtrH (see 2 Kgs 18:4).

[5–17] Various attempts have been made to attribute this section to a late priestly or temple-oriented source,[1] but such attempts overlook the central role

---

1. J. Wellhausen, *Die Composition des Hexateuch* (Berlin: de Gruyter, 1963), 293–98; cf. G. H. Jones, *1 and 2 Kings* (2 vols.; The New Century Bible Commentary; Grand Rapids: William B. Eerdmans; London: Marshall, Morgan, and Scott, 1984), 487–88.

of the temple in ancient Judean religious and national life throughout the monarchic period. Some means had to be devised to keep the temple in repair over the course of some three to four centuries, and the present narrative gives some inkling as to how that might have been accomplished. Some commentators are highly critical of the priests, charging them with embezzlement of the funds collected for the repair of the temple or misuse of funds (e.g., Provan, *1 and 2 Kings* 223–24). Later statements in vv. 12–16 concerning the honesty of the building contractors and use of the funds only for temple repair suggest that the funds had not been properly allocated and spent. The text does not state, however, that the priests were guilty of wrongdoing; the issue is simply the failure to accomplish the purpose for which the funds were collected. It is not entirely clear that the priests themselves would have the expertise to undertake or supervise the repairs themselves. Even at the time of the building of the temple, Solomon was the one who initiated the work, and apparently hired contractors, such as Hiram of Tyre, to play an important role in carrying out the work. Here, Jehoash takes charge much like Solomon to see that the work of temple repair is properly financed and accomplished.

Temple renovation during the reign of Jehoash makes sense in relation to historical and political factors. Judah had been under the rule of the house of Omri since the reign of Jehoshaphat. Now that the Omride dynasty had been overthrown by Jehu, and Athaliah's attempt to take control of Judah had been thwarted, it was time for Jehoash to consider a new status for Judah vis-à-vis its northern Israelite overlord. Temple renovation is frequently a sign of national restoration as well as religious reform. The overthrow of the Omride dynasty and the difficulties experienced by the new Jehu dynasty at the hands of the Arameans would have prompted Jehoash to consider the possibility that Judah might redefine its relationship with Israel, perhaps to be independent or at least on a more equal footing. Second Kings 13:22–25 relates the efforts of Jehoahaz of Israel to push back the threatening Arameans, together with the eventual success of his son Jehoash of Israel. With Israel preoccupied, Judah could improve its own lot. Jehoash's marriage to a woman from Beer Sheba signals his intentions to strengthen his hand by consolidating his relationships with local authorities in the Negeb. No such move is evident during the reign of Jehoash, although his son Amaziah later made a failed move to assert Judean independence following his victories over the Edomites (see 2 Kgs 14:7–14). The Aramean advance against Jerusalem noted in vv. 18–19 is an attempt to ensure that Judah would be unable to assist Israel against Aram.

Jehoash relies heavily on the people's willingness to present offerings to the temple. Literary models for the collection of such funds appear in Exod 32:1–6, which relates the collection of gold to create the golden calf, and Exod 35:20–29, which relates the collection of material for the construction of the tabernacle. The system employed by Jehoash presupposes the development of a cash economy, which began with the rise of the Assyrian empire in the ninth-seventh centuries B.C.E.[2] Deuteronomy 14:22–29 indicates that it is possible to pay tithes to the temple in cash. The present account focuses on the cash value of offerings paid to the temple on behalf of persons who pay due to obligations—for example, the temple tax (Exod 30:11–16), the tithe (see Gen 14:20; 28:22; Lev 27:30–33; Num 18:21–32; Deut 14:22–29; 1 Sam 8:15, 17; Amos 4:4), sin offerings (Lev 4:1–5:13), guilt offerings (Lev 5:14–6:7), or due to free will, thanksgiving, and votive offerings (Lev 27), such as the daily burnt offering (Lev 1) or the peace offering (Lev 3). Many translate the term *makkārô* as "his acquaintance" or "his benefactor," but it signifies "his purchaser"—that is, one who makes an obligatory or voluntary offering to the temple.

Jehoash's role in the collection of funds and their distribution for temple repair appears in vv. 7–9. Jehoiada would be aging, and Jehoash at age thirty would feel less dependent on the priesthood than in his earlier years. Furthermore, the long period of Judah's subjugation to Israel would have drained income from the temple and disrupted any normal repair mechanism that might have been in place. Jehoash's actions, taken at a time of rising Judean power vis-à-vis Israel, redress that situation. Jehoash's fiscal reforms in the temple during his twenty-third year coincide with the death of Jehu and the ascension to the throne of his son Jehoahaz (2 Kgs 13:1). By taking the funds out of the hands of the priests, Jehoash reasserts royal Davidic control over the sanctuary.

The procedure employed by Jehoiada to collect and assign the funds for temple repair appears in vv. 10–17.[3] Some interpreters contend that v. 10 specifies two locations, namely, "beside the altar" and "to the right of the entrance of the Temple of YHWH" (Jones 492; cf. Cogan and Tadmor 138). They note manuscript Alexandrinus, which reads "mazzebah" in place of "altar." The confusion is rooted in the uncertainties of the placement of the altar before the temple: although the altar stands before the temple, its exact location is not stated in the accounts of Solomon's construction of the temple and its furnishings in 1 Kgs 6–8 (cf. Exod 27:1–8; 38:1–7). Second Kings 16:10–16 indicates that King Ahaz of Judah removed the bronze altar from "before YHWH," "before the House," and "the place between the altar and the House of YHWH" (v. 14) to make way for a new altar based on the design of the one he saw in Damascus when he was summoned before the Assyrian monarch, Tiglath-pileser III. Because the bronze altar was placed to the north of "the altar"—that is, the new altar built to the pattern observed in Damascus—the altar must have stood directly before the entrance to the temple. This explains the wording of the text, with the chest for the deposit

2. See J. Betlyon, "Coinage," *ABD* 1:1076–89, esp. 1078, 1079–83.
3. See A. L. Oppenheim, "A Fiscal Practice of the Ancient Near East," *JNES* 6 (1947): 116–20, who notes typical use of a collection box; cf. Victor Hurowitz, "Another Fiscal Practice in the Ancient Near East: 2 Kings 12:5–17 and a Letter to Esarhaddon (LAS 277)," *JNES* 45 (1986): 289–94.

of funds to the right of the altar. One would have to pass by the side of the altar when approaching the temple. Since one approaches the temple from the east, the right would be the north side of the altar where Ahab later placed the bronze altar.

The collection of the funds is supervised by the priestly gatekeepers (see 1 Chr 26:1–19), who were responsible for authorizing passage through the gates of the temple complex. The royal scribe worked together with the high priest to collect, count, and bag the funds when the chest became full. The notice that funds were not employed to manufacture the vessels used in the temple ritual —basins, snuffers, bowls, trumpets, and so on (cf. 1 Kgs 7:38–40, 45–47)— indicates that the funds were used only for repairs. The notice concerning the honesty of the contractors suggests that the priests had not properly allocated the funds in the past. The priests would continue to receive funds from the sin offerings (*ḥaṭṭāʾt*) and the guilt offerings (*ʾāšām*; cf. Lev 4:1–5:19).

[18–19] Although Jehu of Israel had allied with the Assyrian king, Shalmaneser III (858–824 B.C.E.), this did not put an end to the threat posed to Israel and Judah by the Arameans. The Arameans harassed Israel during the reign of Jehu, his son Jehoahaz (2 Kgs 13:3–5), and his grandson Jehoash (2 Kgs 13:22, 24–25). The Aramean threat was contained only in the reign of Jehoash of Israel, who allied with Adad Nirari III (810–783 B.C.E.). The invasion of Philistia and the advance against Jerusalem indicated here during the reign of Jehoash of Judah continues that threat. Coming after the twenty-third year of Jehoash's rule, the same year that Jehoahaz of Israel ascended the northern throne (see 2 Kgs 13:1), Hazael isolated the new northern monarch by cutting off any aid from Egypt and removing his Judean vassal. Gray posits that Adad Nirari's advance against the city of Gath in Philistia in the fifth year of his reign (Gray 589; see *ANET* 282) is a response to the Aramean incursion that would have lent support to his Israelite ally. The location of Gath remains disputed, although most now identify it with Tel Zaphit (Tel es-Safi), located in the western Shephelah, where it commands the Wadi Elah.[4] Interpreters note the absence of Gath from the lists of Philistine cities in Amos 1:6–8; Zeph 2:4, and posit that Hazael destroyed the city at this time. Jehoash's submission to Hazael together with his temple reform is an attempt to distance himself from his northern Israelite overlord. Such a move anticipates a similar action on the part of his son, Amaziah (2 Kgs 14:8–14). In both cases, the price proved to be very high, as both kings were assassinated by elements within their own courts (see vv. 20–22; 2 Kgs 14:19–20).

[20–22] Jehoash's submission to Hazael and the loss of funds collected since the reign of Jehoshaphat undoubtedly played an important role in his demise. The assassination would have steered the nation back to its alliance with Israel, particularly after Adad Nirari had reasserted Assyrian authority—and that of his northern Israelite vassal—in Philistia and elsewhere.

4. See Ephraim Stern, "Tel Safit," *NEAEHL* 4:1522–24.

The location of the assassination is unclear. Although the Millo appears to be the royal citadel built on the northern portion of the city of David, the Sillo descent is less certain. Some view *sillāʾ* as a variant of *mĕsillâ,* "highway," but such a solution is speculative. The term *sillāʾ* is employed only here in the Bible, and it likely represents the name for one of the roadways leading from the Millo to outside the city. The two assassins, Jozacar ben Shimeath and Jehozabad ben Shomer, are unknown. Although 2 Chr 24:26 identifies them as foreigners—as sons of Ammonite and Moabite women, respectively—this appears to be part of the Chronicler's effort to attribute the entire episode to the sins of Jehoash, including his killing of the son of Jehoiada and his apostasy. Jehoash was far more likely killed as a result of his political missteps.

XVIII. Regnal Account of Jehoahaz ben Jehu of Israel 2 Kings 13:1-9

13:1 In the twenty-third year of Joash ben Ahaziah, King of Judah, Jehoahaz ben Jehu ruled over Israel in Samaria for seventeen years. 2 He did evil in the eyes of YHWH, and walked in the sins of Jeroboam ben Nebat, who had caused Israel to sin. He did not turn aside from it.

3 The anger of YHWH burned against Israel, and He gave them into the hand of Hazael, King of Aram, and into the hand of Ben Hadad ben Hazael continuously. 4 Jehoahaz implored YHWH, and YHWH listened to him because He saw the oppression of Israel, for the King of Aram oppressed them. 5 And YHWH gave to Israel a deliverer, and they were freed from the power of Aram, and the people of Israel lived in their tents as formerly. 6 But they did not turn aside from the sins of the house of Jeroboam, who caused Israel to sin. They continued to walk in them, and also the Asherah stood in Samaria, 7 for the King of Aram did not leave Jehoahaz an army; only fifty horses and ten chariots, and ten thousand foot soldiers, for he had destroyed them and made them like dust for trampling.

8 And the rest of the acts of Jehoahaz and all that he did, and his power, are they not written in the book of the Chronicles of the Kings of Israel? 9 Jehoahaz slept with his fathers, and they buried him in Samaria, and Joash his son ruled in his place.

Second Kings 13:1-9 continues to emphasize the Aramean oppression of Israel throughout the reign of the Omride dynasty and the early years of the Jehu dynasty. It follows from YHWH's instructions to Elijah in 1 Kgs 19:15–18 to anoint Hazael as king of Aram and the notice in 2 Kgs 10:32–33 that YHWH employed Hazael to cut off parts of Israel. Although Aramean advances against Israel reflect the historical realities of the late ninth and early eighth centuries B.C.E.,[1] the portrayal of Hazael's continued oppression of Israel serves the interests of the Jehu History.

The passage is easily demarcated by the introductory regnal account in 2 Kgs 13:1–2 and the concluding regnal summary in 2 Kgs 13:8–9. The middle section in vv. 3–7 provides the account of Jehoahaz's reign, which emphasizes Aram's reduction of Israel's power and YHWH's granting of a "deliverer" to ensure Israel's security in their own homes.

[1–2] Interpreters note a problem with the notice that Jehoahaz's seventeen-year reign begins in the twenty-third year of Joash ben Ahaziah of Judah. Since 2 Kgs 10:36 states that Jehu ruled for twenty-eight years and 2 Kgs 12:1 states that Joash ben Ahaziah began his forty-year reign in the seventh year of Jehu, Joash ben Ahaziah would have ruled only for nineteen years after the death of Jehu. Josephus, in an attempt to correct the problem, states that Jehoahaz began his rule in the twenty-first year of Joash (see *Ant.* 9:173). Others posit that Jehoahaz served as coregent with his father for several years, or a shift in the means by which the regnal years of the northern Israelite kings were reckoned (see Cogan and Tadmor 142–43).

[3–7] The narrative portrays Jehoahaz's piety in a manner like that of the period of the Judges, namely, Aram oppresses Israel because of its sins; Jehoahaz implores YHWH; YHWH sends a "deliverer" (*môšî'a*) to save the people from the oppressor. Unfortunately, this redeemer does not appear until the time of Jehoahaz's son, Jehoash, who ultimately defeats the Arameans and restores peace to Israel, thereby paving the way for the reign of his son, Jeroboam. Second Kings 14:27 states specifically that YHWH "redeemed them (Israel) by the hand of Jeroboam ben Joash." Much like his grandfather Jehu, Jehoash ben Jehoahaz was compelled to ally with the Assyrians in order to keep the Arameans off his back.[2] Aramean oppression during the reign of Jehoahaz provides the reason that Jehoash felt compelled to submit to Assyria. The reduction of the Israelite army to ten chariots, fifty horses, and ten thousand foot soldiers indicates that the main striking force of Ahab's once powerful army left Israel virtually defenseless.

---

1. Benjamin Mazar, "The Aramean Empire and Its Relations with Israel," in *The Early Biblical Period: Historical Essays* (Jerusalem: Israel Exploration Society, 1986), 151–72.

2. Adad-Nirari III claims that Jehoash of Israel paid him tribute (Stephanie Page, "A Stele of Adad-Nirari III and Nergal-Ereš from Tell al Rimah," *Iraq* 30 [1968]: 139–53).

XIX. Regnal Account of Jehoash
ben Jehoahaz of Israel
2 Kings 13:10–25

13:10 In the thirty-seventh year of Joash, King of Judah, Jehoash ben Jehoahaz ruled over Israel in Samaria for sixteen[a] years. 11 He did evil in the eyes of YHWH; he did not turn aside from all the sins of Jeroboam ben Nebat which he caused Israel to commit. He continued in them.

12 And the rest of the acts of Joash and all that he did, and his power when he fought with Amaziah, King of Judah, are they not written in the book of the Chronicles of the Kings of Israel? 13 Joash slept with his fathers, and Jeroboam sat upon his throne, and Joash was buried in Samaria with the kings of Israel.

14 Elisha became sick with the illness by which he would die. So Joash, King of Israel, came down to him, wept before him, and said, "My father! My father! The chariotry of Israel and its horses!" 15 And Elisha said to him, "Take a bow and arrows!" And he took for himself a bow and arrows, 16 and said to the King of Israel, "Place your hand upon the bow!" And he placed his hand upon the bow, and Elisha placed his hand upon the hand of the king. 17 And he said, "Open the east window!" And he opened it. And Elisha said, "Shoot!" And he shot. And he said, "An arrow of victory for YHWH! And an arrow of victory against Aram! And you shall utterly destroy Aram at Aphek!" 18 And he said, "Take arrows!" And he took (arrows). And he said to the King of Israel, "Strike the ground!" And he struck three times and stood. 19 And the man of G-d became angry, and said, "If you struck five or six times, then you would utterly destroy Aram. But now three times you will strike Aram."

20 Elisha died, and they buried him. And Moabite raiding bands came against the land at the beginning of the year. 21 While they were burying a man, behold, they saw the raiding band, and they threw the man in the grave of Elisha. When the dead man touched the bones of Elisha, he lived and rose upon his feet.

22 Hazael, King of Aram, oppressed Israel all the days of Jehoahaz. 23 But YHWH showed favor to them, showed them mercy, and turned to them for the sake of His covenant with Abraham, Isaac, and Jacob. He did not want to destroy them and did not cast them out from before His face until now. 24 Hazael, King of Aram, died, and Ben Hadad his son ruled in his place. 25 And Jehoash ben Jehoahaz returned, and took the cities from the hand of Ben Hadad ben Hazael which he took from the hand of Jehoa-

haz his father in war. Three times Joash struck him, and he restored the cities of Israel.

a. Peshitta reads "thirteen."

The regnal account of Jehoash ben Jehoahaz of Israel displays an unusual formulation insofar as it presents intertwined accounts of the death of the prophet Elisha in vv. 14–21 and Jehoash's defeat of the Arameans in vv. 22–25 as an appendix. The technique is analogous to other examples of traditions concerning Elisha. The account of Elisha's succession of Elijah and other traditions about the prophet appear in 2 Kgs 2, immediately following the account of Ahaziah ben Ahab's reign in 1 Kgs 22:51–2 Kgs 1:18. Likewise, the account of Elisha's actions in 2 Kgs 3:4–8:15 appears immediately following the introductory regnal notice concerning Jehoram ben Ahab in 2 Kgs 3:1–3, although a concluding regnal account for Jehoram ben Ahab is lacking due to his assassination by Jehu in 2 Kgs 9–10. The regnal account of Jehoram ben Jehoshaphat appears in 2 Kgs 8:16–24, and the introductory regnal account of Ahaziah ben Jehoram appears in 2 Kgs 8:25–29, which give the impression that the Elisha traditions in 2 Kgs 3:4–8:15 are an appendix to the Jehoram ben Ahab narrative. Such a technique suggests that the Elisha traditions have been worked into an earlier chronicle of the kings of northern Israel.

The appended traditions concerning Elisha and the defeat of Aram demonstrate YHWH's deliverance of Israel as a result of Jehoahaz's repentance in 2 Kgs 13:4–5. The earlier text had indicated that YHWH would send a "deliverer" (*môšîʿa*), and Jehoash, with the backing of the dying Elisha, serves in that role. Jehoash's victory over Aram paves the way for his son, Jeroboam, who is able to restore the borders of Israel to rule over a kingdom like that of Solomon (2 Kgs 14:23–29). Such a portrayal indicates the interests of the Jehu History to portray the dynasty as one that returned the nation to YHWH and thereby restored the united kingdom. The Jehu History was later incorporated into the Hezekian, Josian, and exilic DtrH editions, each of which presents a very negative evaluation of northern Israel as part of their respective agendas.

Jehoash's defeat of the Arameans and recovery of cities lost to them reflects the changed circumstances that would result from his alliance with the Assyrian monarch, Adad Nirari III (810–783 B.C.E.). A stela of Adad Nirari III found at Tel al Rimah in 1967 lists Ia'asu the Samaritan—King Jehoash of Israel—as one of the kings who submitted to the authority of the Assyrian monarch during his campaign to the Hatti land in his first year.[1] This hardly represents a new

1. Stephanie Page, "A Stele of Adad-Nirari III and Nergal-Ereš from Tell al Rimah," *Iraq* 30 (1968): 139–53; for discussion of Adad-Nirari III's reign, see A. K. Grayson, "Adad-Nirari III (810–783 B.C.)," CAH III/1, 271–76.

development, since Jehoash's grandfather, Jehu, had initially submitted to Shalmaneser III of Assyria,[2] but Adad Nirari's campaign would have subdued any Aramean resurgence and placed Jehoash back in the debt of Assyria. The extent of Jeroboam's kingdom may be explained by this alliance, which was designed to keep the common enemy, Aram, in check. Excavations at Samaria indicate that major buildings were rebuilt during the reigns of Jehoash and Jeroboam, which coincides with the resurgence of Israelite power in the accounts of their reigns.[3]

[12–13] Another version of the concluding regnal formula for Jehoash appears unexpectedly in 2 Kgs 14:15–16, where it precedes the notice that Amaziah ben Joash of Judah ruled for fifteen years after the death of Jehoash. The present formula anticipates Jehoash's attack against Jerusalem during the reign of Amaziah, when the latter attempted to challenge his northern Israelite overlord (2 Kgs 14:8–14). Amaziah's revolt was prompted by a combination of his own victory over Edom and his perception that the Arameans would continue to hold the upper hand over Judah, but Jehoash's alliance with the Assyrians gave Jehoash the strength he needed to reassert control over his Judean vassal. Curiously, the succession formula for Jeroboam varies in v. 13 by stating "and Jeroboam sat upon his throne." The variation suggests an earlier formulation that would have appeared within the context of the Jehu History.

[14–21] The appendix to the regnal account of Jehoash's reign in vv. 14–21 constitutes an example of the prophetic legenda.[4] The narrative begins with a conjunctive *waw* joined to the name Elisha, *weʾelîšaʿ*, "and Elisha," to emphasize the leading character. Two episodes appear respectively in vv. 14–19, in which the dying Elisha performs a symbolic act to ensure Jehoash's victory over the Arameans, and in vv. 20–21, which relate the miraculous resurrection of a dead man who is cast into Elisha's tomb.[5] Both episodes emphasize the power of the prophet, but they also relate to the overarching theme of Aramean oppression of Israel in the Omride and Jehu periods. Although they point to Jehoash's defeat of the Arameans in vv. 22–25, they also provide a basis for understanding later Aramean interference in the northern kingdom of Israel in the latter eighth century B.C.E., when King Rezin of Damascus prompted Pekah to assassinate Pekahiah of Israel to instigate the Syro-Ephraimitic War against Judah (see 2 Kgs 15–16). This war had tremendous consequences for northern Israel because it prompted the first Assyrian actions against the northern kingdom and thereby inaugurated a series of encounters that ultimately saw the destruction of northern Israel. Because Jehoash did not utterly destroy Aram, he left the way open for Aram to play an important role in Israel's destruction at a later time.

2. For Shalmaneser's Black Obelisk, see *ANET* 281; *ANEP* 351, 355.

3. See Nahman Avigad, "Samaria," *NEAEHL* 4:1300–1310, esp. 1303.

4. See Alexander Rofé, *The Prophetical Stories* (Jerusalem: Magnes, 1988), 55–58.

5. Cf. Hans-Christoph Schmitt, *Elisa* (Gütersloh: Gerd Mohn, 1972), 80–82, who treats them as independent episodes.

The first episode presents Joash's visit to the dying Elisha. The narrative does not specify where Elisha is located, but the notice that Joash "went down," presumably from Samaria, to see him suggests that Elisha was back in the Jordan Valley where he seems to have been based with the sons of the prophets (2 Kgs 6:1–7). Specific locations might include Abel-meholah, where he was originally from (1 Kgs 19:16); Jericho, where he and the sons of the prophets witnessed Elijah's ascent to heaven (2 Kgs 2:1–18); or Gilgal, where he and the sons of the prophets lived for a time (2 Kgs 2:1; 4:38). Joash's cry, "My father! My father! The chariotry of Israel and its horses!" repeats the cry uttered by Elisha at the ascent of Elijah to heaven (2 Kgs 2:12). The address, "my father," expresses respect for a master, and the reference to "the chariotry of Israel and its horses" acknowledges Elisha's importance as a defender of Israel. Elisha elsewhere is accompanied by a divine army of chariots and horses that fights against Israel's enemies (2 Kgs 6:8–23). The dying prophet performs a symbolic action together with Joash, which both signifies and brings about Israel's defeat of Aram. Although many consider symbolic actions to be a form of magic,[6] they are better understood as ritual drama that symbolizes and ensures the desired result.[7] By shooting an arrow out the eastern window of the house where Elisha resides, Joash dramatizes the arrows that he will shoot against Aram and effectively makes his shot an "arrow of victory" over Aram. Some note that Aphek, where Elisha tells him that he will achieve his victory, lies not to the east where he shoots the arrow, but to the west in the coastal plain, where the Wadi Shiloh provides access to the Israelite hill country.[8] Aphek is a strategic site, where the Philistines struck at Israel in order to ensure their control of the coastal plain and the Israelite hill country (1 Sam 4). There is another site called Aphek in the Transjordan some three miles east of the Sea of Galilee where Ahab defeated Ben Hadad (1 Kgs 20:26–30). Because this site lies to the east of Israel and sits astride the strategic passage from Aram into the Jezreel Valley, this site is more likely the one in question. The prophet's command to strike the ground with the arrows is meant as a symbolic action to represent the number of times that Jehoash would strike Aram. It also provides an opportunity once again to demonstrate the power and danger represented by the man of G-d (v. 19), who upbraids Jehoash for striking only three times. In the immediate context, this motif symbolizes the three victories that Jehoash would achieve against Hazael (see v. 25 below). In the larger DtrH, it points to Aram's survival and its later role in instigating Pekah's revolt against Pekahiah and the subsequent Syro-Ephraimitic War, which proved to be the beginning actions of

6. See, e.g., G. Fohrer, *Die symbolischen Handlungen des Propheten* (Zurich: Zwingli, 1968), 23–25.

7. W. D. Stacey, *Prophetic Drama in the Old Testament* (London: Epworth, 1990), 93–95; cf. W. B. Barrick, "Elisha and the Magic Bow: A Note on 2 Kings xiii 15–17," *VT* 35 (1985): 355–63.

8. For discussion of the various sites of Aphek, see R. Frankel, "Aphek," *ABD* 1:275–77.

a process that would lead ultimately to the destruction of both Aram and northern Israel by the Assyrian empire (2 Kgs 15–16).

The second episode in vv. 20–21 provides another example of the prophet's extraordinary power by portraying the resurrection of a man whose body came into contact with that of the prophet. Moabite raids against Israel would have accompanied Aramean incursions since both nations had an interest in wresting control of the Transjordan from Israel. The resurrection motif is characteristic of the Elijah and Elisha traditions in 1 Kgs 17:17–24 and 2 Kgs 4:8–37.

[22–25] The second appendix to the account of Jehoash's reign in vv. 22–25 emphasizes the threat posed by Hazael of Aram against Israel and Jehoash's defeat of his Aramean nemesis. The previous appendix notes Jehoash's symbolic action of striking the earth three times with arrows, and the present narrative constitutes the realization of that symbolic action. It begins with a *waw*-conjunctive formulation combined with the proper name Hazael, *wahaz-a'el,* "and Hazael," to emphasize the shift of major characters from Elisha to Hazael. The introductory notice in v. 22 recalls Hazael's oppression of Israel during the reign of Jehoahaz, but v. 23 indicates Jehoash's repentance, which then motivates YHWH to act on behalf of Israel. The present narrative recalls once again the typical narrative pattern of the book of Judges in which Israel sins, YHWH brings an oppressor, Israel repents, and then YHWH sends a "deliverer" (*môšî'a*; cf. 2 Kgs 13:5 above from the regnal account of Jehoahaz) to save the people. Some argue that this pattern is a late DtrH redactional interpolation, since it allegedly draws on Judges (see Gray 595, 601–2; Fritz 308, 314; cf. Montgomery and Gehman 435). This position is frequently supported by reference to YHWH's unwillingness to destroy the covenant of Abraham, Isaac, and Jacob, since it presupposes the ancestral promise traditions of Genesis–Numbers and Deuteronomy. Although Abraham, Isaac, and Jacob appear elsewhere in the DtrH only in Josh 24:3–4, which many also take to be a late text, the argument that this statement must be an exilic-period addition does not stand up. The exilic DtrH emphasizes that YHWH is quite willing to set aside the promises to the ancestors in the case of the decision to destroy Jerusalem and to exile the people on account of the sins of Manasseh (2 Kgs 21:1–18). There is no appeal to the covenant with Abraham, Isaac, and Jacob in this passage or in the other instances where Manasseh's sins are cited as the cause of the Babylonian exile (2 Kgs 23:26–27; 24:3–4). Furthermore, the ancestral promise tradition appears throughout Deuteronomy (see Deut 1:8; 6:10; 9:5, 27; 29:12; 30:20; 34:4), which appears to be a monarchic-period composition,[9] and the ancestral promise tradition in Genesis–Numbers appears already in the J and E strata of the Pentateuch. The ancestral promise here func-

---

9. Marvin A. Sweeney, *King Josiah of Judah: The Lost Messiah of Israel* (Oxford and New York: Oxford University Press, 2001), 137–69.

tions as a reason to save Israel in the aftermath of the Omride atrocities, and it underlies the portrayal of the secure kingdom of Jeroboam ben Jehoash, who restored Israel's borders to those of David and Solomon. The citation of the ancestral tradition here does not ensure Israel's return from exile at the end of Kings. Instead, it points to the restoration of Israel under Jehoash and Jeroboam and therefore functions as part of the Jehu History. A key consideration appears in v. 23 that "(YHWH) was not willing to destroy them and to cast them out from before His presence until now." That temporal qualification explains the continued existence of Israel from the standpoint of the author of the narrative, which once again points to the period of the Jehu dynasty in early-eighth-century Israel.

Although Jehoash recovered the cities of Israel lost by his father Jehoahaz, he was not able to destroy Aram completely, which enabled Aram to play a role in Israel's later destruction by backing Pekah's coup against Pekahiah and by drawing Israel into the Syro-Ephraimitic War.

XX. Regnal Account of Amaziah ben Joash of Judah 2 Kings 14:1–22

14:1 In the second year of Joash ben Joahaz, King of Israel, Amaziah ben Joash, King of Judah, ruled. 2 He was twenty-five years old when he began his rule, and he ruled in Jerusalem for twenty-nine years. The name of his mother was Jeho'adan[a] from Jerusalem. 3 He did what was right in the eyes of YHWH, but not like David his father. He acted according to all that Joash his father did. 4 But the high places did not cease. The people were still offering sacrifices and burning incense at the high places.

5 When he took control of the kingdom, he executed his servants who had struck down his father the king. 6 But the sons of the killers he did not put to death as it is written in the book of the Torah of Moses which YHWH commanded, saying, "Fathers shall not be put to death on account of the sons, and sons shall not be put to death on account of the fathers, but each according to his sin [b]shall be put to death."[b]

7 He killed ten thousand Edomites in the Valley of Salt,[c] captured Sela' in the battle, and called it Yokte'el until this day.

8 Then Amaziah sent messengers to Jehoash ben Jehoahaz ben Jehu, King of Israel, saying, "Come, let us meet face to face." 9 And Jehoash, King of Israel, sent to Amaziah, King of Judah, saying, "The bramble in Lebanon sent to the cedar in Lebanon, saying, 'Give your daughter to my

son as a wife, but a wild animal in Lebanon came by, and trampled the bramble.' 10 You have indeed defeated Edom, but you act brashly. Be satisfied and stay at home. Why would you stir up trouble for yourself, so that you and Judah with you would fall?" 11 But Amaziah would not listen, so Jehoash, King of Israel, went up and they met face to face, he and Amaziah, King of Judah, at Beth Shemesh, which belongs to Judah. 12 Judah was defeated by Israel, and they fled, each to his home.[d] 13 And Amaziah, King of Judah, the son of Jehoash ben Ahaziah, Jehoash, King of Israel, captured at Beth Shemesh, and he came to Jerusalem and broke down the wall of Jerusalem from the Ephraim Gate to the Corner Gate, four hundred cubits. 14 He took all the gold and the silver and all the vessels that were found in the House of YHWH and in the storerooms of the house of the king and the hostages, and returned to Samaria. 15 And the rest of the acts of Jehoash which he did and his power and how he fought with Amaziah, King of Judah, are they not written in the book of the Chronicles of the Kings of Israel? 16 And Jehoash slept with his fathers, and he was buried in Samaria with the kings of Israel; and Jeroboam his son ruled in his place. 17 And Amaziah ben Joash, King of Judah, lived for fifteen years after the death of Jehoash ben Jehoahaz, King of Israel.

18 And the rest of the acts of Amaziah, are they not written in the book of the Chronicles of the Kings of Judah? 19 And they conspired against him in Jerusalem, and he fled to Lachish, and they sent after him to Lachish and killed him there. 20 They carried him on horses, and he was buried in Jerusalem with his fathers in the city of David. 21 All the people of Judah took Azariah, who was sixteen years old, and they made him king in place of his father Amaziah. 22 He built Elath and restored it to Judah after the King slept with his fathers.

a. Ketiv, *yehô'adîn,* "Jeho'adin," cf. LXX and Targum Jonathan; read with Qere, *yehô'adan,* "Jeho'adan," cf. 2 Chr 25:1; Peshitta.

b–b. Ketiv, *yāmôt,* "he shall die" (cf. Targum Jonathan); read with Qere, *yûmāt,* "he shall be put to death."

c. Ketiv, *hammelah,* "the salt"; read with Qere, *melah,* "salt."

d. Ketiv, *le'ohālô,* lit., "to his tent"; read with Qere, *le'ohālāyw,* "to his tents."

The regnal account of King Amaziah ben Joash of Judah is demarcated by the introductory regnal form in vv. 1–4 and by the concluding regnal form in vv. 18–22. Although a concluding regnal form for the Israelite King Jehoash ben Jehoahaz (see 2 Kgs 13:10–25) appears in vv. 15–16, it has been incorporated into the larger literary framework of the Amaziah account. It functions as part of the overall portrayal of Jehoash's defeat of Amaziah in vv. 8–14 and as the premise for the statement in v. 16 that Amaziah lived for fifteen years after the death of Jehoash.

The account of Amaziah's reign in vv. 5–16 focuses on Amaziah's attempts to consolidate his power following the assassination of his father Jehoash (the shortened form of the name, Joash, is employed here) ben Ahaziah and his ill-considered attempt to free Judah from Israelite control. The account includes two basic components, distinguished by a combination of syntactical and thematic features. Verses 5–6 relate Amaziah's execution of those responsible for the assassination of his father, and vv. 7–16, which lack an introductory conjunction and begin simply with the pronoun *hûʾ*, "he," comprise an account of Amaziah's victory over the Edomites. This victory in turn prompted Amaziah's failed attempt to renegotiate Judah's relationship with its northern Israelite suzerain. Fifteen years after Jehoash's death, the concluding regnal account states that conspirators in Jerusalem assassinated the Judean king. Many view this as a consequence of Amaziah's failed attempt to throw off northern control, but the lapse of time between Amaziah's failed attempt and the assassination suggests other causes.

The presence of a concluding regnal account form for Jehoash ben Jehoahaz of Israel suggests that the origins of this narrative may be traced to the Jehu History, particularly since it demonstrates how the Jehu monarchy finally put to rest any threat of revolt posed by Judah. Such a demonstration functions as part of a larger scenario in which the Jehu dynasty reestablished the former Davidic-Solomonic kingdom. The narrative provides no hints that the Jehu dynasty had anything to do with the assassination of Amaziah, but his premature death would have functioned as a partial fulfillment of Elijah's prophecy that the house of Ahab/Omri would be entirely wiped out (see 1 Kgs 21:17–29). As a result of the marriage of the Omride princess Athaliah to Jehoram ben Jehoshaphat of Judah (2 Kgs 8:18; cf. 8:26; 11:1–20), all members of the house of David from Ahaziah ben Jehoram on were descendants of the house of Omri. As the last reigning Judean monarch at the time that Jeroboam ben Joash ascended the throne of Israel, Amaziah's death clears the way for the presentation of Jeroboam ben Joash as the promised deliverer who would restore Israel to its former glory.

Within the Hezekian and Josian DtrH editions, the Amaziah narrative presents northern Israel's suppression of Judah, and thereby provides grist for the contention that the restoration of Davidic rule over all Israel would redress the wrongs committed by the northern monarchs. In the exilic DtrH, Israel's suppression of Judah preceded the destruction of Jerusalem and Judah.

[1–4] The origins of Amaziah's mother in Jerusalem suggest an attempt by Joash ben Ahaziah of Judah to consolidate his position in Jerusalem, particularly since he was the grandson of the Omride princess Athaliah, who attempted to supplant the Davidic line. Joash's assassination indicates that such an attempt was both necessary and unsuccessful. Amaziah's assassination indicates that instability in the house of David persisted into the reign of his son as well. Amaziah is judged to be righteous, although his righteousness is compared to his father Joash rather than to his more distant ancestor David. Insofar as Joash was known for supporting the temple, one may surmise that Amaziah gave the temple similar support. His successful campaign against the Edomites and his less-than-successful attempt to renegotiate his relationship with Israel would call for support and perhaps refurbishing of the temple as a symbol of national sovereignty and power. His failure to attain such standing explains the hesitancy in comparing him to David. The notice concerning the continuation of the high places serves Hezekian DtrH interests, since Hezekiah brings this practice to an end (2 Kgs 18:4).

[5–6] The first subunit takes up Amaziah's execution of those responsible for the assassination of his father Joash. The men responsible for the murder, Jozacar ben Shimeath and Jehozabad ben Shomer, are named in 2 Kgs 12:22. The notice that Hazael of Aram threatened Jerusalem and extorted the funds gathered by Joash and his predecessors indicates that they acted because Joash had failed to secure Judah from outside threat. The account of Amaziah's reign, with its emphasis on his victory over Edom and his attempt to remove Judah from its vassal state in relation to Israel, suggests that the new monarch was preoccupied with this very concern. The notice that Amaziah executed those responsible for the death of his father states that he did not take action against their families. The passage cites a principle from Deut 24:16 that "fathers are not put to death on account of the sons, and sons are not put to death on account of the fathers."

[7–17] The introductory pronoun *hû᾿*, "he," both signifies the independence of this subunit with the lack of a conjunction and demonstrates its dependence by relying on the preceding material to identify "he" as Amaziah. The initial statement in v. 7 thereby shifts to its new concern with Amaziah's relationship with Israel, beginning with his victory over Edom.

The notice concerning Amaziah's victory over Edom sets in motion a chain of events that leads ultimately to his defeat by King Joash of Israel. It resolves the long-standing problem of the revolt of Edom against Judean rule that began during the reigns of Solomon (1 Kgs 11:14–22) and Jehoram ben Jehoshaphat (2 Kgs 8:20–22). As 2 Kgs 8:22 suggests, it is not clear that Amaziah was able to defeat the Edomites completely. From the standpoint of the Jehu History, 2 Kgs 14:28 claims that Jeroboam ben Joash of Israel restored Israel's borders to the Sea of the Arabah (v. 25)—which would include Edom—as part of its attempt to portray Jeroboam as "the deliverer" for Israel announced during the reign of Jehoahaz (2 Kgs 13:5). The fact that 2 Kgs 14:28 pointedly notes that

Jeroboam recovered Damascus and Hamath "for Judah in Israel" indicates that the Israelite "deliverer" Jeroboam is portrayed in the Jehu History as a figure who resolves problems left open by incapable Judean kings.

The exact location of the Valley of Salt is unclear,[1] although 2 Sam 8:13 notes that David's victory over the Edomites took place at the same location (cf. 1 Chr 18:12–13). Some identify it with the Wadi el-Milḥ in southern Judah, which bears a similar name. Such identification entails an Edomite incursion into Judah, which is not entirely impossible, although it precludes Amaziah's conquest of Sela. The site of Sela itself is disputed, although many identify it with modern Umm el-Bayyarah in Jordan, east of the Arabah and just north of Petra. This association suggests that the Valley of Salt is identified with the lowlands of es-Sebkah south of the Dead Sea, although military activity would be difficult here. Mazar identifies the Valley of Salt with the Valley of Harashim in the Arabah (1 Chr 4:13–14; see Tadmor and Cogan 155 n. 7).

The account of Amaziah's encounter with Joash in vv. 8–14 begins with the particle *ʾāz*, "then," which ties Amaziah's confrontation with Joash to his victory over the Edomites. As Joash's later comment to Amaziah suggests (v. 10), the victory made the Judean king overconfident and prompted him to commit a rash blunder in relation to his overlord. Amaziah's message to Joash is a proposal to meet so that Amaziah could renegotiate his relationship with Joash. Joash's response, which employs the parable of the bramble that demanded a marriage between its son and the daughter of the cedar,[2] displays a diplomatic art form observable in Canaan as early as the Amarna period (fourteenth century B.C.E.) when King Labayu of Shechem informed the Egyptian pharaoh that even ants bite the hand that slaps them in response to charges that he had attacked neighboring city-states (see EA 252; *ANET* 486; cf. Judg 9:7–21; Isa 5:1–7). Joash's response that Amaziah should content himself with his victory alone shows judicious patience. Joash was allied with the Assyrian monarch Adad Nirari III,[3] which perhaps gave Joash the support necessary to put Amaziah in his place.

The Israelite king surprised Amaziah by sending a military expedition against Judah's flanks at Beth Shemesh at the western border of Judah. This move demonstrates Joash's power and results in the capture of Amaziah and the demolition of the north wall of Jerusalem. The identification of the wall

1. See R. W. Younker, "Valley of Salt," *ABD* 5:907.
2. Ann Solomon, "Jehoash's Fable of the Thistle and the Cedar," in *Saga, Legend, Tale, Novella, Fable. Narrative Forms in OT Literature* (ed. G. W. Coats; JSOTSup 35; Sheffield: Sheffield Academic Press, 1985), 114–32.
3. See the Tell al Rimah stele of Adad Nirari III, which lists Jehoash the Samaritan among the Assyrian king's tributaries (Stephanie Page, "A Stele of Adad-Nirari III and Nergal-Ereš from Tell al Rimah," *Iraq* 30 [1968]: 139–53).

destroyed in Jerusalem is not entirely certain.[4] The "Ephraim gate" points to a gate on the northern side of the city that provides access to a road leading toward the northern Israelite hill country of the tribe of Ephraim (cf. Neh 12:39). The corner gate is mentioned in Jer 31:37 and Zech 14:10, and it defines the western boundary of the city. Because the Temple Mount defines the northern boundary of the city of David, the Ephraim gate would be located along a portion of wall that extended from the Temple Mount westward to the corner gate. Avigad's excavations point to such a wall built by Hezekiah during the eighth century to defend the western hill. Avigad's excavations on the western hill indicate that the broad eighth-century wall was built by Hezekiah over the remains of earlier Israelite houses and that the two gates may have been known in an earlier defensive perimeter. Even if Hezekiah refortified this area, interpreters are still at a loss to define an earlier defensive wall for the western portions of the city. Joash's action left at least this portion of Jerusalem undefended. His pillaging of the Jerusalem treasury—what was left after Hazael had emptied it of funds during the reign of Joash ben Ahaziah—left Amaziah in a vulnerable position much like his father before him.

[15–17] The concluding regnal formula for Joash ben Jehoahaz originally concluded an underlying account of Joash's reign in the Jehu History. Such an account would have emphasized Joash's victory over Amaziah as part of a larger agenda to portray the emergence of the Jehu dynasty's power, culminating in the reign of Jeroboam ben Joash. It appears now as part of the Judean-oriented Hezekian, Josianic, and exilic DtrH editions. The references to Joash within the Amaziah account would help to clarify the setbacks suffered by the Judean king.

[18–22] The regnal summary for Amaziah begins as a typical Judean example of the form, although it shifts into a brief account of the assassination of Amaziah and the succession of his son Azariah. Amaziah's flight to Lachish makes a great deal of sense for an internal revolt, since Lachish, a heavily fortified site identified with Tel Lachish or Tell ed-Duweir in the western Shephelah, served as a sort of a second capital for Judah.[5] Lachish enabled the Davidic kings to control Judah's western borders, to project power into the Philistine regions, and to defend Judah against attack from the coastal plain. It was a likely site for Amaziah to rally support and to defend himself against the conspirators. Interpreters assume that Amaziah's assassination came as

4. For discussion of the walls and gates of Iron Age Jerusalem, see esp. Y. Shiloh, "Jerusalem," *NEAEHL* 2:698–712, esp. 704–9; Nahman Avigad, *Discovering Jerusalem* (Jerusalem: Shikmona and the Israel Exploration Society, 1983), 31–60; P. J. King, "Jerusalem," *ABD* 3:747–66, esp. 755–57; Amihai Mazar, *Archaeology of the Land of the Bible, 10,000–586 B.C.E.* (New York: Doubleday, 1990), 417–24.

5. D. Ussishkin, "Lachish," *NEAEHL* 3:897–911.

a result of his failed attempt to renegotiate his relationship with Israel, but such a view does not explain why he was killed fifteen years after the death of Joash. Because Jeroboam ben Joash controlled an empire that extended from Lebo Hamath to the Sea of Arabah, it is likely that Amaziah's death served northern Israelite interests. The conspiracy is placed in Jerusalem, and the people of Judah take action to make sure that his son Azariah succeeded him. Such a scenario suggests that Amaziah presented some obstacle to Jeroboam's plans, and that Jeroboam had sufficient support in Judah to motivate action that would secure the relationship between Israel and Judah. By all accounts, Azariah—or Uzziah—served as a loyal ally to Jeroboam throughout his reign. His control of the Red Sea port of Eilat not only ensured Judean access to the lucrative trading routes of the Red Sea, but it would also have ensured Azariah's overlord Jeroboam of an empire that extended all the way to the Sea of the Arabah.

XXI. Regnal Account of Jeroboam ben Joash of Israel
2 Kings 14:23–29

14:23 In the fifteenth year of Amaziah ben Joash, King of Judah, Jeroboam ben Joash, King of Israel, ruled in Samaria for forty-one years. 24 He did what was evil in the eyes of YHWH. He did not turn from all the sins of Jeroboam ben Nebat, who caused Israel to sin.

25 He restored the border of Israel from Lebo Hamath to the Sea of Arabah according to the word of YHWH, G-d of Israel, which He spoke by the hand of His servant, Jonah ben Amitai the prophet who was from Gath Hepher. 26 For YHWH had seen that the affliction of Israel was very galling;[a] there was no one bond or free left, and no one to help Israel. 27 But YHWH did not intend to wipe out the name of Israel from under the heavens, so He delivered them by the hand of Jeroboam ben Joash.

28 And the rest of the acts of Jeroboam and all that he did and his power, how he fought and how he recovered Damascus and Hamath for Judah in Israel; are they not written in the book of the Chronicles of the Kings of Israel? 29 And Jeroboam slept with his fathers, with the kings of Israel, and Zechariah his son ruled in his place.

a. Hebrew, *mōreh,* "contentious"; cf. LXX, *pikran,* "bitter," and Peshitta, *dmryr,* "bitter," which presuppose Hebrew, *mar,* "bitter."

The regnal account of Jeroboam ben Joash of Israel is demarcated by the introductory regnal form in vv. 23–24 and the concluding form in vv. 28–29. The brief presentation of the major events of his reign in vv. 25–27 focuses on his restoration of an Israelite empire like that controlled by David and Solomon two centuries earlier.

Many interpreters overlook the significance of this section because of its relatively short and straightforward presentation of a king whose reign saw few major challenges. Like all Israelite monarchs, Jeroboam is judged to be evil because he followed in the sins of his older namesake, but his regnal account serves the interests of the later Judean DtrH editions, which uniformly condemn all northern monarchs. Nevertheless, this brief account indicates that Jeroboam's reign holds utmost significance for the kingdoms of Israel and Judah since he was the first and only monarch ever to restore control over the entire extent of the empire once controlled by David and Solomon.[1] The reign of Jeroboam ben Joash resolves the many problems faced by Israel and Judah from the time of Solomon onward. Lebo Hamath is identified with the region of Hamath in upper Syria, the Sea of the Arabah is identified with the Red Sea to the south, and Jeroboam's control of Hamath and Damascus restores Aram to Israel's control for the first time since the Arameans revolted against Solomon (1 Kgs 11:23–25). Because Joash subdued Amaziah, who in turn had defeated Edom, Jeroboam controlled Edom.

Jeroboam's reign sees an end to the greatest challenge faced by Israel through the ninth and early eighth centuries: the Arameans. Although Joash had allied with the Assyrians, enabling Israel to control Aram, the accounts of the Omride dynasty, the Aramean wars, and the rise of the Jehu dynasty point to YHWH's direct involvement in the affairs of Israel through the prophets Elijah and Elisha. YHWH had sworn to destroy the house of Omri for its idolatry, to employ the Arameans for that purpose, and to replace the Omrides with the house of Jehu. This goal was finally accomplished during the reign of Jeroboam. In keeping with the patterns in the book of Judges, the land has rest for forty years during his reign. YHWH's decision to deliver Israel from oppression is based on YHWH's observation of Israel's oppression in the book of Judges (see also 2 Kgs 13:4, which precedes the promise of a "deliverer" for Israel in 2 Kgs 13:5). Furthermore, the land lacked anyone who was free or bonded, a cryptic reference to YHWH's threats to destroy the entire house of Omri, both free and bond (1 Kgs 21:21; 2 Kgs 9:8), as well as the house of Jeroboam beforehand (1 Kgs 14:10). Furthermore, v. 27 states that YHWH "delivered" Israel by the hand of Jeroboam, which indicates

1. Menahem Haran, "The Empire of Jeroboam ben Joash," *VT* 17 (1967): 267–324.

that Jeroboam is the "deliverer" of Israel mentioned in 2 Kgs 13:5. The restoration is foreseen by the prophet Jonah ben Amitai, about whom we are told nothing else, although a much later prophetic book concerning YHWH's decision to spare Nineveh is attributed to him. When all of these factors are considered, the reign of Jeroboam ben Joash emerges as the culmination of the Jehu History.

XXII. Regnal Account of Azariah (Uzziah) ben Amaziah of Judah
2 Kings 15:1–7

15:1 In the twenty-seventh year of Jeroboam, King of Israel, Azariah[a] ben Amaziah ruled as King of Judah. 2 He was sixteen years old when he ruled, and he reigned for fifty-two years in Jerusalem. The name of his mother was Jecoliah from Jerusalem. 3 He did what was right in the eyes of YHWH according to all that Amaziah his father did. 4 Only the high places were not removed; the people were still sacrificing and burning incense at the high places.

5 YHWH struck the king, and he was leprous until the day of his death. He lived in a separate house, and Jotham, Son of the King who was over the house, was ruling the people of the land.

6 And the rest of the acts of Azariah and all that he did, are they not written in the book of the Chronicles of the Kings of Judah? 7 Azariah slept with his fathers, and they buried him with his fathers in the city of David, and Jotham his son reigned in his place.

a. Cf. Peshitta, "Uzziah," and in vv. 6 and 7.

The regnal account of King Azariah (Uzziah) ben Amaziah of Judah is easily demarcated by the introductory regnal account form in 2 Kgs 15:1–4 and the concluding form in 2 Kgs 15:5–7. The body of the account appears only in v. 5, which mentions Azariah's leprosy and the active role played by his son Jotham in ruling the kingdom. Azariah's rule coincides largely with the reign of Jeroboam ben Joash of Israel. Jeroboam ruled over a kingdom comparable to that of Solomon, and Azariah was his vassal or ally. Despite attempts to identify Azariah with an opponent of Assyria mentioned in the annals of Tiglath-pileser

III (*ANET* 282), recent readings of the cuneiform texts identify him as an Aramean (see Cogan and Tadmor 165–66).

[1–4] Azariah is called Uzziah in 2 Kgs 15:13, 20, 32, 34; Amos 1:1; Hos 1:1; Isa 1:1; 6:1; 7:1, but the similarities in spelling suggest that the name is a simple variant. At sixteen, Azariah is relatively young at the time of his accession to the throne, particularly since his father ruled for twenty-nine years. Azariah was born only one year prior to the death of Jehoash of Israel. Amaziah's older sons may have been killed or taken as hostages when Jehoash put down Amaziah's attempted revolt. His mother Jecoliah is from Jerusalem, which suggests a marriage arranged to consolidate Amaziah's hold on Jerusalem following his failed attempt at revolt.

[5] The body of the regnal account focuses only on Azariah's leprosy and the role played by his son Jotham in administering the kingdom. As a leper, Azariah was considered impure (Lev 13:45) and thereby was unable to carry out the functions of state or to appear at the temple.[1] Lepers lived apart from the rest of the population (Lev 13:46).

Jotham is identified both as "son of the king," which functions as an official title, and as the officer who is "over the house," i.e., the chief administrator of the kingdom.[2] His authority extends to "the people of the land," who were responsible for placing Azariah on the throne following the assassination of his father (see 2 Kgs 14:21).

The present account does not mention Azariah's commercial and military exploits, which played an important role in securing the power of the kingdom. Second Kings 14:21–22 notes that Azariah rebuilt Elath and restored it to Judah, which would have given the kingdom an important commercial link to the Red Sea trading routes with the east coast of Africa, the west coast of the Arabian peninsula, and perhaps areas beyond. Second Chronicles 26 notes Azariah's (Uzziah's) military actions against Philistia, the Arabs of Geur-Baal, the Meunites, as well as his efforts to fortify Jerusalem and to secure his hold on the Shephelah. All of these actions are consistent with those of a long-reigning king who would have seen to his kingdom's security and expansion during a long period of peace, prosperity, and security.

[6–7] The concluding regnal formula includes the typical notices concerning Azariah's acts in the royal chronicles, his death and burial, and the succession of his son Jotham. An Aramaic inscription discovered by E. L. Sukenik

---

1. See Lev 13–14; cf. D. P. Wright and R. N. Jones, "Leprosy," *ABD* 4:277–82.

2. For discussion of both of these titles, see Nili Sacher Fox, *In the Service of the King: Officialdom in Ancient Israel and Judah* (Monographs of the Hebrew Union College 23; Cincinnati: Hebrew Union College, 2000), 43–53, 81–96.

reads, "Here were brought the bones of Uzziah, king of Judah. Do not open!" and once marked Uzziah's tomb outside Jerusalem.[3]

XXIII. Regnal Account of Zechariah ben Jeroboam of Israel
2 Kings 15:8–12

15:8 In the thirty-eighth year of Azariah[a] King of Judah, Zechariah ben Jeroboam ruled over Israel in Samaria for six months. **9** He did what was evil in the eyes of YHWH just as his fathers had done. He did not turn from the sins of Jeroboam ben Nebat, who caused Israel to sin.

10 Shallum ben Jabesh conspired against him and struck him down [b]before the people,[b] and he killed him and ruled in his place.

11 And the rest of the acts of Zechariah, are they not written in the book of the Chronicles of the Kings of Israel? **12** That was the word of YHWH which he spoke to Jehu, saying, "Four generations of your sons will sit upon the throne of Israel," and it was so.

a. Peshitta, "Uzziah."

b–b. Reading with MT, *qābāl-ʿām,* "before (the) people." There are two problems with this reading: (1) *qābāl,* "before," is an Aramaic preposition that presumably has no place in the current Hebrew text; (2) *ʿām,* "people," lacks the definite article. Many interpreters follow other Hebrew manuscripts and LXX Codex Vaticanus that combine the two terms into the place name "Kebla'am"; cf. the Lucianic tradition, which reads the place name as "Ibleam" (Greek, *en Iblaam,* presupposing Hebrew, *bĕyiblĕʿām*), the same location where Ahaziah was killed by Jehu (2 Kgs 9:27). (For discussion, see Tadmor and Cogan 170–71; Montgomery and Gehman 449, 445.)

The regnal account concerning Zechariah ben Jeroboam focuses on his assassination by Shallum ben Jabesh. Zechariah was the last of the Jehu dynasty, and his assassination after only six months on the throne marks the conclusion of the long period of Israel's stability brought about by the nation's alliance with the Assyrian empire. Although the reasons for Shallum's coup against Zechariah are not mentioned, he was likely motivated by an interest in changing Israel's alignment from Assyria to Aram. Shallum's own assassination by Menahem ben Gadi was motivated by an interest in returning to the Assyrian orbit, and the

3. W. F. Albright, "The Discovery of an Aramaic Inscription Relating to King Uzziah," *BASOR* 44 (1931): 8–10.

assassination of Pekahiah ben Menahem was likewise motivated by Pekah's interest in allying with Aram. Israel's break with Assyria proved to be disastrous, as both Aram and Israel were eventually overrun by the Assyrians. Zechariah's regnal account includes the typical introductory regnal formula in vv. 8–9, the body of the regnal account in v. 10, and the concluding regnal formula in vv. 11–12. The text indicates that Zechariah's assassination was carried out in the midst of a public assembly. The speed with which Shallum was dispatched by Menahem ben Gadi suggests that the usurper lacked popular support. Verse 12 notes the fulfillment of YHWH's promise to Jehu that he would see his sons on the throne to the fourth generation (2 Kgs 10:30).

XXIV. Regnal Account of Shallum ben Jabesh of Israel 2 Kings 15:13–16

15:13 Shallum ben Jabesh ruled in the thirty-ninth year of Uzziah[a] King of Judah, and he ruled for one month in Samaria.

14 Menahem ben Gadi went up from Tirzah, came to Samaria. He struck Shallum ben Jabesh in Samaria, killed him, and ruled in his place.

15 And the rest of the acts of Shallum and his conspiracy which he conspired, behold they are written in the book of the Chronicles of the Kings of Israel. 16 Then Menahem attacked Tipsah[b] and all who were in it and its territory from Tirzah, because it did not open. He attacked and ripped open its pregnant women.

a. LXX, "Azariah."
b. Lucianic LXX identifies the city as Tappuah.

The regnal account for Shallum ben Jabesh is necessarily brief, since Shallum ruled only for a month before being assassinated himself. The literary structure includes the introductory regnal form in v. 13, the body of the regnal account in v. 14, and the concluding regnal form in vv. 15–16. Menahem ben Gadi's submission to Assyria (2 Kgs 15:19–20) suggests his efforts to put a stop to an attempted revolt against the Assyrians by Shallum. The identification of Tipsah with the northern Aramean city on the banks of the Euphrates (1 Kgs 5:4) is impossible to reconcile with notices concerning its proximity to Tirzah. This accounts for the Lucianic LXX's identification of the city as Tappuah (cf. Josh 17:8). Tipsah is more likely identified with modern Sheik Abu Zarad, about eight miles northwest of Shiloh ("Tiphsah," *HBD* 1156).

XXV. Regnal Account of Menahem ben Gadi of Israel 2 Kings 15:17–22

15:17 In the thirty-ninth year of Azariah[a] King of Judah, Menahem ben Gadi ruled over Israel for ten years in Samaria. 18 He did what was evil in the eyes of YHWH; he did not turn aside from the sins of Jeroboam ben Nebat which he caused Israel to commit all his days.

19 Pul, King of Assyria, came against the land, and Menahem gave to Pul one thousand talents of silver [b]to support him,[b] i.e., [c]to strengthen the kingdom in his hand.[c] 20 Menahem exacted money from Israel and from all the wealthy men to give to the King of Assyria, fifty shekels of silver for each man. So the King of Assyria returned and did not remain in the land.

21 And the rest of the acts of Menahem and all that he did, are they not written in the book of the Chronicles of the Kings of Israel? 22 Menahem slept with his fathers, and Pekahiah his son ruled in his place.

a. Peshitta, "Uzziah."

b–b. MT, *lihyôt yādāyw ʿittô,* lit., "to be his hands with him," i.e., "so that his hands would be with him," an apparent reference to Menahem's payment for the support of the Assyrian king.

c–c. Lacking in LXX. This phrase is likely an early gloss that explains the preceding expression.

Menahem's ten-year reign indicates a rare period of stability during Israel's last years. The body of the regnal account focuses exclusively on Menahem's actions to pay off the Assyrian monarch, Tiglath-pileser III (745–727 B.C.E.), also known as Pul (cf. *ANET* 272), who threatened Israel. Such a move makes great sense in the aftermath of Shallum's reign, insofar as Shallum's revolt was motivated by an interest in breaking Israel's alliance with Assyria to realign with Aram. Tiglath-pileser responded against the short-lived revolt by reasserting his authority over his vassal (see *ANET* 283–84, where Tiglath-pileser mentions receiving tribute from Menahem and other monarchs in 738 B.C.E.). Assyrian kings typically undertook such expeditions on a regular basis, although the recent coup in Israel would have called for even greater attention on Tiglath-pileser's part. Menahem's levying of a special tax on the propertied men of Israel suggests financial hardship in meeting a heavy assessment. The weight of a talent is uncertain, although it ranges from 66 pounds/30 kilograms to 134.6 pounds/61.2 kilograms.[1] One thousand

1. W. G. Dever, "Weights and Measures," *HBD* 1206–11, esp. 1206.

talents of silver was a considerable sum, comparable to the ten talents of gold and one thousand talents of silver demanded of King Hulli of Tabal (*ARAB* 1:802) and the thirty gold talents and eight hundred silver talents paid by Hezekiah to Sennacherib (*ANET* 288).

XXVI. Regnal Account of Pekahiah ben Menahem of Israel
2 Kings 15:23–26

15:23 In the fiftieth year of Azariah[a] King of Judah, Pekahiah ben Menahem ruled over Israel in Samaria for two years. **24** He did what was evil in the eyes of YHWH; he did not turn from the sins of Jeroboam ben Nebat, who caused Israel to sin.

25 Pekah ben Remaliah, his officer, conspired against him and attacked him in Samaria in the palace of the house of the king, [b]at Argob and the Aryeh.[b] Fifty men were with him from the Gileadites,[c] and he killed him and ruled in his place.

26 And the rest of the acts of Pekahiah and all that he did, behold they are written in the book of the Chronicles of the Kings of Israel.

a. Peshitta, "Uzziah."

b–b. These terms are sometimes taken as the names of Pekah's coconspirators, but the definite article before Aryeh precludes this interpretation. Some argue that they are place names, perhaps displaced from the list of locations taken by Tiglath-pileser in v. 29 below, but the reasons that they would be placed in their present location are lacking. The terms mean "eagle" and "the lion," which would refer to two guardian figures that stand at the entrance to the royal palace.[1]

c. LXX reads "the four hundred," which suggests that Pekah's coconspirators were drawn from a four-hundred-man palace guard. 2 Kgs 11 notes that the Carite "commanders of hundreds" were to control the four sides of the temple forecourt where the king would stand.

The regnal account for Pekahiah in v. 25 mentions only his assassination in a coup led by Pekah ben Remaliah. He likely continued his father's policy of alliance with the Assyrian empire. Pekah's subsequent shift of Israel's alliance to Aram formed the so-called Syro-Ephraimitic coalition, which attempted to garner support among the smaller states of southwest Asia to oppose Assyria's

1. Mordechai Cogan and Hayim Tadmor, *II Kings* (Anchor Bible 11; New York: Doubleday, 1988), 173.

attempts to dominate the region. Pekah is here identified as a military officer, and his support from among the Gileadites indicates that the primary goal of the coup was to realign Israel with Aram. Gilead is located in the Transjordan immediately south of Aram. The region's proximity to Aram and Israel's sense of historic ties with the Arameans (Gen 11:27–32) were major motivating forces for an alliance with Aram during this period.[2]

XXVII. Regnal Account of Pekah ben Remaliah of Israel 2 Kings 15:27–31

15:27 In the fifty-second year of Azariah[a] King of Judah, Pekah ben Remaliah ruled over Israel in Samaria for twenty years. 28 He did what was evil in the eyes of YHWH; he did not turn from the sins of Jeroboam ben Nebat, who caused Israel to sin.

29 In the days of Pekah, King of Israel, Tiglath Pileser King of Assyria came. He took Iyyon, Abel Beth Maacah, Yanoah, Kedesh, Hazor, the Gilead, and the Galilee, all the land of Naphtali, and exiled them to Assyria. 30 Hosea ben Elah conspired against Pekah ben Remaliah, attacked him, killed him, and ruled in his place in the twentieth year of Jotham ben Uzziah.[b]

31 And the rest of the acts of Pekah and all that he did, behold, they written in the book of the acts of the Kings of Israel.

a. Peshitta, "Uzziah."
b. LXX, "Azariah."

[27–28] Although the narrative states that Pekah ruled for twenty years, most interpreters consider this to be far too long a period, since Assyrian records indicate that Menahem paid tribute to Assyria in 738 B.C.E. and Hoshea surrendered to Tiglath-pileser III in 732 B.C.E. The timing of Pekah's assassination of Pekahiah and seizure of the throne indicates that it took place about the time of Azariah's death. This is not coincidental since Pekah's plans were to bring Judah into his alliance with Rezin of Aram to form the Syro-Ephraimitic coalition. The death of the Judean monarch provided an opportune time to begin overtures to Judah.

[29–30] The body of Pekah's regnal account focuses cryptically on Tiglath-pileser III's invasions of Israel in 734–732 B.C.E. and Hosea ben Elah's

---

2. See my commentary on Hosea in *Twelve Prophets* (Berit Olam; Collegeville, Minn.: Liturgical, 2000), 1:3–144.

assassination of Pekah.[1] The Syro-Ephraimitic coalition was instigated by Rezin of Damascus to resist the Assyrians, who threatened the northern territories of Aram. Israel's entry into the coalition thereby constituted another attempt at reversing Israel's long-standing alliance with the Assyrians established by the Jehu dynasty and reestablished by Menahem ben Gadi. The Syro-Ephraimitic war fought against Judah in 734 B.C.E. was designed to remove King Jotham or his son Ahaz from the throne and to replace him with Ben Tabeel, whose name suggests Transjordanian and perhaps Aramean background (see Isa 7:1–25, esp. v. 6). Although Jotham died before the Syro-Ephraimitic attack commenced, his twenty-year-old son Ahaz recognized his isolated position and called for support from his Assyrian suzerain. Tiglath-pileser III carried out a series of campaigns that destroyed Damascus and subjugated Israel, Philistia, and Judah. Israel was stripped of its territory in the Transjordan, the Galilee, and the coastal plain, as each of these regions was incorporated into the Assyrian empire as the provinces Galaza (Gilead), Magiddu (Megiddo), and Duru (Dor), leaving Israel with only the northern Israelite hill country.[2] The cities named in the present text, Ijon (Tell ed-Dibin, located at the northern end of the Huleh Valley near Israel's border with Aram);[3] Abel Beth Maacah (Tell Abel el-Qamh, about four to five miles north-northwest of the city of Dan);[4] Janoah (the exact site is disputed, although it is clearly in the vicinity of Abel Beth Maacah in all proposals);[5] Kedesh (Tell Kedesh, the home of Deborah's companion Barak [see Judg 4–5] in the territory of Naphtali, located northwest of the Huleh Valley in the Galilee where it also overlooks the Jordan Valley);[6] Hazor (Tell Hazor in the northern Galilee, south-west of the Huleh Valley);[7] and the regions of the Gilead, the Galilee, and Naphtali, all correspond to the regions annexed by Tiglath-pileser III. In the face of such an overwhelming miscalculation that brought northern Israel to its knees, Pekah was assassinated by Hoshea ben Elah. Hoshea's prompt surrender to the Assyrians likely avoided further devastation. Tiglath-pileser's deportation of some elements of the population was a standard Assyrian policy in cases of revolt.[8] Such deportations were designed to punish and destabilize the popula-

1. Herbert Donner, "The Syro-Ephraimitic War and the End of the Kingdom of Israel," *Israelite and Judaean History* (ed. J. H. Hayes and J. M. Miller; Philadelphia: Westminster, 1977), 421–34; H. Cazelles, "Syro-Ephraimitic War," *ABD* 6:282–85.

2. Albrecht Alt, "Das System der assyrischen Provinzen auf dem Boden des Reiches Israel," *KS* 2:188–205.

3. R. A. Mullins, "Ijon," *ABD* 3:387–88.

4. V. Fritz, "Abel," *ABD* 1:10.

5. R. Frankel, "Janoah," *ABD* 3:640–41.

6. R. Arav, "Kedesh," *ABD* 4:11.

7. Yadin and A. Ben-Tor, "Hazor," *NEAEHL* 2:594–606.

8. See Bustenay Oded, *Mass Deportations and Deportees in the Neo-Assyrian Empire* (Wiesbaden: O. Harrassowitz, 1979).

tion by removing its leadership, and to apply the skills of the deportees in other regions of Assyria.

[31] The reference to Hoshea's assassination of Pekah in the twentieth year of Jotham contradicts 2 Kgs 15:33, which states that Jotham ruled for only sixteen years. Some maintain, however, that Jotham ruled for a period as coregent since his father suffered from leprosy.

XXVIII. Regnal Account of Jotham ben Uzziah of Judah
2 Kings 15:32–38

15:32 In the second year of Pekah ben Remaliah King of Israel, Jotham ben Uzziah[a] reigned as King of Judah. 33 He was twenty-five years old when he reigned, and for sixteen years he ruled in Jerusalem. The name of his mother was Jarusha bat Zadok. 34 He did what was right in the eyes of YHWH. He acted according to all that Uzziah[a] his father did. 35 Only the high places were not removed; the people were still sacrificing and burning incense at the high places.

He built the upper gate of the House of YHWH.

36 And the rest of the acts of Jotham which he did, are they not written in the book of the Chronicles of the Kings of Judah? 37 In those days, YHWH began to send against Judah Rezin King of Aram and Pekah ben Remaliah. 38 Jotham slept with his fathers. He was buried with his fathers in the city of David his father, and Ahaz his son ruled in his place.

a. LXX, "Azariah."

Jerusha bat Zadok is otherwise unknown, although the name of her father suggests that she could be the daughter of a priest. The body of Jotham's regnal account in v. 35b simply mentions that he built the upper gate of the house of YHWH. This gate may be identified with the upper Benjamin gate of the temple where Passhur placed Jeremiah in stocks (Jer 20:2) and the temple gate that faces north in Ezek 9:2. Because the northern boundary of Jerusalem (and the temple complex) is built over relatively flat terrain, it would have been the most difficult side of Jerusalem to defend. The concluding regnal formula in vv. 36–38 encloses a reference to the beginning of the Syro-Ephraimitic war. Although the cause of Jotham's death is unclear, he seems to have died after the attack commenced, leaving Ahaz to deal with the threat.

XXIX. Regnal Account of Ahaz ben Jotham of Judah 2 Kings 16:1–20

16:1 In the seventeenth year of Pekah ben Remaliah, Ahaz ben Jotham reigned as king of Judah. 2 Ahaz was twenty years old when he reigned, and he ruled for sixteen years in Jerusalem, and he did not do what is right in the eyes of YHWH, his G-d, like David, his father. 3 He walked in the path of the kings of Israel, and he passed his son through fire according to the abominations of the nations whom YHWH expelled before the sons of Israel. 4 He sacrificed and burned incense at the high places and on the hills and under every leafy tree.

5 Then Rezin, King of Aram, and Pekah ben Remaliah, King of Israel, went up to Jerusalem for war, and they besieged Ahaz, but they were not able to overcome (him). 6 At that time, Rezin, King of Aram, restored Elath to Aram, and he cleared out the Judeans from Elath. The Edomites[a] came to Elath, and they settled there until this day.

7 Ahaz sent messengers to Tiglath Pileser, King of Assyria, saying, "I am your servant and your son. Come up and deliver me from the hand of the King of Aram and from the hand of the King of Israel who stand against me." 8 Ahaz took the silver and the gold that was found in the house of YHWH and in the treasuries of the house of the king, and he sent it to the King of Assyria as tribute. 9 The King of Assyria listened to him, and the King of Assyria went up to Damascus, seized it, exiled it to Kir, and killed Rezin. 10 And King Ahaz went to meet Tiglath Pileser, King of Assyria, at Damascus, and saw the altar which was in Damascus. King Ahaz sent to Uriah the Priest the design of the altar and its blueprint for all its construction, 11 and Uriah the Priest built the altar. According to all that King Ahaz sent from Damascus, so Uriah the Priest built, until King Ahaz came back from Damascus. 12 The king came from Damascus, and the king saw the altar, and the king approached the altar, and he made an offering upon it. 13 He burned his whole burnt offering and his grain offering, poured out his libation offering, and sprinkled the blood of his peace offering upon the altar. 14 And the bronze altar which was before YHWH, he moved from before the Temple structure, (from) between the altar and the Temple structure and placed it on the north side of the altar. 15 King Ahaz commanded[b] Uriah the Priest saying, "Upon the great altar burn the whole burnt offering of cattle and the evening grain offering and the whole burnt offering of the king and his grain offering and the whole

burnt offering of the people of the land and their grain offering and their libation offerings, and all the blood of the whole burnt offering and all the blood of the (peace) sacrifice you shall sprinkle. The bronze altar shall be for me ^cto make oracular inquiry.^c 16 And Uriah the Priest did according to all that King Ahaz commanded. 17 King Ahaz cut off the frameworks of the stands, removed the basin from upon them, brought down the sea from upon the bronze cattle which were under it, and placed it upon a pavement of stones. 18 And he removed from the house of YHWH ^ethe Shabbat ^dcovered passage^d which they built in the Temple^e and the outer entrance of the king because of the king of Assyria.

19 And the rest of the acts of Ahaz which he did, are they not written in the book of the Chronicles of the Kings of Judah? 20 Ahaz slept with his fathers, and he was buried with his fathers in the city of David, and Hezekiah his son reigned in his place.

a. Ketiv, *waʾărāmîm*, "and the Arameans"; read with Qere, *waʾădōmîm*, "and the Edomites." Peshitta reads "and the Arameans."

b. Ketiv, *yayiṣawwehû*, "and he commanded him"; Qere, *yayiṣawweh*, "and he commanded."

c–c. LXX reads '*eis toproi*, "in the morning," which presupposes Hebrew, *labbōqer*, "for the morning," a repointing of MT, *lĕbaqqer*, "to make oracular inquiry." The LXX did not recognize the function of altars in oracular interpretation (see Balaam's use of altars in Num 22–24), and read the phrase as a reference to the king's morning offerings.

d–d. Ketiv, *mesak*, "enclosure"; read with Qere, *mûsak*, "covered (passage)."

e–e. MT, *wĕʾet mûsak haššabbăt ʿăšer-bānû babbayit*, "and the Shabbat covered passage which they built in the house (Temple) . . ." Cf. LXX, *Kai ton themelion tes kathedras oikodomesen 'en 'oikoi Kuriou*, "and the base of the throne which he built in the house of the L-rd," presupposes Hebrew, *wĕʾet mûsād haššebet ʿăšer-bānâ babbayit YHWH*. The LXX did not understand the Shabbat passageway and read the text to refer to an unattested royal throne built in the temple.

The regnal account for Ahaz ben Jotham is demarcated by the introductory regnal formula in vv. 1–4 and by the concluding regnal formula in vv. 19–20. The body of the regnal account in vv. 5–18 focuses entirely on Ahaz's actions in relation to the Syro-Ephraimitic War (735–732 B.C.E.) when King Pekah of Israel and King Rezin of Aram attempted to force Judah into its anti-Assyrian coalition. The present account begins in vv. 5–6 with the attacks against Judah launched by the Syro-Ephraimitic coalition, and it continues in vv. 7–19 with an account of Ahaz's appeal to Tiglath-pileser and the consequences that followed from Assyria's intervention.

Interpreters allow the historiographical and theological perspectives of the Kings account and the corresponding account of Isaiah's encounter with Ahaz in Isa 7:1–9:6 to color their evaluations of Ahaz as a sinful monarch who rejected the protection offered him by YHWH. Such a strategy obscures essential historical issues and theological perspectives in this narrative.

Second Kings 16 emphasizes that Ahaz's appeal for assistance was the catalyst for Assyria's entry into the region and its subsequent domination of Judah until the time of Hezekiah's revolt, when YHWH responded to Hezekiah's appeal to defeat the Assyrian invaders and expel them from the land (2 Kgs 18–20). Such a portrayal conflicts with the view of Assyria's role in the region known from Assyrian sources. The Black Obelisk indicates that the Assyrians had already entered into suzerain-vassal relationship with Israel as early as the reign of Jehu in the latter half of the ninth century B.C.E. (see *ANEP* 351–55; *ANET* 281). Judah had been an ally of Israel during the reigns of Jehoshaphat of Judah and the Omride monarchs, although it is uncertain if this relationship held together during the course of Jehu's revolt and subsequent reign. Biblical sources indicate that King Amaziah of Judah attempted to renegotiate Judah's relationship with Israel following his defeat of the Edomites, but Joash's assault against Judah quickly reestablished Israel's hegemony (see 2 Kgs 14:1–22). A stela of the Assyrian monarch Adad Nirari V indicates that Joash of Israel was an Assyrian tributary during the early eighth century B.C.E.[1] Because of Judah's relationship with Israel during the reigns of the Jehu monarchs, Judah would also have been a vassal of Assyria during this time.

Ahaz's appeal to Tiglath-pileser was that of a loyal vassal who called upon his overlord for assistance when his neighboring nations were engaged in revolt. His actions were not motivated by apostasy, but by the desperate situation of isolation in which the twenty-year-old monarch found himself at the outset of his reign. Although Isaiah offered him YHWH's protection in Isa 7:1–9:6, such an offer must have seemed ludicrous, insofar as it did not come with a relief column.[2] Ironically, Isaiah's advice was tactically sound—namely, the Syro-Ephraimitic forces could ill afford to waste much time in a protracted siege of Jerusalem while Aram's borders with Assyria lay open to assault. The practical side of Isaiah's advice was that Jerusalem's defenses would withstand a siege long enough to force the Syro-Ephraimtic forces to withdraw in order to protect Aram against Assyrian attack. Tiglath-pileser hardly needed Ahaz's invitation as an excuse to attack Aram. Ahaz's request did leave him obligated for his life and throne to Tiglath-pileser, but no such obligation would have existed had Tiglath-pileser attacked Aram of his own accord. Tiglath-pileser did not reward Ahaz for his loyalty, but instead imposed further tribute upon him as the price for saving his neck.

The presentation of Ahaz's actions, however, serves the historiographical and theological agenda of the Hezekian and Josianic DtrH editions. By pinning

1. Stephanie Page, "A Stele of Adad-Nirari III and Nergal-Ereš from Tell al Rimah," *Iraq* 30 (1968): 139–53.

2. For discussion of Isa 7:1–9:6, see M. A. Sweeney, *Isaiah 1–39* (FOTL; Grand Rapids and Cambridge: Eerdmans, 1998), 143–88.

on Ahaz the responsibility for Assyria's domination of Judah, the DtrH sets him up as a foil for the righteous Hezekiah and later for Josiah. The DtrH writers have already portrayed Israel's submission to Assyria during the reign of King Menahem (2 Kgs 15:19–20), which will lead ultimately to Israel's destruction when it revolts against Assyria during the reigns of Pekah and Hoshea (2 Kgs 15:29–30; 17). In reflecting upon this destruction, the DtrH makes it very clear that it must be traced ultimately to the apostasy of Jeroboam ben Nebat, who causes Israel to sin. By portraying Ahaz as a Judean monarch who followed in the path of the kings of Israel (2 Kgs 16:3), the present account emphasizes an analogous scenario of apostasy, and backs it up with a description of Ahaz's own acts of apostasy, including passing his son through fire and sacrificing and burning incense at the high places. The Assyrian invasion of Judah in 2 Kgs 18–20 thereby becomes an act of divine punishment for Judah that can only be reversed by the righteous actions of King Hezekiah. The Hezekian DtrH puts forward Hezekiah as a model of piety—in contrast to the apostate Ahaz—whose lack of fidelity placed Judah under the authority of Assyria in the first place. When read in relation to the Josianic DtrH, Ahaz likewise serves as a foil to the righteous Josiah. Although the Assyrian threat is long gone by the time of Josiah's reign, Josiah must act to remove the various foreign cultic installations brought to Jerusalem by his predecessors, including the altars on the roof of the upper chamber of Ahaz (2 Kgs 23:12). When read in relation to the exilic DtrH, Ahaz merely serves as an example of a sinful Judean monarch.

[1–4] The seventeenth year of Pekah's twenty-year reign allows for the three-year period in which the Syro-Ephraimitic coalition began its attacks against Judah and the subsequent Assyrian assaults against Aram and Israel in 735–732 B.C.E. Jotham died at the beginning of the Syro-Ephraimitic War, thereby leaving Ahaz as king of Judah. Tiglath-pileser III refers to a king Jehoahaz (Ia-ú-ha-zi, a longer form of Ahaz) of Judah as one of his tributaries (*ANET* 282).[3]

Ahaz is presented as an apostate who follows the sins of the kings of Israel, indulges in child sacrifice like the pre-Israelite inhabitants of the land, and sacrifices and burns incense at the illicit high places and green trees in opposition to the Dtr requirement for worship at only one central sanctuary (Deut 12:2–7). The high places and green trees are associated with Canaanite worship—for example, the high places are equated with sanctuaries for Baal and the trees represent Asherah imagery.[4] Such a presentation ensures Ahaz's condemnation, since he emulates the actions of three major classes of apostates in the DtrH—namely,

3. See H. Tadmor, *The Inscriptions of Tiglath Pileser III, King of Assyria* (Jerusalem: The Israel Academy of Sciences and Humanities, 1994), 171:11, 277.

4. Susan Ackerman, *Under Every Green Tree: Popular Religion in Sixth-Century Judah* (HSM 46; Atlanta: Scholars Press, 1992).

northern Israelite kings, pre-Israelite nations, and those within Israel who violate YHWH's expectations.

[5–18] The body of the regnal account begins with the basic statement in v. 5 concerning the attack launched against Jerusalem by the two major allies in the Syro-Ephraimitic coalition, Rezin of Aram and Pekah of Israel (see 2 Kgs 15:27–31). The goals of the Syro-Ephraimitic assault were to force Judah to join Aram and Israel (and the other small states of western Asia) in an effort to resist Tiglath-pileser III's attempts to expand the Assyrian empire into western Asia. Pekah's decision to ally with Aram broke the long-standing alliance between Israel and Assyria initiated by the Jehu dynasty, and it completely changed the balance of power in the region by freeing Aram from the combined pressure of Assyria and Israel. With Israel now firmly in the Aramean camp, Rezin was free to confront the Assyrians from a position of strength. Although Israel's shift in alliance freed Aram's southern borders and allowed Rezin to focus on his border with Assyria, Rezin could not proceed in any confrontation with Assyria without also ensuring the allegiance of all small states in western Asia. To do otherwise would have left him with a potentially hostile power at his rear that would undermine his efforts to resist the Assyrians. Although Rezin succeeded in convincing the various small states of the region (e.g., Edom, Moab, Philistia, and Phoenicia), Judah resisted Rezin's overtures. The reasons for Judah's (perhaps Jotham's) reluctance are not difficult to fathom. Breaking an alliance with Assyria would have severe consequences if the effort was unsuccessful, and the history of the two major partners in the alliance, Israel and Aram, was fraught with conflict from the time of the Davidic, Omride, and Jehu dynasties. Jotham must have concluded that it would be foolish to risk his nation's security (and his own life) by joining such a fragile alliance.

The result was the combined assault by the armies of Aram and Israel. With the Syro-Ephraimitic confrontation with Assyria imminent, Rezin and Pekah would have had little time to lose in a protracted siege of Jerusalem. Aram's northern border would have been exposed to Assyrian attack, and Jerusalem's defenses would hold down the Syro-Ephraimitic army for a lengthy period of time. Isaiah 7 portrays Isaiah's encounter with Ahaz while the king was inspecting the weak point of Jerusalem's defenses—that is, the water system of the city which opened at the conduit of the upper pool on the highway to the Fuller's Field (Isa 7:3). As a walled city with valleys along its eastern (the Kidron Valley) and western (the Tyropoean Valley) boundaries, Jerusalem was easily defended against attack. Like most walled cities, Jerusalem's weak point was its water system, which opened outside the eastern defensive walls of the city at the base of the hill in the Kidron Valley.[5] Indeed, 2 Sam 5:8 and 1 Chr 11:6 indicate that David took Jerusalem by sending Joab and his men up the water shaft that

5. Y. Shiloh, "Jerusalem," *NEAEHL* 2:701–12.

provided water for the city. The shaft opened well below the defensive walls. With the water system properly concealed and defended, the Syro-Ephraimitic forces would have had little choice but to place the city under siege. With an assured supply of water, the siege would depend upon Jerusalem's stored food supplies. Like most walled cities, Jerusalem would have enough food to resist for months.

Verse 5 appears in Isa 7:1 in a somewhat different form at the beginning of the Isaian account of the Syro-Ephraimitic War. The statement in Isa 7:1 is part of the Josianic redaction of Isaiah that reworked 2 Kgs 16:5 to introduce its narrative concerning Isaiah's encounter with Ahaz at the time of the Syro-Ephraimitic War.[6] The statement in v. 6 concerning Rezin's actions to take control of Elath has provoked a great deal of text-critical discussion concerning the identity of the nation that captured Elath. Interpreters consider it unlikely that Aram actually took control of Elath and that the Arameans then inhabited the city after having driven out the Judeans. Edom is the far more likely candidate for such an action because of the proximity of its southern boundaries to Elath and because 2 Chr 28:17 mentions an Edomite attack against Judah at the time of the Syro-Ephraimitic War. Second Chronicles 28:5–21 paints a bleak picture in which the Syro-Ephraimitic coalition slaughtered or took captive thousands of Judeans, and smaller countries, such as Philistia and Edom, were able to take large areas of Judean territory and slaughter even more Judeans. Edom had always been subjugated to Judah rather than to Israel, even when Judah was subject to Israel. Working in concert with Israel, Rezin would have been able to instigate the Edomites to attack Elath, and would even have been able to provide support for such an attack by means of the King's Highway that provided Damascus with access to the Transjordan and the Arabian peninsula. Excavations at Tell el-Khaleifeh, located in the vicinity of biblical Elath, indicate the presence of Edomites along the northern shores of the Gulf of Aqaba in the eighth century B.C.E.[7] The reference to the Edomites' remaining in Elath "until this day" would fit any edition of the DtrH from the Hezekian edition onward.

Ahaz's appeal to Tiglath-pileser for assistance and Tiglath-pileser's subjugation of Damascus appear in vv. 7–9. As a vassal of Assyria, Ahaz would be obligated to support Tiglath-pileser against any insurrection. His statement, "Your servant and your son am I," is a very clear statement of loyalty by Ahaz to his Assyrian overlord. Ancient Near Eastern treaties are known to label suzerain monarchs as "father" and vassal monarchs as "son," although Assyrian treaties employ the term "servant" for a vassal.[8] Ahaz's dispatch of funds to

6. Sweeney, *Isaiah 1–39,* 149–59, esp. 150–51.

7. N. Glueck and G. D. Pratico, "Tell el-Kheleifeh," *NEAEHL* 3:867–70.

8. See Dennis McCarthy, "Notes on the Love of G-d in Dt and the Father-Son Relationship between YHWH and Israel," *CBQ* 27 (1965): 144–47; Montgomery and Gehman, 348; M. L. Barré, "Treaties in the ANE," *ABD* 6:653–56.

Tiglath-pileser, here referred to as *šohad*, "bribe," connotes Ahaz's payment of a special tribute to his overlord to provide incentive for assistance in a time of crisis. Tiglath-pileser destroyed Damascus in 734–732 B.C.E. following a protracted siege. His records do not mention the execution of King Rezin of Aram, but there is little reason to doubt that he put Rezin to death. The location of Kir is unknown, although Amos 9:7 identifies Kir as the original homeland of the Arameans, and Isa 22:6 associates it with Elam. Tiglath-pileser also attacked Israel, but Israel's capitulation following the assassination of Pekah (2 Kgs 15:29–30) saved it from destruction at this time.

Ahaz's journey to Damascus to meet with Tiglath-pileser appears in vv. 10–11. The primary purpose for such a meeting would be for Ahaz to demonstrate his loyalty to Tiglath-pileser following the Assyrian victory over the Arameans that had saved Ahaz and his kingdom. The report that Ahaz saw an altar in Damascus and sent instructions to the high priest Uriah in Jerusalem to have a copy of this altar built for the Jerusalem temple is an example of Ahaz's subservience to his Assyrian overlord. Uriah is the same figure mentioned in Isa 8:2 as one of the witnesses to the birth of Isaiah's son Maher Shalal Hash Baz. Early scholars argue that the Assyrians had imposed worship of Assur on Judah and that the new altar was an Assyrian model designed for such worship.[9] Thorough studies of the issue by McKay and Cogan demonstrate that the Assyrians did not impose their own religious worship on conquered nations.[10] A notable feature of this argument is that the altar was used for whole burnt offerings of meat (see vv. 13, 15 below), but the Assyrians did not employ animal sacrifices as part of their worship.[11] The role of this altar as a symbol of Judah's subservience to Assyria in the aftermath of the defeat of the Syro-Ephraimitic coalition cannot be dismissed.[12] The Assyrians were well known for their use of local officials and power structures in their administration of conquered lands within their empire.[13] Assyria itself did not employ animal sacrifice as part of its own religious worship, but it would follow local customs in setting the requirements for cultic expressions of loyalty to the Assyrian empire. YHWH would be subservient to Assur. The replacement of the old altar with the new

9. T. Oestreicher, *Das deuteronomische Grundgesetz* (Gütersloh: Bertelsmann, 1923), 38, 55–56; A. T. Olmstead, *History of Assyria* (Chicago: University of Chicago, 1968), 452.

10. John McKay, *Religion in Judah under the Assyrians* (SBT 2/26; Naperville, Ill.: Allenson, 1973), 5–12; Morton Cogan, *Imperialism and Religion* (SBLMS 19; Missoula, Mont.: Scholars Press, 1974), 55–96.

11. A. Leo Oppenheim, *Ancient Mesopotamia: Portrait of a Dead Civilization* (Chicago: University of Chicago, 1968), 192.

12. Hermann Spieckermann, *Juda unter Assur in der Sargonidenzeit* (FRLANT 129; Göttingen: Vandenhoeck & Ruprecht, 1982), 307–72, esp. 362–69.

13. A. K. Grayson, "Assyrian Rule of Conquered Territory in Ancient Western Asia," *CANE* 2:959–68; cf. Jeffrey Kah-jin Kuan, *Neo-Assyrian Historical Inscriptions and Syria-Palestine* (Jin Dao Dissertation Series 1; Hong Kong: Alliance Bible Seminary, 1995).

one of Damascene design expresses that new relationship.

Ahaz's actions upon his return from Damascus to Jerusalem appear in vv. 12–18. His first act upon his return to Jerusalem is to inaugurate use of the new altar by making the standard range of sacrifices,[14] including the Olah or whole burnt offering (Lev 1), the Minḥa or grain offering (Lev 2), the libation offering (Num 15:5), and the Shelamim or peace offering (Lev 3). Ahaz acts in the role of a priest in offering sacrifice at the new altar. Elsewhere, David's sons are designated as priests (see 2 Sam 8:18); kings typically offered sacrifice at the inauguration of a new altar or temple (see, e.g., David in 2 Sam 6, esp. vv. 17–18; Solomon in 1 Kgs 8, esp. v. 63; Jeroboam in 1 Kgs 12:32; 13:1–10). The present narrative suggests some continuing role for the monarch, as the regular sacrifices of the king are to be offered at the new altar together with the sacrifices of the people of the land in v. 15. The movement of the bronze altar to the north symbolizes Judah's subjugation to Assyria. The king retains the bronze altar for use in oracular inquiry. Although the dynamics of oracular inquiry on behalf of the king are not clear, it calls for the king to make a sacrifice to YHWH in order to receive an oracle from YHWH's prophets. First Kings 22 portrays Ahab's and Jehoshaphat's oracular inquiry of the prophets prior to battle at Ramoth Gilead, although the narrative does not mention a sacrifice (see also 2 Sam 2:1; 2 Kgs 19:1–7; and 2 Kgs 22:11–20). First Kings 14:1–18 portrays the visit by the wife of Jeroboam to Ahijah the prophet, and it notes that she must bring a gift to the prophet in order to receive an oracle concerning the health of her son (see v. 3). Although this is hardly a temple sacrifice, it suggests the need to make an offering as part of the process of oracular inquiry. Second Kings 8:8 indicates Ben Hadad's order to Hazael to take a gift to Elisha for oracular inquiry, and 1 Sam 9:7–9 indicates the need for Saul to bring a gift to the prophet Samuel.

The references in v. 17 to Ahaz's removal of the bronze frameworks for the basin stands of the temple (1 Kgs 7:27–39) and the twelve bulls that supported the molten sea (1 Kgs 7:23–26) indicate his need for the bronze used in their construction to pay his tribute to Tiglath-pileser. The removal of the king's covered Shabbat passageway to the temple probably does not provide him with the means to pay tribute since there is no indication that bronze or any other valuable metal was employed in its construction. It is more likely that the passageway symbolized the intimate relationship between the house of David and YHWH, in which YHWH regarded the Davidic king as a son who would enjoy royal protection (e.g., Ps 2; cf. Pss 46–48; 89; 132). With Assyria as Judah's overlord, symbols of royal privilege and YHWH's protection would now be removed to recognize Assyria's new role as Judah's protector. Although the function of this passageway is not clear, it evidently provides access for the king

14. See Lev 6–7; Num 15; J. Milgrom, "Sacrifices and Offerings, OT," *IDBSup* 763–71.

from his palace to the temple, and suggests the role of the temple as royal chapel and national shrine.

XXX. Regnal Account of Hoshea ben Elah of Israel
2 Kings 17:1–41

17:1 In the twelfth year of Ahaz, King of Judah, Hoshea ben Elah ruled in Samaria over Israel nine years. 2 He did evil in the eyes of YHWH, but not like the kings of Israel before him.

3 Shalmaneser, King of Assyria, came up against him, and Hoshea became his servant to him and paid him tribute. 4 The King of Assyria discovered conspiracy in Hoshea when he sent messengers to So, King of Egypt, and he did not bring up tribute to the King of Assyria as he had done annually. The King of Assyria arrested him and confined him in prison. 5 The King of Assyria went up against the entire land, and he went up against Samaria, and he besieged it for three years.

6 In the ninth year of Hoshea, the King of Assyria captured Samaria, exiled Israel to Assyria, and settled them in Halah, and in Habor, Nahar[a] Gozan, and the cities[b] of the Medes.

7 And this happened because the sons of Israel sinned against YHWH, their G-d, who brought them up from the land of Egypt from under the hand of Pharaoh, King of Egypt, and they feared other gods. 8 They walked in the statutes of the nations whom YHWH expelled from before the people of Israel and the kings of Israel whom they had made. 9 The people of Israel did things secretly that were not right concerning YHWH, their G-d, and they built high places for themselves in all their cities, from watchtowers to fortified cities. 10 They erected masseboth and asherim for themselves on every high hill and under every green tree. 11 They burned incense there in all the high places like the nations whom YHWH had exiled from before them, and they did evil things to provoke YHWH. 12 They served the idols concerning which YHWH had said to them, "You shall not do this thing."

13 YHWH witnessed against Israel and against Judah by the hand of [c]every prophet and every seer,[c] saying, "Return from your evil ways and observe my commandments and my statutes according to all the Torah which I commanded your fathers and which I sent to you by the hand of my servants the prophets." 14 But they did not listen, and they stiffened their neck like the neck of their fathers who did not believe in YHWH

their G-d. 15 They rejected His statutes and His covenant which He cut with their fathers and His testimonies by which He made them swear, and they went after nothingness so that they became nothing and after the nations that were around them that YHWH commanded them not to imitate. 16 They abandoned all the commandments of YHWH, their G-d, and they made for themselves molten image(s), two calves, and they made an asherah, and they worshiped all the host of heaven, and they served Baal. 17 They passed their sons and their daughters through fire, engaged in divination, practiced sorcery, and sold themselves to do evil in the eyes of YHWH to provoke Him.

18 YHWH was very incensed against Israel and removed them from before His face; only the tribe of Judah remained. 19 Judah also did not . observe the commandments of YHWH, their G-d, and they followed in the statutes which Israel had done. 20 So YHWH rejected all the seed of Israel, afflicted them, and gave them into the hand of plunderers until He had cast them out from before Him 21 because Israel had torn away from the house of David and made Jeroboam ben Nebat king, and Jeroboam thrust[d] Israel away from after YHWH and made them commit great sin. 22 The people of Israel walked in all the sins of Jeroboam which he did; they did not turn from it 23 until YHWH removed Israel from before His face just as He spoke by the hand of all His servants the prophets, and He exiled Israel from upon its land to Assyria until this day.

24 And the King of Assyria brought (people) from Babylon, and from Kuthah, and from Avvah, and from Hamath, and from Sepharvaim, and he settled (them) in the cities of Samaria in place of the people of Israel, and they possessed Samaria, and they settled in its cities. 25 They did not fear YHWH when they began to settle there, so YHWH sent lions against them that were killing them. 26 They said to the King of Assyria, saying, "The nations whom you exiled and settled in the cities of Samaria did not know the law of the G-d of the land, and He sent lions against them. Behold, (they are) killing them because they do not know the law of the G-d of the land." 27 And the King of Assyria commanded, saying, "Dispatch there one of the priests whom you exiled from there, and they shall go and settle there, and he shall teach them the law of the G-d of the land." 28 And one of the priests whom they exiled from Samaria came and settled in Beth El, and began teaching them how they should fear YHWH. 29 But each nation continued making its gods, and each nation set them in the temple of the high places which the Samarians had made in their cities where they were settling. 30 The men of Babylon made Sukkoth Benoth, and the men of Kuth made Nergal, and the men of Hamath made Ashima, 31 and the Avvaites made Nibhaz and Tartaq, and the Sepharvites were burning their sons in fire for Adramelek and Anamlek, the gods[e] of

Sepharvaim. ₃₂ They continued to fear YHWH, ᶠand they made priests of the high places from all among themselves, and they continued to officiate on their behalf at the temple of the high places. ₃₃ YHWH they continued to fear and their gods they continued to serve according to the law of the nations from which they had been exiled. ₃₄ Until this day they continued to act according to the former laws; they did not continue to fear YHWH and they did not continue to act according to their statutes, their law, the Torah, and the command which YHWH commanded the sons of Jacob whom he named Israel. ₃₅ YHWH had made a covenant with them, and He commanded them saying, "You shall not fear other gods, and you shall not worship them, and you shall not serve them, and you shall not sacrifice to them. ₃₆ But only YHWH, who brought you up from the land of Egypt with great strength and with outstretched arm, Him you shall fear, Him you shall worship, and to Him you shall sacrifice. ₃₇ And the statutes, the laws, the Torah, and the command which He wrote for you, you shall be careful to do all the days, and you shall not fear other gods. ₃₈ You shall not forget the covenant which I made with you, and you shall not fear other gods. ₃₉ But only YHWH, your G-d, you shall fear, and He will deliver you from the hand of all your enemies." ₄₀ But they did not listen, for they were following only their former custom. ₄₁ And these nations continued to fear YHWH and they continued to serve their images, even their sons and the sons of their sons; just as their fathers had done, they continue to do until this day.

a. Lit., "the river of Gozan"; cf. LXX, "the rivers of Gozan."

b. Cf. LXX, "mountains (of the Medes)," which presupposes Hebrew, *hārê*, "mountains of," in place of *ᶜārê*, "cities of," in the MT. The difference may be explained by observing that the pronunciation of the Hebrew letter *ayin* is sometimes aspirated so it might sound like a *he*.

c–c. Reads with Qere, *kol-nĕbîʾê* (Ketiv, *nĕbîʾô) kol-ḥōzeh*, lit., "all the prophets of (Ketiv, "all his prophet, i.e., every one of his prophets") every seer"; cf. LXX, *panton ton propheton autou pantos horontos*, "all his prophets, every seer"; Targum Jonathan, *kol sĕpār kol mālêp*, "every instructor of every teacher"; Peshitta, *dklhwn ᶜbdwh nbyʾ wkl hzyʾ*, "of all his servants, the prophets, and every seer." The awkward syntactical construction is generally taken to mean "every prophet and every seer."

d. Ketiv, *wayyaddaʾ*, "and he drove away"; read with Qere, *wayyaddah*, "and he thrust away."

e. Ketiv reads, *ʾĕlōah*, "god"; read with Qere, *ʾĕlōhê*, "gods of."

f. Cf. LXX, "and they established their abominations in the houses of the high places which they made in Samaria, each nation in the city in which they dwelt; and they feared the L-rd, and they made for themselves priests of the high places, and they sacrificed for themselves in the house of the high places." The expanded LXX reading draws upon language from v. 29 to interpret the Hebrew term, *miqṣôtām*, "from their ends," i.e., "from throughout themselves." The Greek text presupposes that the term is interpreted as a form of the verb root *qwṣ*, "to be loathsome, disgusting," i.e., *miqquṣôtām*, "from their disgusting things."

The regnal account of Hoshea ben Elah focuses on the Assyrian invasion of Israel in 724–721 B.C.E. that saw the complete destruction of the nation and its capital city at Samaria, the exile and flight of significant elements of the northern Israelite population, and the settlement of northern Israel by foreign populations that were brought in by the Assyrian empire to replace the displaced Israelites. The narrative is formulated largely as a theological treatise that explains the exile of northern Israel as a consequence of the people's apostasy against YHWH and points to a continuing problem of apostasy among the foreign population brought in by the Assyrians.

Such an account must be recognized as an expression of theodicy, insofar as it portrays YHWH as righteous, despite the destruction of the northern kingdom of Israel. By arguing that the people themselves were responsible for their own suffering by violating their covenant with YHWH, the narrative asserts that YHWH is Israel's G-d and protector, but Israel itself must be held accountable for its own demise. The narrative ultimately blames the victims of foreign invasion for their own victimization. Such an attempt thereby avoids questions that might be posed concerning the righteousness or efficacy of YHWH in the aftermath of evil, namely, must YHWH be considered evil? Is YHWH impotent in the face of evil? Is YHWH somehow disengaged or negligent? Such questions have been posed in modern theological discussion in the aftermath of the Shoah or Holocaust, in which some six million Jews (and other groups, such as Gypsies, homosexuals, Slavs, etc.) were deliberately murdered by Nazi Germany and its European supporters.[1]

The question of theodicy is not the only concern of this narrative. The portrayal of continuing apostasy by the foreign population brought in by Assyria points to an intolerable situation from the standpoint of Deuteronomistic historiography in which the people now resident in the land fail to abide by YHWH's expectations. The deliberate contrast between northern Israel destroyed by Assyria in 2 Kgs 17 for its apostasy against YHWH and southern Judah—or at least Jerusalem—spared in 2 Kgs 18–20 because King Hezekiah repented and turned to YHWH as required of northern Israel (2 Kgs 17:13) suggests that Hezekiah serves as a model for what northern Israel should have done in the eyes of the DtrH. Such an attempt at contrast invites speculation as to the means by which the apostasy of northern Israel's foreign population might be addressed.

---

1. Zachary Braiterman, *(G-d) after Auschwitz: Tradition and Change in Post-Holocaust Jewish Thought* (Princeton, N.J.: Princeton University Press, 1998); Clark M. Williamson, *A Guest in the House of Israel: Post-Holocaust Church Theology* (Louisville, Ky.: Westminster/John Knox, 1993).

The DtrH narratives in 2 Kgs 22–23 portray such interest on the part of King Josiah, who destroyed the Beth El altar that symbolized the center of northern Israel's apostasy throughout the DtrH and who died at Megiddo when he went to meet the Egyptian army under Pharaoh Necho of Egypt. Such a portrayal suggests that 2 Kgs 17 was formulated to prepare the reader for action on Josiah's part to restore Davidic rule to the north and thereby to restore adherence to YHWH's torah as defined in the DtrH. The narrative also serves the exilic DtrH, which portrays the destruction and exile of northern Israel as a paradigm for and prelude to the Babylonian destruction and exile of Judah a century and a half later.

The literary structure of 2 Kgs 17 demonstrates the dual concerns with justifying the exile of northern Israel and the continuing problem of apostasy among the foreign population within the framework of Hoshea ben Elah's regnal account.[2] The passage begins in typical form with a syntactically independent introductory regnal account in vv. 1–2. A second syntactically independent section in vv. 3–5 recounts Shalmaneser's invasions of Israel, first to force Hoshea's submission as a tribute-paying vassal and then to punish Hoshea for an overture to King So of Egypt to free Israel from Assyrian hegemony. A lengthy third section in vv. 6–41, introduced by the syntactically independent chronological notice in v. 6 concerning Assyria's capture of Samaria and the exile of its population, then takes up the theological questions of Israel's exile in vv. 7–23 and the continuing problem of apostasy among the foreign population of the land in vv. 24–41. Verses 7–23 emphasize Israel's apostasy, beginning with Jeroboam ben Nebat's establishment of the golden calves at Beth El and Dan as the cause of Israel's problems from the outset of the northern monarchy. Verses 24–41 emphasize the syncretism of the resident foreign population, which is only reinforced when a northern Israelite priest is brought back to the land to instruct the people in YHWH's laws. The fact that the people would continue in their syncretistic ways is hardly surprising to readers of the DtrH, since 1 Kgs 12:31 informs readers that Jeroboam appointed non-Levitical priests from among the people. In such a circumstance, who could be surprised that the foreigners were syncretistic? The northern Israelite priests had presided over a population that was exiled because of its own syncretism according to the DtrH. With such a record, why should the resident foreigners behave any differently from the prior Israelite population? Finally, because King Hoshea was removed by the Assyrians, who then proceeded to destroy northern Israel, the passage lacks a concluding regnal formula.

Second Kings 17 functions as a key text in which the exilic DtrH offers its analysis of Israel's history. Since Noth's initial work on the DtrH, subsequent

---

2. Cf. Burke O. Long, *2 Kings* (FOTL 10; Grand Rapids: William B. Eerdmans, 1991), 180–90; John MacDonald, "The Structure of II Kings xvii," TGUOS 23 (1969–70): 29–41; Pauline A. Viviano, "2 Kings 17: A Rhetorical and Form Critical Analysis," *CBQ* 49 (1987): 548–59.

scholars have attempted to identify the literary history that produced the present form of the chapter.[3] Although such diachronic concerns are necessary, they have tended to blur certain features of the synchronic form of the text. For one, 2 Kgs 17 must be read in anticipation of the Babylonian destruction of Jerusalem and Judah in the present form of the work. The portrayal of the destruction of the northern kingdom of Israel and the contention that such disaster took place because of northern Israel's apostasy presents a model or analogy for understanding the subsequent downfall of the southern kingdom of Judah. For another, the portrayal of the continuing apostasy of the nations brought to Israel by the Assyrians points to a problem that requires resolution from the standpoint of the DtrH—that is, such apostasy continues "until this day" (see vv. 34, 41; cf. v. 23).[4] Later generations, particularly following the restoration of the temple in 520–515 B.C.E. and the reforms of Ezra and Nehemiah in the fifth–fourth centuries B.C.E., would read this concern as an indictment of the Samaritan community in the early Second Temple period.[5]

Although many interpreters argue that much of the material in 2 Kgs 17 is the product of exilic or postexilic writers, the evidence for such a contention is limited. This chapter makes no explicit reference to the Babylonian exile or to the Samaritan community. Only vv. 13 and 18 make any reference to Judah at all, and these references are easily understood in relation to the concerns of the Josianic reform of the late seventh century when the experience of the northern kingdom of Israel was taken as a warning for Judah and Jerusalem to return to YHWH or experience a similar fate. Northern Israel continued as an Assyrian province for a century following its collapse, and Josiah had ambitions to restore Davidic rule over the territory and population of the former northern kingdom. Such a background easily explains the text's concerns with a return to YHWH and YHWH's torah, commandments, and so on (v. 13; cf. vv. 7–20); the continued adherence to foreign gods, even by foreigners who could be incorporated into Israel according to Dtr law (vv. 24–40; cf. Deut 1:16; 10:18–19; 24:14, 19–22; etc.); the adherence to the sins of Jeroboam (vv. 21–23); and the repeated

3. See Martin Noth, *The Deuteronomistic History* (JSOTSup 15; Sheffield: JSOT Press, 1981), 73, who argues that vv. 7–20 are a DtrH composition, and that vv. 21–23, 34b-40 are a later insertion to a section in which various traditions in vv. 24, 25–28, 29–31, and 32–34a had been compiled by the DtrH; cf. Cross, "Themes," 281, who identifies 2 Kgs 17:1–23 as the climactic treatment of northern Israel and Jeroboam in the DtrH, and Walter Dietrich, *Prophetie und Geschichte* (FRLANT 108; Göttingen: Vandenhoeck & Ruprecht, 1972), 41–46, who assigns this material to his exilic DtrG and vv. 21–23 to DtrN; for an overview, see Mark A. O'Brien, *The Deuteronomistic History Hypothesis: A Reassessment* (OBO 92; Freiburg: Universitätsverlag; Göttingen: Vandenhoeck & Ruprecht, 1989), 208–12.

4. Brevard S. Childs, "A Study of the Formula, 'Until this day,'" *JBL* 82 (1963): 279–92.

5. Shemaryahu Talmon, "Polemics and Apology in Biblical Historiography: 2 Kings 17:24–41," *The Creation of Sacred Literature* (ed. R. E. Friedman; Berkeley: University of California Press, 1981), 57–68.

references to the prophets, whose works were edited during the reign of Josiah to lend support to his program of religious reform and national restoration. Such concerns lend a different significance to the repeated concerns with exile and apostasy that continues "until this day"—that is, not only until the time of the exile and the postexilic restoration, but in an earlier age until the time of the anticipated Josianic restoration.

The present form of this text displays evidence of redactional activity. Specifically, the concerns with the apostasy of the foreign population in vv. 24–33, 41 stand in tension with the portrayal of apostasy by those with whom YHWH had made a covenant in vv. 34–40. Verses 34–40 portray a population with whom YHWH had made a covenant (vv. 35, 38), which was brought up from the land of Egypt (v. 36), which was enjoined to observe YHWH's torah, commandments, statutes, and so on (vv. 34, 37), and which had been renamed from Jacob to Israel (v. 34). Although the present form of the text applies this description to the foreigners whom Assyria settled in the land of northern Israel, it clearly refers to Israel itself.[6] This interpretation suggests that vv. 34–40 represent an earlier text and that vv. 24–34, which portray the introduction of the foreigners to the land and their practices, may be a later redaction from the time of the Josianic reform. Such an observation leaves open the possibility that an earlier form of 2 Kgs 17 in vv. 1–21, 34–40 may constitute the basis for a Hezekian edition of this text that was designed to explain the punishment of northern Israel for apostasy and point to the continued apostasy among the inhabitants of the land "until this day." King Hezekiah's revolt against Assyria in 701 B.C.E., which would have led to the reunification of Israel and Judah under Davidic rule, would have provided the impetus for the composition of such a text.

[1–2] Hoshea is regarded as evil, but his evaluation is qualified by the observation that he was not like the other kings of northern Israel. No particular reason is given, although Hoshea assassinated Pekah ben Remaliah (2 Kgs 15:30) and attempted to revolt against the Assyrians. Nothing is said about Hoshea's attitude toward the golden calves at Beth El and Dan.

[3–5] Beginning with the syntactically independent notice of Shalmaneser V's advance against Hoshea, vv. 3–5 recount the main events in Assyria's subjugation and defeat of northern Israel during Hoshea's reign.[7] Unfortunately,

6. Cf. Mordechai Cogan, "Israel in Exile: The View of a Josianic Historian," *JBL* 97 (1978): 4–44, who identifies these verses as an example of *Wiederaufnahme,* a repetition that refers back to the earlier discussion concerning the Israelites, but the framing of vv. 34–40 by concern with the foreign inhabitants of the land in vv. 24–33 and 41 indicates that the passage, although written originally in reference to Israel, now refers to the foreigners.

7. John H. Hayes and Jeffrey K. Kuan, "The Final Years of Samaria (730–720 BC)," *Bib* 72 (1991): 153–81; MacDonald, "The Structure of II Kings xvii"; Nadav Na'aman, "The Historical Background to the Conquest of Samaria (720 BC)," *Bib* 73 (1990): 206–25.

Shalmaneser V's brief reign (726–722 B.C.E.) leaves few records concerning his activities.[8] The initial statement that Shalmaneser had gone up against Hoshea likely refers to the initial forays by the Assyrian monarch throughout the western empire to demonstrate his power and secure his hold over the kingdoms that had formerly submitted to Tiglath-pileser III.[9] The Egyptians would always be ready to exploit any Assyrian weakness during a period of transition by fomenting revolt in southwestern Asia.

The identity of King So of Egypt is hotly debated.[10] Because no pharaoh named So reigned in Egypt during this period, proposals included Pharaoh Shabaka of Egypt (710–696 B.C.E.), a north Arabian monarch named Silhu (Šanda 214–16), and an Egyptian officer named Sibe. These proposals are demonstrably impossible, and interpreters have come to accept that the name refers to Sais (*s'w*), the capital of the Pharaoh Tefnakhte, who ruled in 726–716 B.C.E.[11] The three-year siege of Samaria would have been necessary due to the well-constructed fortifications of the city, which would have been nearly impossible to breach by frontal assault.[12] Basically, the Assyrians chose to starve the Israelites into submission. Although Sargon II claims to have taken Samaria, it appears that Shalmaneser V carried out the siege of the city.[13]

[6–41] The lengthy segment in vv. 6–41 begins in the style of a regnal account with a syntactically independent notice concerning the Assyrian capture of Samaria and the exile of northern Israel's population in the ninth year of Hoshea's reign. It quickly shifts to a sermonic or instructive style that explains the causes of Israel's exile from the land and the consequences of moving in a population of foreigners who do not know YHWH's expectations for life in the land. Although Shalmaneser V conquered the city, Sargon II (721–705 B.C.E.) oversaw the deportation of northern Israel's inhabitants (see *ANET* 284–85). The Assyrians were known for deporting elements of the population of nations that revolted against them.[14] Such deportations punished the nation for revolt, allocated skilled persons to the service of the Assyrian empire,

8. See J. A. Brinkman, CAH 3/2, 85–86, for discussion of the reign of Shalmaneser V.

9. See Hayim Tadmor, "The Campaigns of Sargon II of Assur: A Chronological Historical Study," *JCS* 12 (1958): 22–40, 77–100.

10. E.g, Duane L. Christensen, "The Identity of King So of Egypt (2 Kings xvii 4)," *VT* 39 (1989): 140–53; S. Yeivin, "Who Was King So of Egypt?" *VT* 2 (1952): 164–68.

11. H. Goedicke, "The End of 'So, King of Egypt,'" *BASOR* 171 (1993): 64–66; T. R. Hobbs, *2 Kings* (Word Biblical Commentary 13; Waco, Tex.: Word, 1985), 229; Mordechai Cogan and Hayim Tadmor, *II Kings* (Anchor Bible 11; New York: Doubleday, 1988), 196; G. H. Jones, *1 and 2 Kings* (2 vols.; The New Century Bible Commentary; Grand Rapids: William B. Eerdmans; London: Marshall, Morgan, and Scott, 1984), 546–47.

12. N. Avigad, "Samaria," *NEAEHL* 4:1300–1310, esp. 1302–3.

13. Brinkman, CAH 3/2, 87–88.

14. Bustenay Oded, *Mass Deportations and Deportees in the Neo-Assyrian Empire* (Wiesbaden: O. Harrassowitz, 1979).

destabilized the population, and thereby minimized the possibility of subsequent revolt. Halah is identified with a variety of Mesopotamian sites, such as Chalchitis on the Habor/Khabur River, Chalkitis on the Balikh River, Halahhu on the Tigris River, and others.[15] Habor refers to a river now known as the Khabur, which flows into the Euphrates near the Turkish-Syrian border. Assyrian documents at Gozan along the Khabur River (Tell Halaf) include Israelite names.[16] The "cities of the Medes" refers to the Medean kingdom, located to the east of Assyria in western Iran.[17] The Assyrians moved elements of the northern Israelite population into Philistia as well. Excavations at Tell Miqne/Ekron demonstrate that the Assyrians turned the city into a processing center for olive oil during the late eighth and seventh centuries B.C.E. The many four-horned altars on the site indicate that much of the city's population was Israelite.[18]

Verses 7–23 constitute a lengthy DtrH sermon on the causes of Israel's exile. The language and emphasis on covenant; YHWH's torah, laws, statutes, and so on; worship of foreign gods; the apostasy of Jeroboam; and so forth are all characteristically Deuteronomistic.[19] Although some interpreters argue that emphasis on the legal aspects of covenant is a mark of postexilic composition or redaction, such a view is informed by Wellhausenian polemics that viewed law, cultic, and priestly concerns as a degenerative aspect of Israelite religion. Such contentions fly in the face of evidence that Israelite religion, like that of its neighbors in the Syro-Canaanite region, was based around temples, priesthoods, and cultic observance. The use of law codes as a basis for social conduct appears as early as the late third millennium, which long predates Israel's existence. Indeed, the Hebrew word *tōrâ,* frequently mistranslated as "law" in accordance with Pauline polemics against Judaism, actually means "instruction," and thereby represents the fundamental duty of Israelite priests to "instruct" the people in YHWH's "instruction"—that is, YHWH's expectations for Israel's conduct (see Lev 10:10–11; Deut 33:8–10; Ezek 44:23–24; Hag 2:10–13; cf. Jer 7; Hos 4).

Verses 7–12 emphasize Israel's sins against YHWH by worshiping other gods and by following in the laws of the nations whom YHWH exiled from the land before Israel. The passage reminds its audience of YHWH's identity as the

15. H. O. Thompson, "Halah," *ABD* 3:25.

16. G. A. Herion, "Habor," *ABD* 3:10.

17. T. C. Young Jr., "Media," *ABD* 4:658–59.

18. Seymour Gitin, "Tel-Miqne-Ekron: A Type Site for the Inner Coastal Plain in the Iron Age II Period," *Recent Excavations in Israel: Studies in Iron Age Archaeology* (AASOR 49; Winona Lake, Ind.: Eisenbrauns, 1989), 23–58; Gitin, "Incense Altars from Ekron, Israel and Judah," *Eretz Israel* 20 (1989): 52*–67*.

19. Cf. Weinfeld, *Deuteronomy and the Deuteronomic School,* 320–65.

one who brought Israel up from the land of Egypt. The worship at cultic *bāmôt,* "high places," indicates temple or altar sites apart from the central sanctuary envisioned by Deut 12 where worshipers would bring grain offerings. Because wind must be used as part of the process for threshing grain, a location at a "high place" or hill is especially suitable. Such high places put local offerings out of the reach of the central Israelite or Judean government. The erection of masseboth (stelae or cultic pillars) and asherim (sacred trees) are vestiges of older Canaanite forms of worship, although the practices are well known in Israel (Gen 12:6–7; 28; Judg 4).

Verses 13–17 emphasize YHWH's witness against Israel and Judah by means of the prophets sent to demand Israel's return to YHWH. The inclusion of Judah indicates a Josianic parenetic interest in viewing the experience of northern Israel as an example of what might happen to Judah. The call for repentance is consistent with the roles of the prophets who attempted to persuade their audiences to adapt specified courses of action. The passage speaks to the DtrH interest in theodicy—that is, defending YHWH's righteousness by contending that Israel rejected YHWH's covenant and thereby brought punishment upon itself. The reference to the molten calves in v. 16 harks back to Jeroboam's golden calves at Beth El and Dan in 1 Kgs 12. The hosts of heaven may indicate the influence of an Assyrian pantheon, but local custom would call for foreign gods to be identified with the gods of Canaan, Phoenicia, and perhaps Aram.

Verses 18–23 emphasize YHWH's anger against Israel and subsequent exile of Israel as a means to punish the people. The removal of Israel, leaving Judah alone, points to a monarchic period setting for this text. Other texts indicate that elements of Benjamin are also left in place. Verses 21–23 point to Israel's rebelliousness in rejecting the house of David in favor of Jeroboam (1 Kgs 11–14). Jeroboam's apostasy emerges as the basis for Israel's sins against YHWH, although the rejection of the house of David points to a political dimension as well. The mention of exile to Assyria "until this day" again points to a monarchic-period setting for this text.

Verses 24–41 then shift to the portrayal of the foreigners brought in by Assyria to resettle northern Israel. Foreign settlers were brought in from various locales in Mesopotamia, Aram, Elam, and other areas under Assyrian control. Babylon was an Assyrian vassal during the late eighth and seventh centuries B.C.E., and would later ally with Hezekiah and Josiah to oppose Assyrian interests. Cuth or Cuthah was a city in southern Mesopotamia, perhaps to be identified with Tell Ibraham some twenty miles northeast of Babylon.[20] Avva is identified with the modern Tell Kafr'aya in Syria on the Orontes River southwest of Homs or with

---

20. S. A. Meier, "Cuth," *ABD* 1:1220–21.

the Elamite city of Ama known for its worship of Ibnahaza and Dirtaq.[21] Hamath is the central Aramean city along the Orontes River approximately 128 miles north of Damascus.[22] The identification of Sepharvaim remains a subject of dispute. Potential candidates include Sippar (modern Habbah) around 20 miles southwest of Baghdad, a Mesopotamian city named Sipraani in the Murashu documents, and others.[23] The diversity of the new population indicates Assyria's interest in mixing populations to ensure destabilization among its subjects.

This passage clearly expects that the new foreign inhabitants of the land will be subject to YHWH's laws. It views Israel as one more nation that was expelled for its pagan practices, much like the Canaanite population that preceded it in the land. The emergence of the lions that attack the new inhabitants represents the realization of covenant cursing in which the land itself—or at least the animals in it—responds to the people's failure to live by YHWH's laws. It is perhaps no accident that lions are YHWH's predators, particularly since the lion is the symbol of the tribe of Judah. The solution devised by the Assyrians—namely, returning an Israelite priest to the land to instruct the population in YHWH's laws—is an ill-conceived effort from the standpoint of the DtrH, given the results and Israel's own failure to live according to YHWH's law. The syncretistic practices of the foreign inhabitants of Israel bear this out as each continues to worship YHWH together with its own deities. The Babylonian god, Sukkoth Benoth, appears to refer to "the image of Banitu," a reference to the Mesopotamian creator goddess sometimes associated with Marduk.[24] The Cuthian worship of Nergal refers to "the lord of the Netherworld" during the Neo-Assyrian period.[25] The Hamathian Ashima is derived from the Aramaic term for "name," and may represent a case of hypostatization for a local deity.[26] Nibhaz is an Elamite deity of fresh water known as Ibnahaz,[27] and Tartaq is identified either as the Elamite Dirtaq or more likely the Aramaean fertility goddess Atargatis.[28] Adrammelech appears to be a Canaanite or Phoenician deity,[29] and Anammelech may be identified with the Canaanite goddess Anath.[30] Ironically, the appointment of priests from the foreign population resembles Jeroboam's appointment of non-Levitical priests from Israel (1 Kgs 12:31).

21. G. Herion, "Avva," *ABD* 1:531.
22. Cf. Isa 36:19; see M.-L. Buhl, "Hamath," *ABD* 3:33–36.
23. H. Avalos, "Sepharvaim," *ABD* 5:1090.
24. M. Cogan, "Sukkoth Benoth," *DDD*² 821–22.
25. A. Livingstone, "Nergal," *DDD*² 621–22.
26. M. Cogan, "Ashima," *DDD*² 105–6.
27. A. R. Millard, "Nibhaz," *DDD*² 623.
28. M. Cogan, "Tartak," *DDD*² 836–37.
29. A. R. Millard, "Adrammelech," *DDD*² 10–11.
30. A. R. Millard, "Anammelech," *DDD*² 34–35.

XXXI. Regnal Account of Hezekiah ben Ahaz of Judah
2 Kings 18:1–20:21

The regnal account of King Hezekiah ben Ahaz of Judah is demarcated by the introductory regnal form in 2 Kgs 18:1–7, which provides the initial assessment of Hezekiah's reign (cf. Long 190, 193), and by the concluding regnal form in 2 Kgs 20:20–21, which provides the typical notices concerning Hezekiah's death, burial, and successor. The narrative focuses especially on the invasion of Judah in 701 B.C.E. by the Assyrian king Sennacherib, following Hezekiah's attempted revolt against the Assyrian empire. It emphasizes YHWH's miraculous deliverance of Jerusalem once King Hezekiah turns to YHWH and prays for the deliverance of his beleaguered city. Sennacherib came to terms with Hezekiah after devastating the Judean countryside and its cities so that he could move quickly against Hezekiah's Babylonian ally, Merodach Baladan of Babylon.[1] Although Judah was overrun by the Assyrian army and much of its population was killed or marched off as captives by the Assyrians, Jerusalem was never taken. Consequently, Hezekiah was able to continue on the throne, to claim a great victory, and to begin the process of rebuilding his devastated country. Within 1–2 Kings, Hezekiah's reign marks the end of the Assyrian threat against Judah and Jerusalem, although the Assyrians continued to control Judah through the mid-seventh century B.C.E. Such a portrayal serves the historiographical interests of the DtrH, which portrays YHWH's protection and deliverance in response to those who turn to YHWH and adhere to YHWH's expectations.

A parallel version of this narrative appears in Isa 36–39, where it plays a transitional function within the literary structure of the book.[2] Although the question continues to be disputed, literary analysis of the two versions indicates that the Isaian form of the narrative derives from the present version in Kings. The differences in the Isaian version of this narrative indicate that it was redacted to serve first as a conclusion to a Josianic edition of the book of Isaiah and later as a transitional element within the literary structure of the successive editions of Isaiah in the sixth and fifth centuries B.C.E. Details are discussed in the commentary.

---

1. For discussion of the historical aspects of Sennacherib's invasion of Judah, see esp. CAH 3/2, 109–11; Bustenay Oded, "Judah and the Exile," *Israelite and Judaean History* (ed. J. H. Hayes and J. M. Miller; OTL; Philadelphia: Westminster, 1977) 446–51; G. W. Ahlström, *The History of Ancient Palestine* (Minneapolis: Fortress, 1993), 707–16.

2. For discussion of Isa 36–39, see M. A. Sweeney, *Isaiah 1–39* (FOTL; Grand Rapids and Cambridge: Eerdmans, 1998), 454–511.

The typical elements of the regnal account form—namely, the regnal introduction (2 Kgs 18:1–7), the body of the regnal account (2 Kgs 18:8–20:19), and
the concluding regnal form (2 Kgs 20:20–21)—influence the literary presentation of the text. Although these generic elements appear within the text, a combination of syntactical features and thematic elements determine a different
formal literary structure. The introductory regnal form comprises four subunits
that provide factual information concerning the circumstances of Hezekiah's
accession to the throne, his actions as king, and characterization of his reign.
The text begins in 2 Kgs 18:1 with an introductory regnal statement that Hezekiah's accession to the throne took place during the third year of the reign of
Hoshea ben Elah of Israel. The syntactically independent vv. 2–3 then follow
with a series of linked statements concerning Hezekiah's age at accession,
the duration of his reign, the name of his mother, and general characterization
of his reign as righteous. Verse 4 notes his religious reform, particularly his
removal of pagan cultic installations. Verses 5–7 emphasize his adherence to
YHWH and YHWH's efforts to ensure his success.

Second Kings 18:8–19:37 then turns to Hezekiah's revolt against Assyria
and YHWH's destruction of the Assyrian army following Hezekiah's prayer for
the deliverance. This lengthy unit begins with a brief statement in 2 Kgs 18:8
of Hezekiah's efforts to subdue the Philistines, apparently in preparation for
the revolt.

A second subunit in 2 Kgs 18:9–12 begins with a temporal reference to the
fourth year of Hezekiah's reign introduced by the *waw*-consecutive *wayĕhî*,
"and it came to pass," which links this passage to v. 8. This brief narrative correlates the Assyrian action against Samaria with the seventh year of the last
Israelite monarch, Hoshea ben Elah. The subunit recounts the three-year siege,
conquest, and exile of Samaria by the Assyrian monarch, Shalmaneser V, as an
introduction to the account of Sennacherib's siege of Jerusalem. This passage
also presents the fall of Samaria and the exile of northern Israel's population in
contrast to the deliverance of Jerusalem by YHWH following Hezekiah's
prayer. By setting up this contrast, the narrative pointedly contrasts the consequences of northern Israel's apostasy with the results of Hezekiah's piety and
repentance to demonstrate its hermeneutical viewpoint that adherence to
YHWH brings about deliverance and security, whereas rejection of YHWH
brings about punishment.

The third subunit in 2 Kgs 18:13–19:37 begins with a reference to the fourteenth year of Hezekiah's reign, introduced by a conjunctive *waw* that joins this
text to the preceding subunit. This lengthy narrative relates YHWH's deliverance of Jerusalem at the time of Sennacherib's invasion of Judah, constituting
a form of a prophetic confrontation narrative that pits Sennacherib, represented
by his three officers who call for the surrender of Jerusalem, against Hezekiah
and YHWH, who are likewise represented by three officers who parlay with

the Assyrians from the walls of the besieged city. The narrative emphasizes Hezekiah's turn to YHWH in prayer as the means by which Hezekiah prompted YHWH to intervene.

The next major unit of the Hezekiah regnal account in 2 Kgs 20:1–11 begins with the temporal formula *bayyāmîm hāhēm,* "in those days." Although this formula is syntactically independent, it correlates the narrative with the preceding account of YHWH's defeat of the Assyrian invasion of Judah. This subunit presents an account of Hezekiah's illness and recovery following his prayer to YHWH, and reinforces the need for prayer and reliance on YHWH as a means to realize YHWH's protection from threats of invasion or illness.

The penultimate major unit in Hezekiah's regnal account in 2 Kgs 20:12–19 begins with the temporal formula *bāʿēt hahîʾ,* "at that time." This formula is syntactically independent, and it correlates the narrative with the preceding narratives concerning Sennacherib's invasion and Hezekiah's illness, relating the embassy sent to Jerusalem by Hezekiah's ally in his revolt against Assyria, Merodach Baladan of Babylonia. The narrative emphasizes Isaiah's opposition to Hezekiah's plans for revolt against the Assyrians, and states that Hezekiah's action will result in the removal of Judah's wealth and the deportation of Hezekiah's sons to Babylonia.

Second Kings 20:20–21 sums up the Hezekiah narratives with notices concerning his power, his building of the Jerusalem water system, his death, and his succession by his son, Manasseh.

The Hezekiah regnal account in 2 Kgs 18–20 anticipates the Babylonian exile in the exilic DtrH. When read in relation to the destruction of Jerusalem and the exile of its population at the end of Kings, Isaiah's statement that Hezekiah's sons will be deported to Babylon can only refer to Nebuchadrezzar's exile to Babylon of King Jehoiachin ben Jehoiakim of Judah in 2 Kgs 24:8–17. It is by no means clear that the present text of the narrative is entirely the product of exilic-period composition. Second Chronicles 33:1–20, the alternative version of the narrative concerning Manasseh's reign in 2 Kgs 21:1–18, portrays his forcible removal to Babylon by the Assyrian monarch at the time of Babylon's revolt against Assyria in 652–648 B.C.E. Although many scholars tend to dismiss Chronicles as a late narrative influenced by priestly interests, recent scholarship takes the historical claims of Chronicles much more seriously.[3]

This raises the possibility that the narrative concerning Manasseh's reign in 2 Chr 33:1–20 represents an earlier form of the narrative that once appeared as part of the Josianic DtrH. Manasseh's deportation to Babylon at the time that the Assyrian monarch Assurbanipal put down the Babylonian revolt led by his

---

3. E.g., Andrew Vaughn, *Theology, History, and Archaeology in the Chronicler's Account of Hezekiah* (Archaeology and Biblical Studies 4; Atlanta: Scholars Press, 1999).

brother Shamash Shum Ukin points to Manasseh's change of heart.[4] Whereas Manasseh began his reign by acting against those in Judah who would have opposed his submission to Babylon, the Chronicler portrays the latter years of his reign as a period of consolidation and rebuilding in anticipation of the time when Judah might be able to free itself from the domination of Assyria. Upon his return to Jerusalem in the Chronicler's narrative, Manasseh consolidates his power in Jerusalem and the Negev, although he makes no overt move to free himself from Assyrian control. Within the context of the Josianic DtrH, such a move would be left to Manasseh's grandson, Josiah. Hezekiah's seemingly cavalier remark indicates an interest in pointing to a stage in the process of Judah's liberation from Assyrian control that would culminate in the reign of King Josiah a century later. Such an understanding suggests that this narrative was not written in anticipation of the Babylonian exile, although it may have been edited for such a purpose. It appears instead to have been written in anticipation of Manasseh's forced appearance in Babylon before Assurbanipal as part of the Josianic DtrH.

Other elements of the Hezekiah narratives point to their origins in the Josianic DtrH.[5] The account of YHWH's deliverance of Jerusalem from Sennacherib's invasion can hardly be considered as an exilic-period text. It appears within the exilic DtrH, and it thereby presents Hezekiah's repentance and prayer to YHWH as a model by which Jerusalem might have been saved from Babylonian destruction. The post-Hezekian setting for the composition of this text is made clear by its reference to Sennacherib's assassination by his own sons in the temple of Nisroch and the accession to the Assyrian throne by his son Esarhaddon. Assyrian records confirm that he was assassinated in 681 B.C.E. by one or more of his sons, and that Esarhaddon succeeded him on the throne.[6] Although the Kings account must have been written in the aftermath of 681 B.C.E., no element within this narrative overtly anticipates the Babylonian destruction of Jerusalem. By pointing instead to the means by which Jerusalem was saved from destruction, it provides a model for King Josiah's subsequent return to YHWH and restoration of the Jerusalem temple as the center for worship envisioned in Deuteronomy.

Much the same must be said about the narrative concerning Hezekiah's recovery from illness in 2 Kgs 20:1–11. The narrative does not raise the issues of the Babylonian destruction of Jerusalem, the exile of Jerusalem's and Judah's population to Babylon, or even the potential end of the royal house of David. Instead, it points to Hezekiah's recovery from mortal illness as a result of his

4. For the Chronicler's presentation of Manasseh, see my paper, "King Manasseh of Judah and the Problem of Theodicy in the Deuteronomistic History," *Good Kings and Bad Kings* (LHBOTS 393; ed. L. L. Grabbe; London and New York: T and T Clark, 2005), 264–78.

5. Iain W. Provan, *Hezekiah and the Books of Kings* (BZAW 172; Berlin and New York: Walter de Gruyter, 1988).

6. See CAH 3/2, 119–21.

repentance and prayer to YHWH. Hezekiah's prayer and repentance save him from death and provide a model for Josiah's subsequent prayer and repentance in the Josianic DtrH.

Both narratives concerning YHWH's deliverance of Jerusalem and healing of Hezekiah serve the interests of the Josianic DtrH. Although the narrative concerning the visit to Jerusalem by the emissaries of the Babylonian prince Merodach Baladan currently points to the Babylonian exile, it too may have appeared in an earlier form within the Josianic DtrH to anticipate Manasseh's forced appearance in Babylon before the Assyrian monarch Assurbanipal. If this is the case, an earlier version of the narrative pointed to Manasseh as an instigator of the process by which Josiah's program of religious reform and national restoration was realized.

Finally, interpreters must consider that a Hezekian edition of this text would have formed the culmination of the Hezekian DtrH.[7] Provan points to the account of Hezekiah's reforms in 2 Kgs 18:1–8, particularly his removal of the high places in v. 4, as evidence for a Hezekian narrative. This observation is significant because it constitutes the final notice concerning the destruction of the high places that appear throughout the DtrH as an expression of apostasy against YHWH. Unfortunately, the Assyrian invasion of Judah in 701 B.C.E. and the subsequent composition of the narratives that portray the event would have overshadowed any projected Hezekian narrative that constituted the culmination of a Hezekian DtrH.

2 Kings 18:1–7 The Regnal Introduction: Hezekiah's Accession to the Throne

18:1 In the third year of Hoshea ben Elah, King of Israel, Hezekiah ben Ahaz, King of Judah, became king.

2 He was twenty-five years old when he became king, and he ruled in Jerusalem for twenty-nine years. The name of his mother was Abi bat Zechariah. 3 He did that which is right in the eyes of YHWH, according to all that David his father did.

4 He removed the high places, broke down the masseboth, and cut down the asherah. He ground up the bronze serpent, which Moses had made, for the people of Israel were burning incense to it until that time. It was called Nehushtan.

5 He trusted in YHWH, G-d of Israel, and after him there was no one like him among all the kings of Judah and none who were before him. 6 He

7. Baruch Halpern and David Vanderhooft, "The Editions of Kings in the 7th–6th Centuries," *HUCA* 62 (1991): 179–244; Marvin A. Sweeney, *King Josiah of Judah: The Lost Messiah of Israel* (Oxford and New York: Oxford University Press, 2001).

adhered to YHWH—he did not turn from after Him—and he observed His commandments, which YHWH had commanded Moses. 7 YHWH was with him. Whenever he would go out he would succeed. He rebelled against the king of Assyria, and would not serve him.

The literary structure of this passage includes four syntactically independent statements. Verse 1 notes the date of Hezekiah's accession to the throne. The second statement in vv. 2–3 states his age at the time of his accession to the throne, the duration of his reign, the name of his mother, and an evaluation of his reign. The third statement in v. 4 notes Hezekiah's removal of idolatrous cultic installations. The fourth statement in vv. 5–7 emphasizes Hezekiah's exemplary observance of YHWH's requirements and YHWH's support of the new monarch.

[1] The initial statement concerning the year of Hezekiah's accession to the throne indicates that he begins his rule in the third year of Hoshea ben Elah of Israel (r. 732–724 B.C.E.), suggesting that Hezekiah's twenty-nine-year reign began in 730–729 B.C.E., and continued until the time of Sennacherib's 701 B.C.E. siege of Jerusalem or shortly thereafter. Because Sennacherib did not remove Hezekiah and because Hezekiah is granted fifteen more years of life following his illness (which is correlated with the siege in the text of Kings), most interpreters maintain that Hezekiah ruled during the years 715–687 B.C.E., which would place his reign well beyond the time of Hoshea ben Elah. This would be consistent with the notice in 2 Kgs 18:13 that Hezekiah revolted against Sennacherib in the fourteenth year of his reign. Because Sennacherib's invasion dates to 701 B.C.E., there appears to be a discrepancy in the narrative concerning the dates of Hezekiah's reign. Unfortunately, the various attempts to resolve this discrepancy have failed to persuade most interpreters. Nevertheless, our text demonstrates an interest in contrasting the fate of Israel, which is portrayed throughout Kings as having abandoned YHWH, with that of Judah, which was saved from a similar disaster by Hezekiah's repentance and prayer to YHWH.

[4] The notice that Hezekiah removed the *bāmôt,* "high places," is significant within the larger context of the DtrH. Worship at the high places is a long-standing theme within the DtrH, beginning with the notices in 1 Kgs 3:2 that the people continued to sacrifice at the high places during Solomon's reign and in 1 Kgs 3:3–4 that Solomon continued to sacrifice at the high places as well (see also 1 Kgs 11:17). Notices concerning the continued use of high places appear in the regnal accounts of Jeroboam ben Nebat of Israel (1 Kgs 12:31, 32); Rehoboam ben Solomon of Judah (1 Kgs 14:23); Asa ben Abiam of Judah (1 Kgs 15:14); Jehoshaphat ben Asa of Judah (1 Kgs 22:44); Jehoash ben Ahaziah of Judah (2 Kgs 12:4); Amaziah ben Joash of Judah (2 Kgs 14:4); Azariah (Uzziah) ben Amaziah of Judah (2 Kgs 15:4); Jotham ben Uzziah (Azariah) of Judah (2 Kgs 15:35); Ahaz ben Jotham of Judah (2 Kgs 16:4); all the kings of Israel (2 Kgs

17:9, 11), and the foreigners who were settled in Israel following the destruction of the northern kingdom (2 Kgs 17:29, 32). The notices concerning the northern kings include only Jeroboam and a blanket condemnation of all the northern kings who followed him, although worship at the high places is also mentioned in relation to Samuel (1 Sam 9:12, 13, 14, 25; 10:5, 13; n.b. the references to high places in 2 Sam 1:19, 25; 22:34 are poetic references to hills that do not necessarily denote cultic places). Whether Hezekiah's actions included the demolition of the high places in the former northern kingdom of Israel is not clear, but his action clearly brings to an end an oft-noted problem in Judah.

The notice that Hezekiah destroyed Nehushtan, the bronze serpent that Israel had worshiped since the time of Moses, builds on a reference from Num 21:4–9. The Nehushtan figure likely represents a fixture of the Jerusalem temple prior to the time of Hezekiah. It is probably a typical Canaanite fertility symbol adapted to Judean religious context.

Given the emphasis on building high places, asherim, and masseboth in the time of Rehoboam (1 Kgs 14:23), it seems that Hezekiah dealt with an issue that had plagued Judah in the viewpoint of the DtrH from the time of Rehoboam, if not before. The notices concerning Manasseh's rebuilding the high places (2 Kgs 21:3) and the asherah (2 Kgs 21:4) indicate that Manasseh renewed practices that Hezekiah abolished, and these in turn were removed once again by Josiah (2 Kgs 23:5, 6, 8, 9, 13, 14, 15, 19, 20). Provan is correct to point to this action as a culminating point in the DtrH. Although he attributes the composition of the Hezekiah narratives to the Josianic DtrH, such a notice indicates an early interest in presenting Hezekiah's actions as the culmination of the Hezekian DtrH. In the aftermath of the Assyrian invasions and Josiah's reform of King Josiah, the Hezekiah narrative would have been extensively reworked to present Hezekiah's actions in anticipation of Josiah within the Josianic DtrH.

[5–7] The statements concerning Hezekiah's trust in YHWH, observance of YHWH's commands, and YHWH's support of the monarch articulate a typical Dtr statement of approval. The statement "and after him there was none like him among all the kings of Judah who were before him" indicates Hezekiah's incomparability, although similar statements appear for Solomon (1 Kgs 3:12) and Josiah (2 Kgs 23:5; cf. 22:2). Knoppers argues that the Solomonic statement indicates incomparable wealth and wisdom, the Hezekian statement indicates incomparable trust in YHWH, and the Josian statement indicates incomparable reform.[8] Although such a synchronic reading is justified in considering the final form of the text, such incomparability, especially when expressed in relation to the Josian statement, indicates that Hezekiah was presented as the culmination of the Davidic line in a Hezekian DtrH.

8. Gary N. Knoppers, "'There Was None Like Him': Incomparability in the Books of Kings," *CBQ* 54 (1992): 411–31.

2 Kings 18:8–19:37 The Account of YHWH's
Deliverance of Jerusalem

18:8 He struck the Philistines as far as Gaza and its borders from watch tower to fortified city.

9 In the fourth year of King Hezekiah—it was the seventh year of Hoshea ben Elah, King of Israel—Shalmaneser, King of Assyria, went up against Samaria and besieged it. **10** And they captured it after three years. In the sixth year of Hezekiah—it was the ninth year of Hoshea, King of Israel—Samaria was captured. **11** The King of Assyria exiled Israel to Assyria, and he settled them in Halah, and in Habor, Nahar Gozan, and the cities[a] of the Medes **12** because they did not listen to the voice of YHWH, their G-d, and they violated his covenant—all that Moses, the servant of YHWH, had commanded—and they did not listen and they did not do it.

13 In the fourteenth year of King Hezekiah, Sennacherib, King of Assyria, came up against all the fortified cities of Judah and seized them. **14** And Hezekiah, King of Judah, sent to the King of Assyria at Lachish, saying, "I have sinned. Withdraw from me. Whatever you impose upon me, I will bear," and the King of Assyria imposed upon Hezekiah, King of Judah, three hundred talents of silver and thirty talents of gold. **15** Hezekiah gave all the silver that was found in the House of YHWH and in the treasuries of the house of the king.

16 At that time, Hezekiah stripped the doorposts of the Temple of YHWH and the supports which Hezekiah, King of Judah, had overlaid, and gave them to the King of Assyria. **17** [b]And the King of Assyria sent the Tartan, and the Chief Eunuch, and the Chief Cup Bearer from Lachish to King Hezekiah with a heavy army to Jerusalem. They went up and came to Jerusalem, they went up and came, they stood by the upper channel of the pool which is by the highway of the washers' field,[b] **18** [c]and they called out to the king.[c] So Eliakim ben Hilkiah, who was over the house, Shebna the scribe, and Yoah ben Asaph the secretary came out [d]to them.[d] **19** And the Chief Cup Bearer said to them, "Say now to Hezekiah, 'Thus says the great king, the King of Assyria, "What is this confidence on which you rely? **20** [e]Do you think that mere words are[e] counsel and power for war? Now, on whom do you rely that you have rebelled against me? **21** Now[f] behold, you have relied for yourself on this broken shaft of a reed, on Egypt, upon which a man leans, and it enters his hand and pierces it! Thus is Pharaoh, King of Egypt for all who rely on him! **22** And if you[g] say to me, 'On YHWH, our G-d, we rely,' Is it not He whose high places and altars that Hezekiah removed? And He had said to Judah and to Jerusalem, 'Before this altar you shall worship [h]in Jerusalem'?"[h] **23** And now, make a wager with my lord, the King of Assyria, and I will give to you two thousand horses, if you are able to provide for yourself riders upon them! 24 How will you defy even one governor among the least servants of my lord when you rely for yourself upon Egypt for chariots and horses? 25 Now, was it not because of YHWH that I have come up against this place to destroy it? YHWH said to me, "Go up against this land, and destroy it!"'" 26 And Eliakim ⁱben Hilkiahⁱ and Shebna and Yoah said to the Chief Cup Bearer, "Please speak Aramaic to your servants, because we understand it, and do not speak withʲ us Judean in the ears of the people who are upon the wall." 27 So the Chief Cup Bearer said ᵏto them,ᵏ "Is it to your lord and to you that my lord has sent me to say these things? Is it not to the men who are sitting on the wall to eat their own filthˡ and to drink their own urineᵐ with you?" 28 And the Chief Cup Bearer stood, called out in a great voice in Judean, ⁿand he spokeⁿ and said, "Hear the wordᵒ of the great king, the King of Assyria! 29 Thus says the king, 'Do not let Hezekiah deceive you, because he is not able to save you from hisᵖ hand! 30 And do not let Hezekiah cause you to trust in YHWH, saying, "YHWH will surely save us, and this city will not be given into the hand of the King of Assyria."' 31 Do not listen to Hezekiah, for thus says the King of Assyria, 'Make a truce with me, come out to me, and eat, each his vine and each his fig tree, and drink, each the waters of his well, 32 until I come, and I take you unto a land like your land, a land of grain and wine, a land of bread and vineyards, ۹a land of olive oil and honey, and live, and do not die! And do not listen to Hezekiah, because he will allure you, saying, "YHWH will save us."۹ 33 Did any of the gods of the nations indeed save his own land from the hand of the King of Assyria? 34 Where are the gods of Hamath and Arpad? Where are the gods of Sepharvaim, ʳHena, and Ivvah, that they have saved Samaria from my hand?ʳ 35 Who among all of the gods of theˢ lands have saved their land from my hand that YHWH will save Jerusalem from my hand?'"

36 ᵗAnd the people were silent,ᵗ and they did not answer him a word, for the command of the king was, "Do not answer him." 37 And Eliakim ben Hilkiah, who was over the house, and Shebna the scribe, and Yoah ben Asaph the secretary came to Hezekiah in torn garments, and they declared to him the words of the Chief Cup Bearer. 19:1 And when King Hezekiah heard, he tore his garments, covered himself in sackcloth, and entered the House of YHWH. 2 And he sent Eliakim, who is over the house, and Shebna the scribe, and the elders of the priests covered in sackcloth to Isaiah the prophet ben Amoz. 3 And they said to him, "Thus says Hezekiah, 'Today is a day of distress, punishment, and disgrace, that children come to birth and there is no strength to give birth. 4 Perhaps YHWH, your G-d, will hear allᵘ the words of the Chief Cup Bearer, whose master the

King of Assyria sent to insult the living G-d, and He will punish the words which YHWH your G-d has heard, and you shall raise your prayer on behalf of the remaining remnant.'" 5 So the servants of King Hezekiah came to Isaiah. 6 And Isaiah said to them, "Thus you shall say to your lord, 'Thus says YHWH, "Do not fear these words which you have heard by which the lackeys of the King of Assyria revile me. 7 Behold, I am placing a spirit in him, and he will hear a rumor, and he will return to his land, and I will cause him to fall in his own land."'" 8 And the Chief Cup Bearer returned and found the King of Assyria fighting against Libnah, for he heard that he had departed from Lachish. 9 And he heard concerning Tirhakah, King of Ethiopia, saying, "Behold,^{v} he has gone out to fight with you." And he again^w sent messengers to Hezekiah, saying, 10 "Thus you shall say to Hezekiah, King of Judah, saying, 'Let not your G-d on whom you rely deceive you saying, "Jerusalem shall not be given into the hand of the King of Assyria." 11 Behold, you have heard what the kings of Assyria did to all the lands, to destroy them, and you shall be saved? 12 Did the gods of the nations which my fathers destroyed,^{x} save Gozan and Haran and Rezeph and the sons of Eden in Telassar? 13 Where is the King of Hamath and the King of Arpad and the King of Lair, Sepharvaim, Hena, and Ivvah?'" 14 And Hezekiah took the documents from the hand of the messengers, read them,^{y} and went up to the House of YHWH, and Hezekiah spread it before YHWH. 15 And Hezekiah prayed before YHWH and said,^{z} "YHWH, G-d of Israel who sits upon the Cherubim, You alone are G-d of all the kingdoms of the earth. You have made the heavens and the earth. 16 Incline, YHWH, your ear, and hear. Open, YHWH, your eyes, and see, and hear^{aa} the words of Sennacherib who sent him to insult the living G-d. 17 Surely, YHWH, the kings of Assyria have destroyed the nations^{bb} and their lands. 18 They have consigned their gods to fire because they are not gods, but only the works of human hands, wood and stone, and they destroyed them. 19 And now, YHWH our G-d, Save us please from his hand, and all the kingdoms of the earth will know that you, YHWH, are G-d alone." 20 And Isaiah ben Amoz sent to Hezekiah, saying, "Thus says YHWH, G-d of Israel, 'When you prayed unto me concerning Sennacherib, King of Assyria, I heard.' 21 This is the word which YHWH spoke concerning him, 'She mocks you, you scorns you, the maiden Daughter of Zion, after you she shakes (her) head, Daughter of Jerusalem. 22 Whom do you insult and revile? Against whom do you raise voice and lift on high your eyes? Against the Holy One of Israel! 23 By the hand of your messengers^{cc} you insult my L-rd, and you say, "With my many^{dd} chariots, I have gone up to the high mountains, to the summits of Lebanon, and I will cut down the highest of his cedars and the choicest of his cypresses, and I will enter ^{ee}his highest lodge,^{ee} his choicest forest. **24** I dug and I drank foreign[ff] waters, and I tread with the sole of my feet [gg]all the rivers of Egypt."[gg] **25** Did you not hear it from the past? I did it! From the ancient days, that I created it? Now, I bring it about, and it shall be to destroy into heaps of ruins fortified cities. **26** Their inhabitants are powerless, they are shattered and ashamed. They are grass of the field and underbrush, weeds of the rooftops and scrub brush before the grain. **27** Your sitting, your going out, and your coming in, I know, and your raging to me. **28** Because you have raged against me, and your arrogance has come up to my ears, I will put my hook in your nose and my bridle in your mouth, and I will cause you to return by the path on which you came. **29** And this will be the sign for you. Eat this year what grows on its own, and in the second year the after growth,[hh] and in the third year, sow and harvest, and plant vineyards and eat their fruit. **30** The survivors of the House of Judah will again take root downward, and they will produce fruit above, **31** for from Zion shall the remnant go out and the survivors from Mount Zion. The zeal of YHWH Sebaot[ii] will accomplish this.' **32** Therefore, thus says YHWH to the King of Assyria, 'He shall not enter this city, and he shall not shoot an arrow there, and he shall not advance against it with shield, and he shall not cast up against it siege works. **33** By the path on which he came, he shall return, and into this city he shall not enter,' oracle of YHWH. **34** 'And I shall defend this city to save it for my sake and for the sake of David my servant.'" **35** [jj]And that night[jj] the angel of YHWH went out, and struck the camp of Assyria, one hundred eighty five thousand, and they awoke in the morning, and behold, all of them were dead corpses. **36** Sennacherib, King of Assyria, left, went, returned, and lived in Nineveh. **37** And while he was worshiping in the House of Nisroch, his god, Adrammelech and Sarezer [kk]his sons[kk] struck with the sword, and they fled to the land of Ararat, and Esarhaddon, his son, reigned in his place.

a. Cf. LXX, "(the) mountains of" (*ore*; Hebrew, *hārê*); MT, *ʿārê*, "(the) cities of (the Medes)."

b–b. Cf. Isa 36:2, "And the King of Assyria sent the Chief Cup Bearer from Lachish to Jerusalem to King Hezekiah with a heavy army, and he stood at the channel of the upper pool by the highway of the washers' field."

c–c. Lacking in Isa 36:6.

d–d. Lacking in Isa 36:3.

e–e. MT reads lit., "you say indeed a word of the lips is (counsel and power for war)," i.e., mere talk does not mean that help will come when war begins.

f. Lacking in Isa 36:6.

g. MT reads as plural; cf. LXX, Peshitta, and Isa 36:7, which read as singular.

h–h. Lacking in Isa 36:7.

i–i. Lacking in Isa 36:11.

j. Cf. Isa 36:11, "to (us)."

k–k. Lacking Isa 36:12.

l. Ketiv, *ḥărêhem,* "their dung"; read with Qere, *ṣôʾātām,* "their filth."

m. Ketiv, *šênêhem,* "their urine"; read with Qere, *mêmê raglêhem,* "the waters of their feet," i.e., a somewhat more polite reference to urine.

n–n. Lacking in Isa 36:13.

o. Cf. Isa 36:13, which reads as a plural.

p. Cf. Targum, Peshitta, "my hand"; "from his hand" is lacking in Isa 36:14.

q–q. Cf. Isa 36:17–18, which reads, "lest Hezekiah allure you, saying, 'YHWH will save us.'"

r–r. Cf. Isa 36:19, "and if (*wĕkî*) they delivered Samaria from my hand?" See also Targum Jonathan, "Did they not remove them and exile them?" The Targum's reading is based on an interpretation of *hēnᶜa,* "Hena," as a hiphil form of the verb *nwᶜ,* "to move," and of *ᶜwwâ,* "Ivvah," as a piel form of the verb *ᶜwh,* "to do subvert, lay waste."

s. Cf. Isa 36:20, "these."

t–t. Cf. Isa 36:21 and LXX, "and they were silent."

u. Lacking in Isa 37:4.

v. Lacking in Isa 37:9.

w. Cf. Isa 37:9, which reads, "and he heard (*wayyišmaᶜ*)," instead of "and he returned/again (*wayyāšāb*)."

x. MT, *šiḥătû,* "(they) destroyed"; cf. Isa 37:12, *hišḥîtû,* "(they) caused to destroy."

y. LXX and Isa 37:14 read as a singular.

z. Isa 37:15, "saying."

aa. Isa 37:17 reads, "all"; cf. Targum Jonathan.

bb. Isa 37:18 reads, "lands."

cc. Cf. Isa 37:24, "your servants."

dd. Ketiv, *bĕrōkĕb,* "with the rider of (my chariot)"; read with Qere and Isa 37:24, *bĕrōb,* "with the multitude of (my chariotry)."

ee–ee. MT, *mĕlôn qiṣṣōh* (Qere; Ketiv is *qiṣṣoh*), "his highest lodge," lit., "the lodge of his end"; cf. Isa 37:24, *mĕrôm qiṣṣô,* "his farthest height," lit., "the height of his end."

ff. Isa 37:25 omits.

gg–gg. MT, *kōl yĕʾōrê māṣôr,* "all the rivers of Egypt," which presumes that *māṣôr* represents a form of *miṣrayim,* "Egypt." Others understand *māṣôr* as "fortress, fortified," from the root *nṣr,* "to guard"; cf. LXX, "all the rivers of fortified places"; Targum Jonathan and Peshitta, "all the waters of the deep rivers (i.e., mighty rivers)."

hh. Hebrew, *sāḥîš,* "grain that grows on its own"; cf. Isa 37:30, *šāḥîs,* a different term that refers to the same thing.

ii. Ketiv does not include a term here; read with Qere and Isa 37:32, *ṣĕbāʾôt,* "(YHWH) of Hosts."

jj. Isa 37:36 lacks this phrase.

kk-kk. Ketiv does not include this phrase; read with Qere and Isa 37:38, *bānāyw,* "his sons."

Second Kings 18:8–19:37 is demarcated by the syntactically independent statement in 2 Kgs 18:8 concerning Hezekiah's subjugation of the Philistines in preparation for his revolt against Sennacherib. It comprises three major episodes in 2 Kgs 18:8; 18:9–12; and 18:13–19:37, which are joined by dating formulas that employ either the *waw*-consecutive, *wayĕhî baššānâ hārĕbî'ît,* "and it came to pass in the fourth year (of King Hezekiah)," in 2 Kgs 18:9 or the *waw*-conjunctive, *ûbĕ'arba' 'eśreh šānâ,* "and in the fourteenth year (of King Hezekiah)," in 2 Kgs 18:13 to coordinate the three major elements of the narrative concerning Hezekiah's revolt. The three narrative subunits of this section—Hezekiah's subjugation of the Philistines (18:8), Shalmaneser's defeat of Samaria and his deportation of the Israelite population (18:9–12), and YHWH's deliverance of Jerusalem at the time of Sennacherib's invasion (18:13–19:37)—combine to provide the reader with a view of the three major military events that lead up to YHWH's deliverance of Jerusalem. Although they are held together by their common concern with the military dimensions of the revolt, the full narrative block demonstrates that Hezekiah's revolt is futile until he turns to YHWH. The following narratives concerning Hezekiah's illness in 2 Kgs 20:1–11 and Hezekiah's reception of the Babylonian embassy in 2 Kgs 20:12–19 are correlated with these narratives by their respective temporal formulas, but they do not employ *waw* or other overt syntactical connectors. They are related, but remain structurally separate at this level of the narrative, and thereby provide the reader with an opportunity to look back at associated events that occurred prior to Hezekiah's revolt. They support the contention of 2 Kgs 18:8–19:37 by portraying Hezekiah's prayer to YHWH for healing and Isaiah's condemnation of Hezekiah's reception of the Babylonian embassy that had come to discuss preparations for the revolt.

[8] The rationale for Hezekiah's subjugation of the Philistines is clear, since they sat astride the coastal plain that gave access to Judah and Israel from Egypt to the south and both Mesopotamia/Aram and Phoenicia/Asia Minor to the north. The incursion by the Arameans during the late-ninth-century reign of Jehoash ben Ahaziah of Judah (2 Kgs 12:18–19) demonstrated Judah's vulnerability in this regard. Control of the coastal plain was one of the first goals of Assyrian invasions of the region led by Shalmaneser V, Sargon II and Sennacherib throughout the late eighth century B.C.E. Such moves protected against an Egyptian advance.

Hezekiah's subjugation of the Philistines is corroborated in Sennacherib's account of his invasion of Judah. Sennacherib notes that Hezekiah imprisoned Padi, king of Ekron (*ANET* 287–88; *ARAB* 2:240, 311, 312). He rewards the Philistine kings, Mitinti of Ashdod, Padi of Ekron, Sillibel of Gaza, and an unnamed king of Ashkelon with territory taken from Hezekiah. The present form of the text places the notice concerning Hezekiah's subjugation of the Philistines immediately prior to the report of Samaria's downfall, which suggests that Hezekiah moved against the Philistines prior to the northern revolt against Assyria. There is little evidence to corroborate such a contention since his move appears to be in preparation for his revolt against Sennacherib. The placement of this notice merely highlights Hezekiah's actions during his reign and the implications that the fall of Samaria would have for Hezekiah's own revolt.

[9–12] The notice concerning Shalmaneser's conquest of Samaria and the Assyrian deportation of major elements of the northern Israelite population largely repeats information from the main account of the fall of northern Israel in 2 Kgs 17, esp. 17:1–6. There is some question as to whether Shalmaneser V lived to see the full conquest of Samaria and the deportation of the Israelite population; his successor, Sargon II, claims credit for these actions.[9] There is also some question as to whether Hezekiah was on the throne of Judah at the time of the Assyrian siege of Samaria. For commentary on the background of the revolt, the involvement of Shalmaneser, the deportation of the Israelites, and so forth, see the commentary on 2 Kgs 17.

The placement of this narrative warns the reader of the futility of attempted revolt against the Assyrians without divine support. There is no need to repeat the information of 2 Kgs 17 merely to assert that the fall of Samaria took place during Hezekiah's reign. Instead, the placement of this narrative in its present context serves the overall historiographical perspectives of the Hezekian, Josianic, and exilic editions of the DtrH. This is clear in the first instance by the statement in v. 12 that northern Israel suffered defeat and deportation because the people did not listen to YHWH or observe YHWH's covenant. This statement is a summation of 2 Kgs 17:7–23, which states this perspective in detail. Although the causes for Israel's defeat likely involve Israel's difficulties in raising a coalition that could resist the Assyrian army at this time, such an attempt at theological explanation serves the primary historiographical interests of the DtrH in theodicy, that is, to portray YHWH's righteousness, to defend YHWH's involvement and power in the history of Israel, and to assert the people's responsibilities to abide by divine covenant.

[18:13–19:37] This subunit is the culminating narrative of this section, with its portrayal of Hezekiah's revolt against Sennacherib, the Assyrian devastation of Judah and its demand for Jerusalem's unconditional surrender, and YHWH's deliverance of Jerusalem following Hezekiah's plea for deliverance. The text is demarcated by its chronological formula, which places the revolt in Hezekiah's fourteenth year, and its consistent focus on scenes relevant to the revolt.

A nearly identical version of this narrative appears in Isa 36–37. Together with Isa 38 and 39, which correspond to the narratives in 2 Kgs 20, these chapters form a major narrative block within the book of Isaiah that facilitates the transition between the presentation of the prophet in the first part of the book (chs. 1–33) and in the second part of the book (i.e., the so-called Second and Third Isaiah, in chapters 40–55; 56–66). Considerable debate concerning the

---

9. For discussion, see CAH 3/2, 85–86; H. Tadmor, "The Campaigns of Sargon II of Assur: A Chronological Historical Study," *JCS* 12 (1958): 22–40, 77–100.

priority of the Kings and Isaiah versions of this narrative has taken place, but a comparative analysis indicates that the Isaiah version is derived from the earlier version in Kings.[10] Slight modifications of the text in the Isaian version eliminate or reformulate statements that might be understood to question or criticize Hezekiah. The result is a virtual whitewash of his character in the Isaiah version to facilitate his presentation as an ideal model for piety to readers of the book.[11] Specific points of comparison include the assertive statement in 2 Kgs 18:32, "do not listen to Hezekiah for (*kî*) he will mislead you," and the less accusatory statement in Isa 36:17–18, "unless (*pen*) Hezekiah misleads you"; the statement in 2 Kgs 19:35, "and it came to pass that night," does not appear in Isa 37:36, which eliminates any hint that YHWH delayed in striking at the Assyrians; and most importantly, the portrayal of Hezekiah's submission to Sennacherib in 2 Kgs 18:14–16 is absent in the Isaiah version, which eliminates any hint that Hezekiah would submit to an arrogant, pagan monarch who blasphemes against YHWH. Other differences between 2 Kgs 20 and Isa 38–39 are discussed below.

Many interpreters maintain that this narrative is a combination of several independent literary sources concerning the Assyrian confrontation with Hezekiah that have been combined to form the present narrative.[12] Stade identified the basic narrative sources, based upon the distinctive characters of the narrative concerning Hezekiah's submission to Sennacherib and the two accounts of Assyrian delegations sent to Hezekiah to demand his surrender. Source A is a historically reliable account of Hezekiah's submission to Sennacherib in 2 Kgs 18:13–16; source B$_1$ comprises the first legendary account of a delegation to Hezekiah in 2 Kgs 18:17–19:9ba, 36–37; and source B$_2$ comprises the second legendary account of a delegation to Hezekiah in 2 Kgs 19:9b–20, 32aß–b, 34–35. Although this analysis has been accepted throughout much of the twentieth century, it is based largely on the limited presuppositions of late-nineteenth-century source-critical exegesis that failed to consider the literary interrelationships between materials that it identified as discrete literary sources. An enhanced understanding of plot, characterization, and dramatic tension influences the interpretation of this narrative.[13] The pericope concerning

10. See Christopher R. Seitz, *Zion's Final Destiny: The Development of the Book of Isaiah. A Reassessment of Isaiah 36–39* (Minneapolis: Fortress, 1991); Sweeney, *Isaiah 1–39*, 496–502.

11. Sweeney, *Isaiah 1–39*, 476–85.

12. See B. Stade, "Anmerkungen zu 2 Kö 15–21" *ZAW* 6 (1886): 172–86; Brevard S. Childs, *Isaiah and the Assyrian Crisis* (SBT 2/3; Naperville, Ill.: Alec R. Allenson, 1967); Francolino Gonçalves, *L'expédition de Sennachérib en Palestine dans la literature hébraïque ancienne* (Louvaine-la-neuve: Institute Orientaliste, 1986); Seitz, *Zion's Final Destiny*.

13. See Dana N. Fewell, "Sennacherib's Defeat: Words at War in 2 Kings 18.13–19.37," *JSOT* 34 (1986): 79–90; K. A. D. Smekik, "King Hezekiah Advocates True Prophecy," in *Converting the Past: Studies in Ancient Israelite and Moabite Historiography* (OTS 28; Leiden: Brill, 1992), 93–128.

Hezekiah's submission to Sennacherib need not be read simply as an alternative account of the encounter. Its placement at the outset of the narrative highlights Sennacherib's despicable character as an arrogant and unjust enemy of YHWH by portraying his demands for Hezekiah's surrender and the deportation of the population even after Hezekiah had already submitted to his authority. The report of successive delegations does not mark independent narratives, but points instead to the development of dramatic tension in the midst of a confrontation between the two groups, portrayed at the surface level by the numerically balanced groups of three Assyrian and three Israelite officers, who represent the major characters, namely, the Assyrian king Sennacherib and Hezekiah or YHWH.

This narrative is an example of the typical prophetic confrontation story.[14] The prophetic confrontation story is a literary device that pits a prophet (representing YHWH) against an opponent who would challenge or deny the validity of the prophet or YHWH. Although the terms of the confrontation vary from story to story, the result is inevitably the demise of the opponent, which then validates the prophet's message or YHWH's power (1 Kgs 18:1–46; 22:1–40; Amos 7:10–17; and Jer 27–28; 36). Sennacherib's demise and the deaths of his soldiers validates the claims of YHWH's sovereignty over creation and Jerusalem and comes as a response to the blasphemous statements delivered by the Assyrian officers.

The generic identification of this narrative as a prophetic confrontation narrative and its legendary elements raise questions concerning its historical character. Similar questions emerge in relation to the notice in 2 Kgs 19:9 that the Assyrian army departed to meet an attack by Pharaoh Tirhakah of Egypt, particularly since Tirhakah did not ascend to the Egyptian throne until 690–689, over a decade after Sennacherib's invasion. Some elements appear to be historical: Sennacherib's 701 B.C.E. invasion of Judah and siege of Jerusalem are well known from his own records, the Chief Cup Bearer's argumentation and use of language forms is consistent with Assyrian practice of the period, and Sennacherib was murdered by his own sons. Nevertheless, various elements point to the character of this narrative as a very late, retrospective, and highly propagandistic view of the event that is designed to enhance the reader's estimation of YHWH's power and capacity to protect the city of Jerusalem and the Davidic monarch. Sennacherib was killed by his own sons, but his assassination took place in 681 B.C.E., some twenty years after the siege. The portrayal of a prophet who convinced Hezekiah to abandon his confrontation and submit to YHWH is known elsewhere in biblical tradition, but the account of Jeremiah's trial for sedition in Jer 26:16–19 attributes this role not to Isaiah but to his contemporary, Micah, who announced that Jerusalem would be destroyed. The most

---

14. For a discussion of the prophetic confrontation story, see Sweeney, *Isaiah 1–39*, 518.

telling evidence, however, is Sennacherib's own account of the encounter, in which he claims to have captured forty-six Judean cities, besieged Jerusalem, deported one hundred fifty thousand captives, taken thirty talents of gold and eight hundred talents of silver (cf. the thirty talents of gold and three hundred talents of silver mentioned in 2 Kgs 18:14), and so on.

Although propagandistic, Sennacherib's account agrees with the biblical accounts on several crucial points—that is, Sennacherib devastated Judah, besieged Jerusalem, and exacted tribute from Hezekiah. Furthermore, Sennacherib never claimed to have captured Jerusalem, and he never killed Hezekiah or forced him from the throne. This is a remarkable turn of events for a monarch who led a revolt against the Assyrian empire. The reason for his failure to kill or remove Hezekiah is readily at hand. Hezekiah was allied with Merodach Baladan of Babylon,[15] and key to the revolt was the strategy to hit Sennacherib simultaneously at both the eastern and western edges of his empire, forcing the Assyrians either to divide their forces and risk defeat in both regions or to concentrate on the one while allowing the other free rein to consolidate and to ensure the success of at least one of the partners in this coalition. Sennacherib's stunning success in defeating the western allies, beginning with Tyre and ending with Hezekiah, convinced many of the western allies to abandon the fight and to submit to Assyria. But time was a major factor in Sennacherib's strategy, and he did not have time to wait out a lengthy siege of Jerusalem while Merodach Baladan was loose in the east. It appears that Sennacherib settled with Hezekiah, allowing him to remain on the throne, while the Assyrian army rushed east to put down the Babylonian threat. Both sides could then claim success; Sennacherib's records highlight his devastation of Judah and the forced submission of Hezekiah, while Judean records highlight YHWH's protection of Jerusalem and the house of David (cf. Pss 2; 46; 47; 48).

The literary structure of this narrative emphasizes an interest in portraying YHWH as protector of Jerusalem and the house of David. It is based in a series of scenes that unfold the basic events of the revolt and YHWH's defeat of the Assyrians. The narrative begins in 2 Kgs 18:13 with a brief notice that King Sennacherib of Assyria attacked Judah in the fourteenth year of Hezekiah's reign and seized all the fortified cities of Judah, which builds on the statement in 2 Kgs 18:7 that Hezekiah revolted against the king of Assyria. The second scene, in 2 Kgs 18:14–16, portrays Hezekiah's submission to Sennacherib, including his stripping the temple to pay Sennacherib three hundred talents of silver and thirty talents of gold to end the hostilities. The third scene, in 2 Kgs 18:17–36, portrays the negotiation for the unconditional surrender of Jerusalem between the three Assyrian officers representing Sennacherib and the three

15. See J. A. Brinkman, "Merodach-Baladan II," *Studies Presented to A. Leo Oppenheim, June 7, 1964* (Chicago: Oriental Institute, 1964), 6–53.

Judean officers representing Hezekiah. The Assyrians make it clear that the surrender of Jerusalem will entail the deportation of its population. The fourth scene, in 2 Kgs 18:37–19:7, portrays the report by the Judean officers to Hezekiah concerning the Assyrian terms for surrender and Hezekiah's initial oracular consultation of YHWH through the prophet Isaiah, who informs the king that YHWH will deliver the city. The fifth scene, in 2 Kgs 19:8–13, portrays the second demand by the Assyrians for Jerusalem's unconditional surrender. The sixth scene, in 2 Kgs 19:14–34, presents Hezekiah's prayer to YHWH and YHWH's oracular response. YHWH's lengthy oracle expresses divine indignation at the Assyrians' blasphemy and promises to defeat and humiliate the Assyrian monarch to demonstrate that YHWH is the true sovereign of creation. The final scene, in 2 Kgs 19:35–37, portrays the realization of YHWH's promises, including the deaths of 185,000 Assyrian troops; Sennacherib's return to his capital city, Nineveh; and his assassination by his own sons in the temple of his god, Nisroch.

[18:13] This statement places Sennacherib's invasion in the fourteenth year of Hezekiah. Because Sennacherib's invasion is securely dated to 701 B.C.E., this statement conflicts with 2 Kgs 18:1, which places Hezekiah's accession in the third year of Hoshea ben Elah. Most interpreters accept the present chronology and place Hezekiah's accession in 715 B.C.E.

[18:14–16] Hezekiah's early capitulation heightens narrative tension, particularly with regard to Sennacherib's arrogance and blasphemy, and it prepares the reader for YHWH's oracle against the Assyrian monarch, the destruction of his army, and his assassination at the hands of his own sons in the temple of his own god. Sennacherib's siege of Lachish is represented in a palace relief intended to impress visitors with his power (*ANEP* 371–73).

[18:17–36] The Isaian version of this narrative mentions only the Rab Shakeh, "Chief Cup Bearer," to portray the confrontation between the lone Assyrian representative of Sennacherib and Hezekiah as the lone representative of YHWH. The Kings version includes three Assyrian officers, the Tartan, the Chief Eunuch, and the Chief Cup Bearer, which correspond to the three Israelite officers designated to speak on Hezekiah's behalf. It thereby emphasizes a confrontation between two delegations that represent their respective kings. The Tartan (Hebrew, *tartān*; Akkadian, *turtanu*), "viceroy," is the chief military commander after Sennacherib, and leads the army in the king's absence (cf. Isa 20:1). The Rab Saris (Hebrew, *rab sārîs*; Akkadian, *rab ša reši*), "Chief Eunuch," is a senior officer who also leads military forces on behalf of the king (see *ARAB* 1:803; Jer 39:3, 13). The Rab Shakeh (Hebrew, *rab šāqēh*), "Chief Cup Bearer," is a senior officer, who functions as a diplomat or advisor to the king.

The location of the Assyrian delegation is identified as "the channel of the upper pool by the highway of the Fuller's (launderers') Field." The exact site of this pool is disputed (Gray 679–82). The most likely site is the collection pools associated with the Gihon Spring, which emerges on the eastern slope of the city of David in the Kidron Valley. This spring is one of the main water sources for the city of David, and its waters were collected in pools along the Kidron Valley to provide water for agriculture and other purposes. Hezekiah's tunnel was designed to collect the waters of the Gihon and channel them under the city of David, where they would flow into the Siloam pool, apparently the lower pool, at the southern tip of the city.[16] The Kidron Valley then forms a natural roadway along the eastern side of the city, and it provides a convenient site from which the Rab Shakeh's words could be heard at the Ophel, the site of the royal palace complex, as well as by the men guarding the eastern walls of the city.

The Israelite delegation likewise includes three officers,[17] Eliakim ben Hilkiah, "who is over the house"; Shebna the scribe; and Yoah ben Asaph the secretary. Eliakim and Shebna are mentioned in Isa 22:15–25, where Isaiah denounces Shebna and states that his authority will be given to Eliakim. In Isa 22:15, Shebna is identified as "he who is over the house" (Hebrew, *ʾăšer ʿal habbāyit*), a term that designates the chief administrator over the king's household. Perhaps our texts reflect a power struggle or change in office among Hezekiah's chief administrators in which Eliakim supplanted Shebna. Shebna is identified as "the scribe" (Hebrew, *hassōpēr*), who would play a major role in communicating the will of the king and the affairs of government. Yoah ben Asaph's designation as "the secretary, recorder, royal herald" (Hebrew, *hammazkîr*) indicates a role in records, which would include taxation, accounts, and other obligations.

The Rab Shakeh's speeches employ classic speech forms from Assyrian diplomacy, such as the diplomatic messenger formula with its designation of Sennacherib, "Thus says the great king, the King of Assyria," the portrayal of Egypt as "a broken reed," and the disputational forms of argumentation, particularly the use of rhetorical questions, that are designed to challenge and destroy the confidence of the enemy.[18] The speech heightens the portrayal of Sennacherib's blasphemy against YHWH and the helplessness of Jerusalem and Hezekiah, who had already surrendered to Sennacherib. The Rab Shakeh presents three key arguments for Hezekiah's surrender. The first challenges Hezekiah's confidence in his coalition by pointing out that his alliances are now worthless. Hezekiah's allies failed to show at the crucial moment of the Assyrian assault. The second

16. Yigal Shiloh, "Jerusalem," *NEAEHL* 2:709–12.

17. For discussion of these offices, see Nili Sacher Fox, *In the Service of the King: Officialdom in Ancient Israel and Judah* (Monographs of the Hebrew Union College 23; Cincinnati: Hebrew Union College, 2000), 81–121.

18. See Burke O. Long, *2 Kings* (FOTL 10; Grand Rapids: William B. Eerdmans, 1991), 209–21; Childs, *Isaiah and the Assyrian Crisis*, 80–85; Chaim Cohen, "Neo-Assyrian Elements in the First Speech of the Biblical Rab-Šaqe," *IOS* 9 (1979): 32–48; Peter Machinist, "Assyria and Its Image in First Isaiah," *JAOS* 103 (1983): 719–37.

challenges Hezekiah's reliance upon YHWH, whose shrines and high places Hezekiah's reforms had broken down. The Assyrians portray Hezekiah's reforms as an affront that motivated YHWH to authorize the Assyrian attack. The third is that Hezekiah lacks the men to defend Jerusalem. The Rab Shakeh's offer to provide two thousand horses to Hezekiah is designed to humiliate the Judean king.

The response by the Judean officers highlights their helpless situation as they request that the Assyrians speak Aramaic rather than Judean (i.e., Hebrew) so that the Judean soldiers on the wall will not understand. This presents the Rab Shakeh with a fine opportunity to speak to the men who will bear the brunt of the Assyrian assault. He undermines their morale by addressing them in Judean as "those who will eat their own waste and drink their own urine," to highlight conditions of starvation in a besieged city. Again, he presents a series of arguments. The first is that the Judean soldiers should not trust Hezekiah, who lacks the power to save them. The second is that they should not trust in YHWH either, who likewise lacks the power or will to save them. His argument then turns to more positive images when he makes an offer for the safety of the soldiers—that is, they will drink from their own pools and eat from their own vineyards and fig trees when the Assyrians deport them to a land like their own. Having offered the carrot, he then returns to the stick by pointing out all of the other gods who had failed to save their cities from his power, namely, Hamath, Arpad, Hena, Ivvah, and Samaria. Arpad is a north Aramean city taken by Tiglath-pileser III in 740 B.C.E.,[19] and Hamath was a chief city in northern Aram taken by Sargon II in 720 B.C.E.[20] Sepharvaim, Hena, and Ivvah are unknown. Samaria is the capital of northern Israel conquered by Shalmaneser V and Sargon II in 722/721 B.C.E.

[18:37–19:7] The report of the Judean officers to Hezekiah underscores the desperate situation of Jerusalem. Tearing garments and dressing in sackcloth are typical symbols of mourning for death and disaster. Lacking any clear solution to the situation, Hezekiah turns to an oracular inquiry of YHWH through the prophet Isaiah ben Amoz. Yoah ben Asaph is replaced in the delegation by the elders of the priests. This change is not due to scribal error, but reflects the typical role of priests in the consultation of oracular prophets (see, e.g., Exod 4:1–17; 2 Kgs 22:11–20). Hezekiah's quotation of the proverb, "Today is a day of distress, punishment, and disgrace, that children come to birth and there is no strength to give birth," signals once again Hezekiah's desperation as a prelude for his turn to YHWH.[21] Hezekiah's statement likewise signals his continuing adherence to YHWH, despite the Assyrian blasphemy. The narrative

19. H. Avalos, "Arpad," *ABD* 1:401.
20. M.-L. Buhl, "Hamath," *ABD* 3:33–36.
21. Katheryn Pfisterer Darr, *Isaiah's Vision and the Family of G-d* (Louisville, Ky.: Westminster John Knox, 1994), 205–24.

signals the ultimate outcome: YHWH will hear Hezekiah's prayer. Isaiah's response confirms YHWH's power and willingness to intervene. The prophet employs the classic reassurance formula, "do not fear" (Hebrew, *'al tîrā'*),[22] to confirm YHWH's support.

[19:8–13] Sennacherib first attacked Lachish, the most important city in the region, before moving to smaller targets, such as Libnah. The most likely identification of the site of Libnah is Tell Bornat, located five miles northeast of Lachish.[23] The notice that Sennacherib had gone to fight Tirhaqah is anachronistic, since Tirhaqah did not rule Egypt until 690–689 B.C.E.

The speech by the Assyrian messengers is much shorter than the first speech by the Chief Cup Bearer. It presents a similar argument concerning YHWH's powerlessness against the Assyrians, although it adds a few details. It again points to the failure of foreign gods and kings to defend their cities, namely, Hamath, Arpad, Sepharvaim, Hena, and Ivvah. It adds references to Gozan, Haran, Retzeph, the people of Eden in Telassar, and La'ir. Gozan, an Aramean city identified with Tell Halaph on the Habor River in northern Aram, was conquered by Assyria in the ninth century.[24] Haran, a part of Assyria since 1100 B.C.E., was a Hurrian city located to the northwest of Gozan in northern Mesopotamia some sixty miles north of the confluence of the Balikh and Euphrates rivers.[25] It is identified as the site where Terah, the father of Abram, moved his family from Ur of the Chaldeans (Gen 11:31–32), and in 609 B.C.E., it served as the site of the Assyrian army's last stand against the Babylonians and their Medean allies. Rezeph is modern Rezzafeh, located about a hundred miles south of Aleppo along the Euphrates River.[26] It served as an Assyrian provincial capital after its conquest by Shalmaneser III in 838 B.C.E. The people of Eden are identified with Bit Adini, a region south of Haran along the Euphrates (Tadmor and Cogan 235). Telassar could be a corrupted form of Til Basir, the capital of the region, but may refer to Til Aššuri, located in the Zagros region along the lower Diyala River (Tadmor and Cogan 235). La'ir is Lahiru in northeastern Babylonia (Tadmor and Cogan 235).

[19:14–34] This episode highlights once again the theme of Hezekiah's piety and reliance on YHWH as the essential key to YHWH's deliverance of Jerusalem and the king from the Assyrian threat. His prayer to YHWH employs the address form frequently associated with the ark, "O YHWH, G-d of Israel, who is enthroned above the Cherubim" (cf. 1 Sam 4:4; 2 Sam 6:2; 1 Kgs 6:32; Pss 80:2; 99:1). It highlights the liturgical identification of YHWH as sole G-d

22. Edgard W. Conrad, *Fear Not Warrior: A Study of 'al tîrā' Pericopes in the Hebrew Scriptures* (BJS 75; Chico, Calif.: Scholars Press, 1985); Sweeney, *Isaiah 1–39*, 547.

23. J. L. Peterson, "Libnah," *ABD* 4:322–23.

24. "Gozan," *HBD* 386.

25. Y. Kobayashi, "Haran," *ABD* 3:58–59.

26. H. O. Thompson, "Rezeph," *ABD* 5:708.

of all kingdoms and creator of heaven and earth to petition YHWH to deliver Jerusalem.

Following the narrative introduction in v. 20a, YHWH's oracular response appears in two messenger speeches in vv. 20b–31 and 32–34. The initial statement of the messenger formula, "Thus says YHWH, G-d of Israel, etc.," and another introductory notice concerning YHWH's word introduce the oracle, which comprises a modified prophetic judgment speech that states the grounds for judgment against Sennacherib and the judgment per se. It begins with a metaphorical portrayal of the daughter of Zion's taunt of the Assyrian monarch in v. 21b, followed by accusations in vv. 22–24 in the form of rhetorical questions and quotations of the monarch, that charge Sennacherib with blasphemy against YHWH. The oracle employs claims to ride a chariot to the heights of Lebanon to cut down cedars, enter the uppermost regions of the earth, dig channels, drink waters, and dry up the rivers of Egypt. These images draw upon the classic Assyrian portrayal of the god Assur flying through the heavens on a winged disk at the head of his armies and Assyrian claims to cut down the cedars of Lebanon as a symbol of power.[27] The digging of wells recalls Mesopotamian mythologies in which the gods and their royal representatives put the people to work digging the canals that watered Mesopotamian farmland.[28] The drying of the rivers of Egypt alludes to Assyrian efforts to conquer Egypt in the early seventh century B.C.E. as well as YHWH's defeat of Egypt in the exodus tradition.

Verses 25–28 employ a literary style much like that of Second Isaiah to assert that YHWH is the one who actually does these things from ancient times. This provides the basis for the prophet's claim that YHWH decided long ago to bring the Assyrian king to this point, which means the blasphemous Sennacherib does not understand the basis for his own power.

The announcement of the sign to confirm this word in vv. 29–31 draws on agricultural metaphors, which are pertinent since the Assyrian armies devastated Judah's agricultural base. The sign envisions a three-year process for rebuilding Judean agriculture. In the first year, the people will eat whatever grows wild since the Assyrians stripped the land. In the second year, they eat whatever grows afterward. In the third year, they replant and eat the resulting harvest. Employing a classic Isaian theme, the agricultural metaphor symbolizes the regrowth of the remnant of Judah (Isa 11:1–16). The statement in v. 31 concerning the going forth of the remnant of Judah from Zion and the zeal of YHWH who accomplishes this draws upon Isaian language as well (cf. Isa 2:2–4; 4:2–6; 9:6).

27. For a portrayal of Assur flying through the heavens, see *ANEP* 536. For the cutting of the cedars of Lebanon by Mesopotamian monarchs, see *ANET* 278 (Shalmaneser III), 307 (Nebuchadnezzar); for the metaphor of harvesting fish, see *ANET* 284 (Sargon II).

28. See W. G. Lambert and A. R. Millard, *Atra-Hasis: The Babylonian Story of the Flood* (Oxford: Clarendon, 1969), 55–61 (*Atra Ḥasis* ii. 1–260), which discuss the creation of humankind so that the gods might be relieved from digging the canals.

The second messenger speech in vv. 32–34 presents YHWH's judgment against the Assyrian king that draws upon the classical language and conceptualization of the Zion tradition. The introductory *lākēn,* "therefore," typically introduces the announcement of judgment in the prophetic judgment speech, and the following messenger formula, "thus says YHWH to the king of Assyria," identifies an oracle by YHWH.[29] Arrows, shields, and siege mounds allude to standard Assyrian military tactics that were employed successfully against Lachish. The oracle reiterates the basic themes of the Zion tradition, that is, YHWH defends Jerusalem and the Davidic king (cf. Pss 2; 46; 47; 48). Sennacherib's failure to take Jerusalem and to remove Hezekiah from the throne reinforces the view that YHWH protects Jerusalem and the house of David unconditionally.

[19:35–37] The destruction of 185,000 Assyrian troops by the angel of YHWH recalls the angel of death that destroyed the firstborn of the Egyptians in Exodus. The death of so many Assyrian troops is a legendary embellishment that illustrates the claims of the Zion tradition. Herodotus (2:141) claims that Sennacherib was forced to withdraw from Pelusium at the gates of Egypt due to a plague of mice that destroyed the weapons of his army, although many maintain that this tradition is based in part on the present narrative.

Sennacherib was assassinated in 681 B.C.E. and was succeeded by Esarhaddon. Esarhaddon claims that he was chosen as heir by his father, and that his older brothers later revolted until they were defeated in Khanigalbat (near Urartu/Ararat). The Babylonian Chronicle states that Sennacherib was murdered by his own son in a rebellion that continued until Esarhaddon ascended the throne.[30] The god, Nisroch, has not been securely identified, although Ninurta, the Mesopotamian god of arable land and patron of war, is a likely candidate.[31]

2 Kings 20:1–11 The Account of YHWH's Healing of Hezekiah's Illness

20:1 In those days, Hezekiah became mortally ill, and Isaiah ben Amoz the prophet came and said to him, "Thus says YHWH, 'Command your house, you will die, and you shall not live.'" 2 So he[a] turned his face to the wall and prayed to YHWH, saying,[b] 3 "Please, YHWH, remember how I served before you in truth and with a whole heart, and the good in your eyes that I did," and Hezekiah wept profusely. 4 [c]And Isaiah had not yet left the inner court[d] when the word of YHWH came to him, saying,[c] 5 "Return,[e] and say to Hezekiah, the leader of my people, 'Thus says

---

29. Sweeney, *Isaiah 1–39,* 533–34, 524, respectively.
30. CAH 3/2, 119–21.
31. C. Uehlinger, "Nisroch," *DDD*[2] 630–32.

YHWH, G-d of David your father, "I have heard your prayer. I have seen your tears. ᶠBehold, I am healing you. On the third day you shall go up to the House of YHWH. 6 I will extend your days by fifteen years,ᶠ and from the hand of the King of Assyria I will save you and this city, and I will defend this city ᵍfor my sake and for the sake of David my servant."'"ᵍ 7 ʰAnd Isaiah said, "Take a cake of figs," and they took one and placed it on the boil, and he lived.ʰ 8 ⁱAnd Hezekiah said to Isaiah, "What is the sign that YHWH will heal me, that I will go up on the third day to the House of YHWH?"ⁱ 9 And Isaiah said to him, "This will be the sign to you from YHWH that YHWH will do this thing that he has said. ʲThe shadow has gone ten steps, so it will return ten steps."ʲ 10 ᵏAnd Hezekiah said, "It is easy for the shadow to move ten steps, but not that the shadow would return back ten steps." 11 So Isaiah the prophet called to YHWH, and He caused the shadow to return back ten steps from the ten steps which it had gone down on the steps of Ahaz.ᵏ

a. LXX, Peshitta, and Isa 38:2 add, "Hezekiah."

b. Hebrew, *lēʾmōr,* "saying"; cf. Isa 38:3, *wayyōʾmār,* "and he said."

c–c. Cf. the much shorter text in Isa 38:5, "and the word of YHWH was unto Isaiah, saying."

d. Ketiv, *hāʿîr,* "the (middle) city"; read with Qere, *ḥāṣēr,* "the (middle) court"; cf. LXX; Targum Jonathan; Peshitta.

e. Hebrew, *šûb,* "return"; cf. Isa 38:5, *hālôk,* "go."

f–f. Cf. Isa 38:5–6, which presents a much shorter text, "behold, I am extending your days by fifteen years."

g–g. Lacking in Isa 38:6.

h–h. Cf. Isa 38:21, immediately following the conclusion of Hezekiah's psalm, "And Isaiah said, 'Let them take up a cake of figs, and they will rub it on the boil so that he may live.'"

i–i. Cf. the conclusion of the Isaian version in Isa 38:22, "And Hezekiah said, 'What is the sign that I shall go up to the house of YHWH?'"

j–j. Cf. Isa 38:8, "Behold, I am returning the shadow of the steps that have gone down on the steps of Ahab by the sun backwards ten steps, and the sun will return ten steps on the steps where it had gone down."

k–k. Isaiah omits the statements in 2 Kgs 20:10–11, and proceeds instead with the psalm of Hezekiah in Isa 38:9–20.

Second Kings 20:1–11 presents a prophetic legend that recounts YHWH's healing of Hezekiah from mortal illness as a corollary with the account of YHWH's deliverance of Jerusalem. The introductory formula *bayyāmîm hāhēm,* "in those days," aids in correlating this unit with the preceding narrative together with its larger concerns with YHWH's miraculous deliverance of Hezekiah. YHWH's deliverance of Hezekiah corresponds to YHWH's miraculous deliverance of Jerusalem; the presentation of Hezekiah's piety, particularly his prayers to YHWH and his presence at the Jerusalem temple in both narratives; and the very explicit statement in v. 6 that correlates Hezekiah's illness with the deliverance of Jerusalem, "and I will extend your days by fifteen years, and I will deliver you from the hand of the King of Assyria, and I will defend this city for my sake and for the sake of my servant David" (cf. 2 Kgs 19:34, which includes a similar statement concerning YHWH's defense of Jerusalem). Such a correlation demonstrates a concern with emphasizing the need for piety and a return to YHWH. It also shifts the focus from the deliverance of Jerusalem to the deliverance of Hezekiah, and thereby highlights Hezekiah as a model of personal piety and the ideal qualities of a king in the DtrH.

Although Hezekiah is presented as a model of piety in this version, its counterpart in Isa 38 introduces a number of subtle and blatant modifications that idealize him even more. Whereas 2 Kgs 20:4–5 states, "and Isaiah had not gone out from the middle court when the word of YHWH came to him saying, 'Return, and you shall say to Hezekiah, the leader of my people . . . ,'" Isa 38:4–5 simply states, "and the word of YHWH came to Isaiah, saying, 'Go, and you shall say to Hezekiah. . . .'" The Kings version suggests delay in YHWH's communication to Isaiah, whereas the Isaian version portrays YHWH's oracle as an immediate response to Hezekiah's prayer. Second Kings 20:5–6 states, "Behold, I am healing you, on the third day you shall go up to the house of YHWH, and I shall add fifteen years to your days," but Isa 38:5 states simply, "Behold, I am adding fifteen years to your days." Again, Kings indicates delay in YHWH's response to Hezekiah, whereas the Isaian version eliminates any such suggestion.

Second Kings 20:6–9 differs extensively from its counterpart in Isa 38. Whereas v. 6 states that YHWH will heal Hezekiah "for my sake and the sake of my servant David," Isaiah includes no such concern for the royal house of David, since such a statement would suggest a motivation other than Hezekiah's piety. The references to Isaiah's application of a remedy and Hezekiah's request for a sign in vv. 7–8 appear only at the end of the Isaian narrative in Isa 38:21–22 following Hezekiah's prayer of thanksgiving in Isa 38:9–20, which does not appear in the Kings narrative at all. Their placement in the Isaian narrative eliminates any suggestion that Hezekiah was motivated in his piety by a desire for healing. Second Kings 20:9 indicates that Isaiah states the sign to Hezekiah, whereas Isa 38:6–7 emphasizes that the sign comes from YHWH.

Second Kings 20:9b–11 indicates that Hezekiah calls for a more difficult act to confirm YHWH's sign: the shadow on Ahaz's steps must move backward, which suggests skepticism on Hezekiah's part, whereas the Isaian version lacks the exchange between the prophet and Hezekiah altogether. Isaiah 38:8 presents the return of the shadow as part of YHWH's statement, which emphasizes YHWH's direct response to Hezekiah.

The literary structure of this narrative is based on the sequence of events. Verses 1–3 focus on Hezekiah's prayer to YHWH upon hearing from Isaiah that he would die from his illness. Verses 4–6 present Isaiah's reception of YHWH's oracle promising to heal Hezekiah. Verses 8–10 relate the exchange of conversation between Isaiah and Hezekiah concerning YHWH's healing of Hezekiah and the king's questions concerning the sign that he would be healed. Verse 11 presents the culmination of the narrative with its report of the miraculous sign.

[1–3] The introductory formula, "in those days," correlates Hezekiah's illness with the account of Sennacherib's siege of Jerusalem. When Isaiah delivers an oracle instructing him to set his affairs in order because he will die, Hezekiah prays to YHWH to remember his exemplary deeds. YHWH's response confirms that Hezekiah is portrayed as a righteous king.

[4–6] Isaiah receives the oracle from YHWH while walking through the middle court of the royal palace (1 Kgs 7:8). The addition of fifteen years to Hezekiah's life correlates his illness with Sennacherib's siege, which took place in the fourteenth year (2 Kgs 18:13) of Hezekiah's twenty-nine-year reign (2 Kgs 18:2). Interest in the siege is confirmed by YHWH's statements concerning the defense of the city for YHWH's own sake and that of David.

[7] A cake or plaster of figs is a known remedy for a boil in the ancient world.[32]

[8–11] The steps or dial of Ahaz refers to a sundial by which the time of day could be measured. The backward movement of the shadow would be a miraculous indication of YHWH's promise to heal Hezekiah (cf. Josh 10).

2 Kings 20:12–19 The Account of Isaiah's Condemnation of Hezekiah

20:12 At that time, Berodach[a] Baladan ben Baladan, King of Babylon, sent officials and a present to Hezekiah because he heard [b]that Hezekiah was sick.[b] 13 [c]And Hezekiah listened to them,[c] and showed them all the house of his treasury, the silver and the gold and the spices and the good oil and[d] the house of his vessels and all that was found in his storerooms. There was not a thing that Hezekiah did not show them in his house and in all his kingdom. 14 And Isaiah the prophet came to King Hezekiah and said to him, "What did these men say, and from where did they come to you?" Hezekiah said, "From a far land they came,[e] from Babylon." 15 And he said, "What did they see in your house?" Hezekiah said, "All that is in my house, they saw. There was not a thing which I did not show them in my storerooms." 16 And Isaiah said to Hezekiah, "Hear the word of YHWH,[f] 17 'Behold, the days are coming when all that is in your house and that your fathers stored until this day will be carried off to Babylon. There will not remain a thing,' says YHWH. 18 'And from your own sons whom you sired, [g]they shall be taken,[g] and they will be eunuchs in the

32. Pliny, *Nat.*, 23.7.122.

palace of the King of Babylon.'" 19 And Hezekiah said to Isaiah, "Good is the word of YHWH which you have spoken." And he said, ʰ"Will there not be peace and truth in my days?"ʰ

a. Cf. Isa 39:1; LXX; Peshitta, "Merodach (Baladan ben Baladan)," which is the correct representation of the Babylonian prince's name.

b–b. Cf. Isa 39:1; LXX; and Peshitta, which omit Hezekiah's name (Hebrew, *ḥizqiyyāhû*), but include the phrase "but he had recovered (Hebrew, *wayyeḥĕzaq*)," based on the same root.

c–c. Hebrew, *wayyišmaʿ ʿalêhem hizqîyahû*, "and Hezekiah listened to them"; cf. Isa 39:3, *wayyismaḥ ʿălêhem ḥizqîyyāhû*, "and Hezekiah rejoiced over them"; see also LXX; Peshitta, which follow the Isaian reading.

d. Isa 39:3 adds "all"; cf. Peshitta.

e. Isa 39:3; LXX; Peshitta adds "to me."

f. Isa 39:5 adds "Sebaoth."

g–g. Ketiv, *yiqqāḥ*, "he will take" (cf. Targum Jonathan, which reads with Ketiv); read with Qere, *yiqqāḥû*, "they (your sons) will be taken."

h–h. MT presents Hezekiah's statement as a question, "Will there not be peace and truth in my days (Hebrew, *hălôʾ im šālôm weʾmet yihyeh bĕyāmāy*)?" whereas Isa 39:8 presents it as an assertion, "For there will be peace and truth in my days (Hebrew, *kî yihyeh šālôm weʾĕmet bĕyāmāy*)." Cf. LXX, "Let there be peace in my days"; Peshitta, "Let there be peace and justice in my days."

The temporal formula *bāʿēt hahîʾ*, "at that time," relates this episode to the preceding unit concerning Hezekiah's recovery from illness. It includes two basic episodes: an account of Merodach Baladan's dispatch of an embassy to meet with Hezekiah due to his illness in vv. 12–13 and an account in vv. 14–19 of Isaiah's confrontation of Hezekiah. The dialogue between Isaiah and the monarch includes three exchanges in vv. 14, 15, and 16–19 that culminate in the prophet's announcement that Hezekiah's goods and sons will be carried off to Babylon.

The present text differs from the parallel version in Isa 39. In 2 Kgs 20:19, Hezekiah concludes by observing, "Good is the word which you have spoken. . . .Will there not be peace and truth in my days?" Hezekiah's question suggests doubt, but the corresponding statement in Isa 39:9, "for there will be peace and truth in my days," removes any hint of doubt by Hezekiah as part of an effort to idealize him in the Isaian narrative. There was apparently some discomfort with this verse in the LXX (see also Peshitta), which omits Hezekiah's question.

The historical background of this narrative conflicts with the claims of the text. The occasion for Merodach Baladan's embassy to Hezekiah is not concern for the ill monarch. Rather, it is based in the alliance between Hezekiah and Merodach Baladan and their plans to revolt jointly against the Assyrian Empire following the battlefield death of Sargon II in 705 B.C.E. and the succession to

the throne by Sennacherib.[33] Hezekiah's willingness to show Merodach Baladan's ambassadors all of his wealth indicates preparation for alliance and revolt.

2 Kings 20:20–21 The Concluding Regnal Formula

20:20 And the rest of the acts of Hezekiah and all his power and all that he
did, the pool and the channel, and how he brought the waters to the city,
are they not written in the book of the Chronicles of the Kings of Judah?
21 Hezekiah slept with his fathers, and Manasseh his son ruled in his place.

The concluding regnal formula includes a notice concerning Hezekiah's
construction of the Siloam water tunnel that channeled water from the Gihon
spring under the city of David and into the Siloam pool within the city walls at
the southern edge of Jerusalem (see also 2 Chr 32:3–4).[34] The Siloam inscription describes how two parties of workmen dug the tunnel.[35]

XXXII. Regnal Account of Manasseh ben Hezekiah of Judah
2 Kings 21:1–18

21:1 Manasseh was twelve years old when he became king, and he ruled
in Jerusalem for fifty-five years. The name of his mother was Hephzibah.
2 He did evil in the eyes of YHWH according to the abominations of the
nations which YHWH expelled from before Israel. 3 He rebuilt the high
places that Hezekiah his father had destroyed, established altars for Baal,
made an Asherah like that which Ahab, King of Israel, made, worshiped
to all the host of heaven, and served them.

4 He built altars in the house of YHWH where YHWH had said, "I will
place my name." 5 And he built altars for all the host of heaven in the two
courts of the house of YHWH.

6 He caused his son to pass through the fire, and he practiced sooth-
saying and divination, conjured ghosts, and multiplied sorcerers to do evil
in the eyes of YHWH to provoke (Him). 7 And he placed the image of
Asherah which he had made in the house where YHWH had said, "Unto
David and unto Solomon his son in this house and in Jerusalem which I

33. Brinkman, "Merodach-Baladan II," 22–27.
34. Y. Shiloh, "Jerusalem," *NEAEHL* 2:709–12.
35. See *ANET* 321; R. B. Coote, "Siloam Inscription," *ABD* 6:23–24.

have chosen from all the tribes of Israel, I place my name forever. **8** And I will not again cause the foot of Israel to wander from the land which I have given to their ancestors if only they will be careful to act according to all that I have commanded and to all the Torah that my servant Moses has commanded them." **9** But they did not listen, and Manasseh led them astray to do more evil than the nations which YHWH had destroyed from before the people of Israel. **10** So YHWH spoke by the hand of his servants the prophets, saying, **11** "Because Manasseh, the king of Judah, has committed these abominations—he has done more evil than all that the Amorites who were before him had done and he also caused Judah to sin with his idols—**12** therefore, thus says YHWH, G-d of Israel, 'Behold, I am bringing evil against Jerusalem and Judah so that the ears of ᵃeveryone who hears about itᵃ will tingle. **13** And I will extend over Jerusalem the line of Samaria and the scale of the house of Ahab, and I will wipe Jerusalem just as one wipes a plate, wiping and turning it over. **14** I will forsake the remnant of my inheritance and will give them into the hand of their enemies, and they shall be spoil and plunder for all their enemies **15** because they have done evil in my eyes and they have been provoking me from the day when their ancestors went out from Egypt until this day.'"

16 Manasseh also spilled very much innocent blood until he filled Jerusalem from end to end apart from his sin which he caused Judah to commit, to do evil in the eyes of YHWH.

17 And the rest of the acts of Manasseh and all that he did, and his sin which he committed, are they not written in the book of the Chronicles of the Kings of Judah? **18** Manasseh slept with his fathers and was buried in the garden of his house, in the Garden of Uzza, and Amon his son ruled in his place.

a–a. Read with Qere, *šōmᶜāh,* "he who hears it," which corresponds with *ʾoznāyw,* "his ears"; cf. Ketiv, *šōmᶜāyw,* "those who hear it."

Second Kings 21:1–18 includes the introductory regnal form in vv. 1–3, the body of the regnal account in vv. 4–16, and the concluding regnal form in vv. 17–18 (contra Long 246–47, 250).

The body of the regnal account in vv. 4–16 provides a detailed account of Manasseh's reign. Although much of this material is formulated in the typical *waw*-consecutive narrative form, a series of conjunctive *waw*s followed by finite verbs in vv. 4, 6, 9, and 16 mark the major subunits of this section in vv. 4–5, 6–8, 9–15, and 16. Each subunit begins with an initial statement concerning actions by Manasseh or the people that serves as the premise for the following statements. With the exception of the last subunit in v. 16, each includes a quote by YHWH that illustrates the narrative presentation of Manasseh as one of the worst monarchs of the Davidic line. This sequence of subunits builds a case for YHWH's decision to destroy Jerusalem and the temple and to exile the people from the land.

The charge that Manasseh is responsible for YHWH's decision to destroy Jerusalem and to hand the people over to their enemies is particularly remarkable.[1] The narrative portrays the issue as an analogy to the destruction of Samaria and northern Israel in v. 13 (cf. 2 Kgs 17), but the analogy does not quite fit. Throughout 1–2 Kings, every northern Israelite monarch (with the exception of Hoshea) is portrayed as having followed in the sins of Jeroboam ben Nebat in causing the people of northern Israel to sin. Second Kings 17 makes it clear that the destruction of northern Israel is a collective punishment for the actions of the kings and the people throughout their history. The same cannot be said for the kings of the Davidic line or the people of Judah. Although many of the Davidic monarchs are condemned, others are judged to be righteous (e.g., Asa, Jehoshaphat, Hezekiah, Josiah, etc.). Even those judged as evil are not held responsible for leading the people into sin. The present text identifies a single generation—and, most pointedly, one man—as the party responsible for a disaster that will be realized some fifty-five years after Manasseh's death. Even the repentance and reforms of Josiah do not overcome the decree.

The issue is complicated by the presentation of Manasseh's reign in 2 Chr 33:1–20. Although the Chronicler's text follows Kings in 2 Chr 33:1–9, the balance of the text differs substantially. Second Chronicles 33:10–17 states that Manasseh was dragged in chains to Babylon to appear before the king of Assyria and that he repented from his evil as a result of this experience. The balance of his reign was spent fortifying Judah, removing the idolatrous cultic installations, and worshiping YHWH. The differences between Kings and Chronicles continue through the reign of Josiah. Second Kings 22–23 portrays Josiah in ideal terms, but 2 Chr 35:20–25 states that Josiah died because he resisted the will of YHWH.

Many interpreters sidestep the significance of this issue. Most accept the charges against Manasseh in Kings as a presentation of the corruption that must have run rampant in his reign. He is seen as a loyal vassal of Assyria, and his idolatry is tied to his subservience to the Assyrians and their gods. But studies by Cogan and McKay challenge the notion that the Assyrians imposed their reli-

1. See Marvin A. Sweeney, "King Manasseh of Judah and the Problem of Theodicy in the Deuteronomistic History," in *Good Kings, Bad Kings* (ed. L. L. Grabbe; JSOTSup; Sheffield: Sheffield Academic Press, forthcoming); Marvin A. Sweeney, *King Josiah of Judah: The Lost Messiah of Israel* (Oxford and New York: Oxford University Press, 2001), 52–63; Francesca Stavrakopoulou, *King Manasseh and Child Sacrifice* (BZAW 338; Berlin and New York: Walter de Gruyter, 2004).

gious systems on subject nations.[2] Others point out that the Chronicler's account is likely based in historical events, particularly since Manasseh would have been brought to Babylon during Babylon's revolt against the Assyrian monarch Assurbanipal in 652–648 B.C.E.[3] Judah was allied with Babylon at the time of Hezekiah's revolt against Sennacherib in 705–701 B.C.E. (see 2 Kgs 20:12–19). Nevertheless, the search for a solution to this dilemma on historical grounds misses an important theological point, namely, our sources disagree with each other on Manasseh's (and indeed on YHWH's) moral character.

Both the Kings and the Chronicles presentations of Manasseh's reign require reconsideration. Whereas scholars tend to approach each narrative with historical questions—did he act as the narrative says he did?—our narratives struggle with a theological question: why was Jerusalem destroyed? Without the ability to trace the corruption of the entire house of David as it did for the northern kings, Kings points to Manasseh as the cause and then portrays Josiah's repentance and death along the lines of King Ahab of Israel.[4] Just as Ahab (and the house of Omri) was condemned for his role in the murder of Naboth, and just as Ahab was allowed the mercy of death prior to seeing the destruction of his house (1 Kgs 21), so Josiah's repentance allowed him a death prior to the realization of judgment against Jerusalem and Judah that was imposed on account of Manasseh (2 Kgs 22–23). The analogy with Ahab is no accident. The portrayal of Manasseh in Kings emphasizes his erection of an asherah like that of Ahab in v. 3 to make the analogy clear. All Davidic kings from Joash ben Ahaziah on were descendants of the condemned house of Omri by virtue of their descent from Athaliah bat Ahab/Omri. The presentation in Kings of Manasseh as the cause for the destruction of Jerusalem reprises the condemnation of the house of Omri for the Judean branch of the Omride line.

The fundamental flaw in this argument remains: why should a later generation suffer for the sins of an earlier time? The Chronicler rejects this notion, and instead judges Manasseh as repentant. Such a stance would explain why his fifty-five-year reign made him the longest-ruling monarch of the Davidic line. It likewise provides an explanation for Josiah's early death: he opposed the will of YHWH. The Chronicler points to the generation that revolted against Babylon as the guilty party. Second Chronicles 36:14 charges the priests and people of the time with polluting the temple, vv. 15–16 maintain that the people mocked the messengers and prophets sent by YHWH to turn them, and v. 17

2. Morton Cogan, *Imperialism and Religion* (SBLMS 19; Missoula, Mont.: Scholars Press, 1974); John McKay, *Religion in Judah under the Assyrians* (SBT 2/26; Naperville, Ill.: Allenson, 1973).

3. E.G., McKay, *Religion in Judah*, 25–26; see Sara Japhet, *I & II Chronicles: A Commentary* (OTL; Louisville, Ky.: Westminster John Knox, 1993), 1002.

4. Sweeney, *King Josiah*, 49–50.

claims that YHWH sent the Babylonians against Jerusalem because of the actions of that generation. Chronicles resolves the moral questions left open by Kings—namely, that Jerusalem was not destroyed for the sins of one man from an earlier generation; it was destroyed for the sins of an entire generation that suffered for its actions.

Both Kings and Chronicles offer an interpretation of history that addresses the problem of theodicy. Both struggle to demonstrate that Jerusalem was not destroyed because YHWH lacked the power or will to defend the city. Instead, both choose to assign responsibility for the destruction of Jerusalem on the people, either Manasseh or the generation that suffered the Babylonian conquest. Each of these narratives is written as a defense of YHWH's righteousness.

The present form of the narrative was clearly edited to serve the purposes of the exilic DtrH. The quotation of YHWH's promises to David and Solomon in vv. 7–8 is particularly noteworthy. Although the promise to choose Jerusalem as a place for the divine name to reside is consistent with the portrayal of the establishment of the house of David and the building of the Jerusalem temple in the DtrH, the promise never to allow the people of Israel to wander from the land is enigmatic when considered in this context. The statement is generally taken as a reference to Israel's sojourn in Egypt beginning in the time of Joseph and Jacob, but the quotation of such a statement in the aftermath of the destruction of northern Israel and the deportation of its population precludes such an understanding. It makes far more sense to view this statement as YHWH's promise not to bring about another calamity such as the destruction and exile of northern Israel, suggesting that this text was composed for another purpose that presupposes Israel's security and Jerusalem's centrality in the aftermath of such an event. Thus, this statement seems to have been composed to serve as part of the narrative concerning Josiah's reign in the Josianic DtrH, which would have portrayed Josiah's reunification of Israel and Judah around the Jerusalem temple as the culmination of Israel's history. The early death of Josiah, the failure of his program, and the destruction of Jerusalem raised the very questions that the present version of Manasseh's reign is designed to answer.

The Chronicler's portrayal of Manasseh's forced appearance before the Assyrian king in Babylon presupposes the Babylonian revolt against Assyria in 652–648 B.C.E. led by Shamash Shum Ukin, the brother of Assurbanipal.[5] The revolt prompted a bloody war that severely tested the power of the Assyrian empire, although it was ultimately put down by the Assyrians and Shamash Shum Ukin was killed. Because Hezekiah had been an ally of the Babylonians during the 701 B.C.E. revolt against Sennacherib, Manasseh would have been suspect. The subsequent death of Josiah, at Megiddo while attempting to stop

---

5. For discussion of the revolt, see CAH 3/2, 149–52.

the Egyptian army from supporting the Assyrians against Babylon in 609 B.C.E. indicates that Assyrian suspicions were well-founded.

Such a clear demonstration of Assyrian power, particularly its willingness to act against those who challenged it, helps to explain Manasseh's submission to the Assyrians during his reign.[6] Assyrian power reached its zenith during the reign of Manasseh.[7] Esarhaddon (680–669 B.C.E.) conquered Egypt by 671 B.C.E. Although Esarhaddon died in 669 B.C.E. while leading an army against Egypt to put down disturbances there, the Assyrian conquest of Thebes in 663 B.C.E. reestablished his successor Assurbanipal's (669–635/627 B.C.E.) control. Subsequent events are murky, but the Assyrian withdrawal from Egypt appears to be motivated not by defeat but by the installation of the Saite dynasty under Pharaoh Psamtek I (664–609 B.C.E.), who acted as an Assyrian ally throughout his reign.[8] Manasseh had to contend with Assyria to the north and its ally Saite Egypt to the south; any moves at independence would have been foolhardy.

The danger of Manasseh's situation is further confirmed by archaeological study of the land of Israel during the seventh century B.C.E. Excavations at Tel Miqne, identified as Philistine Ekron, indicate that the Assyrians turned this city into a center for the production of olive oil that could supply the needs of the entire Assyrian empire.[9] Excavations have also uncovered a large number of four-horned altars that are uniquely identified with Israelite religious practice. Such a find indicates that the Assyrians moved many elements of Israel's population into the Philistine region to work in the olive oil industry. Studies of population density in Judah at this time likewise indicate a shift in the population away from the Judean Shephelah, which bordered Philistia, and into the Judean hill country and the Negev desert, away from the areas of direct Assyrian control.[10] The Negev region sees the buildup of Judean sites—for example, Beer Sheba, Tel Masos, Tel Ira, and so on. Although the purpose of this buildup is debated, the sites protect the trade routes through the Negev that provided access from the Philistine plain to Edom, which in turn connected to the King's Highway that led to Aram and Assyria in the north and the Gulf of Aqaba/ Arabian peninsula to the south. The absence of conflict between Judah and

---

6. Cf. *ANET* 291, 294, which list Manasseh as a loyal ally of Esarhaddon and Assurbanipal.

7. For discussion of the reigns of Esarhaddon and Assurbanipal, see CAH 3/2, 122–61.

8. See also Anthony Spalinger, "Assurbanipal and Egypt," *JAOS* 94 (1974): 316–28; Spalinger, "Psammetichus, King of Egypt I," *JARCE* 13 (1976): 133–47.

9. Seymour Gitin, "Tel Miqne-Ekron: A Type Site for the Inner Coastal Plain in the Iron Age II Period," *Recent Excavations in Israel: Studies in Iron Age Archaeology* (ed. S. Gitin and W. G. Dever; AASOR 49; Winona Lake, Ind.: Eisenbrauns, 1989), 23–58; Gitin, "Seventh Century B.C.E. Cultic Elements at Ekron," *Proceedings of the Second International Congress on Biblical Archaeology, June 1990* (Jerusalem: Israel Exploration Society, 1993), 248–58.

10. Israel Finkelstein, "The Archaeology of the Days of Manasseh," in *Scripture and Other Artifacts: Essays on Bible and Archaeology in Honor of Philip J. King* (ed. M. D. Coogan et al.; Louisville, Ky.: Westminster John Knox, 1994), 168–87.

Assyria during this period suggests that these sites were built and manned by Judah to protect Assyrian trading interests. Willingly or not, Manasseh served as a loyal Assyrian ally.

The Chronicler's account may represent an earlier form of the narrative, particularly since it would have fulfilled Isaiah's prediction in 2 Kgs 20:12–19 that Hezekiah's sons would be taken to Babylon. The Chronicler's portrayal of Manasseh's repentance provided a model for his grandson, Josiah, to emulate in the Josianic DtrH.

[1–3] Manasseh was twelve years old when he began to reign, which means that he was born three years after Hezekiah's revolt against Assyria. Sennacherib claims to have carried off Hezekiah's daughters following his siege of Jerusalem (*ANET* 288), but he says nothing about Hezekiah's sons. Either Hezekiah did not have sons prior to his revolt, or any sons born to him prior to the revolt died. Manasseh's fifty-five-year reign is the longest of all the kings of Judah or Israel. Due to chronological difficulties, many contend that Manasseh ruled only for forty-five years, but there is no evidence for this figure. The name of Manasseh's mother, Hephzibah ("my delight is in her"), appears in Isa 62:4 as a name for the restored city of Jerusalem.

The regnal evaluation of Manasseh compares his actions to the abominations of the nations that inhabited the land prior to Israel (cf. Deut 12:2–3; 12:29–13:1; 18:9–14). His idolatry includes rebuilding of high places to Baal, an asherah like that of Ahab,[11] and his worship of the host of heaven. The reference to Ahab's asherah highlights an attempt to portray the enormity of Manasseh's sins by comparing him to one of northern Israel's most notorious monarchs.

[4–16] The body of the regnal account includes four subunits in vv. 4–5, 6–8, 9–15, and 16. They build the case for Manasseh's sins and for YHWH's decision to destroy Jerusalem.

[4–5] The first subunit emphasizes Manasseh's building of idolatrous altars in the temple and its courts. It begins with the conjunctive *waw* verbal statement *ûbanâ,* "and he built . . ." The quote by YHWH emphasizes that Manasseh thereby defiled the holy temple since the temple is the place where YHWH placed the divine name (Deut 12:4–5). Verse 5 continues with the portrayal of Manasseh's desecration of the temple by noting his building altars for the host of heaven. Some argue that the reference to two courts presupposes the second temple, since there is no mention of two courts in the portrayal of Solomon's temple in 1 Kgs 6–8 (see Jones 597). Second Kings 20:4 indicates that the temple had at least two courts.

---

11. See Judith Hadley, "YHWH and 'His Asherah': Archaeological and Textual Evidence for the Cult of a Goddess," *Ein G-tt allein? JHWH-Verehrung und biblischer Monotheismus im Kontext der israelitischen und altorientalischen Religionsgeschichte* (ed. W. Dietrich et al.; OBO 139; Göttingen: Vandenhoeck & Ruprecht, 1994), 235–68.

[6–8] The second subunit begins with the conjunctive *waw* verbal statement *wĕheʿĕbîr,* "and he caused (his son) to pass (through the fire). . ." (cf. Deut 12:31). The following statements indicate Manasseh's consultation of diviners, soothsayers, and the like, together with his establishment of an image of asherah in the temple (cf. Deut 18:9–14). The quote by YHWH emphasizes that the temple represents YHWH's promise never to remove the people of Israel from the land again so long as they observe the torah given them through Moses. The divine promise to David and Solomon recalls the similar statement by YHWH to Solomon in 1 Kgs 6:11–13. The promise not to allow the feet of the people of Israel to wander from the land *again* presupposes that the people have left the land before. Although such a statement may presuppose Jacob's wanderings, either to Aram (Gen 27–35) or Egypt (Gen 37–50), the exile of the northern kingdom of Israel must be considered (2 Kgs 17), suggesting that the statement was originally composed in relation to Josiah's projected reunification of Israel and Judah around the Jerusalem temple.

[9–15] The third subunit constitutes the key element in the sequence insofar as it announces YHWH's decision to destroy Jerusalem despite the promises articulated in the preceding subunit. This subunit begins with a conjunctive *waw* verbal formulation that focuses on the people's refusal to observe YHWH's torah, *wĕlōʾ šāmēʿû,* "and they did not listen . . ." The following references to Manasseh's leading the people astray provide the occasion for the presentation of a prophetic oracle that states YHWH's intention to destroy Jerusalem just as Samaria was destroyed. The prophets remain unidentified, although they are cited once again in 2 Kgs 24:1–4 when Nebuchadnezzar begins to send raiding parties against Judah.

The oracle in vv. 11–15 is formulated as a prophetic judgment speech.[12] The basis for judgment appears in v. 11, which begins with the formulaic expression *yaʿan ʾăšer,* "because Manasseh, King of Judah, did these abominations. . ." The verse speaks generally about the abominations and evil deeds like those of the Amorites by which he caused Judah to sin (cf. vv. 3, 4–8). The announcement of punishment in vv. 12–14 begins with the typical particle, *lākēn,* "therefore," followed by the messenger formula, "thus says YHWH, G-d of Israel." The formula for judgment, "behold I am bringing evil," appears frequently in Jeremiah (see Jer 6:19; 11:11; 19:3; 42:17; 45:5), although it also appears in DtrH oracles condemning the house of Jeroboam (1 Kgs 14:10), Ahab (1 Kgs 21:21), and Jerusalem (Huldah's oracle, 2 Kgs 22:16, 20). The DtrH sequence of oracles employing this formulation ties this passage to the exilic DtrH, which blamed Josiah's death and Jerusalem's destruction on Manasseh by establishing an analogy with Elijah's condemnation of Ahab and the house of Omri. Just as Josiah was granted an early death because of his repentance so that he would not witness

---

12. See Sweeney, *Isaiah 1–39,* 533–34.

the destruction of Jerusalem, so Ahab was granted an early death following his repentance so that he would not witness the destruction of his house. The oracle establishes the analogy between the destruction of Samaria and the destruction of Jerusalem to show a two-stage outworking of judgment in the exilic DtrH—that is, the punishment of northern Israel provides a model for that of Jerusalem and southern Judah, although their causes are very different. Whereas Israel is punished for the sins of its kings who led the people astray throughout its history, Jerusalem is punished for the sins of Manasseh, who only led his own generation astray. The references to the measuring line of Samaria and the scale of the house of Ahab combine Isaian references (Isa 28:17) with those of the Elijah traditions (1 Kgs 21). The metaphorical language concerning the wiping of Jerusalem like a plate is unique. A second statement of the basis for punishment in v. 15, again introduced by the formula *ya^can ^{>}ăšer*, "because. . . ," employs typical DtrH language concerning the doing of evil and provoking YHWH, although it adds a reference to the exodus from Egypt. The concluding formula, "and until this day," refers to the time of Manasseh, since Josiah repented.

[16] The final subunit sums up the account of Manasseh's sins by noting how he filled Jerusalem with innocent blood. Manasseh's sins included murder, much as Ahab was responsible for the murder of Naboth of Jezreel (cf. Deut 19:10, 13; 21:8, 9).

[17–18] The burial of Manasseh departs from past burials in the city of David. Earlier commentators identify Uzza with King Uzziah, but the name refers to Uzza in 2 Sam 6:8. The burial site may be located at Siloam, across the Kidron Valley from the city of David.[13]

XXXIII. Regnal Account of Amon ben Manasseh of Judah 2 Kings 21:19–26

21:19 Amon was twenty-two years old when he became king, and he ruled in Jerusalem for two years. The name of his mother was Meshullemet bat Harutz from Yotebah. 20 And he did evil in the eyes of YHWH just as Manasseh his father had done. 21 He walked in all the way which his father had walked, served the idols which his father had served, and worshiped them. 22 He abandoned YHWH, the G-d of his ancestors, and did

13. Mordechai Cogan and Hayim Tadmor, *II Kings* (Anchor Bible 11; New York: Doubleday, 1988), 270; Benjamin Mazar, *The Mountain of the L-rd* (Garden City, N.Y.: Doubleday, 1975), 187; cf. David Ussishkin, *The Village of Silwan* (Jerusalem: Israel Exploration Society, 1993), 320–32.

not walk in the path of YHWH. 23 And the servants of Amon conspired against him and killed the king in his house. 24 But the people of the land struck down all those who were conspiring against King Amon, and the people of the land made his son Josiah as king in his place.

25 And the rest of the acts of Amon which he did, are they not written in the book of the Chronicles of the Kings of Judah? 26 And (they) buried him in his tomb in the Garden of Uzza, and Josiah his son ruled in his place.

The regnal account of King Amon ben Manasseh of Judah begins with the typical introductory regnal account form in vv. 19–22, which includes the various details of his age, the duration of his reign, his mother's name, and an evaluation of his name. The body of the account in vv. 23–24 focuses on the coup that led to his assassination and the intervention of the people of the land who put down the revolt and placed Amon's eight-year-old son Josiah on the throne. The concluding regnal formula in vv. 25–26 provides the details of death, burial, and succession.

Many speculate that the revolt against Amon was prompted by an interest in revolt against the Assyrian empire.[1] The account provides no reason to think that Amon veered from the submissive policy of his father. Nevertheless, Assyria was in decline by the time of Amon's reign after having put down the bloody Babylonian revolt in 652–648 B.C.E. Assyria was compelled to put down a revolt by Elam in 642–639 B.C.E., which provided impetus for revolt on the part of the conspirators. The revolt originated in the royal court, but it was defeated by the people of the land, who would have paid the bulk of any tribute owed to Assyria in crops and cattle during this period. Although revolt would have lessened their tax burden, the Judean population of the countryside had to be rebuilt following the devastating invasion of Sennacherib and the subsequent shift in population from the Shephelah to the hill country and the Negev.[2]

[19–22] Amon was twenty-two when he became king, which means that he was born when Manasseh was forty-five. We have no explanation for the delay in producing a son, although male members of the Davidic house could easily have been carried off for service by the Assyrians. Many speculate that Amon's mother, Meshullemeth, must have been Arabian since Jotbah is identified in Num 33:33–34 as a Negev site by Ezion Geber and since the name of her father, Haruz, is known from inscriptions from Sinai, Kihyani, and Philistia.[3] Although

1. Abraham Malamat, "The Historical Background of the Assassination of Amon, King of Judah," *IEJ* 3 (1953): 26–29.
2. Baruch Halpern, "Jerusalem and the Lineages in the Seventh Century BCE: Kingship and the Rise of Individual Moral Liability," in *Law and Ideology in Monarchic Israel* (ed. B. Halpern and D. W. Hobson; JSOTSup 124; Sheffield: JSOT Press, 1991), 1–107.
3. John McKay, *Religion in Judah under the Assyrians* (SBT 2/26; Naperville, Ill.: Allenson, 1973), 24.

some identify Jotbah with the Galilean site, Judah's expansion into the Negev in the seventh century would be well served by a marriage with a Negev-based family. The portrayal of Amon's idolatry fits the pattern of Manasseh, who remained a loyal Assyrian vassal.

[23–24] The revolt against Amon came after a long period of subservience to Assyria—and perhaps to Assyria's ally Egypt—during the reign of Manasseh. The Babylonian revolt of 652–648 B.C.E. and the Elamite revolt of 642–639 B.C.E. exposed Assyria's weakness even though both were successfully put down.[4] The time for revolt was not ripe. Having borne the brunt of Sennacherib's earlier attacks, the people of the land put an end to the coup in the royal court and placed Amon's eight-year-old son Josiah on the throne.

XXXIV. Regnal Account of Josiah ben Amon of Judah 2 Kings 22:1–23:30

22:1 Josiah was eight years old when he began to rule, and he ruled for thirty-one years in Jerusalem. The name of his mother was Yedidah bat Adaiah from Bozkath. 2 He did what is right in the eyes of YHWH, walked in all the way of David his father, and did not turn to the right or to the left.

3 In the eighteenth year of King Josiah, the king sent Shaphan ben Azaliah ben Meshullam the scribe to the house of YHWH, saying, 4 "Go up to Hilkiah the high priest, [a]and let him assign them[a] the money that was brought to the house of YHWH that the keepers of the threshold have collected from the people. 5 He shall allocate it to those appointed to oversee the workers of the house[b] of YHWH, and they shall give it to those who do the work who are in the house of YHWH to repair the damage of the house, 6 to the craftsmen and to the builders and to the masons and to purchase wood and quarried stone to repair the Temple. 7 But the money that is allocated to them shall not be accounted for because they deal honestly."

8 Hilkiah the high priest said to Shaphan the scribe, "I have found a book of Torah in the house of YHWH," and Hilkiah gave the book to Shaphan, and he read it.

9 Shaphan the scribe came to the king, brought word to the king, and said, "Your servants have melted down the money that was found in the house, and allocated it to those appointed to do the work of the house of

4. For discussion of the Elamite revolt, see CAH 3/2, 151–54.

YHWH." 10 And Shaphan the scribe stated to the king, saying, "Hilkiah the priest gave a book to me," and Shaphan read it before the king.

11 And when the king heard the words of the book of Torah, he tore his garments. 12 And the king commanded Hilkiah the priest, Ahikam ben Shaphan, Achbor ben Micaiah, Shaphan the scribe, and Asaiah the servant of the king, saying, 13 "Go, inquire of YHWH on my behalf and on behalf of the people and of all Judah concerning the words of this book that was found, for great is the wrath of YHWH that is kindled against us because our fathers did not listen to the words of this book to do according to all that is written concerning us."

14 And Hilkiah the priest, Ahikam, Achbor, Shaphan, and Asaiah went to Huldah the prophet, wife of Shallum ben Tiqvah ben Harhas, keeper of the garments—she was living in Jerusalem—ᶜin the Mishneh,ᶜ and they spoke to her.

15 And she said to them, "Thus says YHWH, G-d of Israel, 'Say to the man who sent you to me, 16 "Thus says YHWH, 'Behold, I am bringing evil to this place and upon its inhabitants, all the words of the book that the king of Judah has read 17 because they abandoned me and burned incense to other gods in order to provoke me with all the work of their hands. My wrath will burn against this place, and it shall not be quenched.' 18 And to the king of Judah who sends you to inquire of YHWH, thus you shall say to him, 'Thus says YHWH, G-d of Israel, "Concerning the words that you have heard, 19 because your heart has softened and you humbled yourself before YHWH when you heard what I said about this place and about its inhabitants, that it will become desolate and cursed, and you tore your garments and wept before me, and indeed I have heard," oracle of YHWH. 20 "Therefore, behold, I am gathering you to your fathers, and you shall be gathered to your tombs in peace, and your eyes shall not see all the evil that I am bringing against this place."'"'"

And they brought word to the king.

23:1 And the king sent, and all the elders of Judah and all the inhabitants of Jerusalem gathered to him. 2 And the king went up to the house of YHWH, and everyone of Judah and all the inhabitants of Jerusalem were with him, and the priests and the prophets and all the people from the smallest to the greatest, and he read in their hearing all the words of the book of the covenant that was found in the house of YHWH. 3 And the king stood by the column and made the covenant before YHWH to walk after YHWH and to observe His commandments and His testimonies and His statutes with full heart and with full soul to establish the words of this covenant that were written in this book, and all the people entered the covenant.

4 And the king commanded Hilkiah the high priest and the priests of the second rank and the keepers of the threshold to bring out from the

Temple of YHWH all the implements that were made for Baal and for
Asherah and for all the Host of Heaven, and he burned them outside of
Jerusalem in the fields of Kidron, and he carried their ashes to Beth El. 5
And he removed the idolatrous priests whom the kings of Judah had
appointed to burn incense at the high places in the cities of Judah and the
environs of Jerusalem and those burning incense to Baal to the sun and
to the moon and to the constellations and to all the host of heaven. 6 And
he brought the Asherah from the house of YHWH out of Jerusalem to the
Kidron Valley, and he burned it by the Kidron Valley, and he crushed it
to ash, and he scattered its ash upon the grave of the people. 7 And he tore
down the houses of the cult prostitutes that were in the house of YHWH
where the women were weaving coverings[d] for Asherah. 8 And he brought
all the priests from the cities of Judah, and he defiled the high places
where the priests had burned incense from Geba to Beer Sheba, and he
tore down the gate enclosures that were by the entrance of the gate of
Joshua, commander of the city, which was on the left as one enters the
gate of the city. 9 But the priests of the high places did not go up to the
altar of YHWH in Jerusalem, but instead they ate unleavened bread
among their brothers. 10 And he defiled the Topheth which was in the valley of Ben[e]-Hinnom to prevent a man from passing his son or his daughter through the fire for Molech. 11 And he removed the horses which the
kings of Judah placed for the sun from the entrance to the house of
YHWH by the chamber of Nathan Melech the eunuch which was in the
colonnade,[f] and he burned the chariots of the sun with fire.

12 And the altars that were on the roof of the upper chamber of Ahaz,
which the kings of Judah made and the altars which Manasseh made in
the two courts of the house of YHWH the king tore down, and he hurried
from there to throw their ashes into the Kidron Valley.

13 And the high places[g] that were before Jerusalem to the right of the
Hill of Destruction[h] which Solomon, King of Israel, built for Ashtoreth,
the atrocity of the Sidonians, and for Chemosh, the atrocity of Moab, and
for Milcom, the abomination of the sons of Ammon, the king defiled.
14 And he broke down the pillars, cut down the Asherah, and filled their
place with human bones.

15 And also the altar which was in Beth El, the altar which Jeroboam
ben Nebat, who caused Israel to sin, made, also that altar and the high place
he tore down, burned the high place, crushed it to ashes, and burned the
Asherah. 16 And Josiah turned, saw the graves there on the hill, sent, took
the bones from the graves, burned them on the altar, and defiled it according to the word of YHWH which the man of G-d proclaimed when he proclaimed these things. 17 And he said, "What is this marker that I see?" And
the men of the city said to him, "The grave of the man of G-d who came

from Judah, who proclaimed these things which you have done against the altar of Beth El." 18 And he said, "Let him be. Let no one touch his bones," and his bones were left with the bones of the prophet who came from Samaria.

19 And also all the temples of the high places that were in the cities of Samaria, which the kings of Israel made to provoke, Josiah removed, and he did with them according to all the actions that he undertook in Beth El. 20 And he sacrificed all the priests of the high places who were there on the altars, and he burned human bones upon them and returned to Jerusalem.

21 And the king commanded all the people, saying, "Observe Passover for YHWH, your G-d, as it is written in this book of the covenant," 22 for Passover like this has not been observed since the days of the judges who judged Israel and all the days of the kings of Israel and the kings of Judah, 23 but in the eighteenth year of King Josiah, this Passover was observed for YHWH in Jerusalem.

24 And also the necromancers, the soothsayers, the idols, the images, the atrocities that were seen in the land of Judah and in Jerusalem, Josiah burned in order to establish the words of the Torah which were written in the book which Hilkiah the priest found in the house of YHWH.

25 And there was never before a king like him who turned to YHWH with all his heart and with all his soul and with all his power according to the Torah of Moses, and after him there did not arise another like him.

26 But YHWH did not turn from His great anger which burned against Judah because of all the provocations by which Manasseh provoked Him. 27 And YHWH said, "Also Judah I will remove from My Presence just as I removed Israel, and I will reject this city which I have chosen, Jerusalem, and the Temple where I said My Name would be."

28 And the rest of the acts of Josiah and all that he did, are they not written in the book of the Chronicles of the Kings of Judah?

29 In his days, Pharaoh Necho,[i] King of Egypt, came up to the King of Assyria by the River Euphrates, and King Josiah went to meet him, and he killed him at Megiddo when he saw him.[j] 30 So his servants transported him dead from Megiddo, brought him to Jerusalem, and buried him in his grave, and the people of the land took Jehoahaz ben Josiah, anointed him, and made him king in place of his father.

a–a. Hebrew, *wĕyattēm,* lit., "and he shall cause to give them," i.e., "and he shall assign"; cf. LXX, *kai sphragison,* "and he shall seal with approval"; Targum Jonathan, *wîtāqēs,* "and he shall arrange/assign (coins)." Although *BHS* contends that the LXX (and perhaps the Targum) presupposes Hebrew, *waḥātom,* "and he shall seal," the Hiphil form of the verb *ntn,* otherwise unattested in biblical Hebrew (although Hophal forms do occur), would convey the meaning "to assign (funds)."

b. Read with Qere, *bêt,* "house of"; cf. Ketiv, *běbbêt,* "in the house of . . ."

c–c. Hebrew, *bammišneh,* "in the mishneh," literally, "in the second," which refers to a neighborhood in the expanded (hence, second) western region of Jerusalem that Hezekiah fortified in the late eighth century B.C.E. Cf. Peshitta, *bthnnt*ʾ, "in prayer"; Targum Jonathan, *běbêt 'ulpānā',* "in the house of study, in school." Both readings presuppose an understanding of the term *mišneh,* "second, repetition," in reference to its rabbinic Hebrew usage as a reference to repeating prayers or lessons, i.e., prayer and study.

d. Hebrew, *bāttîm,* literally, "houses"; cf. LXX, Targum Jonathan, and Peshitta, which interpret the term in relation to tents, curtains, and hangings.

e. Read with Qere, *ben,* "son of"; cf. Ketiv, *běnê,* "sons of."

f. Hebrew, *bapparwārîm,* an obscure Persian loan word that means "in the columns"; cf. LXX, *pharoumim*; Peshitta, *dbprwr*ʾ; Targum Jonathan, *dibparwārāyā',* which simply transliterate the term because they don't know what it means.

g. Hebrew, *bāmôt,* "high places"; cf. LXX, "house" (Hebrew, *bayit*), which is a minor consonantal variation that may indicate a temple.

h. Hebrew, *mašḥît,* "destruction"; cf. Targum Jonathan, *zêtāyā',* "(Mount of) Olives."

i. Hebrew, *někōh,* "Necho," corresponds to Hebrew, *nekeh,* "lame"; cf. Targum Jonathan and Peshitta, which refer to "Pharaoh the Lame."

j. Peshitta adds "(to meet him), to fight against him, and Pharaoh said to him, 'I have not come against you, turn aside from me.' But Josiah did not listen, so Pharaoh killed him at Megiddo when he saw him there." This addition harmonizes the account with 2 Chr 35:20–22.

The regnal account of Josiah ben Amon of Judah is demarcated by the introductory regnal form in 2 Kgs 22:1–2 and the concluding regnal form, which includes a notice of Josiah's early death at Megiddo by the hand of Pharaoh Necho of Egypt, in 2 Kgs 23:28–30.

The body of Josiah's regnal account in 2 Kgs 22:3–23:27 illustrates the initial righteous evaluation of his reign. The narrative structure of this material highlights Josiah's ambitious program of religious reform and national restoration. It focuses respectively on the actions of a series of major characters in the narrative until it culminates in the account of Josiah's reform program in 2 Kgs 23:1–24.[1] Thus, 2 Kgs 22:3–7 recounts Josiah's instructions to the scribe Shapan ben Azaliah ben Meshullam to commission the high priest Hilkiah to undertake the refurbishing of the Jerusalem temple. Second Kings 22:8 recounts Hilkiah's report to Shaphan concerning the discovery of a book of Torah in the temple during the course of renovations. Second Kings 22:9–10 relates Shaphan's report to King Josiah concerning the discovery of the scroll. Second Kings 22:11–13 relates Josiah's distress on hearing the words of the Torah scroll and his command to a delegation including Hilkiah the priest, Shaphan the

1. Contra Norbert Lohfink, "The Cult Reform of Josiah of Judah: 2 Kings 22–23 as a Source for the History of Israelite Religion," in *Ancient Israelite Religion* (ed. P. D. Miller et al.; Philadelphia: Fortress, 1987), 459–75.

scribe, and others to make an oracular inquiry of YHWH to determine the significance of this discovery. Second Kings 22:14 states that the delegation went
to the home of the prophet, Huldah, wife of Shallum ben Harhas, the keeper of
garments, to make the inquiry. Huldah's oracle follows in 2 Kgs 22:15–20a, in
which she acknowledges Josiah's righteousness, but states that it cannot reverse
YHWH's decree of destruction for Jerusalem because of the people's apostasy.
Huldah indicates that Josiah's righteousness earned him the right to a peaceful
death before the catastrophe strikes. Second Kings 22:20b notes the delegation's report to the king. Second Kings 23:1–24 provides a detailed account of
Josiah's reforms despite the decree of judgment announced by Huldah. Second
Kings 23:25–27 provides a concluding evaluation of Josiah, which simultane-
ously lauds him as Israel's most righteous monarch and attempts to explain why
his early death was unavoidable due to YHWH's decision to destroy Jerusalem,
Judah, and the temple on account of the sins of Manasseh.

The narrative concerning Josiah's reforms in 2 Kgs 23:1–24 likewise displays a unique narrative structure that relates the various elements of the king's
reforms, culminating in the first celebration of Passover in the land since the
days of the Judges. It begins in vv. 1–3 with a brief account of Josiah's assembly of the people and their leaders to renew their covenant with YHWH at the
Jerusalem temple. A detailed account of Josiah's specific reforms then follows
in vv. 4–20, including an overview of reforms in Jerusalem and Judah, followed
by specifications concerning the removal of specific installations, most of
which were built by earlier kings. The overview of his reforms in Jerusalem and
Judah appears in vv. 4–11; a specification concerning his removal of cultic
installations built by King Ahaz appears in v. 12; a second specification concerning his removal of Solomon's cultic installations appears in vv. 13–14; a
third specification concerning his destruction of the Beth El altar established by
Jeroboam ben Nebat appears in vv. 15–18; and a fourth specification concerning his removal of the high places in Israel concludes the sequence in vv. 19–20.
The account of Josiah's celebration of Passover in vv. 21–24 then provides the
capstone for his reforms. This conclusion is appropriate since Passover, with its
emphasis on the exodus from Egypt, recounts the foundational events that saw
the creation of the nation Israel and initiated its journey to the promised land.

The regnal account of King Josiah of Judah functions within the context of
the exilic edition of Kings and the DtrH as a whole to aid in explaining the
destruction of Jerusalem and the Babylonian exile. It thereby serves as a form
of theodicy in that it attempts to defend YHWH's righteousness by placing the
blame for the destruction of the city on the people of Judah themselves (beginning with Manasseh, see 2 Kgs 21:10–15 above), despite the obvious righteousness of King Josiah. The importance of such an attempt is apparent when
one considers that Judah's and Jerusalem's foundational theology emphasizes
YHWH's role as unconditional and absolute author of creation and guarantor

of the security of the city of Jerusalem and the ruling house of David. Obviously, the destruction of Jerusalem presents a major challenge to Jerusalem's "Zion" theology, and the attempt to justify the destruction by citing the people's apostasy emerges as an attempt to modify that theology by asserting its conditional character.

In light of Josiah's righteousness, Huldah's oracle promising him an early death "in peace" indicates a particular difficulty—namely, even Josiah's demonstrable righteousness and repentance does not reverse the divine decree. Josiah's early death is presented as an act of mercy by YHWH in recognition of his unimpeachable character, but it points to the difficulties faced by the writers of this narrative who were compelled to rethink the classical Zion theology in relation to the Babylonian exile. Ultimately, the attempt to wrestle with the theological contradictions posed by the exile forced a rethinking of the notion of repentance as well. The problem is accentuated by the fact that the Chronicler presents a very different understanding of this event. Just as Manasseh is presented as the repentant monarch in 2 Chr 33, so Josiah is presented as the rebellious monarch in 2 Chr 34–35. When Josiah opposes Necho's advance at Megiddo, it is hardly a situation of peace as presupposed in the Kings account, but a situation of war. Necho warns Josiah to cease opposing G-d, who has commanded the Pharaoh to march north (2 Chr 35:21; n.b., the following verse emphasizes that Necho's statement did indeed represent the statement of YHWH). Rather than heed Necho's statement, Josiah joins the battle and is killed by the Egyptian archers (2 Chr 35:22). Altogether, Josiah emerges as the recalcitrant figure, who brings about his own death by his refusal to obey YHWH. The Chronicler thereby avoids the theological and moral problems of the Kings narrative.

The parallels between Josiah's repentance in the Kings narrative and his subsequent fate and those of King Ahab ben Omri of Israel are striking. According to 1 Kgs 21, Elijah condemned Ahab and the house of Omri for Ahab's role in the murder of Naboth of Jezreel and the subsequent appropriation of his land. Although these actions become the cause for the fall of the house of Omri at the time of Jehu's assassination of King Jehoram ben Ahab of Israel and King Ahaziah ben Jehoram of Judah (2 Kgs 9–10), Ahab repents upon hearing Elijah's announcement of judgment against his house. YHWH grants him an early death so that he will not have to witness the demise of his house (1 Kgs 21:17–29); Ahab dies by an arrow in battle at Ramoth Gilead against the Arameans, much as Josiah dies by arrow against the Egyptians at Megiddo (see 1 Kgs 22:29–40). Josiah's repentance and death are modeled on those of Ahab.

This parallel is even more striking when one considers that from the time of King Ahaziah ben Jehoram of Judah, all monarchs of the house of David are also descendants of the house of Omri and therefore subject to Elijah's announcement of destruction. Ahaziah's mother was Athaliah, described once as the daughter of Ahab (2 Kgs 8:18) and once as the daughter of Omri (2 Kgs

8:26). Within the exilic DtrH, the house of David, including Josiah, is condemned to punishment by virtue of its identification with the house of Omri.

The idealization of Josiah begins at the outset of the narrative in 2 Kgs 22:2, which asserts Josiah's righteousness. The evaluation of Josiah as a righteous monarch and the comparison to David is adulatory, but it is hardly all that remarkable. A number of Davidic monarchs, including Asa ben Abijam (1 Kgs 15:11), Jehoshaphat ben Asa (1 Kgs 22:43), Jehoash ben Ahaziah (2 Kgs 12:3), Amaziah ben Joash (2 Kgs 14:3), Azariah/Uzziah ben Amaziah (2 Kgs 15:3), Jotham ben Uzziah (2 Kgs 15:34), and Hezekiah ben Jotham (2 Kgs 18:3) are praised for having done what is pleasing to YHWH, followed in the path of David, or both. It is remarkable, though, that 2 Kgs 22:2 specifies that Josiah did not turn aside to the right or to the left, since this qualification is not applied to any of the kings of Judah. It appears frequently in Moses' exhortations to the people to observe YHWH's Torah in Deut 5:29; 17:11; 28:14, and it is especially noteworthy in the torah of the king, which specifies the ideal monarch is to read YHWH's Torah daily and observe it without deviating to the right or to the left (Deut 17:20). Otherwise, this qualification is applied to Joshua, Moses' successor as leader of the people, in Josh 1:7, and he employs it in his own exhortation in Josh 23:6. The qualification that Josiah did not deviate to the right or to the left thereby indicates that Josiah surpasses all of the monarchs of the Davidic line in his righteousness, and that he is to be compared to Joshua, Deuteronomy's ideal king, and to the Deuteronomic ideal of observance of YHWH's Torah.

The second element in Josiah's idealization is the notice in 2 Kgs 23:25 that there was no king like Josiah "who returned to YHWH with all his heart, and with all his soul, and with all his power according to the Torah of Moses." Such a qualification appears for no other monarch of the Davidic line, including those judged to be righteous, but the language employed again expresses the Dtr ideal of adherence only to YHWH in that it appears elsewhere exclusively in Moses' exhortation to the people to acknowledge YHWH as sole G-d of Israel in Deut 6:5.

Josiah is the ideal monarch who corrects problems introduced by earlier monarchs. His religious reforms focus on a general purification of the temple from the various idols and idolatrous practices that had been introduced over the years. The horses dedicated by the kings of Judah are singled out for special mention (2 Kgs 23:11). He also removed the altars made by the kings of Judah on the upper roof by the upper room of Ahaz (2 Kgs 23:12), the altars made by Manasseh in the temple courtyards (2 Kgs 23:12), and the shrines built by Solomon for Ashtoreth, Chemosh, and Milcom (2 Kgs 23:13). Most importantly, he destroyed the sanctuary at Beth El, established with golden calves by Jeroboam ben Nabat of Israel, in 1 Kgs 12:25–13:34 (2 Kgs 23:15–18), and he destroyed the high places and removed the priests in the region of the former northern kingdom of Israel (2 Kgs 23:19–20). Josiah instituted the first observance of Passover since the days of the Judges (2 Kgs 23:21–23), although the

DtrH indicates that the last noted observance of Passover took place at Gilgal in the days of Joshua immediately after the crossing of the Jordan River prior to the conquest of Jericho (Josh 5). Josiah is noted as the first monarch to renew the covenant in 2 Kgs 23:1–3 in a manner strikingly like Joshua's renewal of the covenant at Shechem in Josh 8:30–35. Joshua is modeled on Josiah, which indicates an attempt to idealize Josiah by presenting him as a righteous monarch who unifies the entire people of Israel around YHWH and Torah, much as Joshua did in the conquest of the land of Israel.[2]

The idealization of Josiah stands in tension with the divine decree of judgment against Jerusalem, Judah, the temple, and even the house of David itself. Such tension signals that the account has been redactionally reworked from a narrative that originally lauded Josiah as a monarch comparable to Moses and Joshua to one that anticipates the destruction of Jerusalem and the Babylonian exile despite Josiah's exemplary righteousness. The exilic reworking of the account is limited to the narrative concerning Huldah's oracle in 2 Kgs 22:14–20 and that concerning Josiah's death in 2 Kgs 23:26–30. These elements are the only indications of Josiah's early death in relation to the upcoming Babylonian exile.

Huldah's oracle presupposes Josiah's idealization in maintaining that he would be granted an early death to spare him from witnessing the upcoming punishment. The formula employed to announce judgment, "Behold, I am bringing evil to this place and against its inhabitants" (2 Kgs 23:16; cf. 23:20), recalls the language employed in the condemnation of the house of Jeroboam ben Nebat, "Behold, I am bringing evil to the house of Jeroboam" (1 Kgs 14:10) and of the house of Omri, "Behold, I am bringing evil to you" (1 Kgs 21:21). Similar language appears in relation to YHWH's decision to destroy Jerusalem on account of Manasseh's sins, "Therefore, I am bringing evil against Jerusalem" (2 Kgs 21:12). It would be a mistake to conclude that the entire account of her consultation is a later addition to the present text. The consultation of the prophet provides a foundation for Josiah's reforms. The oracular statement in 2 Kgs 21:7–8 concerning YHWH's promise to David and Solomon to establish the divine name in the Jerusalem temple and to ensure that Israel would never again wander outside of the land granted to their ancestors seems out of place in a context that calls for the destruction and exile mentioned therein. This oracle—or some version of it—may once have stood as all or part of Huldah's oracle in an earlier version of the narrative. Such an oracle would have signaled the security of Israel, the role of the house of David in overseeing such security, and the role of the temple as the symbol of security and divine presence in the portrayal of Josiah's reign.

Huldah's oracle points directly to 2 Kgs 23:26–30, which reiterates YHWH's decision to destroy Jerusalem and Judah due to Manasseh's sins (vv. 26–27) and

---

2. Richard D. Nelson, "Josiah in the Book of Joshua," *JBL* 100 (1981): 531–40.

recounts Josiah's death at the hands of Pharaoh Necho at Megiddo (vv. 28–30). Neither statement presupposes any portion of the Josiah regnal account apart from Huldah's oracle. Each is written as an appendix to conclude the earlier adulatory narrative concerning Josiah's reform with an account of the monarch's early death and the reasons for it. Apart from vv. 29–30a, vv. 28 and 30b are typical examples of the concluding regnal formula.

[22:1–2] Parallels between the regnal accounts of Jehoash and Josiah suggest that Josiah's account was modeled in part on that of Jehoash, who began his reign at the age of seven (2 Kgs 12:1).[3] Because Josiah was only eight years old, interpreters assume that a regent acted on his behalf until he was old enough to rule himself. The revolt that killed his father originated among Amon's servants, and it was put down by "the people of the land," which would refer to the people of Judah living outside of Jerusalem. Although v. 3 points to Josiah's eighteenth year as the beginning of his reform activities, 2 Chr 34:3 states that Josiah began to seek YHWH in the eighth year of his reign when he was sixteen years old (631 B.C.E.) and that he began to purge Judah and Jerusalem of idolatrous shrines in his twelfth year when he was twenty years old (627 B.C.E.). It is no coincidence that these years mark the death of Assurbanipal, the last great monarch of Assyria, and the beginning of the revolt against Assyria led by Nabopolassar, founder of the Neo-Babylonian Empire.[4]

Josiah's mother, Jedidah bat Adaiah, is from Bozkath, a city in the Judean Shephelah located between Lachish and Eglon (Josh 15:39). The location indicates an interest in securing Judah's borders with the Philistines to protect against Egyptian attack. One of Josiah's wives, Hamutal bat Jeremiah, came from Libnah, located in the same region (2 Kgs 23:31; 24:18).

[22:3–7] The narrative begins with Josiah's eighteenth year (621 B.C.E.), but the Chronicler's account appears to be more historically accurate. The Kings account is motivated by an interest in portraying Josiah's adherence to YHWH's Torah in keeping with the overall theology of the DtrH. It employs the verbs "sent" (Hebrew, *šālaḥ,* "he [the king] sent") and "commanded" (Hebrew, *wayĕṣaw,* "and he (the king) commanded"; see 22:12; 23:4, 21), to indicate a repetitive pattern in the literary structure of the narrative that highlights Josiah's initiative in undertaking the reform process (see also 2 Kgs 23:1).[5] The king sends Shaphan ben Azaliah ben Meshullam the scribe (one of his chief administrators) to the temple to command Hilkiah the high priest to begin the work. Shaphan's sons play important roles in Josiah's administration and in relation to Jeremiah during the reigns of Jehoiakim, Zedekiah, and the Babylonian

3. See Walter Dietrich, "Josia und das Gesetzbuch (2 Reg. XXII)," *VT* 27 (1977): 13–35.

4. For discussion of Assurbanipal's death and the demise of the Assyrian empire, see CAH 3/2, 166–71; Kuhrt, *The Ancient Near East,* 2:540–46.

5. Lohfink, "Cult Reform of Josiah." Although Lohfink's pattern accounts for Josiah's initiatives, the present commentary also takes account of action by the other major characters.

administration of conquered Judah.[6] The language employed for the collection
of the money for temple repair, the designation of the workers, and their honesty draws heavily from 2 Kgs 12:7–17, which suggests that the Josian account
was composed in part on the basis of the narrative concerning the collection of
funds in the reign of Joash.

[22:8] Interpreters identify the Torah found by Hilkiah during temple renovations as a version of Deuteronomy, particularly since Josiah's reforms, including
worship of YHWH at only one location, the prohibition of Canaanite religious
practice, and the demand for a righteous monarch versed in Torah correspond
closely to Deuteronomy's instructions. Although many argue that Deuteronomy
presupposes northern origins, its emphasis on cultic centralization, never a feature of northern Israelite practice, presupposes Judean or Davidic ideology.[7]

[22:9–10] The seventh century B.C.E. saw the emergence of a cash economy
in the Assyrian empire. Although the minting of coins began in Asia Minor during this period, the use of coinage became widespread only in the Persian period.
Silver, gold, and other precious metals were melted down into ingots or other
objects that could be easily transferred for payment.[8] Shaphan's reading of the
Torah before the king anticipates the reading of Torah before the people (see
Deut 31:10–13), and it contrasts markedly with the scene portrayed in Jer 36.[9]

[22:11–13] Josiah tears his garments upon hearing the words of the Torah as
a sign of mourning and repentance for the failure to observe YHWH's Torah. He
immediately commissions a delegation to make an oracular inquiry of YHWH,
presumably to learn YHWH's expectations of Judah now that the Torah is
known. The delegation will be led by the high priest Hilkiah, and it includes
high-ranking officials in Josiah's administration. Shaphan the scribe is previously noted as one of Josiah's chief administrators. Ahikam ben Shaphan lacks
an official title, but later emerges as a leading figure who supports Jeremiah's
pro-Babylonian position during the reigns of Jehoiakim. Achbor ben Micaiah
likewise lacks a title, but may be the father of Elnathan, one of Jehoiakim's officials (Jer 26:22–23; 36:12). Asaiah bears the title "the servant of the king," which
signifies that he is authorized to bear the seal of the king—that is, to sign documents or otherwise act on the king's behalf.[10] Josiah's statement expresses the

6. For discussion of the political role of the Shaphan family in late-monarchic-period Judah,
see Jay Wilcoxen, "The Political Background of Jeremiah's Temple Sermon," *Scripture in History
and Theology* (ed. A. L. Merrill and T. W. Overholt; Pittsburgh: Pickwick, 1977), 151–66.
7. See Marvin A. Sweeney, *King Josiah of Judah: The Lost Messiah of Israel* (Oxford and New
York: Oxford University Press, 2001), 137–69.
8. J. W. Betlyon, "Coinage," *ABD* 1:1076–89.
9. Charles D. Isbell, "2 Kings 22:3–23:24 and Jeremiah 36: A Stylistic Comparison," *JSOT* 8
(1978): 33–45.
10. See Nili Sacher Fox, *In the Service of the King: Officialdom in Ancient Israel and Judah*
(Monographs of the Hebrew Union College 23; Cincinnati: Hebrew Union College, 2000), 53–63.

theological position that Judah's ancestors are responsible for the punishment that might come upon Judah and Jerusalem for failing to observe YHWH's Torah. Although this position is consistent with Dtr ideology, Ezekiel, the Chronicler, and others later maintain that punishment comes only upon the generation that actually commits wrongdoing (see Ezek 18; 2 Chr 36:11–21).

[22:14–20] Rabbinic tradition maintains that Josiah consulted Huldah because a woman would be merciful (*b. Meg.* 14b; Kimḥi; Tadmor and Cogan 283), but modern studies demonstrate that Zephaniah and Jeremiah would have supported Josiah's reform. Women prophets are not unusual in ancient Judah, Israel, and the ancient Near East at large (n.b., Miriam, Deborah, Noadiah). Huldah's marriage to Shallum ben Tiqvah ben Harhas may be of significance since he is identified as "keeper of garments," which suggests some official capacity in relation to the temple. The title appears in relation to a figure associated with the Baal temple in Samaria destroyed in Jehu's revolt (2 Kgs 10:22). She is a resident of the Mishneh—that is, the second quarter of Jerusalem located on the hill immediately to the west of the city of David (see Zeph 1:10). This area was walled in by Hezekiah in the mid-eighth century B.C.E. to accommodate the expanded population of Jerusalem that resulted from the Assyrian invasions of Israel.[11]

Huldah's oracle includes two oracular statements. Together, they justify the destruction of Jerusalem and the early death of Josiah, but their respective forms prompt speculation that the passage has undergone redactional reworking. The first appears in vv. 15–17, which present an oracle that announces divine judgment against "this place"—that is, the city of Jerusalem and its inhabitants, although the reference to "the king of Judah" in v. 16 indicates that it is directed against all Judah as well. The oracle employs the typical language of the prophetic messenger formula, "thus says YHWH. . ." in vv. 15 and 16 to identify the oracular speech as a statement by YHWH. The first appears in Huldah's address to the delegation in which she instructs them to deliver YHWH's oracle to "the man who sent you to me." She later specifies this "man" as "the king of Judah" in v. 18 (see also v. 17). The initial anonymity aids in building up the mystique of an oracular consultation. The oracle appears in vv. 16–17, where it is introduced by a second messenger formula. It is a typical example of a prophetic judgment speech, which begins with an announcement of punishment against "this place"—Jerusalem and Judah—followed by a statement of the reasons for the punishment: the people's worship of other gods. The oracle identifies the Torah found in the temple as the basis for the judgment. The charges

---

11. For discussion of Hezekiah's expansion of Jerusalem, see Yigal Shiloh, "Jerusalem," *NEAEHL* 2:704–9; Nahman Avigad, *Discovering Jerusalem* (Jerusalem: Shikmona and the Israel Exploration Society, 1983), 23–60; Amihai Mazar, *Archaeology of the Land of the Bible, 10,000–586 B.C.E.* (New York: Doubleday, 1990), 417–24.

of abandoning YHWH, following other gods, provoking YHWH, and so forth, are typical of the DtrH.

Huldah's second oracle in vv. 18–20 complements the first by focusing on Josiah and justifying his early death. The messenger formula introduces the oracle per se, which is formulated as an example of a prophetic judgment speech, although it is somewhat awkward both in form and content. It begins with a statement of Josiah's repentance upon hearing YHWH's decree of judgment against "this place." This statement is awkward for two reasons. First, the phrase "(concerning) the words which you heard" is syntactically difficult because it is left without the necessary relative particle. Second, it does not make direct reference to the book of the Torah discovered in the temple, but presupposes the word of judgment delivered against "this place" in vv. 16–17. These examples raise suspicions that the oracle has been reworked. The announcement of punishment in v. 20, with its introductory *lākēn,* "therefore," combines elements of mercy and punishment in its announcement of Josiah's early death. Josiah's early death shields him from seeing the destruction of "this place" announced in Huldah's first oracle. Huldah's claim that Josiah will die "in peace" may represent an element of an original oracle, since Josiah's peaceful death may be questioned. The oracular statement of YHWH's choice of the temple and promise never to cause Israel to wander from the land again in 2 Kgs 21:7–8 may have constituted part of an original version of Huldah's oracle prior to its reworking to account for the destruction of Jerusalem and the early death of Josiah.

[23:1–24] The narrative portrayal of Josiah's reform includes a brief account of Josiah's assembly of the people at the temple to renew the covenant in vv. 1–3, an account of Josiah's reform measures in vv. 4–20, and a concluding account of his Passover celebration in vv. 21–24.

[23:1–3] The people are assembled at the Jerusalem temple to renew the covenant with YHWH. The elders refer to the premonarchic leadership structure of the people, which continued to play a role throughout the monarchic period and beyond.[12] Josiah stands by the pillar at the entrance of the temple, which is the designated place for the kings of Judah and their retinue (see 2 Kgs 11:14; cf. Isa 6). Similar covenant or covenant renewal ceremonies appear in Exod 24:3–8; Josh 8:30–35; Josh 24:1–28; and Neh 8–10 (cf. 2 Kgs 11:17–20).

[23:4–20] The account of Josiah's reforms begins in v. 4 with a notice of the king's commands to purify the temple. As "high priest" (lit., "great priest"), Hilkiah has overall charge of the temple and its priesthood. The reference to "the priests of the second order" (Heb., *kōhănê hammišneh*) refers to priests who serve under the supervision of the high priest, and "the keepers of the

---

12. See R. North, "Palestine, Administration of (Postexilic Judean Officials)," *ABD* 5:86–90, esp. 89–90; Fox, *In the Service of the King,* 63–72.

threshold" (Heb., *šōmĕrê hassap*) refers to those who served in support roles to ensure the sanctity of the temple and its courts.

The purification process begins with the removal of the vessels dedicated to the worship of pagan gods, here identified as Baal, Asherah, and the host of the heavens. The Assyrians did not impose the worship of their own gods on subject peoples, but subjugation to Assyria would call into question YHWH's power to defend the nation. It is therefore hardly surprising that the way would have been open for the introduction of other gods or religious practices into the temple. Such gods and practices likely represent popular religious practice outside of Jerusalem. The burning of these vessels to ash in the fields of Kidron recalls Moses' destruction of the golden calf at Mount Sinai following the nation's apostasy while he received the Torah from YHWH (Exod 32–34). The location in the Kidron Valley makes great sense, since the Kidron separates the city of Jerusalem from the burial sites on the Mount of Olives. The notice in v. 4 that the ashes were carried to Beth El portends Josiah's desecration of the Beth El altar in vv. 15–18.

The term *kōmer,* generally translated as "idolatrous priest," is derived from an Aramaic/Syriac and Akkadian loanword that simply means "priest," but it takes on a connotation of idolatry or illegitimacy in biblical Hebrew. The removal of priests in outlying areas aids in centralizing both worship and the collection of revenues dedicated to temple and state in Jerusalem. There are questions, however, as to how effective or extensive Josiah's efforts might have been. The Judean sanctuary at Arad, which preserves a massebah in its holy of holies, shows no evidence of having been destroyed. The portrayed role of these priests in the worship of sun, moon, stars, and hosts of heaven is consistent with Zephaniah's portrayal of idolatry in Jerusalem and Judah in Zeph 1:4–6 and Manasseh's sins as portrayed in 2 Kgs 21:2–7. The removal of the asherah, the Canaanite fertility goddess generally represented by a tree or bush, would reverse an egregious act of Manasseh that emulated the earlier sins of Ahab and the house of Omri. It is difficult to say whether the reference to the *qĕdēšîm,* "cultic prostitutes," meant that cultic prostitution actually took place in the temple. The term is derived from the root *qdš,* "to be holy," and would thereby designate a cultic role, but the ascription of prostitution to the men (and women) so designated may simply indicate a polemical attempt to defame the cultic functionaries who served in some role in the temple (cf. 1 Sam 2:22). The weaving of robes or other garments for the images of deities is a well-attested practice in ancient Mesopotamia, where it honors the gods and goddesses.[13] The reference to these weavings as *bāttîm,* "houses," is very problematic. Some take it as a textual error, although the term may refer to enclosures formed by curtains or tents within the temple structure.

---

13. See Mordechai Cogan and Hayim Tadmor, *II Kings* (Anchor Bible 11; New York: Doubleday, 1988), 286.

The desecration of high places from Geba in Benjamin to Beer Sheba, which generally defines the southern boundary of Judah in the Negev, indicates that Josiah's measures encompassed the entirety of the kingdom of Judah.

Josiah's attempt to bring the priests of the high places from the cities of Judah to Jerusalem is in keeping with Deut 18:6–8, which allows Levites from throughout the land to serve in the central sanctuary. The dismantling of the high places at the gates of the city would have both religious and political economic significance, since it would have attracted worship and revenue from anyone who entered the city. The reference to the gate of Joshua, governor of the city, indicates that local officials played a role in establishing such high places, perhaps with an eye to enhancing local power and revenue. The refusal of the priests to accept Josiah's offer to move to Jerusalem is generally read as an indication of their idolatrous nature, but a priest who so moved would come to Jerusalem as an outsider (see, e.g., Jer 11–12; 18; 20). Many priests throughout the land would have concluded that their interests would be better served by remaining where they were. Unleavened bread (Heb., *maṣṣôt*) was the standard grain offering in Israelite temples that provided food for the priests (Lev 2:4).

The desecration of Topheth in the Ben-Hinnom Valley removes a notorious cultic site associated with human sacrifice. It is located in the Wadi er-Rababi along the southwestern edge of the city of David, just before the er-Rabbabi meets the Wadi Kidron at En-Rogel.[14] Topheth is derived from an Aramaic term, *tepî* or *tapyā*, "hearth" or "fireplace," but it is pointed with the vowels for the Hebrew *bōšet,* "shame." Biblical sources maintain that child sacrifice was carried out at Topheth together with cultic offerings associated with the dead (see Isa 30:33; Jer 7:31, 32; 19:6, 11–14; 2 Chr 28:3; 33:6 [cf. 2 Kgs 16:3; 21:6]). The identity of the god, Molech, is uncertain, since the name is pointed with the vowels for *bōšet,* "shame." The name may be a derivative of *melek,* "king." Molech is associated with child sacrifice (Lev 18:21; 20:2–5; Jer 32:35; cf. Jer 19:5; Ezek 23:37–39), and is generally believed to be of Phoenician origin.[15]

The use of horse-and-chariot imagery is associated with solar worship, although there are examples of the use of such imagery to depict YHWH in the heavens (Hab 3; Pss 18; 68; 104; cf. Deut 33:2; Judg 5:4–5). Sunrise would be the time for morning service of the temple, and the metaphorical depiction of YHWH's chariot traversing the heavens functions as a liturgical portrayal of the rising of the sun. The location is specified as the entrance to the temple by the chamber of Nathan Melek the eunuch. The term *sārîs,* "eunuch," is typically employed to designate officers or officials and need not be taken as a literal indication that Nathan Melek was castrated, especially since castrated eunuchs would be ritually impure (Deut 23:2).

14. P. C. Schmitz, "Topheth," *ABD* 6:600–601.
15. See esp. G. C. Heider, "Molech," *DDD*[2] 581–85, with bibliography.

[23:12] Verse 12 is the first of four specifications concerning Josiah's reform measures, each of which is introduced by a conjunction and direct object particle, *wĕʾet,* in vv. 12 and 13, or *wĕgam,* "and also," in vv. 15 and 19. The present verse specifies Josiah's removal of cultic installations associated with Ahaz and Manasseh, and thereby presents Josiah as a righteous king who corrects problems introduced by kings of the past. The upper chamber of Ahaz is mentioned in 2 Kgs 20:11. Rooftop altars for the worship of heavenly bodies or Baal are noted in Jer 19:13; Zeph 1:5; Jer 32:29. The altars for the host of heaven placed by Manasseh in the temple courtyards are noted in 2 Kgs 21:5. Josiah's haste to dump the ashes of these installations in the Wadi Kidron signals his piety and enthusiasm for the purification of the temple, although some mistakenly read *wāyyāraṣ* as a reference to crushing these installations.

[23:13–14] Solomon built the high places just outside of Jerusalem for his foreign wives (1 Kgs 11:6–8). The term *har hammašḥît,* "mountain of the destroyer," is a polemical reformulation of *har hammišḥâ,* "mountain of anointing/oil"—that is, the Mount of Olives to the east of the city of David. The gods mentioned here, Ashtoreth of the Sidonians, Chemosh of Moab, and Milcom of Amon, appear in 1 Kgs 11:5, 6–8. The desecration of the masseboth and asherim with human bones ensures that they would remain impure and unfit for worship.

[23:15–18] The DtrH portrays the Beth El altar, established by Jeroboam ben Nebat of Israel, as a site for the worship of the golden calf (1 Kgs 12:26–33), which became the basis for condemning all of the kings of northern Israel. Once again, Josiah corrects the problems introduced by the kings of the past and thereby lays the groundwork for the reunification of Israel and Judah around the worship of YHWH in Jerusalem. The destruction of this altar ground to dust resembles Moses' destruction of the golden calf in Exod 32:20. Josiah's desecration of the altar with the bones from the tombs on the hill overlooking Beth El recalls 1 Kgs 13, which recounts the encounter between the lying prophet of Beth El and the man of G-d from Judah. The man of G-d from Judah announced the desecration of the Beth El altar by Josiah in 1 Kgs 13:2. The Beth El prophet's provenance from Samaria is anachronistic since Samaria was only built by Omri, long after the reign of Jeroboam ben Nebat (1 Kgs 16:24).

[23:19–20] The final specification of Josiah's reforms focuses on his desecration of the high places throughout northern Israel. The pattern follows that of the destruction of Beth El in keeping with the commands of Deut 13:13–19 that call for the destruction of towns that commit apostasy (cf. the annals of Shalmaneser III, *ANET* 277–78).

[23:21–24] Passover, which commemorates the exodus from Egypt and the beginning of the spring harvest, is a national celebration of independence. Josiah's destruction of the altars at Beth El and throughout the rest of Samaria signifies the restoration of Davidic rule over these regions and their independence from Assyria. The Egyptians were Assyrian allies in this period, and may have played a role in ruling Judah on Assyria's behalf. Passover is presupposed throughout Deuteronomy (see Deut 16:1–8). The last reference to the celebration of Passover in the DtrH appears in Josh 5:10–11, in which Joshua and the people celebrated Passover at Gilgal before beginning the conquest of the land of Israel. Josiah's removal of the mediums, wizards, teraphim (a form of family idol; see Gen 31:19; Judg 17:5; 1 Sam 19:13), and images emphasizes Josiah's purification of the land from idolatry (Deut 12:29–13:19).

[**23:25–27**] The concluding evaluation of Josiah draws on Deut 6:5 to portray him as the uniquely righteous monarch in his observance of Mosaic torah (Deut 17:18–20). Verses 26–27 explain the anomaly of Josiah's premature death by pointing to YHWH's decision to destroy Judah, Jerusalem, and the temple because of the sins of Manasseh (2 Kgs 21:10–15; cf. 24:1–4).

[**23:28–30**] The perfunctory reference to Josiah's death hides more than it reveals, prompting charges of "a conspiracy of silence."[16] In contrast to the portrayal of Josiah's death in battle and his refusal to heed YHWH in 2 Chr 35:20–26, the present account simply states that Pharaoh Necho put Josiah to death at Megiddo without explanation. Necho was going north to support the Assyrians in their last stand against the Babylonians, but the failure to provide any indication that Josiah's death took place in battle is an effort to portray his death in relation to Huldah's statement that he would die in peace. Although some speculate that Necho executed Josiah as an unsatisfactory vassal,[17] such claims read more into the text than it will bear.

The people of the land place Jehoahaz, Josiah's twenty-three-year-old second son, on the throne, after Josiah's body is returned to Jerusalem for burial (2 Kgs 23:36). Such a move is an assertion of power by the Judean population, and it suggests that Jehoahaz was likely to continue his father's policy of asserting Davidic independence over a reunited Israel and Judah.

XXXV. Regnal Account of Jehoahaz ben Josiah of Judah
2 Kings 23:31–35

23:31 Jehoahaz was twenty-three years old when he began to rule, and he ruled for three months in Jerusalem. The name of his mother was Hamutal bat Jeremiah from Libnah. 32 He did what was evil in the eyes of

---

16. Stanley Brice Frost, "The Death of Josiah: A Conspiracy of Silence," *JBL* 87 (1968): 369–82.

17. M. Miller and J. H. Hayes, *A History of Ancient Israel and Judah* (Philadelphia: Westminster, 1986), 387–402.

YHWH according to all that his fathers had done. 33 Pharaoh Necho imprisoned him in Riblah in the land of Hamath ªto prevent him from ruling^a in Jerusalem, and he imposed a fine upon the land of one hundred talents of silver and a talent of gold. 34 Pharaoh Necho made Eliakim ben Josiah king in place of Josiah his father, and changed his name to Jehoiakim. He took Jehoahaz, who went to Egypt and died there. 35 Jehoiakim gave silver and gold to Pharaoh, and he assessed the land to give the money at the order of Pharaoh. The people of the land brought silver and gold, each according to his assessment, to give to Pharaoh Necho.

a–a. Read with Qere, *mimmĕlōk,* "from ruling"; cf. Ketiv, *bimlōk,* "when he ruled."

The regnal account of Jehoahaz ben Josiah of Judah lacks the typical concluding regnal account. This deviation may be explained by Jehoahaz's three-month reign and his removal from the throne by Pharaoh Necho, who asserted his control over Judah by replacing Jehoahaz with his older brother Jehoiakim. The account is demarcated by the introductory regnal form in 2 Kgs 23:31–32 and Necho's replacement of Jehoahaz with Jehoiakim in vv. 33–35.

Verses 33–34a employ a *waw*-consecutive syntactical sequence to focus on Necho's actions in removing Jehoahaz and replacing him with Jehoiakim, but shift to a conjunctive *waw* sequence in vv. 34b–35 to provide a notice of Jehoahaz's death in Egypt and Jehoiakim's taxation of the people of the land to pay the indemnity required by Necho.

Although Necho might be presumed to be Assyria's heir as suzerain of Judah following the Assyrian withdrawal from Egypt in 661 B.C.E., it was not until Necho killed Josiah at Megiddo in 609 B.C.E. that Egypt's control over Judah became clear. Necho was unable to intervene directly in Judah's affairs following Josiah's death, because he had to hurry to Haran to support his Assyrian allies in their last stand against Babylonia. Necho arrived too late to have much chance at defeating the Babylonians, and spent several months in Aram in a failed attempt to install his Assyrian ally, Assuruballit, on the throne in Haran.[1]

The people of the land in Judah had installed Jehoahaz, Josiah's second son, on the throne. His mother Hamutal was from Libnah in the Shephelah, which suggests that Josiah married her to shore up his southwestern borders against Egyptian pressure. The anti-Egyptian nature of this branch of the royal house is confirmed by Necho's installation of Jehoahaz's older brother, Jehoiakim, whose mother Zebidah was from Rumah in the north, which suggests Josiah's interests in securing control over northern Israel.

[23:31–32] The introductory regnal formula lists Jehoahaz's age as twenty-three when he ascended the throne, which means that he was two years younger

1. CAH 3/2, 182–84.

than Jehoiakim (cf. 2 Kgs 23:36). His mother's origins in Libnah signal an interest in defending Judah from Egypt. Most identify Libnah with Tell Bornat, about five miles north of Lachish in the Judean Shephelah.[2] Nothing is known of Hamutal's father, Jeremiah. Jehoahaz appears to be a throne name for the new king since Jer 22:11; 1 Chr 3:15 list his name as Shallum. The negative regnal evaluation likely reflects his short three-month reign; he had little time to do much evil while on the throne.

[23:33–35] Pharaoh Necho acts decisively to assert control over Judah. His base in Riblah, located in the Lebanese Beqaʿ Valley about seven miles south of Kedesh on the Orontes River, offered a strategic position for the Egyptians to threaten the south and secure himself from any Babylonian threat to the north.[3] Nebuchadrezzar also used Riblah for his headquarters during the 588–87 B.C.E. siege of Jerusalem (2 Kgs 25:6). Necho's installation of Jehoahaz's older brother, Eliakim (Jehoiakim), ensures that the Egyptians would have a monarch on the throne who would owe his loyalty to Egypt since he was clearly rejected by the people of the land. His family's location in the north offered Necho a base of support against Babylonian attempts to move south. Jehoiakim focused especially on the people of the land in collecting the indemnity imposed on Judah by Necho. Such a move would further distance the new monarch from the people, who had placed his younger brother on the throne, and it would also help to ensure his loyalty to Egypt. The amount of the indemnity, one hundred talents of silver and one talent of gold, is modest when compared to the three hundred talents of silver and thirty talents of gold imposed on Hezekiah (2 Kgs 18:14), but Judah at this time would have been far smaller.

XXXVI. Regnal Account of Jehoiakim ben Josiah of Judah
2 Kings 23:36–24:7

23:36 Jehoiakim was twenty-five years old when he began to rule, and he ruled eleven years in Jerusalem. The name of his mother was Zebudah[a] bat Pedaiah from Rumah. 37 He did what was wrong in the eyes of YHWH according to all that his fathers did.

24:1 In his days Nebuchadnezzar, King of Babylon, came up, and Jehoiakim became his vassal for three years; then he turned and rebelled against him. 2 YHWH sent against him raiding parties of the Chaldeans,

---

2. J. L. Peterson, "Libnah," *ABD* 4:322-23.
3. Y. Kobayashi, "Riblah," *ABD* 5:721.

Aram, Moab, and the people of Ammon, and He sent them against Judah to destroy it according to the word of YHWH which He spoke by the agency of His servants the prophets. 3 Indeed, this happened to Judah on the authority of YHWH to remove it from before His presence due to the sins of Manasseh according to all that he did. 4 And also (due to) the innocent blood that he spilled so that he filled Jerusalem with innocent blood; and YHWH was not willing to pardon him.

5 And the rest of the acts of Jehoiakim and all that he did, are they not written in the book of the Chronicles of the Kings of Judah? 6 Jehoiakim slept with his fathers, and Jehoiachin his son ruled in his place. 7 And the King of Egypt did not again go out from his land, because the King of Babylon took, from the Wadi of Egypt until the Euphrates River, all that had belonged to the King of Egypt.

a. Read with Qere, *zĕbûdâ,* "Zebudah"; cf. Ketiv, *zĕbîdâ,* "Zebidah."

The regnal account of Jehoiakim ben Josiah begins with the introductory regnal formula in 23:36–37. The body of the account, beginning with the syntactically independent statement "in his days (*bĕyāmāyw*) Nebuchadnezzar, King of Babylon, came up . . . ," appears in 24:1–4. The literary structure of this section falls into two basic components. Verses 1–2 focus on a simple report of events during the reign of Jehoiakim, including Nebuchadnezzar's subjugation of Judah, Jehoiakim's revolt against the Babylonians, and Nebuchadnezzar's dispatch of raiding parties from various surrounding nations to harass Judah until he was able to mount a full-scale assault against the tiny kingdom (see Jer 35:1, 11; Zeph 2:8–10; Babylonian Chronicle, *ANET* 564).[1] The second major section in vv. 3–4 provides the primary interpretative framework for the presentation of Jehoiakim's reign. This component begins with the particle ʾ*ak,* "indeed," which introduces the statement in the following verses that the judgment leveled against Judah during Jehoiakim's reign was ultimately caused by the sins of Manasseh. The regnal account concludes with the concluding regnal formula in vv. 5–7.

The account of Jehoiakim's reign displays a marked interest in interpreting the subjugation of Judah by Nebuchadnezzar as an act of YHWH. Such a presentation serves the exilic DtrH by pointing to Manasseh's sins as the cause for the Babylonian exile. The formulation of the introductory regnal account for Jehoiakim's reign in 2 Kgs 23:36–37 is consistent with those of Jehoahaz (2 Kgs 23:31–32); Jehoiachin (2 Kgs 24:8–9), and Zedekiah (24:18–19), which points to the typical compositional pattern of the exilic DtrH.[2] With its focus on the

1. See also D. J. Wiseman, *Chronicles of the Chaldean Kings (626–556 B.C.) in the British Museum* (London: British Museum, 1956).
2. Helga Weippert, "Die 'deuteronomistischen' Beurteilungen der Könige von Israel und Juda und das Problem der Redaktion der Königsbücher," *Bib* 53 (1972): 333–34.

sins of Manasseh as the cause of the Babylonian exile, the exilic DtrH deflects questions concerning the righteousness and efficacy of YHWH by maintaining that the disaster was caused not by divine negligence or impotence but by human—specifically Manasseh's—wrongdoing.[3] The house of David was assured of eternal divine support (2 Sam 7). Although this promise is qualified by the expectation that the sons of David will abide by YHWH's will (1 Kgs 2:1–4; 9:1–5), the assertion of Manasseh's responsibility asserts divine righteousness and power by wrestling with the Davidic/Zion tradition in relation to the harsh realities of the Babylonian exile.

The account is very selective in its portrayal of Jehoiakim's reign. Jehoiakim was placed on the throne in 609 B.C.E. by Pharaoh Necho following his return from Haran, where he had marched to support his now-defunct Assyrian allies. At age twenty-five, Jehoiakim was the oldest son of Josiah, who was bypassed by the people of the land when they placed his twenty-three-year-old brother Jehoahaz on the throne following Josiah's death at Megiddo. The reasons for such maneuvering are not difficult to fathom. Jehoiakim and Jehoahaz are born to different mothers, which in turn points to an important political division within the ruling house of David. Jehoahaz was born to Hamutal bat Jeremiah of Libnah, whereas Jehoiakim was born to Zebudah bat Padaiah of Rumah. The locations of their maternal home cities indicate political motivations. Jehoahaz's family was from Libnah, located in the Shephelah along the southwestern border of Judah with Philistia, which is a key area for the defense of Judah against either Philistia or Egypt. Jehoiakim's family was from Rumah, believed to be located in the Galilee region, which points to its strategic significance for enclosing the territory of northern Israel and for defending the nation against threats from Aram or Mesopotamia. Nebuchadnezzar's later removal of Jehoiakim's son Jehoiachin and his placement of Jehoahaz's younger brother Zedekiah—also born to Josiah by Hamutal bat Jeremiah of Libnah—on the throne indicates an interest in restoring the pro-Babylonian branch of the house of David.[4]

Jehoiakim's pro-Egyptian proclivities are apparent throughout his reign. Egyptian domination of Judah was assured at the outset of his reign. Nevertheless, the unfolding events of the confrontation between Egypt and Babylonia in the aftermath of the Assyrian defeat at Haran very quickly saw a shift in the regional balance of power. There was a great deal of skirmishing and maneuvering between the Egyptians and the Babylonians during the years 609–605, but by 605 things began to change.[5] Following some key maneuvering, Neb-

3. Marvin A. Sweeney, King Josiah of Judah: The Lost Messiah of Israel (Oxford and New York: Oxford University Press, 2001), 31–39.

4. Jay Wilcoxen, "The Political Background of Jeremiah's Temple Sermon," in Scripture in History and Theology (ed. A. L. Merrill and T. W. Overholt; Pittsburgh: Pickwick, 1977), 151–66.

5. See esp. Wiseman, CAH 3/2, 229–33.

uchadnezzar defeated the Egyptians at Carchemesh and Hamath in 605, forcing Necho to withdraw from western Asia. Shortly thereafter, Nebopolassar died, and Nebuchadnezzar became king of Babylon. Jehoiakim became a Babylonian vassal in approximately 604 B.C.E. in the aftermath of the Egyptian defeat as Nebuchadnezzar consolidated his hold over the region, but Jehoiakim's loyalty to the Egyptians remained strong. In 601 B.C.E., a battle between the Egyptians and Babylonians near Pelesium along the highway between Egypt and Gaza saw massive casualties for both sides and forced Nebuchadnezzar to withdraw to Babylon to rebuild his forces. Jehoiakim apparently considered this to be a Babylonian defeat, despite the inability of the Egyptians due to heavy losses to move their forces beyond Gaza to reclaim the region. While Nebuchadnezzar rebuilt his forces between 601 and 598, he sent raiding parties to harass Judah. By 598, Nebuchadnezzar laid siege to Jerusalem to force Judah to end its revolt. Jehoiakim died during the siege at the age of thirty-six. His eighteen-year-old son Jehoiachin replaced him on the throne for three months before his own capitulation and deportation to Babylon in 597 B.C.E.

[23:36–37] At age twenty-five, Jehoiakim is two years older than his twenty-three-year-old half-brother Jehoahaz (23:31), which indicates that the people of the land bypassed him to place Jehoahaz on the throne. Jehoiakim is clearly pro-Egyptian, as indicated by his revolt against Nebuchadnezzar in 601 B.C.E. The debate as to whether Judah should ally with Babylon or Egypt is well represented in Jeremiah, who consistently called for a pro-Babylonian policy like that of Josiah, Jehoahaz, and later Zedekiah (see Jer 27–29; cf. Jer 21:8–10; 38:1–3).[6]

Jehoiakim's eleven-year reign ended in 598 B.C.E. during the Babylonian siege of the city following his revolt against Nebuchadnezzar in 601 B.C.E. Because he was only thirty-six years old when he died, speculation has been rampant that he was assassinated. Such a contention is particularly attractive when one considers the disastrous results of his confrontation with the Babylonians. Jeremiah's contention that his burial would be like that of an ass (Jer 22:18–19) suggests the depth of opposition to Jehoiakim.

Jehoiakim's mother, Zebudah bat Padaiah, is from the city of Rumah. Rumah is generally identified with a location in the Galilee region based on Josephus's mention of two Galileans from the city who attacked the Romans (*J.W.* 3.7.21). The town is identified with Abimelech's home town of Arumah (Judg 9:41). Some identify it with Khirbet er-Rumeh to the north of Sepphoris, mentioned as Arumah in the annals of Tiglath-pileser III (*ANET* 283), and others identify it with a site known as Rumah in the Netophah Valley.[7]

[24:1–4] The body of the account focuses on Nebuchadnezzar's invasion of Judah in 598 B.C.E., when he forced the capitulation of Jerusalem following

---

6. Wilcoxen, "Political Background."
7. S. A. White, "Rumah," *ABD* 5:842.

Jehoiakim's death. The account presents Nebuchadnezzar's harassment and invasion of Judah as an act of YHWH prompted by the sins of Manasseh (2 Kgs 21:10–15; 23:26–27). Such an explanation is an example of theodicy in which the exilic DtrH defends YHWH's righteousness and power by claiming that Jerusalem and the temple were destroyed on account of Manasseh's sins rather than YHWH's negligence or impotence. This view is in keeping with the Dtr view of covenant in which human beings have the responsibility to observe YHWH's will in return for YHWH's assurances of well-being in the land. Such a contention creates tremendous theological difficulties insofar as it attempts to explain disaster by claiming that the victims of disaster must have sinned.

[24:5–7] The notice of Jehoiakim's death conflicts with Jeremiah's portrayal of Jehoiakim's burial like that of an ass (Jer 22:19). Jeremiah's statement, however, does not report Jehoiakim's burial; rather, it anticipates Jehoiakim's burial and does not portray what actually took place. The concluding notice of Pharaoh's inability to move out of his own land recognizes Nebuchadnezzar's conquest of the region from the river of Egypt—that is, the Wadi el-Arish (1 Kgs 8:65) that marked the boundary between Egypt and Syria-Israel—to the River Euphrates. This encompasses the territory once controlled by the house of David (1 Kgs 5:1; 8:65; cf. 2 Sam 8:3).

XXXVII. Regnal Account of Jehoiachin ben Jehoiakim of Judah
2 Kings 24:8–17

24:8 Jehoiachin was eighteen years old when he began to rule, and he ruled for three months in Jerusalem. The name of his mother was Nehushta bat Elnathan from Jerusalem. 9 He did what was wrong in the eyes of YHWH according to all that his father had done.

10 At that time, the servants of Nebuchadnezzar, King of Babylon, came up[a] to Jerusalem, and the city came under siege. 11 And Nebuchadnezzar, King of Babylon, came against the city, and his servants were besieging it. 12 Jehoiachin, King of Judah, came out against[b] the King of Babylon, he and his mother and his servants and his commanders and his eunuchs, and the King of Babylon took him in the eighth year of his reign. 13 He brought out from there all the treasuries of the house of YHWH and the treasuries of the house of the King, and he cut up all the vessels of gold which Solomon, King of Israel, had made in the Temple of YHWH just as YHWH had said.

14 He exiled all Jerusalem and all the commanders and all the soldiers—exiling ten[c] thousand—and every artisan and every metal worker; there was no one except for the poor of the people of the land. 15 He exiled Jehoiachin to Babylon, and the mother of the king and the wives of the king and his eunuchs and the leaders[d] of the land he led into exile from Jerusalem to Babylon. 16 And all the men of the army—seven thousand—and artisans and metal workers—one thousand—all of them warriors trained for battle, and the King of Babylon brought them into exile in Babylon. 17 And the King of Babylon made Mattaniah, his uncle, to rule in his place, and he changed his name to Zedekiah.

a. Read with Qere, *ʿālû*, "(they, i.e., the servants of Nebuchadnezzar) went up"; cf. Ketiv, *ʿālâ*, "(he, i.e., Nebuchadnezzar) went up."

b. MT, *ʿal*, "against," which suggests that Jehoiachin confronted Nebuchadnezzar; cf. LXX and Peshitta, which presuppose *ʾel*, "unto," to suggest that Jehoiachin simply surrendered.

c. Read with Qere, *ʿăśeret*, "ten" (feminine grammatical form required by the context); cf. Ketiv, *ʿăśārâ*, "ten" (masculine grammatical form).

d. Qere, *ʾêlê*, "rams of. . . ," metaphorically, "leaders of . . ."; cf. Ketiv, *ʾûlê*, "leaders of. . ."

The regnal account of King Jehoiachin ben Jehoiakim of Judah begins with the introductory regnal form in vv. 8–9. The body of the account follows in vv. 9–17 with a two-part portrayal of the brief three-month reign of the young monarch and his exile to Babylon together with a significant number of the leading figures and artisans of Jerusalem. The body of the account is distinguished formally by the syntactically independent introductory temporal formula *bāʿēt hahîʾ*, "in that time," which introduces the *waw*-consecutive verbal account in vv. 7–13 of Nebuchadnezzar's siege of Jerusalem in 598–597 B.C.E. and Jehoiachin's capitulation. The second portion in vv. 14–17 begins with a converted perfect verbal form, *wĕhiglâ*, "and he exiled," which presents a *waw*-consecutive verbal account of the thousands of people that Nebuchadnezzar exiled to Babylon together with a statement of his installation of Zedekiah ben Josiah, the uncle of King Jehoiachin, as king of Judah. The account lacks the concluding regnal formula since Jehoiachin's reign ended in his exile rather than in his death. The notice in 2 Kgs 25:27–30 of his release during the reign of the Babylonian monarch Evil Merodach indicates that he was still alive at the conclusion of the Kings presentation of Israel's and Judah's history.

Although the account of Jehoiachin's reign portrays Nebuchadnezzar as the primary actor in the exile of the Judean monarch, brief references to YHWH in vv. 9 and 13 indicate the DtrH viewpoint that Nebuchadnezzar acts on behalf of YHWH. These statements present the basic evaluation of Jehoiachin as having done wrong in the eyes of YHWH and the contention that Nebuchad-nezzar's appropriation of gold vessels from the temple and royal treasuries was in accordance with YHWH's word. Such a perspective continues the portrayal of YHWH's role in bringing about the Babylonian invasion as an act of pun-ishment for the sins of Manasseh (2 Kgs 24:3–4). Although Jehoiachin has lit-tle to do with these sins—and his brief reign provided little opportunity to commit many sins on his own account—the DtrH chooses this strategy to explain the Babylonian exile as an expression of YHWH's power and righ-teousness. Contemporary discussion of the Shoah points to the theological flaws in such a contention—namely, Jehoiachin and his generation are punished not for their own wrongdoing but for the sins of a past generation.

The narrative gives great attention to the gold vessels that were taken from the temple and royal treasury, emphasizing that the temple vessels had been made by Solomon at the foundation of the temple (see 1 Kgs 6–7, esp. 7:48–51). Note YHWH's statement to Solomon in his second vision in 1 Kgs 9:1–9 that the house of David and the temple would be swept away if the kings of Judah did not observe YHWH's expectations. Although this statement now antici-pates the destruction of the temple in 2 Kgs 25, the initial exile in the time of Jehoiachin is the first step in the realization of that destruction. Note also Isa-iah's statement to Hezekiah at the time of the king's reception of the Babylo-nian embassy in 2 Kgs 20:12–19 that the contents of the royal treasuries would one day be carried off to Babylon together with Hezekiah's sons.

Such theological perspectives are consistent with the concerns of the exilic DtrH, which presents the Babylonian exile as an act of YHWH intended to pun-ish the sins of Manasseh. The formulation of the introductory regnal account for Jehoiachin's reign in vv. 8–9 is consistent with the formulations of similar introductory regnal forms for Jehoahaz (2 Kgs 23:32); Jehoiakim (2 Kgs 23:37); and Zedekiah (2 Kgs 24:19).[1] They also correspond to the introductory regnal formulas for Manasseh (2 Kgs 21:2; cf. 21:15), Amon (2 Kgs 21:20), and all of the kings of northern Israel.[2] This pattern points to the influence of the exilic DtrH in the accounts of the reigns of Manasseh and Amon and its attempt to establish a correlation between the northern Israelite kings, who are universally condemned in the DtrH, and the last kings of Judah.

Nebuchadnezzar's invasion of Judah and removal of Jehoiachin is noted in the Babylonian Chronicle, which states that the king of Akkad—that is, Neb-uchadnezzar, king of Babylon—besieged "the city of Judah" in the seventh year of his reign, and replaced the reigning monarch with "a king of his own lik-

1. Helga Weippert, "Die 'deuteronomistischen' Beurteilungen der Könige von Israel und Juda und das Problem der Redaktion der Königsbücher," *Bib* 53 (1972): 333–34.

2. Marvin A. Sweeney, *King Josiah of Judah: The Lost Messiah of Israel* (Oxford and New York: Oxford University Pres, 2001), 36.

ing."[3] Babylonian records shed some light on Jehoiachin's exile. Cuneiform tablets dated from the tenth to the thirty-fifth year of Nebuchadnezzar list rations distributed to various foreign exiles.[4] One of the texts dated to Neb-uchadnezzar's thirteenth year (592 B.C.E.) notes the large quantity of rations for King Yaku-kinu of the land of Yahudu, that is, King Jehoiachin of the land of Judah, and his five sons.

[24:8–9] Jehoiachin is the formal throne name for the monarch. Jeremiah 24:1; 28:4; 29:2 identify him as Jeconiah, and Jer 22:24, 28; 37:1 identify him by the abbreviated form of the name as Coniah. Verse 8 states that Jehoiachin was eighteen years old at the beginning of his reign, but 2 Chr 36:9 claims that he was eight. Although the grounds for determining the correct age are diffi-cult, Ezekiel's elegy for Jehoiachin in Ezek 19:5–9 suggests that he was older than eight. Jehoiachin's grandfather Elnathan may be the same Judean official who was sent to recover the prophet Uriah (Jer 26:22) and who protested Jehoiakim's burning of Jeremiah's scroll (Jer 36:25). The formulation of the introductory regnal formula resembles those for Jehoahaz, Jehoiakim, and Zedekiah, and thereby serves as a mark of the exilic DtrH.

[24:10–17] Although the present text states that Jehoiachin's surrender took place in Nebuchadnezzar's eighth year (597 B.C.E.), Jer 52:28 agrees with the Babylonian Chronicle that it took place in Nebuchadnezzar's seventh year, 598 B.C.E.[5] The date mentioned in the present text may represent an alternative Judean reckoning from the time that Nebuchadnezzar took command of the army prior to his father's death and his own accession to the throne.

Verses 14–17 provide a summation of the people exiled to Babylon and the installation of Zedekiah as a replacement for Jehoiachin. Verse 14 begins by stat-ing that Nebuchadnezzar carried off all Jerusalem. Although this is an exaggera-tion, it expresses the fact that Nebuchadnezzar carried off most of Jerusalem's leading figures and artisans. The officials, military men, and artisans would have been put to work in service of the Babylonian government (cf. Dan 1–6). Like-wise, northern Israelite charioteers served in the Assyrian army following Assyria's conquest of northern Israel. The numbers of exiles, 10,000 in v. 14 and 7,000 officers and 1,000 artisans in v. 17, conflict with the 3,023 mentioned in Jer 52:28. Both texts point to relatively large numbers of the leading people of Jerusalem and perhaps Judah. Insofar as Jer 52:28 mentions only 832 deportees in 587 B.C.E. and 745 in 582 B.C.E., Jehoiachin's deportation constitutes the bulk

3. *ANET* 564; D. J. Wiseman, *Chronicles of the Chaldean Kings (626–556 B.C.) in the British Museum* (London: British Museum, 1956), 72.

4. William Foxwell Albright, "King Jehoiachin in Exile," *BA* 5 (1942): 49–55; E. F. Weidner, "Jojachin, König von Juda, in Babylonischen Keilschrifttexten," *Mélanges syriens offerts à M. René Dussard* (Paris: P. Geuthner, 1939), 2.925–26.

5. *ANET* 564; Wiseman, *Chronicles*, 72.

of the Babylonian exile. The lower numbers for the later figures indicate that the Babylonians had already exiled the key figures, and were more intent on killing off the resistance to their rule than in negotiating a surrender.

Mattaniah ben Josiah, Jehoiachin's uncle whom the Babylonians renamed Zedekiah, is a puppet ruler for the Babylonians. The change in name highlights his vassal status.

XXXVIII. Regnal Account of Zedekiah ben Josiah of Judah and the Consequences of His Reign: The Exile of Jerusalem and Judah 2 Kings 24:18–25:30

24:18 Zedekiah was twenty-one years old when he began to rule, and he ruled eleven years in Jerusalem. The name of his mother was Hamutal[a] bat Jeremiah from Libnah. 19 He did what was wrong in the eyes of YHWH according to all that Jehoiakim had done 20 for the anger of YHWH was against Jerusalem and Judah until He cast them out from before His presence when Zedekiah rebelled against the King of Babylon.

25:1 In the ninth year of his reign, in the tenth month on the tenth day to the month that Nebuchadnezzar, King of Babylon, he and all his army, came against Jerusalem and encamped against it, and they built against it bulwarks all around. 2 The city was under siege until the eleventh year of King Zedekiah.

3 On the ninth of the month, the famine had seized the city and there was no food for the people of the land. 4 And the city was breached, and all the men of war (went out) that night by way of the gate between the walls by the garden of the king. The Chaldeans were all around the city, and he went in the direction of the Arabah. 5 The Chaldean army pursued after the King, and they caught him in the Araboth of Jericho, and all his army was scattered from him. 6 And they captured the King, brought him to the King of Babylon at Riblah, and sentenced him. 7 They slaughtered the sons of Zedekiah before his eyes, and he blinded the eyes of Zedekiah, bound him in chains, and brought him to Babylon.

8 In the fifth month, on the seventh[b] of the month, it was the nineteenth year of King Nebuchadnezzar, King of Babylon, Nebuzaradan, Chief of the Guards[c], Servant[d] of the King of Babylon, came to Jerusalem. 9 He

burned the house of YHWH, the house of the King, and all the houses of Jerusalem; ᶜevery house of a nobleᶜ he burned with fire. 10 All the army of the Chaldeans that was with the Chief of the Guards pulled down the walls of Jerusalem round about. 11 And the rest of the people who were left in the city and the deserters who went over to the King of Babylon and the rest of the population, Nebuzaradan, Chief of the Guards, exiled. 12 But the poorest of the land, the Chief of the Guards left for vine dressers and tillers. 13 And the columns of bronze which were before the house of YHWH, the Chaldeans broke down, and they carried their bronze to Babylon. 14 And they took the pots and the scrapers and the snuffers and the ladles and all the vessels of bronze with which they would serve. 15 And the fire pans and sprinkling bowls that were each made of gold or silver, the Chief of the Guards took. 16 And the two columns, the one sea, and the stands that Solomon had made for the house of YHWH—all these vessels were not weighed for bronze. 17 Eighteen cubits was the height of one column, and the capital upon it was bronze, and the height of the capital was three cubits,ᶠ and meshwork and pomegranates were upon the capital round about—the whole was bronze—and the second column was like these together with the meshwork. 18 And the Chief of the Guards took Seraiah the high priest and Zephaniah the deputy priest and three watchers of the threshold. 19 And from the city he took one eunuch who was appointed over the men of war, and five men from those who served before the King who were found in the city, and the scribe, the commander of the army, who drafted the people of the land, and sixty men from the people of the land who were found in the city. 20 Nabuzaradan, Chief of the Guards, took them and brought them before the King of Babylon at Riblah. 21 The King of Babylon struck and killed them in Riblah in the land of Hamath, and he exiled Judah from upon its land.

22 And the people who were left in the land of Judah, whom Nebuchadnezzar, King of Babylon, allowed to remain, he appointed over them Gedaliah ben Ahikam ben Shaphan. 23 When all the commanders of the armies, they and the men, heard that the King of Babylon had appointed Gedaliah, they came to Gedaliah at Mizpah, including Ishmael ben Nathaniah, Yohanan ben Qareh, Saraiah ben Tanhumcth the Netophite, and Yaazniah ben Ha-Maachatite, they and their men. 24 Gedaliah swore to them and to their men and said to them, "Do not fear ᵍthe servants ofᵍ the Chaldeans! Stay in the land and serve the King of Babylon, and it will be well for you!"

25 And in the seventh month, Ishmael ben Nathaniah ben Elishama, of royal lineage, and ten men with him, struck down Gedaliah and he died, and the Judeans and the Chaldeans who were with him in Mizpah. 26 And

all the people, young and old, and the commanders of the armies, rose
and went to Egypt because they feared the Chaldeans.

27 And in the thirty-seventh year of the exile of Jehoiachin, King of
Judah, in the twelfth month, on the seventh day of the month, Evil Merodach, King of Babylon, released in the year of his reign Jehoiachin, King
of Judah, from prison. 28 He spoke with him good things and placed his
chair above the chair of the kings who were with him in Babylon. 29 He
changed his prison garments and ate bread always before him all the days
of his life. 30 And his allotment, a continuous allotment, was given to him
from the King every day for all the days of his life.

a. Read with Qere, *hămûṭal,* "Hamutal"; cf. Ketiv, *hămîṭal,* "Hamital"; see also LXX.

b. Cf. Peshitta and Lucianic LXX, which read "ninth (day)," presupposing the Jewish
observance of the ninth day of the month of Av as the traditional date for the destruction
of the temple; cf. Jer 52:12, "tenth (day)."

c. Hebrew, *rab ṭabbāḥîm,* "chief of the guards." The root *ṭbḥ* means "to butcher,
slaughter"; cf. LXX, *ho archimageiros,* "the chief cook"; Targum Jonathan, *qaṭûlāyā*,
"the chief of the killers."

d. MT, *ʿebed,* "servant"; cf. LXX, *ho archimageiros hestos enopion,* "the chief cook who
was before (the king of Babylon)," which could presuppose Hebrew, *ʿomed,* "standing."

e–e. MT, *wĕʾet-kol bêt gādôl,* lit., "and every house of a great one (he burned with
fire)"; cf. LXX, which takes *gādôl* as the subject of the following verb, "and every house
the chief cook burned with fire"; Peshitta, "and all the houses of the princes (*drwrbyʾ*)
he burned with fire"; Targum Jonathan, "and all the houses of the princes (*rabrĕbāyāʾ*)
he burned with fire."

f. Read with Qere, *ʾammôt,* "cubits"; cf. Ketiv, *ʾammâ,* "cubit."

g–g. MT, *mēʿabdê,* "from the servants of (the Chaldeans)"; cf. LXX, *parodon,* "(the) pas-
sage/incursion of (the Chaldeans)," which seems to presuppose *mēʿabôr,* "from (the) passage of (the Chaldeans)," a reading of *mēʿabôd,* "from (the) service of (the Chaldeans),"
in Jer 40:9.

The regnal account of Zedekiah ben Josiah of Judah varies from the standard regnal form because it constitutes the concluding unit of the books of
Kings and of the entire DtrH. Because Jerusalem was destroyed during his reign
and because no Davidic king succeeded him on the throne, no concluding regnal formula appears. Instead, the unit contains a standard introductory regnal
formula in 2 Kgs 24:18–20 and the body of the account in 2 Kgs 25:1–30. The
body of the account includes accounts of the events of Zedekiah's reign; the
Babylonian deportation of leading figures from Jerusalem; the appointment and
assassination of the governor of the land under Babylonian rule; and the release
of Jehoiachin ben Jehoiakim, the last true monarch of Judah, from captivity by
the Babylonian king Evil Merodach.

The introductory regnal account in 2 Kgs 24:18–20 includes standard information concerning Zedekiah's age at accession, the duration of his reign, the

name of his mother, and an evaluation of his reign. The addition of an explanatory statement introduced by causative *kî* that YHWH's wrath was directed against Jerusalem and Judah at the time of Zedekiah's rebellion against Babylon aids in explaining the negative evaluation of his reign.

The body of Zedekiah's regnal account in 2 Kgs 25:1–30 is complicated due to his exit from the scene in v. 7, but the additional material in vv. 8–30 explains the consequences of his reign. The basic literary structure of this subunit appears in three chronological statements, each introduced by the *waw*-consecutive *wayĕhî,* "and it came to pass," in vv. 1, 25, and 27. These three subunits deal respectively with Nebuchadnezzar's siege and capture of Jerusalem in vv. 1–24, the assassination of Gedaliah ben Ahikam ben Shaphan in vv. 25–26, and the release of King Jehoiachin ben Jehoiakim from prison in vv. 27–30.

The first major subunit begins in v. 1 with the chronological statement, "and it came to pass in the ninth year of his reign, in tenth month, in the tenth of the month. . . ," which introduces both the account of Zedekiah's reign in general and the initial account of Nebuchadnezzar's siege of the city. The account of the siege and its immediate consequences continues through the eleventh year of Zedekiah's reign when the city was finally taken (see v. 11). Following the initial statements concerning the siege in vv. 1–2, two further subunits, each introduced by a chronological reference to the month of the eleventh year, then lay out the various events that began with and followed the Babylonian capture of Jerusalem. The first begins in v. 3 with a simple conjunctive reference to the ninth of the month that omits reference to the month of the year—namely, "and in the ninth of the month. . . ," suggesting that the event took place in the first month of Zedekiah's eleventh year. This subunit comprises vv. 3–7, and it includes accounts of the Babylonian capture of Jerusalem, the escape of Zedekiah and his officers, Zedekiah's capture by Jericho, his sentencing at Riblah (including the execution of his sons and his own blinding), and his deportation to Babylon. The second subunit appears in vv. 8–24, which begin with a *waw*-conjunctive reference to the seventh day of fifth month: "and in the fifth month, on the seventh of the month . . ." This subunit then relates the deportation of leading figures from Jerusalem, together with the Babylonian appropriation of temple fixtures and vessels made of bronze and gold, the execution of a number of leading figures at Riblah, and the appointment of Gedaliah ben Ahikam ben Shaphan as governor of the land.

Verses 25–26 recount the assassination of Gedaliah ben Ahikam ben Shaphan, who had been appointed by the Babylonians as governor of the land in the aftermath of the deportation of Zedekiah, and vv. 27–30 recount the release of Jehoiachin from prison and the allotment of rations to support him as he continued to live in Babylon during the reign of Evil Merodach.

As the concluding unit of the book of Kings, the account of Zedekiah's reign holds special significance. It supports the DtrH viewpoint that the destruction of Jerusalem, the demise of the temple, and the exile of the people is the result of YHWH's condemnation of the sins of Manasseh (2 Kgs 21:10–15). This perspective is made clear in 2 Kgs 24:20, which pointedly refers to the anger of YHWH following the negative evaluation of Zedekiah. The key statements concerning the burning of the temple, the royal palace, and the houses of the city and the destruction of the city walls appear in 2 Kgs 25:9–10. The detailed account of the temple fixtures and vessels dismantled and carried off by the Babylonians offers a striking contrast with the detailed account of Solomon's efforts to build the temple in 1 Kgs 6–8. By harking back to the temple building account, the narrative emphasizes the sense of reversal from the glory days of Solomon to the present reality of a devastated city and a population now exiled from the land. The unit does not limit itself to the portrayal of the destruction of the city and the exile of the people; it also turns to the assassination of Gedaliah and the release of Jehoiachin from prison. Both episodes are important for understanding DtrH historiographical and theological perspective.

The account of Gedaliah's assassination is a case in point. This passage is a very truncated version of a narrative that appears in much fuller form in Jer 39–44, esp. Jer 41. Viewing the narrative simply as a shortened version of the longer Jeremiah account is not sufficient; the text relates the assassination of Gedaliah, but its place in the narrative is secured by the reference to the flight of the people to Egypt. The Kings narrative does not specify the leading figures who convinced the people to flee to Egypt as in Jeremiah; it simply states that all of the people fled to Egypt. This contrast is striking when considered in relation to the historiographical premises of the DtrH—that is, YHWH led the people from Egyptian bondage into the land of Israel, and now the people have returned to Egypt following Manasseh's failure to observe YHWH's Torah.

The account of Jehoiachin's release from prison also carries great significance.[1] Von Rad contends that Jehoiachin's release from prison portends messianic hope for the future of Israel,[2] but their grounds for such optimism must be qualified. Jehoiachin does not return to Jerusalem or to the land of Israel; instead, he is supported by the Babylonian king for the rest of his life. Insofar as this narrative appears to have been composed during the brief reign of Evil Merodach (a.k.a. Amel Marduk), the son and successor of Nebuchadnezzar, it is unaware of the Babylonian king's demise after a brief two-year reign in 562–560 B.C.E. Although Jehoiachin survived, it was only his grandson, Zerubbabel, who returned to Jerusalem in 522 B.C.E., and he never regained the throne

---

1. Bob Becking, "Jehoiachin's Amnesty, Salvation for Israel? Notes on 2 Kings 25, 27–30," *Pentateuchal and Deuteronomistic Studies* (ed. C. Brekelmans and J. Lust; Leuven: Peeters, 1990), 283–93; Jon D. Levenson, "The Last Four Verses in Kings," *JBL* 103 (1984): 353–61.

2. Gerhard von Rad, *Old Testament Theology* (New York: Harper and Row, 1962–65), 1:334–47.

in Jerusalem. Only the slightest glimmer of hope for Davidic restoration could be entertained for a monarch who remained in Babylon, no matter how honored he might have been by his captor-host.

The concluding account of Jehoiachin's release from prison does not point to future Davidic restoration, but to the demise of the house of David as the ruling monarchy of Israel/Judah in Jerusalem. Such a view is consistent with statements concerning the role of the Davidic promise in the books of Kings—that a son of David would sit on the throne only so long as the monarchs observed the will of YHWH (see 1 Kgs 2:1–4; 8:22–26; 9:3–9). Such qualification undermines the unqualified promise of eternal Davidic rule in 2 Sam 7.

David initially came to the throne as the son-in-law of Saul by virtue of his marriage to Saul's daughter Michal. With one exception, all of the sons of Saul perished—some together with their father in battle at Mount Gilboa in 1 Sam 31 and some when David turned them over to the Gibeonites for execution in 2 Sam 21. David's refusal to have relations with Michal (2 Sam 6) left the path open for David to found his own dynasty by his sons through other wives. One descendant of Saul, Mephibosheth ben Jonathan, remained. He is described in 2 Sam 9 as lame and dependent on David for support. When Mephibosheth abandons Jerusalem at the time of Absalom's revolt against David—apparently at the instigation of his servant Ziba, who sought to accuse him falsely to David and claim his property—David suspects him of treason. Only when Mephibosheth swears loyalty to David and renounces all claim to his father's property does David allow him to return (2 Sam 19:25–31). At this point the future of the house of Saul is sealed, and it will never again reclaim the throne. Much the same must be said of the house of David when Jehoiachin is released from prison. Like Mephibosheth, he is dependent on his master for support, and he never again attempts to assert his claims to the throne. Such a portrayal would be particularly important in the early Second Temple period when under the leadership of Nehemiah and Ezra—both of whom served in Jerusalem as Persian-appointed officials—Judah accepted Persian rule in place of the house of David.

As for the potential restoration of the temple, the narrative is silent. One must note that YHWH claims no need for a temple in 2 Sam 7, preferring instead the freedom to move about in tabernacle and tent. Such a contention sets the stage for divine activity once again in Egypt or Babylon, the two locations where the DtrH places the remnant of the people.

These concerns are those of the exilic DtrH. The narrative is an abbreviated version of Jer 39–44; 52. The portrayal of Jehoiachin's release from prison places its composition in the reign of Evil Merodach (Amel Marduk) who ruled Babylon in 562–560 B.C.E.[3]

---

3. For discussion of Amel Marduk, see Wiseman, CAH 3/2, 240–43.

[**24:18–20**] Zedekiah's eleven-year reign extends from the deportation of Jehoiachin in 597 B.C.E. through the Babylonian capture of Jerusalem in 587 or 586 B.C.E. His mother is Hamutal bat Jeremiah of Libnah, which makes him the younger full brother of Jehoahaz. Zedekiah appears like Jehoahaz to be a member of the pro-Babylonian branch of the Davidic house. His installation on the throne represents a Babylonian attempt to restore the branch of the royal house that would have been favorable to its own interests. His role as younger brother both to Jehoahaz and Jehoiakim would have left him unprepared to assume royal authority. He was unable to contain the pro-Egyptian forces in Judah that called for a second revolt against the Babylonians in 588 B.C.E., which of course led to the destruction of Jerusalem, the end of his reign, the deaths of his sons, and his own blinding and exile to Babylon. During the siege, he consults the prophet Jeremiah, whom he had been forced by anti-Babylonian factions to arrest and imprison in a cistern during the course of the Babylonian siege (Jer 38–39), even threatening the prophet with death should he disclose his conversations with the king (Jer 38:24).

The evaluation formula for Zedekiah resembles those for Jehoahaz, Jehoiakim, and Jehoiachin, which marks this unit as the product of the exilic DtrH. The reference to YHWH's anger, resulting in the casting away of Jerusalem and Judah, recalls YHWH's earlier decision to destroy Jerusalem, Judah, and the temple as a result of the sins of Manasseh (2 Kgs 21:10–15).

[**25:1–7**] The account of Nebuchadnezzar's siege of Jerusalem places the onset of the siege on the tenth day of the tenth month of Zedekiah's ninth year. Since the year begins with the month of Nisan, this would be 10 Tevet (=December–January) in 587 B.C.E. The capture of Jerusalem on ninth of the first (?) month in Zedekiah's eleventh year would be 9 Nisan, 586 B.C.E. Jeremiah 52:6 states that the capture of the city took place on ninth day of the fourth month: 9 Tammuz (= June–July), 586 B.C.E. Jerusalem would have endured sixteen months of siege, which would have carried it through two lost harvest seasons. With the exhaustion of food supplies in the city, the Babylonians would finally have been able to force a breach in the city's defenses, most likely along the northern walls of the city where the ground is more level and susceptible to sappers (cf. Ezek 4:2; 8:5–13). Zedekiah and his men would then have fled the city by way of a southern gate, away from the advancing Babylonians. The gate between the walls by the garden of the king appears to be the "Gate of the Spring"—that is, the gate at the southeastern edge of the city by 'Ein Rogel (Rogel Spring; Neh 3:15)—the point where the expanded wall of Jerusalem built by Hezekiah to enclose the western hill met the southern edges of the older defensive wall that enclosed the city of David.[4] Zedekiah and his

---

4. See Nahman Avigad, *Discovering Jerusalem* (Jerusalem: Shikmona and the Israel Exploration Society, 1983), 54–60.

men fled by way of the Wadi Qelt, which would have led them to the fords south of Jericho where the Jordan River flows into the Dead Sea. This route would have enabled them to cross over into the Transjordanian region in an attempt to seek refuge. Zedekiah was captured in the plains of Jericho, where the Wadi Qelt opens into the dry broad plain of the Arabot Jericho. The Babylonians stationed forces in this region to subdue and control Judah outside of Jerusalem.

The final acts of Zedekiah as king take place by Jericho, where Joshua first began the conquest of the land of Israel in the DtrH and where Hiel of Beth El sacrificed his sons to rebuild the city at the onset of the reign of the house of Omri (1 Kgs 16:34). Elijah's condemnation of the house of Omri is only completed when the house of David, itself descended from the house of Omri by the marriage of Athaliah bat Omri or Ahab to Ahaziah ben Jehoshaphat, is removed from the throne in Jerusalem because of the sins of Manasseh ben Hezekiah (2 Kgs 21:10–15). By portraying the capture of Zedekiah and the end of Davidic rule in this manner, the DtrH brings Israel's history full circle from beginning to end at the city of Jericho.[5]

Nebuchadnezzar maintained headquarters at Riblah, along the Orontes River seven miles south of Kadesh in the Beqaʻa Valley. This strategic location allowed Nebuchadnezzar to control Aram and Phoenicia while putting down the revolt in Judah to the south. The site was employed for similar purposes by Pharaoh Necho in 609 B.C.E. (2 Kgs 23:31–35, esp. v. 33). Nebuchadnezzar passed judgment on Zedekiah at Riblah in keeping with the typical treaty curses of the day for failure to comply with the terms of a treaty. After witnessing the execution of his sons, Zedekiah was blinded and led into exile to Babylonia. This act fulfills the statement made by Isaiah to Hezekiah that some of his sons would be taken to Babylon (2 Kgs 20:18).

[25:8–24] Nabuzaradan, chief of the guards, entered the city on seventh day of the fifth month of Nebechadnezzar's nineteenth year—7 Av, 586 B.C.E.—to begin the process of destruction. Jeremiah 52:12 states that it was the tenth day. Rabbinic tradition reconciles these dates by stating that Nebuzaradan entered the temple on the seventh day of Av, set it on fire on the ninth, and the fire burned until the tenth. Hence the traditional day of mourning for the destruction of the temple is the ninth day of Av (*b. Taʿanit* 29a; see also *t. Taʿan* 4:10).

Nabuzaradan, chief of the guards, is mentioned in Jer 40:1–6, where he notes Jeremiah's role in calling for submission to Babylon and offers to take him back to Babylon. Nabuzaradan's title, *rab-ṭabbāḥîm,* literally means "chief of the

---

5. Marvin A. Sweeney, "On the Literary Function of the Notice Concerning Hiel's Reestablishment of Jericho in 1 Kings 16.34," in *Seeing Signals, Reading Signs: The Art of Exegesis* (ed. M. A. O'Brien and H. N. Wallace; JSOTSup 415; Sheffield: Sheffield Academic Press, 2004), 104–15.

slaughterers," which ironically fits his role in the present chapter. The term also refers to cooking (see 1 Sam 8:13; 9:23, 24). Potiphar holds a similar title, *śar haṭṭabbāḥîm,* "chief of the cooks," which indicates his role as an important administrative officer in the Egyptian monarchy (Gen 37:36). Such a designation, like "chief cup-bearer," indicates his administrative role in Nebuchadnezzar's regime.

Verses 9–17 (cf. Jer 52:13–23) describe Nabuzaradan's destruction of the city and temple, including the burning of the temple, the royal palace, and the houses of Jerusalem, as well as the pulling down of the wall. The complete destruction of the city's wall would hardly be necessary. The Babylonians would destroy key points—gate areas, towers, and the like—to render Jerusalem's defensive walls useless without wasting the time and effort to pull down every inch. The notation concerning those exiled in vv. 11–12 includes both those who remained in the city as well as those who had crossed over to the Babylonian side during the lengthy siege. The leading figures of Jerusalem were exiled with Jehoiachin in 597 (see 2 Kgs 24:8–17), so this deportation would presumably involve fewer officials and artisans (see Jer 52:29). Only poor vinedressers and farmers were left in the land, although Jer 52:30 indicates that another 745 were exiled in Nebuchadnezzar's twenty-third year following Gedaliah's assassination. The description of the dismantled temple fixtures and vessels appropriated by the Babylonians should be read in relation to the narratives concerning Solomon's construction of the temple and manufacture of these items. The two pillars appear in 1 Kgs 7:15–22; the stands in 1 Kgs 7:27–37; the bronze sea in 1 Kgs 7:23–26; the pots in 1 Kgs 7:45; the shovels in 1 Kgs 7:40; and the snuffers, spoons, fire pans, and sprinkling bowls in 1 Kgs 7:50. The inventory in vv. 16–17, particularly the details of the columns and their capitals and the notation concerning the quantity of bronze realized from these fixtures and vessels, are derived from 1 Kgs 7:40–47.

Verses 18–21 relate the execution of temple officials, military officers, and others in the aftermath of the fall of the city. Seraiah the high priest is the son of Azariah (1 Chr 5:40) and ancestor of Ezra (Ezra 7:1). Zephaniah the deputy priest is the son of Maaseiah. He handles oracular inquiries and correspondence involving Jeremiah (Jer 21:1; 29:25, 29; 37:3), which suggests that his role involves public communications and appearances. The keepers of the threshold supervised the temple and its courts. The other officers are military men and members of the royal court. The sixty persons from the people of the land indicate that leading figures from the Judean countryside were also executed at Nebuchadnezzar's headquarters in Riblah.

Mizpeh in vv. 22–24 is identified with Tell en-Nasbeh, about eight miles north of Jerusalem in the territory of Benjamin, although some identify it with

Nebi Samwil, about five miles north of Jerusalem.[6] There is little evidence of widespread destruction in Benjamin, which suggests that Benjamin submitted early. Gedaliah ben Ahikam ben Shaphan was from the influential family that plays a very public role in Jerusalem's affairs during the late seventh and early sixth centuries (see the roles of family members in 2 Kgs 22; Jer 26; 29; 36). The family's association with the pro-Babylonian party likely played a role in Gedaliah's appointment. His name appears on a clay seal found at Lachish, "belonging to Gedaliah, who is over the house," which suggests that he served in Zedekiah's administration.[7]

The men mentioned here come to Gedaliah to recognize his authority. Ishmael ben Nathaniah, described as a member of the royal line below, later assassinates Gedaliah in a bid to restore Judean independence and perhaps the Davidic line (see vv. 25–26 and the full account in Jer 41). Johanan ben Kareah led the forces that put down Ishmael's attempted coup (Jer 41:11–18), and later led a faction that took Jeremiah with them to Egypt (Jer 42–43). Seraiah ben Tanhumeth the Netophite was from Netophah and is perhaps to be identified with Ein an-Natuf (Nauph Spring) south of Bethlehem (cf. Ezra 2:22; Neh 7:26). Jaazniah the Ma'achathite comes from the Ma'achah, a Calebite clan from Judah (1 Chr 2:48; cf. 2 Sam 23:34; 1 Chr 4:19). A seal was found at Tell en-Nasbeh reading "belonging to Jaazniah, servant of the king."[8]

[25:26–27] Verses 25–26 place the assassination of Gedaliah in the seventh month, in Tishri (= September–October), but leave the impression that it takes place in the same year as Jerusalem's destruction. Jeremiah 52:30 indicates that the deportation of 745 persons took place in Nebuchadnezzar's twenty-third year, five years after the destruction of Jerusalem. The Kings version appears to be derived from the earlier detailed version in Jer 41–43. Although the historical context indicates an attempt by Ishmael ben Nathaniah to restore Judean independence and the authority of the house of David, the literary portrayal indicates that the people return to Egypt, from which they had escaped at the outset of the DtrH.

[25:27–30] The DtrH concludes with the notice concerning Jehoiachin's release from prison. The passage dates this event to the twenty-seventh day (cf. Jer 52:31, which reads "twenty-fifth day") of the tenth month in the thirty-seventh year of Jehoachin's exile: 27 Adar, 561–560 B.C.E. The narrative states

6. For discussion of the identification of Mizpeh, see P. M. Arnold, "Mizpah," *ABD* 4:879–81; for discussion of Tell en-Nasbeh, see J. Zorn, *NEAEHL* 3:1098–1102.

7. O. Tufnell et al., *Lachish III* (London: Oxford, 1953), 348; cf. S. H. Hooke, "A Scarab and Sealing from Tell Duweir," *PEQ* 67 (1935): 195–97; D. Ussishkin, "Lachish," *NEAEHL* 3:910.

8. W. F. Badè, "The Seal of Jaazniah," *ZAW* 51 (1933): 151–56.

that Evil Merodach (Amel Marduk), the son of Nebuchadnezzar, released Jehoiachin in the year of his succession to the throne following his father's death in 562. His release may have represented an act of amnesty granted at the beginning of the new king's reign. Jehoiachin would have been fifty-five years old, and with his country devastated would have represented no threat to Babylonia. Tablets discovered in Babylon provide the details of his support by the Babylonian king. Amel Marduk was assassinated in the second year of his reign by Nergal-sar-usar, who usurped the throne.

INDEX OF AUTHORS

Castro, F. Pérez, 33
Cazelles, H., 376
Ceriani, A. M., 38
Childs, Brevard S., 391, 411, 415
Chirichigno, G. C., 288
Christensen, Duane L., 393
Churgin, Pinkhos, 38
Clines, David J. A., 231, 282
Coats, G. W., 365
Cogan, Mordechai, 228, 239, 276, 284,
  320, 352, 355, 365, 370, 371, 374,
  392, 393, 396, 432, 445, 447
Cogan, Morton, 384, 427
Cohen, Harold R. [Chaim], 292, 415
Cohn, Robert L., 179, 220, 299
Conrad, Edgar W., 213, 309, 417
Coogan, M. D., 116, 151, 429
Coote, Robert B., 424
Crenshaw, James, 257
Cross, Frank M., Jr., 11, 15, 159, 162,
  179, 391
Crouwel, J. H., 100

Darr, Katheryn Pfisterer, 416
Davies, G. I., 100
Dearman, Andrew, 281
Debus, Jörg, 165
Delekat, Lienhard, 47
de Miroschedji, P., 186
de Pury, Albert, 3
de Vaux, R., 186, 270
Dever, William G., 2, 144, 194, 244, 309,
  311, 312, 373, 429
DeVries, L. F., 97
DeVries, Simon J., 69, 257
Dietrich, Walter, 4, 269, 391, 430, 443
Dijkstra, Meindert, 321
Dirksen, Peter B., 37
Donner, Herbert, 102, 131, 376
Dotan, Aaron, 33
Dothan, T., 269
Dutcher-Walls, Patricia, 342

Edelman, D. V., 92, 93
Ehrlich, C. S., 145, 345

Ephal, Israel, 150
Eynikel, Erik, 78

Fensham, F. C., 102
Fewell, Dana N., 411
Finkelstein, Israel, 136, 185, 429
Fishbane, Michael, 98
Flanagan, J. W., 18
Fohrer, Georg, 29, 160, 210, 221, 269,
  359
Fox, Nili Sacher, 52, 84, 85, 86, 87, 241,
  242, 243, 261, 337, 370, 415, 444, 446
Frankel, R., 229, 359, 376
Freedman, David Noel, 33
Freud, Richard, 194
Friedman, R. E., 391
Frisch, Amos, 79, 172
Fritz, Volkmar, 194, 229, 237, 360, 376
Frost, Stanley Brice, 450

Galil, Gershon, 40
Galling, K., 274
Gastor, T. H., 250
Gehman, Henry Snyder, 77, 164, 198,
  205, 229, 236, 270, 275, 284, 360,
  371, 383
Geva, Hillel, 58, 144
Ginsburg, Christian D., 33
Gitin, Seymour, 269, 394, 429
Glatt-Gilad, David, 138
Glock, A. E., 92
Glueck, Nelson, 146, 211, 212, 243,
  283, 383
Goedicke, H., 393
Gonçalves, Francolino, 411
Gonen, Rivka, 110
Gooding, D. W., 66, 76, 77, 110, 164
Gordon, Robert P., 165, 231
Görg, Manfred, 72, 97, 136
Goshen-Gottstein, Moshe H., 33
Gottlieb, Hans, 38
Grabbe, L. L., 11, 400, 426
Graham, M. Patrick, 281
Gray, John, 215, 229, 237, 274, 353,
  360, 414